Partnership Taxation

ASPEN CASEBOOK SERIES

Partnership Taxation

Third Edition

George K. Yin
Edwin S. Cohen Distinguished Professor of Law and Taxation
University of Virginia School of Law

Karen C. Burke
Professor and Richard B. Stephens Eminent Scholar in Taxation
University of Florida Levin College of Law

Wolters Kluwer

Published by Wolters Kluwer in New York.

Wolters Kluwer Legal & Regulatory US serves customers worldwide with CCH, Aspen Publishers, and Kluwer Law International products. (www.WKLegaledu.com)

To contact Customer Service, e-mail customer.service@wolterskluwer.com, call 1-800-234-1660, fax 1-800-901-9075, or mail correspondence to:

Wolters Kluwer
Attn: Order Department
PO Box 990
Frederick, MD 21705

Printed in the United States of America.

1 2 3 4 5 6 7 8 9 0

ISBN 978-1-4548-7767-7

Library of Congress Cataloging-in-Publication Data

Names: Yin, George K., author. | Burke, Karen C., 1951- author.
Title: Partnership taxation / George K. Yin, Edwin S. Cohen Distinguished Professor of Law and Taxation, University of Virginia School of Law, Karen C. Burke, Professor and Richard B. Stephens Eminent Scholar in Taxation, University of Florida Levin College of Law.
Description: 3rd ed. | New York: Wolters Kluwer, [2016] | Series: Aspen casebook series
Identifiers: LCCN 2016012475 | ISBN 9781454877677
Subjects: LCSH: Partnership — Taxation — Law and legislation — United States. | LCGFT: Casebooks
Classification: LCC KF6452 .Y56 2016 | DDC 343.7305/2662-dc23
LC record available at http://lccn.loc.gov/2016012475

About Wolters Kluwer Legal & Regulatory US

Wolters Kluwer Legal & Regulatory US delivers expert content and solutions in the areas of law, corporate compliance, health compliance, reimbursement, and legal education. Its practical solutions help customers successfully navigate the demands of a changing environment to drive their daily activities, enhance decision quality and inspire confident outcomes.

Serving customers worldwide, its legal and regulatory portfolio includes products under the Aspen Publishers, CCH Incorporated, Kluwer Law International, ftwilliam.com and MediRegs names. They are regarded as exceptional and trusted resources for general legal and practice-specific knowledge, compliance and risk management, dynamic workflow solutions, and expert commentary.

To Mary
G.K.Y.

To K. and L.
K.C.B.

Summary of Contents

Table of Contents

Preface to the Third Edition

This book introduces students to the federal income taxation of partners and partnerships. In general, partnership tax law disregards the partnership as a business entity and treats the partnership's income as if it were earned by the partners. In this sense, partnership tax is a natural extension of principles learned in the introductory income tax course and this book builds upon that common foundation. The universe of businesses subject to partnership tax has been steadily increasing, and includes not only traditional partnerships and limited liability companies but also more exotic arrangements such as domestic and international joint ventures.

We have written this book to help students overcome the many challenges of learning partnership tax. For example, in considering the tax treatment of transactions involving partnerships, we have employed a building-block approach, progressing from an analysis of basic to more complex transactions. This approach enables students to see that the same transaction may be structured in different ways to achieve different tax goals, and that the taxation of complex transactions to some extent flows naturally from how simpler ones are taxed. By avoiding unnecessary detail yet not oversimplifying, the book facilitates mastery of the material and prepares students to think rigorously and creatively about the kinds of problems they will encounter as practitioners of tax and business law.

Partnership tax is characterized by policy choices that lend structure and coherence to the law, and we emphasize these choices and structural features throughout the book. This structure makes the law so much more than a mere collection of rules. Understanding the law's conceptual underpinning provides immeasurable assistance for students, both in helping them to learn and comprehend specific details and in anticipating the need for, and understanding the meaning of, subsequent changes in the law. This knowledge also provides collateral benefits, as the policy structure of partnership tax is replicated to some extent in the tax rules relating to certain other business arrangements.

We have organized the book around major themes that expose the underlying structure of the law. The first six chapters explain how the income of a partnership is taxed, and how the law achieves its objective of disregarding the business entity and taxing the partners directly. Chapters one through three focus on classification of business entities, the passthrough of a partnership's tax items to the partners of the partnership, and the concept of partnership capital accounts. Chapters four through six examine the difficult question of how the partnership's tax items must be shared or "allocated" among the partners.

Building on this foundation, the balance of the book describes the tax treatment of transactions involving partnerships, including transactions between partners and partnerships. Chapters seven through nine consider transfers of partnership interests, contributions to and distributions from partnerships, and potential recharacterization of these transactions. Chapter ten addresses the tax consequences of compensating partners for services and use of capital, and chapter eleven discusses partnership terminations. Finally, chapter twelve explores special anti-abuse rules that limit opportunities for manipulating the flexible provisions of the law. One of the important themes initially introduced in the first half of the book and more fully developed in the latter half is how the tax law reconciles its disregard of the business entity with the respect given the entity for other legal purposes.

Throughout the book, we emphasize the core source material of the law — the statute and regulations — as amplified in interpretive administrative materials and judicial decisions. We have deliberately tried to make background explanations and illustrative examples concise without being cryptic, based on our firm belief that actively engaging students with the material enhances the learning process. We have interspersed many explanations, problems, and questions to help lead the students through the material. Although partnership tax has earned a reputation as an especially daunting field, we are confident that students will emerge from the course equipped to analyze and evaluate the critical issues they will encounter in practice.

In preparing the first edition, we enjoyed the luxury of starting with a clean slate, without being constrained by past editorial, organizational, or pedagogical choices. This revised third edition builds on the approach of the prior editions, and is updated to reflect developments through March 2016. Tax law is dynamic, and we have brought our combined experience in teaching, private practice, and government to bear in taking a fresh look at the subject matter. We have tried to identify the most important issues and themes that will confront future lawyers in this area.

As a matter of editorial prerogative, we have freely edited judicial decisions and other materials to focus attention on essential analysis and holdings. Footnotes are numbered consecutively within each chapter, and many footnotes in the original sources have been deleted or renumbered. Internal citations and cross-references in cases and other authorities have been omitted without so indicating, while substantive omissions are indicated by an ellipsis (". . .").

George K. Yin
Charlottesville, VA

Karen C. Burke
Gainesville, FL

May 2016

Acknowledgments

We gratefully acknowledge the permission extended by the American Law Institute to reprint an excerpt from the material listed below:

Federal Income Tax Project, Taxation of Private Business Enterprises: Reporters' Study copyright © 1999 by The American Law Institute. All rights reserved. Reprinted with permission.

Federal Income Tax Project, Taxation of Pass-Through Entities, Memorandum No. 1 copyright © 1995 by The American Law Institute. All rights reserved. Reprinted with permission.

Partnership Taxation

Chapter 1

Introduction to Partnership Tax

A. Introduction

From prior study, you are already familiar with the basic concepts of income taxation, including what income is, when it arises, and what its character is. No doubt you have also been exposed to the legal concept of a "partnership" and some of the rules and policies pertaining to it. This course explores what happens when income is earned by a business that is organized as a partnership or treated as one for tax purposes.

Let us begin with an example. Assume that your daughter, Laura, decides to invest $10 of her savings to operate a lemonade stand. She uses the $10 to purchase the items necessary to get the business started — the stand, cups, lemons, and so forth. She then proceeds to hawk her drinks out by the curb in front of your house. The day is hot, the drinks are cool, your daughter is cute and efficient, and your neighbors are kind, and she therefore successfully sells a number of drinks by day's end.

If necessary, we might calculate her income for the day using familiar principles. First, she should have income from services, that is, her compensation for sitting out all day in the hot sun peddling her drinks. Further, as the owner of the enterprise, she may have business income equal to her total receipts less properly allowable expenses (including the compensation her business pays to her). The business income might be thought of as the return she obtains from investing her $10 for one day in the manner described. Our principal concern in this course will be with the taxation of the business income, the income from her $10 capital investment.

Should the tax treatment of the business income vary, depending upon the *form of organization* of the business? For example, the foregoing describes how the business profits might be taxed if the lemonade stand is operated as a *sole proprietorship*. But suppose your daughter only has $5 in her piggy bank and therefore seeks out her older sister, Elizabeth, for the remaining capital needed to start up the business. Elizabeth provides the additional $5 but only on condition that the two sisters form a partnership and share equally in any profits from the business. How should the profits of the *L&E partnership* be taxed?

At least in theory, it is difficult to see why the profits of the partnership should be taxed any differently from those of the sole proprietorship. There is simply more than one owner now. But the economic activity undertaken in the two situations is exactly the same. Moreover, taxing the two situations differently would have the effect of either encouraging or discouraging the pooling of capital.

In fact, as we shall see, partnerships *are* taxed essentially along the lines of the sole proprietorship model. This method of taxation is variously referred to as "passthrough," "flowthrough," "conduit," or "aggregate" taxation. The legal entity (the partnership in this case) is generally ignored for purposes of paying tax. Instead, it is treated as a "conduit" and the income tax items relating to the business are passed through to the owners of the enterprise — the partners — who are the real (and only) taxpayers in interest. Under this approach, the partnership is conceived of as an "aggregate" of owners, each of whom is taxed as if she owned an individual interest in the partnership's assets and conducted the partnership's business directly.

Although the rationale for passthrough taxation is straightforward, its implementation is not. The principal reason is the sometimes conflicting treatment of a partnership for tax and nontax purposes. The disregard of the entity for purposes of paying tax must be reconciled with other circumstances in which the legal entity is respected. Partnerships, for example, can own and sell property and incur debt. Moreover, partners generally own interests in the partnership entity and *not* direct interests in the partnership's assets.

As a consequence, we will see that the tax law has compromised its passthrough objective in certain circumstances, so that the legal entity of the partnership is sometimes respected as a taxpayer separate and distinct from its partners for tax purposes. The resulting blend of entity and aggregate approaches produces some of the more difficult issues in this course. As you work through these materials, consider whether a more consistent application of aggregate principles, or a different blend of the entity and aggregate approaches, would simplify the tax law and ease administration.

Roughly the first half of this book deals with how the passthrough scheme is implemented. In chapter two, we describe the basic operation of the passthrough system, including how the income of the partnership is determined and what happens when it is passed through to the partners. Chapter three provides an introduction to partnership accounting, a topic which you may be surprised to discover is of considerable importance to the tax law. Chapters four through six then focus on the difficult question of how the various tax items passed through to the partners are shared by them.

The second half of the book concerns primarily the taxation of *transactions* involving partnerships or between partners and partnerships. Chapter seven focuses on transfers of partnership interests and chapter eight deals with contributions of property to partnerships and distributions of property from partnerships. Chapter nine then explores possible recharacterizations of partnership contributions, distributions, and sales. Chapter ten describes the tax consequences of compensation provided to partners for services or the use of property, and chapter eleven examines the tax ramifications of terminations of partnership interests and the partnership itself.

The book concludes with a chapter describing certain broad provisions designed to prevent abuse of the partnership tax rules, including the partnership "anti-abuse" regulation under section 701. This regulation may come as a rather rude awakening—it authorizes the IRS to reverse the tax consequences of virtually all aspects of partnership tax law presented in the first eleven chapters. We will consider both what this regulation does and why it was added to the law. As you will see, the regulation has an effect similar to the "economic substance doctrine" (now codified in section 7701(o)), which is applicable to the tax law generally and is also discussed briefly in the final chapter.

The taxation of partners and partnerships is governed by subchapter K of the Internal Revenue Code (§§ 701-761) and the relevant Treasury regulations. A threshold issue is classification: what type of business is subject to the rules of subchapter K? This topic is taken up next.

B. Classification

Take a quick look at the first few provisions in subchapter K, sections 701 through 703. As you can see, the law is phrased in terms of the consequences to "partners" and "partnerships," and the balance of subchapter K follows this same pattern. But exactly what businesses and owners are treated as "partnerships" and "partners"? As described below, the term "partnership" for tax purposes is not limited to arrangements constituting a partnership under state law. The term encompasses a joint venture or other contractual arrangement organized in a variety of unincorporated forms. The following sections describe the two principal classification issues. First, to be a partnership, an arrangement must qualify as a "separate entity" for tax purposes. Second, the arrangement must not be taxable as a corporation.

1. *Qualifying as an Entity Separate from Its Owners*

To be eligible to be taxed under subchapter K, an arrangement must first qualify as an entity separate from its owners. This determination is made based on federal tax law and not local business organization law. In general, to constitute a separate entity, a joint undertaking must involve a carrying on of a trade, business, or financial operation and the division of profits therefrom. See Reg. § 301.7701-1(a)(1) and (2).

A common and difficult question is whether a co-ownership arrangement qualifies as a separate entity for tax purposes and therefore may be taxed under subchapter K. Reg. § 301.7701-1(a)(2) provides that a separate entity for tax purposes does not include a joint undertaking merely to share expenses or a mere co-ownership of property that is maintained, kept in repair, and rented or leased. The following ruling, which interprets a prior but virtually identical version of the regulations on this issue, elaborates on this test.

Rev. Rul. 75-374

1975-2 C.B. 261

Advice has been requested whether, under the circumstance described below, the coowners of an apartment project would be treated as a partnership for Federal income tax purposes.

X, a life insurance company, and Y, a real estate investment trust, each own an undivided one-half interest in an apartment project. X and Y entered into a management agreement with Z, an unrelated corporation, and retained it to manage, operate, maintain, and service the project.

Generally, under the management agreement Z negotiates and executes leases for apartment units in the project; collects rents and other payments from tenants; pays taxes, assessments, and insurance premiums payable with respect to the project; performs all other services customarily performed in connection with the maintenance and repair of an apartment project; and performs certain additional services for the tenants beyond those customarily associated with maintenance and repair. Z is responsible for determining the time and manner of performing its obligations under the agreement and for the supervision of all persons performing services in connection with the carrying out of such obligations.

Customary tenant services, such as heat, air conditioning, hot and cold water, unattended parking, normal repairs, trash removal, and cleaning of public areas are furnished at no additional charge above the basic rental payments. All costs incurred by Z in rendering these customary services are paid for by X and Y. As compensation for the customary services rendered by Z under the agreement, X and Y each pay Z a percentage of one-half of the gross rental receipts derived from the operation of the project.

Additional services, such as attendant parking, cabanas, and gas, electricity, and other utilities are provided by Z to tenants for a separate charge. Z pays the costs incurred in providing the additional services, and retains the charges paid by tenants for its own use. These charges provide Z with adequate compensation for the rendition of these additional services.

Section 761(a) of the Internal Revenue Code of 1954 provides that the term "partnership" includes a syndicate, group, pool, joint venture or other unincorporated organization through or by means of which any business, financial operation, or venture is carried on, and which is not a corporation or a trust or estate.

Section 1.761-1(a) of the Income Tax Regulations provides that mere coownership of property that is maintained, kept in repair, and rented or leased does not constitute a partnership. Tenants in common may be partners if they actively carry on a trade, business, financial operation, or venture and divide the profits thereof. For example, a partnership exists if coowners of an apartment building lease space and in addition provide services to the occupants either directly or through an agent.

The furnishing of customary services in connection with the maintenance and repair of the apartment project will not render a coownership a partnership. However, the furnishing of additional services will render a coownership a partnership if the additional services are furnished directly by the coowners or through their agent. In the instant case by reason of the contractual arrangement with Z, X and Y are not furnishing the additional services either directly or through an agent. Z is solely responsible for determining the time and manner of furnishing the services, bears all the expenses of providing these services, and retains for its own use all the income from these services. None of the profits arising from the rendition of these additional services are divided between X and Y.

Accordingly, X and Y will be treated as coowners and not as partners for purposes of section 761 of the Code.

NOTES

1. *Effect of the ruling*. Since Rev. Rul. 75-374 was issued, Reg. § 1.761-1(a) has been amended. Nevertheless, current Reg. § 301.7701-1(a)(2) contains language almost identical to former Reg. § 1.761-1(a).

2. *Sections 7701(a)(2) and 761(a) and (b)*. Read the definition of "partnership" set forth in I.R.C. § 7701(a)(2). This definition is identical to the one provided in the first sentence of section 761(a), which is referenced in the ruling. Because it applies for purposes of all of title 26 of the U.S. Code, section 7701(a)(2) renders redundant the definition in section 761(a) (which applies only for purposes of subtitle A of title 26, the income tax subtitle). Sections 7701(a)(2) and 761(b) (1st sentence) provide that a "partner" is a member of a partnership. In 2015, Congress amended section 761(b) by adding language that determination of who is a partner in a capital-intensive partnership "shall be determined without regard to whether [that person's] interest was derived by gift from any other person." I.R.C. § 761(b) (2d sentence). This new language is virtually identical to the language of former section 704(e)(1), which was originally added to the Code to clarify that a transferee of a partnership interest would be respected as a partner regardless of the motive for an intrafamily transfer.

3. *Electing out of subchapter K*. Section 761(a) (2d sentence) allows certain unincorporated organizations qualifying as partnerships to "elect out" of the rules of subchapter K. Eligible organizations include those formed solely for investment purposes or engaged in certain aspects of the extractive industry. In addition, the election is available only if the income of the organization's members can be

"adequately determined without the computation of partnership taxable income." This election is commonly used by oil and gas firms in order to allow their owners to make separate tax elections and use different taxable years.

An election may be deemed to have been made if the members demonstrate the requisite intent not to be taxed under subchapter K. See Reg. § 1.761-2(b)(2)(ii). The deemed election is designed to protect taxpayers who never intended to be treated as partners. Indeed, since a partnership may be created quite informally, some persons may be treated as partners even though they are unaware of the existence of a partnership. In this situation, application of the subchapter K rules may have rather unexpected consequences. If an election is made or deemed to be made, the organization may nevertheless be treated as a partnership for purposes of Code provisions outside of subchapter K.

4. *Husband and wife partnerships.* Section 761(f) allows a "qualified joint venture" ("QJV") to elect not to be treated as a partnership for all federal tax purposes. A QJV is a joint venture involving the conduct of a trade or business whose only members are a husband and wife who file a joint return; both spouses must materially participate (within the meaning of section 469(h)) in the trade or business and must elect out of partnership treatment. Since all of the income from the venture would be reported on the couple's joint return regardless of whether subchapter K is followed, the provision is intended to reduce complexity by permitting the couple to avoid filing a partnership return. Each spouse must account for his or her share of income or loss of the QJV as if the spouse were a sole proprietor; all items of the QJV must be divided between the spouses in accordance with their respective ownership interest. The provision also helps to clarify that the share of income (or loss) of each spouse is taken into account in determining net self-employment income of that spouse, an important consideration in calculating future Social Security benefits. See I.R.C. § 1402(a)(17).

The IRS previously granted a similar choice to partnerships (or LLCs) wholly owned by a husband and wife as community property. See Rev. Proc. 2002-69, 2002 C.B. 831. The IRS agreed to accept the couple's treatment of the entity as a partnership or sole proprietorship for federal tax purposes. Partnership treatment is available only if the couple files appropriate partnership tax returns.

5. *What do taxpayers prefer?* Co-owners of property sometimes prefer that their arrangement be classified as a partnership for tax purposes to take advantage of the flexible tax outcomes permitted under subchapter K. In other cases, co-owners prefer to avoid the intricacies of subchapter K; they can adequately compute their individual incomes in a separate manner. There may also be tax-planning reasons to avoid characterization as a separate entity. For example, a co-owner who holds an undivided fractional interest in property may be able to exchange it for like-kind property without the recognition of gain or loss. See I.R.C. § 1031(a)(1). If the ownership arrangement is considered a partnership, however, section 1031 treatment is unavailable. See I.R.C. § 1031(a)(2)(D).

6. *Combining labor and capital.* While many economic arrangements involve a cooperative use of labor and capital, only some qualify as separate entities eligible to

be taxed under subchapter K. Read the following case and consider the stakes involved for the taxpayer.

Wheeler v. Commissioner

37 T.C.M 883 (1978)

IRWIN, Judge: [Petitioner entered into an agreement with Perrault to acquire and develop specific tracts of real property. Petitioner was to provide the "know-how" and Perrault the necessary finances. It was agreed that Perrault would first recoup his investment plus a six percent interest factor, and that remaining profits, if any, were to be divided 75 percent to Perrault and 25 percent to petitioner. Pursuant to their agreement, the parties constructed and sold various properties and petitioner reported his share of the profits as long-term capital gain.]

The salient issue which emerges from this set of facts is one of income characterization. This issue must necessarily be resolved by a determination of whether the agreement between petitioner and Perrault was one of joint venture or one of employment. Thus, we must determine the elements necessary to form a valid joint venture and whether those elements existed in the case before us.

. . . In the case of *Commissioner v. Culbertson*, [337 U.S. 733 (1949),] it is stated that the primary consideration in determining whether an entity taxable as a partnership exists is whether:

> the parties in good faith and acting with a business purpose intended to join together in the present conduct of the enterprise. . . . [337 U.S. at 742]

. . . Thus the single most important consideration is the parties' intent to enter into a joint venture. And there are particular elements, none of which are conclusive, which are indicative of the existence or nonexistence of such intent. They are:

> The agreement of the parties and their conduct in executing its terms; the contributions, if any, which each party has made to the venture; the parties' control over income and capital and the right of each to make withdrawals; whether each party was a principal and coproprietor, sharing a mutual proprietary interest in the net profits and having an obligation to share losses, or whether one party was the agent or employee of the other, receiving for his services contingent compensation in the form of a percentage of income; whether business was conducted in the joint names of the parties; whether the parties filed Federal partnership returns or otherwise represented to respondent or to persons with whom they dealt that they were joint venturers; whether separate books of account were maintained for the venture; and whether the parties exercised mutual control over and assumed mutual responsibilities for the enterprise. . . .

The agreement between the parties seems fairly clear in this case. It specifically stated:

> The parties hereto are associated in a joint venture, under the name of "Perrault and Wheeler," for the purpose of holding, developing, and managing real property for investment purposes.[1]

It was further stated:

> The venture shall relate to and include the projects described on Exhibits "A," "B," and "C" attached hereto and such other projects as Perrault and Wheeler shall *mutually agree upon* and designate from time to time . . . [Emphasis supplied.]

The actual conduct of the parties supported the existence of a joint venture agreement between the parties. It was petitioner who exercised his authority on a day-to-day basis in selecting subcontractors, signing subcontracts, approving payrolls, approving interim payments to subcontractors, approving payments for materials, approving change orders in construction, and negotiating the F.H.A. commitments among other things. While any one of these duties may not raise one to the status of a joint venturer, the total authority granted to petitioner was certainly consistent with such status.

Petitioner was to use his best efforts and so much of his time as was reasonably necessary for the successful completion of the projects; his efforts were to be particularly related to the acquisition, ownership, development and operation of real estate and improvements thereon. Perrault was to contribute cash, credit, or other financing for the purchase and development of the projects covered by the agreement.

Little control was exercised over the petitioner's drawing account. He testified that his drawing account was very informal with no restriction as to amount. This seems supported in the record because at the point in time in 1969 when petitioner released his interest in the Villa Roma project he had a debit balance in his drawing account in the amount of $12,162.

Profits were to be allocated 75 percent to Perrault and 25 percent to petitioner. Cumulative losses were to be borne solely by Perrault; however, once operation of the venture resulted in a profit on a cumulative basis, losses on individual projects were to be allocated in accordance with the ratios indicated above.

Business was transacted under the name of "Perrault and Wheeler." The parties maintained an office in which they based their business operations. The stationery

---

1. Paragraph 10 of the agreement between Perrault and petitioner stated:

> The parties stipulate and agree that no partnership has been or is hereby created or intended between them. The parties shall be joint venturers only and only with respect to the projects herein designated and upon the limited basis herein set forth. Pursuant to Section 761(a) of the Internal Revenue Code of 1954, Perrault and Wheeler hereby elect to exclude this venture from the application of all or any part of the Subchapter K . . . to the full extent permitted by regulations. . . . Perrault may cause to be filed with the Internal Revenue Service an appropriate election on behalf of himself and Wheeler to be so excluded.

bore a "Perrault and Wheeler" letterhead. Advertising for the real estate projects also indicated a partnership type relationship between the parties.

Additionally, we believe the manner in which Perrault reported the sales transaction for tax purposes is highly significant in seeking to determine intent. Perrault did not report 100 percent of the profit and then take a deduction for petitioner's share as compensation, even though it would have had significant tax advantages for him to have done so. This indicates to us that Perrault, who for tax purposes had an interest adverse to the existence of a joint venture, intended that a joint venture exist between himself and petitioner. Of course, petitioner likewise reported the transaction as if a joint venture existed between the parties.

Separate books of account were maintained for the venture's operations. Perrault was given the authority to keep those books by means of which the net profits of the venture were to be computed, subject however to Wheeler's right of examination at all reasonable times. . . . The books were required to be kept using a generally accepted method of accounting and petitioner could submit any dispute to Arthur Anderson & Co., certified public accountants, whose determination on the disputed matter would be conclusive on the parties.

Respondent argued at trial that the fact Perrault reported all current operating income and current operating expenses from the operation of the projects was fatal to the finding of a joint venture because it indicated that petitioner did not truly share in the results of the venture's operations. However, this is not so. The agreement stated that petitioner was not to receive any distribution of profits until Perrault received, out of his share of operating income or sales proceeds (from the projects), an amount equal to his capital and advances plus six percent interest thereon. The agreement also provided that Perrault was to bear all losses in connection with each project until operation of the projects, on a cumulative basis, resulted in a profit. In the relatively brief period that the joint venture actually operated each of the projects there was not a sufficient amount of operating income generated to entitle petitioner to begin receiving his share of the profits. As a result, Perrault's reporting of all income and expenses during this period comported perfectly with the agreement between the parties and was not adverse to the existence of a joint venture interest in petitioner.

To be sure, there are factors in the agreement which tend to indicate the relationship between the parties was not that of a joint venture. Title to the properties was held solely in Perrault's name. Cumulative losses of the venture were to be borne solely by Perrault. Petitioner could not borrow or lend money on behalf of the venture, execute a security instrument, release any debt or claim except upon payment in full, compromise or submit to arbitration any controversy involving the venture [or] sell, assign, pledge, or mortgage his net profits interest in the venture. However, these restrictions on petitioner's authority were merely protection for Perrault's capital advances, and characteristics such as Perrault's holding title to the properties or bearing all the losses have been specifically recognized by respondent as insufficient to negate the existence of a joint venture. Rev. Rul. 54-84, 1954-1 C.B. 284. Perrault was also restricted in his authority to deal with assets of the venture, and although he was not restricted as [severely] as petitioner, the restriction on Perrault was designed to accomplish the same purpose as those on the petitioner, that is to protect the other party's share of the joint venture income.

A relationship having salient characteristics similar to the one here at issue has been recognized by respondent as a joint venture. In Rev. Rul. 54-84, supra, respondent held that the combination of service and capital partners, the absence of loss sharing, and title being held to venture property by one venturer (the one who made the capital contributions) was not fatal to the existence of a joint venture. Without specifically passing on the validity of the above ruling, we believe petitioner's contribution of his skill and know-how in developing commercial realty and Perrault's contribution of the capital necessary to get the projects under way were essential elements of the business enterprise. While not entirely free from doubt, we believe the totality of the relationship between the parties must be viewed as a joint venture. . . .

NOTES AND QUESTIONS

1. *Money and brains. Wheeler* makes clear that a common "money and brains" combination may qualify as a partnership for tax purposes. Under what circumstances might the parties involved prefer the arrangement to be characterized as a mere employment relationship? What should Wheeler and Perrault have done differently if that had been their objective?

2. *Tax reporting prior to sales.* The IRS presumably challenged this case in part because of the manner in which the parties had previously reported the tax consequences of the venture. Prior to the sales transactions, Perrault appeared to be the sole owner of the "joint venture." But, as the court explained, the parties' reporting was entirely consistent with their economic arrangement.

3. *Perrault's tax reporting of sales.* The court was also influenced by Perrault's tax reporting of the sales transactions. Because Perrault reported those transactions as if he were a co-venturer with Wheeler, Wheeler might reasonably be treated as a co-venturer as well. As the court noted, for tax purposes, Perrault's interest was adverse to the existence of a joint venture. Do you think Perrault's reporting of the transaction should be determinative of Wheeler's tax consequences?

4. *Footnote 1.* Why did the court apparently disregard the provision in the agreement reproduced in footnote 1? Why did the parties include it in their agreement in the first place?

5. *The tax advantage to Wheeler.* It may seem strange to allow Wheeler to report his income as long-term capital gain when his only contribution to the firm was his labor. Indeed, one might view Wheeler's receipt of a share of future profits in exchange for his promise to render services as itself a taxable event, resulting in ordinary income to Wheeler. But mere receipt of a "profits only" partnership interest in exchange for services does not generally result in any immediate tax consequences to the service partner or the other partners. This combination of

nonrecognition treatment coupled with passthrough characterization of subsequent partnership income, as illustrated in *Wheeler*, has proven quite controversial recently in the context of compensation paid to advisors of large investment partnerships. Transfers of compensatory partnership interests are discussed in further detail in chapter ten.

6. *The* Culbertson *test and tax avoidance transactions.* As explained in *Wheeler*, the Supreme Court in *Culbertson* indicated that a partnership exists only if "the parties in good faith and acting with a business purpose intended to join together in the present conduct of the enterprise." This inquiry has spawned two slightly different analytical approaches in decisions involving the classification of joint undertakings designed with tax avoidance in mind. Under one approach, the key question is whether the joint undertaking is for a bona fide business purpose other than tax avoidance. In ASA Investerings Partnership v. Comm'r, 201 F.3d 505 (D.C. Cir. 2000), aff'g 76 T.C.M. 325 (1998), cert. denied, 531 U.S. 871 (2000), involving a notorious tax shelter transaction that is discussed further in chapter twelve, the D.C. Circuit disregarded for tax purposes a purported partnership arrangement whose sole function was avoidance of taxes. For similar holdings, see Saba Partnership v. Comm'r, 273 F.3d 1135 (D.C. Cir. 2001) and Boca Investerings Partnership v. U.S., 314 F.3d 625 (D.C. Cir. 2003). The *ASA* court conceded that this type of business-purpose analysis is "hazardous" but thought it was essential to a sound-functioning tax system:

> It is uniformly recognized that taxpayers are entitled to structure their transactions in such a way as to minimize tax. When the business purpose doctrine is violated, such structuring is deemed to have gotten out of hand, to have been carried to such extreme lengths that the business purpose is no more than a façade. But there is no absolutely clear line between the two. Yet the doctrine seems essential. A tax system of rather high rates gives a multitude of clever individuals in the private sector powerful incentives to game the system. Even the smartest drafters of legislation and regulation cannot be expected to anticipate every device. The business purpose doctrine reduces the incentive to engage in such essentially wasteful activity, and in addition helps achieve reasonable equity among taxpayers who are similarly situated in every respect except for differing investments in tax avoidance. [201 F.3d at 513.]

The other approach is to focus more on the partners' specific economic arrangement and less on their subjective tax avoidance motivations or purpose. In TIFD III-E, Inc. v. U.S., 666 F.3d 836 (2d Cir. 2012), rev'g 660 F. Supp. 2d 367 (D. Conn. 2009) (sometimes referred to as "*Castle Harbour*"), the court refused to recognize a purported partnership between a U.S. corporation and two Dutch banks. It found that, based on the terms of the arrangement, the banks' interest was "overwhelmingly in the nature of a secured lender's interest." 666 F.3d at 837. The banks were virtually assured of receiving a specified minimum return on their invested capital, were fully protected against risk of loss (except to a *de minimis* extent in highly unlikely circumstances), and had only a very limited upside potential in the event of unexpectedly large partnership earnings. Since the banks were not bona fide equity participants in the venture, there was no valid partnership. Thus, the court rejected the taxpayer's attempt to shift taxable (but not economic) income to the essentially tax-exempt foreign banks, based on an abuse of the partnership "ceiling rule" (discussed in chapter six).

Problem 1-1: A homeowners' association purchases a $2,000 snow blower for use by its members. The members share the use of the blower and chip in to pay for any repairs or maintenance. Subsequently, the association agrees to allow non-member homeowners to use the snow blower for a small fee to defray the cost of gasoline, maintenance, and depreciation. Because some of the non-member homeowners are elderly, the association hires local children to operate the blower and perform snow removal work. The costs of these services are passed along to the non-member homeowners in the form of higher fees. The children, who enjoy the work and extra money, print flyers offering their services to all of the homes within a two-mile radius.

Does the homeowners' association have to report the results of these activities on a partnership tax return? Does it matter that there is no written partnership agreement and the members do not consider themselves to be partners?

2. *Not Taxable as a Corporation*

Read I.R.C. § 7701(a)(2) and (3). As you can see, a "partnership" is defined to include a variety of unincorporated organizations. But the term specifically excludes firms, such as "associations," that are treated as corporations for tax purposes.

The regulations promulgated under section 7701 specify which firms are classified as "associations" for tax purposes. Until 1997, these regulations set forth a mechanical corporate resemblance test, described by the Tax Court in Larson v. Comm'r, 66 T.C. 159, 172 (1976), as follows:

> The starting point of the regulations' definition of an "association" is the principle applied in *Morrissey v. Commissioner*, 296 U.S. 344 (1935), that the term includes entities which resemble corporations although they are not formally organized as such. *Morrissey* identified several characteristics of the corporate form which the regulations adopt as a test of corporate resemblance. For the purpose of comparing corporations with partnerships, the significant characteristics are: continuity of life; centralization of management; limited liability; and free transferability of interests. Other corporate or noncorporate characteristics may also be considered if appropriate in a particular case. An organization will be taxed as a corporation if, taking all relevant characteristics into account, it more nearly resembles a corporation than some other entity. . . . This will be true only if it possesses more corporate than noncorporate characteristics.
>
> The regulations discuss each major corporate characteristic separately, and each apparently bears equal weight in the final balancing. . . . This apparently mechanical

approach may perhaps be explained as an attempt to impart a degree of certainty to a subject otherwise fraught with imponderables.

These classification regulations were developed in response to efforts by taxpayers to *achieve* "association" status for their unincorporated entities. Doctors and other professionals sought that status to take advantage of pension and profit-sharing rules more favorable to *corporate* employees. (Many state laws at the time prohibited professionals from incorporating their practices.) Consequently, the regulations were widely perceived as biased against association status.

By the mid-1970s, changes in state and federal law eliminated the need for professionals to obtain association status for their unincorporated businesses. At the same time, tax shelters started to flourish. These shelters were often organized as limited partnerships in order to permit the passthrough of losses to their investors, and the classification regulations made it easy for such partnerships to avoid association status. See Larson v. Comm'r, supra.

In January 1977, the IRS issued proposed regulations that would have reversed the bias against association classification of entities organized as limited partnerships. The proposed regulations caused a major controversy and were promptly withdrawn. In 1980, the IRS tried again and put forward proposed regulations to the effect that an organization in which no member is liable for the debts of the organization, such as a limited liability company (LLC), would automatically be classified as an association and treated as a corporation for tax purposes. These regulations were also controversial and withdrawn.

By 1988, the IRS had clearly retreated from its prior positions. In Rev. Rul. 88-76, 1988-2 C.B. 360, it concluded that a Wyoming LLC could under certain circumstances be treated as a partnership for tax purposes. This ruling opened the floodgates as state after state authorized a similar form of business organization providing full limited liability protection for the owners of the enterprise while still maintaining enough "noncorporate" characteristics to qualify for partnership tax treatment under the classification regulations. An LLC statute was ultimately enacted by every state in the nation as well as the District of Columbia. The combination of limited liability and partnership taxation made the LLC the entity of choice for many new business ventures despite initial concern about the legal status of an LLC outside its state of organization. The IRS soon found itself flooded with ruling requests for the classification of businesses organized under the state LLC statutes. Although the rulings involved largely mechanical determinations, they nevertheless required a case-by-case analysis and were time-consuming. See, e.g., Rev. Rul. 93-38, 1993-1 C.B. 233 (discussing classification of two Delaware limited liability companies with different provisions in their respective LLC agreements, one classified as a partnership and the other as an association). Meanwhile, the Treasury questioned the utility of using scarce administrative resources for this purpose, given that "taxpayers can achieve partnership tax classification for a non-publicly traded organization that, in all meaningful respects, is virtually indistinguishable from a corporation." Notice 95-14, 1995-1 C.B. 297.

The Treasury therefore changed the classification regulations in 1996 to allow certain domestic, unincorporated business organizations to elect their status for federal tax purposes. The current regulations are commonly referred to as the "check-the-box" regulations because they provide a simple classification election. Read Reg. §§ 301.7701-1(a) and (b), -2(a), (b)(1)-(7), (c)(1) and (2)(i), -3(a), (b)(1) and (3)(i), (f)(1) and (2). The threshold question under the regulations is whether an organization qualifies as an entity separate from its owners for federal tax purposes. In general, an unincorporated organization (other than certain trusts) that is a separate entity with two or more owners may choose to be taxed as either a partnership or corporation. If no election is made, such an entity will generally be treated as a partnership by default. An entity with only one owner can elect corporate status; in the absence of an election, the separate nature of a single-owner entity is "disregarded" for tax purposes, and the entity is treated as a sole proprietorship, branch, or division. Ordinary trusts — arrangements merely to protect or conserve property for beneficiaries — are not provided with a classification choice because they generally do not have associates or an objective to carry on business for profit. A separate set of rules in the Internal Revenue Code (subchapter J) specifies how they are taxed. Business or commercial trusts — which are devices created by beneficiaries to operate profit-making ventures — are permitted, however, to make the classification election.

NOTES AND QUESTIONS

1. *Types of unincorporated business organizations.* The following describes the typical state-law characteristics of some of the most common forms of unincorporated business organizations eligible to make the check-the-box election. In general, the distinguishing feature of these organizations is the extent to which the owners of the organization may be held liable for its obligations. In a *general partnership*, the general partners are ordinarily jointly and severally liable for all of the obligations of the partnership. In contrast, in a *limited partnership*, comprised of both limited partners and at least one general partner, the liability of the limited partners may be limited to the amount of their investment in the venture. In addition, limited partners are generally precluded from being actively involved in the management of the business. In a *limited liability company* (LLC), all of the owners (termed "members") may have limited liability like limited partners but, unlike such partners, may also be involved in management. A *limited liability partnership* (LLP) is a special type of general partnership in which each partner is typically protected from liability for torts committed by those not under such partner's supervision. LLPs are popular among professional service firms because they may serve to insulate each partner from liabilities arising from malpractice committed by other partners. Finally, a *limited liability limited partnership* (LLLP) is a special type of limited partnership in which each general partner typically has no vicarious liability for torts committed

by other partners. Because some of these organizational forms are relatively new, their legal consequences may not be well established.

2. *Corporations.* The election is only available to *unincorporated* firms. Thus, corporations may not choose to be taxed under subchapter K. See Reg. § 301.7701-2(b)(1) and -3(a). How might the states respond to that restriction? Is the restriction likely to move the law in a sensible direction?

3. *Public firms.* In general, firms with publicly traded ownership interests, even though not incorporated, are also ineligible to be taxed under subchapter K. Instead, such firms are taxed as corporations. See I.R.C. § 7704(a); Reg. § 301.7701-2(b)(7) and -3(a). This rule does not apply to firms that derive 90 percent or more of their income from certain categories such as interest, dividends, rent and gain from real property, and income or gain from exploiting natural resources. Firms with such qualifying income may continue to be taxed as partnerships even though their ownership interests are publicly traded. Interests are considered publicly traded if they are traded on an established securities market, a secondary market, or the substantial equivalent thereof. Certain publicly traded private equity funds organized as partnerships have relied upon the qualifying income exception to avoid classification as a corporation. Achieving this objective requires creative structuring to ensure that the bulk of the income of the funds, which is active income from financial management services, is nevertheless treated as passive-type qualifying income. Legislative proposals would reverse the claimed result under section 7704. Avoiding corporate classification is also important to preserve another significant tax advantage relating to the receipt of a profits ("carried") interest by the fund managers; compensatory transfers of profits interests are discussed in chapter ten.

4. *Series LLCs.* Some states have authorized creation of a "Series LLC," which is a special form of LLC typically engaged in more than one business or investment activity. In general, each series of a Series LLC may have different members and managers, different business purposes or investment objectives, and different distribution and other governance rights. In certain circumstances, state law may allow the obligations relating to one series to be enforceable only against the assets of that series and not against those of a different series. For federal tax purposes, the question is whether a Series LLC should properly be treated as a single entity or multiple entities — or some hybrid of the two.

The Service has recently issued proposed regulations under section 7701 classifying series entities. Prop. Reg. § 301.7701-1(a)(5). Subject to general tax principles, each series is treated as a separate entity for federal tax purposes, regardless of its status for state law purposes. A series is defined as "a segregated group of assets and liabilities" established by a "series organization" (including a Series LLC or a series partnership) pursuant to a "series statute." Ownership of interests in the series (and of assets "associated with" the series) is determined based on who bears the economic benefits and burdens of ownership. Once separate entity status is established, each individual series is classified under the normal check-the-box rules, e.g., as a disregarded entity, partnership, or corporation. The proposed regulations thus leave open the possibility, for federal tax purposes, that a Series LLC and all of its series may constitute either a single entity or multiple entities. Collectively, a single tax entity exists if the Series LLC is treated as owning all of the interests in its series, each of which is classified as a single-owner disregarded entity. Alternatively, multiple tax entities exist if members of the Series LLC (who are associated with the series) are treated as owning interests in the series, each of which may separately elect its status.

5. *Validity of regulations.* Are the check-the-box regulations valid? For example, what authorized the Treasury to permit a limited liability company that resembles a corporation in all but name to elect to be taxed as a partnership? On the other hand, who might complain if they aren't valid? Can you think of a situation where a taxpayer might want to challenge the classification of a limited liability company as a partnership, in effect claiming that the entity is an association taxable as a corporation under the Code?

In Littriello v. U.S., 484 F.3d 372 (6th Cir. 2007), in a case of first impression, the Sixth Circuit upheld the validity of the check-the-box regulations. See also McNamee v. U.S., 488 F.3d 100 (2d Cir. 2007) (accord). In *Littriello*, the taxpayer was the sole owner of a limited liability company responsible for about $1 million of unpaid federal employment taxes. Because the company did not elect to be treated as a corporation, its status as a separate entity was disregarded for tax purposes and, therefore, the sole owner was liable for the taxes. Applying the "deferential" analysis of Chevron U.S.A., Inc. v. Natural Res. Def. Council, Inc., 467 U.S. 837 (1984), the court concluded that the regulations represented a reasonable administrative interpretation of section 7701. Revised regulations have since reversed the specific outcome in *Littriello* and treat an entity that is generally disregarded for tax purposes as, nevertheless, a corporation for employment tax purposes. Reg. § 301.7701-2(a) and (c)(2)(i) and (iv). This reversal was intended to conform federal employment tax law with that of the states, which generally continue to make the entity responsible for the reporting, collection, and payment of state employment tax despite the disregarded status of the entity for federal tax purposes.

6. *Classification changes.* Changes in the tax status of a firm may result either from a change in the firm's elected status or, in certain cases, from a change in the number of its owners. If a firm classified as a partnership elects to be treated as a corporation, the partnership is deemed to contribute all of its assets to a corporation in exchange for stock of the corporation and the partnership is then deemed to liquidate. In the reverse situation where a firm classified as a corporation elects to be treated as a partnership, the corporation is deemed to liquidate (in a taxable transaction) and the former shareholders are treated as contributing the distributed corporate assets to a newly formed partnership. Reg. § 301.7701-3(g)(1).

Rev. Rul. 99-5, 1999-1 C.B. 434, describes two possible ways in which a single-owner firm may acquire an additional member and subsequently be treated as a partnership for tax purposes. Under the first method, the single owner sells one-half of her interest in the firm to the new member. Under the second method, the new member contributes cash to the firm in exchange for an interest representing one-half of the firm. The ruling concludes that the first transaction results in a taxable sale by the original owner of half of the entity's assets whereas the second transaction does not trigger immediate taxation to anyone.

7. *Simplification?* As described in Notice 95-14, the check-the-box regulations were adopted as a simplification measure. Do you think that these regulations achieve that objective?

C. Tax Choices Available to Private Unincorporated Firms

The classification rules preclude public firms as well as all corporations from being taxed as partnerships. However, private unincorporated firms, no matter what their organizational characteristics, have a range of tax choices available to them. As we have seen, if they qualify as a "separate entity," they may be taxed as partnerships under subchapter K. Or, they may elect to be taxed as regular corporations under subchapter C, subjecting their income potentially to two taxes — one paid by the firm when the income is earned and another paid by the firm's owners when the income is realized by them. Finally, if they satisfy certain eligibility requirements, private unincorporated firms may be taxed as "S corporations," a special category of corporations described in subchapter S. An S corporation is taxed on a modified passthrough basis, but with generally less flexible rules than those available to partnerships.

The following excerpt describes some important differences between and among these three tax regimes. Consider whether you agree with its critical assessment of the availability of so many different tax choices.

American Law Institute Reporters' Study

Taxation of Private Business Enterprises 35-47 (1999)

As a result of a recent change by the Treasury Department, many private business enterprises, no matter what their organizational characteristics, are provided with an explicit choice regarding how the income of the firm is taxed. For firms engaged in general business activities, the choices under the "check-the-box" regulations of current law are generally the rules contained in subchapters C, K, and S of the Internal Revenue Code. Although incorporated firms are currently not provided with the same choice as unincorporated ones, an unincorporated business with *precisely* the same characteristics as an incorporated firm *is* given that choice. Hence, it seems only a matter of time before all private firms, incorporated and unincorporated, will be afforded the same explicit choice of taxation schemes.

This state of affairs is surprising. . . . [T]he separate entity taxation scheme of subchapter C and the conduit taxation approach of subchapter K can be traced to some extent to theories relating to the legal personality of corporations and partnerships. Corporations, as entities, were taxed independently from owners; partnerships, as aggregates, were not. And important in deciding whether a business organization constitutes an entity or an aggregate were the characteristics of the organization such as centralized management, continuous life, free transferability of ownership interest[s], and limited liability.

Other differences in the substantive rules of subchapters C and K bear out this entity/aggregate distinction. For example, liabilities incurred by a partnership, but not a corporation, are passed through and taken into account in determining the tax consequences of the owners of the firm.

Subchapter S . . . constitutes a middle ground between subchapters C and K. It provides a conduit form of taxation for certain businesses organized in corporate form. Nevertheless, perhaps because of its close relationship to subchapter C (a given business may move easily between the C world and the S world by the mere filing of an election) and because it has been applicable only to corporations, subchapter S retains many "entity" tax characteristics. Probably the most important is the refusal to permit corporate-level debt to pass through to the shareholders of an S corporation for income tax purposes. Furthermore, unlike subchapter K, there is no mechanism in subchapter S for adjusting the inside basis of a firm's assets upon the death of an owner, a transfer of ownership interests, or a distribution from the firm. Finally, S corporations, but not subchapter K firms, can participate in a tax-free reorganization with a C corporation.

Thus, each set of rules — most clearly in the case of subchapters C and K and less obviously in the case of subchapter S — was designed to apply to a particular form of business organization with specific characteristics. Yet, adoption of the check-the-box regulations reflects a policy determination generally to disregard business organization form and characteristics for income tax purposes. Given that, it is difficult to understand why private firms are nevertheless allowed a choice regarding how they are taxed, and why they are given the particular choices that they are.

If the three sets of rules produced more or less the same tax consequences in most situations, the choice among them might not be especially significant. But that is not the case. In any given situation, subchapters C, K or S may provide an advantageous tax result for particular taxpayers. For example, under subchapter C, the firm (and not the owners) is taxed on the business income when it initially arises and the owners are taxed on the same income when it is distributed to them. The possibility of double taxation, and the inability to net business income and losses with other tax items of the owners, is ordinarily unattractive to taxpayers. On the other hand, for many private subchapter C firms, the business income is initially taxed at graduated rates unrelated to the ability to pay of the owners. In addition, the second tax [on] such firms may be deferred or eliminated altogether, or may be levied at preferential rates. In combination with the graduated tax rate schedule, it is therefore possible for business income to be taxed more favorably under subchapter C than either subchapters K or S. Private firms may also select subchapter C because it allows the future conversion to public status to be without tax consequences, and entitles the firm to other special tax provisions.

In contrast, subchapters K and S [offer] a form of conduit taxation under which the firm is not taxed; instead, business income and losses are passed through to the owners of the firm. Thus, double taxation is avoided and owners are permitted to net any business income and losses with their other tax items. On the other hand, the owners must pay tax at their tax rates on the business income as it arises. Obviously, these features of conduit taxation may or may not be advantageous, depending upon the applicable tax rates and other factors. As between subchapters K and S, there are three significant tax differences in addition to the ones previously noted. Subchapter K but not subchapter S firms may specially allocate their tax items among their owners. In addition, the contribution and, especially, the distribution rules of subchapter S are more likely to result in the recognition of gains and losses than their subchapter K counterparts. Only subchapter K firms, however, are subject to a series of complicated rules designed to prevent tax advantages in selected situations. After taking into account all of the differences, subchapter S is usually less advantageous than subchapter K but in certain cases, it may be more advantageous.

There is some evidence that these differences have, in fact, influenced taxpayer behavior. Analysts who have examined this question have typically focused on possible taxpayer responses in the face of a change in the law that shifts the incentives from one method of taxation to another. One study concluded that the tax law changes of the Tax Reform Act of 1986 including, particularly, the change in the relationship between the maximum corporate and individual income tax rates, "had a large effect on how certain corporations chose to be taxed." Another study broke the ten-year period, 1985–1994, into five separate subperiods marked by important changes in the relationship of those tax rates, and found a distinct correlation in the expected direction between the rate relationship during the subperiod and the taxpayer choice of being taxed as an "individual" (sole proprietorship, subchapter K, or subchapter S) or corporation (subchapter C). Other studies of earlier tax years have reached similar conclusions.

The elective tax treatment of private firms under current law undermines both equity and efficiency objectives for the income tax. Although in theory, similarly situated businesses have an equal opportunity to be treated in the same tax-advantageous manner under current law, the practical reality is probably to the contrary, due to disparities in the quality of advice the businesses receive. By permitting such disparate tax choices without any apparent underlying, conceptual foundation, current law has simply provided a tax benefit for the well-advised and a trap for the ill-advised. There is no particular policy reason why the taxation of private business firms should result in the minimization of tax liabilities for only the well-advised. Moreover, current law violates vertical equity norms. By giving well-advised private business owners a range of tax liabilities to choose from, current law by definition cannot impose the "proper" level of tax on them based upon vertical equity principles.

The elective nature of current law fosters inefficiency in several ways. First, not all businesses are provided with the same tax benefit of being able to choose their tax liability within a range of options. Neither public firms nor sole proprietors, for example, are provided with the same degree of flexibility in determining the amount of their income tax liabilities. Thus, current law may distort the economic decisions of firms near the boundary of those eligible for the tax choice, thereby potentially causing deadweight losses. Indeed, private firms were already generally taxed more favorably than either of the other two types of businesses prior to the check-the-box regulations; the new choice for private firms simply tilts the tax scales further in their favor.

Second, as previously noted, not all eligible firms may make the optimal tax choice due to a variety of factors. But if, for whatever reasons, firms differ in their access to the tax minimization techniques, then allocative distortions across firms may result.

Finally and most importantly, current law is unnecessarily complicated and costly. To minimize tax burdens, businesses must consider the consequences of three possible operating rule systems on their anticipated business activities and learn to comply with the rules selected. The IRS must administer and give oversight to the three different systems. Further, the planning, compliance, and administration costs are ongoing in that businesses may have the opportunity to change their choice of rule structure as their business activities evolve or as other aspects of the law change. Reducing the number of choices should simplify the law and improve its efficiency by decreasing transaction costs.

In conclusion, the current system of taxing the income of private business enterprises has evolved into one that is inconsistent with its historical roots and violates important tax policy objectives. With the link between taxes and organizational form broken, there is no longer any clear justification to maintain all three systems of taxation. . . .

NOTES

1. *Eligibility conditions for S corporations.* To qualify as an S corporation, a firm must satisfy a number of conditions. It may not have more than 100 owners nor more than one class of ownership interests. Further, there are restrictions on who can own an S corporation, with nonresident aliens and certain entities specifically barred.

2. *Employment taxes.* In addition to the income tax differences, the choice of business form may affect the employment tax liability of the parties involved. Under current law, individuals are required to pay Social Security and Medicare taxes on their self-employment income. The Social Security tax is 12.4 percent of up to $118,500 (in 2016) of such income, and the Medicare tax is 2.9 percent (3.8 percent for certain high-income earners) of all self-employment income. (There is also a 3.8 percent tax on the net investment income of certain high-income individuals; this tax is intended to mirror the Medicare tax imposed on "earned income.")

How should taxpayers who are not sole proprietors determine their "self-employment income"? In general, owners of S corporations need *not* include their distributive share of the firm's income as part of their self-employment income, on the theory that the distributive share represents a return on their capital investment and not compensation for their labor efforts. The same is generally true of limited partners who, under state law, are ordinarily barred from participating too actively in their limited partnerships. See I.R.C. § 1402(a)(13) (generally exempting the distributive share of a "limited partner" from self-employment taxes). But cf. Renkemeyer v. Comm'r, 136 T.C. 137 (2011) (self-employment tax applies to services income, but not investment income, of LLP members who claimed to be limited partners). General partners, by contrast, must include their distributive share of partnership income as self-employment income. This rule is based on an assumption that a general partner is often actively engaged in the underlying business of the partnership.

Members of LLCs have presented the most difficult question because there is typically no "general" or "limited" distinction among members. Some members participate actively in the company business and others do not. The IRS has proposed regulations that try to distinguish between active and inactive LLC members for purposes of the self-employment tax. But these rules have proven to be highly controversial, and Congress has imposed a temporary moratorium to prevent them from becoming final. Thus, at present, the self-employment tax liability of LLC members is very much up in the air.

3. *Some data.* **Figure 1-1** shows the changing number of partnerships (including LLCs), C corporations, and S corporations between 1980 and 2012. The number of C corporations has generally declined since 1986, whereas the number of each type of passthrough entity has generally increased throughout the period. Both nontax and tax developments have contributed to these trends. The gradual shift in the economy during the period from manufacturing to service industries has reduced the number of firms (typically organized as C corporations) that require large amounts of capital. An important tax development was the adoption in 1986 of an inverted rate structure in which the top individual income tax rate was less than the corporate tax rate; this change fueled an increase in the number of S corporations and a decrease in the number of C corporations. In addition, legislative changes in 1986 curtailing tax shelters generally reduced the attractiveness of partnerships, but adoption of the check-the-box regulations in 1996 led to a sharp growth in the number of LLCs taxed as partnerships. Interestingly, although the LLC may have replaced to some extent the C corporation, the popularity of S corporations has steadily grown throughout the 32-year period. As described in the ALI excerpt, the tax rules for S corporations are less flexible, but simpler and generally more familiar, than those for entities taxed as partnerships. Particularly for firms with one or very few owners, the choice of an S corporation can often satisfy most tax and nontax objectives. The S corporation may also provide an advantage over other business forms in reducing liability for employment taxes and the tax on net investment income (I.R.C. § 1411). The principal category of business entity not represented

in **Figure 1-1** is the nonfarm sole proprietorship. By number, such proprietorships exceeded all of the other categories, increasing from 8.9 million in 1980 to 23.6 million in 2012. By comparison, there were about 4.2 million S corporations, 3.4 million partnerships (including LLCs), and 1.6 million C corporations in 2012. Among partnerships and LLCs, about one-half of all firms (and just under 30 percent of all partners and LLC members) were engaged in real estate or the rental and leasing sector in 2012.

Figure 1-2 shows the average amount of income (less deficits) reported by partnerships (including LLCs), S corporations, and nonfarm sole proprietorships between 1980 and 2012. The use of partnerships as tax shelters prior to 1986 is reflected in the very small amount of net income, or net losses, reported by those entities throughout the 1980s. That pattern has changed, however, and in 2012, partnerships reported income of almost $230,000 per firm, roughly twice the average amount reported by S corporations. The drop in the average income of both partnerships and S corporations during 2008 and 2009 reflected the economic recession. The income reported by C corporations is almost exclusively that of the large, public corporations and tends to fluctuate even more dramatically with the business cycle than the average income of the other business forms shown. In 2012, the average income of C corporations was about $650,000, or almost three times the average income of partnerships.

Figure 1-3 illustrates the increased share of total business income (that reported by C and S corporations, partnerships (including LLCs), and nonfarm sole

Figure 1-1: Number of Partnerships (including LLCs), C Corporations, and S Corporations, 1980-2012

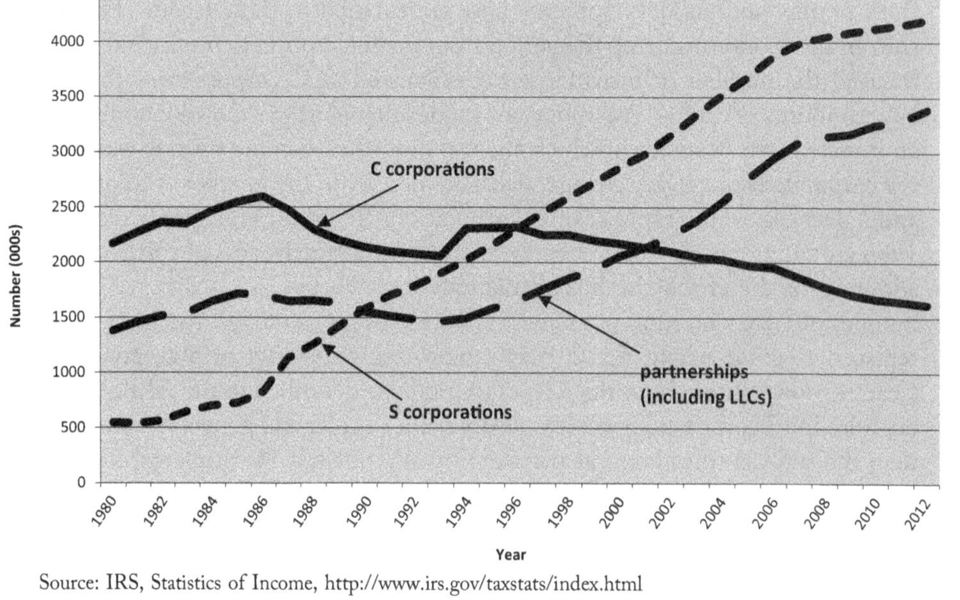

Source: IRS, Statistics of Income, http://www.irs.gov/taxstats/index.html

Figure 1-2: Average Income (Net Deficit) of Partnerships (including LLCs), S Corporations, and Nonfarm Sole Proprietorships, 1980-2012

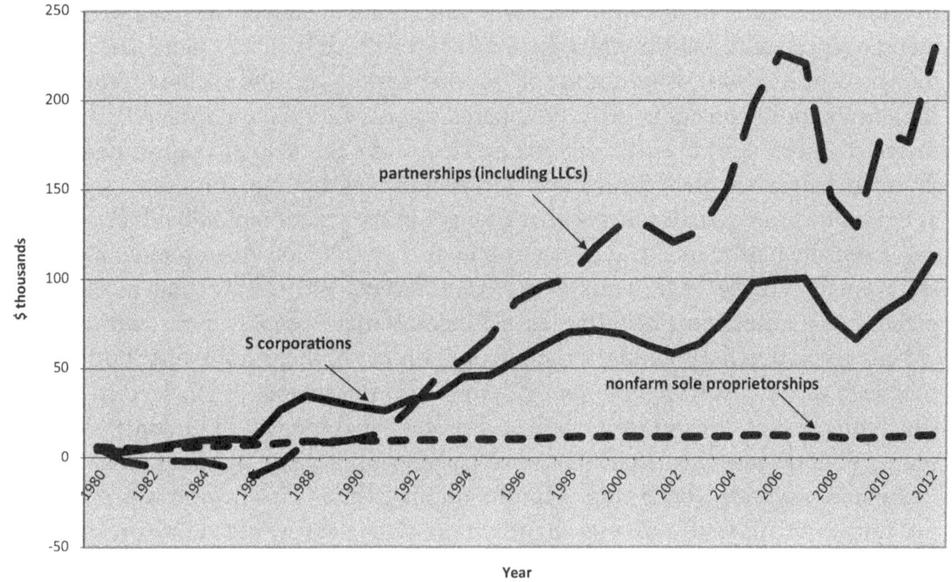

Source: IRS, Statistics of Income, http://www.irs.gov/taxstats/index.html

Figure 1-3: Portion of Total Business Income Reported by Partnerships (including LLCs), S Corporations, and Nonfarm Sole Proprietorships, 1980-2012

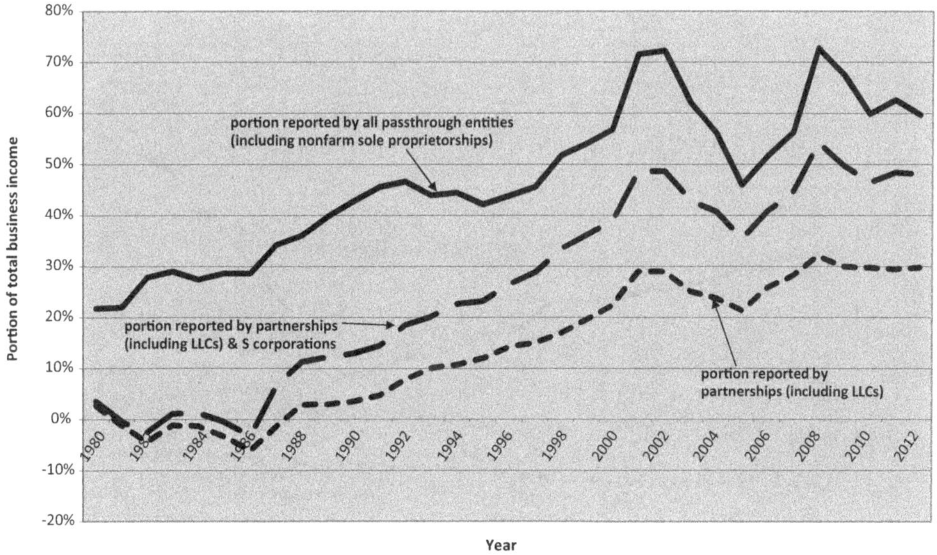

Source: IRS, Statistics of Income, http://www.irs.gov/taxstats/index.html

proprietorships) attributable to passthrough entities. The share of business income reported by partnerships (including LLCs) was about 30 percent in 2012 (compared to under three percent in 1980). If S corporations are included, the share of business income reported by passthroughs was almost 50 percent in 2012 (compared to about four percent in 1980). If nonfarm sole proprietorships are also included, this figure rises to about 60 percent in 2012 (compared to about 22 percent in 1980). Thus, an increasing portion of business income is taxed under the income tax for *individuals*. This fact helps to explain the declining importance of the U.S. corporate income tax as a revenue source. It also means that changes in the taxation of individuals, including especially higher income tax rates on upper-income taxpayers, may spark future shifts in the choice of business entity. One recent study found that in 2011, 69 percent of partnership (including LLC) income that was passed through to individuals accrued to households in the top one percent of the income distribution, and that such income was predominantly derived from partnerships engaged in finance (including real estate and insurance) and professional services. The study also estimated that, despite this large amount of partnership income accruing to very high-income households, the average tax rate on all partnership income was only 15.9 percent; this estimated rate was slightly more than the estimated rate on sole proprietor income (13.6 percent), but considerably lower than the estimated rates on the income of S corporations (24.9 percent) or C corporations (31.6 percent).

Figures 1-4, **1-5**, and **1-6** generally break down this information by type of partnership (including LLCs) for the period between 1986 and 2012. **Figure 1-4**

Figure 1-4: Number of Partnerships and LLCs, by Type, 1986-2012

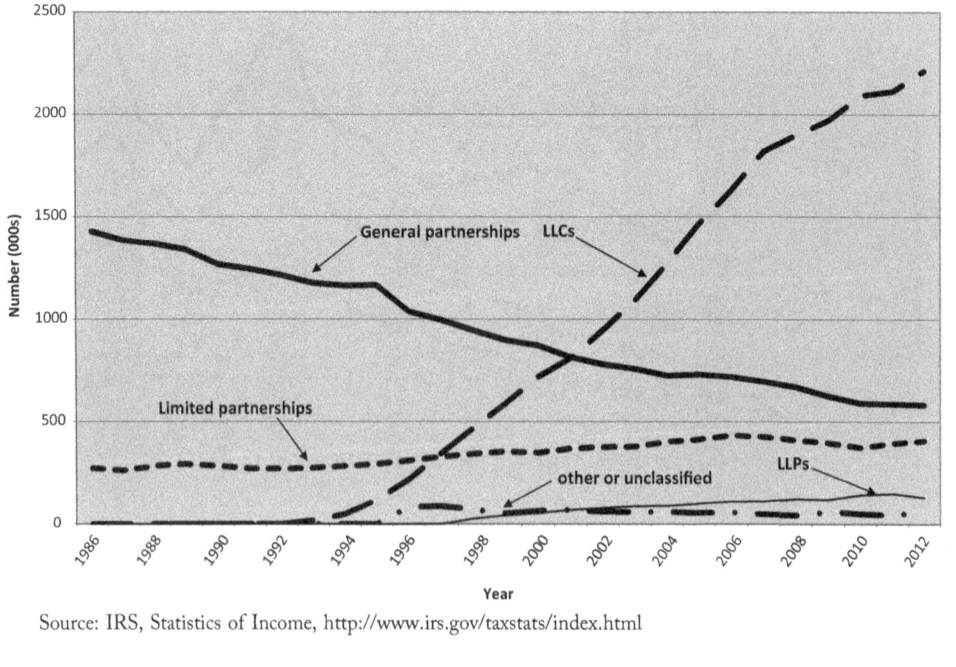

Source: IRS, Statistics of Income, http://www.irs.gov/taxstats/index.html

Figure 1-5: Number of Partners and LLC Members, by Type of Entity, 1986-2012

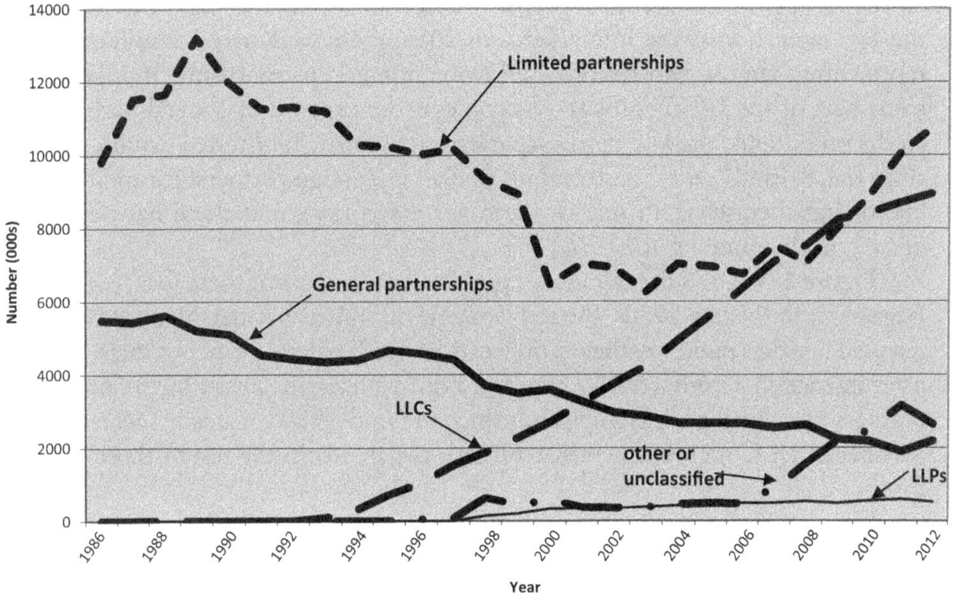

Source: IRS, Statistics of Income, http://www.irs.gov/taxstats/index.html

Figure 1-6: Net Income (Less Deficit) of Partnerships and LLCs, by Type of Entity, 1986-2012

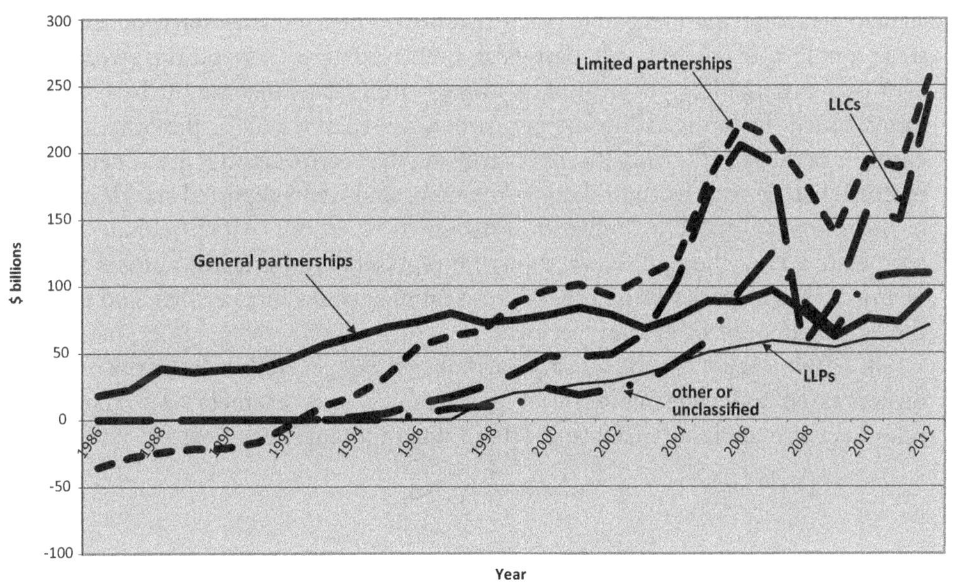

Source: IRS, Statistics of Income, http://www.irs.gov/taxstats/index.html

reveals the dramatic growth in the number of LLCs since the mid-1990s (when use of that form of business entity became widespread among the states and the check-the-box regulations went into effect). In 2012, there were over 2.2 million LLCs, representing almost two-thirds of all firms taxed as partnerships. It appears that some part of the LLC's growth has come at the expense of general partnerships. In the mid-1990s, the IRS began separately accounting for limited liability partnerships (LLPs) and "other" partnerships (including foreign partnerships and those not identifying themselves in one of the other categories), and there has been some growth in the number of LLPs.

Figure 1-5 shows the number of partners or members of these forms of entities. Beginning in the late 1980s, the reduced role of limited partnerships as tax shelters resulted in a decreased number of investors in that business form, but there has been a resurgence in recent years. There has been a steady decrease in the number of partners of general partnerships and, since the mid-1990s, a steady increase in the number of LLC members, consistent with the trends in the use of those business forms.

Figure 1-6 depicts the generally increasing amount of income, net of deficits, reported by all of these partnership forms since 1986. It clearly shows the change in the use of limited partnerships from entities that passed through losses during the 1980s to profit-reporting ventures since then. The erratic results during 2008 and 2009 again reflect the volatile economic conditions during that period.

Finally, **Table 1-1** provides data for 2012 on the average number of owners and income of the principal forms of passthrough business entities. With the principal exception of the limited partnership, which is sometimes used as an investment vehicle for large numbers of passive investors, these entities have on average a small number of owners. Of particular note is that S corporations average just over two shareholders per firm. The average amount of income of these business forms varied. In terms of income per owner, the LLP led all of the other business entities, perhaps reflecting the popularity of that form among firms performing professional services. Both limited partnerships and LLPs reported sizable amounts of income per firm. The "other or unclassified" category (which includes foreign partnerships) may be significant; though it represents the smallest number of firms of any of the categories, it had the highest number of owners per firm and reported the largest amount of income per firm.

4. *Terminology*. In the rest of this book, we will generally refer to the firms and owners taxed under subchapter K as "partnerships" and "partners" even though the rules may also apply to LLCs and other unincorporated ventures.

Table 1-1
Average Number of Owners and Income of Passthrough Business Entities – 2012

Form of organization	*firms (000s)*	*owners (000s)*	*owners/ firm*	*income ($Ms)*	*income/ firm ($)*	*income/ owner ($)*
Sole proprietors (non-farm)	23,554	23,554	1.0	304,896	12,945	12,945
General partnerships	583	2,186	3.7	95,200	163,293	43,550
Limited partnerships	407	10,753	26.4	259,900	638,575	24,170
S corporations	4,205	9,236	2.2	475,998	113,186	51,535
LLCs	2,212	8,947	4.0	242,500	109,629	27,104
LLPs	129	521	4.0	70,600	547,287	135,509
Other or unclassified	59	2,634	44.6	109,500	1,855,932	41,572

Source: IRS, Statistics of Income, http://www.irs.gov/taxstats/index.html

Chapter 2

The Passthrough System

A. Introduction

In this chapter, we examine the basic consequences of the decision to tax partnerships as conduits or passthrough entities. What does it mean to disregard the entity for tax purposes? A partnership, just like a sole proprietorship, is ordinarily not subject to tax. Instead, its income and other tax items are allocated among the partners who must report those items on their own tax returns. Nevertheless, we will discover that the partnership plays an important accounting function and performs virtually all of the tasks of a taxpayer other than paying tax. In that respect, the partnership is really a hybrid — it is respected for some tax purposes and disregarded for others. We will also explore some of the ramifications to the partners when a share of partnership income or loss passes through to them.

But before we parse the specific rules, read the following case involving a simple fact pattern. The case asks the fundamental question of whether the passthrough system provided by subchapter K is consistent with assignment-of-income principles you studied in the basic income tax course. Do any of the opinions in the case provide a satisfactory answer?

Schneer v. Commissioner

97 T.C. 643 (1991)

GERBER, Judge: [Petitioner is a former associate of the BSI law firm who was paid a fixed salary as well as a percentage of the fees received by the firm from clients he had brought to the firm. After he left BSI in 1983, he became a partner at two other law firms, B&K and then SSG&M. At each of them, he agreed to turn over to the firm any legal fees he received after joining the partnership.

In 1984 and 1985, BSI paid petitioner part of the fees it received from clients he had previously referred to the firm. Except for $1,250, the fees related to work done after petitioner left BSI. Although petitioner did a significant amount of consulting to help earn the fees, the court found that "[p]etitioner would have become entitled to his percentage of the fees even if he had not been called upon to consult." Pursuant to his agreements with B&K and SSG&M, petitioner turned the fees over to those firms which treated them as partnership income to be distributed to all of the partners, including petitioner, based on their partnership profit shares.]

. . . There is agreement that the amounts paid to petitioner by [BSI] are income in the year of receipt. The question is whether petitioner (individually) or the partners of petitioner's partnerships (including petitioner) should report the income in their respective shares.

The parties have couched the issue in terms of the anticipatory assignment-of-income principles. See *Lucas v. Earl*, 281 U.S. 111 (1930). Equally important to this case, however, is the viability of the principle that partners may pool their earnings and report partnership income in amounts different from their contribution to the pool. See sec. 704(a) and (b). The parties' arguments bring into focus potential conflict between these two principles and compel us to address both.

. . . The principle of assignment of income, in the context of Federal taxation, first arose in *Lucas v. Earl*, supra, where the Supreme Court . . . held that income from a husband-taxpayer's legal practice was taxable to him, even though he and his wife had entered into a valid contract under State law to split all income earned by each of them. In so holding, Justice Holmes, speaking for the Court, stated:

> There is no doubt that the statute could tax salaries to those who earned them and provide that the tax could not be escaped by anticipatory arrangements and contracts however skillfully devised to prevent the salary when paid from vesting even for a second in the man who earned it. [281 U.S. at 114-15.]

From that pervasive and simply stated interpretation, a plethora of cases and learned studies have sprung forth. Early cases reflected the use of the assignment-of-income principle only with respect to income not yet earned. The theory behind those interpretations was that income not yet earned is controlled by the assignor, even if assigned to another. Such income is necessarily generated by services not yet performed. Because the assignor may refuse to perform services, he necessarily has control over income yet to be earned. . . . This early rationale left open the possibility of successful assignments, for tax purposes, of income already earned. That possibility was foreclosed in *Helvering v. Eubank*, 311 U.S. 122 (1940), where the Supreme Court held that income already earned would also fall within the assignment-of-income doctrine of *Lucas v. Earl*, supra.

Respondent contends that *Helvering v. Eubank*, supra, is controlling in this case because petitioner had already earned the income in question at the time he entered into the partnership agreements. In that case, the taxpayer was an insurance agent who switched jobs and then assigned the future renewal commissions from policies already written. The taxpayer had written the policies and completed all work on them before leaving that job. The renewals and commissions were realized by the taxpayer solely due to the initiative and action of policyholders. . . . We must decide whether petitioner had earned the fees in question prior to assigning them to the B&K or the SSG&M partnerships. . . .

The transaction under consideration is one where petitioner had an agreement under which he would receive a percentage of fees received by BSI from clients who were referred by petitioner while he was an employee of BSI. Inherent in petitioner's unconditional right to payment is the condition precedent that billable services have been performed for the referred client. Additionally, petitioner's right to payment may also be subject to a second condition precedent that he may be required to consult and be involved in performing the services to be billed.

. . . [W]e hold that petitioner had not earned the fees in question prior to leaving BSI, with the exception of the $1,250 received for services performed in an earlier year. More specifically, we hold that petitioner earned the income in question while a partner of a partnership to which he had agreed to pay such income. With respect to substantially all of the fees in issue, BSI records reflect that clients were billed and payment received during the years in issue [1984 and 1985]. Moreover, if petitioner had refused a request for his consultation, it was, at very least, questionable whether he would have received his share of the fee if the work had been successfully completed without him. Petitioner was requested to and did provide further services with regard to clients from which about 90 percent of the fees were generated. . . . Accordingly, with the exception of $1,250 . . . we hold that petitioner had not earned the income in question prior to leaving BSI and did not make an anticipatory assignment of income which had been earned.

Two additional related questions remain for our consideration. First, respondent argues that irrespective of when petitioner earned the income from BSI, "there was no relationship . . . [between] the past activity of introducing a client to . . . [BSI], and the petitioner's work as a partner with . . . [B&K or SSG&M]." According to respondent, petitioner should not be allowed to characterize as partnership income fees that did not have a requisite or direct relationship to a partnership's business. In making this argument, respondent attempts to limit and modify his longstanding and judicially approved position in Rev. Rul. 64-90, 1964-1 C.B. 226 (Part 1). . . . Second, while we generally hold that petitioner did not make an assignment of income already earned, the possibility that this was an assignment of unearned income was not foreclosed.

These final two questions bring into focus the true nature of the potential conflict in this case — between respondent's revenue ruling and the assignment-of-income doctrine. Both questions, in their own way, ask whether any partnership agreement — under which partners agree in advance to turn over to the partnership all income from their individual efforts — can survive scrutiny under the assignment-of-income principles.

Rev. Rul. 64-90 . . . in pertinent part, contains the following:

> . . . several individuals formed a partnership for the purpose of engaging in the general practice of law. Aside from the partnership business, each of the partners has performed services from time to time in his individual capacity and not as a partner. The

several partners have always regarded the fees received for such services as compensation to the recipient as an individual.

The partnership . . . files its Federal income tax returns for fiscal years ending January 31, and the partners file their individual returns . . . for calendar years. Each partner reports his distributive share of the partnership income, gain, loss, deduction or credit for the partnership fiscal year ending within the calendar year for which his individual return is filed. All compensation received by each partner for services performed in his individual capacity is reported in that partner's return for the calendar year when received.

It is proposed to amend the partnership agreement as of the beginning of the partnership's next fiscal year to provide that all compensation received by the partners be paid over to the partnership immediately upon receipt.

The question in the instant case is whether compensation remitted to the partnership pursuant to this provision will constitute partnership income. . . .

In the instant case, the general practice of the partnership consists of rendering legal advice and services. Consequently, fees received by a partner for similar services performed in his individual capacity will be considered as partnership income if paid to the partnership in accordance with the agreement. Those fees need not be reported separately by the partner on his individual return. However, the partner's distributive share of the partnership's taxable income which he must report on his individual return will include a portion of such fees. [Emphasis supplied.]

A key requirement of this ruling is that the services for which fees are received by individual partners must be *similar* to those normally performed by the partnership. . . . Respondent now attempts to add to this requirement by arguing that the fees here in question were earned through activity, which was admittedly legal work, but was not sufficiently related to the work of petitioner's new partnerships. In other words, respondent argues that the income here was earned in BSI's business activity and not B&K's or SSG&M's business activity. . . .

There is no need for us to adopt a broader view of petitioner's partnership in this case. His referral fee income was clearly earned through activities "within the ambit" of the business of his new partnerships. Their business was the practice of law as was petitioner's consulting activity for BSI. His work was incident to the conduct of the business of his partnerships. We decline to adopt respondent's more narrow characterization of the business of petitioner's new partnerships. Neither the case law nor respondent's rulings support such a characterization.

Thus, we arrive at the final question in this case. We have already held that petitioner had not yet earned the majority of the income in question when he joined his new partnerships. Additionally, petitioner's fee income from his BSI clients qualifies, under the case law and respondent's rulings, as income generated by services sufficiently related to the business conducted by petitioner's new partnerships. If we decide that petitioner's partnerships should report the income in question, petitioner would be taxable only to the extent of his respective partnership share. This would allow petitioner, through his partnership agreements with B&K and SSG&M, to assign income not yet earned from BSI. Thus, the case law and respondent's rulings permit (without explanation), in a partnership setting, the type of assignment addressed by *Lucas v. Earl.* We must reconcile the principle behind Rev. Rul. 64-90 with *Lucas v. Earl.* The question is whether income not yet earned and anticipatorily assigned under certain partnership agreements are [outside] the reach of the assignment-of-income principle. . . .

The fundamental theme penned by Justice Holmes provides that the individual who earns income is liable for the tax. It is obvious that the partnership, as an abstract entity, does not provide the physical and mental activity that facilitates the process of "earning" income. Only a partner can do so. The income earned is turned over to the partnership due solely to a contractual agreement, i.e., an assignment, in advance, of income.

The pooling of income is essential to the meaningful existence of subchapter K. If partners were not able to share profits in an amount disproportionate to the ratio in which they earned the underlying income, the partnership provisions of the Code would, to some extent, be rendered unnecessary. . . .

The provisions of subchapter K tacitly imply that the pooling of income is permissible. Said implication may provide sufficient reason to conclude that a partnership should be treated as an entity for the purpose of pooling the income of its partners. Under an entity approach, the income would be considered that of the partnership rather than the partner, even though the partner's individual efforts may have earned the income. If the partnership is treated as an entity earning the income, then assignment-of-income concepts would not come into play.

In this regard, an analysis of personal service corporations (PSC's) may provide, by way of analogy, some assistance in reconciling the principles inherent in Rev. Rul. 64-90 with those underlying *Lucas v. Earl.* . . . In both, a separate entity—the partnership or personal service corporation—is cast as the "earner" for tax purposes. That characterization in both situations is, in essence, an assignment of income. . . .

In analyzing the status of personal service corporations, courts have relied upon the rationale that:

> the realities of the business world present an overly simplistic application of the Lucas v. Earl rule whereby the true earner may be identified by merely pointing to the one actually turning the spade or dribbling the ball. Recognition must be given to corporations as taxable entities which, to a great extent, rely upon the personal services of their employees to produce corporate income. When a corporate employee performs labors which give rise to income, it solves little merely to identify the actual laborer. Thus, a tension has evolved between the basic tenets of Lucas v. Earl and recognition of the nature of the corporate business form.

. . . Thus, an employee of a personal service corporation, or other corporate entity, is outside the holding of *Lucas v. Earl*, supra, to some degree because of the "entity concept." The business entity is cast as the earner of the income, obviating the need to analyze whether there has been an assignment of income.

The same type of approach may be used with respect to partners of a partnership. In the same manner that a corporation is considered the earner of income gained through the labor of its employees, a partnership, with an appropriate partnership agreement, may be considered the earner of income. Income earned prior to such an agreement, of course, remains within the principles and holding of *Lucas v. Earl.* The link between respondent's Rev. Rul. 64-90 and *Lucas v. Earl* must be the entity concept as it relates to partnerships.

The theory concerning partnerships as entities is not easily defined. It is well established that the partnership form is a hybrid—part separate entity, part aggregate. . . . For purposes of an entity concept approach to partnerships, we must consider the type and source of income which should be included. Because we have already determined that the type of activity generating the income is relevant to an assignment-of-income analysis in the partnership setting, we focus our analysis of partnerships as entities on situations where the income is of a type normally earned by the partnership. Only in such situations has a partner acted as part of the partnership entity.

The entity concept as it relates to partnerships is based, in part, on the concept that a partner may further the business of the partnership by performing services in the name of the partnership or individually. The name and reputation of a professional partnership plays a role in the financial success of the partnership business. If the partners perform services in the name of the partnership or individually they are, nonetheless, associated with the partnership as a partner. This is the very essence of a professional service partnership, because each partner, although acting individually, is furthering the business of the partnership. . . .

Accordingly, in circumstances where individuals are not joining in a venture merely to avoid the effect of *Lucas v. Earl,* it is appropriate to treat income earned by partners individually, as income earned by the partnership entity, i.e., partnership income, to be allocated to partners in their respective shares. To provide the essential continuity necessary for the use of an entity concept in the partnership setting, the income should be earned from an activity which can reasonably be associated with the partnership's business activity. In the setting of this case, with the exception of $1,250 in 1984, petitioner was a partner of B&K or SSG&M when the fees were earned. Additionally, about 90 percent of the fees were, in part, earned through petitioner's efforts while he was a partner of B&K or SSG&M.

There is no apparent attempt to avoid the incidence of tax by the formation or operation of the partnerships in this case. Petitioner, in performing legal work for clients of another firm, was a partner with the law firms of B&K and SSG&M. In view of the foregoing, we hold that, with the exception of $1,250 for 1984, the fee income from BSI was correctly returned by the two partnerships in accord with the respective partnership agreements. . . .

Reviewed by the court.

BEGHE, J., concurring: . . . I reach the majority result in the following two steps. Even if the assignment-of-income doctrine requires petitioner to include in his gross income the amounts of the fees he earned and received from BSI after he became a partner in B&K and in SSG&M, his payments of those amounts to B&K and SSG&M, pursuant to his agreements with those firms, entitled him to equivalent concurrent deductions as ordinary and necessary business expenses under section 162(a). . . . Those amounts thereby became partnership income distributable to all the partners, including petitioner, in accordance with the partnership agreements.

WELLS, J., dissenting: . . . The critical threshold issue framed by the majority is whether the fees were paid to petitioner for services he performed prior to leaving BSI or for services he performed after he left BSI. If the fees were for services performed by petitioner prior to the time he left BSI, they are "past services" which should be taxed to petitioner under the rule of *Helvering v. Eubank*, 311 U.S. 122 (1940). On the other hand, if the fees were paid to petitioner for services to be performed by him after he left BSI, they are future services, *Eubank* does not apply, and the income should be taxed to the partners of petitioner's subsequent law firms. . . .

Several considerations support a conclusion that the fees were not earned by petitioner after he left BSI. As found by the majority, the basis of petitioner's entitlement to fees from BSI was the act of having brought or referred clients to BSI. . . . Furthermore, the "consultation" services actually performed by petitioner must have been inconsequential, as the majority does not even take the trouble to detail them. . . . The amount of petitioner's fee was in no way related to the value of the services he performed. To the contrary, the amount of the fee was dependent upon the value of the services BSI rendered to the clients, a matter over which petitioner had little or no control. Finally, the fact that petitioner and BSI did not address whether petitioner's right to the fees would be jeopardized by his failure to consult indicates that BSI's right, and, for that matter, the clients' right to obtain additional services from petitioner was not important to them and was not the reason for the fee arrangement. . . . [T]he majority states that "it was, at very least, questionable" whether petitioner would receive his fee without performing consulting services. The majority's statement, however, is little more than speculation. . . .

[T]he majority's findings concerning the nature of the relationship between petitioner and BSI [show] that the actual event giving rise to the right to the fees was the past services of petitioner in securing the clients for BSI. Accordingly, I would hold that the fee income was taxable to petitioner under assignment of income principles, as required by *Eubank*.

HALPERN, J., dissenting: . . . [The majority's] analysis wholly ignores the doctrine of agency. When a partner, *acting as agent for the partnership*,[1] performs services for a client, the partnership is the earner of the income: the instrumentality (in this case the partner) through which the partnership has earned its fee is of no

1. The Uniform Partnership Act, sec. 9(1), provides that a (general) partner is an agent of the partnership. . . .

consequence. Therefore, the focus of the anticipatory assignment-of-income analysis ought to be on whether the partner acted for himself individually or as agent of the partnership. This is entirely consistent with the [latitude] accorded partnerships to disproportionately distribute partnership income: the pertinent requirement is merely that the partnership income so distributed have been earned by the partnership. In this case, it is quite clear that petitioner earned the fees in question pursuant to an agreement he entered into, on his own behalf, with [BSI] — an agreement that was consummated before petitioner's relationship with [B&K]. Consequently, petitioner is the true earner of the income and should not escape taxation by means of an anticipatory assignment. *Lucas v. Earl*, 281 U.S. 111.

. . . The majority considers the determinative question to be whether the income is "of a type normally earned by the partnership. Only in such situations has the partner acted as part of the partnership entity." The majority requires merely that income "be earned from an activity which can reasonably be associated with the partnership's business activity." Thus, the majority would allow a partner to assign fees to the partnership if the work performed for such fees is similar to that performed by the partnership, but not if the work is different.

The majority's distinction is unprincipled.[2] The majority observes that "The name and reputation of a professional partnership plays a role in the financial success of a partnership business" suggesting that partners, even acting individually, can further the business of the partnership by adding to its reputation. But, that may be so even if the partner acts individually, doing work entirely dissimilar to that normally performed by the partnership. In any event, the majority fails to explain why such an obviously incidental benefit to the partnership should permit us to frustrate the assignment-of-income doctrine. . . . All that matters is whether the partner has acted on his own behalf or on behalf, and as agent of, the partnership. . . . It would make far more sense to ask, with agency principles in mind, whether the income in question was earned by the partnership or by the partner acting as an individual. . . .

NOTES AND QUESTIONS

1. *Core issue*. The majority opinion eventually reaches the core issue: When partners agree to pool the income generated by their future efforts, does the taxation of such income under subchapter K violate assignment-of-income principles? Inherent in this question is an assumption that the income tax consequences under subchapter K for any given year will not exactly reflect each partner's contribution to the income in such year. As the majority states: "If partners were not able to share profits in an amount

---

2. The majority fails to explain why the similarity of the work done by the partner to earn the fees to the work of the partnership is determinative. That failure not only casts doubt upon the correctness of this decision, but foreshadows the difficulty future courts will have in resolving the question: how similar is similar enough? Without any inkling of why similarity has been deemed important, future courts will lack any effective guidelines for answering that question.

disproportionate to the ratio in which they earned the underlying income, the partnership provisions of the Code would, to some extent, be rendered unnecessary."

To resolve this fundamental issue, begin, as the majority does, with the case of a personal service corporation (PSC). A PSC is a corporation whose principal activity is the performance of personal services provided by a shareholder-employee of the corporation, usually the principal or sole shareholder. If the corporation is taxed under subchapter C, it is treated as a taxpayer separate from its shareholders and pays corporate tax on its income. See I.R.C. § 11(a) and (b). Yet a PSC's "income" is often nothing more than the return resulting from the personal efforts of its shareholder. How then can taxing the PSC on such income be reconciled with a no-assignment-of-income principle? What legal principle justifies that outcome? How does the Code try to prevent taxpayers from using a PSC to reduce their income tax liabilities?

Now consider the same questions in connection with a service partnership such as a law or medical firm. Again, what principle permits the conclusion that the partnership as an entity has any income at all? How is that income taxed under subchapter K? Is it easier to reconcile the no-assignment-of-income principle in the PSC context than in the partnership context?

2. *Earned vs. unearned income.* The discussion in both the majority opinion and Judge Wells' dissent concerning whether the taxpayer's income was earned or unearned at the time of the assignment may seem strange in view of the Lucas v. Earl and *Eubank* precedents. As explained in the majority opinion, those two cases seem to prohibit assignment of income *regardless* of whether the income is earned or unearned when assigned. Yet, in the partnership context at least, the tax law seems much less willing to permit assignment of income that has already been earned. For example, you will soon encounter section 704(c), which is intended to prevent the shifting of unrealized but economically accrued income from one partner to another.

3. *What's the holding?* Try to articulate the holding of this case. Under what specific conditions would the majority respect an assignment of income such as Mr. Schneer's in the future?

4. *Rev. Rul. 64-90.* Review closely the facts of Rev. Rul. 64-90, excerpted in the majority opinion. Note particularly the partnership's choice of a fiscal year ending January 31. We will return to the taxable year issue very shortly.

B. Determination and Passthrough of Partnership Tax Items

1. *In General*

Read I.R.C. §§ 701-703. While a partnership is ordinarily not subject to income tax, it nevertheless plays an important accounting role. A partnership must calculate its taxable income and other tax items and make many tax elections for the business, including choosing a method of accounting and taxable year. Can you figure out why? Once the tax items are calculated, the partnership must inform the partners of their "distributive share" of the items and the partners must then report that share on their own tax returns (and pay any applicable tax). "Distributive share" is a bit of a misnomer; the term refers to the share allocated to a particular partner, whether or not any distribution occurs.

Section 703(a) provides that a partnership must compute its taxable income as an individual, except that it may not claim deductions for personal exemptions, foreign taxes, charitable contributions, net operating losses, and certain itemized deductions, among other things. Why not?

The partnership must also state separately the items listed in section 702(a). This is just an illustrative list because of the expansive regulatory authority provided by section 702(a)(7). See if you can determine the purpose for the separate-statement requirement. For example, why is a partnership barred from claiming a charitable contribution deduction (section 703(a)(2)(C)) but required to state separately to the partners their share of the partnership's charitable contributions (section 702(a)(4))? Additional items that must be separately stated, including any specially allocated items, are specified in Reg. § 1.702-1(a)(8)(i), and a "catch-all" requirement is found in Reg. § 1.702-1(a)(8)(ii). Items not required to be separately stated can be lumped together and passed through to the partners as a single, residual item under section 702(a)(8); this amount is commonly referred to as the "bottom-line" item.

In addition to computing its tax items, a partnership must file a tax return (Form 1065) by the 15th day of the third month after the close of the partnership's taxable year. See I.R.C. §§ 6031(a), 6072(b). This is only an "information return" because no tax is assessed on or paid by the partnership. The partnership attaches to its return copies of the information (Schedule K-1) it has provided to the partners to inform them of their distributive share of separately stated and bottom-line items. A copy of Form 1065 and Schedule K-1 are included in the appendix.

In chapters four through six, we will examine in some detail how a partner's "distributive share" of items is determined.

2. *Partnership Taxable Year*

Read I.R.C. § 706(b)(1)(A). As you can see, the partnership must select its own taxable year. This rule is consistent with the partnership's accounting function: to accommodate partners who might have different taxable years, the partnership selects a taxable year and calculates its taxable income accordingly.

But when does a partner report income if her taxable year differs from the partnership's taxable year? The rule of reconciliation is contained in section 706(a). Read it very carefully. The operative portion of the provision says that a partner must include her share of partnership items for the partnership's taxable year "ending within or with the taxable year of the partner." Try to understand what these words mean by applying them to the following problem.

> **Problem 2-1:** Formerly, service partnerships like law firms typically selected a taxable year ending near the beginning of the calendar year, such as a January 31 or February 28 year. (Recall the facts in Rev. Rul. 64-90, discussed in *Schneer* (pp. 31-32).) Why were such taxable years so popular? Was it simply an effort by the partnership's accountants to stagger taxable years and thereby avoid heavy burdens during the busy year-end holiday period?
>
> Assume that a law firm uses a taxable year ending January 31. Joe, a calendar-year taxpayer and an associate of the firm, is admitted as a partner effective February 1 of Year 1. Assume that during his first three years as a partner, Joe's share of partnership income is earned ratably, $20,000 each month beginning in February of Year 1 and ending in January of Year 4. Determine how much taxable income Joe must report in Years 1-3 under the general rule of section 706(a), assuming the partnership's January 31 year is permissible. What would Joe have had to report if the firm had instead used a December 31 taxable year? What result if Joe had practiced as a sole practitioner and earned the income directly in those years?

As **problem 2-1** illustrates, the administrative simplicity of allowing a partnership to choose its own taxable year must be balanced against the need to prevent undue tax deferral to its partners. Congress, therefore, has restricted the taxable years that a partnership may select with three general objectives in mind: (1) allow firms to select a taxable year that serves a legitimate business need; (2) match the partnership's taxable year as closely as possible to that of the partners to minimize the deferral of income; and (3) provide stability by not requiring changes in the firm's taxable year too frequently. To understand how the rules seek to achieve those objectives, read section 706(b) and analyze the following problem.

> **Problem 2-2:** What taxable year may the partnership select in the following situations? Assume that there is no business purpose for any particular year.
>
> (a) A newly formed partnership has five partners: A, a 44 percent partner with a 6/30 taxable year; B, also a 44 percent partner with a 6/30 taxable year; and C, D, and E, each a 4 percent partner with a 12/31 taxable year.
>
> (b) Same as (a), except that at the very end of the partnership's first year, B sells its 44 percent interest to partner F; F uses a 12/31 taxable year.
>
> (c) Same as (b), except that B's sale of its 44 percent interest is to 11 new partners, each of which acquires 4 percent of the partnership and uses a 9/30 taxable year.

NOTES AND QUESTIONS

1. *Business purpose.* A partnership is entitled to use any taxable year for which it can establish a legitimate business purpose. See I.R.C. § 706(b)(1)(C). One example is a "natural business year," defined as any 12-month period if the partnership earns 25 percent or more of its gross receipts in the final two months of the period and that pattern is repeated for three consecutive 12-month periods. See Rev. Proc. 2002-38, 2002-1 C.B. 1037, § 5.05. A toy business, for example, might be able to qualify for a January 31 taxable year under this rule. If this test cannot be satisfied, a partnership may still be able to meet the business purpose standard based on facts and circumstances, but the IRS scrutinizes these cases very closely.

2. *Least aggregate deferral.* Pursuant to its regulatory authority in section 706(b)(1)(B)(iii), the IRS requires partnerships to use a taxable year which produces the "least aggregate deferral" if neither the majority interest nor principal partner rules is applicable. The regulations illustrate this rather complicated trial-and-error method for determining the particular taxable year that minimizes deferral. See Reg. § 1.706-1(b)(3)(i) and (iv) (examples).

To illustrate this method, assume in **problem 2-2(b)** that F uses a 5/31 taxable year. Now what taxable year may the partnership select (again assuming that there is no business purpose for a particular year)? See Reg. § 1.706-1(b)(3)(i) and (iv) (ex. 1).

3. *Section 444 election.* Notwithstanding the restrictions in section 706(b), section 444 permits a partnership to elect any taxable year that does not result in more than three months of deferral at the partner level. Read I.R.C. § 444(a), (b), and (e). Under section 444, what taxable years are permissible for a law firm comprised solely of calendar-year partners?

The price of the section 444 election is that the partnership must make essentially an interest-free deposit with the government that is intended to compensate approximately for the benefit of deferral to the partners. See I.R.C. § 7519. The required payments under section 7519 are recomputed annually and excess payments may be refunded. If section 7519 provides an adequate offset for the deferral benefit, should the tax law expand the section 444 election to permit a partnership to elect *any* taxable year on condition that it make the required deposits?

Assume that a partnership makes a valid election under section 444 to have a taxable year ending on September 30, resulting in a deferral benefit for any partners not using that year. If the partnership's income remains constant during the following year, is there any additional deferral benefit in the later year?

4. *Why so many choices?* Large accounting firms played a pivotal role in urging some form of relief from section 706(b), and their efforts culminated in the enactment of sections 444 and 7519. What concerns may have animated the accounting industry?

5. *Loss acceleration.* Can a partnership manipulate its taxable year in order to accelerate losses?

3. *Partnership Elections*

Read I.R.C. § 703(b). To ensure consistent tax accounting, the tax law generally requires that the partnership make any election affecting computation of its taxable income. The statute provides only three exceptions to this rule. Section 703(b)(1), for example, requires partners to make their own elections under section 108(b)(5) and (c)(3) relating to discharge of indebtedness income. This exception follows from the fact that partnership discharge of indebtedness income passes through to the partners who then apply separately the rules of section 108 depending on their particular circumstances. See I.R.C. § 108(d)(6). The general rule of partnership-level elections can have surprising results if partners are unaware of the existence of a partnership for federal tax purposes. If partners are eligible to elect out of subchapter K under section 761(a), they may be able to make independent elections.

Demirjian v. Commissioner

457 F.2d 1 (3d Cir. 1972)

VAN DUSEN, Circuit Judge: . . . The tax deficiencies [of plaintiffs Anne and Mabel Dermirjian] were based on the failure to report $54,835.00 in gain for the taxable year 1962. Plaintiffs maintain that the gain in question is covered by the nonrecognition provisions of Code Section 1033. . . . [W]e agree with the ruling of the Tax Court that § 703 of the Internal Revenue Code requires that the nonrecognition of gain election and replacement under § 1033 be made by Kin-Bro Realty, a partnership, and that the replacements by plaintiffs individually were thus ineffective.

The facts . . . show that Anne and Mabel Demirjian each owned 50% of the stock of Kin-Bro Realty Corporation, which had acquired title to a three-story office building in Newark, New Jersey, in October 1944. On November 3, 1960, the corporation was dissolved and its chief asset, the office building, was conveyed by deed to "Anne Demirjian . . . and Mabel Demirjian . . . partners trading as Kin-Bro Real Estate Company." Although no formal partnership agreement was executed, Anne and Mabel did file a trade name certificate indicating that they intended to conduct a real estate investment business at the Newark office building under the name of Kin-Bro Real Estate Company. The office building, which constituted Kin-Bro's sole operating asset, was conveyed to the Newark Housing Authority on September 12, 1962, after an involuntary condemnation proceeding. In the deed of conveyance the grantors are listed as "Anne Demirjian and Mabel Demirjian, partners trading as Kin-Bro Real Estate Company." The net proceeds of the sale were distributed to Anne and Mabel in amounts equal to approximately 50% of the total sale price. At this point, both Anne and Mabel apparently elected to replace the property with equivalent property in order to take advantage of the nonrecognition of gain provision contained in § 1033 of the Internal Revenue Code. Normally gain resulting from the sale or exchange of investment real property is taxable, but § 1033 provides that if property is involuntarily converted and the proceeds are used to replace it with substantially equivalent property within one year,[3] then gain is recognized only to the extent that the amount received due to the conversion exceeds the purchase price of the replacement property. The reinvestments, however, were made by Anne and Mabel as individuals and not through the partnership. On April 15, 1963, Anne invested $40,934.05 of her share of the proceeds in property which was similar to the condemned property. Mabel was unable to find suitable replacement property within the one-year replacement period, and, by letter of October 17, 1963, she made a written application to the District Director of Internal Revenue, Newark, New Jersey, for an extension of time in which to make such a replacement. In a letter dated January 16, 1964, the District Director stated:

> . . . [A]n extension of time was requested for the purpose of replacing your share of the partnership property that was owned by Kin-Bro Real Estate Company (a partnership). The property was sold to the Housing Authority of the City of Newark on September 12, 1962 under threat of condemnation.
>
> You have stated that although you have made a continued effort to replace the converted property, you have not been successful to date. . . . Based on the information submitted, together with the data already in our file, extension is hereby granted until December 31, 1964, within which to complete the replacement of the converted property.

On February 7, 1964, Mabel invested $45,711.17 in similar real estate. Neither Anne nor Mabel reported any portion of the gain realized on the condemnation sale in their initial returns for the 1962 tax year. In 1964 Anne and Mabel filed amended 1962 joint returns with their husbands, reporting the excess of their distributive share from the condemnation sale over the cost of their respective replacement property as long-term capital gains. The Commissioner of Internal Revenue disagreed with these computations and assessed deficiencies, reasoning that the § 1033 election for nonrecognition of gain and replacement with equivalent property could only be made by the partnership under the terms of § 703(b) of the Code. The Tax Court affirmed the Commissioner's finding of deficiencies and plaintiffs here appeal that decision. . . .

Petitioners' first contention on this appeal is that the Newark office building was owned by Anne and Mabel as tenants in common, not as partners, and that, therefore, the § 1033 nonrecognition of gain election and replacement was properly made by them in their individual capacities as co-tenants. On the basis of the record before the Tax Court, we find that the property in question was owned by Kin-Bro Realty, a partnership, composed of Anne and Mabel Demirjian. It is noted that several federal cases have ruled that taxpayers such as petitioners who represent, in their dealings

3. Now generally two years. See I.R.C. § 1033(a)(2)(B)(i). — Eds.

with the Internal Revenue Service, that property is owned by a partnership are bound by such representations.

Petitioners next contend that even if the office building was owned by the partnership, the election and replacement with equivalent property under 26 U.S.C. § 1033(a)(3) were properly made by them in their capacity as individual partners. We agree with the Tax Court's determination that 26 U.S.C. § 703(b) requires that the election and replacement under § 1033 be made by the partnership and that replacement by individual partners of property owned by the partnership does not qualify for nonrecognition of the gain. Section 703(b) provides, with exceptions not relevant here, that any election which affects the computation of taxable income derived from a partnership must be made by the partnership. The election for nonrecognition of gain on the involuntary conversion of property would affect such computation and is the type of election contemplated by § 703(b). The partnership provisions of the Internal Revenue Code treat a partnership as an aggregate of its members for purposes of taxing profits to the individual members and as an entity for purposes of computing and reporting income. In light of this entity approach to reporting income, Congress included § 703(b) to avoid the possible confusion which might result if each partner were to determine partnership income separately only on his own return for his own purposes. To avoid the possible confusion which could result from separate elections under § 1033(a), the election must be made by the partnership as an entity, and the failure of the partnership to so act results in the recognition of the gain on the sale of partnership property.

Petitioners' final contention is that the Commissioner is estopped from denying that a valid election and replacement were made under § 1033. Two separate grounds for estoppel are alleged. The first ground, that the petitioners have conformed their conduct to existing interpretations of the law and the Commissioner may not "invoke a retroactive interpretation to the taxpayer's detriment," is clearly without merit. The second alleged ground is that the Commissioner is estopped by the implicit approval of the individual partner's election and replacement by the District Director for Newark in his letter of January 16, 1964. Even if we were to accept the letter as a justifiable basis for detrimental reliance, petitioners have demonstrated no such reliance and, furthermore, the doctrine of estoppel does not prevent the Commissioner from correcting errors of law. . . .

NOTES AND QUESTIONS

1. *Policy of section 703(b). Demirjian* provides an excellent example of why status as a partnership matters as well as the importance of obtaining proper tax advice. The court notes that the requirement concerning partnership-level elections is intended "to avoid the possible confusion which might result if each partner were to determine partnership income separately . . . for his own purposes." Would allowing each partner in *Demirjian* to make separate section 1033 elections have resulted in confusion? Does the result in *Demirjian* seem particularly harsh?

2. *Planning*. Suppose only one of the two partners in *Demirjian* had wished to make a section 1033 election, while the other partner was willing to recognize gain immediately on her share of the condemnation proceeds. Could the partnership have accommodated these differing objectives by first distributing the condemned property to the partners as joint tenants and then allowing them to decide individually whether to reinvest the proceeds in similar property?

3. *Method of accounting*. Under the authority of section 703(b), a partnership selects its own method of accounting. As with the choice of taxable year, Congress has imposed restrictions on what accounting method a partnership may use. Read I.R.C. § 448(a). Because a C corporation generally cannot use the cash method of accounting, partnerships are likewise precluded from using it if any partner is a C corporation. The same prohibition applies to any partnership qualifying as a "tax shelter"; the definition of this term is sufficiently broad to include any partnership that allocates a substantial portion of its losses to passive investors, as well as any publicly offered partnership. The prohibition on use of the cash method does not apply to a partnership (other than a tax shelter) whose average annual gross receipts do not exceed $5 million for the prior three years.

4. *Special passthrough rules for electing large partnerships*. Certain large partnerships may elect to be taxed under a somewhat simplified passthrough system. See I.R.C. §§ 771-777. To be eligible for this system, a partnership generally must not be a service partnership and must have at least 100 members. See I.R.C. §§ 775(a)(1), (b)(2). The large-partnership provisions are intended primarily to simplify reporting and administration by reducing the number of separate partnership items that must be flowed through to the partners. With certain exceptions, a large partnership nets most items of income or loss and reports a single figure to its partners. See I.R.C. § 772(a). Any limitations in computing taxable income are generally applied at the partnership level; most elections (including the large-partnership election) are also made by the partnership. See I.R.C. § 773(a)(2), (3). Streamlined reporting is intended to facilitate computerized matching of partner and partnership returns.

Since their inception, the large-partnership rules have not been widely used. This may reflect the fact that the simplification benefits for eligible firms, which may have fairly sophisticated tax advisors, are outweighed by the imprecision and other disadvantages resulting from use of the rules. In 2015, Congress repealed the large partnership rules, effective for partnership taxable years beginning in 2018. Would it make more sense to try to devise instead a simplified passthrough system for "small" partnerships? How should small partnerships be defined?

4. *Characterization Issues*

How is the character of partnership income determined? For example, suppose a partnership is a dealer with respect to real property but a particular partner is not. What is the character of any income or loss the partner must report from that activity? Read I.R.C. § 702(b). The usual interpretation of this rather opaque provision is illustrated by the following case.

Podell v. Commissioner

55 T.C. 429 (1970)

QUEALY, Judge: . . . In this case, during each of the years 1964 and 1965, petitioner entered into an oral agreement with Young for the purchase, renovation, and sale of certain residential real estate. Profit and loss realized on the sale of such property was shared equally by petitioner and Young.

Petitioner maintains that the properties sold were capital assets and that any gains on those sales should be taxed as capital gains.

Respondent argues that the oral agreements between petitioner and Young established a partnership or joint venture for the purposes of purchasing, renovating, and selling real estate in the ordinary course of business, and that consequently, the gains arose from the sale of noncapital assets and are to be treated as ordinary income.[4]

We have found as an ultimate fact that the agreement between petitioner and Young gave rise to a joint venture. Under section 761(a), a joint venture is included within the definition of a "partnership.". . .

A joint venture has been defined as a "special combination of two or more persons, where in some specific venture a profit is jointly sought without any actual partnership or corporate designation." . . .

The elements of a joint venture are: (a) A contract (express or implied) showing that it was the intent of the parties that a business venture be established; (b) an agreement for joint control and proprietorship; (c) a contribution of money, property, and/or services by the prospective joint venturers; and (d) a sharing of profits, but not necessarily of losses (although some jurisdictions require that there be a sharing of losses). . . .

In many respects, the concept of joint venture is similar to the concept of partnership, and many of the principles of partnership law are applicable to joint ventures. . . . A primary distinction between the two concepts is that a joint venture is generally established for a single business venture (even though the business of managing the venture to a successful conclusion may continue for a number of years) while a partnership is formed to carry on a business for profit over a long period of time. . . .

It is undisputed that petitioner and Young joined in an agreement establishing a joint business venture to acquire, improve, and resell residential property at a profit, and it is immaterial that the petitioner was motivated, in part, by social objectives. There was a contribution to the business of property, services, or money by each of the parties involved. Petitioner and Young also agreed to share equally in any resulting gain or loss.

4. According to section 1221, the term "capital asset" does not include property held by the taxpayer primarily for sale to customers in the ordinary course of his trade or business. — EDS.

The fact that petitioner did not exercise as much managerial control over the day-to-day activities relating to the purchase, renovation, and sale of the real estate as Young is not sufficient reason for this Court to find against the existence of a joint venture. While petitioner gave Young discretion with respect to all aspects of the purchase, renovation, and sale of the real estate in question, petitioner retained the power to approve of the steps undertaken by Young to execute their agreement through his control over his continued contributions of funds to the venture. . . .

The real estate acquired by the joint venture is to be considered partnership property for purposes of taxation. . . . Section 702(b) establishes the "conduit rule" for the income taxation of partnerships. . . .

In essence, the "conduit rule" requires that for the purpose of determining the nature of an item of income, gain, loss, deduction, or credit in the hands of the partnership before distribution or a partner . . . after distribution, the partnership is to be viewed as an entity and such items are to be characterized from the viewpoint of the partnership rather than from the viewpoint of an individual partner. Thus, the phrase "his trade or business" in section 1221(1) clearly refers to the trade or business of the partnership, despite the fact that under section 701 partnerships are not subject to income tax. It is the intent of the partnership and not that of any specific partner which is determinative in characterizing the income for purposes of taxation. . . .

The trade or business of the joint venture or partnership in this case during the years in question was the purchase, renovation, and sale of certain residential real estate irrespective of and separately from the various businesses or professions of the individual joint venturers. The real estate sold by the joint venture was held for sale to the customers of the joint venture in the ordinary course of the joint venture's business with the consequence that the residential real estate parcels were not capital assets in the hands of the joint venture. Consequently, the income realized by the joint venture on the sale of the real estate was ordinary income. Therefore, applying the "conduit rule" of section 702(b), this income remained ordinary income in the hands of the joint venturers. . . .

NOTES AND QUESTIONS

1. *Issue.* The basic issue in *Podell*, like that in *Demirjian* (p. 41) and *Wheeler* (p. 7), is whether the parties had formed a separate entity taxable under the subchapter K rules. Each court found that an entity had been formed, which benefitted Wheeler but not Podell or the Demirjians. Make sure that you understand why.

2. *Planning opportunity?* Suppose an investor and a real-estate developer undertake a joint venture to develop and sell a single piece of property. Do section 702(b) and the *Podell* case mean that the developer's share of income from this investment might be capital gain? Cf. I.R.C. § 724(b).

3. *"Conduit rule."* Although the court refers to section 702(b) as the "conduit rule," the net result in this case (and others) is to respect the partnership as an entity for tax purposes. Similarly, the long-term or short-term nature of partnership gain or loss from the sale of property is determined by how long the partnership holds the

property, and not how long a partner owns an interest in the partnership. See Rev. Rul. 68-79, 1968-1 C.B. 310.

4. *Characterization of management fees in "fund of funds" arrangement.* In Rev. Rul. 2008-39, 2008-2 C.B. 252, an individual owned a limited partnership interest in an upper-tier partnership ("UTP"), which owned limited partnership interests in several lower-tier partnerships ("LTPs"). UTP's activities consisted solely of investing in the LTPs which were engaged in the business of trading in securities. Both the LTPs and the UTP paid annual fees to their respective managers for management services performed on their behalf. Since the LTPs' management fees were incurred in connection with the conduct of a trade or business and deductible under section 162(a), the IRS concluded that the fees could be netted with the LTPs' other bottom-line items in computing the taxable income or loss passed through to the UTP under section 702(a)(8). UTP's distributive share of this amount similarly constituted part of its bottom-line items passed through to the individual limited partner under section 702(a)(8). As a result, the "trade or business" character of the LTPs' management fees passed through to the UTP's individual limited partner who obtained the equivalent of an above-the-line deduction for such fees. In contrast, because the UTP was engaged solely in an investment-type activity (and was not treated as conducting the trade or business of the LTPs), its own management fees were deductible under section 212 rather than section 162(a). Therefore, the UTP's management fees had to be separately stated and were potentially deductible by the individual limited partner only as an itemized deduction subject to various limitations, including the two percent floor under section 67. See I.R.C. §§ 702(a)(7), 703(a)(2)(E); Reg. § 1.702-1(a)(8)(i). See also Rev. Rul. 2008-38, 2008-2 C.B. 249 (interest expense incurred by partnership engaged in trade or business of trading securities retained its "trade or business" character when passed through to limited partner; thus, it was an above-the-line deduction but subject to the investment interest limitation of section 163(d)).

In Dagres v. Comm'r, 136 T.C. 263 (2011), the taxpayer was a shareholder-employee of an S corporation and a member manager of an LLC taxable as a partnership (the "UTP") that advised and managed a venture capital fund (the "LTP"). The UTP held a one percent general partner interest in the LTP and also received a 20 percent profits ("carried") interest and an additional fee for its management services (the latter fee was paid directly to the S corporation, and the taxpayer and other corporate employees actually performed the services). The issue was the character of the taxpayer's bad debt deduction when a loan made by the taxpayer to a third party to obtain business leads for the venture capital fund became worthless. The court found that the UTP's management of the LTP was a trade or business that was deemed carried on by the taxpayer. The court concluded that the primary motivation for the taxpayer's loan was to further that trade or business (rather than advance any investment purpose or his business activity as an employee of the S corporation). 136 T.C. at 290. Accordingly, the taxpayer was entitled to an ordinary, above-the-line deduction for the bad debt, not a miscellaneous itemized deduction (subject to the section 67 limitation) or a "nonbusiness" bad debt deduction allowable only as a short-term capital loss under section 166(d)(1).

5. *Tougher characterization questions.* The proper characterization of the partnership's income is relatively straightforward in *Podell*. In other contexts, however, this question and the treatment of a partnership as an entity or an aggregate can be much more murky. Read the following case and see whether you agree with its holding.

United States v. Basye

410 U.S. 441 (1973)

Mr. Justice POWELL delivered the opinion of the Court: [Permanente, a limited partnership comprised of physicians, agreed to provide medical services to Kaiser, a nonprofit organization offering prepaid medical services to its members. As part of the partnership's "base compensation" for the medical services, Kaiser agreed to pay amounts to a trust to fund retirement benefits on behalf of partner and nonpartner physicians of Permanente who had completed a minimum service requirement and had elected to participate. Under the trust agreement, no portion of the trust fund was treated as vested in any particular beneficiary, and a physician could forfeit his interest in the fund under a variety of circumstances, including separation from Permanente prior to retirement. Under no circumstances, however, could Kaiser recover any of the payments to the trust. Neither Permanente nor any of its partners reported any income as a result of Kaiser's payments to the trust. The Commissioner assessed deficiencies against each partner-respondent for his distributive share of the amount paid by Kaiser.]

The Commissioner premised his assessment on the conclusion that Kaiser's payments to the trust constituted a form of compensation to the partnership for the services it rendered and therefore was income to the partnership. And, notwithstanding the deflection of those payments to the retirement trust and their current unavailability to the partners, the partners were still taxable on their distributive shares of that compensation. Both the District Court and the Court of Appeals disagreed. They held that the payments to the fund were not income to the partnership because it did not receive them and never had a "right to receive" them. . . . They reasoned that the partnership, as an entity, should be disregarded and that each partner should be treated simply as a potential beneficiary of his tentative share of the retirement fund.[5] Viewed in this light, no presently taxable income could be attributed to these cash basis[6] taxpayers because of the contingent and forfeitable nature of the fund allocations. . . .

---

5. The Court of Appeals purported not to decide, as the District Court had, whether the partnership should be viewed as an "entity" or as a "conduit." 450 F.2d 109, 113 n.5, and 115. Yet, its analysis indicates that it found it proper to disregard the partnership as a separate entity. After explaining its view that Permanente never had a right to receive the payments, the Court of Appeals stated:

> When the transaction is viewed in this light, the partnership becomes a mere *agent* contracting on behalf of its members for payments to the trust for their ultimate benefit, rather than a *principal* which itself realizes taxable income. Id., at 115 (emphasis supplied).

6. Each respondent reported his income for the years in question on the cash basis. The partnership reported its taxable receipts under the accrual method.

We hold that the courts below erred and that respondents were properly taxable on the partnership's retirement fund income. This conclusion rests on two familiar principles of income taxation, first, that income is taxed to the party who earns it and that liability may not be avoided through an anticipatory assignment of that income, and, second, that partners are taxable on their distributive or proportionate shares of current partnership income irrespective of whether that income is actually distributed to them. The ensuing discussion is simply an application of those principles to the facts of the present case. . . .

Section 703 of the Internal Revenue Code of 1954, insofar as pertinent here, prescribes that "[t]he taxable income of a partnership shall be computed in the same manner as in the case of an individual." 26 U.S.C. § 703(a). Thus, while the partnership itself pays no taxes, 26 U.S.C. § 701, it must report the income it generates and such income must be calculated in largely the same manner as an individual computes his personal income. For this purpose, then, the partnership is regarded as an independently recognizable entity apart from the aggregate of its partners. Once its income is ascertained and reported, its existence may be disregarded since each partner must pay a tax on a portion of the total income as if the partnership were merely an agent or conduit through which the income passed.

In determining any partner's income, it is first necessary to compute the gross income of the partnership. One of the major sources of gross income, as defined in § 61(a)(1) of the Code, is "compensation for services, including fees, commissions, and similar items." There can be no question that Kaiser's payments to the retirement trust were compensation for services rendered by the partnership under the medical service agreement. These payments constituted an integral part of the employment arrangement. . . . Nor was the receipt of these payments contingent upon any condition other than continuation of the contractual relationship and the performance of the prescribed medical services. Payments to the trust, much like the direct payments to the partnership, were not forfeitable by the partnership or recoverable by Kaiser upon the happening of any contingency.

Yet the courts below, focusing on the fact that the retirement fund payments were never actually received by the partnership but were contributed directly to the trust, found that the payments were not includable as income in the partnership's returns. The view of tax accountability upon which this conclusion rests is incompatible with a foundational rule, which this Court has described as "the first principle of income taxation: that income must be taxed to him who earns it." *Commissioner v. Culbertson*, 337 U.S. 733, 739-740 (1949). The entity earning the income — whether a partnership or an individual taxpayer — cannot avoid taxation by entering into a contractual arrangement whereby that income is diverted to some other person or entity. Such arrangements, known to the tax law as "anticipatory assignments of income," have frequently been held ineffective as means of avoiding tax liability. The seminal precedent, written over 40 years ago, is Mr. Justice Holmes' opinion for a unanimous Court in *Lucas v. Earl*, 281 U.S. 111 (1930). . . .

The principle of *Lucas v. Earl*, that he who earns income may not avoid taxation through anticipatory arrangements no matter how clever or subtle, has been repeatedly invoked by this Court and stands today as a cornerstone of our graduated income tax system. . . . And, of course, that principle applies with equal force in assessing partnership income.

Permanente's agreement with Kaiser, whereby a portion of the partnership compensation was deflected to the retirement fund, is certainly within the ambit of *Lucas v. Earl*. The partnership earned the income and, as a result of arm's-length bargaining with Kaiser, was responsible for its diversion into the trust fund. . . . We may assume . . . that many partnerships would eagerly accept conditions similar to those prescribed by this trust in consideration for tax-deferral benefits of the sort suggested here. We think it clear, however, that the tax laws permit no such easy road to tax avoidance or deferment. Despite the novelty and ingenuity of this arrangement, Permanente's "base compensation" in the form of payments to a retirement fund was income to the partnership and should have been reported as such. . . .

Since the retirement fund payments should have been reported as income to the partnership, along with other income received from Kaiser, the individual partners should have included their shares of that income in their individual returns. 26 U.S.C. §§ 61(a)(13), 702, 704. For it is axiomatic that each partner must pay taxes on his distributive share of the partnership's income without regard to whether that amount is actually distributed to him. . . . Few principles of partnership taxation are more firmly established than that no matter the reason for nondistribution each partner must pay taxes on his distributive share. . . .

The courts below reasoned to the contrary, holding that the partners here were not properly taxable on the amounts contributed to the retirement fund. This view, apparently, was based on the assumption that each partner's distributive share prior to retirement was too contingent and unascertainable to constitute presently recognizable income. It is true that no partner knew with certainty exactly how much he would ultimately receive or whether he would in fact be entitled to receive anything. But the existence of conditions upon the actual receipt by a partner of income fully earned by the partnership is irrelevant in determining the amount of tax due from him. . . . It should be clear that the contingent and unascertainable nature of each partner's share under the retirement trust is irrelevant to the computation of his distributive share. The partnership had received as income a definite sum which was not subject to diminution or forfeiture. Only its ultimate disposition among the employees and partners remained uncertain. For purposes of income tax computation it made no difference that some partners might have elected not to participate in the retirement program or that, for any number of reasons, they might not ultimately receive any of the trust's benefits. . . .

NOTES AND QUESTIONS

1. *When did the income arise?* One of the issues presented in *Basye* concerns the timing of the income. The uncertain receipt of retirement benefits by any particular trust beneficiary, all of whom used the cash method of accounting, raised the question whether any of them received a "cash equivalent" when Kaiser made the payments to the trust. Should taxation instead have been deferred until the rights of any particular beneficiary became vested? Or should the partnership's use of the accrual method of accounting have been determinative?

2. *Whose income was it?* There were at least five possible answers to the question concerning whose income it was: the partnership, the partners, the trust, the trust beneficiaries, and Kaiser. (Kaiser might be taxed by denying it a deduction for the amounts paid to the trust.) Note that the partners and the trust beneficiaries were not identical. Some of the beneficiaries were physicians associated with Permanente who were not partners of the partnership. Conversely, some of Permanente's partners elected not to participate in the retirement trust or might eventually be determined to be ineligible to receive any benefits.

The Court relies in part on Lucas v. Earl to disregard what the Court perceives as an attempted assignment of income to the trust. But is there any irony in relying upon the no-assignment-of-income principle in this case? Recall the *Schneer* case (p. 29). Who earned the income in *Basye*? Under the Court's holding, who is taxed on that income?

3. *Qualified plans. Basye* also raises an issue concerning the proper treatment of pension plans. Contributions to a qualified pension plan are generally deductible by the contributor even though the taxation of the beneficiaries is deferred until they begin to receive benefits at retirement. Furthermore, the investment income of the plan is tax-exempt. This favorable tax treatment arises, however, only if the plan does not discriminate in favor of highly compensated employees and meets a number of other requirements. See I.R.C. § 401(a)(4). The plan in *Basye* presumably did not satisfy those requirements. Yet, the taxpayer sought the equivalent of these benefits.

C. Basis Adjustments and Limitation on the Passthrough of Losses

1. Basis Adjustments

Although the passthrough system disregards the existence of the partnership entity for the important purpose of paying tax on the business income, the entity is nevertheless respected for nontax purposes. Thus, partners generally do not own direct interests in the assets of the partnership; rather, they own interests in the partnership as a whole, which is analogous to owning stock in a corporation. In general, under state law, it is the partnership that owns the assets and earns the business income. A partner obtains direct ownership of such assets only upon their "distribution" by the partnership to the partner.

This inconsistency between tax law and state partnership law creates the need for certain additional rules. Consider the following example:

> **Example 2-1:** Assume that your daughter, Laura, operates a lemonade stand as a sole proprietorship and in Year 1, the business has net profits of $20. In that case, her basis in the business is automatically increased by $20, either in the form of money retained or business assets acquired with the money, because the proprietorship is not legally separate from Laura. The basis increase ensures that upon a subsequent sale of the business, Laura will not have to pay tax again on the same $20.
>
> Now assume the same facts except that the business is conducted through a partnership and Laura's share of its operating profits for the year is $15. Under the passthrough system, the $15 of profits is not taxed to the partnership but instead is passed through to Laura and taxable to her. While the partnership increases *its* basis in its assets by $15 if it retains the profits, some mechanism is also necessary to adjust Laura's basis in her partnership interest. Otherwise, on a subsequent sale of that partnership interest, she might be taxed again on the same profits.

Current law addresses this problem by prescribing a series of increases and decreases to the basis of a partner's interest in a partnership, usually referred to as "outside basis." (The partnership's basis in its assets is usually referred to as "inside basis.") As we will see, these adjustments are part of a broader goal in subchapter K to maintain parity between the partnership's total inside basis and the partners' total outside basis. Read I.R.C. § 705 and do the following problem.

Problem 2-3:

(a) In **example 2-1**, above, what happens to Laura's outside basis under current law when she is allocated a $15 share of the partnership's operating profits? Does your answer change if the partnership's profits consist entirely of capital gains?

(b) Same as (a), except that Laura, for whatever reason, fails to include her $15 distributive share in her taxable income. What is her outside basis now?

(c) Same as (b), except that the reason Laura fails to report the income is that the $15 distributive share consists entirely of tax-exempt interest income. Does your answer reach a sound policy outcome?

(d) Suppose that the partnership distributes the $15 of earnings to Laura currently. What are the tax consequences to Laura? See I.R.C. §§ 731(a)(1), 733(1).

Example 2-1 and **problem 2-3** illustrate that outside basis adjustments are a fundamental part of any passthrough system. Now test your understanding of the purpose of basis adjustments in a slightly more complicated setting.

Problem 2-4: Suppose that A and B are equal partners of partnership PRS. PRS makes a charitable contribution of property X whose value is $100*x* and whose basis in PRS's hands is $60*x*. Assume that, under section 170(a), a charitable contribution deduction equal to the fair market value of the appreciated property would normally be allowed to an individual contributor. As a result of the partnership's charitable contribution, what adjustment, if any, should be made to the outside bases of A and B? Consider the following possibilities: each partner should reduce her outside basis by (a) $50*x*, (b) $30*x*, or (c) $0. Which is the correct solution? In your reasoning, consider whether the possible answers reach the proper tax result if A (or B) sells her partnership interest subsequent to the partnership's charitable contribution.

To evaluate your intuition in **problem 2-4**, above, read the following excerpt from Rev. Rul. 96-11, on which the problem was modeled.

Rev. Rul. 96-11

1996-1 C.B. 140

... The adjustments to the basis of a partner's interest in a partnership under § 705 are necessary to prevent inappropriate or unintended benefits or detriments to the partners. Generally, the basis of a partner's interest in a partnership is adjusted to reflect the tax allocations of the partnership to that partner. This ensures that the income and loss of the partnership are taken into account by its partners only once. In addition, as provided in § 705(a)(1)(B) and (a)(2)(B), adjustments must also be made to reflect certain nontaxable events in the partnership. For example, a partner's share of nontaxable income (such as exempt income) is added to the basis of the partner's interest because, without a basis adjustment, the partner could recognize gain with respect to the tax-exempt income, for example, on a sale or redemption of the partner's interest, and the benefit of the tax-exempt income would be lost to the partner. Similarly, a partner's share of nondeductible expenditures must be deducted from the partner's basis in order to prevent that amount from giving rise to a loss to the partner on a sale or a redemption of the partner's interest in the partnership. . . .

In determining whether a transaction results in exempt income within the meaning of § 705(a)(1)(B), or a nondeductible, noncapital expenditure within the meaning of § 705(a)(2)(B), the proper inquiry is whether the transaction has a permanent effect on the partnership's basis in its assets, without a corresponding current or future effect on its taxable income. Pursuant to § 703(a)(2)(C), the contribution of X by PRS is not taken into account by PRS in computing its taxable income. Consequently, the contribution results in a permanent decrease in the aggregate basis of the assets of PRS that is not taken into account by PRS in determining its taxable income and will not be taken into account for federal income tax purposes in any other manner. Therefore, for purposes of § 705(a)(2)(B), the contribution of X, and the resulting permanent decrease in partnership basis, is an expenditure of the partnership not deductible in computing its taxable income and not properly chargeable to capital account. . . .

Reducing the partners' bases in their partnership interests by their respective shares of the permanent decrease in the partnership's basis in its assets preserves the intended benefit of providing a deduction (in circumstances not under § 170(e)) for the fair market value of appreciated property without recognition of the appreciation. By contrast, reducing the partners' bases in their partnership interests by the fair market value of the contributed property would subsequently cause the partners to recognize gain (or a reduced loss), for example, upon a disposition of their partnership interests, attributable to the unrecognized appreciation in X at the time of this contribution.

Under the PRS agreement, partnership items are allocated equally between A and B. Accordingly, the basis of A's and B's interests in PRS is each decreased by $30x. . . .

NOTES AND QUESTIONS

1. *"Losses of the partnership."* Section 705(a)(2)(A) provides that outside basis must be reduced by a partner's share of "losses of the partnership." The reference to partnership "losses" is interpreted broadly to include any deduction or loss passed through to the partner. For example, a partner who is allocated a $100 share of the partnership's interest deduction must reduce outside basis by $100 as a result of that allocation.

2. *Section 1031 exchanges.* Suppose that a partnership exchanges Blackacre for Whiteacre in a transaction qualifying under section 1031, when Blackacre is worth $1,000 and has a basis of $700 in the partnership's hands. Under section 1031(a), the partnership's realized gain of $300 is not recognized. What effect, if any, should this transaction have on the outside basis of E, a 50 percent partner?

3. *Section 1032 exchanges.* The basis adjustment rules in conjunction with section 1032 exchanges afforded an opportunity for a "corporate tax shelter" until the IRS shut down the ploy. Under section 1032(a), corporations do not recognize gain or loss on the exchange of their stock for money or other property. This rule applies equally to a transaction carried out by a partnership of which the corporation is a partner. For example, suppose a partnership sells stock in X Corporation (its only asset) for $1,000. Assume that the partnership's basis in the stock prior to sale was $0. If X is a 50 percent partner in the partnership, then X's share of the $500 gain from the sale is not taxable to X by virtue of section 1032(a). Nevertheless, X's outside basis is increased by $500. See Rev. Rul. 99-57, 1999-2 C.B. 678. The reason is that the $500 income, though "exempt" to X, nevertheless results in a permanent increase in the partnership's aggregate basis in its assets. It is just as if the partnership had earned $500 in tax-exempt income allocable to X. Think again of

how much gain or loss should be recognized by X if it were to sell its partnership interest following the partnership's sale of the X stock.

Suppose, however, that X *purchases* a 50 percent interest in the partnership at a time when the partnership's only asset is the X stock worth $1,000. If X pays $500 for a one-half partnership interest, X's initial outside basis is $500. See I.R.C. §§ 742, 1012. Now, what should happen if the partnership sells the X stock for $1,000 and allocates one-half of the gain to X? X again is not taxed on the gain by virtue of section 1032(a) but, under the authority of Rev. Rul. 99-57, supra, X would seem to increase its outside basis to $1,000. Does that seem like the right result? If X were to sell its partnership interest immediately following these events, what would be the tax consequences to X? How much would a purchaser pay for X's interest?

In Notice 99-57, 1999-2 C.B. 693, the IRS announced that a basis increase would *not* be appropriate in this last situation, and it has since promulgated regulations to that effect. See Reg. § 1.705-2(a) and (b) (denying any basis increase (or decrease) for amount of built-in gain (or loss) allocable to purchasing corporation from sale of such corporation's stock). Try to articulate the theory behind this rule. What is the IRS authority to promulgate such a rule?

4. *Section 705(b).* In order to determine her outside basis at any given time, section 705(a) requires a partner to keep track of the entire history of her participation in the partnership up to that time, including the amount of any contributions to and distributions from the partnership and her share of any partnership items triggering basis increases or decreases. Obviously, this could be a daunting task. As an alternative, the regulations under section 705(b) permit a partner's outside basis to be determined, in appropriate circumstances, "by reference to the partner's share of the adjusted basis of partnership property." This alternative rule reflects the fundamental relationship between the aggregate outside basis of the partners and the aggregate inside basis of the partnership's assets, and between a particular partner's outside basis and her share of the partnership's aggregate inside basis. This important theme will recur throughout your study of subchapter K. Chapter three provides a basic introduction to the partners' "capital accounts," something that most partners keep close track of. Although not permitted by the regulations, outside basis can often be determined by making appropriate adjustments to a partner's capital account; this can be a useful check on the partner's determination of outside basis under the other methods.

5. *Importance of outside basis.* As explored below and later in the course, outside basis is important in determining the consequences of a partnership's passthrough of losses, partnership distributions, and sales or liquidations of a partnership interest.

2. *Limitation on the Passthrough of Losses*

Review I.R.C. § 705(a)(2) and note the parenthetical phrase "but not below zero" found there. This statutory prohibition on "negative basis" requires an additional rule limiting the passthrough of losses in excess of outside basis. Read I.R.C. § 704(d) and Reg. § 1.704-1(d)(1) and do the following problem.

Problem 2-5: Laura's sister, Elizabeth, contributes $5 to be a partner in the family lemonade stand business. In the first year of operation, the business loses money and Elizabeth's distributive share of the loss is $8. (At this point, do not be concerned with how these events would likely arise as a practical matter. The impact of partnership liabilities on partnership losses and outside basis is considered later.) In the second year, the business is profitable and Elizabeth's share of income is $8. At the end of the second year, Elizabeth sells her interest in the partnership for $5.

(a) What are the economic consequences of these events to Elizabeth?
(b) What are the corresponding tax consequences to her? See I.R.C. §§ 722, 702(a) and (c), 704(d), 705(a), 741. What difference would it make if section 704(d) were not in the Code?

As **problem 2-5** illustrates, section 704(d) is intended to prevent mismeasurement of income that would otherwise result from the prohibition against negative basis. Losses not allowed by reason of section 704(d) are generally suspended until such time as the partner has enough outside basis to claim such losses.

The existence of section 704(d) heightens the importance of ordering and timing issues relating to the basis adjustments authorized by section 705(a). The amount of partnership losses that may be currently claimed by a partner on her tax return is limited to her outside basis. But outside basis is also important for other reasons; in particular, cash distributed to a partner is not taxed if the cash does not exceed the partner's outside basis immediately prior to the distribution. See I.R.C. §§ 731(a)(1), 733(1). Since cash distributions and partnership losses "vie" for the same outside basis, rules are needed to assign priority in a year when both events occur. Further, section 705(a) authorizes adjustments to a partner's outside basis; it is necessary to determine when and in what order those adjustments occur.

While the timing and ordering rules generally function relatively well, not all of the details have been worked out very precisely. Read Reg. § 1.704-1(d)(2) and the following ruling. The problems following the ruling illustrate some of the continuing uncertainties in this area.

Rev. Rul. 66-94

1966-1 C.B. 166

. . . During the taxable year, A, a member of the partnership, contributed 50x dollars to the partnership as his initial capital contribution, and received 30x dollars as a cash distribution from the partnership. A's distributive share of partnership losses at the end of its taxable year was 60x dollars. . . .

Section 1.704-1(d)(1) of the Income Tax Regulations provides, in part, that a partner's distributive share of partnership loss will be allowed only to the extent of the adjusted basis (before reduction by current year's losses) of such partner's interest in the partnership at the end of the partnership taxable year in which such loss occurred.

Section 1.704-1(d)(2) of the regulations provides, in part, that in computing the adjusted basis of a partner's interest for the purpose of ascertaining the extent to which a partner's distributive share of partnership loss shall be allowed as a deduction for the taxable year, the basis shall first be increased under section 705(a)(1) of the Code and decreased under section 705(a)(2) of the Code, except for losses of the taxable year and losses previously disallowed.

Section 1.731-1(a) of the regulations provides, in part, that where money is distributed by a partnership to a partner, no gain or loss shall be recognized to the partner except to the extent that the amount of money distributed exceeds the adjusted basis of the partner's interest in the partnership immediately before the distribution. For purposes of sections 731 and 705 of the Code, advances or drawings of money or property against a partner's distributive share of income shall be treated as current distributions made on the last day of the partnership taxable year with respect to such partner.

Based on the foregoing, it is concluded that:

(1) In computing A's adjusted basis for his interest in the partnership under section 705(a) of the Code, A's original basis, which is determined under section 722 relating to contributions to the partnership, should be decreased by first deducting distributions made to A by the partnership and thereafter, by deducting his distributive share of partnership losses. However, A's basis for his interest in the partnership may not be reduced below zero. Thus:

A's contribution to the partnership—	50x dollars
Deduct cash distributions made to A by the partnership—	−30x dollars
	20x dollars
Deduct A's distributive share of losses (60x dollars) but only to the extent that A's basis is not reduced below zero—	−20x dollars
A's basis for his interest in the partnership under section 705 of the Code—	-0-

(2) In order to determine the extent to which A's distributive share of partnership losses will be allowed as a deduction, A's basis for his interest in the partnership computed in accordance with section 705(a) of the Code, should be determined without taking into account his distributive share of partnership losses for the taxable year. Thus:

A's contribution to the partnership—	50x dollars
Deduct cash distribution made to A by the partnership—	−30x dollars
	20x dollars
A's distributive share of partnership losses for the taxable year are not taken into account—	-0-
A's basis for determining the amount of his allowable partnership losses—	20x dollars

(3) In order to determine the extent to which gain will be realized by A upon the distribution of cash to him by the partnership, A's basis for his interest in the partnership computed in accordance with section 705(a) of the Code, should be determined without taking into account cash distributions made to him by the partnership during its current taxable year. Thus:

A's contribution to the partnership—	50x dollars
Cash distributions made by the partnership to A during the taxable year are not taken into account—	-0-
	50x dollars
Deduct A's distributive share of partnership losses to the extent allowed by section 704(d) of the Code. (See examples (1) and (2).)—	−20x dollars
A's basis for determining the amount of gain he realized upon the distribution of cash to him by the partnership—	30x dollars

A may deduct his distributive share of the partnership loss to the extent of 20x dollars (see example 2) and he realizes no gain from the cash distribution of 30x dollars because his basis for determining the amount of gain upon such distribution is 30x dollars (example 3).

Problem 2-6: After toiling as an associate at the Nox Ox & Pox firm for ten years, you are finally admitted as a partner to the partnership. No cash or property contribution is required upon entry to the firm. As a partner, you are promised a share of the firm's profits instead of your fixed associate's salary. You have always paid personal expenses out of your monthly salary, but now you no longer receive one. Instead, you are entitled to draw $20,000 each month from your anticipated share of the firm's profits for the year. What are the tax consequences of your receipt of this money? See I.R.C. § 731(a)(1) and Reg. § 1.731-1(a)(1)(ii). What happens if, after drawing $20,000 payments monthly throughout the year ($240,000 total), it turns out that your share of the firm's profits is only $200,000?

Problem 2-7:

(a) At the beginning of the partnership's taxable year, partner A has an outside basis of $6,000; A's share of partnership ordinary income for the year is $1,000 and her share of partnership long-term capital loss is $5,000; and A receives a cash distribution of $7,000 on the last day of the partnership's taxable year. What are the tax consequences to A?

(b) Same as (a), except that A's share of partnership long-term capital loss is only $3,000 and her share of partnership charitable contributions is $2,000. Do your conclusions seem correct from a policy standpoint?

(c) Same as (a), except that A's $1,000 share of income is long-term capital gain rather than ordinary income. Do your conclusions seem correct from a policy standpoint?

NOTES

1. *Interim cash distributions.* The tax consequences of distributions occurring prior to year end are normally determined at the time of the distribution (and before any year-end basis increase for the passthrough of a partner's share of income). Thus, an interim cash distribution may be taxable under section 731(a)(1) even though no gain would be recognized if the distribution were deferred until the end of the year.

2. *Planning.* Reg. § 1.704-1(d)(2) and Rev. Rul. 66-94 make clear that the section 704(d) limitation is tested after all other year-end adjustments to the partner's outside basis. In a year in which a partnership makes a distribution and has a loss, this ordering rule maximizes the chance that the distribution will be received tax free but that any loss passed through will be suspended. Partners can reverse this consequence by deferring the distribution until after the loss year. Of course, the deferred distribution may be taxable in the later year if the partner's outside basis is still insufficient.

3. *"Suspended" losses.* Losses disallowed by section 704(d) are considered "suspended" because they are caught in midstream. Suspended losses are not currently deductible by the partner to whom the loss is allocated. Such losses are not disallowed entirely, however, but instead remain designated for later use by the particular partner. At such time as the partner has enough outside basis, the loss passes through to her, with an accompanying decrease in outside basis.

Other provisions catch losses in midstream before a partner can claim a current deduction for them. For example, as we will see in chapter five, losses not barred by section 704(d) may nevertheless be suspended by the at risk or passive activity loss rules. A current deduction may also produce no immediate tax benefit because of the capital loss limitation or because the partner to whom the loss is allocated has insufficient income to use the loss currently and no carryback is possible.

4. *Some partnership tax consequences of the section 199 "manufacturing" deduction.* Section 199(a) allows a deduction generally equal to nine percent of a taxpayer's "qualified production activities income" ("QPAI"), a very rough proxy for taxable income from domestic manufacturing activities. For a taxpayer in the 35 percent bracket with qualifying income, the section 199 deduction is equivalent to a tax rate reduction equal to 3.15 percentage points. For example, if the taxpayer has $100 of QPAI, the taxpayer reports only $91 of taxable income taxed at 35 percent; the result is equivalent to taxing the $100 of QPAI at a 31.85 percent rate ($91 × 35% = $100 × 31.85% = $31.85). Because the subsidy was intended to promote jobs, the deduction is generally limited to 50 percent of the wages paid by the taxpayer to generate the QPAI.

When QPAI is earned by a partnership, the amount of the section 199(a) deduction must be determined separately by each partner. The partnership must allocate and pass through to each partner a share of all items relevant to the calculation of the deduction, including the amount of gross receipts from qualifying production activities, related deductions, and the wages paid by the partnership to generate its QPAI. Each partner's share of items is then added to any other relevant items the partner may have from nonpartnership production activities in order to calculate the partner's permissible section 199(a) deduction. See I.R.C. § 199(d)(1)(B). If partnership deductions relating to QPAI are allocated to a partner but suspended by reason of section 704(d) or the at risk or passive activity loss rules, the deductions are taken into account for purposes of section 199(a) in the subsequent year in which the suspended deductions are allowed. See Reg. § 1.199-5(b)(2). By analogy to tax-exempt income, the section 199(a) deduction has no effect on a partner's outside basis. See Reg. § 1.199-5(b)(1)(i); see also I.R.C. § 705(a)(1)(A) and (B).

When a partner sells a partnership interest, any gain or loss is generally not considered qualifying income from domestic manufacturing activities and hence does not qualify as QPAI. A limited exception applies, and the gain or loss may be considered QPAI if, as discussed in chapter seven, the partnership tax rules recharacterize a sale of a partnership interest as a sale of the partnership's assets. See I.R.C. § 751(a); Reg. § 1.199-5(f). The section 199 deduction is widely viewed as poor policy and inordinately complex; a recurrent reform proposal is to repeal the deduction and use the revenue savings to reduce corporate tax rates.

Chapter 3

Introduction to Partnership Accounting

A. Introduction

In this chapter, we discuss the basic rules of partnership accounting—how partnerships must maintain their financial accounts (or "books"). An obvious question is why the federal tax law (and this course) should be concerned with these issues. It might seem that the rules for financial accounts are a purely private matter to be determined by the parties who join together to form the partnership. Whatever "rules" they consider satisfactory to describe their economic rights vis-à-vis one another would seem to be determinative, including the absence of any formal books altogether if that is acceptable to them. To be sure, the parties may wish to maintain their accounts in conformity with conventional accounting principles if they at some point plan to involve outsiders—creditors or new investors, for example—in the venture. But why should the *tax law* have any role in setting these rules?

The answer lies in a dilemma fundamental to the passthrough system of taxation. As we have discussed, under the passthrough system, the partnership is generally not taxed when it conducts its operations and earns income. Instead, the partnership is generally disregarded and the partners are taxed on their share of the partnership income.

But how is each partner's share of income determined? Bear in mind that each partner is taxed on her share of income whether or not it is distributed to her. Thus, the tax law must determine how the income *would have been shared* by the partners had there been an actual division of profits.

As we will see in chapter four, for a variety of reasons, the tax law allows considerable flexibility in allocating partnership tax items among the partners. Tax items, including individual items of partnership income, gain, deduction, or loss, may generally be allocated however the parties desire, and the allocation of any given item need not be consistent with the manner in which other items are shared. Further, each of these arrangements can be modified from one year to the next. It does not take much to figure out how such flexibility could result in minimizing tax liabilities for all concerned.

Yet the purpose of subchapter K's flexibility is not to allow the parties to achieve tax minimization. Rather, the purpose is to permit the tax consequences from the venture to conform to the economic consequences to the parties. Because economic shares are determined in a flexible manner, shares for tax purposes must necessarily be determined with the same degree of flexibility if the two are to be consistent with one another.

Thus, the tax law imposes a key condition on the validity of an allocation of tax items: it must be consistent with the economic allocation of the parties. (As we shall see, the tax law imposes other conditions as well, but this is the principal one.) But how is the "economic allocation" determined? The tax law's answer is to look to the financial accounts of the partnership. The sharing of items shown on the partnership's books represents the tax law's best idea of what constitutes the partners' economic shares.

The tax law could have stopped right there. It could have simply articulated a general rule that "allocations of tax items must be consistent with the economic allocation of the partners as reflected on the partnership's books." But it didn't. The law was concerned that if partnerships kept their books in different ways and tax consequences always followed the book entries, then there would be no uniformity in how individual partnerships are taxed. The familiar tax policy goal of taxing similarly situated taxpayers in a similar way would not be met. The tax system would also lack the ability to monitor the partners' tax allocations for possible abuses. Further, some partnerships might not keep any formal books, in which case the tax consequences to the partners would be uncertain.

The tax law, therefore, has created a set of rules that *requires* partnerships to keep formal books and dictates how they must be maintained, if the partnership's allocations are to be insulated from IRS challenge. In addition, as discussed in chapter four, the tax law imposes a key additional condition: the books of the partnership must be respected by the partners in determining their economic rights vis-à-vis one another. In other words, the books required by the tax law cannot be ignored at the moment of reckoning when the partners actually divide up their economic interests in the venture.

This chapter describes the required rules for maintaining the partnership's financial accounts. In some important respects, these rules may differ from those imposed by conventional accounting principles. They also may differ from rules developed by the parties themselves regarding how they will keep track of their economic interests. Thus, many partnerships may end up maintaining several sets of books.

This chapter is organized around a series of examples that walk you through common events in the life of a small business partnership. At each step, we stop to consider what the tax law says the partnership books must look like. Virtually all of the rules are contained in a portion of the regulations, Reg. § 1.704-1(b)(2)(iv) (captioned "maintenance of capital accounts" and sometimes referred to as the "eye-vee" rules). Skim that section now to get a sense of how it is organized, what issues it addresses, and how long it is. You will need to carefully review specific portions of the section in the following discussion.

A final thought before we begin: suppose a partnership fails to keep its books in the manner described in this chapter. Indeed, suppose a partnership fails to keep any formal books whatsoever. What do you think should happen, from a tax standpoint, in that situation? What do you think actually happens, as a practical matter?

B. Starting the Partnership

Consider the following example.

Example 3-1: Individuals A and B decide to form a partnership to engage in a business venture together. As an initial matter, each person contributes $100 to the venture.

How could we depict the economic status of this venture and the rights of A and B immediately after the formation of the venture? Accountants typically use a balance sheet to provide a snapshot at any given time of the well-being of a firm. Immediately after the firm's formation, its balance sheet would appear as follows:

Partnership AB

Assets	*Book*	*Liabilities*	*Book*
cash	200		
		Capital	*Book*
		A	100
		B	100
total	200	total	200

In a balance sheet, the entries on the left side (assets) must equal the entries on the right side (liabilities and capital). This relationship follows from the definition of "capital" as the equity or net worth of the business, i.e., the excess, if any, of assets over liabilities. Thus, assets less liabilities equals capital, so assets must necessarily equal liabilities plus capital.

The left-side/right-side balance also tells you that any change in the assets of the venture that is not attributable to a change in liabilities must be reflected in a change in capital. Thus, for example, if the firm were to make money, thereby increasing its assets without changing its liabilities, then capital must be increased to take account of the earnings. Read Reg. § 1.704-1(b)(2)(iv)(*b*)(*3*). Similarly, if there is an additional contribution to the firm, again increasing assets without affecting liabilities, then capital must be increased by the amount of the contribution. Read Reg. § 1.704-1(b)(2)(iv)(*b*)(*1*) and (*2*), (*d*)(*1*).

Separate capital accounts are maintained for each partner. This keeps track of their economic rights vis-à-vis one another. In the simple example so far, the "100" in the capital accounts for A and B represents the contribution each has made to the firm. It also signifies the amount each partner would be entitled to receive if the partners should immediately change their minds and fold up their venture.

> **Example 3-2:** Assume the same facts as in **example 3-1** except that instead of contributing $100 in cash, B contributes a piece of land worth $100. Assume that B's basis in the land prior to the contribution is $100.

The partnership balance sheet following the facts in **example 3-2** would be as follows:

Partnership AB

Assets	*Book*	*Liabilities*	*Book*
cash	**100**		
land	**100**		
		Capital	*Book*
		A	100
		B	100
total	200	total	200

As you can see, except for a change in the amount of cash and a new entry for the land, the balance sheet appears identical to the first situation. It is what we would expect. The balance sheet depicts *economic* accounts and, as an economic matter, there is very little difference between **examples 3-1** and **3-2**. The land is "booked" at $100, its value at the time of contribution, and B is given credit for having contributed $100 of value to the venture, the same as A. Read Reg. § 1.704-1(b)(2)(iv)(*b*)(*2*).

> **Example 3-2(a):** Following the contributions in **example 3-2**, the land appreciates in value to $150.

What would the partnership balance sheet look like now? There would be no change. The reason is that balance sheet entries are typically recorded at historical cost or "book value," which generally means the value of each item when it was acquired by the partnership. Here, the land was worth $100 when it was acquired by the partnership from B. The fact that the land subsequently increases in value to $150 is not generally reflected on the balance sheet.

This means, of course, that the balance sheet may not accurately reflect the value of the enterprise, or the value of each partner's interest on an ongoing basis. So why isn't fair market value used instead of book value? Principally because of the difficulty of determining reliably what fair market value is. In **example 3-2**, we had some reasonable indication that the land was worth $100 at the time of contribution because A and B presumably had adverse interests at that time. How reliable, however, is the claim that the land is now worth $150? Financial accounting offers a very practical solution to the uncertainties of valuation. In general, balance sheet entries remain recorded at book value until such time as more accurate values are needed, at which time appraisals are undertaken (if necessary) and entries are "booked-up" or "booked-down" to reflect their then-current fair market values. One important exception to this treatment is depreciation. Write-offs of book depreciation are reflected immediately — in other words, the book value of depreciable property is gradually reduced over time — while the book value of other items remains unchanged.

QUESTION

When depreciable property is written down for book purposes, what other account of the balance sheet must be adjusted at the same time? In general, what is the relationship between the partnership's depreciation method for book and tax purposes? See Reg. § 1.704-1(b)(2)(iv)(*g*)(*3*).

Example 3-2(b): Following the contributions in **example 3-2**, the partnership borrows $100.

The partnership balance sheet will now appear as follows:

Partnership AB

Assets	*Book*	*Liabilities*	*Book*
cash	**200**	**debt payable**	**100**
land	100		
		Capital	*Book*
		A	100
		B	100
total	**300**	total	**300**

The proceeds of the borrowing show up on the left side of the balance sheet as additional cash, but that entry is offset by the new entry under liabilities. Thus, the balance sheet remains in balance without any change to the partners' capital accounts. Cf. Reg. § 1.704-1(b)(2)(iv)(*c*) (in general, capital accounts unaffected by changes in a partner's share of partnership liabilities). Once again, this outcome conforms with economic intuition: borrowing generally does not change a firm's net worth (the borrowed amount is offset by a liability of equal amount) and therefore capital accounts should also be unchanged. We can think of a partner's capital account as reflecting (1) the value of her initial and subsequent contributions to the partnership plus (2) her share of any income earned by the partnership less (3) the value of any distributions made to her and less (4) her share of any partnership losses (including depreciation). Read Reg. § 1.704-1(b)(2)(iv)(*b*).

C. Contributions of Appreciated Property and the Concept of "Tax Capital"

Consider the following facts.

Example 3-3: Assume the same facts as in **example 3-2** except that B's basis in the land contributed to the partnership is only $40 rather than $100.

Before we can construct the balance sheet based on the facts in **example 3-3**, we must first ascertain the tax consequences of B's transfer to the partnership. After all, if the transfer were fully taxable to B, with B having to pay tax on the $60 of gain realized in the transfer, then **example 3-3** would effectively be the same as **example 3-2**. Having paid tax on the potential gain, B should be treated as if she had contributed property whose value and basis were both $100.

In fact, however, perhaps to mitigate the "lock-in" effect of taxing contributions to partnerships, current law treats virtually all such transfers as nonrecognition events to both the partners and the partnership. Read I.R.C. § 721(a). The usual conditions for nonrecognition treatment apply—any gain or loss not recognized in the transaction must be preserved for future recognition through the basis rules. The partnership inherits the same $40 basis in the contributed land and B takes a $40 basis in the partnership interest received. Read I.R.C. §§ 722, 723. The partnership's basis in the property is commonly referred to as "inside basis" and B's basis in her partnership interest is commonly referred to as "outside basis."

With that understanding, what would the partnership balance sheet look like following the facts in **example 3-3**? One possibility is the *same* balance sheet as the one following the facts in **example 3-2**. As an economic matter, B has still contributed a piece of land *worth* $100. Thus, the fact that B's (and therefore, the partnership's) tax basis in the land is less than $100 might seem irrelevant to what appears on the balance sheet.

But is it? If you were a partner presented with this balance sheet by the partnership's accountant as a snapshot of the partnership's (and the partners') well-being immediately following the contributions, what would you think? Does it fairly represent what the partners have contributed to the venture?

A has contributed $100 in cash and B has contributed land worth $100. But B's land has associated with it a future tax liability. If the land were sold by the partnership the following day for $100, someone would be taxed on the $60 of gain remaining in the land. Thus, it might appear that A has made a larger contribution than B to the venture.

But the book capital accounts seem to indicate that A and B intend to be equal partners based on the value of their contributions irrespective of the tax bases of the contributed property. If they intend to be equal partners, one possibility is to require B (and only B) to bear the future tax liability on the built-in gain of $60 when and if such gain is recognized. In effect, B has contributed two things to the venture: land subject to a tax liability and a promise to pay the tax liability when and if it becomes due. As long as only B bears the potential tax liability, A should apparently be indifferent as to whether B contributes $100 cash or appreciated property worth $100.

As we will discover, the tax law in fact requires the built-in gain, when recognized, to be taxed to B in this situation. This treatment applies whenever there is a contribution to a partnership of property whose value differs from the partnership's basis in the property following the contribution. Read I.R.C. § 704(c)(1)(A). Such property is commonly referred to as "section 704(c) property" after the operative Code provision mandating this treatment. The reason is to prevent income-shifting between partners of gains and losses that accrued prior to the partnership's acquisition of the property. While this treatment was once optional among the parties, it has been mandatory since 1984.

Furthermore, when a partnership holds section 704(c) property, its balance sheet might be expanded for tax purposes to include that additional piece of information.

Partnership AB

Assets	*AB*	*Book*	*Liabilities*	*Tax*	*Book*
cash	**100**	100			
land	**40**	100			
			Capital	***Tax***	*Book*
			A	**100**	100
			B	**40**	100
total	**140**	200	total	**140**	200

On the left side, an additional column (labeled here as "AB" for "adjusted basis") is added to show that the partnership's inside basis in the land differs from the book value of the property. On the right side, we similarly add an additional "tax" column. Thus, each partner has both a "book capital" and a "tax capital" amount.

What does "tax capital" represent and how must it be adjusted? While the regulations include many examples referring to this concept (see, e.g., Reg. § 1.704-1(b)(5) (ex. 13(i)), they offer precious little specific guidance. The best starting point is perhaps Reg. § 1.743-1(d)(1), which describes a partner's interest in "previously taxed capital," a closely related concept. Previously taxed capital is generally equal to the partner's share of inside basis less the partner's share of partnership liabilities. In **example 3-3**, B has book capital of $100 (the value of her property contribution) but her share of previously taxed capital (or "tax capital") is only $40 (B's contribution to the inside basis of the partnership). B's obligation to pay the potential tax liability attributable to the built-in gain in the land is reflected in the $60 difference between B's book and tax capital accounts shown on the balance sheet, commonly referred to as a "book-tax disparity." The reason we maintain tax capital accounts is to highlight the special section 704(c) obligations of the partners. Note that despite the book-tax disparity, the balance sheet remains in balance: the aggregate book value of the assets on the left-hand side ($200) still equals the total of the "book" entries on the right-hand side ($200), and the aggregate inside basis of the partnership's assets on the left-hand side ($140) equals the total of the "tax" entries on the right-hand side ($140).

Example 3-3(a): Following the contributions in **example 3-3**, the land is sold by the partnership for $100.

As we would expect, immediately after the sale, the book-tax disparity in B's capital accounts disappears.

Partnership AB

Assets	*AB*	*Book*	*Liabilities*	*Tax*	*Book*
cash	200	200			
			Capital	*Tax*	*Book*
			A	100	100
			B	100	100
total	200	200	total	200	200

The $60 of tax gain from the sale of the property would all be allocated to B, increasing her tax capital account from $40 to $100. Since B has been taxed on the $60 gain, B's share of the firm's previously taxed capital increases to $100.

QUESTION

Should the sale of the land result in any change to B's (or A's) *book* capital account? Why or why not? Read Reg. §§ 1.704-1(b)(2)(iv)(*b*)(*3*) and (*d*)(*3*) and

1.704-1(b)(4)(i) to see whether the guidance in the regulations conforms with your intuition.

Example 3-3(b): Following the contributions in **example 3-3** but prior to any sale of the land, the partnership borrows $100 from a bank.

As we have discussed, the adjustments to the book capital accounts for partnership borrowing are straightforward: the proceeds of the loan increase partnership assets, but this change is offset by an increase in liabilities. Accordingly, book capital accounts are unchanged.

Tax capital accounts are also unchanged. Tax capital is a partner's share of inside basis *net* of liabilities. You can back into this result by remembering that tax capital accounts serve to highlight the partners' special section 704(c) obligations measured by the disparity between their book and tax capital accounts. Since borrowing does not affect book capital, it also must leave tax capital unchanged; otherwise, the amount of any book-tax disparity would no longer be correct. Thus, the balance sheet following the borrowing would appear like this:

Partnership AB

Assets	*AB*	*Book*	*Liabilities*	*Tax*	*Book*
cash	200	200	debt payable	100	100
land	40	100			
			Capital	*Tax*	*Book*
			A	100	100
			B	40	100
total	240	300	total	240	300

We include a "100" in the tax column for liabilities to balance the tax entries on the balance sheet.

Finally, we should consider another account that is important for tax purposes — each partner's tax basis in her partnership interest, i.e., the partner's "outside basis." Unlike capital accounts, outside basis *is* affected by partnership liabilities. As we will discuss in much greater detail later, the tax law tries to equate the tax consequences of borrowing by the partnership with those of direct borrowing by one or more of the partners. If a taxpayer acquires property in part with borrowed money, the taxpayer's basis in the acquired property typically includes the amount of the borrowing. Section 752 generally reaches the same result even though the transaction is carried out through a partnership which borrows the money and acquires the property. Increases in a partner's share of partnership liabilities are treated as deemed cash contributions by the partner to the partnership, which increase the partner's outside basis. Conversely, decreases in a partner's share of partnership liabilities are treated as deemed cash distributions to the partner by the partnership, which reduce the partner's outside basis. Read I.R.C. §§ 752(a), (b), 722, 733(1).

Determining a partner's "share" of partnership liabilities can be complicated and depends in part on the nature of the liability. Let us simply assume that the $100 liability in **example 3-3(b)** is shared equally by partners A and B. In that case, the partnership balance sheet might be supplemented with outside basis information as follows:

Partnership AB

Assets	*AB*	*Book*	*Liabilities*	*Tax*	*Book*	
cash	200	200	debt payable	100	100	
land	40	100				
			Capital	*Tax*	*Book*	*OB*
			A	100	100	150
			B	40	100	90
total	240	300	total	240	300	240

Problem 3-1: Construct the partnership balance sheet (including outside basis information) after partnership AB repays its $100 liability.

D. Sales of Partnership Interests and Potential Imbalances

The expanded balance sheet in **example 3-3(b)**, above, reveals an important relationship between inside and outside basis. The aggregate outside bases of the partners ($240) is equal to the aggregate inside basis of the partnership in its assets ($240). This equality makes sense given the goal of passthrough taxation to impose only a single level of tax on business income. Business gain or loss may be realized in either of two ways—"inside" the firm (for example, through a sale by the partnership of one of its assets) or "outside" the firm (for example, through a sale by a partner of her partnership interest). Aggregate inside and outside basis should generally be the same, therefore, in order to harmonize the amount of gain or loss realized and recognized in each situation. Inside and outside basis will generally be identical upon formation of the partnership. If this relationship is to be preserved afterwards, the rules need to make corollary adjustments to basis ("outside" taxable events should result in adjustments to "inside" basis and "inside" taxable events should result in adjustments to "outside" basis). These corollary adjustments are necessary to ensure that the same gain or loss is recognized once and only once. For example, we examined in chapter two the outside basis adjustments mandated by section 705.

Another important relationship follows from the equality of inside and outside basis. Note that each partner's outside basis is equal to the partner's tax capital plus her share of partnership liabilities. For example, A's outside basis ($150) is equal to her tax capital ($100) plus her share of the liability ($50). This relationship naturally follows from the fact that a partner's tax capital is generally equal to her share of inside basis, net of liabilities.

Do these relationships always hold true? Unfortunately not. To see how discrepancies may arise, consider the following example.

> **Example 3-4:** Individuals A, B, C, and D form a partnership as equal partners with A, B, and C each contributing $100 cash and D contributing land worth $100. D's basis in the land prior to the contribution is $40. At a time when the value of the partnership's assets remains unchanged, D sells his one-fourth partnership interest to E.

How much should E pay for D's interest? The answer depends in part on how a sale of a partnership interest is taxed. Under current law, a sale of a partnership interest is generally taxed much like a sale of corporate stock: the seller recognizes gain or loss equal to the difference between the amount realized and the seller's basis in the interest, and the buyer obtains a cost basis in the interest. Read I.R.C. §§ 741, 742, 1012.

The purchase price for D's interest also depends upon what happens to the lurking, section 704(c) tax obligation attributable to the $60 of built-in gain when D contributed the land to the partnership. As we discussed, so long as D remains a partner in the partnership, the tax law requires the partnership to make a special allocation of such gain to D when and if the gain is recognized. But D has now departed from the partnership. D will be taxed indirectly on the built-in gain when he sells his partnership interest. Will such built-in gain be taxed again to the partnership when the land is sold? If so, which partner will bear the tax burden that belonged to D?

The tax law provides that upon the transfer of a partnership interest, the transferee must inherit the transferor's capital accounts. E, therefore, inherits D's section 704(c) obligation. Read Reg. § 1.704-1(b)(2)(iv)(*l*) (1st sentence), -3(a)(7). E (rather than A, B, or C) takes over that responsibility from D because E can presumably take it into account in his dealing with D. Thus, the built-in gain will be taxed to E (as D's successor). To compensate for the potential tax liability, E might insist on paying D something less than $100 for D's partnership interest. Assume that E offers to pay D $88 for the partnership interest and D agrees to that amount. (The actual purchase price will be potentially affected by a number of factors.) Following E's purchase, the partnership balance sheet will appear as follows:

Partnership ABCE

Assets	*AB*	*Book*	*Liabilities*	*Tax*	*Book*	
cash	300	300				
land	40	100				
			Capital	*Tax*	*Book*	*OB*
			A	100	100	100
			B	100	100	100
			C	100	100	100
			E	40	100	88
total	340	400	total	340	400	388

As you can see, aggregate outside basis ($388) is no longer equal to aggregate inside basis ($340). Furthermore, E's outside basis ($88) is no longer equal to the amount of his tax capital ($40) plus his share of partnership liabilities ($0).

What has gone wrong here? One way to understand the source of the imbalance is to recognize that although A, B, C, and E have collectively invested $388 in the venture, which amount is properly reflected in their outside bases, aggregate partnership inside basis remains $340. Had the partners made their investment directly, they presumably would own cash and property with an aggregate basis of $388, not $340. In short, tax events occurring outside the partnership (the sale of D's interest) have not triggered appropriate corollary adjustments inside the partnership. Section 754 provides a procedure to rectify the situation. Just as section 705 operates to adjust outside basis for events occurring inside the partnership, section 754 seeks to adjust inside basis for events occurring outside the partnership. In this case, the procedure would provide E with the equivalent of a cost basis in E's share of the partnership's assets. Thus, the $60 of built-in gain would be taxed only once — to D upon sale of his partnership interest — and not again to E when the land is sold. (In this event, E should presumably be willing to pay $100 (rather than $88) for D's interest.) But the procedure is generally *elective*; for reasons we will discuss later, the election is often not made. The important point to understand now is that when a section 754 election is not in effect, parity between inside and outside basis will not necessarily be preserved.

E. Partnership Income, Loss, and Distributions

Let us next consider the accounting implications of partnership income, loss, and distributions.

Example 3-5: Individuals J and K form partnership JK, with J contributing $100 cash and K contributing land worth $100. K's basis in the land is $100. Subsequently, the partnership has $60 of income.

What effect does the income have on the partnership balance sheet? We know that the income increases partnership assets (cash). Therefore, with no change in liabilities, there must be an equal increase to the partnership capital accounts. The amount of increase to each partner's book capital account will depend upon how the income is shared economically by the partners, as determined by their partnership agreement. As we have discussed, the general objective of subchapter K is to make sure that the allocation of income for *tax* purposes is consistent with whatever economic allocation the parties agree to ("tax must follow book").

Read, however, Reg. § 1.704-1(b)(2)(iv)(*b*)(*3*) very carefully. The regulation provides that a partner's capital account must be increased by the allocation to such partner of "partnership income and gain . . . including income and gain exempt from tax. . . ." In other words, the regulation seems to specify that the adjustment for book purposes must be consistent with the allocation determined for tax purposes and not vice-versa.

You should not view this as a departure from the general principle that "tax must follow book." The regulation is generally addressing a situation where the tax and book items are the same, such as when the partnership has $100 of both book and taxable income. In that case, the regulation states, in effect, that allocation of the tax item will generally be respected so long as a consistent adjustment is made to the partner's book capital account. In cases where the tax and book items are not the same, such as when tax gain is recognized from the sale of section 704(c) property but there is no corresponding book gain, book capital accounts must be adjusted to reflect the book item and not the tax item. See Reg. § 1.704-1(b)(4)(i). More generally, book capital accounts must be adjusted by the amount of book items allocated to each partner and tax capital accounts must be adjusted by the amount of tax items allocated.

Returning to **example 3-5**, if J and K agree to share the $60 income equally, the partnership balance sheet will then appear as follows:

Partnership JK

Assets	*AB*	*Book*	*Liabilities*	*Tax*	*Book*	
cash	160	160	-40			
land	100	100				
			Capital	*Tax*	*Book*	*OB*
			J	130	130	130
			K	130	130	130 -30
total	260	260	total	260	260	260

QUESTIONS

1. Identify the specific statutory or regulatory provisions that authorize the adjustments to outside basis, book capital, and tax capital shown on this balance sheet.

2. On this balance sheet, outside basis, book capital, and tax capital are all the same. We know that outside basis can never be less than zero. See, e.g., I.R.C. §§ 705(a)(2), 733. Can book (or tax) capital ever be negative? If so, what might a negative amount signify?

Example 3-5(a): After partnership JK earns the $60 income in **example 3-5**, it distributes $20 cash to each of the partners.

Once again, before constructing the partnership balance sheet, we must determine the tax consequences of the distribution. On a nonliquidating cash distribution, gain is recognized only to the extent that the amount of cash exceeds the distributee's outside basis immediately before the distribution; loss is never recognized. Read I.R.C. § 731(a).

Problem 3-2: Construct the partnership balance sheet immediately after the distribution in **example 3-5(a)** and find support for your conclusions.

Example 3-5(b): After partnership JK earns the $60 income in **example 3-5**, there is no cash distribution. Instead, assume that the land increases in value to $160. At that point, the partnership distributes one-fourth of the land (with a value of $40 and an allocable basis of $25) to each of the partners J and K.

Nonliquidating property distributions are also generally tax free to both the partnership and the distributee. In general, the distributee inherits the partnership's basis in the property distributed and must reduce outside basis by the amount of basis so inherited. Read I.R.C. §§ 731(a), (b), 732(a)(1), 733(2). Assuming that the distributions in **example 3-5(b)** are taxed in this manner, what would the partnership balance sheet look like after the distribution?

The tax law provides that a partner's book capital account must be reduced by the fair market value of property distributed to the partner. Read Reg. § 1.704-1(b)(2)(iv)(*b*)(*5*). Recall, however, that no change was made to the balance sheet when the land increased in value from $100 to $160. Thus, a portion of the distributed land's value ($30, half of the total appreciation) has not yet been "booked" or included on the balance sheet. To address this problem, the partnership is required to take account of any book gain or loss in the distributed property as if there were a sale of such property for its fair market value immediately before the distribution. Any book gain or loss must then be allocated between the partners, resulting in adjustments to their book capital accounts. (This deemed sale has no effect on the partners' *tax* capital accounts because the distribution does not result in any gain recognized for *tax* purposes.) Finally, the partners' book capital accounts must then be reduced to reflect the value of the distributed property.

Under the facts of **example 3-5(b)**, the partnership realizes $30 of book gain on the deemed sale of the distributed land (its $80 fair market value less its $50 book value). How should the book gain be allocated? As noted, there is no *tax* gain from the distribution so we cannot simply allocate the book gain in the same manner as the tax gain. Instead, the book gain must be shared in the same manner that any tax gain *would have been allocated* had there been a taxable disposition of the property. Read Reg. § 1.704-1(b)(2)(iv)(*e*)(*1*), -1(b)(5) (ex. 14(v)). Assume that J and K intended to divide any profits from eventual sale of the land equally for tax purposes. The book gain should then be allocated equally to each partner.

In short, each partner's book capital account would initially be increased by her share of the book gain ($15) and then reduced by the value of the distributed property ($40), a net reduction of $25. Thus, the post-distribution balance sheet would appear as follows:

Partnership JK

Assets	*AB*	*Book*	*Liabilities*	*Tax*	*Book*	
cash	160	160				
land	50	50				
			Capital	*Tax*	*Book*	*OB*
			J	105	105	105
			K	105	105	105
total	210	210	total	210	210	210

Note that the portion of the land retained by the partnership is still booked at its historical cost of $50, even though it is worth $80. Note also that the net reduction in each partner's book capital account ($25) is equal to one-fourth of the partnership's total tax basis in the land ($100) prior to the distribution.

QUESTIONS

1. Explain the rationale for the adjustments to the tax capital accounts shown on the balance sheet in **example 3-5(b)**.

2. What difference would it make in **example 3-5(b)** if the parties had agreed to allocate all of the profits from sale of the land to K and none to J? What would the post-distribution balance sheet look like then?

F. Entry of New Partners and the Need for Revaluations

Example 3-6: Following the property distribution in **example 3-5(b)**, J and K agree to admit individual L to the partnership. L agrees to make an appropriate cash contribution in exchange for a one-third interest in the venture.

How much must L contribute? The balance sheet indicates that the book capital accounts of J and K are $105 apiece. Yet a $105 contribution by L for a one-third interest in the partnership would presumably be insufficient. Do you understand why?

In a revaluation, a partnership changes the book value of all of its assets to fair market value. Individual assets are "booked-up" or "booked-down," depending upon whether their fair market value is greater or less than recorded book value, and corresponding changes are made to the partners' book capital accounts. See Reg. § 1.704-1(b)(2)(iv)(*g*)(*1*). Revaluations are permitted only in certain limited circumstances, generally when the partners are expected to have sufficiently adverse interests. The tax law is wary of permitting revaluations too liberally because they result in book changes without any corresponding taxable event. In other words, they represent another situation where book and tax adjustments cannot be consistent. (Once again, the adjustments to the book capital accounts of the partners must be made in the same manner as the corresponding tax items would have been shared had they arisen at the time of the revaluation. Read Reg. § 1.704-1(b)(2)(iv)(*f*)(*2*).) On the other hand, sound business practice may demand that a book-up or book-down occur at certain times, including when a new partner joins the partnership. Read Reg. § 1.704-1(b)(2)(iv)(*f*)(*5*).

Thus, prior to the entry of L as a partner, partnership JK would ordinarily be entitled to revalue its books. Assuming that the remaining unrealized appreciation in the land ($30) would be shared equally by J and K for both book and tax purposes, here is how the partnership balance sheet would appear following the revaluation:

Partnership JK

Assets	*AB*	*Book*	*Liabilities*	*Tax*	*Book*	
cash	160	160				
land	50	80				
			Capital	*Tax*	*Book*	*OB*
			J	105	120	105
			K	105	120	105
total	210	240	total	210	240	210

Note that the effect of the revaluation is to create a book-tax disparity for both J and K. Conceptually, this situation is comparable to one where a partner contributes section 704(c) property to a partnership. As discussed earlier, the built-in gain or loss in such contributed property is specially allocated to the contributor and is reflected in the disparity between the contributor's book and tax capital accounts. In the same way, the $30 of unrealized appreciation in the land following the revaluation must be specially allocated, for tax purposes, to the existing partners, J and K, and not to L, the incoming partner. This special section 704(c) obligation is shown by the book-tax disparity in the accounts of J and K. The revalued property is referred to as "reverse section 704(c) property."

Following the revaluation, we can see that L should contribute $120 to the partnership in exchange for a one-third interest. Following L's contribution, the partnership balance sheet will look like this:

Partnership JKL

Assets	*AB*	*Book*	*Liabilities*	*Tax*	*Book*	
cash	280	280				
land	50	80				
			Capital	*Tax*	*Book*	*OB*
			J	105	120	105
			K	105	120	105
			L	120	120	120
total	330	360	total	330	360	330

QUESTIONS

1. Under what circumstances do the tax rules permit a partnership to revalue its books? Explain why revaluations are permitted at these times. Is a partnership ever *required* to revalue its books?
2. When a revaluation occurs, should any adjustment be made to the partners' tax capital accounts or outside bases? Why or why not?
3. Explain the concepts of book value, book capital account, tax capital account, inside basis, and outside basis. Describe the relationships that usually exist in a partnership balance sheet.

Problem 3-3: A, B, and C receive equal one-third interests each in the newly formed ABC general partnership. A contributes $30,000 cash, B contributes land (land #1) with a basis of $15,000 and a fair market value of $30,000, and C contributes securities with a basis and fair market value of $30,000. Construct the partnership's opening balance sheet. Reconstruct the partnership's balance sheet (including outside basis information) to reflect the following consecutive events:

(a) The partnership borrows $60,000 recourse to purchase land #2 worth $60,000. Assume that the partners share the liability equally.

(b) The partnership sells land #1 for $30,000 and the securities for $45,000; the partnership also repays the $60,000 of liabilities.
(c) When land #2 has appreciated in value to $105,000, the partnership admits a new partner, D, in exchange for a contribution of $50,000 cash.

Chapter 4

Partnership Allocations: General Rules

A. Introduction

This chapter begins our examination of how partnership tax items are shared or "allocated" among the partners of the partnership. This is the most important topic of this course and the most significant issue for many partnerships. This chapter describes the general allocation rules applicable to most partnership tax items. The next chapter deals with the allocation of an important class of partnership deductions known as "nonrecourse deductions." A subsequent chapter concerns the allocation of other special items such as partnership gain and loss from section 704(c) property.

In general, subchapter K allows partners considerable flexibility in dividing the tax items of a partnership among themselves. As we have seen, section 702(a) directs each partner to take into account for tax purposes her "distributive share" of the partnership's tax items. Under section 704(a), a partner's distributive share of items is generally determined by the partnership agreement. Thus, as a starting point, the partners can privately agree as to how they will share and report amounts of taxable income, gain, deduction, loss, or tax credit that the partnership may have in a given year. They can agree to different sharing arrangements for each item of the partnership, and can change their arrangements from one year to the next. Moreover, because the "partnership agreement" is defined to include amendments adopted after the end of the taxable year in question (see I.R.C. § 761(c)), partnership allocations can be made with hindsight. The partners can generally decide on how to share a particular tax item *after* the actual amount of such item is known.

This flexibility may seem puzzling to you and inconsistent with basic income tax principles. After all, one of those principles stresses the importance of making sure that only the *proper* taxpayer reports the income or other tax item in question. Indeed, in the classic case of Lucas v. Earl, 281 U.S. 111 (1930), the Supreme Court denied the tax effect of an agreement between two persons to share in the reporting of taxable income earned by only one of them. It might seem, then, that the flexibility afforded the partners of a partnership is fundamentally at odds with this no-assignment-of-income principle. You may recall that the Tax Court in *Schneer* (p. 29) struggled hard to reconcile this seeming inconsistency.

Why does subchapter K allow such flexibility? The answer lies in the desire to conform the tax reporting of partnership items to the *economic* shares of the partners in their common venture. Because partners determine their economic rights and obligations with respect to one another in a flexible manner, the tax law must provide comparable flexibility in the allocation of tax items or else tax consequences will differ from economic consequences.

Consider a real estate development partnership in which some partners provide capital while others mostly perform services. The capital might be invested in a range of properties offering different profit potential and risks. In this case, the partners might decide to share their profits and losses from individual investments disproportionately, depending upon the partner's involvement with the particular investment generating the profit or loss. If partnership tax items could not be divided in the same flexible manner as the sharing of the economic benefits and burdens of the enterprise, then tax shares would deviate from economic shares. Indeed, it could be argued that any tax rule permitting *less* flexibility than that used in the calculation of economic shares would necessarily violate assignment-of-income principles. One partner might then be entitled to a share of profits that is taxed to another.

At the same time, it doesn't take too much imagination to realize how the flexibility of subchapter K may simply lead to tax minimization. Is there anything wrong with that? The concern is that taxpayers, operating through a partnership, will be able to obtain tax results more favorable than had they simply operated on their own or through some other arrangement not entitled to the same flexible rules. The desired "neutral" tax treatment of income earned through different business forms—an objective underlying passthrough taxation—will have been lost. The tax law must therefore achieve a difficult balance: it must provide flexibility but only within certain limits to prevent unjustified tax advantages.

Read I.R.C. § 704(b). As you can see, if the partnership agreement does not specify how a tax item is to be shared, or if the sharing arrangement does not have "substantial economic effect," then the share must be determined in accordance with the "partner's interest in the partnership" ("PIP"). We will shortly encounter both of these concepts in rather excruciating detail in the regulations interpreting section 704(b).

But first, read the *Orrisch* case. *Orrisch* was decided under the pre-1976 version of section 704(b), which required the reallocation of a tax item if "the principal purpose" of the taxpayer's allocation was tax avoidance or evasion. Despite the difference in statutory language, both the courts and the Treasury tended to adopt the notion of "substantial economic effect" as the touchstone for determining the validity of partnership allocations. *Orrisch* furnishes an excellent introduction to both the evolution of the substantial-economic-effect test and the emergence of a capital-account analysis as the cornerstone of the current section 704(b) regulations.

Orrisch v. Commissioner

55 T.C. 395 (1970), aff'd per curiam, 31 A.F.T.R. 1069 (9th Cir. 1973)

FEATHERSTON, J.: [The partners (the Orrisches and Crisafis) initially agreed orally to share profits and losses in the OC partnership equally. In 1966, the partnership agreement was amended to specially allocate all of the depreciation from the partnership's two buildings entirely to the Orrisches. Simultaneously, the partners agreed to allocate any gain on sale of the buildings to the Orrisches up to the amount of the depreciation deductions allocated to them (a "gain chargeback"); any remaining gain was to be divided equally between the partners. During the years in question, the Orrisches had substantial outside income, while the Crisafis had substantial depreciation deductions from other real estate projects and reported no net taxable income. The partners' capital accounts reflected their initial capital contributions and any partnership profits and losses allocated to them. By the end of 1967, the Orrisches had a deficit capital account of $25,187 due mainly to the depreciation deductions, while the Crisafis had a positive capital account of $406. The only issue before the court was whether the special allocation of depreciation deductions to the Orrisches should be disregarded because it was made with the principal purpose of tax avoidance.]

The only issue presented for decision is whether tax effect can be given the agreement between petitioners and the Crisafis that, beginning with 1966, all the partnership's depreciation deductions were to be allocated to petitioners for their use in computing their individual income tax liabilities. In our view, the answer must be in the negative, and the amounts of each of the partners' deductions for the depreciation of partnership property must be determined in accordance with the ratio used generally in computing their distributive shares of the partnership's profits and losses.

Among the important innovations of the 1954 Code are limited provisions for flexibility in arrangements for the sharing of income, losses, and deductions arising from business activities conducted through partnerships. The authority for special allocations of such items appears in section 704(a), which provides that a partner's share of any item of income, gain, loss, deduction, or credit shall be determined by the partnership agreement. That rule is coupled with a limitation in section 704(b),[1] however, which states that a special allocation of an item will be disregarded if its "principal purpose" is the avoidance or evasion of Federal income tax. . . . In case a special allocation is disregarded, the partner's share of the item is to be determined in

1. [Section 704(b), as it existed prior to the 1976 amendment, provided as follows:]

(b) Distributive Share Determined by Income or Loss Ratio. — A partner's distributive share of any item of income, gain, loss, deduction, or credit shall be determined in accordance with his distributive share of taxable income or loss of the partnership, as described in section 702(a)(9), for the taxable year, if—

(1) the partnership agreement does not provide as to the partner's distributive share of such item, or

(2) the principal purpose of any provision in the partnership agreement with respect to the partner's distributive share of such item is the avoidance or evasion of any tax imposed by this subtitle.

accordance with the ratio by which the partners divide the general profits or losses of the partnership. . . .

The report of the Senate Committee on Finance accompanying the bill finally enacted as the 1954 Code . . . explained the tax-avoidance restriction prescribed by section 704(b) as follows:

> Subsection (b) . . . provides that if the principal purpose of any provision in the partnership agreement dealing with a partner's distributive share of a particular item is to avoid or evade the Federal income tax, the partner's distributive share of that item shall be redetermined in accordance with his distributive share of partnership income or loss described in section 702(a)(9) [i.e., the ratio used by the partners for dividing general profits or losses].
>
> Where, however, a provision in a partnership agreement for a special allocation of certain items has substantial economic effect and is not merely a device for reducing the taxes of certain partners without actually affecting their shares of partnership income, then such a provision will be recognized for tax purposes. . . .

This reference to "substantial economic effect" did not appear in the House Ways and Means Committee report . . . discussing section 704(b), and was apparently added in the Senate Finance Committee to allay fears that special allocations of income or deductions would be denied effect in every case where the allocation resulted in a reduction in the income tax liabilities of one or more of the partners. The statement is an affirmation that special allocations are ordinarily to be recognized if they have business validity apart from their tax consequences. . . .

In resolving the question whether the principal purpose of a provision in a partnership agreement is the avoidance or evasion of Federal income tax, all the facts and circumstances in relation to the provision must be taken into account. Section 1.704-1(b)(2), Income Tax Regs., lists the following as relevant circumstances to be considered:

> Whether the partnership or a partner individually has a business purpose for the allocation; whether the allocation has "substantial economic effect," that is, whether the allocation may actually affect the dollar amount of the partners' shares of the total partnership income or loss independently of tax consequences; whether related items of income, gain, loss, deduction, or credit from the same source are subject to the same allocation; whether the allocation was made without recognition of normal business factors and only after the amount of the specially allocated item could reasonably be estimated; the duration of the allocation; and the overall tax consequences of the allocation. . . .

Applying these standards, we do not think the special allocation of depreciation in the present case can be given effect.

The evidence is persuasive that the special allocation of depreciation was adopted for a tax-avoidance rather than a business purpose. Depreciation was the only item which was adjusted by the parties; both the income from the buildings and the expenses incurred in their operation, maintenance, and repair were allocated to the partners equally. Since the deduction for depreciation does not vary from year to year with the fortunes of the business, the parties obviously knew what the tax effect of the special allocation would be at the time they adopted it. Furthermore, as shown by our Findings, petitioners had large amounts of income which would be offset by the additional deduction for depreciation; the Crisafis, in contrast, had no taxable income from which to subtract the partnership depreciation deductions, and, due to depreciation deductions which they were obtaining with respect to other housing projects, could expect to have no taxable income in the near future. On the other hand, the insulation of the Crisafis from at least part of a potential capital gains tax was an obvious tax advantage. The inference is unmistakably clear that the agreement did not reflect normal business considerations but was designed primarily to minimize the overall tax liabilities of the partners.

Petitioners urge that the special allocation of the depreciation deduction was adopted in order to equalize the capital accounts of the partners, correcting a disparity ($14,000) in the amounts initially contributed to the partnership by them ($26,500) and the Crisafis ($12,500). But the evidence does not support this contention. Under the special allocation agreement, petitioners were to be entitled, in computing their individual income tax liabilities, to deduct the full amount of the depreciation realized on the partnership property. For 1966, as an example, petitioners were allocated a sum ($18,904) equal to the depreciation on the partnership property ($18,412) plus one-half of the net loss computed without regard to depreciation ($492). The other one-half of the net loss was, of course, allocated to the Crisafis. Petitioners' allocation ($18,904) was then applied to reduce their capital account. The depreciation specially allocated to petitioners ($18,412) in 1966 alone exceeded the amount of the disparity in the contributions. Indeed, at the end of 1967, petitioners' capital account showed a deficit of $25,187.11 compared with a positive balance of $405.65 in the Crisafis' account. By the time the partnership's properties are fully depreciated, the amount of the reduction in petitioners' capital account will approximate the remaining basis for the buildings as of the end of 1967. The Crisafis' capital account will be adjusted only for contributions, withdrawals, gain or loss, without regard to depreciation, and similar adjustments for these factors will also be made in petitioners' capital account. Thus, rather than correcting an imbalance in the capital accounts of the partners, the special allocation of depreciation will create a vastly greater imbalance than existed at the end of 1966. In the light of these facts, we find it incredible that equalization of the capital accounts was the objective of the special allocation.[2]

2. We recognize that petitioners had more money invested in the partnership than the Crisafis and that it is reasonable for the partners to endeavor to equalize their investments, since each one was to share equally in the profits and losses of the enterprise. However, we do not think that sec. 704(a) permits the partners' prospective tax benefits to be used as the medium for equalizing their investments, and it is apparent that the economic burden of the depreciation (which is reflected by the allowance for depreciation) was not intended to be the medium used.

This case is to be distinguished from situations where one partner contributed property and the other cash; in such cases sec. 704(c) may allow a special allocation of income and expenses in order to reflect the tax consequences inherent in the original contributions.

Petitioners rely primarily on the argument that the allocation has "substantial economic effect" in that it is reflected in the capital accounts of the partners. Referring to the material quoted above from the report of the Senate Committee on Finance, they contend that this alone is sufficient to show that the special allocation served a business rather than a tax-avoidance purpose.

According to the regulations, an allocation has economic effect if it "may actually affect the dollar amount of the partners' shares of the total partnership income or loss independently of tax consequences." The agreement in this case provided not only for the allocation of depreciation to petitioners but also for gain on the sale of the partnership property to be "charged back" to them. The charge back would cause the gain, for tax purposes, to be allocated on the books entirely to petitioners to the extent of the special allocation of depreciation, and their capital account would be correspondingly increased. The remainder of the gain, if any, would be shared equally by the partners. If the gain on the sale were to equal or exceed the depreciation specially allocated to petitioners, the increase in their capital account caused by the charge back would exactly equal the depreciation deductions previously allowed to them and the proceeds of the sale of the property would be divided equally. In such circumstances, the only effect of the allocation would be a trade of tax consequences, i.e., the Crisafis would relinquish a current depreciation deduction in exchange for exoneration from all or part of the capital gains tax when the property is sold, and petitioners would enjoy a larger current depreciation deduction but would assume a larger ultimate capital gains tax liability. Quite clearly, if the property is sold at a gain, the special allocation will affect only the tax liabilities of the partners and will have no other economic effect.

To find any economic effect of the special allocation agreement aside from its tax consequences, we must, therefore, look to see who is to bear the economic burden of the depreciation if the buildings should be sold for a sum less than their original cost. There is not one syllable of evidence bearing directly on this crucial point. We have noted, however, that when the buildings are fully depreciated, petitioners' capital account will have a deficit, or there will be a disparity in the capital accounts, approximately equal to the undepreciated basis of the buildings as of the beginning of 1966. Under normal accounting procedures, if the building were sold at a gain less than the amount of such disparity petitioners would either be required to contribute to the partnership a sum equal to the remaining deficit in their capital account after the gain on the sale had been added back or would be entitled to receive a proportionately smaller share of the partnership assets on liquidation. Based on the record as a whole, we do not think the partners ever agreed to such an arrangement. On dissolution, we think the partners contemplated an equal division of the partnership assets which would be adjusted only for disparities in cash contributions or withdrawals.[3] Certainly

3. We note that, in the course of Orrisch's testimony, petitioners' counsel made a distinction between entries in the taxpayers' capital accounts which reflect actual cash transactions and those relating to the special allocation which are "paper entries relating to depreciation."

there is no evidence to show otherwise. That being true, the special allocation does not "actually affect the dollar amount of the partners' share of the total partnership income or loss independently of tax consequences" within the meaning of the regulation referred to above.

Our interpretation of the partnership agreement is supported by an analysis of a somewhat similar agreement, quoted in material part in our Findings, which petitioners made as part of a marital property settlement agreement in 1968. Under this agreement, Orrisch was entitled to deduct all the depreciation for 1968 in computing his income tax liability, and his wife was to deduct none; but on the sale of the property they were to first reimburse Orrisch for "such moneys as he may have advanced," and then divide the balance of the "profits or proceeds" of the sale equally, each party to report one-half of the capital gain or loss on his income tax return. In the 1969 amendment to this agreement the unequal allocation of the depreciation deduction was discontinued, and a provision similar to the partnership "charge back" was added, i.e., while the proceeds of the sale were to be divided equally, only Orrisch's basis was to be reduced by the depreciation allowed for 1968 so that he would pay taxes on a larger portion of the gain realized on the sale. Significantly, in both this agreement and the partnership agreement, as we interpret it, each party's share of the sales proceeds was determined independently from his share of the depreciation deduction.

In the light of all the evidence we have found as an ultimate fact that the "principal purpose" of the special allocation agreement was tax avoidance within the meaning of section 704(b). Accordingly, the deduction for depreciation for 1966 and 1967 must be allocated between the parties in the same manner as other deductions. . . .

NOTES AND QUESTIONS

1. *The importance of capital accounts.* Note the role of capital accounts in *Orrisch.* The Orrisches maintained that the tax allocations had substantial economic effect because they were consistent with the adjustments made to the partners' capital accounts that reflected their business deal. Why wasn't this enough in the court's view?

To understand the court's position, consider a somewhat simplified version of the facts in *Orrisch.* Assume that O and C contribute $1,000 each to the OC partnership which purchases five-year depreciable property for $2,000. They agree to share all tax items equally except for depreciation which is to be allocated entirely to O. In addition, any tax gain upon disposition of the property will be allocated disproportionately to O up to the amount of the depreciation deductions (a "gain chargeback" provision), with any remaining gain shared equally. Finally, they agree that all tax allocations will be accompanied by corresponding adjustments to the partners' book capital accounts.

Suppose that in Years 1-3, partnership income exactly offsets deductions except for annual depreciation deductions of $400. Under these facts, at the end of Year 3, O has a deficit capital account balance of $200 and C has a positive balance of $1,000.

Suppose the property is sold at the beginning of Year 4. The court considered two possible scenarios: sale of the property for an amount (1) equal to or greater than its original cost or (2) less than its original cost. Suppose, consistent with the first scenario, the property is sold for $2,000. What impact would this sale have upon the partners' capital accounts? What was the court's reaction to this possible outcome? Did it believe this situation would have any economic effect on the parties apart from tax consequences?

Now suppose, consistent with the second scenario, the property is sold for $800. Again, what would the partners' book capital accounts look like after this sale? Did the court think this situation would have any economic effect? Why or why not?

2. *Would "partial" economic effect have been enough?* Suppose O and C had agreed that a partner with a deficit capital account balance on liquidation would not receive anything but would not be required to make up the deficit. Suppose they also intended to respect all positive account balances as much as possible on liquidation. Finally, suppose their partnership agreement did not contain a special gain chargeback provision. Based on its reasoning in *Orrisch*, do you think the Tax Court would have validated a special allocation of depreciation to O under these circumstances? Why or why not? Use the same two scenarios in the previous question to help explain your answer. Does your answer depend upon what the parties expected the sales price for the property to be?

3. *Tax-avoidance purpose.* In *Orrisch*, the court found that there was "persuasive" evidence that the special allocation of depreciation was for a tax-avoidance purpose. Still, the court seemed at least willing to consider whether the allocation might nevertheless be approved if it had substantial economic effect. Should the presence of a tax-avoidance purpose be the end of the inquiry? As you learn more about the existing substantial-economic-effect test for validating partnership allocations, consider whether it would be preferable to rely simply upon a no-tax-avoidance-purpose test.

4. *"Bottom-line" allocations.* Prior to 1976, there was some question whether a special "bottom-line" allocation, i.e., the allocation of *residual* amounts of income or loss after taking into account the allocation of any separately stated partnership tax items (see current I.R.C. § 702(a)(8)), could be invalidated even if the principal purpose of the special allocation was tax avoidance or evasion. Cf. Kresser v. Comm'r, 54 T.C. 1621, 1631 n.5 (1970). By its terms, former section 704(b) seemed to apply only to the special allocation of specific tax *items* and it authorized a reallocation only in accordance with the manner of the bottom-line allocation. (See footnote 1 of the *Orrisch* opinion, which reproduces the pre-1976 version of section 704(b).) The statute was amended in 1976 to clarify this issue. See also Reg.

§ 1.704-1(b)(1)(vii) (current regulations apply to bottom-line allocations as well as allocations of specific partnership items).

B. The Section 704(b) Regulations: General Rules

1. *Overview*

Read Reg. § 1.704-1(b)(1)(i). This provision sets forth three ways in which a partnership's tax allocations may be respected: (1) the allocation has substantial economic effect, (2) the allocation is in accordance with the partners' interests in the partnership, or (3) the allocation is deemed to be in accordance with the partners' interests in the partnership under special rules. The regulations contain three parts corresponding to each of these tests.

The first part, Reg. § 1.704-1(b)(2), defines substantial economic effect by reference to a strict and detailed set of rules that provide, in effect, a safe harbor to ensure that a partnership's allocations will be respected. The safe harbor consists of two independent requirements, termed "economic effect" and "substantiality," both of which must be satisfied to qualify for the safe harbor.

The second part, Reg. § 1.704-1(b)(3), defines the term "partners' interest in the partnership" ("PIP"). This concept serves essentially as a default rule for allocations that fail to meet the safe harbor for substantial economic effect. Unlike the latter, the PIP test is much less well defined and fraught with uncertainty. Both the substantial-economic-effect safe harbor and the PIP definition, however, have the same, fundamental objective: both seek to ensure that the partnership's allocations of tax items are consistent with the partners' sharing of the economic benefits and burdens corresponding to the tax items.

The final part, Reg. § 1.704-1(b)(4), contains special rules for certain tax items whose allocation inherently lacks economic effect because there is no economic benefit or burden corresponding to the item. Under specified conditions, allocation of such items will be deemed to be consistent with the PIP and therefore valid. Formerly, this part contained the rules for allocating deductions attributable to nonrecourse debt. However, these rules are now dealt with separately in Reg. § 1.704-2 and are considered in chapter five of this book.

Regulation § 1.704-1(b)(5) contains examples illustrating the operation of these rules. While occasionally daunting, these examples provide useful guidance and are cross-referenced throughout the other portions of the regulations.

In the remainder of this part, we describe first the "economic effect" and "substantiality" requirements of the substantial-economic-effect safe harbor. We then turn to the PIP definition. We conclude this part with a brief discussion of tax items whose allocation is deemed to be consistent with the PIP.

2. *Economic Effect*

Read Reg. § 1.704-1(b)(2)(i) and (ii)(*a*). As you can see, the substantial-economic-effect safe harbor consists of two independent requirements: economic effect and substantiality. A tax allocation has economic effect only if it is "consistent with the underlying economic arrangement of the partners." In general, this means that a partner who is allocated a particular tax item must also share in the economic benefit or burden associated with such item. The regulations provide three specific ways for an allocation to have economic effect: it can meet the basic or alternate test for economic effect, or it can be deemed to be equivalent to economic effect (sometimes referred to as the "dumb but lucky" rule).

a. Basic Test for Economic Effect

The basic test for economic effect is quite straightforward. Read Reg. § 1.704-1(b)(2)(ii)(*b*)(*1*)-(*3*). As a technical matter, the basic test for economic effect contains three conditions:

(1) Capital-Account Maintenance. The partnership must maintain capital accounts strictly in accordance with the rules of Reg. § 1.704-1(b)(2)(iv), discussed in chapter three;
(2) Liquidating Distributions. Distributions in liquidation of the partnership (or any partner's interest in the partnership) must be made in accordance with the partners' positive capital account balances; and
(3) Unlimited Deficit Make-Up. If any partner has a deficit balance in her capital account following liquidation of her partnership interest, she must be unconditionally obligated to restore the amount of such deficit.

As you can see, the basic test merely requires that the partners maintain their book capital accounts in the manner described in chapter three and respect their account balances upon liquidation. The amount of any positive balance must actually be distributed to the partner, and the amount of any deficit balance must be contributed to the partnership by the partner with the deficit.

The key portion of the capital account maintenance rules, of course, is the requirement that amounts allocated to a partner for tax purposes also be allocated to the partner's capital account. Review Reg. § 1.704-1(b)(2)(iv)(*b*)(*3*) and (*7*). Thus, if partner A is allocated $100 of taxable income in a given year, A's capital account must also be increased by $100 to reflect an economic profit share of that amount. Further, if A were to liquidate her partnership interest at the end of the year, the proceeds received by A must take into account that $100 increase. These requirements are intended to ensure a one-to-one correspondence between the tax and economic effects of the partnership's activities to the partners. By focusing on liquidating distributions, the economic-effect test provides an opportunity to determine whether a partner will ultimately receive the economic benefit (or bear the economic burden) of tax items allocated to that partner.

The theory behind the required matching of taxable and economic amounts allocated to a partner is that assuming positive marginal income tax rates of less than 100 percent, no partner would accept the allocation of a $100 economic loss merely to obtain a tax deduction of the same amount. Likewise, no partner would be willing to accept the allocation of a $100 economic gain to another partner merely to save taxes on the same amount. Thus, the economic allocation should drive the tax allocation and not vice-versa.

QUESTION

Reconsider the *Orrisch* case. Did the partnership agreement in that case satisfy the basic test for economic effect? Why not?

b. Alternate Test for Economic Effect

Many partners are unwilling to comply with the third condition of the basic test for economic effect—the requirement that a partner have an unlimited deficit restoration obligation ("DRO"). This requirement is inconsistent with the economic commitment a limited partner or LLC member is ordinarily willing to make to a venture. Furthermore, although under state law, general partners are personally liable for the partnership's debts to creditors, they may in some cases wish to limit their obligation to repay losses attributable to another partner's capital.

The regulations take this practical reality into account by providing an alternate means of satisfying economic effect. The logic of the alternate test is very simple to understand. The failure of a partner to have an *unlimited* DRO is a problem only when such partner has, in fact, a deficit in her capital account balance that exceeds the amount (if any) of her limited obligation to restore deficits. Thus, so long as an allocation does not cause a partner with a limited DRO to have a deficit balance in excess of such limited obligation, the allocation can be respected. This conclusion assumes, of course, that the partners maintain their capital accounts correctly and respect all *positive* balances.

> **Example 4-1:** Assume that partner C is obligated to restore a deficit in her capital account balance only up to $100. In other words, if C's account deficit should exceed $100 upon liquidation, she could contribute $100 to the venture and then be rid of any further responsibility. In this situation, a tax allocation causing C to have a deficit of no more than $100 is unobjectionable because the allocation still affects the amount C will receive from (or have to contribute to) the partnership. On the other hand, an allocation would be invalid to the extent that it gives rise to a deficit in excess of $100. The portion of the allocation

creating a deficit in excess of $100 would have to be reallocated to other partners.

Read Reg. § 1.704-1(b)(2)(ii)(*d*). As you can see, to satisfy the alternate test for economic effect, a partnership must still maintain capital accounts properly and respect positive balances. The third requirement (unlimited DRO), however, is not obligatory. An allocation to a partner who does not have an unlimited DRO may, nevertheless, have economic effect so long as (1) the allocation does not cause the partner to have a current or anticipated deficit in her capital account (in excess of any limited DRO), and (2) the partnership agreement contains an additional provision known as a qualified income offset ("QIO"). The purpose of the QIO is to eliminate, as quickly as possible, any *unexpected* deficit in excess of a partner's limited DRO, e.g., as a result of an unexpected distribution. Read Reg. § 1.704-1(b)(2)(ii)(*d*)(6), flush language (2d sentence), for the definition of a QIO. Note that a QIO provision may require an allocation of *gross* income or gain to a partner who receives an unexpected distribution that drives her capital account impermissibly negative.

Problem 4-1: G (the general partner) and L (the limited partner) contribute $100,000 each to the GL partnership, which purchases ten-year depreciable property for $200,000. The partnership meets the first two requirements of the basic economic-effect test. L is not required to restore any deficit in her capital account, but the partnership agreement contains a QIO. Under the partnership agreement, all depreciation deductions are allocated to L and all other tax items are to be shared equally by the two partners.

(a) During the first six years, the partnership breaks even except for its deductions attributable to depreciation ($20,000 annually). Determine whether all of the partnership's allocations in these years satisfy the economic-effect requirement.
(b) Same as (a), except that L agrees to restore up to a $25,000 deficit in her capital account. Does this fact change any of your responses to question (a), and if so, how?
(c) Same as (a), except that the partners anticipate, prior to the end of Year 5, that the partnership will have $30,000 in net profits in Year 6 and that such money will be distributed equally to G and L, $15,000 each, in that year. Do these facts change any of your responses to question (a), and if so, how? Read Reg. § 1.704-1(b)(2)(ii)(*d*)(6).
(d) Same as (c), except that the profits in Year 6 never materialize. The partnership realizes $50,000 of gross income in that year but also has $50,000 in business deductions as well as a $20,000 depreciation deduction. Despite the absence of any net profits, the partnership makes the $30,000 distribution in Year 6, funded by the proceeds of a partnership

recourse borrowing of that amount. How must the partnership's tax items be allocated in Years 1-6 in order to have economic effect?

(e) Same as (d), except that the partnership did not anticipate any net profits in Year 6. Instead, the partnership expected from the outset to fund the $30,000 distribution in Year 6 by a partnership recourse borrowing of that amount. How must the partnership's tax items be allocated in Years 1-6 in order to have economic effect?

NOTES AND QUESTIONS

1. *"Expected" vs. "unexpected" distributions.* In determining whether an allocation will cause a deficit balance in excess of a partner's limited obligation to restore deficits, the regulations require the partnership to distinguish between expected and unexpected distributions. How is that assessment made, as a practical matter?

2. *"Wait-and-see" approach?* Some critics maintain that the rule for expected distributions is excessively burdensome. To what extent does this rule introduce an element of uncertainty into the otherwise mechanical test for economic effect? Would a wait-and-see approach be preferable?

3. *Partners with unlimited DROs.* Why is no special rule for distributions (expected or otherwise) needed in the case of partners with unlimited DROs? Note that allocations to such partners will be governed by the basic economic-effect test, even if allocations to other partners must qualify under the alternate test.

4. *Reversing the effect of a QIO.* A QIO may alter rather dramatically the partners' business deal by forcing gross income to one partner, thereby increasing the bottom-line loss allocated to other partners. Experienced partnership practitioners may try to draft around this problem by "reversing" the effect of a QIO in later years. Care is needed to ensure that the subsequent allocations do not unintentionally violate the section 704(b) regulations.

Rev. Rul. 97-38

1997-2 C.B. 69

ISSUE

If a partner is treated as having a limited deficit restoration obligation under § 1.704-1(b)(2)(ii)(*c*) of the Income Tax Regulations by reason of the partner's liability to the partnership's creditors, how is the amount of that obligation calculated?

FACTS

In year 1, GP and LP, general partner and limited partner, each contribute $100x to form limited partnership LPRS. In general, GP and LP share LPRS's income and loss 50 percent each. However, LPRS allocated to GP all depreciation deductions and gain from the sale of depreciable assets up to the amount of those deductions. LPRS maintains capital accounts according to the rules set forth in § 1.704-1(b)(2)(iv), and the partners agree to liquidate according to positive capital account balances under the rules of § 1.704-1(b)(2)(ii)(*b*)(*2*).

Under applicable state law, GP is liable to creditors for all partnership recourse liabilities, but LP has no personal liability. GP and LP do not agree to unconditional deficit restoration obligations as described in § 1.704-1(b)(2)(ii)(*b*)(*3*) (in general, a deficit restoration obligation requires a partner to restore any deficit capital account balance following the liquidation of the partner's interest in the partnership); GP is obligated to restore a deficit capital account only to the extent necessary to pay creditors. Thus, if LPRS were to liquidate after paying all creditors and LP had a positive capital account balance, GP would not be required to restore GP's deficit capital account to permit a liquidating distribution to LP. In addition, GP and LP agree to a qualified income offset, thus satisfying the requirements of the alternate test for economic effect of § 1.704-1(b)(2)(ii)(*d*). GP and LP also agree that no allocation will be made that causes or increases a deficit balance in any partner's capital account in excess of the partner's obligation to restore the deficit.

LPRS purchases depreciable property for $1,000x from an unrelated seller, paying $200x in cash and borrowing the $800x balance from an unrelated bank that is not the seller of the property. The note is recourse to LPRS. The principal of the loan is due in 6 years; interest is payable semi-annually at the applicable federal rate. GP bears the entire economic risk of loss for LPRS's recourse liability, and GP's basis in LPRS (outside basis) is increased by $800x. See § 1.752-2.

In each of years 1 through 5, the property generates $200x of depreciation. All other partnership deductions and losses exactly equal income, so that in each of years 1 through 5 LPRS has a net loss of $200x.

LAW AND ANALYSIS

Under § 704(b) of the Internal Revenue Code and the regulations thereunder, a partnership's allocations of income, gain, loss, deduction, or credit set forth in the partnership agreement are respected if they have substantial economic effect. If allocations under the partnership agreement would not have substantial economic effect, the partnership's allocations are determined according to the partners' interests in the partnership. The fundamental principles for establishing economic effect require an allocation to be consistent with the partners' underlying economic arrangement. A partner allocated a share of income should enjoy any corresponding economic benefit, and a partner allocated a share of losses or deductions should bear any corresponding economic burden. See § 1.704-1(b)(2)(ii)(*a*).

To come within the safe harbor for establishing economic effect in § 1.704-1(b)(2)(ii), partners must agree to maintain capital accounts under the rules of § 1.704-1(b)(2)(iv), liquidate according to positive capital account balances, and agree to an unconditional deficit restoration obligation for any partner with a deficit in that partner's capital account, as described in § 1.704-1(b)(2)(ii)(*b*)(*3*). Alternatively, the partnership may satisfy the requirements of the alternate test for economic effect provided in § 1.704-1(b)(2)(ii)(*d*). LPRS's partnership agreement complies with the alternate test for economic effect.

The alternate test for economic effect requires the partners to agree to a qualified income offset in lieu of an unconditional deficit restoration obligation. If the partners so agree, allocations will have economic effect to the extent that they do not create a deficit capital account for any partner (in excess of any limited deficit restoration obligation of that partner) as of the end of the partnership taxable year to which the allocation relates. Section 1.704-1(b)(2)(ii)(*d*)(*3*) (flush language).

A partner is treated as having a limited deficit restoration obligation to the extent of: (1) the outstanding principal balance of any promissory note contributed to the partnership by the partner, and (2) the amount of any unconditional obligation of the partner (whether imposed by the partnership agreement or by state or local law) to make subsequent contributions to the partnership. Section 1.704-1(b)(2)(ii)(*c*).

LP has no obligation under the partnership agreement or state or local law to make additional contributions to the partnership and, therefore, has no deficit restoration obligation. Under applicable state law, GP may have to make additional contributions to the partnership to pay creditors. However, GP's obligation only arises to the extent that the amount of LPRS's liabilities exceeds the value of LPRS's assets available to satisfy the liabilities. Thus, the amount of GP's limited deficit restoration obligation each year is equal to the difference between the amount of the partnership's recourse liabilities at the end of the year and the value of the partnership's assets available to satisfy the liabilities at the end of the year.

To ensure consistency with the other requirements of the regulations under § 704(b), where a partner's obligation to make additional contributions to the partnership is dependent on the value of the partnership's assets, the partner's deficit restoration obligation must be computed by reference to the rules for determining the value of partnership property contained in the regulations under § 704(b). Consequently, in computing GP's limited deficit restoration obligation, the value of the partnership's assets is conclusively presumed to equal the book basis of those assets under the capital account maintenance rules of § 1.704-1(b)(2)(iv). See § 1.704-1(b)(2)(ii)(*d*) (value equals basis presumption applies for purposes of determining expected allocations and distributions under the alternate test for economic effect); § 1.704-1(b)(2)(iii) (value equals basis presumption applies for purposes of the substantiality test); § 1.704-1(b)(3)(iii) (value equals basis presumption applies for purposes of the partner's interest in the partnership test); § 1.704-2(d) (value equals basis presumption applies in computing partnership minimum gain).

The LPRS agreement allocates all depreciation deductions and gain on the sale of depreciable property to the extent of those deductions to GP. Because LPRS's partnership agreement satisfies the alternate test for economic effect, the allocations of depreciation deductions to GP will have economic effect to the extent that they do not create a deficit capital account for GP in excess of GP's obligation to restore the deficit balance. At the end of year 1, the basis of the depreciable property has been reduced to $800x. If LPRS liquidated at the beginning of year 2, selling its depreciable property for its basis of $800x, the proceeds would be used to repay the $800x principal on LPRS's recourse liability. All of LPRS's creditors would be satisfied and GP would have no obligation to contribute to pay them. Thus, at the end of year 1, GP has no obligation to restore a deficit in its capital account.

Because GP has no obligation to restore a deficit balance in its capital account at the end of year 1, an allocation that reduces GP's capital account below $0 is not permitted under the partnership agreement and would not satisfy the alternate test for economic effect. An allocation of $200x of depreciation deductions to GP would reduce GP's capital account to negative $100x. Because the allocation would result in a deficit capital account balance in excess of GP's obligation to restore, the allocation is not permitted under the partnership agreement, and would not satisfy the safe harbor under the alternate test for economic effect. Therefore, the deductions for year 1 must be allocated $100x each to GP and LP (which is in accordance with their interests in the partnership).

The allocation of depreciation of $200x to GP in year 2 has economic effect. Although the allocation reduces GP's capital account to negative $200x, while LP's capital account remains $0, the allocation to GP does not create a deficit capital account in excess of GP's limited deficit restoration obligation. If LPRS liquidated at the beginning of year 3, selling the depreciable property for its basis of $600x, the proceeds would be applied toward the $800x LPRS liability. Because GP is obligated to restore a deficit capital account to the extent necessary to pay creditors, GP would be required to contribute $200x to LPRS to satisfy the outstanding liability. Thus, at the end of year 2, GP has a deficit restoration obligation of $200x, and the allocation of depreciation to GP does not reduce GP's capital account below its obligation to restore a deficit capital account.

This analysis also applies to the allocation of $200x of depreciation to GP in years 3 through 5. At the beginning of year 6, when the property is fully depreciated, the $800x principal amount of the partnership liability is due. The partners' capital accounts at the beginning of year 6 will equal negative $800x and $0, respectively, for GP and LP. Because value is conclusively presumed to equal basis, the depreciable property would be worthless and could not be used to satisfy LPRS's $800x liability. As a result, GP is deemed to be required to contribute $800x to LPRS. A contribution by GP to satisfy this limited deficit restoration obligation would increase GP's capital account balance to $0.

HOLDING

When a partner is treated as having a limited deficit restoration obligation by reason of the partner's liability to the partnership's creditors, the amount of that obligation is the amount of money that the partner would be required to contribute to the partnership to satisfy partnership liabilities if all partnership property were sold for the amount of the partnership's book basis in the property.

QUESTIONS

1. As a conceptual matter, why is the allocation of depreciation deductions to GP valid in Year 2 but invalid in Year 1? What is the difference between those deductions?

2. Based on the facts in the ruling, did the parties agree to respect positive capital account balances *in all cases* upon liquidation of the partnership or any partner's interest in the partnership? Cf. Reg. § 1.704-1(b)(2)(ii)(*b*)(*2*).

c. Economic Effect Equivalence

Even if an allocation fails to satisfy either the basic or alternate test for economic effect, it may nevertheless be deemed to have economic effect under the "economic effect equivalence" test. See Reg. § 1.704-1(b)(2)(ii)(*i*). This exception is quite narrow, because it applies only if the partners can demonstrate that the partnership's arrangements produce the same economic results as would have occurred if all three requirements of the basic economic-effect test had been satisfied. Thus, the economic-effect-equivalence test is unlikely to be helpful except in the case of a general partnership with relatively simple sharing arrangements. In that case, a failure to comply with some technical requirement will be overlooked so long as the substantive outcome after every taxable year is the one the regulations mandate. Partnerships with sharing ratios that are at all complicated, or that have some partners with limited DROs, will almost certainly have to comply with either the basic or alternate test in order to meet the economic-effect requirement.

3. *Substantiality*

a. Introduction

In addition to having "economic effect," an allocation must satisfy a second requirement, termed "substantiality" (in a curious use of the word), in order to qualify for the substantial-economic-effect safe harbor. These two requirements are independent of one another: failure to meet either one means loss of the safe harbor protection.

Why is a second requirement needed? There are at least two reasons. For one thing, the economic-effect test merely requires a matching of the *pre-tax* consequences of tax and book allocations. In other words, if $100 of income is allocated to a particular partner for tax purposes, then that partner must also be allocated the $100 economic benefit corresponding to that income. Unfortunately, there are different *characters* of income which, depending upon the tax attributes of the partner, may vary the after-tax consequences of these allocations. Thus, to a taxable partner, an allocation of $100 of ordinary income may have very different tax consequences than, for example, an allocation of the same amount of capital gain or tax-exempt income; yet each represents the same $100 economic benefit and increases a partner's capital account by the same amount. In short, the substantiality requirement is needed because capital-account analysis fails to consider how the tax character of partnership items interacts with the tax attributes of the partners and, therefore, the after-tax consequences of an allocation.

> **Example 4-2:** A and B are equal partners in partnership AB which earns $100 in taxable income and $100 in tax-exempt income in a given year. The capital-account effect of allocating $50 of each item to each partner, or allocating all of the taxable income to A and all of the tax-exempt income to B, is identical. In either case, each partner's book capital account will increase by $100 to reflect an economic entitlement of that amount. Yet if A is a zero-bracket taxpayer and B is a high-bracket taxpayer, the after-tax effects of those two allocations would be considerably different.

A second reason for substantiality is illustrated by the following example which is similar to one of the scenarios considered by the court in *Orrisch*.

> **Example 4-3:** O and C contribute $1,000 each to the OC partnership which purchases five-year depreciable property for $2,000. Because C anticipates being temporarily in a low marginal income tax bracket during the next two years, the parties agree to allocate all of the partnership depreciation deductions in those two years to O. In addition, any tax gain upon disposition of the property will be allocated disproportionately to O up to the amount of the depreciation deductions allocated to him, with any remaining gain and all other items to be shared equally. The parties anticipate that the value of the property will never fall below $2,000, its original purchase price. In Years 1 and 2, the partnership's only net tax item is a $400 annual depreciation deduction. At the beginning of Year 3, the property is sold for $2,000.

If they are maintained correctly, the capital accounts of O and C as a result of the foregoing events are as follows:

	O	C
initial contribution	1,000	1,000
depreciation, Yrs. 1-2	(800)	-0-
end of Year 2	200	1,000
gain, Year 3 sale	800	-0-
balance after sale	1,000	1,000

As the court observed in *Orrisch*, the effect of the allocations in **example 4-3** may simply be a "trade of tax consequences." Following the sale, the capital account balance of each partner is back to $1,000, the same place it would have been had they simply shared all items equally in all years. Thus, there may be no economic consequences to the allocations apart from tax considerations. For tax purposes, however, C is relieved of having to pay tax on the capital gain in Year 3 in exchange for giving up his share of depreciation deductions in Years 1 and 2, and O is in the opposite situation. This trade is mutually beneficial to O and C because of their particular tax situations.

In this case, the flaw of the economic-effect requirement is its failure to make book capital accounts time-sensitive. For *tax* purposes, O may be better off in part because of the timing effect of the special allocation. The tax savings from O's "early" deductions may more than offset the tax detriment from the disproportionate share of gain O must report in Year 3. Meanwhile, C may also be better off from a tax standpoint, despite the special allocation to O. C's tax savings from depreciation deductions in Years 1 and 2 might not be as large as C's potential tax savings from avoiding an equivalent amount of gain in Year 3. Alternatively, any tax detriment to C may be more than offset by the tax benefit to O, in which case the parties can negotiate to improve their combined situation.

But there is no similar timing effect of the allocations on the partners' capital accounts. While O's capital account balance is lower than C's in the first two years, O may not suffer any corresponding economic detriment. For example, O is not required to pay any interest for, in effect, borrowing some of C's capital. Nor does C earn any interest despite having a $1,000 balance throughout the three years. Thus, when O is finally allocated the gain upon sale of the property in Year 3, his capital account balance is restored exactly equal to C's, and the timing effects of the allocations are ignored. The substantiality requirement is needed to overcome this additional inadequacy of the economic-effect requirement. (As we shall see shortly, however, although the allocations described in **example 4-3** are theoretically problematic, they in fact are valid under current law.)

In summary, the focus of substantiality is on the after-tax consequences of an allocation. The general intent is to ferret out and invalidate allocations that allow taxpayers, operating through a partnership, to achieve greater tax savings than had they simply operated on their own.

b. "Shifting," "Transitory," and "Overall-Tax-Effect" Tests for Substantiality

In general, the substantiality requirement will be satisfied if "there is a reasonable possibility that the allocation (or allocations) will affect substantially the dollar amounts to be received by the partners from the partnership, independent of tax consequences." Reg. § 1.704-1(b)(2)(iii)(*a*). This general rule, sometimes termed the "dollar-effect" test, seems to validate an allocation if it has a substantial pre-tax effect. But do not be deceived; the rule, in fact, is trumped by the "overall-tax-effect" test for substantiality which focuses on after-tax consequences. In addition, the tax law describes two other substantiality tests: "shifting" and "transitory." Shifting or transitory allocations, or ones flunking the overall-tax-effect test, are considered insubstantial and therefore in violation of the substantial-economic-effect safe harbor.

Read Reg. § 1.704-1(b)(2)(iii)(*b*) and (*c*). The shifting and transitory tests are quite similar: the principal difference is that the shifting test applies to allocations taking place in the same taxable year (like **example 4-2** above) and the transitory test applies to allocations in more than one year (like **example 4-3** above). Each test, however, asks the same two questions about the allocations at issue:

(1) after taking account of the allocations, do the partners' capital account balances not differ substantially from what they would have been had the allocations not been made? and
(2) do the allocations reduce the collective tax liability of the partners after considering their particular tax situations?

The first question is simply a reiteration of the dollar-effect test. If the allocations *do* have a substantial impact on the partners' capital accounts, it suggests the likelihood of some economic reason for the allocations, apart from saving taxes. In that case, the allocations will not be treated as "shifting" or "transitory," although they may still be subject to challenge under the overall-tax-effect test. On the other hand, if the response to both questions is affirmative—that is, if the dollar-effect is not substantially different *and* the allocations also reduce the partners' collective tax liabilities—then the allocations will be treated as invalid under the shifting or transitory tests.

As a technical matter, both the shifting and transitory tests require a prognostication of future events. They ask whether, at the time the allocations were agreed to, there was a "strong likelihood" that they would have no significant dollar-effect and would reduce taxes. But the tax law also creates a presumption, sometimes termed the "hindsight" presumption, that there was a strong likelihood of these consequences occurring if they, in fact, do occur. Read the flush language immediately following part (*2*) of Reg. § 1.704-1(b)(2)(iii)(*b*) and (*c*). This presumption may be rebutted by evidence showing bona fide uncertainty that these consequences would occur at the time the allocations were agreed to.

The "overall-tax-effect" test for substantiality is slightly different. Read Reg. § 1.704-1(b)(2)(iii)(*a*). It also asks two questions:

(1) is the after-tax position of at least one partner improved as a result of the allocations (determined from a present value standpoint)? and
(2) was there a strong likelihood at the time the allocations were agreed to that the after-tax position of no partner would be substantially diminished by the allocations (again determined from a present value standpoint)?

An affirmative answer to each question causes the allocations to flunk the overall-tax-effect test. As a result, the allocation will be deemed insubstantial.

The overall-tax-effect test inquires whether the allocations improve at least one partner's after-tax position without substantially diminishing the after-tax position of any other partner. The purpose of the overall-tax-effect test is thus to invalidate allocations that achieve a net after-tax benefit for one or more partners at the expense solely of the government. Note that the overall-tax-effect test specifically incorporates present value concepts. In contrast, the shifting and transitory tests do *not* include a present value analysis.

There is significant overlap between the shifting and transitory tests, on the one hand, and the overall-tax-effect test, on the other. By doing the following problem, see if you can identify the principal similarities and differences among the three tests.

Problem 4-2: Identify which substantiality test(s), if any, are violated by the following allocations:

(a) A is a U.S. corporation which is taxed on its worldwide income at the marginal tax rate of 35 percent. B is a foreign corporation which is taxed by the U.S. only on its domestic (U.S.)-source income, also at a rate of 35 percent. B is not taxed by the U.S. on any foreign-source income. Assume that A and B are partners of the AB partnership and they agree to share all partnership items equally except for any net domestic-source income (which is allocated all to A) and any net foreign-source income (which is allocated all to B). At the time these allocations are agreed to, there is a strong likelihood that the partnership will have $150 of net domestic-source income and $120 of net foreign-source income in the coming year. In fact, the partnership realizes these amounts and allocates them in accordance with the agreement.

(b) Same as (a), except that at the time the allocations are agreed to, there is a strong likelihood that the partnership will have $125 of net domestic-source income and $120 of net foreign-source income in the coming year. In fact, the partnership realizes these amounts and allocates them in accordance with the agreement.

(c) Same as (a), except that at the time the allocations are agreed to, the partnership is unsure how much foreign- and domestic-source income it will have in the coming year. The partnership ends up realizing $125 of net domestic-source income and $120 of net foreign-source income and allocates these amounts according to the agreement.

(d) C and D are corporate partners in partnership CD. C anticipates being in the 35 percent marginal income tax bracket in Year 1 and future years. D expects to be subject only to the corporate alternative minimum tax in those years; thus, D will be taxed at a marginal rate of 20 percent. The partnership owns a single piece of depreciable property with a remaining recovery period of one year. The partnership agreement allocates all the depreciation (of $100) to C in Year 1 and provides further that C will be specially allocated an equal amount of income as soon as possible after Year 1. All other items of the partnership are to be shared equally. Assume that at the time of the allocations, in addition to the $100 depreciation deduction in Year 1, the parties anticipate that the partnership will have $200 of net income in both Years 1 and 2. Finally, assume that all of the parties' expectations for Years 1 and 2 actually come to pass and that the partnership allocates all items consistent with the parties' agreement.

(e) A partnership consists of several major partners and one extremely minor one with an interest in the partnership of less than one percent. In the same year, several special allocations improve the after-tax position of all of the major partners, but leave the minor one substantially worse off after taxes.

c. The "Value-Equals-Basis" and Five-Year Rules

Review again **example 4-3**, which is similar to the *Orrisch* facts. Do the allocations in that example violate the transitory test for substantiality?

Note that following the sale in Year 3, the capital account balances of the partners do not differ from what they would have been if the parties had divided all items equally. Moreover, given the particular tax situations of O and C, the allocations reduce the partners' collective tax liabilities. Thus, it might seem that this example represents a classic case of an invalid transitory allocation.

But that conclusion would be wrong. Read the last three sentences of the long, long "flush language" immediately following Reg. § 1.704-1(b)(2)(iii)(*c*)(*2*). The sentences describe an important, and *conclusive*, presumption in the tax law to the effect that the value of partnership property is equal to its adjusted tax basis (the "value-equals-basis" rule). Thus, in **example 4-3**, there could not have been a strong likelihood at the time the allocations were agreed to that O would eventually be allocated gain upon sale of the depreciable property to offset the initial allocation of depreciation deductions. This is true notwithstanding the fact that the parties expected the property to hold its value (so that a sale would generate sufficient gain to offset the prior depreciation) and such expectation eventually proved to be true. Hence, a gain chargeback can never give rise to a transitory allocation. See Reg. § 1.704-1(b)(2)(iii)(*c*), -1(b)(5) (ex. 1(vi), (xi)).

Why is the value-equals-basis presumption in the tax law? The standard explanation is administrative convenience; the presumption avoids the many valuation controversies that would otherwise ensue. If there were no such presumption, then in common cases like the one described in **example 4-3**, both taxpayers and the government would have to assemble evidence regarding the parties' expectations concerning future property values at the time the allocations were agreed to. Indeed, the value-equals-basis rule is an integral part of the capital accounting rules, which might otherwise be unworkable as a practical matter. But presumably, there were also other considerations dictating inclusion of the rule. For example, real estate investments make frequent use of sharing arrangements similar to the one described in **example 4-3**. Absent the value-equals-basis presumption, such arrangements might be invalidated for tax purposes.

A second, important and conclusive presumption is the "five-year rule." Read the fourth sentence of the same long "flush language" immediately following Reg. § 1.704-1(b)(2)(iii)(*c*)(*2*). Under this rule, two allocations will not be considered transitory if, at the time the allocations are agreed to, there is a strong likelihood that the original allocation(s) will not be "largely offset" within the following five-year period (determined on a first-in, first-out basis). For example, assume that the parties in **example 4-3** expect to depreciate the property fully in Years 1-5 but plan to hold the property indefinitely. They also expect to have sufficient income in Year 11 to offset the prior depreciation deductions and agree at the outset to specially allocate such income to O. The special allocation of income in Year 11 would be insulated under the five-year rule, even though the parties expected it to occur. The logic behind the five-year rule is apparently that, if an offsetting allocation is deferred for a sufficient period of time, an appreciable economic risk exists that the original allocation may never be neutralized. The five-year rule is essentially arbitrary but partnership allocations are often drafted with an eye toward coming within this safe harbor.

Rev. Rul. 99-43

1999-2 C.B. 506

ISSUE

Do partnership allocations lack substantiality under § 1.704-1(b)(2)(iii) of the Income Tax Regulations when the partners amend the partnership agreement to create offsetting special allocations of particular items after the events giving rise to the items have occurred?

FACTS

A and B, both individuals, formed a general partnership, PRS. A and B each contributed $1,000 and also agreed that each would be allocated a 50-percent share of all partnership items. The partnership agreement provides that, upon the contribution of additional capital by either partner, PRS must revalue the partnership's property and adjust the partners' capital accounts under § 1.704-1(b)(2)(iv)(*f*).

PRS borrowed $8,000 from a bank and used the borrowed and contributed funds to purchase nondepreciable property for $10,000. The loan was nonrecourse to A and B and was secured only by the property. No principal payments were due for 6 years, and interest was payable semi-annually at a market rate.

After one year, the fair market value of the property fell from $10,000 to $6,000, but the principal amount of the loan remained $8,000. As part of a workout arrangement among the bank, PRS, A, and B, the bank reduced the principal amount of the loan by $2,000, and A contributed an additional $500 to PRS. A's capital account was credited with the $500, which PRS used to pay currently deductible expenses incurred in connection with the workout. All $500 of the currently deductible workout expenses were allocated to A. B made no additional contribution of capital. At the time of the workout, B was insolvent within the meaning of § 108(a) of the Internal Revenue Code. A and B agreed that, after the workout, A would have a 60-percent interest and B would have a 40-percent interest in the profits and losses of PRS.

As a result of the property's decline in value and the workout, PRS had two items to allocate between A and B. First, the agreement to cancel $2,000 of the loan resulted in $2,000 of cancellation of indebtedness income (COD income). Second, A's contribution of $500 to PRS was an event that required PRS, under the partnership agreement, to revalue partnership property and adjust A's and B's capital accounts. Because of the decline in value of the property, the revaluation resulted in a $4,000 economic loss that must be allocated between A's and B's capital accounts.

Under the terms of the original partnership agreement, PRS would have allocated these items equally between A and B. A and B, however, amend the partnership agreement (in a timely manner) to make two special allocations. First, PRS specially allocates the entire $2,000 of COD income to B, an insolvent partner. Second, PRS specially allocates the book loss from the revaluation $1,000 to A and $3,000 to B.

While A receives a $1,000 allocation of book loss and B receives a $3,000 allocation of book loss, neither of these allocations results in a tax loss to either partner. Rather, the allocations result only in adjustments to A's and B's capital accounts. Thus, the cumulative effect of the special allocations is to reduce each partner's capital account to zero immediately following the allocations despite the fact that B is allocated $2,000 of income for tax purposes. . . .

ANALYSIS

. . . A and B amended the PRS partnership agreement to provide for an allocation of the entire $2,000 of the COD income to B. B, an insolvent taxpayer, is eligible to exclude the income under § 108, so it is unlikely that the $2,000 of COD income would increase B's immediate tax liability. Without the special allocation, A, who is not insolvent or otherwise entitled to exclude the COD income under § 108, would pay tax immediately on the $1,000 of COD income allocated under the general ratio for sharing income. A and B also amended the PRS partnership agreement to provide for the special allocation of the book loss resulting from the revaluation. Because the two special allocations offset each other, B will not realize any economic benefit from the $2,000 income allocation, even if the property subsequently appreciates in value.

The economics of PRS are unaffected by the paired special allocations. After the capital accounts of A and B are adjusted to reflect the special allocations, A and B each have a capital account of zero. Economically, the situation of both partners is identical to what it would have been had the special allocations not occurred. In addition, a strong likelihood exists that the total tax liability of A and B will be less than if PRS had allocated 50 percent of the $2,000 of COD income and 50 percent of the $4,000 book loss to each partner. Therefore, the special allocations of COD income and book loss are shifting allocations under § 1.704-1(b)(2)(iii)(*b*) and lack substantiality. (Alternatively, the allocations could be transitory allocations under § 1.704-1(b)(2)(iii)(*c*) if the allocations occur during different partnership taxable years.)

This conclusion is not altered by the "value equals basis" rule that applies in determining the substantiality of an allocation. See § 1.704-1(b)(2)(iii)(*c*)(*2*). Under that rule, the adjusted tax basis (or, if different, the book value) of partnership property will be presumed to be the fair market value of the property. This presumption is appropriate in most cases because, under § 1.704-1(b)(2)(iv), property generally will be reflected on the books of the partnership at its fair market value when acquired. Thus, an allocation of gain or loss from the disposition of the property will reflect subsequent changes in the value of the property that generally cannot be predicted.

The substantiality of an allocation, however, is analyzed "at the time the allocation becomes part of the partnership agreement," not the time at which the allocation is first effective. See § 1.704-1(b)(2)(iii)(*a*). In the situation described above, the provisions of the PRS partnership agreement governing the allocation of gain or loss from the disposition of property are changed at a time that is after the property has been revalued on the books of the partnership, but are effective for a period that begins prior to the revaluation. See § 1.704-1(b)(2)(iv)(*f*).

Under these facts, the presumption that value equals basis does not apply to validate the allocations. Instead, PRS's allocations of gain or loss must be closely scrutinized in determining the appropriate tax consequences. Cf. § 1.704-1(b)(4)(vi). In this situation, the special allocations of the $2,000 of COD income and $4,000 of book loss will not be respected and, instead, must be allocated in accordance with the A's and B's interests in the partnership under § 1.704-1(b)(3).

Close scrutiny also would be required if the changes were made at a time when the events giving rise to the allocations had not yet occurred but were likely to occur or if, under the original allocation provisions of a partnership agreement, there was a strong likelihood that a disproportionate amount of COD income earned in the future would be allocated to any partner who is insolvent at the time of the allocation and would be offset by an increased allocation of loss or a reduced allocation of income to such partner or partners.

HOLDING

Partnership special allocations lack substantiality when the partners amend the partnership agreement to specially allocate COD income and book items from a related revaluation after the events creating such items have occurred if the overall economic effect of the special allocations on the partners' capital accounts does not differ substantially from the economic effect of the original allocations in the partnership agreement.

NOTES AND QUESTIONS

1. *Why are the special allocations invalid?* The facts and reasoning of this ruling are a little tricky. To help your understanding, assume that there had been no special allocation, and that the parties had simply shared equally (consistent with their original agreement) both the $2,000 of COD income and the $4,000 book loss arising from the revaluation. In that case, immediately following the allocations, the partnership balance sheet should have appeared as follows:

Assets	*AB*	*Book*	*Liabilities*	*Tax*	*Book*
property	10,000	6,000	debt payable	6,000	6,000
			Capital	*Tax*	*Book*
			A	2,000	0
			B	2,000	0
total	10,000	6,000	total	10,000	6,000

Each partner's book capital account would be zero ($1,000 initial balance increased by $1,000 share of the COD income and decreased by $2,000 share of book loss) and each partner's tax capital account would be $2,000 ($1,000 initial balance increased by $1,000 share of the COD income). Although A also contributed an additional $500, A was allocated $500 of the deductible workout expenses (a wash). Remember that the revaluation results in a $4,000 book loss but no corresponding tax loss. As a result of the revaluation, the partnership property is considered "reverse section 704(c) property." (See part F of chapter three (p. 76).) If the property were sold for $6,000, the $4,000 tax loss would be allocated equally to A and B, eliminating any book-tax disparity.

Now, try to construct the partnership balance sheet immediately following the allocations that were actually made by the parties in the ruling. Does a comparison of the two balance sheets help you to understand the reason for the conclusion in the ruling?

2. *What are the offsetting allocations?* Identify the offsetting allocations that were held to be invalid in the ruling. Would it have made any difference if there had

been a strong likelihood at the time of the loan workout and revaluation that the $4,000 built-in tax loss would not be recognized within five years?

3. *Special allocation of future book gain.* Suppose that at the time of the loan workout and revaluation, there was a strong likelihood that the property would eventually be sold for at least $10,000, its original purchase price, and the parties agreed to allocate any book gain from such sale disproportionately to B to make up for the prior disproportionate allocation of book loss to B. Would these additional facts have affected the conclusion of the ruling?

4. *Special allocations in the initial agreement.* Suppose that at the time the partnership acquired the property, the parties had agreed that if the property were ever to decline in value and a portion of the debt were discharged, any COD income and corresponding book loss would be allocated disproportionately to B in the manner described in the ruling. If these events had actually occurred (with the same allocations to A and B as in the ruling), would the substantiality requirement have been violated?

5. *Applicability of value-equals-basis and five-year rules.* Reread carefully the value-equals-basis and five-year rules contained in the regulations. Do they apply to all three substantiality tests? If not, which ones do they apply to?

6. *Offsetting allocation of income.* Suppose a two-person partnership expects to have net losses for three years and thereafter to have net income. The partnership agreement provides that all net losses will initially be allocated to one partner and then all net income will be allocated to such partner until such time as the partnership's cumulative net income equals its cumulative net losses; thereafter, all income and losses will be allocated equally. Is the bottom-line allocation of loss valid under the section 704(b) regulations? Is there any reason to treat such a bottom-line allocation of loss differently from a special allocation of depreciation?

7. *Risky activities.* Are some activities so inherently risky that offsetting chargebacks should not be considered transitory even if they occur within five years of the original allocation(s)? See Reg. § 1.704-1(b)(5) (exs. 3 (research and development), 19(ii) (oil drilling)).

8. *Whose tax attributes must be taken into account?* If a partnership is owned by another passthrough entity such as another partnership, the substantiality of an allocation is determined by looking through such entity to the tax attributes of its owners or beneficiaries in order to ascertain the after-tax consequences of the allocation. If the partner is a member of a consolidated group of corporations, the tax attributes of the consolidated group must be taken into account. See Reg. § 1.704-1(b)(2)(iii)(*d*).

d. Testing Allocations for Substantiality

To determine whether an allocation satisfies the substantiality tests, the consequences of the allocation must be compared to those of some other sharing arrangement. The goal is to ascertain the "normative" or baseline arrangement the parties would have used to share the item had they not agreed to the special allocation in question. But in any given case, it may be quite difficult to determine what this other, normative arrangement is. The regulations describe the alternative arrangement as the one the parties would have used had the allocations under scrutiny not been included in the partnership agreement. The baseline is the "partners' interests in the partnership" ("PIP"), i.e., the parties' sharing agreement for the economic benefit or burden corresponding to the particular tax item, but without taking into account the manner in which the agreement actually allocates the item under scrutiny. Read Reg. § 1.704-1(b)(2)(iii)(*a*) (last sentence).

The following example, adapted from one contained in the regulations (see Reg. § 1.704-1(b)(5) (ex. 5)), explores the uncertainties that arise in testing substantiality:

> **Example 4-4:** Individuals I and J make equal contributions to form an investment partnership. Over the next several years, they expect to be in the marginal income tax brackets of 50 percent and 15 percent, respectively. The partnership invests in a combination of taxable and tax-exempt investments, and expects to earn about $550 of taxable interest and about $450 of tax-exempt interest in the forthcoming year. The parties agree to allocate 80 percent of the tax-exempt interest to I and the rest of such interest and all of the taxable interest to J, and to distribute cash from such income in those same proportions. They will share equally, however, any gain or loss from the sale of the partnership's investments. Assume that in the first year, all of the expectations regarding the earnings of the partnership and the tax brackets of the partners come to pass, and the partnership allocates all items in accordance with the agreement.

Based on the following comparison, the regulations conclude that the allocations fail the overall-tax-effect test and are therefore insubstantial:

allocation	I(50%)	J(15%)	test	I(50%)	J(15%)
tax-ex. inc.	360	90	tax-ex. inc.	225	225
tax. income	-0-	550	tax. income	275	275
pre-tax	360	640	pre-tax	500	500
tax	-0-	83	tax	138	41
after-tax	360	557	after-tax	362	459

As can be seen, the pre-tax and after-tax consequences of the parties' allocations are tested against the same consequences had the parties simply shared all items equally. Because the allocations make J better off after taxes and do not make I substantially worse off, the overall-tax-effect test is violated.

The "test" case is an equal sharing of both the tax-exempt and taxable income. Because the parties made equal capital contributions and agreed to share equally in any gains and losses from the sale of the investments, the assumption is that they would also have shared equally these particular types of income absent the special allocations. In other words, the "partners' interests in the partnership," for purposes of testing substantiality, is a 50-50 split of these items. In prescribing a remedy for the invalid allocations, however, the regulations do not force the parties to share the income items equally, since otherwise the partners' capital accounts would fail to reflect the total dollar amounts actually allocated to them under the agreement. Instead, the regulations treat 36 percent of each item as allocable to I with the balance allocated to J, consistent with the partners' pre-tax division of the total dollar amounts. As shown below, the pre-tax results of the original allocations and the prescribed reallocations are the same in terms of total dollar amounts (but not character of income): I and J wind up with $360 and $640, respectively.

allocation	I(50%)	J(15%)	reallocation	I(50%)	J(15%)
tax-ex. inc.	360	90	tax-ex. inc.	162	288
tax. income	-0-	550	tax. income	198	352
pre-tax	360	640	pre-tax	360	640
tax	-0-	83	tax	99	53
after-tax	360	557	after-tax	261	587

This outcome is potentially confusing because when an allocation of a tax item fails to satisfy the substantial-economic-effect safe harbor, the regulations require that the item be reallocated in accordance with the "partners' interests in the partnership." In other words, the prescribed reallocation must also reflect the partners' normative arrangement for sharing the item. In the example above, however, the regulations confirm that there are two *different* normative sharing arrangements for the taxable and tax-exempt income: a 50-50 split (for purposes of testing substantiality) and one providing I with a 36 percent share and J with a 64 percent share of each item (for purposes of actual reallocation). The larger point of this example is that in all but the simplest cases, identifying the proper comparative sharing arrangement for applying the substantiality tests is likely to be difficult.

NOTES AND QUESTIONS

1. *PIP for purposes of testing substantiality.* The regulations now expressly provide that the PIP, for purposes of testing substantiality, disregards the manner in which the partnership agreement actually allocates the item under scrutiny. See Reg. § 1.704-1(b)(2)(iii)(*a*) (last sentence). This guidance should put an end to the controversy over applying the PIP test that arose in TIFD III-E, Inc. v. U.S., 342 F. Supp. 2d 94, 117-21 (D. Conn. 2004), rev'd and remanded, 459 F.3d 220 (2d Cir. 2006). In that case, the District Court agreed with the government that it was appropriate to look to the PIP as the baseline arrangement to determine whether a particular allocation was insubstantial. However, in identifying the PIP, the District Court relied upon how the parties had actually allocated the item in their

agreement, and therefore concluded that the allocation was not insubstantial. The government argued that the court's inquiry was essentially circular and threatened to render the substantiality test meaningless. On appeal, the Second Circuit held for the government on other grounds, without addressing the technical issue under section 704(b). Even with this helpful regulatory clarification, properly identifying the PIP remains daunting in many cases.

2. *Should allocation by character be permitted?* In view of the difficulty of applying the substantiality tests and their general complexity, do you think it would be preferable to prohibit altogether any allocation based on the tax characterization of the item, such as its "tax-exempt" or "taxable" nature or its "domestic-source" or "foreign-source" origin?

3. *Comparison to tax-avoidance standard.* It might be stated that the substantial-economic-effect test merely articulates (sometimes in excruciating detail) what was already implicit in the tax-avoidance standard found in the prior regulations and case law. Even if the current section 704(b) regulations are more precise and detailed than their predecessors, is this necessarily an advantage? For whom?

4. *How much economic effect is enough?* Would it be fair to characterize the substantial-economic-effect test as meaning just enough economic effect as needed to sustain the partners' allocations? How can you tell how much is enough?

4. *Reallocation in Accordance with the Partners' Interests in the Partnership ("PIP")*

If the allocation of a partnership tax item lacks economic effect (or the effect is insubstantial), the item must be reallocated in accordance with the PIP. In general, this means that the item must be shared in the same manner that the partners share the economic benefit or burden corresponding to the item. See Reg. § 1.704-1(b)(1)(i) and -1(b)(3)(i). Since this is also the objective generally underlying the substantial-economic-effect safe harbor, the PIP rule does not provide particularly helpful guidance for taxpayers who, for one reason or another, have failed to meet the terms of that safe harbor.

The regulations elaborate to a limited extent on the meaning of the PIP. First, the PIP is determined item-by-item; the PIP for a particular item may or may not correspond to the overall economic sharing arrangement of the partners. Second, the PIP is determined by taking into account all of the facts and circumstances relating to the economic arrangement of the partners. Among the factors to consider are the partners' (1) relative contributions, (2) shares of economic profits and losses, (3) interests in cash flow and nonliquidating distributions, and (4) rights upon liquidation. See Reg. § 1.704-1(b)(3)(ii).

The PIP standard is relatively easy to apply if the partners have agreed to share all items in a particular ratio (e.g., 50:50), except for a special allocation of a particular item such as depreciation. If the special allocation is invalid, the particular item will be reallocated in accordance with the partners' overall sharing ratio. See Reg.

§ 1.704-1(b)(5) (ex. 1(i)). In more complex sharing arrangements, however, the PIP may be quite difficult to ascertain with certainty.

Finally, read Reg. § 1.704-1(b)(3)(iii). This provision contains a special rule for identifying the PIP if an allocation lacks economic effect but otherwise satisfies the first two parts of the basic economic-effect test (maintain capital accounts properly and respect positive balances upon liquidation). If the special rule applies, an item must be reallocated based on a comparison of the amount each partner would receive (or be required to contribute) if the allocation under scrutiny were allowed and the partnership sold all of its assets for their book value and liquidated (1) at the end of the taxable year to which the allocation relates and (2) at the end of the prior taxable year, respectively. The results of this special rule are respected, however, only if they also pass the substantiality requirement.

See if you can understand the meaning of this special rule by working through the following problem which is a slight variant of **problem 4-1**.

> **Problem 4-3:** G (the general partner) and L (the limited partner) contribute \$100,000 each to the GL partnership, which purchases ten-year depreciable property for \$200,000. The partnership meets the first two requirements of the basic economic-effect test. L is not required to restore any deficit in her capital account in excess of \$8,000, but the partnership agreement contains a QIO. Under the partnership agreement, all depreciation deductions are allocated to L and all other tax items are shared equally by the two partners.
>
> (a) During the first six years, the partnership breaks even except for its deductions attributable to depreciation (\$20,000 annually). Determine how the Year 6 depreciation deduction must be allocated.
> (b) Suppose the partnership agreement failed to include a QIO. How must the Year 1 depreciation deduction be allocated?

QUESTIONS

1. Is the hypothetical liquidation approach of the PIP special rule implicit in the basic concept of economic effect? For example, assume that a partner is allocated a tax deduction in a year in which the economic-effect requirement is satisfied. What is the economic significance of that allocation?

2. Should there be a "no harm, no foul"-type rule to the effect that if all partners of a partnership are in the same marginal income tax bracket for a given year, the allocations for the year will all be respected regardless of whether the economic-effect or substantiality requirements are satisfied?

5. *Special Rules for Tax Items That Cannot Satisfy the Economic-Effect Requirement*

Finally, the allocation of certain items, such as tax credits and excess percentage depletion, cannot satisfy the economic-effect requirement because there is no economic benefit or burden corresponding to the item that can be reflected in the partners' capital accounts. If special rules are satisfied, the allocation of these items is deemed to be in accordance with the PIP. For example, if a partnership expenditure (such as certain research expenditures) that gives rise to a tax credit also gives rise to a valid allocation of a partnership deduction (or other downward capital account adjustment), then a sharing of the credit in the same manner as the deduction (or other downward capital account adjustment) will generally be respected for tax purposes. See Reg. § 1.704-1(b)(4)(ii).

Two other special situations are explored in greater detail in subsequent chapters. The allocation of deductions attributable to the partnership's nonrecourse debt similarly falls outside of economic-effect analysis because, as a practical matter, no partner may bear the economic burden corresponding to the deduction. The special rules for nonrecourse deductions are discussed in chapter five. Finally, section 704(c) property and reverse section 704(c) property (resulting from a revaluation) present a special problem because book value and tax basis are not the same. As a result, the allocation of a tax item from such property cannot be matched with an equal, corresponding book capital account adjustment. The special provisions dealing with this problem are described in chapter six.

6. *Target Allocations*

The "target allocation" method of drafting partnership allocations does not follow the traditional notion (incorporated in the section 704(b) regulations) that liquidating distributions are determined by positive capital account balances. Rather, the target allocation method starts with the partners' economic arrangement as expressed in the partnership's distribution provisions and then "backs into" the allocation of profits, losses, and other items needed to achieve as closely as possible the desired distributions. Target allocations have become increasingly popular. By explicitly linking annual allocations to the partnership's distribution priorities, target allocations attempt to track the partners' pre-tax economic arrangement and to avoid unintended results. Generally, target allocations are not considered well suited to the type of tax-motivated shifting of income and loss among partners targeted by the section 704(b) regulations. Thus, many believe that target allocations should be permitted under the section 704(b) regulations even though they deviate from those rules in important respects.

Target allocations compare each partner's capital account at the beginning of the year with the amount the partner would receive if, at the end of the year, the partnership sold all of its assets for their book value and distributed the proceeds in liquidation (the target capital account). The target allocation then "plugs" the difference between the two amounts by allocating items of income, loss, and deduction to the partner. To illustrate, assume that A and B each contributes $500 to the AB partnership, which purchases nondepreciable property worth $1,000. The partners agree that, over the life of the partnership, cash will be distributed according to the following priorities: (1) first to A in the amount required to return A's capital plus a ten percent preferred return on that capital; (2) then to B in the amount required to return B's capital; and (3) then equally to A and B. At the end of Year 1, the partnership sells the property for $1,250 and has no other assets or liabilities. Under the target allocation approach, $1,250 is the amount available at the end of the year to satisfy the partnership's distribution priorities if the partnership liquidated: (1) A would receive $500 return-of-capital plus $50 preferred return ($550 total); (2) B would receive $500 return-of-capital; and (3) A and B would split the remaining $200 equally ($100 each). Thus, A's target capital account would be $650 ($550 plus $100) and B's target capital account would be $600 ($500 plus $100). To reconcile the partner's beginning capital account ($500 for each of A and B) with the target capital account, the partnership's taxable income must be allocated $150 to A ($650 less $500) and $100 to B ($600 less $500).

There is considerable controversy among sophisticated partnership drafters concerning whether target allocations should be respected under the section 704(b) regulations. Well-drafted target allocations typically attempt to mimic the results that arise if the partnership followed the section 704(b) capital-accounting rules, thereby maximizing the likelihood that such allocations will be respected. Neither the basic nor the alternate test for economic effect is likely to be satisfied, however, since partnerships using such allocations typically do not explicitly liquidate based on capital accounts or require partners to restore deficits. Thus, the question is whether such allocations can pass muster under the "economic-effect test" or must rely on the PIP test for their validity. While subject to some dispute, target allocations likely also fall outside the quite narrow exception under the economic-effect-equivalence test for allocations deemed to have economic effect. Because target allocations are intended to track the partners' economic arrangement, though, there may be a strong argument that they should ultimately be treated as valid under the general PIP test. Given the widespread use of target allocations, the Treasury may be expected to provide guidance in the near future clarifying how such allocations fit within the section 704(b) regulations. Until then, however, target allocations must be approached warily, since they trade off some tax certainty for the desired economic advantages.

Problem 4-4: A contributes $80 and B contributes $120 to the newly formed AB limited partnership. A (the limited partner) is not required to restore any deficit in her capital account. B (the general partner) has an unlimited deficit restoration obligation. The partnership purchases equipment for $200 cash, which the partnership depreciates under the straight-line method over a four-year period. The partnership agreement allocates all items of income and loss 40 percent to A and 60 percent to B, except that all depreciation deductions are allocated to A unless otherwise indicated. The partnership agreement satisfies the first two requirements of the basic economic-effect test (maintenance of capital accounts and liquidating distributions) and contains a qualified income offset provision. In Years 1-3, the partnership has annual operating income of $50 and annual operating expenses of $50.

(a) Under the regulations, what must be the partners' respective capital account balances at the end of Year 1? Year 2?
(b) Answer the same question as (a), assuming that A has a deficit restoration obligation of $35.
(c) Assume that the partnership agreement contains a gain chargeback provision. How must the partners' capital accounts be adjusted if the equipment is sold at the beginning of Year 2 (before any Year 2 depreciation) for $250? $175?
(d) Same as (c), except that the equipment is sold for only $150. In Year 2, the partners amend the partnership agreement to provide that liquidating distributions will be shared in the ratio 40:60. Does it matter that the amendment occurs after the partnership's tax return for Year 1 has been filed? See Reg. § 1.704-1(b)(4)(vi).
(e) May the partnership validly allocate all depreciation deductions to B in Years 1-3? What if B were obligated to restore any deficit in her capital account only to the extent necessary to pay third-party creditors?

C. Outside Basis and the Allocation of Partnership Recourse Liabilities

1. *What Is a Partnership Liability?*

Even if a partnership tax deduction or loss is validly allocated to a particular partner, the partner may or may not be entitled to claim the item on her tax return. As we saw in chapter two, a partner may claim a loss allocated to her only if the partner has sufficient outside basis at the end of the year in which the loss is passed through. Review I.R.C. § 704(d). Any losses in excess of outside basis are suspended and may be claimed in a future year if the partner then has enough outside basis.

The presence of partnership liabilities potentially affects a partner's outside basis. Read I.R.C. §§ 752(a) and (b), 722, and 733(1). An increase in a partner's share of partnership liabilities or an increase in a partner's individual liabilities by reason of the assumption by such partner of partnership liabilities is treated as a cash contribution by the partner to the partnership, resulting in an increase in the partner's outside basis. Similarly, a decrease in a partner's share of partnership liabilities or a decrease in a partner's individual liabilities by reason of the assumption by the partnership of such individual liabilities is treated as a cash distribution by the partnership to the partner, resulting in a decrease in the partner's outside basis (among other potential tax consequences). As we have discussed, these rules attempt to conform the tax consequences of debt-financed partnership investments with those of similar investments made directly by the partners. Put another way, they help to achieve one of the continuing themes in subchapter K — the equivalence of aggregate inside basis with aggregate outside basis. If the proceeds of the debt are included in inside basis, they should similarly be included in outside basis. This ensures the ability of partners to claim currently deductions and losses resulting from the partnership's inside basis and passed through to the partners.

What exactly is a partnership "liability" for purposes of section 752? As described in the following ruling, the underlying rationale for section 752 also helps to identify the existence of a liability.

Rev. Rul. 88-77

1988-2 C.B. 128

. . . A is a partner in P partnership. P files returns on a calendar year basis and uses the cash receipts and disbursements method of accounting. At the close of the taxable year at issue, P's accrued expenses and accounts payable consisted of 100x dollars for interest expense and accounts payable of 200x dollars for services received.

LAW AND ANALYSIS

Section 722 of the Code provides that a partner's basis is increased by the amount of money the partner contributes to the partnership.

Section 752(a) of the Code provides that any increase in a partner's share of the liabilities of a partnership, or any increase in a partner's individual liabilities by reason of the assumption by the partner of partnership liabilities, is treated as a contribution of money by the partner to the partnership.

. . . Under P's method of accounting, P's obligations to pay amounts incurred for interest and services are not deductible until paid. For purposes of section 752 of the Code, the terms "liabilities of a partnership" and "partnership liabilities" include an obligation only if and to the extent that incurring the liability creates or increases the basis to the partnership of any of the partnership's assets (including cash attributable to borrowings), gives rise to an immediate deduction to the partnership, or, under section 705(a)(2)(B), currently decreases a partner's basis in the partner's partnership interest. The preceding sentence uses the term "assets" to include capitalized items that are properly allocable to future periods, such as organizational expenses and construction period expenses.

The liabilities incurred by P for interest expense and services do not create or increase the basis of a partnership asset or give rise to a deduction when incurred. Therefore, for purposes of computing A's adjusted basis in P, A may not treat P's accrued expenses and accounts payable as a liability of the partnership.

HOLDING

For purposes of computing the adjusted basis of a partner's interest in a cash basis partnership, accrued but unpaid expenses and accounts payable are not "liabilities of a partnership" or "partnership liabilities" within the meaning of section 752 of the Code. . . .

NOTE AND QUESTIONS

1. *Parity between inside and outside basis.* In common parlance, the payables described in the ruling would ordinarily be considered "liabilities." Nevertheless, based on the rationale for section 752 — the desire to maintain parity between aggregate inside basis and aggregate outside basis — the ruling concludes that such payables are *not* liabilities for purposes of that provision. This rationale also explains all three situations in which the ruling concludes that a "liability" does exist. For example, suppose the partnership in the ruling had used the accrual method of accounting. In that case, the partnership would have deducted the unpaid expenses and accounts payables in the year of accrual, and the deduction would have passed through to the partners and reduced their outside bases. I.R.C. § 705(a)(2)(A). Yet, because the items were accrued but not yet paid, there would be no corresponding decrease in aggregate inside basis. Therefore, in that situation, the accrued items would have been properly classified as liabilities of the partnership, increasing aggregate outside basis by the amount accrued. As a consequence, there would be no net change to aggregate outside basis in the year of accrual (increase in outside basis resulting from creation of partnership liability offset by decrease in outside basis resulting from passthrough of deduction); aggregate inside basis would also remain unchanged. Upon payment of the items in a subsequent year, aggregate inside basis would be reduced by the amount of the payment. Aggregate outside basis would be correspondingly reduced due to the reduction in partnership liabilities. The revised section 752 regulations restate almost verbatim the definition of a liability provided in Rev. Rul. 88-77. See Reg. § 1.752-1(a)(4)(i).

2. *Short sales.* In Rev. Rul. 95-26, 1995-1 C.B. 131, a partnership sold short certain securities. In a "short sale," the seller disposes of property borrowed for that purpose and is then obligated to return the property to the lender at some future time. Ordinarily, the short seller hopes that the value of the property sold will decline during the interim, thereby enabling the seller to profit from the spread. The ruling concluded that the short sale created a partnership liability for purposes of section

752. This conclusion followed from the fact that the proceeds of the sale (or, alternatively, the property borrowed) increased the partnership's aggregate inside basis. See Salina Partnership v. Comm'r, 80 T.C.M. 686 (2000) (partnership's short position constituted a liability for section 752 purposes); Kornman & Assoc. Inc. v. U.S., 527 F.3d 443 (5th Cir. 2008) (same); Marriott Int'l Resorts v. U.S., 586 F.3d 962 (Fed. Cir. 2009) (same). The section 752 regulations have since been revised to address contingent obligations under a short sale. See Reg. § 1.752-1(a)(4)(i) and (ii).

3. *More liability controversies.* In recent years, tax shelters have focused attention on issues concerning which obligations properly constitute "liabilities" for purposes of section 752, and how such liabilities should be measured. For example, suppose a taxpayer purchases a "call option," which is a right to acquire something under certain circumstances for a certain period of time, and also writes an offsetting option with virtually identical terms. Aside from transaction costs and any slight difference in the amount the taxpayer pays and receives for the purchased and written options, the transaction is an economic wash to the taxpayer. Should the taxpayer's obligation under the offsetting option be considered a "liability" for purposes of section 752? What difference might it make? Read the following notice that the IRS issued in an attempt to shut down a tax shelter popularly known as "Son of BOSS." The particular shelter closely resembled an earlier shelter, known as "Bond and Option Sales Strategy" (or "BOSS") that relied on a similarly aggressive interpretation of the meaning of "liability" for corporate tax purposes.

Notice 2000-44

2000-2 C.B. 255

... The Service and the Treasury have become aware of ... arrangements that have been designed to produce noneconomic tax losses on the disposition of partnership interests. These arrangements purport to give taxpayers artificially high basis in partnership interests and thereby give rise to deductible losses on disposition of those partnership interests.

One variation involves a taxpayer's borrowing at a premium and a partnership's subsequent assumption of that indebtedness. As an example of this variation, a taxpayer may receive $3,000x in cash from a lender under a loan agreement that provides for an inflated stated rate of interest and a stated principal amount of only $2,000x. The taxpayer contributes the $3,000x to a partnership, and the partnership assumes the indebtedness. The partnership thereafter engages in investment activities. At a later time, the taxpayer sells the partnership interest.

Under the position advanced by the promoters of this arrangement, the taxpayer claims that only the stated principal amount of the indebtedness, $2,000x in this example, is considered a liability assumed by the partnership that is treated as a distribution of money to the taxpayer that reduces the basis of the taxpayer's partnership interest under § 752 of the Internal Revenue Code. Therefore, disregarding any additional amounts the taxpayer may contribute to the partnership, transaction costs, and any income realized or expenses incurred at the partnership level, the taxpayer purports to have a basis in the partnership interest equal to the excess of the cash contributed over the stated principal amount of the indebtedness, even though the taxpayer's net economic outlay to acquire the partnership interest and the value of the partnership interest are nominal or zero. In this example, the taxpayer purports to have a basis in the partnership interest of $1,000x (the excess of the cash contributed ($3,000x) over the stated principal amount of the indebtedness ($2,000x)). On disposition of the partnership interest, the taxpayer claims a tax loss with respect to that basis amount, even though the taxpayer has incurred no corresponding economic loss.

In another variation, a taxpayer purchases and writes options and purports to create substantial positive basis in a partnership interest by transferring those option positions to a partnership. For example, a taxpayer might purchase call options for a cost of $1,000x and simultaneously write offsetting call options, with a slightly higher strike price but the same expiration date, for a premium of slightly less than $1,000x. Those option positions are then transferred to a partnership which, using additional amounts contributed to the partnership, may engage in investment activities.

Under the position advanced by the promoters of this arrangement, the taxpayer claims that the basis in the taxpayer's partnership interest is increased by the cost of the purchased call options but is not reduced under § 752 as a result of the partnership's assumption of the taxpayer's obligation with respect to the written call options. Therefore, disregarding additional amounts contributed to the partnership, transaction costs, and any income realized and expenses incurred at the partnership level, the taxpayer purports to have a basis in the partnership interest equal to the cost of the purchased call options ($1,000x in this example), even though the taxpayer's net economic outlay to acquire the partnership interest and the value of the partnership interest are nominal or zero. On the disposition of the partnership interest, the taxpayer claims a tax loss ($1,000x in this example), even though the taxpayer has incurred no corresponding economic loss.

The purported losses resulting from the transactions described above do not represent bona fide losses reflecting actual economic consequences as required for purposes of § 165. The purported losses from these transactions (and from any similar arrangements designed to produce noneconomic tax losses by artificially overstating basis in partnership interests) are not allowable as deductions for federal income tax purposes. The purported tax benefits from these transactions may also be subject to disallowance under other provisions of the Code and regulations. In particular, the transactions may be subject to challenge under § 752, or under § 1.701-2 or other anti-abuse rules. . . .

Appropriate penalties may be imposed on participants in these transactions or, as applicable, on persons who participate in the promotion or reporting of these transactions, including the accuracy-related penalty under § 6662, the return preparer penalty under § 6694, the promoter penalty under § 6700, and the aiding and abetting penalty under § 6701. . . .

NOTES

1. *Criminal penalties.* The Notice also indicated that criminal penalties might be applicable to those who promote carrying out these transactions in a manner designed to conceal the claimed tax benefits.

2. *Loan premium transaction.* The "premium loan" described in Notice 2000-44 is clearly a liability for purposes of section 752 to the extent of the principal amount ($2,000*x*). Under Rev. Rul. 88-77, the additional borrowed amount ($1,000*x*), which represents the discounted present value of the taxpayer's obligation to pay interest at an inflated rate, should also be treated as a section 752 liability. Since inside basis is increased by all $3,000*x* of borrowed proceeds, the amount of the liability must also be $3,000*x*, i.e., the principal amount of the loan ($2,000*x*) and the loan premium ($1,000*x*). In tax shelter cases, however, taxpayers sought to ignore the loan premium ($1,000*x*) as "too contingent," thereby avoiding a downward adjustment to outside basis and creating an artificial loss of equal amount on sale of their partnership interests. In Klamath Strategic Inv. Fund, LLC v. U.S., 472 F. Supp. 2d 885 (E.D. Tex. 2007), aff'd in part and vacated in part, 568 F.3d 537 (5th Cir. 2009), the court denied the claimed losses from a loan premium transaction because the transaction lacked economic substance, but refused to impose any penalties. The same lower court had earlier concluded that the loan premium did not constitute a liability for purposes of section 752 and invalidated retroactive application of contrary regulations to transactions (like the one in *Klamath*) carried out before the issuance of Notice 2000-44. See 440 F. Supp. 2d 608 (2006). The retroactive reach of the same regulations was upheld in Cemco Investors, LLC v. U.S., 515 F.3d 749 (7th Cir.), cert. denied, 555 U.S. 823 (2008), excerpted in chapter twelve, involving a transaction that postdated Notice 2000-44 (but predated issuance of the regulations at issue).

3. *Offsetting options transaction.* The "offsetting options" transaction described in Notice 2000-44 has also attracted litigation. See *Cemco*, supra (denying losses and upholding retroactive application of regulation). Other courts have unanimously rejected the offsetting options transactions on their merits. See, e.g., Fidelity Int'l Currency Advisor A Fund, L.L.C. v. U.S., 661 F.3d 667 (1st Cir. 2011); Jade Trading, L.L.C v. U.S., 598 F.3d 1372 (Fed. Cir. 2010). Despite these impressive victories on the merits, the government has had more mixed success on the penalties issue, as discussed in chapter twelve.

4. *Other contingent obligations and cash-method payables.* Subsequent to Notice 2000-44, the IRS revised the section 752 regulations to address the treatment of all fixed or contingent "obligations" (a broader term than "liabilities") to make a payment, including debt, environmental, tort, and contractual obligations. Special rules deal with partnership obligations that are *not* section 752 liabilities (referred to as

"non-section 752 liabilities"). The goal generally is to prevent these non-liability obligations from producing any tax benefit except to the contributing partner upon satisfaction of the obligation by the partnership. See Reg. § 1.752-7(a). Because these non-liability obligations are treated in a similar manner as built-in loss property under section 704(c), more detailed discussion of these rules is deferred until chapter six.

Problem 4-5: Determine the effect, if any, of the following events on the aggregate outside basis of the partners of partnership PS, which is engaged in the business of owning and operating music stores:

(a) PS, a cash-basis taxpayer, agrees to pay Landlord $25,000 rent for the leasing during the current year of Landlord's property housing one of PS's stores.
(b) PS, an accrual-basis taxpayer, agrees to pay Jones $1,000 as compensation for janitorial services he performed last month at certain of PS's stores.
(c) PS, an accrual-basis taxpayer, sells one of its stores to Smith. At the time of the sale, the fair market value of the store is $100,000, PS's basis in the store is also $100,000, and the store is subject to a $20,000 recourse mortgage. In the transaction, Smith pays PS $80,000 cash and assumes the mortgage.
(d) PS, a cash-basis taxpayer, promises to pay Landowner $30,000 in the future for a small real estate lot acquired from Landowner during the past month. PS intends to build a new store on the lot.
(e) PS, an accrual-basis taxpayer, agrees to contribute $10,000 to a local charity.

2. *Allocating Partnership Recourse Liabilities*

a. Introduction

Once partnership liabilities are identified, it becomes important to determine how such liabilities are shared by the partners. *Whose* outside basis is increased or decreased when the amount of partnership liabilities changes?

In this section, we consider how *recourse* liabilities of a partnership are shared by the partners. "Recourse" liabilities are defined as liabilities for which some partner (or related person) bears the economic risk of loss. See Reg. § 1.752-1(a)(1). The sharing of partnership "nonrecourse" liabilities—liabilities for which no partner (or related person) bears the economic risk of loss—is discussed in chapter five.

Under prior law, the liability-sharing rules potentially gave rise to uncertainty and invited manipulation. In particular, the rules failed to resolve problems arising from collateral arrangements such as guarantees, assumptions, and indemnities. The current regulations under section 752 were a direct response to a lower-court decision, overturned in *Raphan* below, holding that the general partners' guarantee of a nonrecourse liability did not create personal liability within the meaning of the former section 752 regulations.

Raphan v. United States

759 F.2d 879 (Fed. Cir. 1985), rev'g 83-2 USTC ¶9613 (Cl. Ct. 1983)

KASHIWA, Circuit Judge: [A partnership ("Associates") was formed between the general partners (the Pomponios) and the limited partners (the Tenzer group, which included the Raphans) to construct an apartment building. The taxpayers argued that the general partners had acted in a nonpartner capacity in guaranteeing a nonrecourse construction loan for the apartment building, and that therefore the guarantee did not convert the nonrecourse loan to a recourse loan for purposes of the liability-sharing rules in existence at that time.]

. . . The Treasury Regulations govern the allocation of a partnership's liabilities. Sec. 1.752-1(e) [prior to 1984 amendments] provides:

> (e) *Partner's share of partnership liabilities.* A partner's share of partnership liabilities shall be determined in accordance with his ratio for sharing losses under the partnership agreement. In the case of a limited partnership, a limited partner's share of partnership liabilities shall not exceed the difference between his actual contribution credited to him by the partnership and the total contribution which he is obligated to make under the limited partnership agreement. However, where none of the partners have any personal liability (as in the case of a mortgage on real estate acquired by the partnership without the assumption by the partnership or any of the partners of any liability on the mortgage), then all partners including limited partners, shall be considered as sharing such liability under section 752(c) in the same proportion as they share the profits.

When no partner has any personal liability for a partnership debt, therefore, all partners, including limited partners, "share" that debt in the proportion they share profits, and each partner's basis reflects his debt share. When, however, a partner has "any personal liability" for that debt, the general partners share in it. The limited partners' share, if at all, will depend on the difference between his actual contribution to the partnership and the total contribution that he is "obligated" to make under the limited partnership agreement.

Personal liability for a debt ("recourse indebtedness") means all of the debtor's assets may be reached by creditors if the debt is not paid. Personal liability is normally contrasted with limited liability ("nonrecourse indebtedness"), against which a creditor's remedies are limited to particular collateral for the debt. Indeed, a partner's guarantee of a partnership's "nonrecourse debt" makes him personally liable because the partner has exposed his assets to pay the debt if the partnership defaults, precluding the limited partners from sharing in the debt. . . .

The Claims Court held that the Pomponios guaranteed the construction loan in a nonpartner capacity, and assumed that personal liability of partners is to be accounted for in allocating basis only if that liability is incurred in their capacity as partners. It reasoned that if the general partners, the Pomponios, were called on to meet their guarantee, they would become creditors of the partnership, and viewed that status as distinct from their relationship as partners.

The view that a partner cannot guarantee partnership debt in his capacity as partner because he then becomes a creditor is insupportable. A general partner, who is liable *as such* for the recourse debts of the partnership, has incurred that liability in his capacity as partner. That a general partner compelled to pay those debts also becomes a creditor does not conflict with his continuing liability as general partner. . . . See also Uniform Partnership Act §§ 18(a)-(c) and 40(b). Acquisition of creditor status, after meeting the guarantee, does not mean that the guaranteeing general partner did not make the guarantee, and thus incur the liability in his capacity as partner.

The Regulations provide that the capacity in which a partner acts is to be determined, not by *a priori* reasoning, but by examination of "the substance of the transaction." See Reg. § 1.707-1(a). Examining the substance here establishes that the Pomponios did not act at arm's length in guaranteeing the construction loan. They did not charge Associates for the guarantee, as would an unrelated person, nor did Associates agree to pay the Pomponios interest if they were called upon to meet their guarantee.

The Pomponios acted not as unrelated guarantors or creditors might, but in guaranteeing the loan they acted in their capacity as partners. . . . The Pomponios thus guaranteed the construction loan so that they could profit from that project through their resulting partnership interests. As the Claims Court found: "The guarantee was a prerequisite to obtaining the loan, which, in turn, was *sine qua non* of the deal between the Tenzer group and the Pomponios." 3 Cl. Ct. at 465. . . .

That the guarantee was not mentioned in the partnership agreement is insignificant. A partnership agreement does not cover every conceivable act the partners might take in the course of their partnership activity. Moreover, the guarantee was known to the Tenzers. It is common, because of the risk, for lenders to refuse a construction loan to a closely held corporation without the principals' personal guarantee. . . . The Tenzers, sophisticated real estate investors, obviously knew of that common practice. . . .

The Raphans contend that a guarantee can never create personal liability, under the Regulations, because it is only a conditional or secondary liability. . . . The Raphans' contention confuses unrelated concepts. The first concept involves personal liability (creditor can reach all debtor's assets) and limited liability (creditor can reach only specific assets). The second concept involves primary and secondary liability, which merely refer to the order in which a creditor must pursue his remedies.

Under the guarantee, a creditor could reach all the Pomponios' assets if Associates defaulted. . . . [T]he Pomponios personally guaranteed a loan that was nonrecourse against Associates and thus, became personally liable, regardless of whether they were also primarily liable.[4] . . .

The Pomponios, as general partners, were personally liable for the construction loan when they guaranteed its payment. The Raphans, as limited partners, do not share in that liability. . . .

NOTES

1. *Former regulations.* The former section 752 regulations (pre-1988), quoted in *Raphan*, allocated liabilities in a relatively straightforward manner. Recourse liabilities were generally shared by general partners in accordance with their shares of partnership losses, while nonrecourse liabilities were shared by all partners, including limited partners, in accordance with their shares of partnership profits. Limited partners were entitled to share in recourse liabilities only to the extent of their obligation (if any) to contribute additional capital to the partnership. As we study the current version of the section 752 regulations, you should consider how it differs from the prior version.

2. *Legislative reversal of the* Raphan *trial court opinion.* Concerned that the trial court decision in *Raphan* might further open the door to tax shelters, Congress in 1984 mandated that the section 752 regulations be revised "to ensure that the partner receiving basis with respect to a partnership liability . . . bears the economic risk of loss with respect to such liabilities." H.R. Rep. No. 98-861, 98th Cong. 2d Sess. 869 (1984). As we have seen, the trial court decision was subsequently overturned on appeal. Nevertheless, the Treasury revised the regulations in response to the Congressional directive.

3. *"Recourse" vs. "nonrecourse" liabilities for purposes of section 752.* Whether a firm's liability is classified as "recourse" or "nonrecourse" for purposes of section 752 depends upon the relationship of the firm's owners to the liability and *not* just upon the terms of the debt instrument itself. For example, a loan which by its terms is "recourse" to the firm, meaning that the creditor may seek repayment from any of the assets of the debtor-firm, may nevertheless be classified as a "nonrecourse" liability if no owner, such as the members of an LLC, has any personal liability for repayment of the debt. Conversely, a loan which by its terms is "nonrecourse" to the firm, meaning that the creditor may obtain repayment only from the firm's property

---

4. A general partner liable as partner for a partnership recourse debt is "personally liable" for that debt. However, a partnership creditor can reach the partner's assets only after exhausting its remedies against the partnership. . . . The Pomponios "unconditionally" guaranteed the loan, and a creditor may therefore proceed against the Pomponios without first exhausting its remedies. . . . The Pomponios thus had a more direct, immediate liability for the loan than a general partner liable for a partnership debt. Acceptance of that more direct and immediate liability did not, as above indicated, mean that the guarantee was not undertaken in the Pomponios' partnership capacity.

serving as security for the loan, may be classified as a "recourse" liability if some owner personally guarantees its repayment.

4. *Bifurcation.* If a liability is part recourse and part nonrecourse, the liability is bifurcated for purposes of section 752. See Reg. § 1.752-1(i), -2(f) (ex. 5).

b. The Economic Risk of Loss Concept

The current rules for the sharing of recourse liabilities operate in tandem with the section 704(b) regulations. As you know, the substantial-economic-effect test attempts to allocate partnership tax deductions and losses to the partner who bears the economic burden corresponding to those items. The liability allocation rules under section 752 employ a similar concept (the "economic risk of loss") to ensure that recourse liabilities are allocated to the partner who bears the economic burden of repayment of the liability.

Read Reg. § 1.752-2(a) and (b)(1). In general, a partner's share of recourse liabilities equals the portion of such liabilities for which she bears the economic risk of loss. To determine how much that is for a particular partner, the tax law poses the following question: If the partnership were unable to pay its obligations, to what extent (if any) would the partner be obligated to pay the liability from personal funds, without any right of reimbursement from any other partner? The partner's share of the partnership's recourse liabilities is equal to the net payment she would be obligated to make in this worst-case scenario.

As a technical matter, the tax law hypothesizes a most extraordinary event, analogous to a nuclear bomb hitting all of the partnership's assets. In general, when the bomb hits, the following events are all deemed to occur:

(1) all of the partnership's assets (including cash) become worthless;
(2) all of the partnership's liabilities become due and payable in full;
(3) the partnership disposes of all of its assets for no consideration (other than satisfaction of nonrecourse liabilities secured by the property);
(4) the partnership allocates its items of income, gain, loss, or deduction from the sale among its partners; and
(5) the partnership liquidates.

Following this hypothetical sale and liquidation, a partner's share of the partnership's recourse liabilities is generally equal to the amount that she would be required to contribute to the partnership to satisfy a deficit in her capital account, or obligated to pay directly to the partnership's creditors, without any right of reimbursement from any other partner.

Example 4-5: A contributes $10,000 and B contributes $90,000 to the AB general partnership; A and B agree to share partnership profits and losses 10:90. The partnership purchases a building (worth $1,000,000) for $100,000 cash and a $900,000 recourse purchase-money note. To determine the partners' share of this liability, the partnership is deemed to liquidate following a sale of the building for no consideration. The sale results in a $1,000,000 loss ($0 amount realized less $1,000,000 basis) which, under the agreement, is allocated $100,000 to A and $900,000 to B. A and B therefore have capital account deficits of $90,000 and $810,000, respectively, after the sale and liquidation. They are required to contribute these amounts to the partnership, either as the result of an explicit deficit make-up provision or by operation of state law, to pay off the liability that is due and payable. Accordingly, A and B share the recourse liability 10:90, the same ratio in which they share partnership losses, and A and B have outside bases of $100,000 and $900,000, respectively.

Example 4-6: The facts are the same as in **example 4-5**, except that the partnership incurs two different liabilities to purchase the property: a $500,000 recourse purchase-money note and a $400,000 note that is secured by the property but is otherwise nonrecourse. Upon the hypothetical liquidation, the building is still considered worthless but the partnership is deemed to realize an amount equal to the nonrecourse liability. The sale therefore results in a loss of $600,000 ($1,000,000 basis less $400,000 amount realized). Under the agreement, this loss is allocated $60,000 to A and $540,000 to B, leaving each partner with a capital account deficit of $50,000 and $450,000, respectively. Once again, they share the $500,000 recourse liability in a 10:90 ratio. (Their share of the nonrecourse liability is discussed in chapter five.)

It might seem odd that the tax law requires the imagining of this totally unlikely event in order to determine how the parties should share a partnership's recourse liabilities. As a practical matter, in the vast majority of cases, recourse liabilities will be satisfied out of the partnership's profits or the proceeds of a sale of partnership assets. Why, then, must we hypothesize this worst-case scenario where all of the partnership's assets are sold for nothing and creditors must be paid off through additional contributions by the partners?

The answer lies in an important policy judgment made by the Treasury in drafting the section 752 regulations. The Treasury decided that the section 704(b) rules adequately policed the allocation of partnership tax items, including deductions and losses, among the partners of the partnership. There was no need, therefore, for section 704(d) to serve as an additional hurdle. Thus, if a particular allocation of losses to a partner passes muster under section 704(b), the partner whenever possible should be provided, through the liability-sharing rules, with a sufficient amount of outside basis to be able to utilize the losses in a timely manner.

Under this view, section 704(d) plays a very limited and pragmatic role in the passthrough of partnership losses. Its function is limited to implementing the policy decision prohibiting the existence of negative basis. Recall that under section 705(a)(2)(A), a partner's outside basis is reduced by the share of losses passed through to the partner. If this basis reduction were without limit, section 704(d) would not be needed. But, in fact, basis cannot be reduced below zero (see the parenthetical in section 705(a)(2)). Hence, the tax law needs a rule that cuts off the amount of losses that may be passed through to a partner until the partner has enough outside basis. Section 704(d) is that rule. But the role of the liability-sharing rules is to prevent the section 704(d) limitation from coming into play, if at all possible.

Thus, return to the worst-case scenario hypothesized by the section 752 regulations. Under section 704(b), partnership tax losses are generally allocated to the partner who bears the corresponding economic burden, as reflected in the partner's capital account. For a partnership with recourse financing, the *maximum* amount of tax losses that could be allocated to a particular partner is generally equal to the economic burden suffered by that partner if all of the partnership's assets became worthless and the recourse financing had to be satisfied out of nonpartnership assets. True, the partnership is unlikely ever to realize that amount of losses. Nevertheless, to ensure that a partner who is allocated a loss has a sufficient outside basis to cover the loss, the section 752 regulations allocate partnership recourse liabilities in the same manner that the tax loss is allocated—to the partner bearing the economic burden of the loss as reflected in the partner's capital account—in the circumstances that would produce the maximum possible loss to the partner. By definition, the partner then should have sufficient outside basis to cover her allocable share of losses under less draconian circumstances.

Finally, note the difference between the treatment of recourse and nonrecourse liabilities in **examples 4-5** and **4-6**, above. The different treatment serves principally to isolate the partnership's recourse liabilities from its nonrecourse liabilities. As illustrated in **example 4-6**, upon disposition of property securing both types of liabilities, the resulting deficit balances in the partners' capital accounts equal the amount of the partnership's recourse liabilities and *only* its recourse liabilities.

NOTES AND QUESTIONS

1. *Significance of outside basis.* Although the liability-sharing rules are closely coordinated with the passthrough of losses, a partner's outside basis may have additional tax consequences. For example, outside basis determines how much cash may be extracted from the partnership in a tax-free manner and how much gain or loss must be recognized upon a disposition of a partnership interest. See I.R.C. §§ 731(a)(1), 741.

2. *Book value vs. tax basis.* Suppose at the time of the hypothetical sale and liquidation, the partnership holds section 704(c) or reverse section 704(c) property whose book value is different from its tax basis. For purposes of the section 752 calculation, which figure—book value or tax basis—should be used in determining the partnership's gain or loss from the sale? Why?

c. Determining the Payment Obligation

Read Reg. § 1.752-2(b)(3)-(6). Following the destruction of the partnership's property from the nuclear bomb, a partner's share of partnership recourse liabilities is determined by calculating the partner's "payment obligation." This payment obligation is measured by taking into account all of the facts and circumstances including the terms of the partnership agreement, obligations imposed by side arrangements such as guarantees and indemnification agreements, and obligations imposed by state law. A partner's payment obligation is reduced by the amount of any right to reimbursement belonging to the partner. In addition, contingent payment obligations are ignored if it is unlikely they will ever have to be discharged.

Except in abusive situations, partners are generally assumed to discharge their payment obligations, regardless of their net worth. Thus, if a partner who must pay a creditor is entitled to reimbursement from another partner, only the partner who is ultimately liable may include the recourse liability in basis. For example, a limited partner who guarantees a recourse liability of a partnership is generally subrogated to the creditor's rights against the general partners. In that case, the guarantee does not count as part of the limited partner's payment obligation and would not increase outside basis. Rather, the guarantee would generally be considered "phony," since the limited partner would be entitled to reimbursement from the general partners who are deemed to satisfy their obligations. See Reg. § 1.752-2(f) (exs. 3, 4).

NOTES AND QUESTIONS

1. *Improvement?* Do you think the current section 752 regulations have been faithful to Congress's intent in 1984 to reverse the trial court's decision in *Raphan*? Why or why not? Do they represent an improvement over the earlier version?

2. *Indemnities.* Under a typical "indemnity agreement," one partner may agree to reimburse another partner for payment of a liability, and the indemnitor generally becomes ultimately liable for payment to the extent of the indemnity. In a two-person limited partnership, suppose the limited partner agrees to indemnify the general partner for one-half of any payments to creditors. Should the limited partner be allocated half of the partnership's recourse liabilities? Would it make any difference if the limited partner merely agrees to pay the creditor half of the partnership's recourse obligations in the event that the general partner fails to discharge her obligation?

3. *Pledges and similar arrangements.* A partner may also bear the economic risk of loss for a partnership liability to the extent that she pledges her own separate property (other than her partnership interest) as security for the liability. See Reg. § 1.752-2(h)(1). Alternatively, a partner may transfer property to a partnership that uses the transferred property ("contributed security") solely to secure a partnership liability; the transferor is treated as bearing the economic risk of loss for the liability to the extent of the fair market value of the contributed security (determined as of the

date of the transfer). See Reg. § 1.752-2(h)(2)-(3). For purposes of the constructive liquidation, the contributed security is not deemed to be worthless. See Reg. § 1.752-2(b)(1)(ii). Substantially all items of income, gain, loss and deduction attributable to the contributed security must be allocated to the transferor; in essence, the transfer leaves the transferor in the same position as if she had continued to own the contributed security outside the partnership but pledged it directly to the creditor.

4. *Shares of general partners.* In the absence of side agreements and similar arrangements, general partners in a "straight-up" partnership (e.g., one in which capital, profits and losses are all shared proportionately) will share recourse liabilities proportionately; indeed, you might even be tempted to dispense with the constructive liquidation test since the correct allocation can be easily intuited. But suppose the partners agree to share profits and losses disproportionately to their capital contributions and are obligated to restore deficits in their capital accounts? In this situation, the constructive liquidation may produce surprising results. Read carefully Reg. § 1.752-2(f) (exs. 1, 2).

5. *Shares of limited partners.* Recall that, under the section 704(b) regulations, a limited partner generally can be allocated losses only to the extent of her capital contribution plus the amount of any limited DRO. What is the effect of a limited DRO on the allocation of recourse liabilities under the section 752 regulations? Logically, a limited partner should be entitled to share in recourse liabilities to the extent that she would be obligated to contribute an amount to the partnership as a result of her limited DRO. Verify that the current section 752 regulations reach this result, which is essentially the same as under the former section 752 regulations. Accordingly, a limited partner should have sufficient outside basis to absorb her share of losses attributable to her initial capital contribution plus her limited DRO. What happens if a limited partner is allocated losses in excess of such amounts? Under the special PIP rule, the excess losses must be reallocated to other partners, i.e., the general partners who bear the economic risk of loss attributable to the partnership's recourse liabilities. Thus, the reallocated losses and liabilities will continue to track each other.

6. *Disregard of purported economic risk of loss.* The regulations make clear that state law limitations must be taken into account in determining a partner's purported payment obligation and economic risk of loss. For example, suppose a taxpayer is the sole owner of an LLC which in turn is a general partner of a limited partnership. The limited partnership agreement provides that the LLC has an unlimited obligation to restore deficits in its capital account. If the LLC is treated as a "disregarded entity" for tax purposes, then the taxpayer, as sole owner of the LLC, would normally be treated as a general partner of the limited partnership with an unlimited DRO.

Under local law, however, the taxpayer may have no liability for the LLC's debts and the LLC may lack any right to contribution from the taxpayer. Thus, as a practical matter, the taxpayer has no exposure to any of the limited partnership's liabilities except to the extent of the net value of any assets owned by the LLC (apart from its equity interest in the limited partnership). In that situation, the regulations properly conclude that the taxpayer's economic risk of loss for the partnership's liabilities is limited to the net value of the LLC's assets, overriding the general assumption that partners are deemed to satisfy all obligations regardless of net worth. See Reg. § 1.752-2(k)(1).

More generally, the regulations include an "anti-abuse rule" that provides authority to disregard a purported arrangement to share the economic risk of loss if a principal purpose of the arrangement is to create the appearance of one person bearing such loss when, in fact, the substance of the arrangement is otherwise. For example, a corporate general partner may have an unlimited DRO but be capitalized with an amount significantly less than the potential losses that might be generated. If a principal purpose of the arrangement is to allow such a partner to benefit from tax losses in excess of its real economic exposure, the partnership's liabilities must be reallocated in accordance with the economic substance of the arrangement. See Reg. § 1.752-2(j)(1) and (4) (example).

7. *Revising liability-sharing rules.* Controversial proposed regulations under section 752 would fundamentally alter the rules for sharing partnership recourse liabilities. REG-119305-11, 2014-8 I.R.B. 524. According to the preamble, the proposed regulations "turn off" the presumption that partners will satisfy their payment obligations. Id. at 529. The current approach under Reg. § 1.752-2 focuses on a worst-case scenario in allocating recourse liabilities. The preamble explains that this approach may be unrealistic since partnership liabilities will generally be satisfied with partnership profits, partnership assets seldom become worthless, and partners' payment obligations are often not called upon. Id. The proposed regulations would impose new "recognition" and "net value" requirements to ensure that only "commercially reasonable" payment obligations are respected. Id. at 528.

As a condition for respecting a payment obligation, a partner or related person would be required to maintain a commercially reasonable net worth during the term of the payment obligation (or be subject to commercially reasonable restrictions on asset transfers for inadequate consideration). Prop. Reg. § 1.752-2(b)(3)(ii)(A).The net value requirement, contained in Prop. Reg. § 1.752-2(b)(3)(iii)(B), would apply to all partners other than individuals or a decedent's estate. For purposes of determining economic risk of loss, a payment obligation would be recognized only to the extent of the net value of the partner (or related person) that is allocated to the particular partnership liability. Thus, the net value requirement currently applicable only to disregarded entities, discussed in note 6 above, would apply much more broadly.

In general, a payment obligation would be respected only if the guarantor (or indemnitor) would be liable up to the *full amount* of the payment obligation to the extent that any portion of the liability is not otherwise satisfied. See Prop. Reg. § 1.752-2(b)(3)(ii)(F) (guarantee) and (G) (indemnity). This rule is aimed at "bottom-dollar" guarantees and similar arrangements that may not reflect commercial reality. For example, assume a partner guarantees only the "bottom" $200,000 of a $500,000 nonrecourse liability, i.e., the guarantor would be liable to make a payment only if, and to the extent that, the collateral is worth less than $200,000 on a foreclosure. The proposed regulations would disregard this bottom-dollar guarantee, since there may be little risk that the guarantor would be required to make a payment. See Prop. Reg. § 1.752-2(f) (exs. 10, 11(iii)). By contrast, a "top-dollar" guarantee is likely to impose greater risk, even though limited in amount. For example, assume the guarantor instead agreed to make up any deficiency up to $200,000 if the collateral were worth less than $500,000 upon foreclosure. The proposed regulations would respect this top-dollar guarantee, assuming the net value and other recognition requirements are satisfied. See id.; Prop. Reg. § 1.752-2(f) (exs. 10, 11(ii)). An anti-abuse rule would prevent splitting a single liability into multiple liabilities. Prop. Reg. § 1.752-2(j)(4).

If finalized in their current form, the proposed regulations would often convert recourse obligations under the current regulations into nonrecourse obligations (because no partner would be treated as having a payment obligation and thus bearing the economic risk of loss). Any change to the section 752 liability-sharing rules would require coordination with the section 704(b) rules for allocating deductions if Treasury wishes to continue the policy goal of ensuring that a partner has sufficient outside basis to use such deductions currently. Before considering whether it would be desirable to treat more liabilities as nonrecourse, you will need to understand the current rules for allocating nonrecourse liabilities (and deductions), the subject of chapter five.

Problem 4-6: In the following situations, assume that the partnership agreement requires that capital accounts be maintained in accordance with the section 704(b) regulations and provides for liquidating distributions in accordance with the partners' positive capital accounts. Unless otherwise stated, each partner has an unconditional deficit restoration obligation.

(a) M, N, and O contribute $40, $60, and $100, respectively, to the newly formed MNO general partnership. The partnership purchases equipment (worth $1,000) for $200 cash and an $800 recourse purchase-money note. Under the partnership agreement, profits and losses are allocated 20 percent to M, 30 percent to N, and 50 percent to O. Determine the proper allocation of the $800 recourse liability immediately after formation of the partnership. What is each partner's outside basis?

(b) A and B contribute $200 and $600, respectively, to the AB general partnership and agree to share profits and losses equally. The partnership purchases land (worth $1,200) for $800 cash and a $400 recourse purchase-money note. How is the partnership's $400 recourse obligation allocated? See Reg. § 1.752-2(f) (ex. 2). Why do the regulations provide for this outcome?

(c) The facts are the same as (b), except that A is a limited partner and does not have an unconditional deficit make-up obligation; A nevertheless agrees to restore any deficit in her capital account to the extent of $400. The partnership does not expect to make any distributions prior to liquidation and contains a QIO provision. What is the maximum loss that A may be validly allocated under the section 704(b) regulations? Does A have sufficient outside basis to absorb her share of the loss? What difference would it make if A had no obligation to restore any deficit in her capital account?

(d) The facts are the same as in (c), except that A does not agree to restore any deficit in her capital account. Instead, A transfers additional securities worth $400 (with a basis of $400) to the partnership solely for the purpose of securing the partnership's $400 liability. The partnership allocates all items of income, gain, loss and deduction attributable to the additional securities entirely to A. What is A's share of the partnership's $400 recourse liability? See Reg. § 1.752-2(h). What difference would it make if A instead contributed her promissory note in the principal amount of $400, bearing adequate stated interest?

(e) A and B each contribute $200 to the AB general partnership. The partnership purchases land (worth $600) for $400 cash and a $200 recourse purchase-money note. Profits and losses are allocated 10 percent to A and 90 percent to B. How is the partnership's $200 recourse liability shared? Will both partners have enough outside basis to cover any possible losses allocated to them under the agreement? If not, how might the parties restructure their transaction to avoid suspension of losses under section 704(d)?

(f) The facts are the same as in (e). In Year 1, the partnership has $200 of operating income allocated 10 percent to A and 90 percent to B. At the end of Year 1, the partnership distributes $160 to A and $40 to B. How is the $200 recourse liability shared at the beginning of Year 2?

Chapter 5

Partnership Allocations: Nonrecourse Deductions

A. Introduction

In the previous chapter, we discovered that in general, partnership tax deductions may be validly allocated only to the partner who bears the economic burden corresponding to the deduction. This chapter deals primarily with an important exception to the general rule. In the case of "nonrecourse deductions," which are deductions attributable to nonrecourse liabilities, the economic burden corresponding to the deduction is not borne by any partner. Consequently, the allocation of these deductions cannot have "economic effect." The tax law therefore provides a special set of rules to specify how these deductions may be allocated.

To illustrate the need for the special rules, consider a general partnership that purchases a building for $300,000. The partnership pays $60,000 down and finances the balance of the purchase with the proceeds of a $240,000 nonrecourse liability secured by the building. Under current law, the partnership, as owner of the building, obtains a $300,000 basis in the building and therefore may claim up to $300,000 in deductions with respect to the property. See Crane v. U.S., 331 U.S. 1 (1947). Yet the partnership's (and the partners') economic exposure in this investment is limited to the $60,000 of equity invested. The remaining exposure is the creditor's. If the building became worthless, the partnership's (and the partners') loss would be $60,000 and the creditor's would be $240,000. Thus, after the first $60,000 of tax deductions, the partnership cannot allocate deductions to the partner who bears the corresponding economic burden (as required by "economic effect") because no partner bears that burden.

As a conceptual model, the special rules for the allocation of nonrecourse deductions draw on the holding of Comm'r v. Tufts, excerpted below. In *Tufts*, the Supreme Court considered whether the full amount of a nonrecourse liability should be included in the amount realized upon a sale or other disposition of the property serving as security for the liability, even though the value of such property had declined below the amount of the nonrecourse liability.

Commissioner v. Tufts

461 U.S. 300 (1983)

Justice BLACKMUN delivered the opinion of the Court: [A general partnership obtained nonrecourse financing to build and operate an apartment complex. Each of the general partners subsequently sold his partnership interest to an unrelated party. Based on the facts in the case, the tax consequences from the sale of partnership interests were the same as those from the sale by the partnership of its property, and the Court analyzed the transaction as if the latter had occurred. At the time of the transfer, the fair market value of the partnership property did not exceed $1,400,000. The property had an adjusted basis of approximately $1,450,000 in the partnership's hands and was subject to a nonrecourse liability of approximately $1,850,000, which the purchaser assumed. The purchaser paid no additional consideration, or boot, for the property. The government determined that the partnership recognized a gain of approximately $400,000 in the transaction, i.e., the amount of the nonrecourse liability ($1,850,000) less the adjusted basis of the property ($1,450,000). The individual partners asserted that the partnership recognized a loss of approximately $50,000, i.e., the excess of the adjusted basis of the property ($1,450,000) over its fair market value ($1,400,000).]

Over 35 years ago, in *Crane v. Commissioner*, 331 U.S. 1 (1947), this Court ruled that a taxpayer, who sold property encumbered by a nonrecourse mortgage (the amount of the mortgage being less than the property's value), must include the unpaid balance of the mortgage in the computation of the amount the taxpayer realized on the sale. The case now before us presents the question whether the same rule applies when the unpaid amount of the nonrecourse mortgage exceeds the fair market value of the property sold. . . .

Section 1001 governs the determination of gains and losses on the disposition of property. Under § 1001(a), the gain or loss from a sale or other disposition of property is defined as the difference between "the amount realized" on the disposition and the property's adjusted basis. Subsection (b) of § 1001 defines "amount realized": "The amount realized from the sale or other disposition of property shall be the sum of any money received plus the fair market value of the property (other than money) received." At issue is the application of the latter provision to the disposition of property encumbered by a nonrecourse mortgage of an amount in excess of the property's fair market value. . . .

In *Crane v. Commissioner*, supra, this Court took the first and controlling step toward the resolution of this issue. [In that case, Mrs. Crane sold a building encumbered by a nonrecourse liability to a buyer who took the property subject to the liability and paid an additional $2,500 in cash. Crane argued, among other things, that unlike a recourse liability, the amount of the nonrecourse liability should not be included in her amount realized in the sale.] . . . [T]he Court concluded that Crane obtained an economic benefit from the purchaser's assumption of the mortgage identical to the benefit conferred by the cancellation of personal debt. Because the value of the property in that case exceeded the amount of the mortgage, it was in Crane's economic interest to treat the mortgage as a personal obligation; only by doing so could she realize upon sale the appreciation in her equity represented by the $2,500 boot. The purchaser's assumption of the liability thus resulted in a taxable economic benefit to her, just as if she had been given, in addition to the boot, a sum of cash sufficient to satisfy the mortgage.

In a footnote, pertinent to the present case, the Court observed:

> Obviously, if the value of the property is less than the amount of the mortgage, a mortgagor who is not personally liable cannot realize a benefit equal to the mortgage. Consequently, a different problem might be encountered where a mortgagor abandoned the property or transferred it subject to the mortgage without receiving boot. That is not this case.

Id., at 14, n. 37. . . .

This case presents that unresolved issue. We are disinclined to overrule *Crane*, and we conclude that the same rule applies when the unpaid amount of the nonrecourse mortgage exceeds the value of the property transferred. *Crane* ultimately does not rest on its limited theory of economic benefit; instead, we read *Crane* to have approved the Commissioner's decision to treat a nonrecourse mortgage in this context as a true loan. This approval underlies *Crane*'s holdings that the amount of the nonrecourse liability is to be included in calculating both the basis and the amount realized on disposition. That the amount of the loan exceeds the fair market value of the property thus becomes irrelevant.

When a taxpayer receives a loan, he incurs an obligation to repay that loan at some future date. Because of this obligation, the loan proceeds do not qualify as income to the taxpayer. When he fulfills the obligation, the repayment of the loan likewise has no effect on his tax liability.

Another consequence to the taxpayer from this obligation occurs when the taxpayer applies the loan proceeds to the purchase price of property used to secure the loan. Because of the obligation to repay, the taxpayer is entitled to include the amount of the loan in computing his basis in the property; the loan, under § 1012, is part of the taxpayer's cost of the property. Although a different approach might have been taken with respect to a nonrecourse mortgage loan,[1] the Commissioner has

---

1. The Commissioner might have adopted the theory, implicit in *Crane*'s contentions, that a nonrecourse mortgage is not true debt, but, instead, is a form of joint investment by the mortgagor and the mortgagee. On this approach, nonrecourse debt would be considered a contingent liability, under which the mortgagor's payments on the debt gradually increase his interest in the property while decreasing that of the mortgagee. . . . Because the taxpayer's investment in the property would not include the nonrecourse debt, the taxpayer would not be permitted to include that debt in basis. . . .

We express no view as to whether such an approach would be consistent with the statutory structure and, if so, and *Crane* were not on the books, whether that approach would be preferred over *Crane*'s analysis. We note only that the *Crane* Court's resolution of the basis issue presumed that when property is purchased with proceeds from a nonrecourse mortgage, the purchaser becomes the sole owner of the property. . . . Under the *Crane* approach, the mortgagee is entitled to no portion of the basis. . . . The nonrecourse mortgage is part of the mortgagor's investment in the property, and does not constitute a coinvestment by the mortgagee. . . .

chosen to accord it the same treatment he gives to a recourse mortgage loan. The Court approved that choice in *Crane*, and the respondents do not challenge it here. The choice and its resultant benefits to the taxpayer are predicated on the assumption that the mortgage will be repaid in full.

When encumbered property is sold or otherwise disposed of and the purchaser assumes the mortgage, the associated extinguishment of the mortgagor's obligation to repay is accounted for in the computation of the amount realized. See *United States v. Hendler*, 303 U.S. 564, 566-567 (1938). Because no difference between recourse and nonrecourse obligations is recognized in calculating basis,[2] *Crane* teaches that the Commissioner may ignore the nonrecourse nature of the obligation in determining the amount realized upon disposition of the encumbered property. He thus may include in the amount realized the amount of the nonrecourse mortgage assumed by the purchaser. The rationale for this treatment is that the original inclusion of the amount of the mortgage in basis rested on the assumption that the mortgagor incurred an obligation to repay. Moreover, this treatment balances the fact that the mortgagor originally received the proceeds of the nonrecourse loan tax-free on the same assumption. Unless the outstanding amount of the mortgage is deemed to be realized, the mortgagor effectively will have received untaxed income at the time the loan was extended and will have received an unwarranted increase in the basis of his property. The Commissioner's interpretation of § 1001(b) in this fashion cannot be said to be unreasonable. . . .

The Commissioner in fact has applied this rule even when the fair market value of the property falls below the amount of the nonrecourse obligation. Reg. § 1.1001-2(b). . . .

Respondents received a mortgage loan with the concomitant obligation to repay. . . . The only difference between that mortgage and one on which the borrower is personally liable is that the mortgagee's remedy is limited to foreclosing on the securing property. This difference does not alter the nature of the obligation; its only effect is to shift from the borrower to the lender any potential loss caused by devaluation of the property. If the fair market value of the property falls below the amount of the outstanding obligation, the mortgagee's ability to protect its interests is impaired, for the mortgagor is free to abandon the property to the mortgagee and be relieved of his obligation.

This, however, does not erase the fact that the mortgagor received the loan proceeds tax-free and included them in his basis on the understanding that he had an obligation to repay the full amount. See *Woodsam Associates, Inc. v.*

---

2. The Commissioner's choice in *Crane* "laid the foundation stone of most tax shelters," Bittker, Tax Shelters, Nonrecourse Debt, and the *Crane* Case, 33 Tax L. Rev. 277, 283 (1978), by permitting taxpayers who bear no risk to take deductions on depreciable property. Congress recently has acted to curb this avoidance device by forbidding a taxpayer to take depreciation deductions in excess of amounts he has at risk in the investment. [§ 465(a)]. . . . Although this congressional action may foreshadow a day when nonrecourse and recourse debts will be treated differently, neither Congress nor the Commissioner has sought to alter *Crane*'s rule of including nonrecourse liability in both basis and the amount realized.

Commissioner, 198 F.2d 357, 359 (CA2 1952). . . . When the obligation is canceled, the mortgagor is relieved of his responsibility to repay the sum he originally received and thus realizes value to that extent within the meaning of § 1001(b). From the mortgagor's point of view, when his obligation is assumed by a third party who purchases the encumbered property, it is as if the mortgagor first had been paid with cash borrowed by the third party from the mortgagee on a nonrecourse basis, and then had used the cash to satisfy his obligation to the mortgagee.

Moreover, this approach avoids the absurdity the Court recognized in *Crane*. Because of the remedy accompanying the mortgage in the nonrecourse situation, the depreciation in the fair market value of the property is relevant economically only to the mortgagee, who by lending on a nonrecourse basis remains at risk. To permit the taxpayer to limit his realization to the fair market value of the property would be to recognize a tax loss for which he has suffered no corresponding economic loss. Such a result would be to construe "one section of the Act . . . so as . . . to defeat the intention of another or to frustrate the Act as a whole." 331 U.S. at 13.

In the specific circumstances of *Crane*, the economic benefit theory did support the Commissioner's treatment of the nonrecourse mortgage as a personal obligation. The footnote in *Crane* acknowledged the limitations of that theory when applied to a different set of facts. *Crane* also stands for the broader proposition, however, that a nonrecourse loan should be treated as a true loan. We therefore hold that a taxpayer must account for the proceeds of obligations he has received tax-free and included in basis. Nothing in either § 1001(b) or in the Court's prior decisions requires the Commissioner to permit a taxpayer to treat a sale of encumbered property asymmetrically, by including the proceeds of the nonrecourse obligation in basis but not accounting for the proceeds upon transfer of the encumbered property. . . .

When a taxpayer sells or disposes of property encumbered by a nonrecourse obligation, the Commissioner properly requires him to include among the assets realized the outstanding amount of the obligation. The fair market value of the property is irrelevant to this calculation. . . .

[Concurring opinion by Justice O'Connor omitted.]

NOTES

1. *Correspondence between depreciation deductions and subsequent gain*. Under the Court's holding, the disposition of property subject to a nonrecourse liability results in the realization of gain at least equal to the amount by which the liability exceeds the adjusted basis of the property (the "*Tufts* gain"). *Tufts* therefore ensures that any depreciation deductions taken on the portion of property financed by nonrecourse debt will eventually be offset by matching gain (i.e., the excess of the nonrecourse debt over the adjusted basis of the property) upon disposition of the underlying property. As we shall see, the partnership allocation rules for nonrecourse

deductions rely on this one-to-one correspondence to ensure that partners who are allocated nonrecourse deductions are also allocated the matching amount of *Tufts* gain.

2. *Section 7701(g).* The Court holds that the shortfall in the value of the underlying property is irrelevant in determining the amount realized and corresponding gain on disposition of the property. This holding preceded enactment of section 7701(g) ("clarifying" that the fair market value of property shall be deemed to be not less than the amount of any nonrecourse liability secured by such property). See also Reg. § 1.1001-2(b).

3. *Section 752(c) and (d).* In an omitted portion of the decision, the Court discusses at some length the function of section 752(c). The Court found that, based on its legislative history, section 752(c) only applies to situations where encumbered property is either contributed to or distributed from a partnership. In those situations, Congress was apparently concerned that the existence of debt in excess of fair market value might result in the artificial inflation of outside basis under section 752(a) and (b). Hence, under section 752(c), a partnership (or a distributee partner) is treated as assuming a liability to which property is subject only "to the extent of the fair market value of such property." See Reg. § 1.752-1(e). The Court found that this "fair-market-value" limitation does not apply to a sale of a partnership interest; instead, section 752(d) requires the selling partner to include the full amount of the debt in the amount realized even if the debt exceeds the fair market value of the underlying property.

B. Allocation of Nonrecourse Deductions

In this part, we describe the special rules for allocating nonrecourse deductions. The first two sections of this part provide a general overview of these rules — they describe what nonrecourse deductions are and the conditions that must be satisfied for their valid allocation. The remaining sections of this part discuss in a little more detail some of the steps taxpayers must follow in order to meet those conditions. Although the bottom line in this area is fairly straightforward — in a word, taxpayers are allowed to allocate nonrecourse deductions almost any way they wish — taxpayers and their advisors must jump through a number of hoops, and learn a lot of jargon in the process, before reaching that outcome. The purpose of this part is to expose you to the principal hoops (and jargon) without burying you in excessive detail. As you delve into this material, try not to lose sight of the larger principles set forth in the first two sections of this part. Part C of this chapter then describes how nonrecourse *liabilities* are shared by the partners, and part D serves as a reminder that although nonrecourse deductions may be allocated quite freely, other aspects of the tax law may restrict the corresponding tax benefits.

1. *What Are Nonrecourse Deductions?*

Read Reg. §§ 1.704-2(b)(1) and (3), 1.752-1(a)(2). "Nonrecourse deductions" are those attributable to a partnership liability that no partner is obligated to repay in a worst-case scenario. The classic example of such a deduction is illustrated below:

> **Example 5-1:** A partnership purchases some depreciable property for $300,000 using $60,000 cash and the proceeds of a $240,000 liability. The liability, which is secured by the property, is not a general obligation of the partnership. Rather, by the terms of the debt instrument, the lender's only recourse in the event of default by the partnership is to foreclose on the property. Assume that the partnership claims tax depreciation deductions of $10,000 per year and the principal amount and terms of the debt remain unchanged. In that case, depreciation deductions in excess of the first $60,000 are treated as "nonrecourse deductions." Those deductions are attributable to the debt financing of the property, and no partner has any obligation to repay the debt in a worst-case scenario.

Notice, however, that the definition of the term also encompasses deductions that do not conform to this classic type:

> **Example 5-2:** An LLC, which is taxed under subchapter K, borrows $300,000 to help finance some of its operating expenses for the year. The liability, which is not secured by any property, is a general obligation of the LLC. Nevertheless, in the absence of any personal guarantee or assumption by any of the LLC members, the lender may look under state law for its right to repayment only to the LLC's assets, and not to the personal assets of the LLC members. Thus, any deductions generated by this borrowing are also classified as "nonrecourse deductions." Those deductions are attributable to a liability of the company that no owner has any obligation to repay in a worst-case scenario.

As we shall see, the rules do not provide much guidance concerning the allocation of nonrecourse deductions attributable to the type of liability (sometimes referred to as an "exculpatory liability") described in **example 5-2**. As you learn the rules, consider how they should be applied to this increasingly common form of nonrecourse deduction.

2. *The Nonrecourse-Deduction Safe Harbor*

Because nonrecourse deductions have no corresponding economic burden borne by any partner, their allocation cannot satisfy the "economic effect" requirement of the substantial-economic-effect safe harbor. As a result, the tax law provides a *different* safe harbor applicable only to the allocation of nonrecourse deductions.

If the conditions of this safe harbor are met, the allocation is deemed to be consistent with the PIP and therefore valid. If the safe harbor is not satisfied, then the allocation must be made in accordance with the partners' overall economic interests in the partnership. Given the uncertainty of this last standard, most partnerships try to qualify their allocations within the terms of the safe harbor.

Read Reg. § 1.704-2(e). There are four conditions to the nonrecourse-deduction safe harbor:

(1) the requirements of the basic or alternate test for economic effect must be met;
(2) all other material allocations of the partnership must be valid;
(3) the nonrecourse deductions must be allocated in a manner "reasonably consistent" with allocations, which have substantial economic effect, of some other "significant" partnership item attributable to property securing the nonrecourse liability; and
(4) the partnership agreement must contain a "minimum gain chargeback" ("MGC") provision.

The first two conditions are mechanical in nature. The first condition, which essentially requires that the capital accounts of the partnership be maintained properly and be respected upon liquidation, simply ensures that compliance with the safe harbor is in harmony with the rules specifying the allocation of partnership items other than nonrecourse deductions. The second condition provides the IRS with additional flexibility in the event a partnership allocates a material item incorrectly. In that case, of course, the IRS would have the authority to reallocate the item. But because of the second condition of the safe harbor, the IRS would *also* have the authority to reallocate the partnership's nonrecourse deductions in order to rectify the error.

The third condition, referred to as the "significant item consistency" rule, tries to anchor the allocation of nonrecourse deductions to some other allocation having substantial economic effect. This rule is not particularly stringent, however; partnerships often have a fair amount of freedom to determine what other allocation should serve as the anchor. Moreover, whether an allocation is "reasonably consistent" with the anchoring allocation is interpreted by the tax law quite liberally, as illustrated by the following example.

> **Example 5-3:** A partnership allocates its income and losses (other than its nonrecourse deductions) in an initial ratio of 90:10. The ratio flips to 50:50 upon the satisfaction of certain future conditions. Assuming that both the 90:10 and 50:50 allocations have substantial economic effect and it is reasonably likely the future conditions causing the flip will someday occur, an allocation of nonrecourse deductions in any ratio between 90:10 and 50:50 satisfies the significant item consistency rule, but a 99:1 allocation ratio does not. See Reg. § 1.704-2(m) (ex. 1(ii)-(iii)).

The final condition—the required inclusion of an MGC provision in the partnership agreement—is the centerpiece of the nonrecourse-deduction safe harbor. Its function is to allow an allocation of nonrecourse deductions to a partner only if the partner is also allocated a matching amount of income or gain whenever the partnership disposes of property subject to nonrecourse liabilities (or upon the occurrence of certain other events). The MGC is the provision in the agreement that specifies under what circumstances a partner who has been allocated nonrecourse deductions must be allocated a matching amount of income or gain.

The operation of the MGC can be illustrated by returning to the facts of **example 5-1**. In that example, a partnership purchases depreciable property for $300,000 using $60,000 cash and the proceeds of a $240,000 nonrecourse liability, and claims depreciation deductions of $10,000 per year. The first six years' worth (or $60,000) of depreciation deductions are not nonrecourse deductions; accordingly, their allocation is controlled by the substantial-economic-effect safe harbor. Beginning in Year 7, however, the deductions are nonrecourse; this is because the hypothetical economic loss represented by the $10,000 tax deduction in the seventh and subsequent years would be suffered by the creditor and not by any of the partners.

Suppose the partnership allocates the entire $10,000 deduction arising in Year 7 to partner A. Assuming that the first three conditions of the nonrecourse-deduction safe harbor are met, this allocation would be valid only if A agrees in the MGC provision to be allocated $10,000 of income or gain in the future. The holding in *Tufts* assures us that there *will be* such amount of income or gain at a minimum. For example, even if the property's value fell to zero by the end of Year 7, any disposition or foreclosure of the property at that time would result in partnership gain of $10,000 ($240,000 nonrecourse liability less $230,000 adjusted basis). Hence, because of *Tufts*, we know that the promise made by A is not an empty one. Moreover, the MGC provides that if at any time there is an insufficient amount of future *Tufts* gain to support A's promise, then A must immediately be allocated an amount of income or gain equal to any shortfall.

QUESTIONS

1. *Application to exculpatory liabilities.* How should the significant item consistency rule and the MGC requirement be interpreted when the nonrecourse deductions being allocated are of the type described in **example 5-2**, i.e., deductions attributable to exculpatory liabilities?

2. *What about the substantiality requirement?* We have seen that allocations of nonrecourse deductions cannot have "economic effect," as that term is defined in the section 704(b) regulations. Do they have to pass the substantiality requirement? If they did, would an allocation of nonrecourse deductions pursuant to the four-part safe harbor just described be considered "substantial"? Why or why not?

3. *Liberal test?* Review the conditions necessary for making a valid allocation of nonrecourse deductions. Would it be fair to conclude that partnerships are free to allocate such deductions virtually any way they wish? Why do you think the Treasury has permitted partnerships to have this much freedom?

3. *Partnership Minimum Gain*

Read Reg. § 1.704-2(d)(1). The operational linchpin of the nonrecourse-deduction safe harbor is a concept called "partnership minimum gain" ("PMG"). PMG is the future *Tufts* gain, the amount of gain a partnership will realize when it disposes of its property securing nonrecourse liabilities in full satisfaction thereof and for no other consideration. In general, PMG for any particular property is equal to the excess (if any) of the nonrecourse liability over the basis of the property securing the liability. The amount of PMG is then aggregated for each of the properties of the partnership.

One can think of PMG as the account that keeps track of the size of a partner's promise to be allocated future income or gain equal to the nonrecourse deductions previously allocated to her. At any given time, a partner's share of PMG must generally equal the cumulative amount of nonrecourse deductions allocated to such partner (and, as discussed in section B4 below, her share of certain "nonrecourse distributions") that have not yet been offset by partnership income or gain (or "charged back" in the jargon of tax mavens in this area). See Reg. § 1.704-2(g)(1). In the aggregate, PMG is equal to the sum of the partners' shares of PMG.

> **Example 5-4:** In Year 1, partner A is allocated \$100 of nonrecourse deductions. To be valid, A must promise to be allocated a future amount of income or gain equal to \$100, as shown by a share of PMG equal to \$100. If, in Year 2, A's share of PMG falls to \$80, A must be allocated partnership income or gain of \$20. The size of A's promise has, in effect, shrunk and therefore A must make good on a portion of her promise in the current year. Thus, at the end of Year 2, the amount of nonrecourse deductions allocated to A and not yet offset by partnership income or gain (\$80) equals A's share of PMG.

It follows that there is generally a one-to-one correspondence between the amount of PMG and the amount of nonrecourse deductions not yet offset by partnership income or gain. A net increase in PMG from one year to the next means a corresponding increase in the amount of nonrecourse deductions for the year. A net decrease in PMG means that there must be allocated income or gain for the year equal to the amount of the net decrease, and this allocation is dictated by the terms of the MGC provision. See Reg. § 1.704-2(c), (f)(1). Net increases and decreases in PMG are significant events in the operation of the safe harbor, so we consider them in (just a little) more detail below.

a. Net Increases in PMG

Because PMG is generally equal to the excess of nonrecourse liabilities over the basis of property securing the liabilities, the amount of PMG increases from one year to the next for either one of two reasons. First, the basis of the property might be reduced during the year by an amount greater than any reduction in the nonrecourse liability (as a result of, for example, a repayment of principal). Any basis reduction, of course, is normally a consequence of depreciating the property. Thus, depreciation deductions causing an increase in PMG (i.e., widening the gap between the amount of a nonrecourse liability and the adjusted basis of the property securing the liability) are nonrecourse deductions.

Second, PMG might increase because the amount of the nonrecourse liability might increase by more than any basis increase. For example, the partnership might obtain additional debt proceeds by using the property as security for a second nonrecourse loan. In this case, the tax law generally assumes that the additional debt proceeds generate additional nonrecourse deductions for the partnership, unless the proceeds are distributed to the partners. See Reg. § 1.704-2(c), 1st sentence.

b. Net Decreases in PMG

The amount of PMG decreases because of the opposite two phenomena: either the secured property's basis increases by more than any increase in the nonrecourse loan, or the amount of the nonrecourse loan decreases by more than any decrease in basis. The most common cause of a PMG decrease is a disposition of the secured property in satisfaction of the nonrecourse liability. Recall that PMG is a measure of the partnership's *future Tufts* gain: the disposition reduces the future amount of *Tufts* gain to zero, triggering an allocation of current *Tufts* gain. Other common reasons for a PMG decrease are a loan repayment in excess of any annual depreciation taken on the secured property, or discharge of the nonrecourse debt (with the partnership retaining the secured property).

A PMG decrease triggers the MGC provision. As we have seen, because the future amount of *Tufts* gain that the partnership will realize has shrunk, partners who have been allocated nonrecourse deductions must be allocated income or gain in the current year equal to their share of the shrinkage. If the cause of the PMG decrease is a disposition of the secured property, the effect of the MGC is simple: the partners are allocated shares of the current *Tufts* gain resulting from the disposition equal to their share of the PMG decrease. If nonrecourse debt is discharged and the partnership retains the secured property, the COD income relating to the discharged debt is similarly covered by the MGC provision and allocated to the partners in the same manner. If there is some other cause for the PMG decrease, then the partners must be allocated a pro rata share of other items of partnership income or gain. See Reg. § 1.704-2(f)(1) and (6).

In summary, net PMG *increases* generally signal the existence of nonrecourse deductions whose allocation must comply with the conditions of the nonrecourse-deduction safe harbor. Net PMG *decreases* generally signal the need for a special allocation of income or gain to the partners who have previously been allocated nonrecourse deductions. As a practical matter, a PMG chart is a useful way of keeping track of net increases and decreases in PMG. Review carefully the facts of the following extended **example 5-5**, which illustrates the use of a PMG chart and the consequences of increases and decreases in PMG. We rely on the same facts, but change the Year 4 events, in **examples 5-6** and **5-7**.

Example 5-5: G and L form the GL limited partnership. G (the general partner) contributes $50 and L (the limited partner) contributes $200. GL purchases depreciable property for $250 cash and a $750 nonrecourse purchase-money note, with no principal repayment required for five years. In Years 1-3, GL breaks even except for $200 of annual depreciation deductions. The partnership agreement satisfies the first two requirements of the basic economic-effect test (maintenance of capital accounts and respect for positive balances on liquidation) and contains a QIO and MGC. G has an unlimited obligation to restore deficits but L does not. Except for nonrecourse deductions, all partnership items are allocated in the ratio 20:80 (to G and L, respectively) until such time as the partnership's cumulative profits equal its prior cumulative losses; thereafter, all such partnership items are allocated in the ratio 60:40. Nonrecourse deductions are allocated in the ratio 50:50 throughout the life of the partnership. The partnership does not expect to make any distributions prior to liquidation. Finally, at the beginning of Year 4, when the basis of the property is $400, the partnership sells the property for $1,000, with the buyer paying $250 in cash and taking the property subject to the $750 nonrecourse liability. The partnership has no other tax items in Year 4.

In allocating the partnership's recourse and nonrecourse deductions and its gain from the sale, the first step is to construct a PMG chart as follows:

	Adjusted Basis	*Nonrecourse Liabilities*	*PMG*	*Net Increase (Decrease) in PMG*
End Year 1	800	750	-0-	—
End Year 2	600	750	150	150
End Year 3	400	750	350	200
End Year 4	-0-	-0-	-0-	(350)

At the end of Year 1, PMG is zero, since the adjusted basis of the property ($800) exceeds the amount of the nonrecourse liability ($750). Accordingly, all of the partnership's deductions for Year 1 are recourse deductions allocated 20:80 to G and L. At the end of Year 2, the partnership has PMG of $150 ($750 nonrecourse liability less $600 adjusted basis). During Year 2, the partnership therefore has a $150 net increase in PMG (zero PMG at the end of Year 1 compared to $150 PMG at the end of Year 2). Therefore, $150 of the depreciation deductions are nonrecourse (equal to the net increase in PMG for Year 2) and $50 are recourse ($200 total depreciation deductions less $150 classified as nonrecourse). At the end of Year 3, the partnership has $350 PMG so that the partnership has a $200 net increase in PMG during the year. Accordingly, all of its depreciation deductions for Year 3 are nonrecourse. Finally, at the end of Year 4, having sold the property, the partnership has no PMG ($0 liability less $0 basis) and there is a $350 net decrease in PMG during the year. This means that of the partnership's $600 gain from the sale in Year 4 ($1,000 amount realized less $400 adjusted basis), $350 must be allocated in accordance with the MGC provision.

Next, it is necessary to allocate the partnership's depreciation deductions and gain from the sale in accordance with the partners' sharing agreement. At the end of Year 4, the partners' capital accounts will be as follows:

	G	*L*
Initial balance	50	200
Year 1: recourse deductions (20:80)	(40)	(160)
End Year 1	10	40
Year 2: nonrecourse deductions (50:50)	(75)	(75)
recourse deductions (20:80)	(10)	(40)
End Year 2	(75)	(75)
Year 3: nonrecourse deductions (50:50)	(100)	(100)
End Year 3	(175)	(175)
Year 4: $350 gain from sale (MGC)	175	175
$250 gain from sale (20:80)	50	200
End balance	50	200

The validity of the allocation of the recourse deductions in Years 1 and 2 and the $250 of Year 4 gain in excess of the PMG is tested under the substantial-economic-effect safe harbor. The nonrecourse deductions are tested separately under the nonrecourse-deduction safe harbor. Assuming that the partnership reasonably expects someday to have substantial profits and losses allocated in the ratio 60:40, the partners' equal division of the nonrecourse deductions should satisfy the significant item consistency rule, and the other conditions of the safe harbor are satisfied. Accordingly, the allocation of nonrecourse deductions is valid. At the end of Year 2, there is total PMG of $150 and each partner's share of it is $75 (50% of $150). At the end of Year 3, total PMG is $350 and each partner's share is $175. In each year, the partner's share of PMG exactly equals the amount of nonrecourse deductions allocated to the partner and not yet charged back. Finally, upon the sale in Year 4, $350 of the gain must be charged back to the partners in accordance with their shares of the PMG decrease, $175 to each. The additional $250 of gain is allocated in the same ratio (20:80) as the partnership's prior recourse deductions, restoring the partners' capital accounts to positive $50 and $200, respectively.

If the property were sold for more than $1,000, any additional gain would be allocated according to the "flip" ratio (60:40) in which the partners have agreed to share partnership items once cumulative profits equal prior cumulative losses. For example, assume the property is sold for $1,200, with the buyer paying $450 in cash and taking the property subject to the $750 nonrecourse liability. The total gain would be $800 (rather than $600), and the last $200 of gain would be allocated $120 to G (60%) and $80 to L (40%), increasing G's capital account to $170 and L's capital account to $280. Under the partnership agreement, the flip in sharing ratios occurs once the partners' original contributions have been restored. The additional $200 of gain represents true "economic" gain, i.e., gain in excess of the prior depreciation deductions.

QUESTIONS

1. *Permissible deficits?* In **example 5-5**, the parties apparently tried to satisfy the alternate test for economic effect because L did not have an unlimited obligation to restore deficits. But review the Year 2 capital account adjustments resulting from the facts in the example. Note that if the $75 nonrecourse deduction in Year 2 is taken into account first, then both its allocation and that of the $40 recourse deduction to L in that year caused and increased a deficit in L's capital account balance. If the recourse deduction is taken into account first, then the allocation of the $75 nonrecourse deduction to L caused a deficit balance in her account. Either result would seem to violate the key condition of the alternate test for economic effect—an allocation of an item may not "cause or increase" a deficit balance in excess of a partner's obligation to restore deficits. See Reg. § 1.704-1(b)(2)(ii)(*d*)(*3*) (flush language). Given that satisfaction of the alternate test for economic effect is, under the facts of this example, a requirement for *both* the substantial-economic-effect and nonrecourse-deduction safe harbors, why is the allocation of either of the deductions in Year 2 valid? See Reg. § 1.704-2(g)(1) (flush language). Can you articulate the rationale for this outcome?

2. *Calculation of PMG.* Suppose that in **example 5-5**, the property had declined in value to $500 over the first three years. Furthermore, suppose the partnership simply surrendered the property at the beginning of Year 4 to the creditor in complete satisfaction of the nonrecourse liability but for no other consideration. What tax items would have arisen in Year 4 and how would they have been allocated? Would these changed facts have placed in jeopardy the validity of any of the deductions allocated in the first three years?

3. *Effect on PMG.* As described, PMG is generally equal to the excess (if any) of the amount of the nonrecourse liability over the basis of the property securing the liability. Assume that, at the beginning of the year, a partnership owns

nondepreciable property with a basis of $200, subject to a nonrecourse liability of $250. What effect do the following alternative events have on PMG? On the obligation of the partnership to make a special allocation of income or gain pursuant to the MGC provision?

(a) During the year, the partnership obtains additional nonrecourse financing of $200 secured by the property, and the partnership uses the $200 to improve the property.
(b) The partnership uses its cash reserves to repay $50 of the nonrecourse liability.
(c) The same as (b), except that the property is depreciable and the partnership has $50 of annual depreciation deductions attributable to the property.
(d) The same as (b), except that the cash originates from one of the partners who makes an additional contribution of $50. See Reg. § 1.704-2(f)(3). Explain the logic behind this rule.
(e) The same as (b), except that the creditor requires one of the partners to guarantee the nonrecourse liability. See Reg. § 1.704-2(f)(2). Explain the logic behind this rule.

4. *Section 704(c) property as security*. How should PMG be measured if the property secured by the nonrecourse liability is either section 704(c) property or reverse section 704(c) property (i.e., revalued property)? See Reg. § 1.704-2(d)(3). Explain the reason for this rule.

5. *Effect of revaluation*. Suppose at the end of Year 1, a partnership owns nondepreciable property whose tax basis and book value are both $100, and the property is subject to a nonrecourse liability of $130. During Year 2, a new partner joins the partnership and the partnership books are revalued. See Reg. § 1.704-1(b)(2)(iv)(*f*)(*5*)(*i*). At the end of Year 2, the debt is still $130 but the restated book value of the property is $150. What effect do these events have on PMG? On the obligation of the partnership to make a special allocation of income or gain pursuant to the MGC provision? See Reg. § 1.704-2(d)(4). Explain the reason for this rule.

6. *Waivers of the MGC requirement*. The partners may also request a waiver of the MGC under appropriate circumstances. See Reg. § 1.704-2(f)(4) (waiver to avoid unintended economic distortions). When might a waiver be appropriate? See Reg. § 1.704-2(f)(7) (ex. 1) (prior income allocations that offset nonrecourse deductions allocated to the partners made the required chargeback under the MGC unnecessary and contrary to the economic agreement of the parties).

Example 5-6: Assume the same facts as in **example 5-5**, except that there is no sale of the building at the beginning of Year 4. Instead, G contributes at that time $250 to the partnership which uses the money to repay $250 of the nonrecourse liability. The partnership again breaks even in Year 4 except for its $200 depreciation deduction.

As the PMG chart shows, there is only $300 of PMG at the end of Year 4:

	Adjusted Basis	*Nonrecourse Liabilities*	*PMG*	*Net Increase (Decrease) in PMG*
End Year 3	400	750	350	200
End Year 4	200	500	300	(50)

During Year 4, there is a net decrease in PMG of $50 ($300 PMG at the end of Year 4 compared to $350 PMG at the end of Year 3). The net decrease is attributable to the excess of the loan repayment ($250) over the Year 4 depreciation ($200). Each partner's share of the net decrease in PMG is $25 (50% of $50). See Reg. § 1.704-2(g)(2). Since G's capital contribution is used to repay the debt, no MGC is triggered with respect to G. See Reg. § 1.704-2(f)(3). The MGC does apply to L, however, since she did not contribute any additional funds to the partnership. Since the building is not disposed of, there is no gain to allocate to L. Instead, the MGC requires a special allocation of partnership operating income of $25 to L during Year 4. See Reg. § 1.704-2(f)(6).

During Year 4, assume that the partnership has operating income of $175 and operating expenses of $175 in addition to the $200 depreciation deduction. The priority allocation of $25 of gross income to L increases the partnership's bottom-line loss to $225 ($150 balance of operating income less $175 of operating expenses less $200 of depreciation). The Year 4 bottom-line loss is classified as a recourse deduction, since the partnership had no net increase in PMG for the year. L cannot be allocated any of the Year 4 bottom-line loss, since she is not required to restore any deficit in her capital account (after taking into account her deemed DRO of $150 attributable to her remaining share of PMG). See Reg. § 1.704-2(g)(1), flush language. Thus, the entire $225 bottom-line loss must be allocated to G. Verify this result by examining the partners' capital accounts following the Year 4 allocations:

	G	*L*
End Year 3	(175)	(175)
Year 4: G's contribution	250	
MGC		25
bottom-line loss	(225)	
End Year 4	(150)	(150)

At the end of Year 4, each partner has a capital account deficit of $150 equal to her share of the remaining PMG. In effect, G's $250 contribution in Year 4 was used partly to repay G's share of the net decrease in PMG ($25) and partly to fund the partnership's recourse deductions ($225). Under the substantial-economic-effect test, G bears the economic burden corresponding to the Year 4 bottom-line loss as a result of her capital contribution. Upon a foreclosure at the beginning of Year 5, the partnership would recognize gain of $300 ($500 nonrecourse liability less $200 basis), allocated $150 to each partner (50% × $300).

QUESTION

What happens in **example 5-6** if the partnership has no gross income in Year 4? See Reg. § 1.704-2(f)(6) and (7) (ex. 2).

4. *Nonrecourse Distributions*

In this section, we consider one last concept that is part of the nonrecourse-deduction safe harbor, referred to as "nonrecourse distributions." These are distributions attributable to the proceeds of nonrecourse borrowing to the extent that the borrowing gives rise to an increase in PMG. See Reg. § 1.704-2(h)(1). To understand the reason for this concept and the corresponding special treatment, review the following example.

> **Example 5-7:** Return to the facts of **example 5-6**, but assume that there is no contribution by G nor repayment of any part of the liability in Year 4. Instead, at the beginning of that year, the partnership borrows an additional $200 nonrecourse, secured by the building, and distributes the borrowed proceeds equally to G and L.

In this example, the partnership has a $400 net increase in PMG during Year 4, as shown by the PMG chart:

	Adjusted Basis	*Nonrecourse Liabilities*	*PMG*	*Net Increase (Decrease) in PMG*
End Year 3	400	750	350	200
End Year 4	200	950	750	400

Despite this increase, the partnership has only $200 in nonrecourse deductions during the year (the depreciation deduction). The other $200 increase is attributable to additional debt, the proceeds of which have been distributed by the partnership to the partners. Accordingly, the proceeds have not generated any deductions for the partnership. See Reg. § 1.704-2(c). Thus, at the end of Year 4, there is a minimum amount of future gain to be recognized by the partnership of $750, but only a total of $550 in nonrecourse deductions ($350 as of the end of Year 3 plus the additional

$200 arising in Year 4) have been allocated to any partner. In other words, the full amount of the minimum future gain has not been "promised" to any partner.

No problem, right? After all, the tax law's concern is that the promise of future income or gain be *large enough* to support a current allocation of nonrecourse deductions. In **example 5-7**, that clearly is true. So why do we need to provide any special treatment for the distribution?

The answer is revealed by the partners' capital accounts:

	G	*L*
End Year 3	(175)	(175)
Year 4: nonrecourse deductions (50:50)	(100)	(100)
distribution	(100)	(100)
End Year 4	(375)	(375)

A partner's share of PMG is added to the partner's limited DRO. See Reg. § 1.704-2(g)(1), flush language. But absent a special rule, L's share of PMG is only *$275* (the aggregate amount of nonrecourse deductions allocated to L during the first four years). As you can see, by the end of Year 4, L has a deficit of *$375*. Under the alternate test for economic effect, a deficit balance of this size would be impermissible. It would result either in some reallocation of deductions away from L or an immediate allocation of $100 of income or gain to L pursuant to the QIO to "restore" L's deficit balance to no more than $275.

The Treasury decided that neither of these two outcomes should occur so long as L agrees to be allocated the unpromised portion of the PMG equal to the amount of the nonrecourse proceeds distributed to L. In effect, by promising to be allocated a greater amount of income or gain in the future, L avoids the necessity of a current allocation of income or gain (pursuant to the QIO) or a current loss of partnership deductions. A partner's share of PMG is therefore equal to the *sum* of the nonrecourse deductions previously allocated to her *plus* her nonrecourse distributions, to the extent those amounts have not already been charged back. Read Reg. § 1.704-2(g)(1)(i). In **example 5-7**, L's share of PMG at the end of Year 4 is $375, and therefore the deficit balance in L's capital account is permissible. Upon a foreclosure at the beginning of Year 5, the partnership would recognize gain of $750 ($950 nonrecourse liability less $200 basis), of which $375 would be allocated to L under the MGC.

QUESTIONS

1. How does a partnership determine whether a distribution made during a year is attributable to the proceeds of nonrecourse financing or some other source (such as accumulated profits)? See Reg. § 1.704-2(h)(2) (any reasonable method of allocation is allowed).

2. In **example 5-7**, what is G's share of PMG at the end of Year 4? See Reg. § 1.704-2(h)(3).

Problem 5-1: G and L form a limited partnership. G (the general partner) contributes $60,000 and L (the limited partner) contributes $140,000. The partnership purchases equipment for $200,000 cash and a $300,000 nonrecourse purchase-money note. The partnership agreement satisfies the first two requirements of the basic economic-effect test (maintenance of capital accounts and liquidating distributions) and contains a qualified income offset provision and a minimum gain chargeback provision. G has an unlimited deficit restoration obligation, but L is not required to restore any deficit in her capital account. The partnership allocates all income and loss to G and L in the ratio 30:70 until such time as the partnership's cumulative profits equal its prior cumulative losses; thereafter all partnership items are allocated in the ratio 50:50. The partnership does not expect to make any distributions prior to liquidation. The partnership depreciates the equipment over a five-year period using the straight-line method. In Years 1-5, annual operating income ($200,000) equals annual operating expenses ($200,000).

(a) Will the partnership's allocations be respected? Why or why not? What must be the partners' respective capital account balances at the end of Year 3?
(b) Same as (a), except that the partnership agreement allocates all depreciation to G and L in the ratio 10:90.
(c) Same as (a), except that the partnership agreement allocates all nonrecourse deductions to G and L in the ratio 50:50.

Problem 5-2: The facts are the same as in **problem 5-1**, except that the partnership allocates all income and loss to G and L in the ratio 30:70 throughout the life of the partnership. At the end of Year 3, the basis of the equipment is $200,000 ($500,000 less $300,000 depreciation); G has a deficit capital account of $30,000 and L has a deficit capital account of $70,000. If the following alternative events occur, what must be the partners' respective capital account balances at the end of Year 4?

(a) At the beginning of Year 4, G contributes $45,000 and L contributes $105,000, which the partnership uses to repay $150,000 of the nonrecourse liability.
(b) At the beginning of Year 4, G guarantees payment of up to $200,000 of the partnership's nonrecourse liability if the creditor is unable to recover the full $300,000.
(c) At the beginning of Year 4, the partnership borrows an additional $200,000 nonrecourse, secured by the equipment, and immediately distributes the borrowed proceeds $60,000 to G and $140,000 to L.

C. Outside Basis and the Allocation of Nonrecourse Liabilities

1. *Introduction*

In chapter four, we described the potentially important role that outside basis, and a partner's share of partnership liabilities, may play in determining whether losses allocated to a partner can be currently utilized. In addition, we explained that, in general, *recourse* liabilities are allocated to the partner who bears the economic risk of having to repay the liability in a worst-case scenario. This part considers how partnership *non*recourse liabilities are shared. Because no partner bears the risk of having to repay these liabilities in a worst-case scenario, a different test must be provided for their allocation. As in the case of recourse liabilities, nonrecourse liabilities are shared in a way that ensures that a partner who is allocated nonrecourse deductions has sufficient outside basis to utilize the deductions in a timely manner.

Read Reg. § 1.752-1(a)(2). As we have seen, a nonrecourse liability is defined as any liability (or portion thereof) for which no partner bears the economic risk of loss. In general, these liabilities are allocated among the partners in accordance with their share of partnership profits. The underlying assumption is that if these liabilities are ever satisfied by the partnership, they will be paid out of partnership profits.

Read Reg. § 1.752-3(a). The tax law provides that a partner's share of nonrecourse liabilities is determined in three stages or "tiers." First, partners are allocated nonrecourse liabilities equal to their share of partnership minimum gain (PMG). Second, additional nonrecourse liabilities are allocated up to the partners' share of *minimum* section 704(c) gain, i.e., the amount of taxable gain that would be allocated to the partner if the partnership disposed of its section 704(c) or reverse section 704(c) property for no consideration other than satisfaction of nonrecourse liabilities secured by such property. Finally, any nonrecourse liabilities left unallocated by the first two tiers (termed "excess nonrecourse liabilities") are divided in accordance with the partners' share of partnership profits.

As you can see, each tier generally allocates nonrecourse liabilities consistent with an item of income or gain allocable to the partner. The first two tiers represent special allocations of income or gain to the partner, and the third is a more general profit share. We describe each of these tiers in somewhat more detail below.

2. *Tier 1: Partner's Share of PMG*

Recall that PMG is the future *Tufts* gain of a partnership, the amount of gain the partnership will realize upon disposition of its property securing nonrecourse liabilities in full satisfaction thereof and for no other consideration. See Reg. § 1.704-2(d)(1). We learned that a partner's share of PMG represents, in effect, the size of the partner's promise to be allocated a future amount of income or gain equal to her share of prior nonrecourse deductions and nonrecourse distributions not yet charged back. This "promise" is embodied in the MGC provision that must be included in the partnership agreement to qualify allocations under the nonrecourse-deduction safe harbor.

As we discussed, a partner's share of PMG already plays two crucial roles under the safe harbor because it supports the front-end allocation of nonrecourse deductions to that partner and also counts as a limited DRO for partners without an unlimited obligation to restore deficits. By allocating nonrecourse liabilities first up to a partner's share of PMG, the tax law provides a *third* essential function for this "promise." The tier 1 rule ensures that a partner who is allocated nonrecourse deductions is also allocated the *same* amount of the nonrecourse liability. Thus, the partner will generally have enough outside basis to be able to utilize the nonrecourse deductions currently.

> **Example 5-8:** At the beginning of the year, a partnership holds depreciable property with an adjusted basis of $800. The property is security for a nonrecourse liability of $800. During the year, the property is depreciated and the $200 depreciation deduction is allocated entirely to partner E. There is no change in the principal amount of the debt.

Assuming that the conditions of the nonrecourse-deduction safe harbor are satisfied, this allocation is valid and E's share of PMG is increased by $200. See Reg. § 1.704-2(g)(1)(i). Thus, based on the tier 1 allocation, E also has at least a $200 share of the nonrecourse liability, increasing her outside basis by $200. E's outside basis should, therefore, be sufficient to absorb her share of the nonrecourse deductions. The increase in E's outside basis is deemed to occur immediately before taking into account the downward adjustment to reflect the $200 of depreciation deductions allocated to her.

The tier 1 rule may have another important ramification. If a partner's share of PMG results from nonrecourse distributions previously made to the partner, the tier 1 allocation generally ensures that the partner has enough outside basis to avoid paying tax on the distribution.

> **Example 5-9:** Assume the same facts as **example 5-8**, except that the property is not depreciable and there is no change to either the basis of the property or the principal amount of the original debt. During the year, the partnership borrows an additional $100 on a nonrecourse basis, which liability is secured by the property, and distributes the proceeds all to partner F.

As a result of these facts, F's share of PMG is generally increased by $100, which means, based on the tier 1 allocation, that F has at least a $100 share of the liabilities. See Reg. §§ 1.704-2(g)(1)(i), 1.752-3(a)(1). Therefore, the distribution generally does not trigger gain to F under section 731(a)(1) because F's outside basis is increased (immediately before the distribution) by her share of the nonrecourse borrowing. See I.R.C. §§ 752(a), 722.

3. *Tier 2: Partner's Share of Minimum Section 704(c) Gain*

You may recall that "section 704(c) property" or "reverse section 704(c) property" is partnership property whose value differs from basis at the time the property is either contributed to, or revalued by, the partnership. In general, the built-in gain or loss in such property at the time of the contribution or revaluation must be specially allocated by the partnership when the gain or loss is realized in order to prevent income shifting among the partners. Under tier 2, any nonrecourse liabilities not allocated by the tier 1 rule must be allocated to partners up to their share of minimum section 704(c) gain in such property.

> **Example 5-10:** Partnership owns an asset whose book value and basis are both \$50. During the year, the value of the asset appreciates to \$90; the partnership incurs an \$80 nonrecourse liability which is secured by the asset. Assume that an event occurs during the year that permits the partnership to book up the asset to its fair market value of \$90, and under section 704(c), the booked-up amount (\$40) is allocated equally to partners C and D.

Under the tier 2 rule, \$30 of the nonrecourse liability must be allocated to C and D, \$15 each. The \$30 is the *minimum* amount of future gain that would be allocated to C and D in the future pursuant to section 704(c). For example, even if the asset's value were to fall to zero, a foreclosure of the asset by the creditor would result in recognition of gain of \$30 by the partnership (\$80 nonrecourse liability less \$50 basis), which would be shared equally by C and D. The rest of the liability is allocated under tier 3, discussed below.

It might seem from the facts in **example 5-10** that there is also some PMG. In general, PMG is equal to the excess of the nonrecourse liability over the tax basis of property securing the liability. See Reg. § 1.704-2(b)(2). Thus, there would seem to be PMG of \$30 in **example 5-10**.

But remember that where the secured property's book value and basis are different, PMG is measured by the excess, if any, of the nonrecourse liability over the *book value* of the property. See Reg. § 1.704-2(d)(3). Thus, there is no PMG in this example and there would be no allocation of the liability under tier 1. Logically, the same gain cannot be "promised" more than once. Because the \$30 gain has already been promised to C and D under section 704(c), it cannot be promised again to some other partner to support an allocation of nonrecourse deductions to that partner. This rule, therefore, prevents any overlap between PMG and minimum section 704(c) gain.

Finally, in **example 5-10**, there is, in fact, *\$40* of built-in gain that must be specially allocated to C and D under section 704(c), not just \$30. Should C and D get credit for this greater amount of gain in determining their share of the nonrecourse liability? Under the tier 2 rule, the answer is "no." The logic is that, although C and D are obligated to receive a special allocation under section 704(c) of as much as $40 of gain, the partnership may never realize that amount of gain. Only the $30 of *minimum* section 704(c) gain will definitely be allocated to C and D in the future. As we shall see below, however, the additional $10 of potential section 704(c) gain may be taken into account under tier 3.

QUESTIONS

1. As you may remember, partnerships are entitled to revalue the property on their books only in certain circumstances, such as upon entry of a new partner. See Reg. § 1.704-1(b)(2)(iv)(*f*)(*5*)(*i*). Suppose none of those events occurs in **example 5-10** and therefore there is no book-up of the asset in the year of the borrowing. Now, how will the partnership nonrecourse liability be shared?

2. Suppose in **example 5-10**, the asset appreciates further and the partnership incurs an additional $20 nonrecourse liability that is secured by the asset. Assume that the book value and basis of the asset, and the principal amount of the original liability, are unchanged from the example. How must the total nonrecourse liabilities of $100 be shared?

4. *Tier 3: Partner's Share of Partnership Profits*

The excess nonrecourse liabilities — those left unallocated by the tier 1 and 2 rules — must be divided in accordance with the partners' share of partnership profits. If a partnership has no PMG or minimum section 704(c) gain, all nonrecourse liabilities are allocated under this third tier.

In theory, one might think that this third tier should focus on the *overall* profit shares of the partners because that may be the best guess of how the nonrecourse liability will be paid off. Instead, the parties have extraordinary latitude in allocating any excess nonrecourse liabilities. First, the parties may specify what their profit shares are, solely for purposes of allocating excess nonrecourse liabilities, so long as the designated share is reasonably consistent with an allocation, which has substantial economic effect, of some significant item of partnership income or gain. See Reg. § 1.752-3(a)(3), 3d sentence. It is common practice, for example, for partners to state in their agreement that their profit share is 50:50, or any other ratio, "for purposes of section 752." This provision designates how they have agreed to share nonrecourse liabilities *under tier 3*, because general profit shares are irrelevant for purposes of allocating nonrecourse liabilities under tiers 1 or 2 (or allocating recourse liabilities). This designation is valid so long as the designated share is reasonably consistent with how the parties share some significant item of income or gain.

Second, to the extent nonrecourse liabilities are not already taken into account under tier 2, partnerships may specifically allocate such liabilities under tier 3 up to a partner's share of section 704(c) gain or reverse section 704(c) gain. See Reg. § 1.752-3(a)(3). In **example 5-10**, above, this flexibility means that an additional $10 of the nonrecourse liability, representing the potential section 704(c) gain in excess of the minimum amount, may be allocated to C and D under tier 3.

Finally, partnerships may bypass profit shares altogether and allocate nonrecourse liabilities under tier 3 in the manner in which they reasonably expect the deductions attributable to such liabilities to be allocated. See Reg. § 1.752-3(a)(3), 4th sentence. This last alternative is the clearest evidence of the policy objective to ensure that a partner who is allocated nonrecourse deductions has sufficient outside basis to utilize the deductions in a timely fashion. Furthermore, the alternative provides an easy way to avoid changes in liability shares each year, which may have unexpected and undesirable tax consequences. The following two examples, which track the basic facts of **example 5-5**, illustrate:

> **Example 5-11:** A and B form the AB partnership, with A contributing $50 and B contributing $200. AB purchases depreciable property for $250 cash and a $750 nonrecourse purchase-money note, with no principal repayment required for five years. In Years 1-5, AB breaks even except for $200 of annual depreciation deductions. Except for nonrecourse deductions, all partnership items are allocated in the ratio 20:80 (to A and B, respectively) until such time as the partnership's cumulative profits equal its prior cumulative losses; thereafter, all such partnership items are allocated in the ratio 60:40. Nonrecourse deductions are allocated in the ratio 50:50 throughout the life of the partnership.

During Year 1, there is no PMG or minimum section 704(c) gain. Accordingly, the partnership's nonrecourse liability of $750 must be allocated under tier 3 in accordance with the partners' profit shares. Assume that A and B specify 20:80 as the ratio in which they share partnership profits for purposes of section 752, the same ratio that they share all items other than nonrecourse deductions. Based on that assumption, A's share of the liability is $150 (20% of $750) and B's share is $600 (80% of $750).

During Year 2, there is a $150 increase in PMG (allocated 50:50, the same manner in which the nonrecourse deductions are allocated) and a corresponding $150 decrease in the amount of liabilities shared under the third tier (allocated 20:80). Therefore, there is a shift in the allocation of the nonrecourse liability. At the end of Year 2, A's share of the nonrecourse liability is $75 (50% × $150 PMG) plus $120 (20% × $600 excess nonrecourse liability), or a total of $195. B's share of the nonrecourse liability is $75 (50% × $150 PMG) plus $480 (80% × $600 excess nonrecourse liability), or a total of $555. Thus, A's share is increased, and B's share is decreased, by $45 from Year 1 to Year 2. In subsequent years, additional increases in PMG cause further shifts in the partners' shares of the liability. When the partnership property is fully depreciated, A's and B's share of the PMG is each $375 and therefore they will share equally in the nonrecourse liability, corresponding to the total nonrecourse deductions allocated to each partner.

Note that A's share of the liability continually increases in this example to provide her with sufficient outside basis to absorb the nonrecourse deductions allocated to her. In the process, however, B's share continually decreases. These changes are caused by the initial allocation of the liability in a 20:80 ratio even though the liability must eventually be shared 50:50, consistent with the manner in which the nonrecourse deductions are allocated. In addition to the nuisance created by these constant changes, B's decreasing share of partnership liabilities, which is treated as a constructive cash distribution to B under section 752(b), could cause unexpected and adverse tax consequences to B.

> **Example 5-12:** Assume the same facts as in **example 5-11**, except that the partners agree to allocate nonrecourse liabilities under tier 3 in the same manner in which they expect the corresponding nonrecourse deductions to be allocated (50:50).

In this case, in Year 1, A and B are allocated $375 each of the nonrecourse liability. In Year 2, the $150 increase in PMG does not trigger any shift in the partners' shares of the liability, since the PMG is shared in the same ratio (50:50) as the tier 3 allocation. Thus, allocating nonrecourse liabilities under tier 3 in the same manner that the partners reasonably expect the nonrecourse deductions to be allocated avoids changes in the partners' shares of such liabilities as PMG changes.

> **Problem 5-3:** A and B are equal partners of partnership AB, which owns one asset, *x*, whose book value and tax basis are both $40. Prior to C's joining the firm, the partnership revalues *x* to its fair market value of $100, with the booked-up amount shared equally by A and B. C then joins the firm by contributing asset *y* whose value is $100 and basis is $60. Thus, C is a 50 percent partner after joining the firm and A and B are each 25 percent partners. Thereafter, the partnership borrows $90. Assume that for purposes of section 752, the partners validly designate their overall profit shares in the ratio 25:25:50.
>
> (a) If the liability is nonrecourse and secured by asset *x*, how is it shared by the partners?
> (b) Same as (a), except that the liability is secured by asset *y* and not *x*.
> (c) Suppose the partnership is an LLC taxed under subchapter K, and the partners are members of the firm. If the liability is an unsecured, general obligation of the firm, how is it shared by the members? See Reg. § 1.752-3(b)(1) and (c) (ex. 3).

Problem 5-4: The facts are the same as in **problem 5-1**.

(a) In **problem 5-1(a)**, assume that the partners agree to allocate nonrecourse liabilities under tier 3 in the ratio 30:70. What is each partner's outside basis at the end of Year 3?
(b) In **problem 5-1(c)**, assume that the partners agree to allocate nonrecourse liabilities under tier 3 in the ratio 50:50. What is each partner's outside basis at the end of Year 3?

Problem 5-5: The facts are the same as in **problem 5-2**.

(a) In **problem 5-2(b)**, how does G's guarantee affect the sharing of liabilities? What is each partner's outside basis at the end of Year 4?
(b) In **problem 5-2(c)**, does each partner have sufficient outside basis to absorb her share of the distribution attributable to the nonrecourse borrowing? What is each partner's outside basis at the end of Year 4?

NOTES

1. *Less flexibility?* Proposed regulations under section 752 would curtail some of the flexibility in allocating "excess" nonrecourse liabilities. Prop. Reg. § 1.752-3(a)(3). Partners would still be allowed to specifically allocate liabilities under tier 3 up to a partner's share of section 704(c) gain or reverse section 704(c) gain, but they would no longer be permitted to use the "significant item" method or the "alternative method" relating to expected allocations of future nonrecourse deductions. Under a new "liquidation value" approach, the partners' interests in partnership profits could be specified based on the partners' "liquidation value percentages." The proposed regulations provide an example illustrating operation of the liquidation value approach. Prop. Reg. § 1.752-3(c) (ex. 2). Elimination of the alternative method might make it more difficult to avoid unintended changes in liability shares each year, while the determination of liquidation value percentages would introduce new complexity.

2. *Sharing of nonrecourse liabilities in a Series LLC.* As mentioned in chapter one, some states have authorized creation of a "Series LLC," a special type of LLC typically engaged in multiple activities in which the obligations incurred in connection with one activity or series may not be enforceable against the assets of another series. The tax consequences of transactions involving this type of entity will depend upon whether a Series LLC and all of its series are treated as a single entity or multiple entities for tax purposes. The Treasury's proposed classification regulations provide some guidance on that question. See Prop. Reg. § 301.7701-1(a)(5). For example, suppose each of three series of a Series LLC borrows money and the lender's right of recovery in each instance is limited to the assets belonging to the series incurring the debt. If the Series LLC is treated

as a single entity, should each member of the LLC share in the nonrecourse liabilities of each series? Would the result differ if each series were treated as a separate entity owned by only certain of the Series LLC's members?

D. At Risk and Passive Loss Limitations

1. *Introduction*

In this part, we discuss briefly two other potential restrictions on the ability of a partner to claim losses properly allocated to her. The "at risk" and "passive activity loss" provisions are two "super-rules" that apply broadly to taxpayers, including many partners of a partnership. Although these rules are not limited to partnerships, they owe their existence in no small part to partnership investments and transactions. It was largely the failure of subchapter K to curtail tax shelters carried out through partnerships that led to their enactment. These rules apply in addition to the subchapter K limitations. Thus, losses properly allocated to a partner who has sufficient outside basis to claim the loss, as determined under sections 704 and 752, may nevertheless be disallowed under the at risk or passive loss rules. While adding considerable complexity and perhaps being overly broad, these rules succeeded in curbing the targeted class of tax shelters.

The at risk and passive loss limitations may significantly affect the tax consequences of a partnership investment — thus making successful navigation of the section 704/752 maze seem all for naught. Nevertheless, it is important to keep firmly in mind their limited reach; in many circumstances, sections 704 and 752 alone are controlling. In general, the at risk and passive loss rules apply only to losses claimed by individuals and certain closely held corporations. See I.R.C. §§ 465(a)(1), 469(a). Thus, a widely held corporate joint venturer is exempt from these restrictions. In addition, these rules generally do not restrict the use of losses against the active business income of closely held corporations that are not personal service corporations. See I.R.C. §§ 465(c)(7), 469(e)(2). This limited scope reflects Congress's desire to prevent the sheltering of income from only certain activities, such as personal services or portfolio investments, through the use of losses from completely unrelated activities. Both the at risk and passive loss rules limit the use of "losses" from certain activities, i.e., deductions in excess of income from that activity. The principal difference between the two sets of rules is that the at risk limitation generally restricts tax losses for which a taxpayer bears no economic risk, while the passive loss limitation applies much more bluntly: it potentially defers both economic and non-economic losses if they are derived from activities in which the taxpayer does not materially participate. Both sets of rules apply to partnership losses at the partner level (not the entity level), once such losses have been passed through under section 704.

The following sections describe these provisions in somewhat greater detail and then consider their overall relationship to sections 704 and 752.

2. *"At Risk" Limitation*

Read I.R.C. § 465(a), (b)(1)-(5), and (d). Even if a partner has sufficient outside basis to deduct her share of partnership losses, the at risk rules of section 465 may defer the deduction. Under the at risk rules, losses allocated to a partner from a particular partnership activity are generally deductible only up to the amount that the taxpayer has "at risk" in the activity. A partner's amount at risk is generally determined in a manner similar to her outside basis, with two important differences. First, amounts borrowed for use in an activity generally increase a partner's at risk amount only to the extent that she is personally liable for the borrowed amount. Second, borrowed amounts are not considered at risk if the lender has an interest (other than as a creditor) in the activity or is related to a person (other than the taxpayer) who has such an interest. See I.R.C. § 465(b)(2) and (3). Thus, the at risk rules generally place a tighter lid than outside basis on the amount of partnership losses that may be deducted by a partner. Although partners obtain basis for the portion of their investments financed by nonrecourse debt, see Crane v. Comm'r, 331 U.S. 1 (1947), the at risk rules may nevertheless deny them the tax benefit of losses attributable to nonrecourse financing.

As under the section 704(d) limitation, losses in excess of a partner's amount at risk are "suspended" and carried over indefinitely to subsequent years until the partner's at risk amount is sufficient to absorb them. The section 704(d) limitation is applied before determining whether a loss is suspended under section 465. Thus, if losses pass muster under section 704(d), outside basis is correspondingly reduced even though such losses are nevertheless suspended by section 465.

The at risk limitation applies only to losses resulting from a particular "activity" of the taxpayer. This is a key limitation because it delineates the circumstances in which netting of income and losses may (or may not) be allowed. Thus, there is no restriction on a taxpayer's netting of deductions (including deductions resulting from nonrecourse financing) and income from the same activity; the reason is that the income itself increases the taxpayer's at risk amount available to absorb the loss. But losses from one activity that are suspended by the at risk rules may not be used to shelter income from a different activity. Despite its potential significance, the term "activity" is rather amorphous. Ownership and management of two buildings may be considered one or two activities based on the degree of interrelationship between the investments. When a partnership engages in multiple activities, partners must keep track of their at risk amount and other partnership items on an activity-by-activity basis.

An important exception permits taxpayers engaged in real estate activities to count their share of "qualified nonrecourse financing" (QNF) as part of their at risk amount with respect to such activity. Read I.R.C. § 465(b)(6). QNF is nonrecourse financing secured by real property used in the activity. In general, the nonrecourse borrowing must be from a normal commercial lender who is not related to the borrower (and must not be from the seller of the property or a promoter who receives fees with respect to the taxpayer's investment). See I.R.C. §§ 465(b)(6)(B)(ii) and (D)(i), 49(a)(1)(D)(iv). A loan from a related party may nevertheless qualify for the QNF exception if the loan is "commercially reasonable and on substantially the same terms as loans involving unrelated persons." I.R.C. § 465(b)(6)(D)(ii). A partner's share of QNF is generally the same as the partner's share of the liability under section 752. See I.R.C. § 465(b)(6)(C). These restrictions are intended to exclude artificially inflated nonrecourse debt (a fertile source of overvaluation abuses) from qualifying for the QNF exception. The existence of the QNF exception itself can be explained by the common use of nonrecourse financing in commercial real estate activities.

For purposes of section 752, a nonrecourse liability is treated as recourse debt to the extent a partner (or related person) is the lender and bears the economic risk of loss. See Reg. §§ 1.752-2(c)(1); 1.704-2(b)(4) (partner nonrecourse debt). In applying this rule, the regulations provide a special *de minimis* exception for loans from partners (or related persons) that also meet the QNF requirements. If the lender holds only a *de minimis* interest in the partnership (generally a ten percent or smaller interest), a nonrecourse loan will not be recharacterized as recourse for purposes of section 752 even though the lender bears the economic risk of loss. See Reg. § 1.752-2(d)(1). Thus, a commercial lender who holds a relatively minor interest in a partnership may provide nonrecourse financing with respect to real estate activities without recharacterization of the loan as recourse. This rule ensures that such borrowing will generate both outside basis and at risk amounts for non-lender partners who are allocated a share of the QNF under the normal section 752 sharing rules for nonrecourse liabilities.

In the case of an LLC, a general obligation that is recourse to the entity may be equivalent to nonrecourse financing, if none of the members has guaranteed or otherwise assumed the liability. In this situation, the at risk rules provide that the personal liability of the entity is disregarded for purposes of determining whether the liability is QNF. See Reg. § 1.465-27(b)(4). Thus, such a recourse liability may be treated as QNF if the other QNF requirements are met. Similar rules apply to entities that are disregarded for federal tax purposes. See Reg. § 1.465-27(b)(5) and (6) (ex. 6).

Section 465 *defers* losses until a subsequent year when a partner has a sufficient amount at risk to absorb the loss, e.g., as a result of income from the activity or additional capital contributions. Any remaining suspended losses may be deducted when either the partnership disposes of the activity or the partner disposes of her partnership interest. See Prop. Reg. § 1.465-66(a).

3. *Passive Loss Limitation*

Read I.R.C. § 469(a), (b), (c)(1), (d), (e)(1)(A) and (3), and (h)(1). Even if a loss successfully passes through the subchapter K and at risk filters, it may nevertheless be trapped by the passive loss filter. The loss passthrough reduces a partner's outside basis and at risk amount even though the loss is ultimately blocked under section 469.

The passive loss rules generally require taxpayers to segregate their tax items, including any items passed through by a partnership, into three categories or baskets: a passive basket, portfolio basket, and residual basket consisting generally of tax items relating to personal service or active business income. In general, net losses and unused credits from the passive basket may not be used to offset income and tax liability from the other two baskets. Any disallowed loss or credit is carried forward indefinitely to subsequent years when it is subject to the same limitation. Unlike the at risk rules, losses may be restricted under section 469 even though they represent amounts for which the taxpayer bears real economic risk.

While the at risk rules require segregation of items into a potentially unlimited number of activities, the passive loss rules break down items into only three baskets. But whether a tax item belongs in a particular basket depends, in part, on the extent of the taxpayer's involvement in the activity generating the item. The tax items from an activity in which the taxpayer does not "materially participate" generally belong in the passive or portfolio baskets. (Portfolio income generally includes interest, dividends, annuities, or royalties not derived from a trade or business, and gains from disposing of investments producing such income. See I.R.C. § 469(e)(1)(A).) If the material participation test is met, the items belong in the residual basket. Thus, just like the at risk rules, the passive loss rules require taxpayers to divide income (or loss) into various activities, and the passive loss rules make the further inquiry whether the taxpayer's involvement with a particular activity is active or passive. The regulations are quite flexible in permitting taxpayers to identify which economic undertakings may be grouped together to constitute an activity, subject to a duty of consistent groupings over time. See Reg. § 1.469-4(c)(2) (taxpayer may use any reasonable method), -4(e)(1). For reporting purposes, the initial aggregation of activities occurs at the partnership level; partners may then further aggregate activities that the partnership treated as separate, but cannot segregate activities that the partnership has aggregated. See Reg. § 1.469-4(d)(5)(i).

The statute defines "material participation" as involvement which is regular, continuous, and substantial. See I.R.C. § 469(h)(1). The regulations interpret this term generally to require over 500 hours of participation in an activity during the course of a year. Fewer hours may constitute material participation in special situations, such as when the taxpayer is virtually the only participant in an activity or has greater involvement in it during the year than anyone else. See Temp. Reg. § 1.469-5T(a)(1)-(3).

Unless a taxpayer is engaged in a real estate business on a substantial basis, losses from rental activities are generally treated as belonging in the passive basket. See I.R.C. § 469(c)(2) and (7); Reg. § 1.469-2(f)(6) (net *income* from rental activities may be placed in the passive *or* residual baskets, depending upon the level of taxpayer's involvement in the activity). This "passive" presumption reflects the traditional use of losses from real estate investments to shelter other, unrelated income of the taxpayer. Nevertheless, up to $25,000 of losses from rental real estate activities may escape the passive loss limitation under certain conditions. See I.R.C. § 469(i). Except as provided in the regulations, losses passed through by a limited partnership to limited partners are also precluded from being placed in the residual basket. See I.R.C. § 469(h)(2). When the passive loss rules were enacted, passive treatment of limited partners reflected the general state law prohibition against a limited partner's active involvement in partnership activities if she wished to preserve limited liability protection. State law has generally moved in the direction, however, of allowing limited partners to participate in management of the partnership's business without jeopardizing their limited liability shield, and proposed regulations (described below) now attempt to take into account this trend. Because there is generally no state law limitation on the permissible activities of LLC members, such members should be treated as analogous to general partners for this purpose. Indeed, courts have rejected the government's attempt to treat LLC members as limited partners under the current regulations. See, e.g., Garnett v. Comm'r, 132 T.C. 368 (2009) (since LLC members could participate in management, the tax items passed through to them qualified as nonpassive income).

Proposed regulations amend the definition of a limited partnership interest (LPI) for purposes of the passive loss rules. Prop. Reg. § 1.469-5(e). Under the proposed regulations, an interest in an entity classified as a partnership for federal tax purposes is an LPI if the holder of the interest lacks "rights to manage the entity at all times during the entity's taxable year" under local law and under the partnership agreement. Prop. Reg. § 1.469-5(e)(3)(i)(B). Consistent with the purpose of section 469, the proposed regulations abandon limited liability as the litmus test in favor of a test based on the individual partner's ability to participate in management of the entity. An interest in an entity that is not a limited partnership under state law may nevertheless be treated as an LPI provided the entity is a partnership for federal tax purposes. An LLC member would generally not be treated as a limited partner, however, since LLC members have management rights by default. The proposed LPI definition is expressly limited to section 469, with no inference that a similar definition applies for other Code purposes.

Losses suspended by the passive loss rules are generally deductible upon a complete taxable disposition of the activity generating the loss. See I.R.C. § 469(g)(1)(A). In the case of a partnership, the suspended loss may thus be freed up upon a disposition of the activity by the partnership or upon a complete disposition of a partner's partnership interest.

4. *Relationship of Sections 704 and 752 to the At Risk and Passive Loss Rules*

Sections 704 and 752, coupled with the at risk and passive loss rules, provide increasingly fine filters that potentially trap losses and prevent their current utilization at the partner level. Despite this similar general consequence, the rules serve different purposes that may help to explain some existing differences among them. As previously discussed, the purpose of section 752 (as well as much of the rest of subchapter K) is to provide consistent tax results regardless of whether a taxpayer invests directly or through a partnership. Since borrowing (including nonrecourse borrowing) outside of subchapter K gives rise to tax basis, section 752 generally provides the same result for financing taking place through a partnership. The bottom line is that one partner or another *must* obtain a share of the partnership's liability and the corresponding outside basis in order to preserve parity with a direct investment; the only question is *which* partner receives the share of liability and outside basis. Section 752 generally allocates recourse liabilities based on which partner bears the economic risk of loss in a worst-case scenario; nonrecourse liabilities are allocated based generally on the partner's profit-sharing ratios (subject to refinements for the various minimum gain layers). The main goal is to ensure that that each partner has sufficient outside basis to support her share of partnership losses under section 704(b).

The purpose of the at risk and passive loss rules is different. The at risk rule, for example, tries to determine whether a taxpayer's economic risk with respect to a liability is sufficiently fixed and certain to justify an immediate claiming of a tax loss resulting from that liability. In certain situations, such as liabilities attributable to nonrecourse financing (other than QNF), there may be no person other than the lender who bears the economic risk in any given year and who would therefore be treated as at risk for that year. In the partnership context, therefore, the question is not which of all of the partners must be treated as being at risk with respect to a partnership liability; rather, the question is more basic — whether *any* partner sufficiently bears the economic risk in order to be treated as satisfying the at risk requirement. The passive loss inquiry in the partnership context is similar — does any partner materially participate in the partnership activity? — with "all," "some," or "none" of the partners all being feasible responses.

NOTES

1. *Guarantees*. Generally, a limited partner's guarantee of a nonrecourse debt generates an additional amount at risk. As under the section 752 rules with respect to recourse liabilities, the test is generally whether the guarantor has a fixed and definite obligation to pay the obligation in a worst-case scenario. See, e.g., Pritchett v. Comm'r, 827 F.2d 644 (9th Cir. 1987); Abramson v. Comm'r, 86 T.C. 360 (1986).

2. *DROs*. Should LLC members be treated as at risk for the entity's recourse borrowing if they agree to DROs but do not guarantee (or otherwise assume) the liability? In Hubert Enterprises, Inc. v. Comm'r, T.C. Memo 2008-46 (2008), the Tax Court held that such DROs were not sufficient to generate at risk amounts. The court found that the LLC members were not the payor of last resort because the DROs would be triggered only if the LLC were liquidated and, under state law, a default on the recourse debt would not have caused a liquidation of the LLC.

The DROs were thus not unavoidable, since the members could avoid any additional capital contribution simply by continuing the LLC. Instead, the lender, who had originally agreed to seek repayment solely from the assets of the LLC, was the payor of last resort. The court did not address the different question of whether the DRO resulted in the liability being treated as a "recourse liability" for purposes of section 752.

3. *Loans from persons with an interest in the activity.* As previously noted, a taxpayer's at risk amount does not include borrowing, even borrowing for which the taxpayer has personal liability, from persons with an interest in the taxpayer's activity (other than a mere creditor's interest). See I.R.C. § 465(b)(3). Suppose a general partnership borrows $10,000 from a nonpartner key employee whose compensation is determined in part by the level of the partnership's net profits. Under the at risk rules, the employee would be considered a person with an interest in the activity of the partnership. See Reg. § 1.465-8(b)(1), (3) and (4) (ex. 1). As a result, the general partners would not be considered at risk with respect to this debt even though they may be personally liable. Nevertheless, for purposes of section 752, they would be entitled to include the $10,000 liability in outside basis.

The disparate purposes of section 752 and the at risk rules help to explain this difference. Since the borrowing produces a basis for the partnership in the form of the $10,000 proceeds, the liability must give rise to outside basis of some partner under section 752. Nevertheless, the employee's financial interest in the partnership's business (other than merely as a creditor) means that the employee may never seek to enforce his rights as a creditor. Thus, section 465 refuses to treat any partner as having a sufficiently fixed and definite obligation to pay the liability.

4. *Tax on net investment income.* In the case of an individual, section 1411(a)(1) imposes a 3.8 percent tax on the lesser of net investment income (NII) or the amount by which an individual's modified adjusted gross income exceeds a threshold amount ($200,000 for single filers and $250,000 for joint filers). I.R.C. § 1411(a)(1) and (b). NII includes items such as capital gain, interest, dividends, annuities, royalties, and rents, as well as income from a trade or business that is a passive activity (within the meaning of section 469) or a trade or business of trading in financial instruments or commodities (less properly allocable deductions). Thus, it generally does not include income (including passive-type income) derived in the ordinary course of a trade or business. I.R.C. § 1411(c)(1) and (2). The IRS has issued lengthy regulations providing guidance on application of the section 1411 tax, although many issues remain unresolved.

Under section 702, NII items (and allocable deductions) that pass through to a partner must be separately stated. As just noted, trade or business income is generally excluded from NII unless derived from a passive activity or trading in financial instruments or commodities. The regulations apply the "passive activity" test (using general principles of section 469) at the partner level. By contrast, the characterization of a trade or business as one of trading in financial instruments or commodities is made at the partnership level and the income retains its character when passed through to the partner. As a result, income from such trading is included in NII even though passed through to a partner who materially participates in the activity. Likewise, income derived from any other trade or business that passes through to a partner who does not materially participate in the activity is also NII. See Reg. § 1.1411-4(b)(2) and (3) (exs. 3, 4).

In general, the section 1411 tax does not apply to items of income and deduction that are taken into account in computing self-employment income. Reg. § 1.1411-9. For this purpose, a limited partner's distributive share of income that is excluded under section 1402(a)(13) is not treated as taken into account in computing self-employment income. Thus, the distributive share will be subject to the section 1411 tax unless the limited partner satisfies the material participation test. Reg. § 1.469-5(e).

Section 1411(c)(4) limits the amount of net gain subject to the section 1411 tax upon disposition of an interest in a partnership (or S corporation) to the net gain that would be taken into account by the transferor if all property of the partnership (or S corporation) were sold for fair market value immediately prior to the disposition. Proposed regulations generally limit the amount of net gain taxed under section 1411 to the *lesser* of (i) the amount of gain recognized by the seller on disposition of the interest or (ii) the seller's share of net gain from the deemed sale of the pass-through entity's property that would be subject to section 1411. See Prop. Reg. § 1.1411-7(b)(1)(i). Significantly, this limit applies only if the passthrough entity is engaged in a trade or business (other than the trading of financial instruments or commodities) and the transferor is not a passive participant (within the meaning of section 469) in such trade or business. Prop. Reg. § 1.1411-7(a)(3)(i). The proposed regulations also provide special rules for certain kinds of partnership payments. See Prop. Reg. § 1.1411-4(g)(10) and (11) (section 707(c) guaranteed payments and section 736 payments).

Final regulations also address the interaction between the section 1411 tax and the section 469(c)(7) exception for real estate professionals. Real estate professionals may qualify under a safe harbor, provided they participate in rental real estate activities for more than 500 hours per year. See Reg. § 1.1411-4(g)(7) (excluding gross rental income and gain or loss on sale derived from such rental activities). Even if this safe harbor is not met, the section 1411 tax will not apply if the rental activity constitutes a trade or business (within the meaning of section 162). See I.R.C. § 1411(c)(1)(A)(i) (exception for income, including rents, "derived in the ordinary course of a trade or business").

Chapter 6

Partnership Allocations: Special Anti-Income-Shifting Rules

A. Introduction

We have previously described the potential conflict between the no-assignment-of-income doctrine and the flexibility generally permitted by subchapter K in the allocation of tax items. This chapter focuses on three areas where income-shifting concerns trump partnership flexibility. Part B deals with the allocation of tax items attributable to contributed or revalued property, what we have referred to as section 704(c) or reverse section 704(c) property. As you will discover, allocations involving such property must generally take into account the variation between the property's basis and value at the time of the contribution or revaluation. Part C introduces special rules that require allocations to take into account the varying interests of the partners in a partnership during a taxable year. Finally, part D briefly describes a provision dealing specifically with allocations by family partnerships.

You might wonder why these particular areas have been singled out for anti-income-shifting rules. The first two areas share a common concern about assignment of income (or loss) that is economically accrued at the time of the assignment. You may recall that in *Schneer* (p. 29), the court evidenced enhanced vigilance toward the assignment of earned (as opposed to unearned) income. The third area of concern, family partnerships, is part of the larger problem of income-shifting among members of a family. Over the years, the courts and Congress have paid close attention to such family arrangements because of the ease (and low transaction costs) of the income-shifting techniques and the potential tax savings. Other legislation (such as enactment of the "kiddie tax" in section 1(g)) has addressed this problem more broadly, thereby reducing the significance of anti-income-shifting rules in the family area that are specific to subchapter K.

B. Allocations Involving Contributed or Revalued Property

1. *Introduction*

You may remember that when property is contributed to a partnership, the section 704(b) regulations require that the property be stated on the partnership's books at its fair market value even though the contributor does not recognize any gain or loss for tax purposes. Similarly, revalued property must be restated on the partnership's books at fair market value even though there is no recognition for tax purposes of gain or loss inherent in the property at the time of the revaluation. Consequently, the tax items attributable to contributed or revalued property may not be the same as the corresponding book items. In this situation, a partnership cannot follow the "general rule" of section 704(b) requiring tax items to be allocated in the same manner as the corresponding book item. To illustrate, consider the following facts:

> **Example 6-1:** A and B form partnership AB as equal partners. A contributes property worth $10,000 with a basis of $6,000. B contributes $10,000 cash. The property is subsequently sold for $11,000.

Although A does not recognize any gain on the transfer of property to the partnership, with the partnership simply inheriting A's $6,000 tax basis, the property is nevertheless booked at its fair market value of $10,000. Thus, when the property is sold, the partnership has $5,000 of tax gain but only $1,000 of book gain. The partnership therefore cannot allocate the tax gain in the same manner that the book gain is allocated.

How, then, should the tax gain be allocated? Read I.R.C. § 704(c)(1)(A). The partnership must allocate the gain in a manner that takes into account the difference between the property's value and basis at the time of the contribution. In other words, partner A, who contributed the property, must be allocated at least $4,000 of the tax gain, the amount of tax gain built into the property when it was contributed. The remaining $1,000 of tax gain must be allocated in accordance with the partnership agreement (and the section 704(b) regulations). If the partners agree to split the book gain equally, then A and B must be allocated $4,500 and $500 of the tax gain, respectively. Such an allocation eliminates the initial "book-tax disparity" in A's capital accounts:

Cap. Accts.	*A*		*B*	
	tax	*book*	*tax*	*book*
initial	6,000	10,000	10,000	10,000
sale — § 704(c) allocation	4,000	-0-	-0-	-0-
sale — balance of transaction	500	500	500	500
end	10,500	10,500	10,500	10,500

Note that the required section 704(c) allocation of the tax gain does not really deviate from the general rule that tax allocations must follow book allocations. By booking the property initially at $10,000, the partnership gave A economic credit of $4,000 in excess of her $6,000 contribution to the partnership's inside basis. Thus, the section 704(c) allocation of $4,000 of tax gain to A simply catches up with this economic credit already given to her. The section 704(c) allocation also prevents A from shifting to B any of the tax gain of $4,000, the amount economically accrued at the time the partnership was formed.

A simple rule you might take from this example is to allocate specially to the contributing partner an amount of tax gain (or loss) equal to the book benefit (or detriment) already credited to the partner in excess of her contribution to inside basis, with the sharing of any remaining tax and book items determined by the agreement. An alternative rule, which will prove more helpful as a general approach, is to allocate to the *non*contributing partner(s) only those tax items that match the book items allocated to such partner(s), with all remaining items allocated to the contributing partner. In **example 6-1**, B (the noncontributing partner) is allocated $500 of tax gain to match her $500 of book gain, with everything else allocated to partner A.

Example 6-2: Same as **example 6-1**, except that the property is subsequently sold for $9,000.

This example is more complicated because the only tax item arising from the sale is tax gain of $3,000. Thus, there is not enough tax gain to match the $4,000 in economic benefit already credited to A in excess of her contribution to inside basis. Further, the sale results in a book *loss* of $1,000. If B, the noncontributing partner, is allocated one-half of that book loss, there is no corresponding tax loss to allocate to B, in contravention of our alternative rule. Finally, even if all of the tax gain is allocated to A, and none to B, a book-tax disparity remains for both partners:

Cap. Accts. — Option 1	*A*		*B*	
	tax	*book*	*tax*	*book*
initial	6,000	10,000	10,000	10,000
sale — § 704(c) allocation	3,000	-0-	-0-	-0-
sale — balance of transaction	-0-	(500)	-0-	(500)
end	9,000	9,500	10,000	9,500

The disparity in the partners' capital accounts under option 1 shown above reflects an income shift of $500 from A to B. As evidenced by her tax capital account and share of inside basis, A has paid tax on $9,000 (the $6,000 basis of her contribution plus $3,000 of tax gain on the sale). But A has an economic credit of $9,500, as shown by her ending book capital account. B is in the opposite situation: she has a tax-paid basis of $10,000 (the cash contributed) but has an economic credit of only

$9,500. Moreover, since the property creating the book-tax difference has been disposed of, future allocations cannot easily eliminate the disparity.

A fairly straightforward way to avoid this outcome would be to follow the alternative rule strictly: thus, B would be allocated a tax loss of $500 to match her book loss of $500. Since the partnership has no actual tax loss to allocate, however, an offsetting tax gain of $500 would need to be allocated to A, the contributing partner, in accordance with the alternative rule:

Cap. Accts. — Option 2	*A*		*B*	
	tax	*book*	*tax*	*book*
initial	6,000	10,000	10,000	10,000
sale — § 704(c) allocation	3,000	-0-	-0-	-0-
sale — balance of transaction	500	(500)	(500)	(500)
end	9,500	9,500	9,500	9,500

The allocations under option 2 seem consistent with what has happened to the partnership and its property. Partner A received economic credit for $4,000 more than her contribution to inside basis. She should therefore be allocated $4,000 of tax gain to match that benefit. But subsequent to the contribution of the property, the partnership suffered an economic loss of $1,000. Assuming that this book loss is shared equally by the partners and is matched by an equal amount of tax loss, then A should be allocated a net tax gain of $3,500 and B should be allocated a tax loss of $500, as shown.

As described in the following sections, the allocation methods authorized by the regulations to deal with section 704(c) and reverse section 704(c) property differ primarily in how they handle the facts of **example 6-2**. The "remedial method" requires that allocations to A and B follow the approach of option 2, whereas the "traditional method" mandates that allocations follow the approach of option 1. A third method, the "traditional method with curative allocations," achieves essentially a middle ground between these two outcomes.

Why doesn't the tax law mandate the outcome under option 2, which prevents the income-shifting and eliminates any book-tax disparity in the partners' capital accounts? In part, there was concern that some partnerships would find the remedial method too onerous to comply with. But there was also concern that the approach under option 2 requires fictitious allocations, whose validity depends entirely on the proper initial valuation of the property. Thus, the parties might be able to manipulate value to achieve a preferred tax outcome. (As you review the examples and problems that follow, keep this issue in mind. What would be the effect of an erroneous initial valuation on the situations you encounter in this chapter?) The traditional method therefore defers to what is known as the "ceiling rule": the partnership may allocate only tax items that actually arise. Thus, in **example 6-2** under the traditional method, the only item that may be allocated is tax gain of $3,000. Allocations subject to the ceiling rule are sometimes said to be "ceiling-limited."

NOTE

Section 704(c)(1)(A) is the key statutory provision governing allocations with respect to contributed property. Congress has also enacted other provisions that backstop section 704(c)(1)(A). For example, as discussed in chapter nine, section 704(c)(1)(B) deals with the situation in which section 704(c) property is contributed to a partnership and later (within seven years of the original contribution) distributed to another partner. Recently, Congress added section 704(c)(1)(C) to prevent the potential "duplication" of built-in losses upon a transfer (or liquidation) of the contributing partner's interest prior to the partnership's realization of the built-in loss. Section 704(c)(1)(C) is discussed briefly in this chapter and again in later chapters.

2. *Traditional Method*

Read Reg. § 1.704-3(b)(1). For nondepreciable property, the section 704(c) allocations attributable to contributed and revalued property are taken into account only when the property is sold or otherwise disposed of. The mechanical operation of the traditional method tracks the alternative rule described above (subject to the ceiling-rule limitation) and can be summarized as follows. First, determine the tax gain (or loss) and book gain (or loss) upon sale of the contributed or revalued property. Second, allocate the book gain (or loss) among the partners based on their sharing ratios under the partnership agreement. Third, allocate (to the extent possible) matching tax gain (or loss) to the noncontributing partner(s) equal to their share of the book gain (or loss) in accordance with the principle that tax follows book. Finally, allocate any remaining tax gain (or loss) to the contributing partner. Thus, the results in **example 6-2** (option 1) can be expressed as follows:

Cap. Accts. — traditional method	*A*		*B*	
	tax	*book*	*tax*	*book*
initial	6,000	10,000	10,000	10,000
sale — book gain (loss)	-0-	(500)	-0-	(500)
sale — tax gain (loss)	3,000	-0-	-0-	-0-
end	9,000	9,500	10,000	9,500

Test your understanding of the traditional method by doing the following problem.

Problem 6-1:

(a) A contributes land (basis $120, value $200) and B contributes $200 cash in exchange for equal partnership interests. The parties agree to share all items equally except as otherwise required by the traditional method under section 704(c). How must the partnership allocate the tax items resulting from a sale of the land for $30?

(b) Same as (a), except that the partnership sells the land for $180.

For *depreciable* section 704(c) or reverse section 704(c) property, the special allocations required by the traditional method follow the same steps except that the discrepancy between value and basis must be taken into account as the property is depreciated, rather than waiting until sale of the property. In determining the amount of its tax depreciation deduction with respect to contributed property, a partnership steps into the shoes of the contributor of the property. See I.R.C. § 168(i)(7). In addition, under the section 704(b) regulations, the amount of a partnership's book depreciation must bear the same ratio to the adjusted book value of the depreciable property as the amount of tax depreciation bears to the adjusted tax basis of the property. See Reg. § 1.704-1(b)(2)(iv)(*g*)(*3*).

Read Reg. § 1.704-3(b)(2) (ex. 1) and do the following problem.

Problem 6-2:

(a) The facts are the same as in **problem 6-1(a)** except that A contributes depreciable property instead of land and the property is not sold. A used the straight-line method to depreciate the property, which has a remaining recovery period of four years at the time of contribution. What allocations are required by the traditional method when the partnership depreciates the property in Years 1-4? Try to articulate the rationale for these consequences: How do they comply with the statutory mandate that allocations to partner A must take into account the built-in gain in the contributed property?

(b) Same as (a), except that the basis of the depreciable property at the time of contribution is only $80.

(c) Same as (a), except that the parties agree to allocate the depreciation 90 percent to A and 10 percent to B (or, alternatively, 10 percent to A and 90 percent to B). Assume that the special allocations of depreciation have substantial economic effect. See Reg. § 1.704-1(b)(5) (ex. 17).

NOTES AND QUESTIONS

1. *Temporary effect of ceiling rule.* Income shifts resulting from ceiling-limited allocations may eventually be reversed. For example, review the tax consequences under option 1 of **example 6-2**. Because of the ceiling rule, $500 of A's gain is shifted to B. As a result, however, A's outside basis is increased to only $9,000 ($6,000 initial basis plus $3,000 gain allocated to A) and B's outside basis remains at $10,000 ($10,000 cash contributed and no loss allocated to B). Thus, if the partnership were to liquidate and distribute $9,500 each to A and B equal to their book capital

accounts, A would recognize gain of $500 and B would recognize a loss of $500. I.R.C. § 731(a). Thus, the ceiling-rule disparity would eventually be reversed.

Nevertheless, the ceiling rule permits a misallocation of income pending the reversing event. Furthermore, the reversal may be imperfect once income character is taken into account. The initial income shift may be of ordinary income or loss, whereas the reversed amount of gain or loss is almost always capital in nature.

2. *Scope of section 704(c).* Suppose a lawyer transfers her solo law practice to a newly formed partnership that assumes certain deductible accounts payable attributable to the former practice. Assume that any assumption of the liabilities is not a taxable event and that both the lawyer and the partnership use the cash method of accounting. How must the partnership allocate any deduction when it pays off the payables? See I.R.C. § 704(c)(3). Try to articulate the reason for this rule.

3. *Traditional Method with Curative Allocations*

Read Reg. § 1.704-3(c)(1)-(3) and (4) (exs. 1, 2). To reduce or eliminate ceiling-rule distortions, the regulations permit partnerships to use the "traditional method with curative allocations." Under this method, a partnership is permitted to deviate from the principle that "tax must follow book" for an item (other than the ceiling-limited one) in order to overcome the ceiling-rule distortion. For example, the partnership might allocate taxable income to one partner even though the corresponding book income is allocated to another partner. As you might expect, permission to depart from the basic tax-follows-book principle of the section 704(b) rules is severely constrained. Curative allocations are closely scrutinized to ensure that the amount, character, and timing of the item subject to the allocation conform to those characteristics of the ceiling-limited item. The restriction on the *character* of an item subject to a curative allocation is relaxed in one situation: a curative allocation of gain from the sale of section 704(c) or reverse section 704(c) property is permitted to offset ceiling-limited depreciation of such property. See Reg. § 1.704-3(c)(3)(iii)(B).

> **Example 6-3:** C and D form partnership CD as equal partners. C contributes depreciable property worth $10,000 with a basis of $4,000, and D contributes $10,000 cash. C used the straight-line method to depreciate the property, which has a remaining recovery period of five years at the time of contribution. Assume that in its first year, the partnership has no tax items other than depreciation of the property contributed by C, and that at the beginning of Year 2 (before any further depreciation is taken), the partnership sells the property for $9,000.

In Year 1, the partnership has book depreciation of $2,000 ($10,000 × 20%) and tax depreciation of $800 ($4,000 × 20%). In Year 2, the sale results in book gain of $1,000 ($9,000 less the adjusted book basis of $8,000) and tax gain of $5,800 ($9,000 less the adjusted tax basis of $3,200). If one-half of the book depreciation and book gain is allocated to D (the noncontributing partner), then under the traditional method, D must be allocated all of the tax depreciation and $500 of the tax gain and C is allocated everything else. The partners' capital accounts would appear as follows:

Cap. Accts. (trad. method)	*C*		*D*	
	tax	*book*	*tax*	*book*
initial	4,000	10,000	10,000	10,000
Year 1—depreciation	-0-	(1,000)	(800)	(1,000)
Year 2—gain on sale	5,300	500	500	500
end	9,300	9,500	9,700	9,500

If elected by the partners, a curative allocation of $200 of the tax gain on the sale is permitted to offset the ceiling-rule impact on the depreciation allocated in Year 1. While C would be allocated additional tax gain of $200 (and D $200 less of tax gain), the allocations of book gain would remain unchanged. Further, this is the one case where a curative allocation is permissible even though the character of the item subject to the curative allocation (possible capital gain from the sale) may be different from the character of the ceiling-limited item (ordinary deduction for depreciation).

Cap. Accts. (w/ curative allocation)	*C*		*D*	
	tax	*book*	*tax*	*book*
initial	4,000	10,000	10,000	10,000
Year 1—depreciation	-0-	(1,000)	(800)	(1,000)
Year 2—gain on sale	5,500	500	300	500
end	9,500	9,500	9,500	9,500

Problem 6-3: Assume that the partners in the following questions agree to share all items equally except as required by the traditional method with curative allocations under section 704(c). How may they allocate the items identified?

(a) A contributes land (basis $120, value $200) and B contributes $200 cash in exchange for equal partnership interests. The partnership invests the cash in some securities. In Year 2, the land is sold for $180. In Year 3, the securities are sold for $400.

(b) A contributes depreciable property (basis $80, value $200) and B contributes $200 cash in exchange for equal partnership interests. A used the straight-line method to depreciate the property, which has a remaining recovery period of four years at the time of contribution. At the very beginning of Year 2 (before any Year 2 depreciation is taken), the depreciable property is sold for $200.

4. *Abusive Use of the Traditional Method and Traditional Method with Curative Allocations*

Read Reg. § 1.704-3(a)(10). The section 704(c) regulations contain an anti-abuse rule aimed at a partnership's use of an unreasonable method for allocating book-tax differences with respect to contributed property. An allocation is impermissible if the contribution of property and corresponding tax allocation "are made with a view to shifting the tax consequences of built-in gain or loss among the partners in a manner that substantially reduces the present value of the partners' aggregate tax liability." Reg. § 1.704-3(a)(10). While the scope of the anti-abuse rule is potentially quite expansive, it clearly encompasses attempts to exploit ceiling-rule limitations under the traditional method or to manipulate curative allocations. Under the anti-abuse rule, the effect of allocations on all direct and indirect partners must be considered.

> **Example 6-4:** C and D agree to be equal partners in the CD partnership. C is a corporation with substantial, expiring net operating losses, and D is a high-bracket taxpayer. C contributes $1,500 cash and D contributes depreciable property with a basis of $300 and a fair market value of $1,500; D's property has a remaining depreciation recovery period of one year (though a much longer remaining economic life). The partners elect to use the traditional method of allocating items from section 704(c) property. They expect to be able to sell D's property at the beginning of Year 2 for $1,500 and to shift some of the built-in gain to C, thereby taking advantage of C's expiring net operating losses to reduce their aggregate tax liability.

In Year 1, if the partners share equally the book depreciation of $1,500, then C must be allocated the entire tax depreciation of $300. At the end of Year 1, the difference between the book value and tax basis of the contributed property has been eliminated (i.e., both the tax basis and book value are zero). Thus, there is no further obligation under the traditional method to make a special allocation of items from the contributed property. See Reg. § 1.704-3(b)(1), -3(a)(3)(ii). If the property is sold for $1,500 at the beginning of Year 2, C and D may share equally the $1,500 of gain which the partnership recognizes for both tax and book purposes. Assuming that the allocations are respected, the partners will have the following tax and book capital accounts after the sale:

Cap. Accts.	*C*		*D*	
	tax	*book*	*tax*	*book*
initial	1,500	1,500	300	1,500
Year 1—depreciation	(300)	(750)	-0-	(750)
Year 2—gain on sale	750	750	750	750
end	1,950	1,500	1,050	1,500

As you can see, the traditional method results in a shift of $450 of built-in gain from D to C (C's $750 share of gain from the sale less $300 of tax depreciation). Since the partners have undertaken the allocation with a view to reducing their aggregate tax liability, use of the traditional method is impermissible. See Reg. § 1.704-3(b)(2) (ex. 2). A reasonable method of handling the book-tax disparity would be to require a curative allocation of gain upon sale of the property, i.e., D would be allocated $1,200 of the tax gain ($750 book share plus $450 additional tax gain), and C would be allocated only $300 of tax gain ($750 book share less $450 tax gain reallocated to D). As a result, the partners would be left with identical tax and book capital accounts of $1,500.

QUESTIONS

1. Observe that the abusive shifting of built-in gain depends on the interplay between the traditional method and the short one-year cost-recovery period for C's contributed property. Why should the partners be permitted to recover the entire book value of the contributed property over a one-year period, even though the remaining economic life is significantly longer?

2. Suppose the contributed property had an adjusted tax basis of $1 (but still a $1,500 value) and a remaining recovery period of one year at the time of contribution. Is there any reason not to require that substantially all of the built-in gain be allocated to the contributor upon the sale of the property for $1,500? Should it matter whether the partners have differing outside tax attributes?

Use of the traditional method with curative allocations may also be abusive. Read Reg. § 1.704-3(c)(4) (ex. 3). The cited example is quite similar to the one above, except that the partner contributing depreciable property with value greater than basis (J) has net operating losses due to expire, and the other partner (K) is in a high bracket. The partnership does not sell the contributed property but instead uses a curative allocation of ordinary income from sale of different property to offset the ceiling-limited depreciation from Year 1. The curative allocation is impermissible because it has the effect of shifting taxable income away from K (the high-bracket partner) to J (the loss partner). In this situation, a special curative allocation of the ordinary income over the remaining economic life of the depreciable property (rather than its remaining cost recovery period) would have been permissible.

NOTE AND QUESTIONS

1. *Measure of the tax advantage.* In Reg. § 1.704-3(c)(4) (ex. 3), suppose K had instead purchased one half of J's property immediately before formation of the partnership, and each partner contributed half of the property to the partnership.

The partnership would take a cost basis in the purchased portion of the property, and would depreciate that half of the property over the recovery period of newly purchased property of the same class life (longer than one year). K would recover her portion of the basis of the purchased property over this recovery period. By contrast, the abusive curative allocation in example 3 of the regulations diverts other income away from K, thereby allowing K to "expense" a portion of her investment in the partnership immediately.

2. Is it possible to define more precisely the type of abuse that warrants overriding a partnership's use of the traditional method or the traditional method with curative allocations? If so, should the Treasury simply have mandated use of a "proper" method?

5. *Remedial Allocation Method*

Curative allocations may be made only with respect to tax items that the partnership actually has. Thus, if the partnership lacks appropriate items to overcome the ceiling-rule distortion, then no curative allocation is possible and the distortion will persist. The remedial allocation method solves this problem by authorizing the *creation* of notional tax items necessary to overcome the distortion. The notional tax item, which is allocated to the noncontributing partner(s), must be of the same character and type as the ceiling-limited item and may not exceed the amount necessary to overcome the ceiling-rule limitation. Further, to avoid misreporting its taxable income, the partnership must create an offsetting tax item of the same amount, character, and type and allocate it to the contributing partner.

Review option 2 of **example 6-2** and read Reg. § 1.704-3(d)(1), (3)-(6), and (7) (exs. 2, 3). The following problem illustrates use of the remedial method on the sale of nondepreciable section 704(c) property.

> **Problem 6-4:** A contributes land (basis \$120, value \$200) and B contributes \$200 cash in exchange for equal partnership interests. What allocations are required upon sale of the land for \$180 if the partners agree to share all items equally except as required by the remedial method under section 704(c)?

The remedial method also cures ceiling-rule distortions with respect to depreciable property. For purposes of depreciating the partnership's book basis, the method divides such basis into two components: a "carryover" portion (equal to the adjusted tax basis of the property) and a "purchased" portion (equal to the excess of book over tax basis). The carryover portion is depreciated in the same manner as the adjusted tax basis; thus, tax and book depreciation deductions will be identical with respect to the carryover portion. The purchased portion is recovered as if the partnership had newly purchased such portion (i.e., using a depreciation method and recovery period for new property of the same class as the contributed property). Read Reg. § 1.704-3(d)(2) and (7) (ex. 1).

Example 6-5: A contributes depreciable property (basis $80, value $200) and B contributes $200 cash in exchange for equal partnership interests. The parties agree to share all items equally except as required by the remedial method under section 704(c). A used the straight-line method to depreciate the property, which has a remaining recovery period of four years at the time of contribution.

Under the remedial method, the partnership steps into the contributing partner's shoes with respect to the carryover portion of the property (with a tax and book basis of $80), resulting in annual depreciation deductions of $20 ($80 × 25%) for both tax and book purposes over the remaining four-year recovery period of the property. The partnership may recover the $120 purchased portion of book basis ($200 total book basis less $80 carryover portion) as if it were newly purchased property. Assume that the partnership recovers the $120 purchased portion in a straight-line manner over ten years, resulting in annual depreciation deductions of $12 for book purposes (and zero for tax purposes). The partnership has the following tax and book depreciation deductions for Years 1-10:

	(1) Tax depreciation ($80/4 years)	(2) Carryover portion of book depreciation ($80/4 years)	(3) Purchased portion of book depreciation ($120/10 years)	(4) Total book depreciation: Col. (2) + (3)
Year 1	20	20	12	32
Years 2-4	60	60	36	96
end Year 4	80	80	48	128
Year 5	-0-	-0-	12	12
Years 6-10	-0-	-0-	60	60
end Year 10	80	80	120	200

As under the traditional method, the partnership must first allocate book items in accordance with the partnership agreement and the section 704(b) regulations, and then allocate tax items to the noncontributing partner(s) in accordance with the tax-follows-book principle. Remedial allocations are permitted only to the extent necessary to correct ceiling-limited allocations under the traditional method. At the end of Year 4, the partners have the following tax and book capital accounts:

Cap. Accts.	*A*		*B*	
	tax	*book*	*tax*	*book*
initial	80	200	200	200
Years 1-4: depreciation	(16)	(64)	(64)	(64)
end Year 4	64	136	136	136

As you can see, by the end of Year 4, there is not yet any book-tax disparity in the capital accounts of B, the noncontributing partner, because B has been allocated tax depreciation equal to her share of book depreciation. At that point, however, the partnership's tax basis in the property is zero but there is still $72 remaining of book basis, generating annual book depreciation of $12. In Years 5-10, therefore, B is allocated $36 of book depreciation and no tax depreciation, creating a book-tax disparity in those years. To cure the ceiling-rule limitation in Years 5-10, the partnership allocates notional ordinary deductions of $36 to B (and offsetting notional ordinary income of $36 to A). The allocations of notional items are for tax purposes only. At the end of Year 10, the partners have the following tax and book capital accounts:

Cap. Accts.	*A*		*B*	
	tax	*book*	*tax*	*book*
end Year 4	64	136	136	136
Years 5-10: depreciation	-0-	(36)	-0-	(36)
Years 5-10: remedial allocation	36	-0-	(36)	-0-
end Year 10	100	100	100	100

The remedial method has the effect of slowing down the partnership's book depreciation, thereby postponing ceiling-rule distortions until later years (i.e., when the tax and book basis of the carryover portion have been fully recovered). Thus, the ceiling-rule limitation is not triggered until Year 5 when the partnership's actual tax depreciation is exhausted. The book-tax disparity is entirely eliminated only at the end of Year 10.

NOTES AND QUESTIONS

1. *Curative allocations compared.* Contrast the result in **example 6-5** with that under the traditional method with curative allocations (assume the partnership has sufficient gross income to offset any ceiling-limited depreciation). In Years 1-4, the partnership would have $80 of tax depreciation ($20 annually) and $200 of book depreciation ($50 annually). B's share of the tax depreciation would be ceiling-limited to the extent of $20 ($100 share of book depreciation less $80 total tax depreciation). The traditional method with curative allocations would allow the partnership to allocate $20 additional gross income to A (and away from B) to cure the ceiling-rule distortion. Thus, A's built-in gain would be recognized in Years 1-4, while the remedial method defers a portion of that gain until Years 5-10. On the other hand, the remedial method also defers a portion of B's depreciation deductions to the later years. Depending upon the tax situations of the partners, these two effects may not cancel themselves out. For example, if the partner contributing property with built-in gain is a high-bracket taxpayer and the noncontributing partner is tax-exempt, it may be advantageous for the partners to use the remedial method.

Another important difference between the two methods is that a curative allocation of gain from the sale of property is allowed to overcome ceiling-limited depreciation of the same property. A remedial allocation must match income character in this situation: thus, only remedial allocations of ordinary income or deductions may be used to offset ceiling-limited depreciation.

Of course, the potentially most significant difference between the two methods concerns whether the partnership has actual items sufficient to make the appropriate curative allocations. If the partnership lacks such items, the two methods can produce dramatically different outcomes.

2. *Abusive use of the remedial method?* Regulation § 1.704-3(d)(5) generally prohibits partnerships from using any method other than the remedial method to create notional tax items, and bars the IRS (in exercising its authority to prevent abuse under Reg. § 1.704-3(a)(10)) from requiring use of the remedial method (or any other method creating notional items). The IRS may, however, prevent an abusive use of the remedial method under the authority of the general partnership anti-abuse rule under section 701 (discussed in chapter twelve). Regulation § 1.704-3(a)(1) provides that a purported contribution may be recast "as appropriate to avoid tax results inconsistent with subchapter K" and lists use of the remedial allocation method by related parties as one factor to be considered in disregarding a purported contribution. This provision was aimed partly at abusive tax shelters engaged in by Enron that also led to enactment of section 755(c), discussed in chapter eight. The regulation makes clear that the various section 704(c) allocation methods apply only to "contributions of property that are otherwise respected."

6. *Revalued Property*

Although all of the examples and problems in this chapter thus far have involved contributed property, the section 704(c) allocation methods apply equally to items attributable to revalued or reverse section 704(c) property. See Reg. §§ 1.704-1(b)(2)(iv)(*f*), 1.704-1(b)(4)(i), and 1.704-3(a)(6)(i).

Example 6-6: In exchange for equal partnership interests, A and B each contribute $60 cash to the newly formed AB partnership which purchases land for $120. When the land has appreciated to $200, C contributes $200 in exchange for a 50 percent partnership interest, and the partnership revalues its property.

Immediately prior to C's admission, the AB partnership has the following balance sheet:

Assets	*AB*	*Book*	*Capital*	*Tax*	*Book*
land	120	120	A	60	60
			B	60	60
total	120	120	total	120	120

Following C's admission, the partnership has the following balance sheet:

Assets	*AB*	*Book*	*Capital*	*Tax*	*Book*	
cash	200	200	A	60	100	+40
land	120	200	B	60	100	+40
			C	200	200	
total	320	400	total	320	400	

In this example, A and B each receive a $40 "book-up adjustment" to reflect their share of the unrealized appreciation in the land at the time of C's entry into the partnership. The book-up affects their book (but not tax) capital accounts. Thus, the revalued balance sheet shows that A and B are in the same position substantively as if they had contributed an undivided interest in section 704(c) property (with a basis of $120 and a fair market value of $200) to the new ABC partnership in exchange for a 50 percent partnership interest at the very same time C contributed $200 cash for the remaining 50 percent partnership interest. Moreover, the allocation of tax items attributable to the revalued land is controlled by the identical section 704(c) allocation methods previously described.

Problem 6-5:

(a) If the land in **example 6-6** is subsequently sold for $400, how must the resulting tax gain be allocated under the traditional and remedial methods?

(b) A contributes land (basis $90, value $100) and B contributes $100 cash in exchange for equal partnership interests. When the land has increased in value to $170, C contributes $135 cash in exchange for a one-third interest in the partnership, and the partnership revalues its property. Assume that both the AB partnership and the ABC partnership use the traditional method under section 704(c). How must the partnership allocate any gain or loss if the land is subsequently sold for $140?

NOTES AND QUESTIONS

1. *Section 704(b) alternative.* In situations where they are permitted, revaluations are nevertheless optional. If there is no revaluation, the section 704(b) regulations provide an alternative way of accomplishing a similar result. See Reg. § 1.704-1(b)(5) (ex. 14(iv)). For example, if there were no revaluation in **problem 6-5(a)**, the partnership could specially allocate the $280 tax gain from the sale ($400 less $120 basis) to take into account the built-in amount at the time of C's

entry into the partnership. The partners' capital accounts would then appear as follows:

Cap. Accts.	*A*		*B*		*C*	
	tax	*book*	*tax*	*book*	*tax*	*book*
balance after C's entry	60	60	60	60	200	200
sale—§ 704(b) special allocation	90	90	90	90	100	100
balance after sale	150	150	150	150	300	300

If a partnership fails to revalue its assets and also fails to make a special allocation of any built-in gain (or loss), the result may be a capital shift. The regulations warn that such a capital shift may be recharacterized—for example, as compensation for services or a disguised gift—to reflect the economic substance of the transaction. Cf. Reg. § 1.704-1(b)(2)(iv)(*f*)(*5*).

2. *The risk of not making a revaluation.* Suppose there were no revaluation in **problem 6-5(a)**, but the partners agreed to specially allocate any built-in gain arising prior to C's admission. If the land declines in value and is subsequently sold for $180, how much gain or loss must be allocated to each partner? If the partnership were liquidated immediately after the sale, how much would each partner receive in liquidation? Does this scenario suggest why the existing partners might insist on a book-up when C is admitted?

3. *Failure to apply section 704(c) principles.* What are the consequences if a partnership revalues its assets but fails to apply section 704(c) principles to take into account the resulting book-tax disparity? Presumably, the partnership's other allocations can no longer qualify for safe harbor treatment under the section 704(b) regulations. See Reg. § 1.704-1(b)(5) (ex. 14(i)) (last sentence) (violates capital-account maintenance requirements).

4. *Should there be so many choices?* In addition to the section 704(c) methods already described, the regulations clearly indicate that other allocation methods may be permissible in appropriate circumstances. See Reg. § 1.704-3(a)(1). Moreover, partnerships may elect to use different methods for different property and may even use different methods for the *same* property. For example, since the land in **problem 6-5(b)** is both section 704(c) and reverse section 704(c) property, the partnership may allocate the built-in amounts using different section 704(c) methods. See Reg. § 1.704-3(a)(2) and (6)(i). If a partnership has multiple contributed or revalued properties at the same time, it quickly becomes exceedingly difficult to determine how section 704(c) allocations must be made for items from any given property. Would it be simpler to require mandatory application of the remedial method? Proposed regulations provide that a partnership must track separately different "layers" of built-in gain or loss arising from each contribution (a forward section 704(c) layer) and each revaluation (a reverse section 704(c) layer). Prop. Reg. § 1.704-3(a)(6)(i). Any "reasonable method" may be used to allocate tax items across various section 704(c) layers. Prop. Reg. § 1.704-3(a)(6)(iii).

5. *Section 704(c)(1)(C).* In 2004, Congress enacted section 704(c)(1)(C), which provides that any built-in loss in contributed property may be taken into account only in determining the amount of items allocated to the contributing partner. Congress enacted the provision specifically to prevent potential duplication of built-in loss in contributed property when the contributing partner exits the partnership before the built-in loss has been realized. Congress was concerned that the built-in loss might be realized both by the contributing partner (on sale or liquidation of her interest) and by the other partners upon a subsequent sale of the built-in loss property.

Proposed regulations clarify the operation of section 704(c)(1)(C). A partner who contributes built-in loss property (a "section 704(c)(1)(C) partner") is treated as having a special basis adjustment (a "section 704(c)(1)(C) basis adjustment") with respect to the contributed built-in loss property ("section 704(c)(1)(C) property.") Prop. Reg. § 1.704-3(f)(2). The special basis adjustment, which belongs exclusively to the contributing partner and represents a portion of that partner's total basis in the contributed property, is initially equal to the amount of the built-in loss in the property. The amount is then adjusted for subsequent depreciation and other events affecting the property. Upon disposition of the property, the section 704(c)(1)(C) partner reports a tax loss (or less tax gain) to account for any remaining basis adjustment. Prop. Reg. § 1.704-3(f)(3)(ii). The proposed regulations treat the common tax basis of the contributed property in the partnership's hands as equal to its fair market value upon contribution for all purposes, rather than only for purposes of "determining the amount of items allocated to the other partners" as specified in the statute. See I.R.C. § 704(c)(1)(C)(ii). In many respects, the introduction of a section 704(c)(1)(C) adjustment previews the special basis adjustment under section 743 for a purchaser of a partnership interest (discussed in chapter seven).

Consider the following simple scenario. Assume that A contributes land with a basis of $1,000 and a fair market value of $800 and B contributes cash of $800 to the equal AB partnership. The land appreciates in value to $1,000 and the partnership sells it for that amount. A is a section 704(c)(1)(C) partner and has an initial section 704(c)(1)(C) adjustment of $200 (equal to the built-in loss) with respect to the contributed property. The partnership's tax basis in the contributed property is treated as only $800 (the fair market value of the section 704(c)(1)(C) property at the time of the contribution). Since the book value of the property is also $800, the partnership recognizes $200 of both tax and book gain on sale of the property and allocates $100 of each to A and B. After taking into account the section 704(c)(1)(C) adjustment, A reports a net tax loss of $100 ($100 allocable tax gain less $200 basis adjustment). A's outside basis is reduced to $900 ($1,000 less $100 net tax loss), and B's outside basis is increased to $900 ($800 plus $100 tax gain). A and B each increase their book capital accounts from $800 to $900 to reflect their $100 share of the post-contribution book gain. The section 704(c)(1)(C) adjustment has no economic consequences and is not taken into account in adjusting the partners' book capital accounts. The economic result is correct for both partners, since they share equally in the post-contribution gain. Only A benefits from the section 704(c)(1)(C) adjustment of $200, which is netted against A's $100 share of the post-contribution gain.

6. *Small disparity property*. One minor relief provision allows partnerships to disregard section 704(c) principles for property whose disparity between value and basis is small. A disparity is considered small if the value of all properties contributed by a partner during the year is not more than 115 percent or less than 85 percent of the aggregate tax basis of the properties, and the total gross disparity does not exceed $20,000. See Reg. § 1.704-3(e)(1). For example, this provision might allow the partnership in **problem 6-5(b)** to ignore section 704(c) with respect to A's initial contribution, depending upon what other properties she contributes to the partnership in the same year.

> **Problem 6-6:** Test your understanding of section 704(c)(1)(C) by doing this problem: A contributes land (FMV $45, AB $90), and B contributes $45 cash for equal shares of partnership AB. Assume that C joins the partnership when the land has increased in value to $75 (and the partnership revalues the property at that point). Accordingly, C contributes $60 cash for a one-third interest in the partnership. How should gain or loss be allocated if the partnership uses the traditional method and the property is sold for $75 after C's admission?

7. *Collateral Impact of Section 704(c) on Other Subchapter K Issues*

This part describes the impact of section 704(c) principles on the allocation of nonrecourse liabilities and the tax treatment of non-liability obligations.

a. Allocation of Nonrecourse Liabilities

You may recall that nonrecourse liabilities are generally shared by the partners in accordance with their shares of partnership profits, but that the determination is made in three stages or "tiers." First, partners are allocated nonrecourse liabilities equal to their share of partnership minimum gain. Second, additional nonrecourse liabilities are allocated up to the partners' share of *minimum* section 704(c) gain, i.e., the amount of taxable gain that would be allocated to the partner if the partnership disposed of its section 704(c) or reverse section 704(c) property for no consideration other than satisfaction of nonrecourse liabilities secured by such property. Finally, any remaining nonrecourse liabilities are allocated in accordance with the partners' share of partnership profits. Within limits, partners may designate their overall profit shares for this purpose.

Read the following excerpt which describes how the first two tiers are determined when the property subject to a nonrecourse liability is section 704(c) property. As the ruling indicates, the second tier calculation depends upon the partnership's choice of section 704(c) allocation methods. Following the excerpt, do **problem 6-7**, which builds upon **problem 5-3**.

Rev. Rul. 95-41

1995-1 C.B. 132

... A and B form a partnership, PRS, and agree that each will be allocated a 50 percent share of all partnership items. A contributes depreciable property subject to a nonrecourse liability of $6,000, with an adjusted tax basis of $4,000 and a fair market value of $10,000. B contributes $4,000 cash. ...

(1) First Tier Allocation:

Under § 1.752-3(a)(1), a partner's share of the nonrecourse liabilities of PRS includes the partner's share of partnership minimum gain determined in accordance with the rules of § 704(b) and the regulations thereunder. Section 1.704-2(d)(1) provides that partnership minimum gain is determined by computing, for each partnership nonrecourse liability, any gain the partnership would realize if it disposed of the property subject to that liability for no consideration other than full satisfaction of the liability, and then aggregating the separately computed gains. Pursuant to § 1.704-2(d)(3), partnership minimum gain is determined with reference to the contributed property's book value rather than its adjusted tax basis.

In contrast, § 704(c) requires that allocations take into account the difference between the contributed property's adjusted tax basis and its fair market value. Thus, because partnership minimum gain is computed using the contributed property's book value rather than its tax basis, allocations of nonrecourse liabilities under § 1.752-3(a)(1) are not affected by § 704(c). Moreover, because the book value of the property at the time of contribution ($10,000) exceeds the amount of the nonrecourse liability ($6,000), there is no partnership minimum gain immediately after the contribution, and neither A nor B receive (sic) an allocation of nonrecourse liabilities under § 1.752-3(a)(1) immediately after the contribution.

(2) Second Tier Allocation:

Under § 1.752-3(a)(2), a partner's share of the nonrecourse liabilities of the partnership includes the amount of taxable gain that would be allocated to the contributing partner under § 704(c) if the partnership, in a taxable transaction, disposed of the contributed property in full satisfaction of the nonrecourse liability and for no other consideration. If PRS sold the contributed property in full satisfaction of the liability and for no other consideration, PRS would recognize a taxable gain of $2,000 on the sale ($6,000 amount of the nonrecourse liability less $4,000 adjusted tax basis of the property). Under § 704(c) and § 1.704-3(b)(1), all of this taxable gain would be allocated to A. The hypothetical sale also would result in a book loss of $4,000 to PRS (excess of $10,000 book value of property over $6,000 amount of the nonrecourse liability). Under the terms of the partnership agreement, this book loss would be allocated equally between A and B. Because B would receive a $2,000 book loss but no corresponding tax loss, the hypothetical sale would result in a $2,000 disparity between B's book and tax allocations.

If PRS used the traditional method of making § 704(c) allocations described in § 1.704-3(b), A would be allocated a total of $2,000 of taxable gain from the hypothetical sale of the contributed property. Therefore, A would be allocated $2,000 of nonrecourse liabilities under § 1.752-3(a)(2) immediately after the contribution.

If PRS adopted the remedial allocation method described in § 1.704-3(d), PRS would be required to make a remedial allocation of $2,000 of tax loss to B in connection with the hypothetical sale to eliminate the $2,000 disparity between B's book and tax allocations. PRS also would be required to make an offsetting remedial allocation of tax gain to A of $2,000. Thus, A would be allocated a total of $4,000 of tax gain ($2,000 actual gain plus the $2,000 allocation of remedial gain) from the hypothetical sale of the contributed property. Therefore, if the partnership adopted the remedial allocation method, A would be allocated $4,000 of nonrecourse liabilities under § 1.752-3(a)(2) immediately after the contribution.

If PRS used the traditional method with curative allocations described in § 1.704-3(c), PRS would be permitted to make reasonable curative allocations to reduce or eliminate the difference between the book and tax allocations to B that resulted from the hypothetical sale. However, PRS's ability to make curative allocations would depend on the existence of other partnership items and could not be determined solely from the hypothetical sale of the contributed property. Because any potential curative allocations could not be determined solely from the hypothetical sale of the contributed property, curative allocations are not taken into account in allocating nonrecourse liabilities under § 1.752-3(a)(2). Therefore, if PRS used the traditional method with curative allocations, A would be allocated $2,000 of nonrecourse liabilities under § 1.752-3(a)(2) immediately after the contribution. . . .

Problem 6-7: A and B are equal partners of partnership AB, which owns one asset, *x*, whose book value and tax basis are both $40. Prior to C's joining the firm, the partnership revalues *x* to its fair market value of $100, with the booked-up amount shared equally by A and B. C then joins the firm by contributing asset *y* whose value is $100 and basis is $60. Thus, C is a 50 percent partner after joining the firm and A and B are each 25 percent partners. Thereafter, the partnership borrows $90. Assume that the partners validly designate their overall profit shares in the ratio 25:25:50 for purposes of section 752, and that they agree to use the remedial method.

(a) If the liability is nonrecourse and secured by asset *x*, how is it shared by the partners?
(b) Same as (a), except that the liability is secured by asset *y* and not *x*.

b. Tax Treatment of Non-Liability Obligations

Suppose partner A contributes a piece of land with a basis of $2 million to a partnership for a 50 percent partnership interest. Unencumbered, the land is worth $2 million. The land, however, is subject to an uncertain, environmental remediation obligation on the part of the owner, and the partnership takes the land subject to this contingent obligation. Suppose that the contingent obligation is reasonably valued at $600,000 at the time of the contribution of the land to the partnership so that the net value of A's contribution is only $1.4 million. Simultaneously, partner B contributes cash of $1.4 million for the remaining 50 percent partnership interest.

Since the contingent obligation did not create basis in any property including cash (or give rise to an immediate deduction), it is not considered a liability for purposes of section 752. See Rev. Rul. 88-77, 1988-2 C.B. 128 (p. 113); Reg. § 1.752-1(a)(4)(i). Instead, the section 752 regulations defer classification of this obligation as a "liability" until the partnership eventually satisfies the obligation and receives the corresponding deduction. If the contingent obligation is satisfied by a deductible payment of $600,000 when A is still a partner, the deduction must be allocated to A under section 704(c) principles. For purposes of section 704(c), the contingent obligation is treated as a "negative asset," i.e., as built-in loss property with a book-tax disparity at the time of contribution. See Reg. §§ 1.704-3(a)(12) and 1.752-7(c)(1)(i). In effect, the contingent obligation is considered "property" with a tax basis generally equal to zero and a negative value equal to the cost (in present value terms) of satisfying the obligation in the future.

Applying these rules, the initial balance sheet of the AB partnership is as follows:

Assets	*AB*	*Book*	*Capital*	*Tax*	*Book*
cash	1,400,000	1,400,000	A	2,000,000	1,400,000
land	2,000,000	2,000,000	B	1,400,000	1,400,000
non-liab. obligation	0	−600,000			
total	3,400,000	2,800,000	total	3,400,000	2,800,000

Under the section 704(b) regulations, the partners' book capital accounts must be properly adjusted to reflect all obligations to which the contributed property is subject, not just section 752 liabilities. See Reg. § 1.704-1(b)(2)(iv)(*b*). Thus, A's book capital account is initially $1.4 million ($2 million less $600,000 obligation) and A's tax capital account is $2 million (the basis of the contributed property). See Reg. § 1.752-7(c)(2) (example). The book-tax disparity ($600,000) reflects the built-in deduction attributable to the contingent obligation that must be allocated to A when the amount is eventually paid. A's initial outside basis ($2 million) is not reduced by the contingent obligation, since it is not treated as a section 752 liability until it matures.

If the partnership eventually pays $600,000 to satisfy the obligation, A's book capital account remains $1.4 million (and there is no book gain or loss). The passthrough of the $600,000 tax deduction, allocable entirely to A under section 704(c) principles, reduces A's tax capital account from $2 million to $1.4 million, eliminating any book-tax disparity. Simultaneously, A's initial outside basis of $2 million is first increased to $2.6 million to reflect the $600,000 liability under section 752(a) and then decreased to $1.4 million to reflect both the passthrough of the $600,000 deduction and relief of the $600,000 liability under section 752(b). The purpose of these rules is to ensure that the contingent obligation does not provide any tax benefit except to the contributing partner upon satisfaction of the obligation by the partnership. Reg. § 1.752-7(a).

What happens if A leaves the partnership before the $600,000 obligation is satisfied? If A's outside basis is $2 million (the basis of the contributed land unreduced by the contingent obligation), there would appear to be a built-in loss in A's partnership interest (worth only $1.4 million). Thus, a prompt sale of A's partnership interest for $1.4 million might generate a tax loss of $600,000. In this situation, the IRS was justifiably concerned that the sale of the contributing partner's interest might accelerate the deduction for the contingent obligation before its actual payment and potentially allow a duplicated deduction to some other partner when the obligation is satisfied. Indeed, tax shelters were structured precisely for the purpose of exploiting these potential mismatches. See Notice 2000-44 (p. 115) and chapter twelve.

The section 752 regulations now expressly put an end to such gambits by requiring the contributing partner's outside basis to be reduced by the contingent obligation if the partner leaves the partnership before the obligation is satisfied. Reg. § 1.752-7(d)-(f). Thus, on a sale of A's interest before the obligation matures, A's outside basis would be reduced to $1.4 million, preventing any acceleration of the built-in loss. In that situation, the regulations also prevent a shifting of the built-in loss to the remaining partners. If the partnership eventually satisfies the obligation after A is no longer a partner, the partnership may notify A (who may be entitled to the deduction at that time). The partnership is not permitted to claim any loss, deduction, or capital expenditure to the extent of the remaining built-in loss.

NOTES AND QUESTION

1. *Obligations associated with a trade or business.* The special basis-reduction rules may be draconian in situations in which an obligation that is not recognized as a section 752 liability is assumed by a partnership as part of a contribution of the trade or business with which the obligation is associated and the partnership continues to carry on that trade or business. Recall, for example, that accounts payable of a cash-method taxpayer are not treated as section 752 liabilities because they do not create basis in any property (or give rise to an immediate deduction). See chapter four. The section 752 regulations provide an exception from the basis-reduction rules for such obligations when assumed by the partnership in connection with a transfer of the associated trade or business that the partnership carries on. Reg. § 1.752-

7(d)(2)(i)(A). Even if the trade or business exception applies, however, any such obligations are treated as built-in loss property for purposes of section 704(c). Accordingly, the deduction resulting from the partnership's payment of the accounts payable must be allocated to the contributing partner, assuming that she remains a member of the partnership. See I.R.C. § 704(c)(3).

2. *Duplication of built-in losses.* The section 752 regulations are directed at curbing potential acceleration *or* duplication of built-in losses. Recent statutory changes are also designed to prevent a duplication of losses through use of the partnership tax rules. Given the passthrough nature of partnerships, how serious is the problem of duplication (as opposed to acceleration) of built-in losses associated with contingent obligations?

C. Allocations When Partners' Interests Change During the Year

1. *The Basic Rules*

Suppose a taxpayer becomes a member of an existing partnership part way through the partnership's taxable year. What tax items may be allocated to the new partner at the end of the partnership's taxable year?

The answer may be surprising. Read I.R.C. § 706(d)(1). As you can see, partnership allocations must take into account the "varying interests of the partners in the partnership" during the taxable year. In general, these rules try to prevent the partnership from allocating to the new partner any items that economically accrued prior to the time the new partner joined the firm, a type of retroactive allocation. In other words, the goal is similar to that of section 704(c). In this section, we will briefly review the basic rules. The next section will discuss why these rules might be considered anomalous in light of other provisions of subchapter K.

> **Example 6-7:** PRS is a calendar year, cash-basis partnership which pays deductible business rent for the entire year of $12,000 on June 1 of Year 1. On December 1 of Year 1, taxpayer E contributes cash to PRS and obtains a one-fourth interest in the firm.

Absent special rules, PRS must allocate its tax items to its partners, including new partner E, as of December 31 of Year 1, the end of its taxable year. It might thus seem that PRS could allocate all or any part of the $12,000 deduction to E, subject to the rules of section 704(b).

Section 706(d)(1) prescribes a different result, however. As the legislative history of section 706(d) makes clear, PRS's allocations must take into account E's late entry as a partner. The regulations contain a step-by-step process for making allocations when there is a change (referred to as a "variation") in the partners' interests during the year. Reg. § 1.706-4(a)(1) and (3). The partnership must use one of two methods to account for the partners' varying interests: (1) the interim closing of the books method (the default rule) or (2) the proration method (by agreement of the partners). The regulations also specify certain conventions for determining when events are deemed to occur. Reg. § 1.706-4(c).

A partnership may use different methods (interim closing or proration) for different "segments" of the partnership's taxable year. Reg. § 1.706-4(a)(3)(iii). Segments are specific portions of the partnership's taxable year created by interim closings of the partnership's books. Reg. § 1.706-4(a)(3)(vi). The first segment commences with the beginning of the partnership's taxable year and ends at the time of the next interim closing (but no later than the end of the partnership's taxable year). If the partnership does not use the interim closing method, it will have only one segment which corresponds to its entire taxable year. Id. Within that single segment, however, the partnership may have more than one "proration period," which is a portion of a segment created by a variation for which the partnership uses the proration method. Reg. § 1.706-4(a)(3)(viii).

Under the proration method, E could be allocated about $1,000 (1/12 × $12,000) of the deduction; the remainder would be treated as falling into the first proration period which ends at the time of E's entry. The partnership's taxable year would be treated as a single segment with two proration periods (before and after E's entry). By contrast, under the interim closing of the books method, the partnership's taxable year would be divided into two segments, with the first segment ending at the time of E's entry. E could not be allocated any part of the deduction since payment of the rent on June 1 occurred prior to E's admission. The result would be the same as if the partnership's taxable year had actually closed on December 1, the date E joined the firm.

Standing alone, the interim closing of the books method could be easily manipulated. In this example, if PRS were able to delay paying the rent until sometime in December, then the entire deduction could potentially be allocated to new partner E. To forestall that possibility, the statute requires cash-basis partnerships to spread certain items — so-called "allocable cash basis items" such as deductions for rental payments — over the period in which the item economically accrued. Such items must then be allocated among the partners strictly in proportion to their interests in the partnership during the relevant period. Read I.R.C. § 706(d)(2)(A) and (B). Since the June 1 rental payment was for the use of property throughout Year 1, only $1,000 of the deduction may be prorated to December. Moreover, only $250 of the deduction may be allocated to E, a one-fourth partner during that month.

Suppose the payment on June 1 of Year 1 related to PRS's use of property from July 1 of Year 0 through June 30 of Year 1? Read I.R.C. § 706(d)(2)(C) and (D). In that case, the statute treats the $6,000 portion of the deduction which economically accrued during Year 0 as, nevertheless, arising on the first day of Year 1 for purposes of determining when PRS may deduct that amount. (Since PRS is a cash-basis taxpayer and payment of all $12,000 is made in Year 1, PRS is treated as having a $12,000 deduction in Year 1.) But the *allocation* of that portion of the deduction may only be made to partners who owned interests in PRS during the last half of Year 0, in proportion to their interests during that period. PRS must capitalize any portion of the deduction allocable to a person who is no longer a PRS partner during Year 1. In any event, E would be out of luck if the entire deductible cash basis item accrued prior to E's entry into the partnership.

Under the regulations, each segment is treated as a separate period for purposes of allocating the partners' distributive shares. For example, under the interim closing of the books method, a partner may be allocated a net capital loss for a particular segment, even though the partnership has a net capital gain for the entire year. Reg. § 1.706-4(a)(3)(vii). There is a safe harbor for non-capital intensive partnerships, such as a law firm, which may use any reasonable method to account for varying interests. Reg. § 1.706-4(b)(2). In addition, "extraordinary items" — including gain from sale of most capital assets, discharge of indebtedness income, and other items whose ratable allocation would substantially distort income — must generally be allocated among the partners in proportion to their interests at the time of the day on which the item is taken into account, regardless of the method (interim closing or proration) or conventions otherwise used by the partnership. See Reg. § 1.706-4(e)(1).

The following problem requires you to apply section 706(d)(3), a provision relating to tiered partnerships. It is intended to foil the ingenuity of late entrants such as E who might otherwise seek to obtain a share of previously accrued deductions by using more complicated partnership structures. Do you understand why the provision was needed and how it reaches the intended outcome?

> **Problem 6-8:** Suppose that in **example 6-7**, nearly all of PRS is owned throughout Year 1 by calendar-year partnership ABC. Instead of acquiring an interest in PRS, taxpayer E contributes cash and acquires a one-fourth interest in ABC on December 1 of Year 1. How much of PRS's $12,000 Year 1 business deduction may be allocated to E as a result of E's ownership interest in ABC?

2. *Planning Under the Basic Rules*

What is so surprising or anomalous about these rules prohibiting certain types of retroactive allocations? For one thing, subchapter K expressly permits another type of retroactive allocation: partners in a partnership are permitted to wait until *after* the end of the partnership's taxable year before determining their distributive shares of the partnership's tax items for the year. The partners need merely specify their desired shares of each item in an amendment to their partnership agreement made prior to the time when the partnership tax return must be filed. See I.R.C. §§ 704(a), 761(c).

As a technical matter, it might be argued that any amendment changing a partner's share of an item causes a "varying interest" in the partnership during the year, thereby implicating the section 706(d) restrictions. But section 706(d) has never been interpreted to apply to this situation. According to the regulations, the varying interests rule does not apply to changes in allocations among contemporaneous partners for the partnership's entire year (or for a segment to which an item is entirely allocable), provided that the changes are not attributable to additional capital contributions (or distributions that represent a return of capital) and the allocations pass muster under section 704(b). Reg. § 1.706-4(b)(1). Moreover, with the exception of the quite restrictive rules pertaining to allocable cash basis items, section 706(d) might not have much force even if it were applicable. Provided that the partners own *some* interest in the partnership throughout the year, a mandatory proration of partnership items throughout the year would not necessarily affect the amount of each item potentially allocable to any partner.

Even for *new* partners, and again leaving aside restrictions on allocable cash basis items, section 706(d) may not be very effective in prohibiting retroactive allocations. Here, it is important to understand that, while the section 704(b) regulations defer to section 706(d) (see Reg. § 1.704-1(b)(1)(iii)), the partnership may nevertheless make a special, disproportionate allocation to the new partner of items deemed to arise under section 706(d) subsequent to the new partner's admission. The following example illustrates this point.

> **Example 6-8:** Calendar-year partnership PRS has $12,000 of net operating income (prior to depreciation) during the year and a $24,000 depreciation deduction. Thus, PRS incurs a $12,000 net tax loss for the year. Taxpayer F contributes cash to PRS and joins the firm as a one-third partner on October 1 of the year.

How much of the loss may be allocated to new partner F? Absent section 706(d), the partnership might try to allocate one-third of the loss, or $4,000, to F. But as you now know, section 706(d) tries to prevent that outcome. It would require the partnership to take F's short-term status into account in allocating its tax items. Absent a section 704(b) special allocation, F may be allocated under the proration method a maximum of $1,000 of the partnership's net tax loss under section 706(d). Under that method, only $3,000 of the net tax loss would be deemed to arise during the last three months of the year, and F's share would be limited to one-third of that amount.

But the result to F may be improved if the partnership makes a valid section 704(b) special allocation to F of items deemed to arise during the last three months of the year. Thus, the partnership could specially allocate all $3,000 of the last three months' net tax loss to her.

Perhaps the partnership could allocate yet more losses to F. For example, again subject to section 704(b), F could receive a special allocation of the entire $6,000 of depreciation deemed to arise during the last three months. If this special allocation were combined with F's pro rata share of the partnership's operating income

($12,000 × 1/4 × 1/3, or $1,000), F would effectively be allocated a net tax loss of $5,000 for the year. Or, if F's $1,000 share of the partnership's operating income were allocated to the other partners, F could be allocated a total loss of $6,000 for the year. In short, section 706(d) places some limitations on the flexibility of partnership allocations, but such restrictions may prove quite minimal in any particular case.

NOTES

1. *Unavailability of cash method.* As noted, the allocation rules applicable to allocable cash basis items are quite restrictive. But, shortly after these rules were enacted, Congress diminished their significance by barring partnerships classified as "tax shelters" from using the cash method of accounting altogether. See I.R.C. § 448(a).

2. *Closing the partnership year.* The scope of retroactive allocations is more limited if the event triggering a change in the partners' percentage interests causes the partnership's taxable year to close with respect to some or all of the partners. In this situation, a share of partnership items must then be allocated to such partners based on the partnership's short taxable year. As discussed in chapter eleven, certain major transfers of partnership interests over a 12-month period cause the partnership's taxable year to close for all partners. See I.R.C. §§ 706(c)(1), 708(b). The partnership taxable year also ends for any partner who sells or liquidates her entire interest in the partnership. I.R.C. § 706(c)(2)(A). If a partner sells only a portion of her partnership interest (or her interest is otherwise reduced, e.g., upon admission of a new partner), however, the partnership taxable year does not close. I.R.C. § 706(c)(2)(B). The section 706(d) restrictions are likely to be most significant in these situations.

D. Family Partnerships

Read I.R.C. §§ 704(e) and 761(b) and Reg. § 1.704-1(b)(1)(iii), -1(e)(1)(v), and -1(e)(3). Even though an allocation has substantial economic effect, it may not be respected under section 704(e), which has generally related to family partnerships. As you may recall from the *Schneer* case in chapter two, courts have struggled to reconcile the allocative flexibility of the partnership rules with assignment-of-income principles. In the context of partnerships involving family members, the opportunities for deflecting income attributable to capital or services to lower-bracket taxpayers are particularly ripe. Prior to enactment of section 704(e), the Service challenged income-shifting efforts through the use of family partnerships by arguing that membership in such partnerships required a contribution of either "vital services" or "original capital." Under the government's view, a family member (such as a child) who provided neither to the partnership was not a partner and therefore could not be allocated any of the partnership's tax items. In Culbertson v. Comm'r, 337 U.S. 733 (1949), the Supreme Court rejected this position and instead articulated a standard based on the parties' intent: "whether, considering all the facts . . . the parties in good faith and acting with a business purpose intended to join together in the present conduct of the enterprise."

Congress enacted the predecessor to former section 704(e)(1) to reduce the uncertainty of the *Culbertson* test by providing a safe harbor for determining partner status if capital is a material income-producing factor in a partnership. In this situation, a person owning a capital interest was recognized as a partner for tax purposes, regardless of whether the interest was acquired by gift or purchase. In 2015, Congress relocated this safe harbor in the general definition of a partner under section 761(b). I.R.C. § 761(b) (2d sentence). In addition to striking former section 704(e)(1), Congress also renumbered former sections 704(e)(2) and (3) to become current sections 704(e)(1) and (2), respectively. It is not clear that these changes have any substantive effect, since former section 704(e)(1) applied for purposes "of this subtitle," the identical scope as section 761(b). The scant legislative history suggests that Congress intended to reject the taxpayer's position in *TIFD III-E*, excerpted below. Of course, the references in the regulations do not yet reflect the 2015 changes.

A capital interest is defined as a right to receive a share of assets upon liquidation of the partnership. Reg. § 1.704-1(e)(1)(v). Note that the safe harbor does not apply to a person who acquires only an interest in future partnership profits or an interest in a non-capital intensive partnership. In these situations, the *Culbertson* intent test continues to govern whether the partnership and its members will be respected for tax purposes.

If a valid partnership interest exists, section 704(e)(1) (formerly section 704(e)(2)) nevertheless permits the Service to reallocate partnership items in narrowly defined circumstances to backstop assignment-of-income principles. If a partnership interest is created by gift, reallocation between the donor and donee is permitted if (i) the donor fails to receive adequate compensation for services rendered to the partnership or (ii) the distributive share allocated to the donee's capital is disproportionately greater than the distributive share allocated to the donor's capital. Section 704(e)(2) (formerly section 704(e)(3)) permits the same reallocation in the case of partnership interests resulting from a purchase and sale between family members. An interest may be created by gift or intrafamily purchase either directly or indirectly. Reg. § 1.704-1(e)(3)(ii)(*a*) and (*b*).

The significance of the family partnership rules has been reduced as a result of enactment of the "kiddie tax," which effectively taxes the income of children under a specified age at their parents' rate. See I.R.C. § 1(g). Congress has also enacted special rules to curb the potential advantages of certain estate-planning techniques involving family partnerships designed to shift value from an older generation to a younger generation outside the estate tax. See I.R.C. §§ 2701-2704. Nevertheless, family partnerships continue to represent an important estate-planning tool, particularly in connection with valuation discounts and buy-sell agreements.

NOTES AND QUESTIONS

1. *Reasonable allowance for services.* If a donor fails to receive adequate compensation for services, partnership income must be reallocated by first allocating a reasonable allowance for the donor's services and then attributing the balance of the income to the donor and donee in proportion to their share of partnership capital. Reg. § 1.704-1(e)(3)(i)(*b*). If there are other partners in the partnership, the reallocation affects only the portion of the partnership income attributable to the donor and donee. In determining the reasonableness of compensation and the resulting reallocation, the regulations list certain factors to be considered, including participation in management, the value of comparable services by a nonpartner, and whether an interest is that of a general or limited partner. Reg. § 1.704-1(e)(3)(i)(*c*) and (ii)(*c*).

2. *Capital as a material income-producing factor.* If income from the partnership's business consists principally of fees or other compensation for personal services, capital is not considered a material income-producing factor; thus, the safe harbor of section 761(b) (2d sentence) (formerly section 704(e)(1)) is unavailable for service partnerships. Reg. § 1.704-1(e)(1)(iv); but see Bateman v. U.S., 490 F.2d 549 (9th Cir. 1973) (partnership income was attributable to goodwill of service partnership). In other situations, whether capital is a material income-producing factor depends on the facts and circumstances. One court has held that capital was not a material income-producing factor where a real estate partnership was financed mostly by borrowing. See Carriage Square, Inc. v. Comm'r, 69 T.C. 119 (1977).

3. *Disproportionate loss allocation.* In addressing required reallocations, the regulations refer only to partnership "income," not losses. Does this mean that a disproportionate loss allocation that passes muster under the general rules of section 704(b) should be outside the purview of section 704(e)(1) (formerly section 704(e)(2))? Should it matter whether the disproportionate allocation is of specific loss items or of net losses?

4. *Estate-tax inclusion.* Under section 2036(a), property transferred by a decedent, other than by a bona fide sale for full consideration, may be included in the decedent's gross estate if the decedent retained possession or enjoyment of the property. For example, section 2036(a) may apply when property transferred to the family partnership remains available to satisfy the transferor's post-transfer living expenses and other needs. If the bona fide sale exception applies, only the discounted value of the decedent's retained interest in the partnership (rather than the property transferred to the partnership) is includible in the decedent's estate. While courts have not yet reached a consensus concerning how to apply the bona fide sale exception, it seems clear that some significant nontax purpose for the transfer to the

partnership is required. Thus, transfers that lack an independent business purpose and are intended solely to reduce estate taxes should fall outside this exception.

The following case involves a very sophisticated attempt to exploit the ceiling rule prior to the effective date of the anti-abuse rule under section 704(c). Although the government ultimately prevailed, it lost three times in the District Court. In the opinion below, the Second Circuit reverses the District Court's second opinion holding that purported partners qualified under former section 704(e)(1) — the family partnership provision — even though the *Culbertson* test was not satisfied.

TIFD III-E, Inc. v. United States

666 F.3d 836 (2d Cir. 2012)

LEVAL, Circuit Judge: [Two subsidiaries of General Electric Capital Corp. ("GECC") purportedly formed a partnership ("Castle Harbour") with two Dutch banks not subject to U.S. tax. The GECC partners contributed a rental fleet of fully depreciated airplanes, while the Dutch banks invested cash and were essentially guaranteed a fixed rate of return on their investment. Nearly all (98 percent) of the partnership's operating book and tax income was allocated to the Dutch banks but large book depreciation deductions offset most of the operating income, leaving the banks with only a much smaller share of economic income. By sheltering most of the rental income, the arrangement effectively allowed the GECC partners to "redepreciate" the value of the airplanes. Rather than attack the underlying section 704(c) abuse directly, the government argued that the Dutch banks were essentially lenders and that the taxable income allocated to them should be reallocated to the GECC partners.

Applying the totality-of-the-circumstances test of Comm'r v. Culbertson, 337 U.S. 733 (1949), the Second Circuit agreed with the government and concluded that the banks' interest was not a "bona fide equity participation," but instead "overwhelmingly in the nature of a secured lender's interest." It found that the partnership agreement was designed essentially to guarantee the reimbursement of the Dutch banks' cash investment plus an annual rate of return referred to in the agreement as the "Applicable Rate." It remanded to the District Court to determine whether the banks nevertheless qualified as partners under former section 704(e)(1) (now section 761(b) (2d sentence)). On remand, the District Court so held and the government again appealed. The Second Circuit once again reversed the District Court in the opinion that follows.]

. . . [W]e conclude that the same evidence which, on our last review, compelled the conclusion that the banks' interest was so markedly in the nature of debt that it does not qualify as bona fide equity participation also compels the conclusion that the banks' interest was not a capital interest under § 704(e)(1). . . .

Our previous ruling was essentially to the effect that, because a holding of partnership debt does not qualify as a partnership participation and the banks' interest in the partnership was overwhelmingly in the nature of debt, they did not qualify for tax purposes as partners in Castle Harbour. The argument that the banks nevertheless qualify as partners under § 704(e)(1) implicitly assumes that after passage of this section, debt could qualify as a partnership interest. We believe the passage of § 704(e)(1) made no such change in the law.

Section 704(e)(1) provides:

> A person shall be recognized as a partner for purposes of this subtitle if he owns a capital interest in a partnership in which capital is a material income-producing factor, whether or not such interest was derived by purchase or gift from any other person. I.R.C. § 704(e)(1).

For purposes of the section, the Treasury regulations define a "capital interest" as

> an interest in the assets of the partnership, which is distributable to the owner of the capital interest upon his withdrawal from the partnership or upon liquidation of the partnership. Treas. Reg. § 1.704-1(e)(1)(v).

. . . The question is whether the term "capital interest in a partnership" was intended to, and does, include a holding of debt. Our first reference must be to the terms of the statute and regulations to determine whether a literal reading provides an unambiguous answer. We conclude that it does not. The terms "capital" or "capital interest" are reasonably subject to multiple interpretations. However, the ambiguity as to whether the term "capital interest" includes a debt-holder's interest distinctly favors the government's position that the banks' interest, which is overwhelmingly in the nature of debt, does not qualify as partnership interest under § 704(e)(1).

Our consultation of various dictionaries, both specialized in the area of finance and general, reveals that, while the word "capital" can be used to refer to a firm's available resources regardless of whether they represent equity or debt, the more favored usage refers to an ownership, or equity, interest. . . . The pertinent regulation, § 1.704-1(e)(1)(v), similarly tends to favor the government, while perhaps leaving the matter ambiguous. [T]he regulation states that a "capital interest" is "an interest in the assets of the partnership." According to common understanding, a holder of a firm's debt does not own an interest in the firm's assets. To be sure, the holder of a firm's debt, as a creditor, has a claim to be paid out of the firm's general assets. But, absent a contractually negotiated right, the holder of the firm's debt has no right even to be consulted as to whether or how the firm disposes of its assets. Furthermore, so long as the partnership has resources dependably sufficient to pay the debt, the value of the creditor's interest does not rise and fall with the value of the partnership's assets.

Notwithstanding that they tend to favor the government's position, the governing statute and regulation leave some ambiguity as to whether the holder of partnership debt (or an interest overwhelmingly in the nature of debt) shall be recognized as a partner. Therefore, we may consult the legislative history to see whether it sheds light on their interpretation. . . . The reports of the House and the Senate accompanying the passage of § 704(e) make clear that the provision did not intend to broaden the character of interests in partnerships that qualify for treatment as a partnership interest to include partnership debt.

The purpose of the statute was to address an altogether different question. The concern of § 704(e)(1) was whether it matters, for the determination of whether a person is a partner for tax purposes, that the person's purported partnership interest arose through an intrafamily transfer. The section was passed to reject court opinions that refused to recognize for tax purposes transfers of partnership interests because the transfers were effectuated by intrafamilial gift, as opposed to arm's length purchase.[1] Its focus is not on the nature of the investment in a partnership, but rather on who should be recognized for tax purposes as the owner of the interest.

Thus, the legislative reports accompanying passage of the statute do not discuss at all whether different types of interests (debt as opposed to equity) will qualify as a capital interest. They do not suggest that the statute changed the type of interest that will qualify. Their focus is entirely on the *transfer* of an interest and whether the purported transfer effectuated a true change in ownership. The reports thus assert that the amendment was designed to "leave[] the Commissioner and the courts free to inquire in any case whether the donee or purchaser *actually owns the interest* in the partnership which the transferor purports to have given or sold him." . . . The reports of the House and Senate made clear that "[a]ll the facts and circumstances . . . may be taken into consideration in determining the bona fides or lack of bona fides of a purported gift or sale," and that "where there is a real transfer of ownership, a gift of a family partnership interest is to be respected for tax purposes without regard to the motives which actuated the transfer." . . . Nothing in the reports suggests any intention that the amendment alter the eligibility of a holding of partnership debt to be deemed a partnership interest.[2]

Nor has litigation under the section addressed the question whether its passage changed the type of interest that qualifies as a partnership interest. The cases have focused, appropriately, on the purpose of the provision — to dispel any relevance of the fact that a partnership interest, concededly in the nature of equity, arose from a gift, in determining whether a purported transferee of an interest is in fact its true

1. The steeply graduated tax rates of the 1940's created an incentive for families to divide a single partner's interest among two or more members, so that the total income from the interest would be taxed at a lower rate. *See Comm'r v. Tower*, 327 U.S. 280 (1946). . . .

2. The limited purpose is reflected in the title given to § 704(e) — "Family partnerships" — and to § 704(e)(1) — "Recognition of interest created by purchase or gift." . . .

owner for tax purposes. . . . None of the decisions suggest in any way that § 704(e)(1) should be construed as drastically altering the pre-existing law of partnership taxation by allowing an interest properly characterized as debt to be recognized as a partnership interest.

We do not understand either the district court, or for that matter the taxpayer, to argue otherwise. The district court's analysis was not that § 704(e)(1) changed the law to allow debt to be considered a partnership interest, but rather that the banks' interest should be deemed to be in the nature of equity, and thus a "capital interest" for the purpose of § 704(e)(1), because the banks' return could vary with the performance of the partnership. . . . The district court found that the banks incurred what it characterized as "real risk" that their capital accounts, as defined by the partnership agreement, would be negative upon dissolution, requiring them to restore the deficit. . . . Because the payout to the banks upon liquidation of the partnership was thus linked, in some degree, to the value of the banks' capital accounts, and because the value of those accounts was in turn linked, in some degree, to the value of Castle Harbour's assets, the court reasoned that the payout to the banks upon liquidation was "tied to the availability of partnership capital." . . . The court concluded that the banks' interest was therefore an "interest in the assets of the partnership" distributable to them upon liquidation. Treas. Reg. § 1.704-1(e)(1)(v). . . . The district court's finding that the banks' interest qualified as a capital interest was thus premised entirely on the significance it accorded to the possibility that the banks would be required to bear 1% of partnership losses exceeding $7 million, or 100% of partnership losses exceeding $541 million.

We respectfully disagree. The "risks" in question were in the nature of appearance of risk, rather than *real* risk. The risks do not justify treating the banks' interest as a capital, or equity, interest. . . . In its decision following remand, the district court did not suggest that it, or we, had underestimated the significance of these risks. Rather, it concluded that the banks' overall downside risk, although "minimal," was "still possible, and therefore not meaningless." . . . In our prior opinion, however, we explicitly considered the extent of the banks' downside risk and concluded that they "incurred no meaningful downside risk." . . . The district court's new conclusion that the banks' downside risk was "not meaningless" was squarely at odds with our previous ruling. Our conclusion that the banks ran no meaningful risk of a return below the Applicable Rate (together with our conclusion that they enjoyed no meaningful prospect of a return above the Applicable Rate) was a part of our holding, as this conclusion was essential to our ruling that their interest was not a bona fide equity interest. . . .

The district court was perhaps reading § 704(e)(1) to mean that the addition to a debt interest of any possibility that the holder's ultimate entitlement will vary, based on the debtor's performance, from pure reimbursement plus a previously fixed rate of return will qualify that interest as a partnership interest, no matter how economically insignificant the potential deviation and how improbable its occurrence. We disagree with any such reading of the statute. No such interpretation is compelled by the plain language of § 704(e)(1). And the fact that the statute was intended to serve an altogether different purpose is confirmed by the legislative reports.

In explaining our conclusion that the banks' interest was not a genuine equity interest, we repeatedly emphasized that, as a practical matter, the structure of the partnership agreement confined the banks' return to the Applicable Rate regardless of the performance of Castle Harbour. . . . We found that the partnership agreement's effective decoupling of the banks' rate of return from the value of Castle Harbour's assets compelled the conclusion that the banks' interest "was overwhelmingly in the nature of a secured lender's interest, which would neither be harmed by poor performance of the partnership nor significantly enhanced by extraordinary profits." . . .

The banks' interest was therefore necessarily not a "capital interest," which is "an interest in the assets of the partnership . . . distributable to the owner . . . upon withdrawal . . . or liquidation." Treas. Reg. § 1.704-1(e)(1)(v). . . . Because the banks' interest was for all practical purposes a fixed obligation, requiring reimbursement of their investment at a set rate of return in all but the most unlikely of scenarios, their interest rather represented a liability of the partnership. . . . Accordingly, for the same reasons that the evidence compels the conclusion that the banks' interest was not bona fide equity participation, it also compels the conclusion that their interest was not a capital interest within the meaning of § 704(e)(1).[3]

. . . The government argues that the taxpayer is subject to a penalty for substantial understatement of income for the years 1997 and 1998 because it has not demonstrated substantial authority for treating the banks as partners in Castle Harbour for tax purposes. We agree. The district court found otherwise because it mistakenly concluded that several of our decisions supported treatment of the banks as partners in Castle Harbour. . . . The taxpayer has failed to point to substantial authority supporting its treatment of the banks as partners. We find that a penalty for substantial understatement of income was therefore properly assessed.

. . . The judgment of the district court is reversed.

---

3. The taxpayer argues that the banks' interest may qualify as a capital interest under § 704(e)(1) despite failing to qualify as bona fide equity participation under *Culbertson*'s totality-of-the-circumstances test because the *Culbertson* test is ultimately focused on the parties' intent, while the § 704(e)(1) inquiry is limited to an assessment of the objective nature of the interest. . . . Even assuming, however, that there may be circumstances in which the application of *Culbertson* and § 704(e)(1) yields different results as to whether the purported holder of a partnership interest qualifies as a partner, we see no reason why the results should differ in this case. In our prior opinion, we ruled that the objective facts of the structure that the parties had created (and intended to create) indicated that the banks' interest was "overwhelmingly in the nature of a secured lender's interest," and therefore required that the banks' interest be treated as debt for tax purposes, regardless of the parties' desire to have it treated as equity. . . . Even if the taxpayer is correct that the tests of partner status under *Culbertson* and § 704(e)(1) conceivably yield different results in some circumstances, that possibility has no bearing on this case.

NOTES AND QUESTIONS

1. *Former section 704(e)(1) vs.* Culbertson. As the Second Circuit's opinion indicates, section 704(e)(1) was enacted to resolve the controversy surrounding use of "family partnerships" to shift income among family members. In *TIFD III-E*, the taxpayer argued that this provision could essentially "trump" the *Culbertson* doctrine by conferring partner status in a capital-intensive partnership even though the partner lacks a "bona fide equity interest." Although the final footnote leaves open the possibility that *Culbertson* and section 704(e)(1) may "yield different results in some circumstances," how realistic is this possibility? Is there any inherent conflict between this provision and *Culbertson*?

In 2015, Congress "clarified" that former section 704(e)(1) was not intended "to provide an alternative test for whether a person is a partner in a partnership," the argument advanced by the taxpayer in *TIFD III-E*. Given the Second Circuit's decision in 2012, do you think any change was needed? Does it make any difference now that the language of former section 704(e)(1) appears instead in section 761(b)?

2. *Partnership debt vs. equity.* In its first opinion, the Second Circuit referred to the banks' interests as overwhelmingly debt-like but carefully refrained from actually classifying them as debt. See TIFD III-E, Inc. v. U.S., 459 F.3d 220 (2d Cir. 2006). If the banks' interests were debt for tax purposes, they would clearly not qualify as equity interests. How easy is it to distinguish between debt and equity in the partnership context? Should debt-equity principles derived in the corporate context apply?

3. *Partnership allocations.* By holding that the banks were not valid partners, the Second Circuit found it unnecessary to consider whether the district court erroneously determined that the partnership's allocations were valid under section 704(b). See 459 F.3d at 241 n.19. Under current law, the section 704(c) anti-abuse rule would curb such tax-motivated shifting of income upon a contribution of low-value, high-basis property by requiring "curative" allocations. Should *Culbertson* be used to backstop these technical provisions? Do you think penalties were justified? See TIFD III-E, Inc. v. U.S., 604 Fed. Appx. 69 (2d Cir. 2015), cert. denied, 136 S. Ct. 796 (2016).

Chapter 7

Sales of Partnership Interests

A. Introduction

Beginning with this chapter, we shift our attention to the taxation of *transactions* involving partnerships and between partners and partnerships. The first type of transaction we consider is a sale of all or a portion of a partnership interest.

How should this transaction be analyzed for tax purposes? Should the seller be treated as disposing of an interest in the partnership entity as a whole, analogous to a sale of corporate stock? Or should she instead be viewed as transferring an undivided interest in each of the individual assets of the partnership? These two possibilities represent once again the "entity" versus "aggregate" conceptions of a partnership.

What are the different tax implications of these two approaches? For one thing, the character of the seller's gain or loss might be affected. For example, assume that one of the partnership's assets is appreciated property that would generate ordinary income if sold. (This type of property is often referred to as a "hot asset.") In that case, an aggregate approach to the sale of a partnership interest would result in some ordinary income to the seller. In contrast, an entity approach would result in capital gain if the partnership interest is a capital asset in the seller's hands.

But would an entity approach to the transaction really provide the seller with an advantage? After all, the buyer should presumably be aware of the fact that she is purchasing an interest in a partnership with a hot asset and might, therefore, be allocated in the future some of the ordinary income built into the asset at the time of her purchase. Thus, the transferee might take this potential future tax liability into account by reducing the purchase price. If the buyer and seller were both in more-or-less the same tax situation, such bargaining might eliminate any advantage to the transferor.

Of course, the transferee might *not* be in a similar tax situation as the transferor. For example, a tax-exempt transferee might not be concerned with a future share of ordinary income. Moreover, as we will see in part C of this chapter, in certain circumstances the purchaser of a partnership interest is provided with the equivalent of a cost basis in her share of the partnership's assets. In that case, there would not be any built-in gain for the purchaser to take into account in her purchase price.

Current law determines the tax consequences to the transferor of a partnership interest in a pragmatic way. In general, current law adopts the simpler, entity approach and treats a sale of a partnership interest similar to a sale of corporate stock. The amount and character of gain or loss, basis, and holding period are all based on the partnership interest held by the seller and *not* on the underlying assets of the partnership.

But this general rule is overridden, and the partnership is looked through, in order to prevent a mischaracterization of the transferor's gain or loss. Thus, an aggregate approach is generally adopted if the partnership has any hot assets at the time of the sale of the partnership interest. The same approach is used if the partnership at that time holds other assets — such as "collectibles" or property with "section 1250 capital gain" — gain from the sale of which is taxed less favorably than long-term capital gain (although more favorably than ordinary income). (We might label such property as "lukewarm assets.") Part B of this chapter describes the tax treatment of the transferor.

Current law's treatment of the transferee of a partnership interest is also based on pragmatic considerations, although the end result is not always as satisfactory as the treatment of the transferor. The buyer is generally treated as if she purchased an interest in the partnership entity as a whole, with no change in her share of the partnership's inside basis. In certain cases, however, the buyer "looks through" the partnership and obtains a share of inside basis as if she purchased the partnership's assets directly. This result occurs if the partnership so elects or if it has a "substantial built-in loss," i.e., if the aggregate inside basis of its assets exceeds their fair market value by more than $250,000 immediately after the purchase. The transferee's tax consequences are examined in part C of this chapter.

B. Consequences to the Transferor

1. *The Entity Approach*

Read I.R.C. §§ 741, 752(d). The "entity" treatment of a transfer of a partnership interest is very straightforward. The transferor recognizes capital gain or loss measured by the difference between the amount realized and the transferor's basis in the interest. Generally, the transferor's outside basis must be adjusted to reflect her distributive share of partnership items up to the date of disposition. See Reg. § 1.705-1(a)(1) (6th sentence). Such interim adjustments prevent a partner from converting her distributive share of income or loss from hot or lukewarm assets into long-term capital gain or loss. In addition, because outside basis includes the transferor's share of partnership liabilities, the transferor's amount realized must also include the share of partnership liabilities assumed (or taken subject to) by the purchaser. See I.R.C. § 752(d); Reg. § 1.1001-2(a)(4)(v); and Comm'r v. Tufts (p. 132).

If the transferor owns more than one type of partnership interest at the time of the transfer, the partner is treated as having a unitary basis in all of her partnership interests. Thus, if she disposes of less than her entire interest, she must apportion her single unitary basis between the sold and retained interests based on their relative fair market values. The tax consequences become a bit more complicated if the partner owns interests, such as both a general and limited partnership interest, with different shares of the partnership's liabilities. As you recall, a partner's share of partnership liabilities affects outside basis, but a limited and general partner may share such liabilities differently. Rev. Rul. 84-53, 1984-1 C.B. 159, explains how the transferor's basis is determined in that situation:

> In cases where the partner's share of all partnership liabilities does not exceed the adjusted basis of such partner's entire interest (including basis attributable to liabilities), the transferor partner shall first exclude from the adjusted basis of such partner's entire interest an amount equal to such partner's share of all partnership liabilities. . . . A part of the remaining adjusted basis (if any) shall be allocated to the transferred portion of the interest according to the ratio of the fair market value of the transferred portion of the interest to the fair market value of the entire interest. The sum of the amount so allocated plus the amount of the partner's share of liabilities that is considered discharged on the disposition of the transferred portion of the interest (under section 752(d) of the Code and section 1.1001-2 of the regulations) equals the adjusted basis of the transferred portion of the interest.

Example 7-1: A is both a general and limited partner in the same partnership. A's unitary basis in both partnership interests is $60, which includes A's $45 share of partnership liabilities in her capacity as general partner. Assume that A receives $20 cash on sale of her limited partnership interest, worth one-third of the total net value of her combined interests.

Under Rev. Rul. 84-53, A's allocable basis in the sold interest is $5, consisting of one-third of A's net unitary basis of $15 ($60 less $45 share of all liabilities) plus zero share of liabilities considered discharged on disposition of the limited partner interest. A thus recognizes gain of $15 ($20 cash less $5 allocable basis) on sale of her limited partnership interest.

If A instead sold her general partnership interest for $40 cash, A's allocable basis in the sold interest would be $55, consisting of $10 (two-thirds of A's net unitary basis of $15) plus A's $45 share of liabilities considered discharged on disposition of the general partnership interest. A's amount realized would be $85 ($40 cash plus $45 liabilities relieved) and A would recognize gain of $30 ($85 amount realized less $55 allocable basis) on sale of her general partnership interest. The total gain recognized if A sells the interests separately ($45) is thus the same as if she had sold the interests together for $60 cash plus $45 relief of liabilities ($105 amount realized less $60 unitary basis). The important point to remember is that a partner's share of liabilities is included both in her outside basis and her amount realized.

NOTES

1. *Unitary basis.* Rev. Rul. 84-53 treats a selling partner as having a unitary basis in her partnership interests even if the interests were acquired at different times and represent different legal entitlements. In contrast, each share of corporate stock, albeit of the same class and acquired at the same time as other shares, is sometimes viewed as a separate ownership interest. See Fink v. Comm'r, 789 F.2d 427 (6th Cir. 1986), rev'd, 483 U.S. 89 (1987). The issue of unitary versus fragmented basis of partnership interests arises again in connection with the taxation of partnership distributions.

2. *Holding period.* Despite the general "unitary" treatment of a partnership interest, a partner must fragment her interest for holding period purposes. Thus, upon the sale or exchange of a partnership interest with a split holding period, the seller must calculate her long-term and short-term capital gain or loss from the sale based on the portion of the interest held for more than one year and the portion held for one year or less. Reg. § 1.1223-3(c)(1). Partners obviously have split holding periods in their interests if they acquire the interests at different times. In addition, however, partners obtain "tacked" holding periods when they contribute capital gain or section 1231 property to a partnership in exchange for a partnership interest, but not if they contribute other types of property. I.R.C. § 1223(1). Thus, if a partner contributes cash and a capital asset to a partnership in exchange for a partnership interest, the holding period of the portion of the interest received in exchange for the capital asset will include the contributing partner's holding period in that asset; the portion of the interest received for cash will have a new holding period. Going forward, the contributing partner will then need to keep track of these split holding periods.

3. *Closing of the partnership year.* If a partner sells her entire interest in a partnership, the taxable year of the partnership closes for the seller and she is allocated her distributive share of partnership items as of the time of the sale. See I.R.C. § 706(c)(2)(A); Reg. § 1.706-1(c)(2)(i). The passthrough of these items is then taken into account in determining the amount of her outside basis at that time. If the seller only sells a portion of her interest, the partnership taxable year does not end with respect to such partner. See I.R.C. § 706(c)(2)(B). As discussed in chapter six, however, the allocation of items must take into account such partner's varying interest in the partnership during the year, with the passthrough of items again affecting her outside basis and amount of gain or loss on the sale.

4. *Gifts.* Even a gift of a partnership interest may trigger recognition of gain, since the transferor is deemed to be discharged of her share of partnership liabilities. See Reg. § 1.1001-2(a)(4)(iii).

2. *The Look-Through Exception*

Read I.R.C. § 751(a). If a partnership holds hot assets consisting of "unrealized receivables" or "inventory items" at the time the partnership interest is transferred, the amount and character of the transferor's gain or loss is determined in part by looking through the partnership. A similar procedure is followed if the partnership holds lukewarm property—such as collectibles or section 1250 capital gain property—sale of which generates gain taxed at a higher rate than long-term capital gain. Such higher-taxed capital gain is referred to as "look-through capital gain." See I.R.C. § 1(h)(1), (5)(B), (6)(A), (9), and (10)(D); Reg. § 1.1(h)-1(a) and (b).

a. Definition of Unrealized Receivables and Inventory Items

Read I.R.C. § 751(c) and (d). As you can see, the terms "unrealized receivables" and "inventory items" are defined quite expansively to include essentially all assets that would generate ordinary income (including certain recapture items) or ordinary loss. The following case explores the potential breadth of these definitions.

Ledoux v. Commissioner

77 T.C. 293 (1981), aff'd per curiam, 695 F.2d 1320 (11th Cir. 1983)

STERRETT, Judge: [Petitioner was a partner of the Collins-Ledoux partnership whose principal asset was a long-term agreement to manage and operate a dog track owned by the Sanford-Orlando Kennel Club, Inc. Under the agreement, the partnership was obligated to pay the owner the first $200,000 of annual net profits from operating the track, with any remaining profits belonging to the partnership. The partnership's operation of the track was highly successful, with its net income increasing from $72,000 to over $550,000 between 1955 and 1972.

In 1972, petitioner sold his interest in the partnership to the other partners for $800,000, which represented five times his share of the partnership's 1972 earnings. Petitioner reported his gain from the sale as capital gain. The respondent determined that approximately $225,000 of the purchase price was attributable to petitioner's share of the tangible assets of the partnership. He claimed, however, that the income from the balance (about $575,000) related to petitioner's interest in the dog track agreement and should be reported as ordinary income as a result of section 751.]

... [W]e must decide whether any portion of the sales price is attributable to "unrealized receivables" of the partnership....

Petitioner contends that the dog track agreement gave the Collins-Ledoux partnership the right to manage and operate the dog track. According to petitioner, the agreement did not give the partnership any contractual rights to receive future payments and did not impose any obligation on the partnership to perform services. Rather, the agreement merely gave the partnership the right to occupy and use all of the [Sanford-Orlando] corporation's properties (including the racetrack facilities and the racing permit) in operating its dog track business; if the partnership exercised such right, it would be obligated to make annual payments to the corporation. . . . Thus, because the dog track agreement was in the nature of a leasehold agreement rather than an employment contract, it did not create the type of "unrealized receivables" referred to in section 751.

Respondent, on the other hand, contends that the partnership operated the racetrack for the corporation and was paid a portion of the profits for its efforts. As such, the agreement was in the nature of a management employment contract. When petitioner sold his partnership interest . . . in 1972, the main right that he sold was a contract right to receive income in the future for yet-to-be-rendered personal services. This, respondent asserts, is supported by the fact that petitioner determined the sales price for his partnership interest by capitalizing his 1972 annual income (approximately $160,000) by a factor of 5. Therefore, respondent contends that the portion of the gain realized by petitioner that is attributable to the management contract should be characterized as an amount received for unrealized receivables of the partnership. Consequently, such gain should be characterized as ordinary income under section 751.

The legislative history is not wholly clear with respect to the types of assets that Congress intended to place under the umbrella of "unrealized receivables." The House report states:

> The term "unrealized receivables or fees" is used to apply to any rights to income which have not been included in gross income under the method of accounting employed by the partnership. The provision is applicable mainly to cash basis partnerships which have acquired a contractual or other legal right to income for goods or services. . . .

In addition, the regulations elaborate on the meaning of "unrealized receivables" as used in section 751. Section 1.751-1(c), Income Tax Regs., provides:

> Sec. 1.751-1(c) Unrealized receivables. (1) The term "unrealized receivables," . . . means any rights (contractual or otherwise) to payment for—
>
> (i) Goods delivered or to be delivered (to the extent that such payment would be treated as received for property other than a capital asset), or
>
> (ii) Services rendered or to be rendered, to the extent that income arising from such rights to payment was not previously includible in income under the method of accounting employed by the partnership. Such rights must have arisen under contracts or agreements in existence at the time of sale or distribution, although the partnership may not be able to enforce payment until a later time. For example, the term includes trade accounts receivable of a cash method taxpayer, and rights to payment for work or goods begun but incomplete at the time of the sale or distribution. . . .

The language of the legislative history and the regulations indicates that the term "unrealized receivables" includes any contractual or other right to payment for goods delivered or to be delivered or services rendered or to be rendered. Therefore, an analysis of the nature of the rights under the dog track agreement, in the context of the aforementioned legal framework, becomes appropriate. A number of cases have dealt with the meaning of "unrealized receivables" and thereby have helped to define the scope of the term. Courts that have considered the term "unrealized receivables" generally have said that it should be given a broad interpretation. . . .

In *Roth v. Commissioner,* 321 F.2d 607 (9th Cir. 1963), affg. 38 T.C. 171 (1962), the Ninth Circuit dealt with the sale of an interest in a partnership which produced a movie and then gave a 10-year distribution right to Paramount Pictures Corp. in return for a percentage of the gross receipts. The selling partner claimed that his right to a portion of the payments expected under the partnership's contract with Paramount did not constitute an unrealized receivable. The court rejected this view, however, reasoning that Congress "meant to exclude from capital gains treatment any receipts which would have been treated as ordinary income to the partner if no transfer of the partnership interest had occurred." 321 F.2d at 611. Therefore, the partnership's right to payments under the distribution contract was in the nature of an unrealized receivable.

. . . [Another] example of the broad interpretation given to the term "unrealized receivable" is *United States v. Eidson,* 310 F.2d 111 (5th Cir. 1962), revg. an unreported opinion (W.D. Tex. 1961). The court there considered the nature of a management contract which was similar to the one at issue in the instant case. The case arose in the context of a sale by a partnership of all of its rights to operate and manage a mutual insurance company. The selling partnership received $170,000 for the rights it held under the management contract, and the Government asserted that the total amount should be treated as ordinary income. The Court of Appeals agreed with the Government's view on the ground that what was being assigned was not a capital asset whose value had accrued over a period of years; rather, the right to operate the company and receive profits therefrom during the remaining life of the contract was the real subject of the assignment. 310 F.2d at 116. . . .

In *United States v. Woolsey,* 326 F.2d 287 (5th Cir. 1963), revg. 208 F. Supp. 325 (S.D. Tex. 1962), the Fifth Circuit again faced a situation similar to the one that we face herein. . . . There, the court was faced with the sale of interests in a partnership which held, as one of its assets, a 25-year contract to manage a mutual insurance company. As in the instant case, the contract gave the partners the right to render services for the term of the contract and to earn ordinary income in the future. In holding that the partnership's management contract constituted an unrealized receivable, the court stated:

> When we look at the underlying right assigned in this case, we cannot escape the conclusion that so much of the consideration which relates to the right to earn ordinary income in the future under the "management contract," taxable to the assignee as ordinary income, is likewise taxable to the assignor as ordinary income although such income must be earned. Section 751 has defined "unrealized receivables" to include any rights, contractual or otherwise, to ordinary income from "services rendered, or to be rendered," (emphasis added) to the extent that the same were not previously includable in income by the partnership, with the result that capital gains rates cannot be applied to the rights to income under the facts of this case, which would constitute ordinary income had the same been received in due course by the

> partnership. . . . It is our conclusion that such portion of the consideration received by the taxpayers in this case as properly should be allocated to the present value of their right to earn ordinary income in the future under the "management contract" is subject to taxation as ordinary income. . . . [326 F.2d at 291.]

. . . The dog track agreement at issue in the instant case is similar to the management contract considered by the Fifth Circuit in *Woolsey*. Each gives the respective partnership the right to operate a business for a period of years and to earn ordinary income in return for payments of specified amounts to the corporation that holds the State charter. Therefore, based on our analysis of the statutory language, the legislative history, and the regulations and relevant case law, we are compelled to find that the dog track agreement gave the petitioner an interest that amounted to an "unrealized receivable" within the meaning of section 751(c).

Petitioner further contends that the dog track agreement does not represent an unrealized receivable because it does not require or obligate the partnership to perform personal services in the future. The agreement only gives, the argument continues, the Collins-Ledoux partnership the right to engage in a business.

We find this argument to be unpersuasive. The words of section 751(c), providing that the term "unrealized receivable" includes the right to payment for "services rendered, or to be rendered," do not preclude that section's application to a situation where, as here, the performance of services is not required by the agreement. As the Fifth Circuit said in *United States v. Eidson, supra*:

> The fact that . . . income would not be received by the [partnership] unless they performed the services which the contract required of them, that is, actively managed the affairs of the insurance company in a manner that would produce a profit after all of the necessary expenditures, does not, it seems clear, affect the nature of this payment. It affects only the amount. That is, the fact that the taxpayers would have to spend their time and energies in performing services for which the compensation would be received merely affects the price at which they would be willing to assign or transfer the contract. . . . [310 F.2d at 115.]

Consequently, a portion of the consideration received by Ledoux on the sale of his partnership interest is subject to taxation as ordinary income.

Having established that the dog track agreement qualifies as an unrealized receivable, we next consider whether all or only part of petitioner's gain in excess of the amount attributable to his share of tangible partnership assets should be treated as ordinary income. Petitioner argues that this excess gain was attributable to goodwill. . . .

With respect to goodwill, we note that petitioner's attorney drafted, and petitioner signed, the agreement for sale of partnership interest, dated October 17, 1972, which contains the following statement in paragraph 7:

> 7. In the determination of the purchase price set forth in this agreement, the parties acknowledge no consideration has been given to any item of goodwill.

The meaning of the words "no consideration" is not entirely free from doubt. They could mean that no thought was given to an allocation of any of the sales price to goodwill, or they could indicate that the parties agreed that no part of the purchase price was allocated to goodwill. The testimony of the attorney who prepared the document indicates, however, that he did consider the implications of the sale of goodwill and even did research on the subject. He testified that he believed, albeit incorrectly, that, if goodwill were part of the purchase price, his client would not be entitled to capital gains treatment.

Petitioner attempts to justify this misstatement of the tax implications of an allocation to goodwill not by asserting a mistake, but by pointing out that his attorney "is not a tax lawyer but is primarily involved with commercial law and real estate." We find as a fact that petitioner agreed at arm's-length with the purchasers of his partnership interest that no part of the purchase price should be attributable to goodwill. The Tax Court long has adhered to the view that, absent "strong proof," a taxpayer cannot challenge an express allocation in an arm's-length sales contract to which he had agreed. . . .

NOTES AND QUESTIONS

1. *What was the source of the taxpayer's income?* To be an unrealized receivable, a right to receive income from the performance of services or the sale of non-capital assets "must have arisen under contracts or agreements in existence at the time of sale." Reg. § 1.751-1(c)(1)(ii). Thus, for example, the sale of a partner's interest in a law practice does not result in ordinary income to the seller merely because, had the seller continued in the practice, she would have earned ordinary income from future services. On the other hand, if one of the assets of the partnership at the time of sale was a contractual agreement by a client of the firm to pay certain fees upon the firm's completion of a task, then the amount of the purchase price attributable to such asset would be subject to section 751(a).

What was the source of the taxpayer's income in *Ledoux*? Was it from a contract or agreement in existence at the time of the sale?

2. *Allocations in the sales agreement.* The section 751 regulations no longer give any deference to agreements between the parties allocating the purchase price to particular section 751(a) or non-section 751(a) assets. See T.D. 8847, 1999-2 C.B. 701. As discussed below, the amounts allocated to hot or lukewarm assets is based on a hypothetical sale of such assets by the partnership for fair market value. Any premium or discount in the overall purchase price is allocated entirely to assets other than hot or lukewarm ones, thereby increasing or decreasing the amount of the transferor's capital gain or loss.

3. *Depreciation recapture, section 1250 capital gain, and collectibles gain.* For purposes of sections 741, 751, and certain other provisions dealing with partnership distributions, the term unrealized receivables also includes potential depreciation

recapture from section 1245 property or section 1250 property. See I.R.C. § 751(c) (flush language, 1st sentence); Reg. § 1.751-1(c)(4)(iii) and (v). Section 751(c) treats such property as two separate assets: (1) a section 751(a) asset with a zero basis and a fair market value equal to the amount of the potential recapture, and (2) a non-section 751(a) asset consisting of the rest of the property. See Reg. § 1.751-1(c)(5). Rules similar to these also apply to determine the amount of section 1250 capital gain and collectibles gain upon a sale or exchange of a partnership interest because these gains are also taxed at a rate different from long-term capital gain. Section 1250 capital gain is essentially gain attributable to the unrecaptured portion of depreciation previously claimed with respect to section 1250 property, and collectibles gain is gain from the sale or exchange of a collectible, such as a work of art, an antique, a gem, stamp, or coin, held for more than one year. See Reg. § 1.1(h)-1(b)(1), (2)(i), and (3)(i).

4. *Overlapping definitions.* The section 751(d) definition of inventory items is quite broad and includes many unrealized receivables defined in section 751(c). See I.R.C. § 751(d)(2); Reg. § 1.751-1(d)(2)(ii). Under prior law, section 751 applied to a partnership's inventory items only if they were, in the aggregate, "substantially appreciated," and it was therefore important to know whether a particular asset constituted an inventory item, an unrealized receivable, or both. Congress has now repealed the "substantial appreciation" requirement, but only for purposes of section 751(a). Proposed regulations would also eliminate any overlap for purposes of section 751(b), which concerns partnership distributions. Prop. Reg. § 1.751-1(d)(1) (substantially appreciated inventory does not include unrealized receivables). Chapter eight discusses section 751(b).

5. *Installment sales.* Generally, a partner may report gain from an installment sale of a partnership interest under the installment method of section 453. If the partnership has appreciated section 751(a) assets, however, a portion of the selling partner's gain may not be eligible for installment reporting, on the theory that such assets would be ineligible if sold directly. See I.R.C. § 453(b)(2)(B) (gain from sale of inventory not eligible for installment reporting); Rev. Rul. 89-108, 1989-2 C.B. 100 (same result when interest in partnership holding inventory is sold). In Mingo v. U.S., 773 F.3d 629 (5th Cir. 2014), the court relied on the legislative history of section 751 to deny installment-sale treatment of gain from the sale of a partnership interest to the extent such gain was attributable to the partnership's unrealized receivables (an account receivable for services previously rendered). The court found that a disposition of "property," as required by section 453 (I.R.C. § 453(b)(1)), did not include disposition of an ordinary-income asset like the unrealized receivables. The extent of the required fragmentation for installment-sale purposes remains unclear, however. A full-fragmentation approach would seem to render superfluous provisions such as section 453(i)(2) that mandate only partial fragmentation (for recapture items) in determining installment-sale treatment of partnership interests. See also I.R.C. §§ 453A(e)(2) and 751(f).

b. Mechanics of the Look-Through Exception

Read Reg. § 1.751-1(a)(2). If, upon sale of a partnership interest, the partnership holds any unrealized receivables or inventory items, the character of the transferor's gain or loss is determined in the following manner. First, the transferor determines her overall gain or loss based on a pure entity approach to the transaction. Next, the transferor must look through the partnership to determine the amount of ordinary income or loss that would be allocated to her—taking into account any remedial allocations under Reg. § 1.704-3(d)—upon a "hypothetical sale" for cash of her share of the partnership's hot assets. Finally, the difference between the amount of the transferor's overall gain or loss under the entity approach and the amount of section 751 "look-through" ordinary income or loss is the residual capital gain or loss to the transferor. A similar procedure applies if the partnership holds lukewarm assets at the time of the sale. See Reg. § 1.1(h)-1(b)(2)(ii) and (3)(ii), -1(c).

Read Reg. §§ 1.751-1(g) (ex. 1) and 1.1(h)-1(f) (exs. 1, 2) and test your understanding of the mechanics of the look-through process by doing the following problem.

Problem 7-1:

(a) A (whose outside basis is $45) sells her partnership interest to D for $75 cash, when the ABC partnership has the following assets and no liabilities:

Assets	*Basis*	*BV*	*FMV*
Capital asset	30	30	60
Inventory #1	15	15	90
Inventory #2	90	90	75
Total	135	135	225

Assume that A has a one-third interest in all of the partnership's assets, income, and loss.

(i) What are the tax consequences of the sale to A?
(ii) Same as (i), except that Inventory #1 has a fair market value of $15 and the capital asset is worth $135 at the time of the sale.
(iii) Same as (i), except that Inventory #1 is a work of art qualifying as a "collectible."

(b) E (whose outside basis is $150) sells her partnership interest in the ABCDE accrual-method general partnership to F for $150 cash, when the partnership has recourse liabilities of $250 (allocated one-fifth to each partner) and the following assets:

Assets	*Basis*	*BV*	*FMV*
Cash	$100	$100	$100
Securities	100	100	250
Equipment*	50	50	80
Accts. Rec.	200	200	170
Inventory	300	300	400
Total	$750	$750	$1000

* includes $30 of depreciation recapture

The accounts receivable relate to services previously rendered by the partnership. Assume that E has a one-fifth interest in all of the partnership's assets, income, and loss.

(i) Determine the tax consequences of the sale to E.
(ii) Same as (i), except that the partnership originally purchased the equipment for $70 and had taken $20 of depreciation deductions by the time of the sale. See Reg. § 1.1245-1(a).

(c) A contributes inventory with a basis of $30 and a fair market value of $75 to the ABC partnership. B and C contribute $75 cash each to the partnership which purchases a capital asset for $150. When the value of the capital asset is $60 and the value of the inventory is $15, A sells her one-third partnership interest (with a basis of $30) for $25 cash. Assuming the partnership uses the remedial allocation method under section 704(c), what are the tax consequences of the sale to A?

C. Consequences to the Transferee

1. *The Entity Approach*

Read I.R.C. §§ 742, 1012, and 743(a). As with the transferor's tax consequences, the starting point for determining the consequences to the transferee is the entity approach. The transferee is treated as having acquired an interest in the partnership as a whole, analogous to corporate stock. If the transferee purchases the interest, the transferee obtains a cost basis in the interest (including her share of the partnership's liabilities). Unless the partnership makes an election or has a substantial built-in loss immediately after the transfer, the transaction has no effect on the transferee's share of the partnership's basis in its assets. Under the entity approach, the transferee simply "steps into the shoes" of the transferor with respect to those assets.

As illustrated by **example 7-2**, the entity approach may distort both the character and the timing of the transferee's income and loss:

Example 7-2: D acquires C's one-third interest in partnership ABC for $75 cash. At the time of the acquisition, ABC has the following assets and no liabilities:

Assets	*Basis*	*BV*	*FMV*
Capital asset	30	30	60
Inventory #1	15	15	90
Inventory #2	90	90	75
Total	135	135	225

Under the entity approach, D obtains a $75 basis in her partnership interest, but her share of inside basis remains unchanged. Thus, if the partnership were to sell all of its assets immediately following D's entry into the partnership, D would be allocated $10 of capital gain and $20 of ordinary income, representing D's one-third interest in the income and loss of the partnership. This result occurs even though there has been no change in the value of any of the assets since D's joining the partnership. Because the $30 of total income allocated to D increases her outside basis to $105, D has an offsetting, potential capital loss of $30 upon disposition of her interest ($105 outside basis less $75 value of the interest). But the timing and character of D's tax consequences are both incorrect.

What is the remedy for this problem? Note that while D in effect paid $30 for a one-third interest in inventory #1, D's share of the partnership's basis in that asset is only $5. Thus, there seems to be a shortfall in inside basis of $25 with respect to that asset. Suppose, therefore, the partnership's basis in each of its assets were adjusted to reflect the purchase price paid by D. For example, if the partnership's basis in inventory #1 were increased by $25 to $40 to take into account the shortfall, would the above distortions be eliminated?

The answer depends upon how the remaining $50 of income in inventory #1 ($90 value less $40 basis) would be shared. If upon sale of the inventory, D still must report a one-third share of the income, then it is clear that the problem persists. On the other hand, requiring the entire $50 of income to be allocated to the partners other than D would seem to remedy D's tax problem. Prior to D's entry into the partnership, the other partners owned a two-thirds interest in the partnership and were responsible for $50 of the $75 of gain inherent in inventory #1. The amount of their responsibility should not change when D purchases an interest in the partnership. Thus, following D's entry into the partnership, a $50 special allocation to the other partners of the income from inventory #1 would appear to be appropriate.

But a special allocation approach might be cumbersome if there are many partners in the partnership. Thus, as described in the next section, current law opts to make the basis adjustment personal to D, the purchaser. Instead of specially allocating income and loss to the other partners, current law in effect permits a special allocation of basis to the purchasing partner to give her the equivalent of a cost basis in her share of the partnership's assets.

NOTES AND QUESTIONS

1. *Effect on capital accounts.* When a taxpayer purchases a partnership interest from an existing partner, what is the effect of the transaction on the partnership's books and capital accounts? In particular, is there a required or permissible revaluation of the partnership's assets to fair market value? What is the purchasing partner's initial tax and book capital account? Read Reg. § 1.704-1(b)(2)(iv)(*f*) and (*l*) (1st sentence), -3(a)(7). Explain why the treatment of capital accounts in this situation differs from the result when a new partner joins a partnership through a contribution of cash or other property.

2. *Continuing distortions.* Suppose in **example 7-2**, immediately after purchasing her partnership interest (and there has been no change in the partnership's balance sheet), D sells the interest to E for $75. E, in turn, immediately sells the interest to F for $75, again when the balance sheet is unchanged. What is the amount and character of any gain or loss that D and E must report from their sales?

2. *The Look-Through Approach*

Read I.R.C. §§ 743(b) and 754. Similar to the tax treatment of the transferor, the consequences to the transferee may be determined by looking through the partnership. The transferee is treated as if she acquired an undivided interest in each of the partnership's assets, providing her with a special basis adjustment ("SBA") which increases or decreases her share of the common basis of the partnership in its assets. Unless the partnership has a substantial built-in loss immediately after the transfer, the look-through treatment of the transferee arises only if the section 754 election is in effect. When look-through treatment does not apply, the entity approach determines the transferee's tax consequences and may give rise to potential distortions to the character and timing of income.

Why isn't the look-through approach always required? One concern is that a completely mandatory look-through approach would impose excessive administrative burdens. As explained in the previous section, the SBA is personal to each purchaser and does not apply to the partnership's common basis in its assets. Partnerships therefore must potentially keep track of a separate SBA in each property for every partner who acquires a partnership interest from another partner. The look-through approach also requires that there be a valuation of all of the partnership's assets in order to allocate properly the total amount of the adjustment among the assets. Obviously, the administrative burden may be quite severe, depending upon how widely held the partnership is, the number and type of assets owned by the partnership, and the frequency of transfers.

Although the SBA normally affects only the transferee, the section 754 election must be made by the partnership. Thus, an election may be subject to negotiations between the transferor, the transferee, and the other partners of the partnership. Once made, the election applies to all subsequent transfers of partnership interests (and distributions of partnership property) unless revoked with permission of the IRS. Each subsequent purchaser calculates her SBA independently of prior transfers by reference to her outside basis and share of inside basis. Thus, a section 754 election can serve to eliminate disparities between inside and outside basis attributable to prior transfers when the partnership did not have a section 754 election in effect.

The section 754 election is generally beneficial if the partnership's assets have appreciated in value: a positive SBA reduces or eliminates the purchasing partner's share of built-in gain on a subsequent sale of such assets. Conversely, an election may be disadvantageous if the partnership's assets have declined in value: a negative SBA reduces or eliminates the purchasing partner's share of built-in loss on a subsequent sale of such assets. As previously noted and discussed in the last section of this chapter, however, look-through treatment is mandatory where the partnership has a substantial built-in loss at the time of the transfer. Thus, the overall tax effect of making a section 754 election is likely to be advantageous under current law. Moreover, the failure to make an election on transfer of a partnership interest (or death of a partner) can have undesirable consequences if a subsequent distribution triggers a mandatory downward basis adjustment, as discussed in chapter eight. In addition, as described in chapter twelve, the IRS has tools to scrutinize closely the collateral consequences of any failure to use the look-through approach.

Mechanically, the look-through approach is implemented in three steps. First, the overall amount of the transferee's SBA is determined. Second, the overall amount must then be allocated among each of the partnership's assets to determine the transferee's SBA with respect to each one. Finally, the transferee must take the SBA into account in determining her share of tax items arising from the partnership's property. We briefly discuss each step below.

a. Calculating the Overall SBA

Read I.R.C. § 743(b) and Reg. § 1.743-1(d). The overall SBA is equal to the difference between the purchasing partner's outside basis and her share of inside basis. The overall adjustment is positive if the purchasing partner's outside basis exceeds her share of inside basis and negative if the former is less than the latter.

The regulations define a partner's share of inside basis as the sum of her share of "previously taxed capital" plus her share of any partnership liabilities. The regulations posit a "hypothetical transaction," in which (immediately after the purchase) the partnership is deemed to sell all of its assets for their fair market value in a fully taxable transaction. The purchasing partner's share of previously taxed capital is equal to (i) the amount of cash she would receive on liquidation of the partnership following this hypothetical transaction and satisfaction of all of the partnership's liabilities, (ii) increased by her share of tax loss from the hypothetical transaction, and (iii) decreased by her share of tax gain from the hypothetical transaction. The net amount should generally be equal to the purchasing partner's inherited tax capital account. (Recall that "tax capital" also represents a partner's share of inside basis net of liabilities.)

Problem 7-2:

(a) Assume the same facts as **example 7-2**; at the time of D's acquisition of C's one-third interest for $75 cash, the partnership has the following expanded balance sheet:

Assets	*IB*	*BV*	*FMV*	*Capital*	*Tax*	*Book*	*FMV*
Capital asset	30	30	60	A	45	45	75
Inventory #1	15	15	90	B	45	45	75
Inventory #2	90	90	75	C	45	45	75
Total	135	135	225	Total	135	135	225

If the partnership has a section 754 election in effect, what is the overall amount of D's SBA?

(b) Same as (a), except that immediately before C's sale to D, the partnership borrowed $30 recourse and used the proceeds to purchase land worth $30. Assume that all partners share the liability equally.

(c) A contributes land with a basis of $100 and a fair market value of $600 and B and C contribute $600 cash each to the ABC general partnership in exchange for equal one-third partnership interests. The partnership borrows $300 recourse, which it uses to purchase securities; the partners share the recourse liability equally under section 752. When the land has appreciated in value to $900 and there is no other change in any of the other partnership assets and liabilities, D purchases A's partnership interest for $700 cash. Assuming that the partnership has a section 754 election in effect, what is the overall amount of D's SBA?

(d) Same as (c), except that D purchases B's one-third interest in the partnership instead of A's interest.

b. Allocation of Inside Basis Adjustments

Read I.R.C. §§ 743(c), 755(a) and (b); Reg. § 1.755-1(a)(1) and (b)(1)-(3). The rules governing the allocation of the overall section 743(b) adjustment (and basis adjustments resulting from a distribution) are found in section 755. That provision divides partnership assets into two classes, *viz.* "capital gain property" (capital assets and section 1231 quasi-capital assets) and "ordinary income property" (all other assets). The overall adjustment is initially allocated (i) between the two classes (capital and ordinary) and then (ii) among particular assets within each class. To determine the proper allocation, the section 755 regulations posit a hypothetical sale (analogous to the section 743(b) hypothetical transaction) in which the partnership, immediately after the transfer, sells all of its assets for fair market value. Reg. § 1.755-1(b)(1)(ii). The purchasing partner's distributive share of gain or loss on the hypothetical sale (including any remedial allocations under Reg. § 1.704-3(d)) then furnishes the starting point for allocating the overall adjustment.

Problem 7-3: F purchases E's one-fifth partnership interest for $150 cash when the partnership has recourse liabilities of $250 (allocated one-fifth to each partner) and the following assets:

Assets	*IB*	*BV*	*FMV*
Cash	240	240	240
Securities	10	10	80
Equipment*	50	50	110
Account receivable for services rendered	200	200	170
Inventory	300	300	400
Total	800	800	1000

* includes $30 of depreciation recapture

The partnership does not have any section 704(c) assets. At the time of the sale, E's tax capital account is $110. How much is F's overall SBA and how is the basis adjustment allocated among the partnership's assets?

When a buyer pays a premium for a partnership interest, i.e., an amount in excess of the seller's share of the fair market value of the assets shown on the balance sheet, a likely explanation is that the partnership has some zero-basis goodwill or going concern value not stated on its books. For purposes of allocating basis adjustments under sections 743(b) and 755, the "residual method" of valuing goodwill (or going concern value) applies. See I.R.C. § 1060(d); Reg. § 1.755-1(a)(2). Thus, if the purchase price exceeds the total fair market value of all identifiable tangible and intangible assets (other than goodwill and going concern value), the "excess" purchase price is allocated to goodwill and going concern value.

Problem 7-4:

(a) Same as **problem 7-3**, except that F pays $160 cash for E's interest.
(b) Same as **problem 7-3**, except that F pays $140 cash for E's interest.

c. Using the SBA

Under sections 703 and 704, the partnership determines and allocates its income or loss without regard to any section 743(b) adjustments. Once the partnership-level allocations are made, however, the partnership must adjust a partner's share of tax items to take into account any SBA the partner has with respect to the item allocated. The adjustment may increase or decrease the partner's share of the tax item. See Reg. § 1.743-1(j)(2) and (3). For example, if a partner is allocated $100 of gain from the sale of an asset and the partner has a positive $30 SBA with respect to that asset, the partner reports only $70 of gain from the sale and increases her outside basis by the same amount. If the partner's SBA were instead a negative $30, the partner would report $130 of gain from the sale and increase her outside basis by the same amount. The SBA is also taken into account in determining the partner's share of depreciation deductions and the basis of property distributed to her. See Reg. § 1.743-1(g), -1(j)(4) (treating any special basis increase as newly purchased property for depreciation purposes).

The section 743(b) adjustments are *for tax purposes only*. The purchasing partner reports her distributive share of partnership items (net of any section 743(b) adjustments) and adjusts her outside basis accordingly. The section 743(b) adjustments have no effect on the purchasing partner's tax or book capital accounts. Thus, in the preceding example, the partner would increase her tax and book capital accounts by her distributive share of gain from the sale of the asset (without regard to any section 743(b) adjustment). For capital account purposes, the positive or negative SBA is simply ignored. See Reg. § 1.743-1(j)(2). More generally, the impact of a transfer of interests on the partnership's capital accounts is the same, regardless of whether the partnership has a section 754 election in effect at the time of the transfer. See Reg. § 1.704-1(b)(2)(iv)(*m*)(*1*) and (*2*).

3. *Prevention of Loss Duplication*

The look-through approach is mandatory if the partnership has a "substantial built-in loss" immediately after the transfer, i.e., if the aggregate inside basis of its assets exceeds their fair market value by more than $250,000. See I.R.C. § 743(d)(1). The purpose of this rule is to prevent loss duplication. For example, suppose A and B each contributes $500,000 to form partnership AB which uses the money to purchase a $1 million piece of land. Suppose the land falls in value to $600,000 and B then sells her one-half interest in the partnership to C for $300,000, resulting in a $200,000 loss to B. In this situation, look-through treatment is mandatory to prevent the same built-in loss from being recognized by C if the partnership subsequently sells the land. Upon sale of the land for $600,000, C's negative SBA would eliminate her $200,000 share of the partnership's loss. C's outside basis would remain $300,000, since no loss would pass through to her. Of course, if the look-through approach had not applied and a loss had been passed through to C, it would have reduced her outside basis, potentially triggering offsetting gain upon the liquidation of the partnership or C's partnership interest. Current law, however, attempts to prevent even a temporary duplication of loss.

The threshold built-in loss amount of $250,000 is determined at the partnership level after netting together all of the partnership's assets. In the above example, even though B's share of the loss is only $200,000, the look-through approach is mandatory because the partnership has an aggregate built-in loss of $400,000. As illustrated by **example 7-3**, if a partnership holds assets with largely offsetting amounts of unrealized gains and losses at the time of a transfer of interests, the $250,000 threshold may not be satisfied even though a duplicate loss arises.

Example 7-3: A contributes $10 million and B contributes Blackacre (FMV of $10 million and AB of $2 million) for equal shares of partnership AB. The partnership uses the $10 million cash to purchase Whiteacre. A sells her partnership interest to C for $7 million when the value of the partnership's assets are as follows:

Assets	*Basis*	*FMV*
Blackacre	2,000,000	10,000,000
Whiteacre	10,000,000	4,000,000
Total	12,000,000	14,000,000

Since the unrealized built-in gain in Blackacre exceeds the built-in loss in Whiteacre, the partnership does not have a "substantial built-in loss" immediately after the transfer. Yet, A recognizes a $3 million loss upon sale of her partnership interest. If the partnership subsequently sells Whiteacre for $4 million, C (as A's successor) would be allocated a $3 million share of the partnership's loss in the absence of a section 754 election. The Treasury Department has broad regulatory authority to determine when a substantial built-in loss exists, including authority to disregard the "stuffing" of appreciated property into a partnership to circumvent mandatory application of the look-through approach. See I.R.C. § 743(d)(2); Prop. Reg. § 1.743-1(m) (anti-abuse rule).

Finally, even if look-through treatment is not elected (or required), section 704(c)(1)(C) prevents loss duplication in the hands of the transferee if the transferor previously contributed property to the partnership with a built-in loss. This provision applies if the contributed property contained a built-in loss of any amount; there need not be a "substantial" built-in loss at the time of the contribution or a later transfer of the partnership interest. As discussed in chapter six (pp. 181-82), a partner who contributes built-in loss property receives a section 704(c)(1)(C) adjustment (analogous to an SBA) that is equal to the amount of the built-in loss at the time of contribution. Prop. Reg. § 1.704-3(f)(2) and (3)(ii). Upon a taxable disposition of the section 704(c)(1)(C) partner's entire partnership interest, any remaining section 704(c)(1)(C) adjustment is eliminated, and the transferee does not step into the shoes of the section 704(c)(1)(C) partner. Prop. Reg. § 1.704-3(f)(3)(iii)(A). Read Prop. Reg. § 1. 704-3(f)(1), (2), (3)(ii)(A), (3)(iii)(A) and (C) (ex. 1) and do the following problem.

> **Problem 7-5:** A contributes land (FMV $60,000, AB $100,000) and B contributes $60,000 cash for equal shares of partnership AB. A then sells her one-half partnership interest to C for $60,000, when the value of the partnership's assets is unchanged. Assume that the partnership does not have a section 754 election in effect and has agreed to use the traditional method of allocation for purposes of section 704(c). What are the tax consequences of a subsequent sale of the land by the partnership for $50,000?

NOTES AND QUESTIONS

1. Suppose in **problem 7-5**, the land were subsequently sold for $70,000 instead of $50,000. Applying the proposed regulations, what would the results be to B and C upon sale of the land by the partnership? What result to A if the partnership sold the land for $70,000 before A's sale of her interest to C?

2. *Fair market value "at the time of contribution."* The proposed regulations treat the common tax basis of contributed built-in loss property in the partnership's hands as equal to its fair market value upon contribution for all purposes. Prop. Reg. § 1.704-3(f)(3)(ii)(A). In **problem 7-5**, suppose after its contribution to the partnership, the land fell in value to $50,000 and C then bought A's interest for $55,000, not $60,000. Under the proposed regulations, what result to B and C upon sale of the land by the partnership for $50,000? Compare your result to the outcome if there had been a section 754 election in effect at the time of the sale to C.

3. *Depreciable property.* If the contributed built-in loss property is depreciable, the section 704(c)(1)(C) adjustment will be recovered over time, and any cost recovery deductions attributable to the adjustment will be added to the section 704(c)(1)(C) partner's distributive share of partnership items. Prop. Reg. § 1.704-3(f)(3)(ii)(A) and (D)(*1*). Suppose A contributes depreciable property (FMV $50,000, AB $80,000) and B contributes $50,000 cash in exchange for one-half interests in the AB partnership. If the contributed property is depreciated under the straight-line method and has a remaining recovery period of five years, A and B will share equally the $10,000 of annual tax and book depreciation attributable to the common basis of the property ($50,000). In addition, A's section 704(c)(1)(C) adjustment ($30,000) will generate $6,000 of depreciation annually,

which will be taken into account only by A. Each year, A will report depreciation deductions of $11,000 ($5,000 plus $6,000) and B will report depreciation deductions of $5,000. At the end of five years, the partnership's common basis in the contributed property and the section 704(c)(1)(C) adjustment will both be reduced to zero. See Prop. Reg. § 1.704-3(f)(3)(ii)(D).

4. *Nonrecognition transfers.* A donee does not succeed to any portion of the contributor's section 704(c)(1)(C) adjustment. If a section 704(c)(1)(C) partner's interest is transferred in certain other nonrecognition transactions (including section 351, 721, and 731 transfers), the transferee succeeds to the transferor's section 704(c)(1)(C) adjustment and is treated as the section 704(c)(1)(C) partner. Prop. Reg. § 1.704-3(f)(3)(iii)(B)(*1*) and (*2*). The transferee partner's section 704(c)(1)(C) adjustment must be reduced, however, by any negative section 743(b) adjustment allocable to the transferee, regardless of whether the partnership has a section 754 election or a substantial built-in loss. See Prop. Reg. § 1.704-3(f)(3)(iii)(C) (ex. 3).

5. *Electing investment partnerships.* Mandatory look-through treatment is not required in the case of interests transferred in certain electing investment partnerships. Instead, the transferee's distributive share of losses is disallowed except to the extent the share exceeds the loss recognized by the transferor in the transfer. I.R.C. § 743(e)(1) and (2). Such loss disallowance achieves essentially the same result (albeit more crudely) than requiring the partnership and the transferee to determine an SBA with respect to each of the partnership's assets. The electing investment partnership must furnish to the transferee the necessary information concerning the amount of disallowed losses.

Chapter 8

Property Contributions and Distributions

A. Introduction

This chapter concerns the taxation of two common transactions—contributions of property by partners to partnerships and distributions of property by partnerships to partners. We consider these transactions together for two reasons. First, the policies behind their tax treatment are similar; in very general terms, Congress has tried to ensure that such transactions defer recognition of gains and losses to the maximum extent possible. As a result, the rules applicable to contributions and distributions are often quite similar and it is helpful to consider them together. Second, certain common transactions may implicate both the contribution and distribution rules at the same time. For example, a transaction involving encumbered property is often treated as in part, a contribution and in part, a distribution, with the ultimate tax consequences determined by netting the two effects.

Part B describes the basic rules for contributions and nonliquidating distributions, including contributions and distributions of encumbered property, and part C extends the discussion to consider distributions that completely liquidate the distributee's interest in the partnership. Parts D and E then discuss additional rules designed to prevent a distribution from changing the amount, character, and allocation of the partnership's gains and losses prior to the distribution.

This chapter concentrates on the governing rules when the form of the taxpayer's transaction—a contribution or distribution—is respected. To take advantage of favorable nonrecognition treatment, taxpayers sometimes seek to disguise other transactions as a contribution or distribution. The next chapter presents some responses aimed at unmasking these disguises.

B. Contributions and Nonliquidating Distributions

1. *Contributions*

Read I.R.C. §§ 721(a), 722-724. Under section 721(a), a contribution of property to a partnership in exchange for a partnership interest is generally a nonrecognition transaction with respect to both the contributor and the partnership. Any gain or loss realized but not recognized is preserved through the rules for determining inside basis (section 723) and outside basis (section 722). In certain situations, section 724 preserves the pre-contribution character of gain or loss inherent in the contributed property. This rule applies in varying ways to inventory items, unrealized receivables, and built-in capital loss property contributed to the partnership, as well as to "substituted basis property" (see I.R.C. § 7701(a)(42)) subsequently acquired by the partnership in exchange for such contributed property.

A partner generally takes a "tacked" holding period for a partnership interest acquired in a section 721 transaction, i.e., a holding period determined by reference to the holding period for the contributed property, if such property constitutes a capital asset or section 1231 asset. See I.R.C. § 1223(1). Regardless of the character of the contributed property, a partnership interest will generally be a capital asset in the contributor's hands. The partnership may also tack the contributor's holding period in determining its holding period in each transferred asset. See I.R.C. § 1223(2).

Problem 8-1:

(a) A, B, C, and D form the equal ABCD general partnership. Assume that all taxpayers use the cash-method of accounting. In exchange for their respective partnership interests, each partner contributes the following assets, each of which has been held for two years:

Partner	*Asset*	*Basis*	*FMV*
A	cash	5,000	5,000
	land	1,000	5,000
B	inventory	3,000	6,000
	equipment	0	4,000
C	securities	15,000	10,000
D	building	4,000	8,000
	installment note from sale of goodwill	0	2,000

(i) How much gain or loss is recognized by each partner and the partnership as a result of this transaction? What is each partner's outside basis and the partnership's basis in its assets immediately following the exchanges?

(ii) What is the character of any gain or loss recognized by the partnership upon sale of these assets two years after their contribution to the partnership? Six years after the contribution?

(iii) What is each partner's holding period in her partnership interest? The partnership's holding period in each asset? See Reg. § 1.1223-3(a), (b)(1), (e), and (f) (ex. 1).

(b) A, B, and C are equal partners in the ABC general partnership. The fair market value of a one-third interest in the ABC partnership is $15,000 and each partner has an outside basis of $5,000. Each partner contributes an additional $15,000 cash to the partnership, increasing the fair market value of each partner's interest to $30,000. How is the holding period of each partner's partnership interest determined following the additional contributions? See Reg. § 1.1223-3(f) (ex. 4).

NOTES

1. *Theory.* Neither an entity nor aggregate conception of a partnership requires that a partnership contribution be treated as a nonrecognition event. Under an entity theory, the transaction would seem generally to be a taxable event. There might properly be an exception to this result if the contributor has a sufficiently large interest in the partnership to warrant its treatment as her alter ego. Cf. I.R.C. § 351(a) (nonrecognition treatment of transfers to corporation where, immediately after the transfers, the transferors are in control of the corporation). But section 721(a) bestows a nonrecognition result no matter how large or small the contributor's interest in the partnership. Under an aggregate theory, the transaction would also seem to be a taxable event, at least to some extent—in part, it is an exchange of property by the contributor with the other partners of the partnership.

Nevertheless, nonrecognition treatment is often justified as necessary to mitigate lock-in concerns. Treating partnership contributions as taxable events might impose a barrier to the pooling of capital through partnership ventures.

2. *Contributions of "property" by persons acting as partners.* Section 721 only applies to contributions of "property" in exchange for a partnership interest. The term "property" is construed quite broadly to include cash, accounts receivables, installment obligations, and goodwill. If a partner contributes services rather than property, section 721 does not apply and the service partner may recognize ordinary income under section 61 upon receipt of a partnership interest. See chapter ten. Section 721 also only applies to transfers by persons acting in their capacity as partners of the partnership. See Reg. § 1.721-1(a). The tax consequences of transfers by partners acting in some other capacity is considered in chapter nine.

3. *Tax-free diversification.* Congress was also concerned that partnerships might serve as "swap funds" to permit taxpayers to achieve a tax-free diversification of their investments by contributing appreciated stock, securities or similar assets in exchange for a partnership interest. Section 721(b) blocks such attempts by requiring

the contributing partner to recognize gain (but not loss) on the contribution (with appropriate adjustments to inside and outside basis to reflect any gain recognized).

4. *Transfers to partnerships with related foreign partners.* Section 721(c) authorizes regulations overriding nonrecognition treatment under section 721(a) on certain transfers of property if the gain from such property, when recognized, will be includible in income of a non-U.S. person. See also I.R.C. § 367(d)(3). Recently, the Treasury announced that it plans to exercise this authority to require gain recognition on certain transfers to partnerships with related foreign partners unless specified conditions are satisfied. Notice 2015-54, 2015-34 I.R.B. 210. Future regulations would require immediate gain recognition, for example, when a U.S. person contributes appreciated intangibles to an offshore partnership (or a domestic partnership) with related foreign partners unless the partnership agrees to use the remedial allocation method and complies with other rules to prevent inappropriate shifting of built-in gain to the foreign partners.

2. *Nonliquidating Distributions*

A nonliquidating distribution is one that does not liquidate the distributee's entire interest in the partnership. Following a nonliquidating distribution, the distributee retains a continuing interest in the partnership, although her percentage interest may be reduced as a result of the distribution.

Read I.R.C. §§ 731(a) and (b), 732(a), 733, and 735. The provisions governing partnership nonliquidating distributions seek to defer the recognition of gain or loss, both to the partnership and the distributee partner, to the maximum extent possible. Hence, the provisions largely mirror those relating to partnership contributions. Similar to section 721(a), section 731(a) and (b) generally provides for the nonrecognition of gain (or loss) except to the extent any cash distributed exceeds the distributee's outside basis. Section 732(a)(1) then parallels section 723 by providing that the distributee generally takes a basis in distributed property equal to its former basis in the partnership's hands. Just as outside basis is increased under section 722 to reflect the basis of contributed property, section 733 requires a decrease in the distributee's outside basis (but not below zero) to reflect the amount of cash and the basis of other property distributed. Finally, by preserving the pre-distribution character of certain types of distributed property, section 735 plays a role similar to that of section 724 in connection with partnership contributions.

Problem 8-2: A and B are equal partners of partnership AB and each has an outside basis of $100. Determine the tax consequences of the following events to all parties.

(a) AB distributes capital assets *x* and *y*, each worth $90, to A and B, respectively. Just prior to the distributions, AB's basis in the two assets is $40 and $75, respectively.

(b) AB distributes $90 cash to each of A and B.

(c) AB distributes capital asset *z*, worth $150, to A. AB's basis in *z* is $40 prior to the distribution. Following the distribution, A and B share all partnership items in a 40:60 ratio.

(d) Same as (c), except that *z* is an "inventory item" (within the meaning of section 751(d)) that AB distributes equally to A and B. What are the tax consequences to A if she sells *z* three years after the distribution for $200? Seven years after the distribution? Does it matter whether *z* continues to be an "inventory item" in A's hands following the distribution?

NOTE AND QUESTION

1. *Section 732(a)(2).* In a nonliquidating distribution, the distributee's basis in any property received is the same as the partnership's basis, except that the basis of such property may not exceed the distributee's outside basis immediately prior to the distribution reduced by any cash received in the same transaction. See I.R.C. § 732(a)(2). The purpose and effect of this limitation is considered in connection with liquidating distributions, where the identical limitation exists. See I.R.C. § 732(b).

2. *Policy justification?* Is there a sufficient policy justification to support treating partnership distributions generally as nonrecognition events? What arguments might support full (or partial) recognition treatment for distributions? Keep these questions in mind particularly in studying this chapter and the following chapter.

3. Contributions and Distributions of Encumbered Property

a. Contributions of Encumbered Property

Review I.R.C. § 752 and read Reg. § 1.752-1(e). When encumbered property is contributed to a partnership, the partnership is treated as having assumed the liability (to the extent of the fair market value of the contributed property), which has two consequences. First, the decrease in the contributing partner's share of individual liabilities is treated as a deemed distribution of cash to her under section 752(b). It is as if the partnership had incurred the liability directly and distributed the proceeds to the contributing partner.

Second, the corresponding increase in partnership liabilities gives rise to an increase in the share of those liabilities on the part of some partners (including, possibly, the contributing partner). Under section 752(a), an increase in a partner's share of partnership liabilities is treated as a deemed contribution of cash. For the contributing partner, the deemed section 752(b) distribution and the deemed section 752(a) contribution are netted against one another. See Reg. § 1.752-1(f). As a result, a contribution of encumbered property is treated as a distribution of cash to the contributing partner only to the extent of her net decrease in liabilities (i.e., the decrease in the contributing partner's share of individual liabilities less any increase in her share of partnership liabilities).

Problem 8-3: A, B, and C form the equal ABC general partnership. A and B contribute $75 cash each and C contributes land with a fair market value of $150 and an adjusted basis of $50, subject to a recourse liability of $75. Assume that the partnership's recourse liabilities are allocated equally among the partners based on the economic risk of loss.

(a) What are the tax consequences of this transaction to A, B, and C?
(b) Same as (a), except that C's basis in the contributed property is $40 rather than $50.
(c) In (b), how might C avoid recognizing any gain in the transaction?
(d) Following the contributions in (a) and (b), determine the aggregate outside bases of the partners and compare that amount to the aggregate inside basis of the partnership in its assets. Are inside and outside basis equal in both cases? If not, can you explain the reason for any imbalance?

NOTES AND QUESTIONS

1. *Effect of the netting rule.* The effect of the netting rule is to minimize the possibility that a contributing partner will recognize gain under section 731 because of a shortfall in outside basis. See whether you can confirm that impact by determining the tax consequences to partner C in **problem 8-3(a)** if netting were not permitted.

2. *Impact on book and tax capital accounts.* Immediately after formation of the partnership in **problem 8-3(a)**, each partner should have a *book* capital account of $75, i.e., the value of each partner's contribution net of liabilities. See Reg. § 1.704-1(b)(2)(iv)(*b*).

The section 704(b) regulations unfortunately do not provide much guidance concerning the determination of a partner's *tax* capital account when encumbered property is contributed to a partnership. Recall that the spread between a partner's book and tax capital account should reflect the amount of section 704(c) gain attributable to that partner. Since a partner's book capital account must be reduced by the full amount of liabilities encumbering contributed property, a partner's tax capital account must presumably be reduced in a similar manner to preserve the proper section 704(c) spread. Following the contribution in **problem 8-3(a)**, therefore, C's tax capital account should be *negative* $25 ($50 basis of contributed property less $75 of liabilities encumbering the contributed property). The difference between C's tax capital account (negative $25) and C's book capital account ($75) is thus equal to the $100 of section 704(c) gain allocable to C.

3. *Share of the partnership liability.* Recall that a partner's share of partnership recourse liabilities is determined by how each partner would bear the economic risk of loss under a worst-case scenario in which the partnership disposes of all of its assets for no consideration in a taxable transaction, and then the partnership liquidates. See Reg. § 1.752-2(a) and (b)(1). Because the test attempts to measure a partner's share of *economic* loss, the amount of the loss from the deemed disposition is determined by the book value, rather than the tax basis, of the partnership's assets whenever those two amounts are different. See Reg. § 1.752-2(b)(2)(ii). See whether you can determine each partner's share of the liability in **problem 8-3(a)** under the assumption that the partners agree to share all losses equally.

A partnership is treated as assuming a liability encumbering contributed property even though the partnership does not become personally liable for the underlying obligation. See Reg. § 1.752-1(e). Thus, the rules described above are equally applicable to contributions of property subject to *nonrecourse* liabilities. The only difference concerns how the nonrecourse liability is shared. As explained in chapter five, nonrecourse liabilities are allocated according to three tiers: partnership minimum gain (PMG), minimum section 704(c) gain, and excess nonrecourse liabilities. In the case of property contributed to a newly formed partnership, only the second and third tiers are relevant since no PMG exists immediately after formation.[1]

> **Example 8-1:** In **problem 8-3(a)**, above, assume that the $75 liability encumbering C's property is nonrecourse. C is again deemed to be relieved of individual liabilities of $75 under section 752(b), since the partnership takes the property subject to the nonrecourse liability. Under the second tier, assuming that the partnership uses the traditional method for section 704(c) purposes, C is allocated $25 of the partnership's nonrecourse liability equal to her share of minimum section 704(c) gain ($75 liability less $50 basis of contributed property). Under the third tier, C may be allocated the remaining amount of the nonrecourse liability ($50) since it does not exceed her total remaining section 704(c) gain of $75 ($100 less $25 minimum section 704(c) gain). See Reg. § 1.752-3(a)(3). If C is allocated the entire $75 nonrecourse liability under the second and third tiers, C has no net increase or decrease in her share of liabilities ($75 relief of individual liabilities offset by $75 increase in share of

1. Recall that PMG is the amount of future *Tufts* gain that the partnership will realize upon disposition of its property securing nonrecourse liabilities in full satisfaction thereof and for no other consideration. See Reg. § 1.704-2(d)(1). But to prevent overlap between PMG and minimum section 704(c) gain, PMG is measured by the excess of the nonrecourse liability over the book value, and not the tax basis, of the property securing the liability, where tax basis and book value differ. See Reg. § 1.704-2(d)(3). Because the book value of contributed property is its fair market value at the time of contribution, and because any encumbrance on the property is taken into account only up to such fair market value, there cannot be any PMG in contributed property at the time of the contribution. Cf. Reg. § 1.752-1(e).

partnership liabilities). Thus, C's outside basis is equal to her basis in the contributed property ($50) and A and B have an outside basis of $75 each equal to their cash contribution.

Problem 8-4: In **example 8-1**, assume that the partners agree to allocate the excess nonrecourse liability according to their overall profit-sharing ratios (one-third each). Determine the tax consequences of the transaction to C (including C's outside basis after the transaction). How does your answer change if the partnership uses the remedial method for section 704(c) purposes?

b. Distributions of Encumbered Property

The rules for distributions of encumbered property mirror the rules for contributions of encumbered property. A distribution of encumbered property may trigger both a decrease in the distributee's share of partnership liabilities and an increase in her share of individual liabilities. Under section 752, any increases and decreases in the distributee's share of partnership liabilities are again netted against each other. Reg. § 1.752-1(f). The outside basis of the partners, including the distributee, is adjusted upward (or downward) to reflect the net increase (decrease) in the partners' share of liabilities. The following ruling explains the timing of these adjustments for purposes of determining the amount of gain recognized by the distributee and the amount of the distributee's outside basis available for allocation to the distributed property.

Rev. Rul. 79-205

1979-2 C.B. 255

ISSUES

When a partnership makes a nonliquidating distribution of property, (1) is a partner permitted to offset the increase in the partner's liabilities against the decrease in the partner's liabilities in determining the extent of recognition of gain or loss, and (2) is partnership basis adjusted before or after the property distribution?

FACTS

A and B are general partners in M, a general partnership, which was formed for the purposes of owning and operating shopping centers.

On December 31, 1977, M made nonliquidating distributions in a single transaction of a portion of its property to A and B. A and B are equal partners in M. M,

A and B are calendar year taxpayers. No assets of the type described in section 751(a) of the Internal Revenue Code of 1954 were distributed by M to either A or B.

Immediately prior to the distribution A had an adjusted basis for A's interest in M of 1,000*x* dollars, and B had an adjusted basis for B's interest in M of 1,500*x* dollars. The property distributed to A had an adjusted basis to M of 2,000*x* dollars, and was subject to liabilities of 1,600*x* dollars. The property distributed to B had an adjusted basis to M of 3,200*x* dollars and was subject to liabilities of 2,800*x* dollars. A's individual liabilities increased by 1,600*x* dollars by reason of the distribution to A. B's individual liabilities increased by 2,800*x* dollars by reason of the distribution to B. A's share and B's share of the liabilities of M each decreased by 2,200*x* dollars (1/2 of 1,600*x* + 1/2 of 2,800*x* dollars) by reason of the distributions. The basis and fair market value of the properties distributed were greater than the liabilities to which they were subject.

LAW

Section 705(a) of the Code provides, in part, that the adjusted basis of a partner's interest in a partnership shall be the basis of such interest determined under section 722 decreased (but not below zero) by partnership distributions as provided in section 733.

Section 722 of the Code provides, in part, that the basis of a partnership interest acquired by a contribution of money shall be the amount of such money.

Section 731(a)(1) of the Code provides that in the case of a distribution by a partnership to a partner gain shall not be recognized to such partner, except to the extent that any money distributed exceeds the adjusted basis of such partner's interest in the partnership immediately before the distribution.

Section 732(a)(1) of the Code provides that the basis of property (other than money) distributed by a partnership to a partner other than in liquidation of the partner's interest shall, except as provided in section 732(a)(2), be its adjusted basis to the partnership immediately before such distribution.

Section 732(a)(2) of the Code provides that the basis to the distributee partner of property to which section 732(a)(1) is applicable shall not exceed the adjusted basis of such partner's interest in the partnership reduced by any money distributed in the same transaction.

Section 733 of the Code provides that in the case of a distribution by a partnership to a partner other than in liquidation of a partner's interest, the adjusted basis to such partner of the interest in the partnership shall be reduced (but not below zero) by the amount of any money distributed to such partner and the amount of the basis to such partner of distributed property other than money, as determined under section 732.

Section 752(a) of the Code provides that any increase in a partner's share of the liabilities of a partnership, or any increase in a partner's individual liabilities by reason of the assumption by such partner of partnership liabilities, shall be considered as a contribution of money by such partner to the partnership.

Section 752(b) of the Code provides that any decrease in a partner's share of the liabilities of a partnership, or any decrease in a partner's individual liabilities by reason of the assumption by the partnership of such individual liabilities, shall be considered as a distribution of money to the partner by the partnership.

Section 752(c) of the Code provides that for purposes of section 752 a liability to which property is subject shall, to the extent of the fair market value of such property, be considered as a liability of the owner of the property.

ANALYSIS AND HOLDING

In general, partnership distributions are taxable under section 731(a)(1) of the Code only to the extent that the amount of money distributed exceeds the distributee partner's basis for the partner's partnership interest. This rule reflects the Congressional intent to limit narrowly the area in which gain or loss is recognized upon a distribution so as to remove deterrents to property being moved in and out of partnerships as business reasons dictate. See S. Rep. No. 1622, 83rd Cong., 2nd Sess., page 96 (1954). Here, since partner liabilities are both increasing and decreasing in the same transaction offsetting the increases and decreases tends to limit recognition of gain, thereby giving effect to the Congressional intent. Consequently, in a distribution of encumbered property, the resulting liability adjustments will be treated as occurring simultaneously, rather than occurring in a particular order. Therefore, on a distribution of encumbered property, the amount of money considered distributed to a partner for purposes of section 731(a)(1) is the amount (if any) by which the decrease in the partner's share of the liabilities of the partnership under section 752(b) exceeds the increase in the partner's individual liabilities under section 752(a). The amount of money considered contributed by a partner for purposes of section 722 is the amount (if any) by which the increase in the partner's individual liabilities under section 752(a) exceeds the decrease in the partner's share of the liabilities of the partnership under section 752(b). The increase in the partner's individual liabilities occurs by reason of the assumption by the partner of partnership liabilities, or by reason of a distribution of property subject to a liability, to the extent of the fair market value of such property.

Because the distribution was part of a single transaction, the two properties are treated as having been distributed simultaneously to A and B. Therefore, all resulting liability adjustments relating to the distribution of the two properties will be treated as occurring simultaneously, rather than occurring in a particular order.

TREATMENT OF PARTNER A

A will be deemed to have received a net distribution of 600*x* dollars in money, that is, the amount by which the amount of money considered distributed to A (2,200*x* dollars) exceeds the amount of money considered contributed by

A (1,600x dollars). Since 600x dollars does not exceed A's basis for A's interest in M immediately before the distribution (1,000x dollars), no gain is recognized to A.

Under section 732(a) of the Code, the basis of A of the property distributed to A is the lesser of (i) the adjusted basis of the property to the partnership (2,000x dollars), or (ii) the adjusted basis of A's partnership interest (1,000x dollars) reduced by the amount of money deemed distributed to A (600x dollars). Therefore, the basis of the property in A's hands is 400x dollars. Under section 733, the adjusted basis of A's partnership interest (1,000x dollars) is reduced by the amount of money deemed distributed to A (600x dollars) and by the basis to A of the distributed property (400x dollars). The adjusted basis of A's partnership interest is therefore reduced to zero.

TREATMENT OF PARTNER B

B will be deemed to have made a net contribution of 600x dollars, that is, the amount by which the amount of money considered contributed by B (2,800x dollars) exceeds the amount of money considered distributed to B (2,200x dollars). In applying sections 732(a) and 733 of the Code to B, the adjustment to B's basis in B's partnership interest attributable to the liability adjustments resulting from the distributions will be treated as occurring first, and the distribution of property to B as occurring second. By so doing, B's basis for the distributed property is increased and B's basis in B's partnership interest is decreased. This allocation gives greater effect to the general rule of section 732(a)(1), which provides for the partner to have the same basis in distributed property as the partnership had for that property.

Therefore, the first step is that B's basis for B's partnership interest (1,500x dollars) is increased under sections 722 and 705(a) by the amount of the net contribution deemed made by B (600x dollars), and is equal to 2,100x dollars. Next, under section 732(a) of the Code, the basis to B of the property distributed to B is the lesser of (i) the adjusted basis of the property to the partnership (3,200x dollars), or (ii) the adjusted basis of B's partnership interest (2,100x dollars) reduced by the amount of money deemed distributed to B (zero). Therefore, the basis of the property in B's hands is 2,100x dollars. Under section 733, the adjusted basis of B's partnership interest (2,100x dollars) is reduced by the amount of money deemed distributed to B (zero) and by the basis to B of the distributed property (2,100x dollars). The adjusted basis of B's partnership interest is therefore zero.

NOTE

Timing of deemed distributions resulting from decrease in liability shares. Rev. Rul. 94-4, 1994-1 C.B. 196, holds that the deemed cash distribution resulting from a decrease in a partner's share of partnership liabilities is treated as an advance or draw up to the amount of the partner's distributive share of income for the taxable year. Thus, the distributee's outside basis is first increased at year end by her distributive share of partnership income for the year before determining the consequences of the deemed distribution. Cf. Reg. § 1.731-1(a)(1)(ii).

Problem 8-5:

(a) Partner A, whose outside basis is $120, receives a nonliquidating distribution of $50 cash and a capital asset worth $175 (basis of $120), subject to a recourse liability of $90 (the partnership's only liability, which was formerly allocated one-third to A). As a result of the distribution, A's interest in the partnership is reduced from one-third to one-fifth. What is A's basis in the distributed property? How much gain or loss, if any, does A recognize under section 731(a)(1)? What is the effect of the distribution on the other partners?

(b) The ABC partnership has excess nonrecourse liabilities of $15,000 allocated equally to A, B and C. Each partner has an outside basis of $30,000 before taking into account any income, loss or distributions during the current year. At year end, A receives a nonliquidating distribution of $30,000 cash, which reduces her interest in the partnership (and her share of the partnership's excess nonrecourse liabilities of $15,000) from one-third to one-fifth. A's distributive share of income for the year is $2,000. What are the tax consequences of these events to A?

C. Liquidating Distributions

1. *Introduction*

A liquidating distribution is one that terminates the distributee's interest in the partnership. It may or may not involve a termination of the partnership itself. The tax consequences of partnership terminations are considered in chapter eleven.

Review I.R.C. § 731(a) and (b) and read I.R.C. § 732(b). Like the treatment of nonliquidating distributions, the provisions governing the taxation of liquidating distributions generally defer the recognition of gain or loss to both the partnership and the distributee. Because the distributee's interest in the partnership is terminated by the distribution, however, liquidating distributions sometimes present a special problem. **Example 8-2** illustrates this situation:

Example 8-2:

(a) In liquidation of her interest in the partnership, A receives a distribution of $200 cash and some capital-gain property worth $1,000. Just prior to the distribution, the partnership's basis in the property was $500 and A's outside basis was $1,100.

(b) Same as (a), except that the distribution is of ordinary-income property.

If these transactions were both *non*liquidating distributions, it would be (and is) easy to implement the policy of deferring the recognition of all gains and losses. In each case, A would simply inherit the partnership's basis ($500) and the character (capital gain or ordinary income) of the property distributed, and reduce her outside basis by $700 to $400. The $700 reduction equals the amount of the cash and the basis of the property distributed to her. See I.R.C. §§ 732(a)(1), 733, and 735.

It is also (fairly) easy to defer the recognition of gains and losses in **example 8-2(a)** even though it is a *liquidating* distribution. A's remaining outside basis of $400 can simply be added to her basis in the capital-gain property, giving A a $900 basis in such property. See I.R.C. § 732(b). In the transaction, A *realizes* capital gain of $100 (A receives cash and property worth $1,200 in exchange for a capital asset (her partnership interest) with a basis of $1,100), but does not *recognize* such gain. Instead, A ends up with $200 of cash and property with a lurking capital gain of $100 (A's $900 basis in capital-gain property worth $1,000). (As we will see in part D of this chapter, there should also be a change in the basis of the partnership's other assets to make sure the remaining partners are taxed correctly.)

This same solution may not be feasible, however, in **example 8-2(b)**. If A is given a $900 basis in the distributed ordinary-income asset, the amount of ordinary income built into the property might improperly be reduced, from $500 prior to the distribution ($1,000 value less partnership's basis of $500) to $100 after the distribution ($1,000 value less A's basis of $900).

To prevent this possible reduction in the amount of ordinary income, current law retreats from its general nonrecognition objective by requiring A to recognize a capital loss of $400 in **example 8-2(b)**. See I.R.C. § 731(a)(2). A's basis in the ordinary income property is thus limited to $500, the partnership's basis in such property. See I.R.C. § 732(c)(1)(A).

In this situation, recognition of a $400 capital *loss* may seem counterintuitive because, as we have seen, the distributee actually realizes an overall *gain* of $100 from the distribution. Nevertheless, the purpose of the loss-recognition rule of section 731(a)(2) is to prevent a distribution from reducing potential ordinary income in the future. This rule only applies where necessary to achieve that particular end. Thus, section 731(a)(2) allows recognition of loss only in the case of a *liquidating* distribution, and even then only when the distributee receives solely cash, section 751(a) assets (i.e., unrealized receivables and inventory), or a combination thereof. If the distributee receives any non-section 751(a) assets other than cash in a liquidating distribution, the basis of such other property is increased to account for any remaining outside basis. The next section describes how such basis increases are allocated. (In contrast, in a *non*liquidating distribution, loss is never recognized and the distributee can never obtain a basis in the distributed property greater than the partnership's basis in the property.)

Finally, the discussion thus far has focused on the situation where the distributee's outside basis is greater than the amount of cash plus the inside basis of any property distributed. What happens in the opposite situation, where outside basis is less than the sum of cash and the inside basis of property distributed? In that case, nonrecognition treatment applies but the inside basis of the properties distributed must be reduced to conform to the amount of available outside basis. The allocation of such decreases in basis, which may arise in either a liquidating or nonliquidating distribution, is also described in the next section.

Problem 8-6: Partner B, whose outside basis is $250, receives a liquidating distribution of $100 cash and inventory with a basis of $50 and a fair market value of $100. What are the tax consequences of the distribution to B?

2. *Basis of Distributed Property*

Consistent with the general nonrecognition objective, the starting point of the distribution rules is to provide the distributee with a transferred basis (if possible) in any distributed property equal to the partnership's basis in such property. As you recall, this "starting point" is also the ending point for many (perhaps most) nonliquidating distributions. See I.R.C. § 732(a)(1).

For liquidating distributions, this starting point must be adjusted upward or downward to take into account the amount of the distributee's outside basis at the time of the distribution. Since a liquidating distribution terminates the distributee's interest in the partnership, the distributee must end up ultimately with a total basis in any properties distributed (other than cash) equal to outside basis less any cash distributed. Indeed, the statute so provides. Read I.R.C. § 732(b). As a conceptual matter, however, it may be helpful to think of this ending point as equal to transferred basis with appropriate upward or downward adjustments. As illustrated in **example 8-2(a)**, an upward adjustment arises when outside basis exceeds the amount of cash plus the sum of the transferred bases of the properties distributed; the upward adjustment equals the amount of such excess. A downward adjustment occurs in the opposite situation; the downward adjustment equals the amount of the shortfall in outside basis. A downward adjustment is also necessary in a nonliquidating distribution when there is insufficient outside basis. See I.R.C. § 732(a)(2). An upward adjustment never occurs in a nonliquidating distribution. Be sure that you understand why.

Example 8-3: Partner C, with an outside basis of $180, receives a distribution of $100 cash and a capital asset whose basis to the partnership was $30 just prior to the distribution.

(a) If the distribution is nonliquidating, C first reduces her outside basis to $80 to reflect the cash distributed. She then takes a transferred basis in the capital asset of $30 and has a remaining outside basis of $50 after the distribution. I.R.C. §§ 732(a)(1), 733.

(b) If the distribution is liquidating, C takes an $80 basis in the capital asset. I.R.C. § 732(b). This basis might be thought of as the transferred basis in the asset ($30) increased by the "excess" outside basis ($50).

(c) In the case of either a liquidating or nonliquidating distribution, if C's outside basis is only $110, C takes a $10 basis in the capital asset. I.R.C. §§ 732(a)(2), 732(b). This basis might be thought of as the transferred basis in the asset ($30) reduced by the "shortfall" in outside basis ($20), i.e., the amount by which outside basis is less than the sum of the cash and the transferred basis of the capital asset. If the distribution is non-liquidating, outside basis is reduced to zero. I.R.C. § 733.

The following sections briefly describe how the upward and downward adjustments are allocated when the distributee receives more than one property eligible for an adjustment.

a. Allocation of Upward Adjustments

Read I.R.C. § 732(c)(1) and (2). As discussed previously, an upward adjustment may only occur in a liquidating distribution where the distributee receives a non-section 751(a) asset other than cash. In that case, the adjustment applies only to the non-section 751(a) asset. If more than one non-section 751(a) asset is received, the amount of the increase is first allocated to such assets in proportion to their unrealized appreciation (to the extent thereof), and any remaining increase is allocated to such assets in proportion to their relative fair market values. The theory of the allocation rule is to try to spread any basis increase as much as possible among *appreciated* non-section 751(a) assets, thereby eliminating built-in gains. Of course, if there are no appreciated non-section 751(a) assets, the upward adjustment may actually increase the difference between basis and value (i.e., increase the amount of any built-in loss).

b. Allocation of Downward Adjustments

Read I.R.C. § 732(c)(1) and (3). Unlike upward basis adjustments, downward adjustments may apply to both section 751(a) assets and non-section 751(a) assets. The statute provides an ordering rule that requires the distributee to allocate her outside basis first to any cash distributed, then to any section 751(a) assets distributed (up to the partnership's basis in such assets), and finally to any non-section 751(a) assets distributed. Implicitly, this means that downward adjustments to the basis of distributed property (below the partnership's basis in such property) must be made to non-section 751(a) assets before they are made to section 751(a) assets. Read carefully the convoluted statutory provision to confirm these results.

The ordering rule seeks to preserve the distributee's basis in section 751(a) assets as much as possible.[2] Thus, the basis of section 751(a) assets will be unchanged in the distributee's hands as long as the distributee's total outside basis (reduced by any cash received in the distribution) is at least equal to the partnership's basis in distributed section 751(a) assets. If outside basis is insufficient, the distributee will assign all of her available outside basis (after taking into account any cash received) to distributed section 751(a) assets. At this point, the distributee's outside basis will be "exhausted" and any distributed non-section 751(a) assets will necessarily take a zero basis in the distributee's hands.

Within any particular class of assets, any decrease (below the partnership's basis in the distributed assets) is allocated first to assets with unrealized depreciation (i.e., built-in loss) in proportion to their unrealized depreciation (to the extent thereof), and then to all of the assets in the class in proportion to their adjusted basis (after reduction for any unrealized depreciation). The allocation rule therefore attempts as much as possible to eliminate built-in losses.

Example 8-4: Partner A, whose outside basis is $40, receives a liquidating distribution of two non-section 751(a) assets: X worth $20 (partnership basis of $30) and Y worth $60 (partnership basis of $30). Since A's outside basis ($40) is less than the partnership's total basis in both assets ($60), A must reduce (by the $20 shortfall) her basis in the distributed assets whose total basis in A's hands cannot exceed $40. Because X and Y belong to the same class (non-section 751(a) assets), they can be considered together. Tentatively, X and Y are each assigned a $30 basis in A's hands (their pre-distribution basis in the partnership's hands) and then the basis of each asset is reduced to reflect the $20 shortfall in A's outside basis. The total basis decrease ($20) is allocated first to X to the extent of X's unrealized depreciation ($10), initially reducing A's basis in X to $20. The remaining decrease ($10) is allocated $4 to X ($10 × ($20/$50)) and $6 to Y ($10 × ($30/$50)) in proportion to their bases (after reduction for any unrealized depreciation). Accordingly, A takes a basis of $16 in X ($30 less $14 decrease) and a basis of $24 in Y ($30 less $6 decrease).

If A received solely section 751(a) assets with the same basis and fair market value as X and Y, the result would be identical. If, instead, X were a section 751(a) asset and Y a non-section 751(a) asset, then it would be necessary to consider each class of assets separately. A's outside basis ($40) would be assigned first to X (the section 751(a) asset); A, thus, would take a $30 basis in X equal to the partnership's pre-distribution basis. A's remaining unused outside basis ($10) would then be assigned to Y (the non-section 751(a) asset), reducing Y's basis in A's hands from $30 to $10. Thus, the

2. This basis could be fully preserved by requiring the distributee to recognize capital gain in lieu of reducing the basis of section 751(a) assets below their pre-distribution basis; the gain would be the amount of any basis decrease in such assets that would otherwise occur. Such gain recognition would be the mirror image of loss recognition under section 731(a)(2) but is not authorized by the law.

downward basis adjustment (to account for the $20 shortfall in A's outside basis) would fall entirely on asset Y (the non-section 751(a) asset).

Problem 8-7:

(a) Assume the same facts as in **example 8-4**, except that A receives cash of $5 and inventory worth $40 (basis of $40) in addition to the two non-section 751(a) assets, X and Y. What is A's basis in the assets distributed to her?

(b) Same as (a), except that A's outside basis is $143 prior to the distribution.

(c) Partner B, whose outside basis is $50, wishes to liquidate her interest in the ABC partnership. Her ratable share of the partnership's assets consists of nonmarketable securities worth $36 (basis of $15) and depreciable property worth $9 (basis of $15). (Assume that there is no depreciation recapture in this property.) What is B's basis in each asset if she receives a single liquidating distribution? If she were to receive a nonliquidating distribution of the securities in the current year and a liquidating distribution of the depreciable property in the next year? Assume that, in the latter case, the two distributions are not collapsed into a single liquidating distribution.

NOTES

1. *Prior law.* The current version of section 732(c) was enacted in 1997. Although the pre-1997 version was simpler, it potentially provided an opportunity for tax-advantageous shifting of basis among different assets. See Reg. § 1.701-2(d) (exs. 10, 11) (reflecting the pre-1997 version of section 732(c)). For example, a portion of the distributee's outside basis might be shifted from nondepreciable assets to depreciable assets or an artificially high basis might be allocated to an asset that the distributee planned to sell. Since the pre-1997 version of section 732(c) clearly contemplated uneconomic results for the sake of administrative convenience, it is possible that such basis manipulation could not be curbed by the general anti-abuse rules of section 701.

2. *Determining fair market values.* Note that the section 704(b) capital-account rules require the partnership to determine the fair market value of distributed property. Such a determination is necessary to book up or down any unrealized appreciation or depreciation inherent in such property immediately before the distribution. In light of this requirement, how much more burdensome is current section 732(c) than its predecessor? How accurate are such determinations of fair market value likely to be?

3. *Special basis adjustments (SBAs) and possible basis shifts.* Remember SBAs? These are the section 743(b) basis adjustments in partnership assets that are personal to a particular partner who acquires an interest in the partnership when the

partnership has a section 754 election in effect or has a substantial built-in loss. When property subject to an SBA is distributed to the purchasing partner, the distributee's initial transferred basis in the property takes into account the amount of the SBA. See Reg. §§ 1.732-2(b), 1.743-1(g)(1)(i). If such property is distributed to a different partner, however, that distributee cannot take into account the purchasing partner's SBA. Instead, the SBA remains personal to the purchasing partner and may be shifted to other retained partnership property. Reg. §§ 1.743-1(g)(2), 1.732-2(b) (example). Finally, if the purchasing partner's interest is completely liquidated, the amount of any SBA allocable to undistributed property is reallocated to property received in the liquidating distribution. If such reallocation is impossible (for example, the liquidating distribution consists solely of cash), then the amount of the SBA left behind is added to the common basis of the partnership's retained property for the benefit of all of the remaining partners. Reg. §§ 1.743-1(g)(3), 1.734-2(b)(1). Care must be taken in applying all of these rules. Other partnership distribution rules are designed to prevent such basis shifts from changing the character of any income or loss recognized or preserved following the distribution.

4. *Distributions of section 704(c)(1)(C) property.* Recall that a partner who contributes built-in loss property receives a personal basis adjustment (equal to the amount of the built-in loss) with respect to the contributed section 704(c)(1)(C) property. If the built-in loss property is distributed to the contributing partner, the section 704(c)(1)(C) basis adjustment is taken into account in determining the basis of the distributed property in the distributee's hands. Prop. Reg. §§ 1.704-3(f)(3)(v)(A) and (C); 1.732-2(c)(1). If the section 704(c)(1)(C) property is distributed to another partner, the basis adjustment does not carry over to the distributee; except to the extent that the distribution triggers the "mixing bowl" rules (discussed in chapter nine), the basis adjustment is instead reallocated to other partnership property for the benefit exclusively of the contributing partner. Prop. Reg. § 1.704-3(f)(3)(v)(B) and (D) (ex. 2). If the contributing partner's interest is completely liquidated, any basis adjustment allocable to undistributed section 704(c)(1)(C) property must generally be reallocated to distributed property of like character to the undistributed property. Prop. Reg. § 1.704-3(f)(3)(v)(C). If no such reallocation is possible, the common basis of the partnership's property is increased by the amount of the basis adjustment. If the distribution also results in a negative adjustment to partnership basis under section 734(b) (discussed in part D below), only the net amount of the two adjustments is allocated to the partnership's assets. Prop. Reg. § 1.734-2(c)(2) and (3) (exs. 3(ii), 4(ii)).

5. *Section 732(d).* What happens if no elective (or mandatory) section 743(b) adjustments were made when the purchasing partner acquired her interest? Read I.R.C. § 732(d). This provision permits a distributee who receives a distribution within two years of acquiring her interest to obtain by election the same SBA she would have received if section 743(b) adjustments had been made. This is a minor relief provision for taxpayers who, for example, buy into a partnership without a section 754 election and are thereby forced to forgo a favorable basis adjustment. If property that would have been subject to the favorable adjustment is distributed to

them within two years of their acquisition, they can elect independently to obtain the favorable basis adjustment.

The adjustment permitted by section 732(d) is mandatory (whether or not the distribution occurs within two years of the acquisition) if the fair market value of partnership property (other than money) exceeds 110 percent of its basis at the time of the acquisition and certain other conditions are satisfied. See I.R.C. § 732(d) (last sentence); Reg. § 1.732-1(d)(4) (setting forth additional conditions). As suggested by the additional conditions in the regulations, mandatory application of section 732(d) is intended to prevent a shifting of basis from nondepreciable property to depreciable property in connection with a distribution. The 1997 changes in section 732(c) should lessen the need for mandatory section 732(d) basis allocations.

D. Partnership Basis Adjustments

1. *Introduction*

The distribution rules described thus far have focused almost exclusively on the consequences of the transaction to the *distributee*. In general, the distributee's outside basis just prior to the distribution controls the amount of gain or loss recognized by her and her basis in any properties distributed. The upward or downward basis adjustments, for example, ensure that any gain or loss not recognized by the distributee in the transaction is preserved for future recognition. But a distribution may also affect the tax consequences of the other partners, as illustrated by **example 8-5**:

Example 8-5: Equal partnership ABC distributes $300 cash to partner A in complete liquidation of her partnership interest. Immediately before the distribution, each partner had a basis of $200 in her partnership interest and the partnership's balance sheet was as follows:

Assets	*IB*	*BV*	*FMV*	*Capital*	*Tax*	*Book*	*FMV*
cash	300	300	300	A	200	200	300
land #1	90	90	300	B	200	200	300
land #2	210	210	300	C	200	200	300
Total	600	600	900	Total	600	600	900

As we have discussed, A must recognize $100 gain in the distribution. See I.R.C. § 731(a)(1). This result is precisely correct for A, whose $100 of realized gain in the transaction cannot be deferred for later recognition. But what about B and C, the remaining partners? Prior to the distribution, they each had a $100 share of the unrealized gain in the partnership's assets. Following the distribution, however, the partnership's only assets are the two parcels of land, which have total unrealized gain of $300. The distribution has therefore increased B's and C's share of the partnership's unrealized gain from $100 to $150 each.

Suppose that instead of the cash, the partnership distributes land #1 to A in complete liquidation of her interest. In that case, as discussed in part C, A does not recognize any gain or loss but must increase her basis in land #1 to $200. See I.R.C. §§ 731(a), 732(b). Once again, this result is precisely correct for A, given the underlying nonrecognition policy. Her realized gain of $100 is not recognized in the transaction but is preserved for future recognition in land #1. Moreover, the character of the preserved gain (capital gain) corresponds to the character of the gain realized (capital gain). But what about B and C? As you can see, each continuing partner's share of the partnership's remaining unrealized gain after the distribution is now only $45 (half of the built-in gain in retained land #2).

Example 8-5 illustrates that when a disproportionate amount of the partnership's "high-basis" property (like the cash in the first situation) is distributed, the amount of basis that remains behind in the partnership is "too little." The remaining partners' share of the partnership's unrealized gain therefore increases (or their share of unrealized loss decreases). Conversely, when a disproportionate amount of "low-basis" property (like land #1 in the second situation) is distributed, the remaining partners' share of the partnership's unrealized gain decreases (or their share of unrealized loss increases). Under current law, a distribution generally carries out a "disproportionate" amount of basis whenever the total basis of the distributed property is more or less than the distributee's outside basis. In the first situation, A received $300 in cash even though her outside basis was only $200. In the second situation, she received land with a basis of $90 even though her outside basis was again $200.

To address this problem, current law provides a mechanism for the partnership to adjust the basis of its assets following a distribution to reflect any gain (or loss) recognized by the distributee and any changes (upward or downward) to the basis of distributed assets. These basis adjustments are triggered only if (1) the partnership has a section 754 election in effect or (2) the partnership has a "substantial basis reduction" as discussed below. Read I.R.C. §§ 734, 754. Unlike the section 743(b) adjustment we encountered earlier, the section 734(b) adjustment is easier to administer; rather than being personal to a particular partner, it applies instead to the common basis of the partnership in its assets.

The following two sections briefly discuss the amount of the authorized adjustment and its allocation among the assets of the partnership. The last section briefly describes a technical defect in the current section 734(b) adjustment.

2. *Amount of Section 734(b) Adjustment*

Review I.R.C. § 734(b). If a section 754 election is in effect, a partnership must *increase* the basis of its assets by (1) the amount of any gain recognized by the distributee in the distribution, and (2) any amount by which the distributee is required to reduce her basis in the distributed properties below their transferred basis. Since the partnership has distributed a disproportionate amount of "high-basis" property in both situations, it must increase the basis of its remaining assets. Conversely, partnerships must *decrease* the basis of their assets by (1) the amount of any loss recognized by the distributee, and (2) any amount by which the distributee is required to increase her basis in the distributed properties above their transferred basis. Since the partnership has distributed a disproportionate amount of "low-basis" property in both situations, it must reduce the basis of its remaining assets. The reduction in the partnership's basis in its assets may arise as a result of a section 754 election or may be required, even in the absence of an election, if the distribution would otherwise leave the partnership with "too much basis." Thus, a mandatory basis adjustment is required to the extent that a section 754 election (if one were in effect) would result in a net downward adjustment under section 734(b) to the partnership's remaining property in excess of $250,000. I.R.C. § 734(d)(1) (defining "substantial basis reduction").

3. *Allocation of Section 734(b) Adjustment Among the Assets of the Partnership*

Read I.R.C. § 755(a) and (b) and Reg. § 1.755-1(c). The general objective of the allocation rules is to preserve the proper character of any gains or losses following the distribution. The partnership property is first divided between capital gain property (capital assets and section 1231 quasi-capital assets) and ordinary-income property (all other assets). The amount of any basis increase or decrease is then allocated to a particular class based upon the reason for the section 734(b) adjustment. If the adjustment is triggered by the distributee's recognition of gain or loss, which necessarily is *capital* gain or loss, then the amount of the adjustment is allocated exclusively to the partnership's capital gain property. Similarly, if the adjustment is triggered by the distributee's increasing or decreasing the basis of distributed capital gain property above or below its transferred basis, then the amount of the adjustment is likewise allocated exclusively to the partnership's capital gain property. Finally, if the adjustment is triggered by the distributee's decreasing the basis of distributed ordinary-income property, then the amount of the adjustment is allocated exclusively to ordinary-income property.

The allocation of an adjustment among assets within the same class (capital gain or ordinary income) follows the same rules as in section 732(c). The amount of any basis *increase* is first allocated to the assets of the same class in proportion to their unrealized appreciation (to the extent thereof), with any remaining increase allocated to such assets in proportion to their relative fair market values. The amount of any basis *decrease* is first allocated to the assets of the same class in proportion to their unrealized depreciation (to the extent thereof), with any remaining decrease allocated to such assets in proportion to their relative bases. Like section 732(c), the theory behind this allocation rule is to eliminate built-in gain (or loss) in the partnership's assets as much as possible. Like section 732(c), the section 734(b) adjustment also appropriately permits a "wrong-way adjustment," i.e., an adjustment that increases the disparity between basis and fair market value of partnership assets. If, for example, a basis decrease is required but the only properties eligible for basis adjustment all have built-in gains, the downward adjustment will increase the amount of the built-in gains. Finally, the basis of any partnership asset may not be reduced below zero; the adjustment is held in abeyance (and applied to subsequently acquired property) if the partnership lacks assets of the requisite character or such property has an insufficient basis to absorb the adjustment.

Problem 8-8:

(a) Review the facts of **example 8-5**. If the partnership has a section 754 election in effect, what is the basis of its assets following the cash distribution to A? Does this result treat the remaining partners appropriately?

(b) Same as (a), except that the partnership distributes land #2 instead of the cash.

(c) Same as (a), except that the partnership distributes land #1 instead of the cash.

(d) Suppose that in lieu of a liquidating distribution to A, the partnership in **example 8-5** makes three *non*liquidating distributions: $100 cash to A, a $100 portion of land #1 (with an inside basis of $30) to B, and a $100 portion of land #2 (with an inside basis of $70) to C. Answer the same questions as in part (a) and then read Reg. § 1.704-1(b)(2)(iv)(*e*)(*1*) and (*f*)(*5*)(*ii*). Do the cited regulations suggest another way to address this situation?

(e) Partnership ABC distributes $400 cash to partner A in complete liquidation of her partnership interest. Immediately before the distribution, A has a basis of $700 in her partnership interest and the partnership's balance sheet is as follows:

Assets	*IB*	*BV*	*FMV*	*Capital*	*Tax*	*Book*	*FMV*
cash	450	450	450	A	700	700	400
inventory	150	150	150	B	700	700	400
land #1	600	600	300	C	700	700	400
land #2	900	900	300				
Total	2100	2100	1200	Total	2100	2100	1200

If a section 754 election is in effect, what is the partnership's basis in its assets after the distribution?

NOTES AND QUESTIONS

1. *The need for wrong-way adjustments.* Consider the basis consequences of nonrecognition treatment for like-kind exchanges under section 1031. Is it clear why wrong-way adjustments are necessary under section 734(b) to preserve unrealized appreciation (or depreciation) in retained assets?

2. *Should basis adjustments be made mandatory?* As a result of recent amendments to sections 734 and 743, the basis adjustments under sections 734(b) and 743(b) remain elective generally only in those situations in which an election would be advantageous to taxpayers. Do partially mandatory basis adjustments represent a reasonable compromise between protecting the government's interest while still allowing taxpayers some flexibility to avoid the complexities associated with such adjustments? A purchasing partner who is disadvantaged by the absence of a section 754 election should take that consequence into account in negotiating the terms of the purchase. Perhaps, experience with partially mandatory basis adjustments will gradually demonstrate that the administrative burdens are manageable enough to justify fully mandatory adjustments.

3. *Basis shifts.* Partnership distributions often result in a shift in basis from one property to another of similar character. From a policy standpoint, some object to this outcome because it enables taxpayers to shift basis to property where the basis may provide a more immediate tax benefit. For example, if one property is likely to be sold soon and another is not, taxpayers would ordinarily benefit from shifting basis from the latter to the former. Congress has denied nonrecognition treatment for like-kind exchanges in circumstances where this type of basis shifting is likely to occur, see I.R.C. § 1031(f), but it has thus far continued to tolerate the pervasive basis shifting permitted by the partnership rules.

4. *Sections 755(c) and 732(f).* The background of sections 755(c) and 732(f) illustrates well the potential risk to the tax system presented by basis shifts. Section 755(c) does not allow any basis decrease in partnership assets under section 734(b)(2) to be allocated to stock held by a partnership in a corporation which is a partner in the partnership, or stock in a corporation related to such corporate partner. This provision was enacted in reaction to a tax shelter used by Enron. Under section 1032(a), no gain or loss is recognized by a corporation on receipt of money or other property in exchange for its stock. Enron arranged for a distribution of depreciable partnership property that resulted in an increase in the basis of such property and a corresponding decrease in the basis of stock held by the partnership in a corporation which was a partner of the partnership. In other words, Enron used the partnership distribution rules to shift basis from the corporate stock to the distributed depreciable property. This basis shift was advantageous because it allowed higher depreciation deductions at no tax cost; Enron's plan envisaged that any gain from the low-basis corporate stock would eventually be allocated to the corporate partner and therefore entitled to nonrecognition treatment under section 1032(a). In response, section 755(c) now requires a partnership to decrease the basis of partnership property other than the corporate stock if a section 734(b) basis

reduction would otherwise be allocated to corporate stock; gain is recognized to the extent of any prevented basis reduction.

Section 755(c) is intended to backstop section 732(f), which was enacted to prevent a similar tax shelter involving a distribution by a partnership of corporate stock to a corporate partner. In the shelter, as a result of the distribution, the corporate partner obtained a reduced basis in the distributed corporate stock, thereby entitling the partnership to increase its basis in other partnership property. In other words, the transaction resulted in a shifting of basis from the corporate stock to other partnership property similar to the Enron shelter discussed above. This shift was advantageous because, following the distribution, the corporation whose stock was distributed qualified as a controlled subsidiary of the corporate partner. Therefore, a subsequent liquidation of the subsidiary into the parent did not result in the recognition of any gain or loss under sections 332(a) and 337(a). Thus, similar to the shelter underlying section 755(c), the transaction produced a basis increase at no tax cost.

To combat such a transaction, Congress might have disallowed any basis increase under section 734(b)(1)(B) to the retained partnership property. Instead, section 732(f) when applicable requires a decrease in the *controlled subsidiary corporation's* basis in its assets, leaving intact the partnership's increased basis in its assets.

4. *Section 734(b) "Trap"*

The section 734(b) adjustment suffers from an important technical defect: the amount of the adjustment is determined by reference to the distributee's outside basis rather than her share of inside basis. A distribution of high or low basis property should be viewed as carrying out a disproportionate amount of basis only to the extent that the aggregate basis of the distributed property is more or less than the distributee's share of *inside* basis. Yet, the basis adjustment rules do not operate precisely in this fashion: rather, the amount of the upward or downward adjustment is determined by reference to the distributee's *outside basis.* Where the distributee's outside basis differs from her share of inside basis, the section 734(b) adjustment invariably produces the incorrect result.

Example 8-6: A, B and C contribute $200 cash each to the newly formed ABC partnership in exchange for one-third partnership interests. The partnership retains $400 cash and purchases land #1 for $50 and land #2 for $150. Partner A dies when the partnership has the following balance sheet and no section 754 election is in effect:

Assets	*IB*	*BV*	*FMV*	*Capital*	*Tax*	*Book*	*FMV*
cash	400	400	400	A	200	200	400
land #1	50	50	200	B	200	200	400
land #2	150	150	600	C	200	200	400
total	600	600	1200	total	600	600	1200

Immediately after A's death, the partnership distributes $400 cash to A's estate (or A's successor in interest) in complete liquidation of A's partnership interest. Because outside basis is stepped up to the fair market value of the partnership interest under section 1014, there is no gain or loss realized or recognized in the cash liquidating distribution ($400 cash distribution less $400 outside basis). Thus, the partnership is not entitled to a section 734(b) adjustment, even if a section 754 election is in effect at the time of the distribution.[3]

Yet, an upward basis adjustment in the partnership's assets is clearly appropriate in this situation. Prior to A's death and the subsequent distribution, each partner had a $200 share of the partnership's unrealized gain. Section 1014 eliminates A's share of that gain on the liquidating distribution. There is no reason, however, why A's share of unrealized gain left behind in the partnership should be shifted to B and C. But that is precisely what happens: following the distribution, the partnership has $600 of unrealized gain, shared equally by B and C. Thus, each continuing partner's share of such gain has increased from $200 to $300. The obvious solution would be to allow a $200 upward adjustment to the retained assets for the benefit of B and C, but section 734(b) does not authorize any such adjustment.

Recall that a distribution may trigger a mandatory section 734(b) adjustment to the extent that there would be a net downward adjustment to the basis of the partnership's remaining property of over $250,000 if there were a section 754 election in effect. This situation could easily arise if the outside basis of a deceased partner is stepped up under section 1014 and the partnership then distributes low-basis property in liquidation of the deceased partner's interest. Thus, the partnership may be required to step down the basis of its retained property to the extent that the basis of the distributed property is stepped up in the hands of the distributee.

E. Distributions Affecting the Allocation of Income Character

The nonrecognition and basis adjustment rules described thus far ensure that, following a distribution, the *amount* of gains and losses in existence just prior to the transaction are generally either recognized or preserved. The rules also require either recognition or preservation of the *total amount of the character* of income or loss

3. If a section 754 election had been in effect at the time of the *death*, A's estate or successor would have been entitled to a section 743(b) basis adjustment of $200 ($400 outside basis less $200 share of inside basis). If A's former interest had then been liquidated in exchange for $400 cash, the distributee's unused special basis adjustment would have been applied to adjust the basis of the partnership's retained assets by $200. Reg. § 1.734-2(b)(1). This situation is an exception to the general rule that a transferee's special basis adjustment may not benefit partners other than the transferee. The $200 upward basis adjustment to the retained partnership property would eliminate the section 734(b) trap.

existing prior to the transaction. They do not, however, preserve the proper *allocation of the character* of income or loss among the partners. This defect is illustrated in **example 8-7**:

Example 8-7: Assume the same facts as in **example 8-5**, except that land #1 is an ordinary-income asset such as inventory, and the partnership has a section 754 election in effect. Immediately before the liquidating distribution to A, each partner has an outside basis of $200 and the partnership has the following balance sheet:

Assets	*IB*	*BV*	*FMV*	*Capital*	*Tax*	*Book*	*FMV*
cash	300	300	300	A	200	200	300
inventory	90	90	300	B	200	200	300
land	210	210	300	C	200	200	300
total	600	600	900	total	600	600	900

If the partnership distributes the inventory to A in complete liquidation of her interest, A would recognize a $110 capital loss and would inherit the partnership's $90 basis in the inventory (ignoring section 751 (discussed below)). I.R.C. §§ 731(a)(2), 732(a)(1). Since the section 754 election is in effect, the partnership would also reduce its basis in the land by $110, to $100. I.R.C. § 734(b)(2)(A). If the amount of the loss ($110) is netted against the $210 unrealized gain A has in the distributed inventory (and the character of the two items is ignored), these results preserve the proper amount of gain or loss for all three partners ($100 of gain each before and after the transaction). The total amount of unrealized ordinary income ($210 before and after the transaction) is also preserved.

Yet the distribution has shifted around the ordinary-income tax liabilities of the partners. Prior to the distribution, they each had a one-third share of ordinary income, or $70 each. After the distribution, A has the entire share of $210 and B and C have none.

Read I.R.C. § 751(b). The purpose of this provision is to prevent a distribution from resulting in a misallocation of the character of income or loss. The provision first identifies two familiar classes of assets: unrealized receivables and substantially appreciated inventory items (otherwise known as "hot assets" or "section 751(b) assets") and all other assets ("cold assets" or "non-section 751(b) assets"). (Inventory is "substantially appreciated" only if, in the aggregate, the fair market value of such property exceeds 120 percent of its basis to the partnership. See I.R.C. § 751(b)(3).) The provision potentially applies whenever a distribution alters the distributee's pre-distribution share of hot assets. Not surprisingly, this is likely to be a frequent occurrence. Even a simple cash distribution is potentially subject to section 751(b) if, as a result, the distributee reduces her share of the partnership's hot assets. But an important threshold condition is the presence of a hot asset; partnerships with no hot assets may make distributions free of section 751(b) considerations.

The rules implementing section 751(b) are presently in a state of flux. The existing regulations have long contained significant flaws and have not been updated for important statutory changes since their promulgation in 1956. In 2014, following an eight-year study, the Treasury issued a set of proposed regulations that likely represent the future substance of operating rules in this area. Therefore, the following discussion is based on the approach under these proposals, even though they are not yet the law.

If a partnership making a distribution owns a hot asset, the proposals determine the applicability of section 751(b) using a "hypothetical sale" approach similar to that specified in the section 751(a) regulations. The hypothetical sale assumes that the partnership's hot assets (and any distributed hot assets) are sold in a taxable transaction for cash immediately before and after the distribution (taking into account any special allocations and the consequences of a revaluation of partnership assets). Prop. Reg. § 1.751-1(b)(2)(ii) and (iii). The purpose is to compare the amount of ordinary income (or loss) that would be allocated to a partner before and after the distribution. If the distribution does not alter any partner's share of ordinary income or loss, then section 751(b) does not apply and the distribution is governed by the normal distribution rules. If, on the other hand, there is a change in such share, then the distribution is a "section 751(b) distribution" and, immediately prior to the distribution, each partner must generally recognize ordinary income equal to the partner's net decrease in ordinary income or net increase in ordinary loss (known as the "section 751(b) amount"). Prop. Reg. § 1.751-1(b)(2)(i) and (3)(i). The income must be recognized using "a reasonable approach that is consistent with the purpose of section 751(b)." Prop. Reg. § 1.751-1(b)(3)(i).

Although the proposed regulations do not mandate a particular "reasonable approach," certain examples illustrate use of a "deemed gain" approach under which the partnership recognizes hot asset gain equal to the aggregate section 751(b) amount of all partners and allocates the ordinary income to partners based on their share of that amount. See, e.g., Prop. Reg. § 1.751-1(g) (ex. 3(v), (vi)). As a result, either the distributee or the other partners (but not both) must recognize ordinary income immediately prior to the distribution to compensate for the decrease in their share of ordinary income (or increase in their share of ordinary loss) that would otherwise result from the distribution. Appropriate adjustments must be made to the basis of hot assets (retained or distributed) and the partners' outside bases to reflect the recognized hot asset gain. A distributee partner is also permitted (and sometimes required) to recognize gain (generally capital gain) in order to preserve the partnership's basis in distributed hot assets. Prop. Reg. § 1.751-1(b)(3)(ii). Once the section 751(b) consequences are determined, the remainder of the distribution is taxed under the normal distribution rules. Prop. Reg. § 1.751-1(b)(1)(iii).

The proposed rules rely heavily on partnership revaluations immediately before the distribution to minimize the likelihood that section 751(b) will apply. By freezing the allocation of unrealized ordinary income or loss prior to the distribution (using reverse section 704(c) principles), the revaluation makes it more likely that the distribution will not change any partner's share of ordinary income or loss (and therefore will not be a section 751(b) distribution). Under the proposed regulations, revaluations are generally mandatory if the partnership owns hot assets following the distribution. Prop. Reg. §§ 1.704-1(b)(2)(iv)(*f*), 1.751-1(b)(2)(iv). Partnerships that do not maintain capital accounts are required to make future allocations of partnership items to achieve a similar result as if capital accounts were maintained and partnership property revalued in connection with a section 751(b) distribution.

Applying the proposed rules, the following sections illustrate the operation of section 751(b) in the context of liquidating and nonliquidating distributions.

1. *Liquidating Distributions*

Return to **example 8-7** and assume that the partnership distributes the inventory to A (whose outside basis is $200) in complete liquidation of her interest in the partnership when the partnership does not have a section 754 election in effect, and the partnership revalues its assets. Because the substantial appreciation test is satisfied (i.e., the value of the inventory exceeds 120 percent of its basis to the partnership), the partnership has a hot asset and section 751(b) potentially applies. Prior to the distribution, if the partnership's hot assets had been sold for cash, each partner would have had a $70 share of hot asset gain (one-third of the unrealized appreciation in the inventory). Following the distribution, the partnership has no hot assets and (before taking into account section 751(b)) the inventory held by A has hot asset gain of $210 ($300 value of distributed inventory less $90 basis in A's hands). Thus, the distribution increases A's share of hot asset gain from $70 to $210 and reduces B's and C's total share of such gain from $140 to zero. Because the distribution changes the partners' shares of hot asset gain, it is a section 751(b) distribution and the aggregate section 751(b) amount is $140 (the total decrease in B's and C's hot asset gain).

Under the deemed gain approach, immediately prior to the distribution, the partnership must recognize ordinary income equal to the aggregate section 751(b) amount ($140), allocated entirely to B and C ($70 each). Both inside and outside basis must be adjusted accordingly. Thus, B and C each increase their outside basis to $270 ($200 pre-distribution basis plus recognized ordinary income of $70). Also, immediately before the distribution, the partnership increases its basis in the distributed inventory to $230 ($90 pre-distribution basis plus total ordinary income of $140 recognized by B and C). Prop. Reg. § 1.751-1(g) (ex. 3(v), (vi)) (illustrating deemed gain approach).

The result is the same as if B and C had received a fictional distribution of a hot asset with a basis of zero and a fair market value equal to the section 751(b) amount of $140. B and C would be deemed to sell the distributed asset back to the partnership for $140 cash (triggering ordinary income of $140 to B and C), and to re-contribute the cash to the partnership. Following those steps, the partnership would have a $230 basis in the inventory ($140 basis of purchased inventory plus $90 pre-distribution basis of inventory) and B and C would each have an outside basis of $270 ($200 pre-distribution basis plus $70 deemed cash contribution). See Prop. Reg. § 1.751-1(g) (ex. 3(vii), (viii)) (illustrating "deemed hot asset sale" approach). By comparison, the deemed gain approach accomplishes the identical result in a single step (by taxing B and C on ordinary income equal to their section 751(b) amount and adjusting accordingly their outside bases and the partnership's basis in the inventory).

Following the required section 751(b) adjustments, the remaining tax rules for distributions must be applied. Thus, A is treated as receiving a distribution of inventory (worth $300) with a stepped-up basis of $230 in the partnership's hands. Under section 732(b), A's basis in the distributed inventory is limited to $200 (A's outside basis), or $30 less than the partnership's inside basis. If A sold the inventory immediately for $300, A would recognize $100 of ordinary income ($300 amount realized less $200 basis). Although the nondistributee partners (B and C) have properly taken into account their relinquished share of ordinary income ($140), A still winds up with $30 too much ordinary income ($100 compared to A's pre-distribution share of $70). The $30 reduction to the basis of the inventory in A's hands corresponds to A's relinquished one-third share of the appreciation in the land.

In this situation, the proposed regulations allow A to elect to recognize capital gain of $30 immediately prior to the distribution. If A so elects, A's outside basis would be increased from $200 to $230. Prop. Reg. § 1.751-1(b)(3)(ii)(B) and -1(g) (ex. 7(iii)). As a result, A would take a basis of $230 in the distributed inventory (equal to A's entire outside basis), reducing A's outside basis to zero. If the inventory were immediately sold, A would recognize ordinary income of $70 ($300 less $230 basis) equal to A's pre-distribution share of hot asset gain. If A elects to recognize the capital gain, the partnership's basis in the retained land would be increased from $210 to $240. As the following post-distribution balance sheet illustrates, total inside basis ($540) would equal B's and C's total outside basis ($540):

Assets	*IB*	*BV*	*Capital*	*Tax*	*Book*
cash	300	300	B	270	300
land	240	300	C	270	300
total	540	600	Total	540	600

In this case, the *principal* tax consequences fall on B and C, not A. Although B and C may appear to be innocent bystanders, they must each nevertheless recognize $70 of ordinary income (equal to the net decrease in their pre-distribution share of ordinary income). The reason is that once the partnership's inventory is distributed to A, their share of ordinary income disappears. Thus, section 751(b) imposes tax consequences on them when the inventory is distributed. The partnership's $240 basis in the land ($210 basis increased by $30 to reflect A's recognized capital gain) ensures that B and C each continue to have a $30 share of built-in gain in the retained land. A is also taxed properly: A realizes $100 of overall gain, recognizes $30 of capital gain in the transaction, and has $70 of preserved ordinary income in the distributed inventory.

Consider the tax consequences if the partnership has a section 754 election in effect. In this situation, the proposed regulations *require* A to recognize capital gain of $30, with the identical results as described above. Prop. Reg. § 1.751-1(b)(3)(ii)(A) and -1(g) (exs. 5, 6). Do you understand why gain recognition is mandatory in this situation? (Hint: Consider how the section 734(b) basis adjustment would be allocated if A does not recognize gain and A's basis in the inventory is reduced under section 732(b).) Should the distributee partner be required to recognize capital gain whenever the basis of distributed hot assets would otherwise be stepped down in the distributee's hands?

Problem 8-9:

(a) Determine the tax consequences to all parties if, in **example 8-7**, A receives a liquidating distribution of $300 cash (rather than inventory) when the partnership has a section 754 election in effect.
(b) In (a) above, what would be the tax consequences to all parties if A receives a liquidating distribution of land (worth $300) rather than cash?

2. *Nonliquidating Distributions*

Section 751(b) also applies to nonliquidating distributions that alter the distributee's share of the partnership's hot asset gain. Since the distributee remains a partner (with a reduced interest in the partnership), a complicating factor is the need to take into account the distributee's continuing share of hot asset gain inside the partnership (as well as the distributee's share of hot asset gain, if any, outside the partnership) following the distribution. Apart from this additional complication, section 751(b) operates generally as described above.

Example 8-8: Assume the same facts as **example 8-7**, except that A receives a distribution of only $150 cash and, as a result, her interest in the partnership is reduced from one-third to one-fifth. The partnership revalues its assets immediately before the cash distribution to A. See Reg. § 1.704-1(b)(2)(iv)(*f*)(*5*)(*ii*); Prop. Reg. § 1.751-1(b)(2)(iv).

The revaluation freezes the partners' pre-distribution shares of unrealized hot asset gain, thereby preventing a hot asset shift. See Prop. Reg. § 1.751-1(g) (ex. 2). Since there is no net change in any partner's share of unrealized ordinary income, the distribution is not a section 751(b) distribution. Accordingly, the normal distribution rules of sections 731-736 apply. Following the revaluation and distribution, the partnership would have the following balance sheet:

Assets	*IB*	*BV*	*Capital*	*Tax*	*Book*
cash	150	150	A	50	150
inventory	90	300	B	200	300
land	210	300	C	200	300
total	450	750	Total	450	750

Even though A has retained only a one-fifth interest in the partnership ($150/$750), A has a one-third share of the partnership's booked-up gain in the inventory and land. Application of reverse section 704(c) principles ensures that the booked-up gain will be properly taxed when eventually recognized. In effect, A is treated as a one-fifth partner only for purposes of any allocations of tax (and book) items that accrue after the distribution.

Problem 8-10:

(a) Determine the rest of the tax consequences of **example 8-8** to all parties. Following the distribution, what are the tax consequences if the partnership sells the inventory for $300? $375? Is the income from the sale allocated properly?

(b) In **example 8-8**, what would be the tax consequences to all parties if A received a distribution of one-half of the inventory (or one-half of the land) rather than $150 cash?

(c) Assume that the equal ABC partnership has three zero-basis assets: unrealized receivable #1 (worth $150), unrealized receivable #2 (worth $300), and a capital asset (worth $450). Each partner has an outside basis of zero. When no section 754 election is in effect, ABC revalues its assets and distributes unrealized receivable #1 to A in a current distribution, reducing A's partnership interest from one-third to one-fifth. Should section 751(b) apply to the distribution? Why or why not? See Prop. Reg. § 1.751-1(g) (ex. 5).

NOTES AND QUESTIONS

1. *Substantially appreciated inventory items.* Unlike section 751(a), section 751(b) only treats inventory items as hot assets if they are in the aggregate "substantially appreciated" (i.e., value exceeds 120 percent of basis). See I.R.C. § 751(b)(1)(A)(ii) and (3). Because of this requirement, it is necessary under the existing regulations to ascertain whether a particular ordinary-income asset

constitutes an unrealized receivable, an inventory item, or both. See Reg. § 1.751-1(d)(2)(ii) (unrealized receivables are also inventory items). Fortunately, the proposed regulations sensibly exclude unrealized receivables in determining whether the partnership's inventory is substantially appreciated. See Prop. Reg. § 1.751-1(d)(1). Thus, unrealized receivables would no longer count toward the substantial appreciation test.

2. *Admission of new partners.* Under existing law, section 751(b) may apply in unexpected situations, such as upon the admission of a new partner. Recall that changes in a partner's share of partnership liabilities are treated as a deemed contribution or distribution of cash. If a new partner assumes a share of the partnership's liabilities, the deemed cash distribution to the existing partners potentially implicates section 751(b) whenever the partnership holds hot assets.

In Rev. Rul. 84-102, 1984-2 C.B. 119, a new partner (D) was admitted to a partnership that held zero-basis unrealized receivables. Prior to D's admission, each of the partners was allocated one-third of the partnership's liabilities of $100x ($33.3x each). D's admission (in exchange for a cash contribution) reduced each partner's share of the partnership's liabilities from one-third to one-fourth ($25x each), resulting in a deemed cash distribution to the existing partners ($8.3x each). The IRS ruled that section 751(b) applied to the transaction because the existing partners received non-section 751(b) property (cash) in exchange for their share of section 751(b) property (unrealized receivables).

In Rev. Rul. 84-102, the partners might have avoided this outcome if the partnership had revalued its property upon admission of the new partner (or specially allocated any built-in gain), thereby freezing the existing partners' share of the appreciation and value (identical) of the zero-basis receivables. Thus, admission of the new partner would have left unchanged the existing partners' share of the partnership's gain in its hot assets. Under the proposed regulations, mandatory revaluation of the partnership's assets should eliminate any concern about triggering section 751(b) in this situation. Prop. Reg. § 1.751-1(b)(2)(iv).

3. *Exceptions and "safe harbors."* It is also important to identify those situations in which section 751(b) does *not* apply. One situation is where a partner receives a distribution of property that she previously contributed to the partnership. See I.R.C. § 751(b)(2)(A); Prop. Reg. § 1.751-1(b)(5) (successor rules). What is the reason for this exception? Another situation is a pro rata distribution of the same property (such as cash). Do you understand why such a pro rata distribution is not subject to section 751(b)? The proposed regulations expand the situations in which section 751(b) will not apply. For example, a current distribution solely of non-hot assets should generally not trigger section 751(b) since the mandatory revaluation should preserve the partners' pre-distribution share of hot asset gain or loss in the retained (and revalued) partnership assets. Finally, as previously noted, distributions by a partnership with no hot assets are generally outside the scope of section 751(b).

4. *Basis shifts.* Suppose the equal ABC partnership owns two depreciable assets (both section 1245 property): X (basis $30, value $180) and Y (basis $60, value $60). Each partner owns a one-third interest and has an outside basis of $30. If

X were sold for $180, the partnership would recognize $150 of recapture income attributable to prior depreciation deductions. In a current distribution, the partnership distributes asset Y to partner A, and the basis of Y is reduced from $60 to $30 (A's outside basis) under section 732(a). The partnership revalues its assets immediately before the distribution. Does the distribution trigger section 751(b)? Does your answer depend on whether the partnership has a section 754 election in effect? See Prop. Reg. § 1.755-1(c)(2)(iii), (vi), and (c)(6) (exs. 2, 3).

5. *Regulatory authority.* Even though the statutory language has not been amended, the proposed regulations change the mechanics of taxing section 751(b) distributions. The statute contemplates an exchange of hot assets for cold assets but provides that the transaction will be considered a sale or exchange "under regulations." This language would seem to give the Treasury authority to update the regulations to reflect fundamental changes that have occurred in subchapter K since the existing section 751(b) regulations were issued in 1956. In particular, the proposed regulations premise the Treasury's authority on Congress's decision in 1984 to require mandatory section 704(c) allocations. In 1999, Treasury amended the section 751(a) regulations to reflect the section 704(c) changes. In identifying the partners' shares of hot asset gain before and after a distribution, the proposed section 751(b) regulations specifically incorporate the principles of section 704(c).

6. *Remedying flaws in section 751(b).* Suppose a partnership's only assets consist of three equally valuable items of inventory: one item has a basis equal to value and the other two have very low bases. Assume that, in the aggregate, the items are substantially appreciated. Under the proposed regulations, a distribution of any of the three items in complete liquidation of one partner's interest triggers section 751(b) because there is necessarily a shift in the partners' shares of unrealized appreciation. The proposed regulations thus fix an important flaw under the existing regulations which focus on shifts in the *gross value* (not unrealized appreciation) of hot assets.

The proposed regulations also improve the operation of section 751(b) by eliminating the concept of a reciprocal exchange of hot and cold assets (and the need to identify specific assets deemed exchanged). Under the proposed regulations, ordinary income is taxed only to those partners whose share of ordinary income is reduced. The section 751(b) distribution itself will generally not trigger recognition of capital gain, except in very limited situations. For example, a distributee may elect (or sometimes may be required) to recognize capital gain if the distributee's outside basis would otherwise be insufficient to absorb the partnership's basis in distributed hot assets (as adjusted to reflect the consequences of the section 751(b) distribution).

7. *Anti-abuse rule.* If a principal purpose of a transaction is to avoid section 751(b) by exploiting the ability to defer gain under section 704(c), the IRS can recast the transaction to achieve results that are consistent with the purpose of section 751(b). Prop. Reg. § 1.751-1(b)(4). One example of an abusive situation is when a partner retains a *de minimis* economic interest in a partnership while deferring tax on a large amount of booked-up hot asset gain. To illustrate, assume in **example 8-8**

that the partnership revalues its assets and distributes cash of $297 to A in a current distribution, triggering capital gain of $97 to A (when no section 754 election is in effect). If revaluation of the partnership's assets prevents section 751(b) from applying, tax on A's share of ordinary income may be deferred until A's remaining interest (worth $3) is entirely liquidated. Yet, A has effectively cashed out 99 percent of the value of her interest. Does it make sense for the Treasury to provide elaborate rules allowing partners to defer ordinary income by booking-up hot asset gain but then impose anti-abuse rules if the partners use this ability too aggressively?

8. *Interplay between sections 751(a) and 751(b).* Since sections 751(a) and 751(b) were enacted simultaneously and address similar problems, the regulations under each provision should generally be interpreted in tandem. Assume that partner A receives a current distribution of cold assets and retains a partnership interest worth $15 (with a basis of zero) and a $25 share of booked-up hot asset gain attributable to zero-basis unrealized receivables. If the distribution of cold assets does not trigger section 751(b), A's share of ordinary income will be taxed later when the partnership collects the receivables or A sells her retained interest. On a sale of her interest for $15, A would be required under section 751(a) to recognize $25 of ordinary income and a $10 capital loss ($15 overall gain less $25 ordinary income). See Prop. Reg. § 1.751-1(a)(2) and (g) (ex. 1).

9. *Future.* Although the proposed regulations are generally designed to reach results consistent with the purpose of section 751(b), the complexity of the rules may make them inaccessible for many partnerships. Moreover, the effectiveness of the proposed rules depends on accurate determinations of value in the hypothetical sale and revaluation, even though there may often be little or no market evidence of such value. Thus, it remains unclear whether the proposed rules will ultimately achieve their intended result or, instead, be exploited by the well-advised (and ignored by nearly everyone else). As in the case of other tax rules applicable to partnership distributions, the challenge of section 751(b) and its implementing regulations is to prevent tax abuse within the context of a broad nonrecognition rule that essentially invites such abuse.

Chapter 9

Recharacterizing Contributions, Distributions, and Sales

Partnership transactions that follow the form of a partnership contribution, distribution, or sale may be economically indistinguishable from some other transaction with disparate tax consequences. The first three parts of this chapter describe statutory provisions that resolve the overlap of different tax rules with respect to economically similar transactions. Part A deals with contributions and related distributions that are sometimes recharacterized as "disguised sales," part B concerns other anti-"mixing bowl" rules in the case of linked contributions and distributions, and part C discusses the special treatment of marketable securities. The final part of this chapter is a reminder that, in the absence of a statutory rule, common-law principles continue to play a role in potentially recharacterizing partnership transactions.

A. Disguised Sales or Exchanges

1. *Introduction*

The broad nonrecognition provisions of subchapter K encouraged some taxpayers to structure a sale or exchange of property as, instead, a partnership contribution and related distribution. Such planning techniques might permit the taxpayer to exchange one type of property for another type without recognition of gain. Congress enacted the disguised sale rules of section 707(a)(2)(B) to ensure the proper tax treatment of these transactions. The following two cases, which involve transactions occurring prior to the effective date of section 707(a)(2)(B), illustrate both the nature of the problem and the difficulty encountered by courts in analyzing disguised sales.

Otey v. Commissioner

70 T.C. 312 (1978), aff'd per curiam, 634 F.2d 1046 (6th Cir. 1980)

HALL, J.: . . . Petitioner is in the real estate business. In 1963 petitioner inherited from his uncle real property at 2612-14 Heiman Street in Nashville (Heiman Street property). At the time petitioner acquired the property, its fair market value was $18,500.

. . . [P]etitioner and Marion Thurman (Thurman), a real estate developer, decided to develop the Heiman Street property into a moderate-income apartment complex, a type of complex for which there was then available FHA-insured financing. On October 19, 1971, petitioner and Thurman formed a partnership under the name of Court Villa Apartments for the purpose of building a 65-unit FHA-insured residential apartment on the Heiman Street property. Thurman, through his construction company, Marion Thurman Builders, was to build the rental units, and petitioner was to manage them.

On December 30, 1971, petitioner and his wife transferred title to the Heiman Street property to the partnership. At the time of the transfer, petitioner's basis in the property was $18,500 and the fair market value of the property was $65,000.[1] This transfer was pursuant to the partnership agreement, which provided:

> John H. Otey, Jr. has contributed the land to the Joint Venture and the parties agree that the said Otey shall draw the first Sixty Five Thousand ($65,000) Dollars of loan proceeds from the Joint Venture as soon as the loan closes. Moreover the parties have together borrowed Fifteen Thousand ($15,000) Dollars from the Third National Bank and opened up a bank account in the name of COURT VILLA APARTMENTS. After the Sixty Five Thousand ($65,000) Dollars has been repaid to Otey, the parties agree that this loan shall be repaid to the Third National Bank.

The agreement further provided that profits and losses would be shared equally. Similarly, withdrawals and distributions of cash were to be made equally, except that as previously noted the first $65,000 of the loan proceeds was to be paid to petitioner.

On January 11, 1972, the partnership obtained a construction loan of $870,300 from the Third National Bank. Both petitioner and Thurman were jointly and severally liable for the loan. Pursuant to the partnership agreement, petitioner was paid $64,750[2] from the loan proceeds in four installments. . . .

Marion Thurman Builders built the apartment units for the partnership and was paid by the partnership from the construction loan. Thurman contributed no cash or

---

1. Petitioner and Thurman determined that $65,000 was the fair market value of the property by reference to comparable rental properties in Nashville. . . . Similarly, in its partnership returns for 1972 through 1976, the partnership listed the value of the land as $64,750. However, several days before trial, the partnership filed amended returns for 1972 through 1976 which listed the value of the land as $18,500.

2. The joint venture agreement provided that the partnership would pay petitioner $65,000; in fact he received only $64,750. The parties agree that the $250 difference is not material.

other assets to the partnership. His contribution was his ability to get financing for the partnership through his good credit. During 1972, 1973, and 1974 the partnership reported losses on its Form 1065 (U.S. Partnership Return of Income).

The partners intended that petitioner's transfer of the Heiman Street property to the partnership was a contribution to the capital of the partnership and not a sale of the property to the partnership. On receipt of the $64,750 cash from the partnership in 1972, petitioner reduced his basis in his capital in the partnership. Since his basis, consisting of his $18,500 basis in the land contributed plus his liability for one-half of the borrowed construction money, exceeded the money distributed to him, he reported no income from this transaction on his 1972 return. Respondent, in his statutory notice, determined that petitioner realized gain from the "sale" of the Heiman Street property to the partnership in 1972 which should have been reported by petitioner on his 1972 return.

OPINION

Petitioner made a contribution of property worth $65,000 to a partnership of which he was a partner. Within a short period after such contribution, the partnership borrowed funds on which petitioner was jointly and severally liable, and pursuant to agreement distributed $64,750 of such borrowed funds to petitioner, retaining petitioner's property. The distribution of $64,750 did not exceed petitioner's basis in the partnership. The question presented is whether petitioner in reality "sold" his property to the partnership. Respondent, relying on section 707, contends that he did.

Section 707 provides that "If a partner engages in a transaction with a partnership other than in his capacity as a member of such partnership, the transaction shall . . . be considered as occurring between the partnership and one who is not a partner," and section 1.707-1(a), Income Tax Regs., provides that "In all cases, the substance of the transaction will govern rather than its form."

Petitioner relies on section 721—"No gain or loss shall be recognized to a partnership or to any of its partners in the case of a contribution of property to the partnership in exchange for an interest in the partnership"—and section 731—"In the case of a distribution by a partnership to a partner . . . gain shall not be recognized to such partner, except to the extent any money distributed exceeds the adjusted basis of such partner's interest in the partnership immediately before the distribution."

We are cautioned, however, by section 1.731-1(c)(3), Income Tax Regs., as follows:

> (3) If there is a contribution of property to a partnership and within a short period:
>
> (i) Before or after such contribution other property is distributed to the contributing partner and the contributed property is retained by the partnership, or

(ii) After such contribution the contributed property is distributed to another partner,

such distribution may not fall within the scope of section 731. Section 731 does not apply to a distribution of property, if, in fact, the distribution was made in order to effect an exchange of property between two or more of the partners or between the partnership and a partner. Such a transaction shall be treated as an exchange of property.

Thus we are faced with the question whether this transaction, which was in form a contribution of property to a partnership followed by a distribution of loan proceeds to the contributing partner, was in substance a sale of the property to the partnership by the partner. . . .

[R]espondent contends that because neither partner contributed any cash to the partnership, and all available cash had to come from borrowing, "it is unconvincing that a partner would withdraw funds for his personal use, when these funds were needed for the project." Respondent also points out that on the Department of Housing and Urban Development Mortgagor's Certificate of Actual Cost, the cost of the land was stated to be $64,750. Respondent then concludes that "considered as a whole, the facts portray a sale of property to the partnership." We disagree.

Subchapter K provides two possible methods of analyzing the transfer by petitioner of his Heiman Street property to the partnership, with sharply divergent tax consequences depending upon which analysis applies. Using the contribution approach, sections 721 and 731 treat a partner's contribution of property to his partnership as a [nonrecognition] transaction, producing neither gain nor loss, and withdrawals from the partnership are treated as reductions in basis rather than as taxable events. If these sections are applicable, we must sustain petitioner, because the immediate recourse borrowing by the partnership would (like most other borrowing) be a nontaxable event, increasing the basis of the parties in their partnership interest under sections 752(a) and 722. The distribution to a partner (petitioner) of part of the borrowed funds would not generate gain but would simply reduce pro tanto the distributee's basis under sections 731(a)(1) and 733. This approach treats petitioner in a manner rather similar to a proprietor. Had petitioner simply decided to use his Heiman Street property as a proprietor for an FHA housing project and had he been able to obtain an FHA construction loan in an amount exceeding the cost of building the proposed structure, and diverted to his personal use $64,750 of the loan, no gain or loss would have been realized. This would be the case even had he been able to borrow the money only by agreeing to pay half his profits over to Thurman for acting as the cosigner on the loan. Sections 721 and 731 parallel this treatment.

But the Code also recognizes that in some cases partners do not deal with a partnership in their capacity as partners. Even though they are personally on both sides of a transaction with the partnership to the extent of their partnership interest, partners may on occasion deal with the partnership in a capacity other than as a partner and must treat such dealings with the partnership accordingly under section 707. This section, among other things, prevents use of the partnership provisions to render nontaxable what would in substance have been a taxable exchange if it had not been "run through" the partnership. For example, respondent has ruled that if two parties contribute to their partnership their equal interest in stock of two corporations and then liquidate the partnership with each taking all of the stock of one corporation, a taxable exchange has occurred. . . . The partnership form may not be employed to evade the limitations in section 1031, and section 707 is the mechanism for guarding this gate.

Neither the Code and regulations nor the case law offers a great deal of guidance for distinguishing whether transactions such as those before us are to be characterized as a contribution (nontaxable) under section 721, as petitioner contends, or as a sale to the partnership other than in the capacity of a partner (taxable) under section 707, as respondent urges. It is at least clear from the above-quoted regulation under section 731 that application or not of section 707 is not always merely elective with a taxpayer. Occasions exist on which he must be thrust unwillingly within it in order for it to serve its above-described prophylactic function. And the regulations provide that "In all cases, the substance of the transaction will govern rather than its form." Sec. 1.707-1(a), Income Tax Regs.

. . . [S]ection 1.721-1(a), Income Tax Regs., [sheds] some light on the applicable rule:

> Thus, if the transfer of property by the partner to the partnership results in the receipt by the partner of money or other consideration, including a promissory obligation fixed in amount and time for payment, the transaction will be treated as a sale or exchange under section 707 rather than as a contribution under section 721.

. . . Turning to the facts before us, a number of circumstances militate in favor of a conclusion that section 721 rather than section 707 should govern. In the first place, the form of the transaction was a contribution to capital rather than a sale, and there are no elements of artificiality in the form selected which should induce us to be particularly astute to look behind it. . . . Second, and most importantly, the capital in question (borrowed funds aside) was emplaced in the partnership at its inception and as a part of the very raison d'etre of the partnership. Without this transfer, the partnership would have had no assets and no business. It is therefore most difficult for us to agree with respondent that the transaction was between petitioner and the partnership other than in petitioner's capacity as a partner. . . . Third, the capital in question was the only contributed capital of the partnership. To treat this as an outside transaction would require us to hold in effect that no nonborrowed capital was contributed at all. While such partnerships can of course exist, they are unusual and it would seem very strained to contend that this is such a case. The property had to be in the partnership to make the borrowing possible. Fourth, petitioner enjoyed here no guarantee by the partnership that he would be paid (and get to keep) the $65,000 in all events. . . . True, most of that sum was distributed to him almost at once out of borrowed funds, but he remained personally liable for the entire borrowing. Accordingly, we do not consider the transaction to be one described in section 1.721-1(a), Income Tax Regs., resulting "in the receipt by the partner of money or other consideration, including a promissory obligation fixed in amount and time for payment," and causing applicability of section 707. Provisions for preferential distributions out of borrowed funds to restore capital accounts to equality after non-pro rata partnership contributions do not necessarily demonstrate that the contributions were really sales. An important feature distinguishing transfers in the capacity of a partner from section 707 transactions is whether payment by the partnership to the partner is at the risk of the economic fortunes of the partnership. In the present case, whether partnership cash flow would ever suffice to repay the distributed $64,750 to the bank would depend on the partnership's subsequent economic fortunes. If they were adverse, petitioner could be called on to repay the loan himself. Fifth, the pattern here is a usual and customary partnership capitalization arrangement, under which the partner who put up a greater share of the capital than his share of partnership profits is to receive preferential distributions to equalize capital accounts. The only unusual feature here is the immediate availability of the equalizing distribution out of excess borrowed funds. The normality of this general pattern would make it most unsettling were we to accept respondent's invitation to recharacterize the capitalization of the partnership on account thereof. Finally, although respondent relies briefly on the early cash distribution to petitioner of the excess borrowed funds, this payment does not constitute the kind of attempted end-run around the limitations of section 1031 which the regulations properly seek to block. Were there no partnership at all, a taxpayer could borrow funds on the security of appreciated property and apply them to his personal use without triggering gain. Had the distributed funds come directly from the other partner, respondent's case would be stronger. While it may be argued that the funds have come indirectly from Thurman because his credit facilitated the loan, the fact is that the loan was a partnership loan on which the partnership was primarily liable, and both partners were jointly and severally liable for the full loan if the partnership defaulted. We do not view the factual pattern here as constituting a disguised sale of the land to Thurman or the partnership. For all the above reasons, we cannot sustain respondent in his attempted recharacterization of the transfer as a sale. . . .

We hold that the transfer constituted in substance what it was in form — the initial capitalization of the partnership. The early withdrawal of borrowed cash in an amount substantially equivalent to the agreed value of the contributed property reduced petitioner's basis in the partnership but did not create income to him. Secs. 731(a)(1) and 733. . . .

NOTES AND QUESTIONS

1. *Where "sales" characterization is desired.* Unlike the taxpayer in *Otey*, a partner sometimes prefers to characterize her transfer of property to a partnership as a "sale."

For example, a partner may seek to recognize a loss without surrendering control of the property. Alternatively, a partner may wish to sell depreciable property to a partnership to achieve a stepped-up basis, while potentially deferring recognition of gain under the installment sale rules of section 453.

Read I.R.C. §§ 707(a)(1), (b); 267(d); 453(g), (i); 1239(a). In general, section 707(a)(1) treats a transaction between a partnership and a partner acting in a non-partner capacity as if it were a transaction between third parties. Section 707(b) overrides this treatment in the case of sales or exchanges between a partnership and a partner owning (directly or indirectly) more than 50 percent of the capital or profits interests in such a partnership (or between commonly controlled partnerships). See also I.R.C. §§ 267, 1239(a). In these situations, section 707(b)(1) disallows any loss with respect to the sale or exchange, while section 707(b)(2) treats gain from such a sale as ordinary income if the property is a non-capital asset in the transferee's hands. In addition, section 453(g) generally disallows installment sale treatment with respect to sales of depreciable property between related parties. See also I.R.C. § 453(i) (accelerating recapture income in the case of an installment sale).

If a loss is disallowed under section 707(b)(1), the loss does not disappear entirely. Instead, the disallowed loss may be allowed as an offset against subsequent gain realized by the transferee upon a sale of the property. See I.R.C. §§ 707(b)(1) (flush language), 267(d). Appropriate adjustments to outside basis, under section 705, are necessary to preserve the intended benefit or detriment of section 707(b)(1). See Rev. Rul. 96-10, 1996-1 C.B. 138.

2. *The court's reasoning*. In *Otey*, the court lists six factors that militate in favor of finding that no disguised sale occurred. Which factors seem to be the most persuasive?

The court concludes that the transaction did not represent an end-run around the restrictions of section 1031, since Otey could have borrowed against the property prior to the contribution without recognizing any gain. If the partnership had defaulted on the loan, how would the partners have shared the economic risk of loss?

Why would the government's case have been stronger if the distributed funds had come directly from the other partner? How easy is it to trace the source of a distribution?

3. In enacting section 707(a)(2)(B), Congress expressly disapproved of the result in *Otey*. The *Jacobson* case excerpted below suggests, however, that courts were not helpless in combating disguised sales even under the prior regulations.

Jacobson v. Commissioner

96 T.C. 577 (1991)

PARR, J.: . . . Messrs. Jacobson and Larson were general partners of JWC, which in turn owned the McDonald properties. JWC actively tried to sell the McDonald properties outright for about 2 years before forming a partnership with

Metropolitan. JWC contributed the McDonald properties having a net agreed value of $8,036,311 ($15 million less $6,963,689 in mortgages) and Metropolitan contributed $6,027,233 in cash. This amount of cash equals 75 percent of the net agreed value of the McDonald properties ($6,027,233/$8,036,311 = 75%). On the same day, all of the cash was then distributed to or for the benefit of JWC. JWC recognized gain on the distribution, but only to the extent that the distribution was greater than the adjusted basis of its partnership interest. The venture then elected under section 754 to increase the adjusted basis of the McDonald properties by the amount of gain recognized by JWC upon the cash distribution. When the dust finally settled, Metropolitan owned 75 percent in the venture and JWC owned 25 percent, and the venture had increased its depreciable basis in the McDonald properties.

Petitioners argue that the transfer of the McDonald properties to the venture was a nontaxable capital contribution under section 721, and that section 731 requires that gain be recognized only to the extent the amount of cash distributed exceeded the adjusted basis of JWC's partnership interest in the venture. Respondent argues that the transaction should be treated as a nontaxable capital contribution of 25 percent of the McDonald properties in exchange for a 25-percent partnership interest in the venture, and a taxable sale of 75 percent of the McDonald properties for cash. . . .

In *Otey*, one of the taxpayers formed a partnership with another party for the purpose of constructing FHA-financed housing on property owned by the taxpayer. The taxpayer transferred the property to the partnership at an agreed value of $65,000, and the other party contributed no capital, but his credit worthiness was essential to obtaining a construction loan. The partnership took out a loan in an amount greater than needed for the construction, of which the taxpayer would draw about $65,000. We held that the taxpayer's transfer of property to the partnership was, in substance and in form, a contribution to capital under section 721(a), and not a taxable sale to the partnership under section 707(a). . . .

Congress expressed its disapproval of our decision in *Otey* by enacting section 707(a)(2)(B) as part of the Deficit Reduction Act of 1984, which was generally effective for property transferred after March 31, 1984. . . . [T]he legislative history states:

> [I]n the case of disguised sales, the committee is concerned that taxpayers have deferred or avoided tax on sales of property (including partnership interests) by characterizing sales as contributions of property (including money) followed (or preceded) by a related partnership distribution. Although Treasury regulations provide that the substance of the transaction should govern, court decisions have allowed tax-free treatment in cases which are economically indistinguishable from sales of property to a partnership or another partner. The committee believes that these transactions should be treated in a manner consistent with their underlying economic substance. . . .

Respondent acknowledges that section 707(a)(2)(B) does not apply to this case, since it became effective for transfers of property occurring after the year in issue, 1982. . . .

. . . [W]e believe that the facts present in *Otey* differ materially from the facts of this case, but that a similar analysis is helpful in determining the tax consequences of the transaction in issue. Both parties have analyzed this case under six specific factors discussed by the Court in *Otey*. See *Otey v. Commissioner*, 70 T.C. at 319-321. In cases decided after *Otey*, however, we have not subscribed to a mechanical application of these "six factors." . . . Instead, we have utilized the factors as a guide in reviewing the particular facts presented to decide whether the economic substance of the property transfers were in accord with their form. . . .

In determining the substance of the transaction before us, we must thus focus upon "whether what was done, apart from the tax motive, was the thing which the statute intended." Cf. *Gregory v. Helvering*, 293 U.S. 465 (1934). Stated otherwise, "in order to fit within a particular provision of the statute a transaction must comply not only with the letter of the section, but must have a business purpose (other than to avoid taxes) that falls within its spirit as well." See B. Bittker &J. Eustice, Federal Income Taxation of Corporations and Shareholders, par. 14.51, p. 14-170 (5th ed. 1987). Accordingly, in order for the nonrecognition provisions of sections 721 and 731 to apply in this case, there must have been a valid business purpose (or purposes) supporting the contribution of the McDonald properties by JWC to the venture and the distribution of cash by the venture to JWC.[3]

The facts of the present case show, however, that the business purpose was for JWC to sell a 75-percent interest in the McDonald properties to Metropolitan for cash and, thereafter, for JWC and Metropolitan to contribute their 25-percent and 75-percent interests, respectively, to the venture. . . . [T]he transaction in issue is in part a sale, but is not governed by section 707(a) because the sale occurred between partners.

. . . [W]e have stated that we will look behind the chosen form of a transaction where "elements of artificiality" are present. See *Otey v. Commissioner*, 70 T.C. at 319-320 (the first *Otey* factor). When the substance of the transaction in this case is exposed by examining its manifest business purpose, it becomes clear that the transaction should be treated in part as a sale for tax purposes.

JWC had attempted to sell the McDonald properties outright for about 2 years before its transaction with Metropolitan. Petitioners contend that they abandoned their intent to sell the properties when Metropolitan came along and decided instead to form a joint venture. We find that petitioners' intent to sell at least part of the McDonald properties never wavered. All that changed, upon the advice of tax professionals, was the form in which the transaction would be cast.

---

3. In the *Otey* . . . line of cases, we did not expressly state that we were applying a business purpose requirement. Nevertheless, the factors we have discussed represent facts which indicate the presence or absence of a valid business purpose. . . .

We also believe that no reasonable inference can be drawn from the objective facts in this case other than that the business purpose for the transaction was to accomplish a "part sale." JWC owned 100 percent of the McDonald properties before the transaction took place. JWC transferred the McDonald properties to the venture and Metropolitan transferred cash equal to 75 percent of the net agreed value of the properties. The respective ownership percentage interests of JWC and Metropolitan under the partnership agreement, however, were 25 percent and 75 percent. Thus, JWC transferred more assets to the venture than Metropolitan in exchange for less of an ownership percentage interest. The venture immediately "distributed" all of the cash it received from Metropolitan to JWC, causing the relative value of assets contributed and the ownership percentage interests to equalize. After the "distribution," JWC had cash equal to 75 percent of the net value of the McDonald properties, and Metropolitan received a 75-percent interest in the properties through its ownership percentage interest in the venture.

We have previously described equalizing distributions as "a usual and customary partnership capitalization arrangement, under which the partner who put up a greater share of the capital than his share of the partnership profits is to receive preferential distributions to equalize capital accounts." *Otey v. Commissioner*, 70 T.C. at 321 (the fifth *Otey* factor). In the present case, however, the amount of cash Metropolitan transferred to the venture was obviously arrived at by first figuring out how much cash would then need to be distributed to equalize capital accounts (expressed at fair market value) and ownership percentage interests. Thus, the "distribution" was actually disguised consideration in the sale of part of the McDonald properties.

In *Otey*, we stated that the transaction there in issue was not an attempted end-run around the limitations of section 1031 because, were there no partnership at all, the taxpayer could borrow funds on the security of appreciated property and apply them to his personal use without triggering gain. *Otey v. Commissioner*, 70 T.C. at 321 (the sixth *Otey* factor). We warned, however, that "Had the distributed funds come directly from the other partner, respondent's case would be stronger." *Otey v. Commissioner*, supra at 321. In the present case, respondent's case is stronger because the "distributed" funds came from Metropolitan, and not from a lender or some other third party. . . .

Nevertheless, petitioners argue that there was no sale because they remained liable on the two mortgages subject to which the McDonald properties were transferred. In *Otey*, we stated that the taxpayer enjoyed no guarantee that he would be paid (and be able to retain) the money distributed to him by the partnership. *Otey v. Commissioner*, supra (the fourth *Otey* factor). There was no "guarantee" because the distribution was to be paid out of funds to be borrowed by the partnership and the taxpayer was personally liable for the entire borrowing. Here, however, the mortgage debt did not give rise to the cash "distributed" to JWC. Moreover, while petitioners were ultimately liable for the mortgage debt on the McDonald properties, Metropolitan's basis in its partnership interest was increased by 75 percent of the mortgage debt. See sec. 752. Moreover, if petitioners had been required to pay the debt, they would have been entitled to a contribution from Metropolitan of 75 percent. Accordingly, petitioners were effectively relieved of 75 percent of the mortgage debt.

The most important factor in *Otey* was that the real property "was emplaced in the partnership at its inception and as a part of the very raison d'etre of the partnership," which was the construction of housing. *Otey v. Commissioner*, 70 T.C. at 320 (the second *Otey* factor). Petitioners argue that one of the business objectives of the venture was to continue to operate the McDonald properties as they were being operated before the venture was formed. We agree, but only to the extent of the 25-percent interest we find was actually contributed by petitioners.[4]

For all of the foregoing reasons, we hold for respondent. . . .

NOTES AND QUESTIONS

1. *Stakes.* What were the stakes in *Jacobson*? Assume that JWC had a $6 million basis in the McDonald properties, worth $16 million and encumbered by an $8 million mortgage, and that Metropolitan was willing to put up $6 million in cash for a three-fourths interest in the encumbered properties. What would have been the tax consequences to all parties if the form of the taxpayer's transaction had been respected? Under the court's holding? Another possibility, applicable to section 1031 and section 351 transactions, is to require the transferor to recognize gain to the extent of any boot received in an otherwise nonrecognition transaction. See, e.g., I.R.C. §§ 1031(b), 351(b).

2. *Was section 707(a)(2)(B) necessary?* In light of *Jacobson*, consider whether a statutory change was necessary in order to address the problem of disguised sales. Why does the court reject the taxpayers' argument that there was no sale because they remained liable for the mortgages encumbering the transferred property? Is this consistent with the court's rationale in *Otey*?

3. *Disguised sales of partnership interests.* In enacting section 707(a)(2)(B), Congress also made clear that certain contributions and related distributions would be treated for tax purposes as disguised sales of *partnership interests.* See Colonnade Condominium, Inc. v. Comm'r, 91 T.C. 793 (1988) (admission of new partners coupled with deemed section 752(b) distribution constituted sale of a partnership interest under prior law).

---

4. We note that the third factor in *Otey* was that the taxpayer's property was the only capital contributed to the partnership, and to treat the transaction "as an outside transaction would require us to hold in effect that no nonborrowed capital was contributed at all." *Otey v. Commissioner*, supra at 320. Since we hold that there was, in substance, a sale between the partners, followed by contributions by those partners, this factor does not apply to this case.

2. *Section 707(a)(2)(B)*

a. In General

Read I.R.C. § 707(a)(2)(B); Reg. § 1.707-3(a) and (b). Under section 707(a)(2)(B), a transaction taking the form of a partnership contribution and distribution is taxed as a sale or exchange if "properly characterized" as such. The regulations under section 707(a)(2)(B) provide detailed guidance concerning when such a transaction should be recharacterized as a sale of property by a partner to a partnership. The basic test is whether the transfer of money or other consideration by a partnership to a partner "would not have been made but for" the transfer of property by the partner to the partnership. Reg. § 1.707-3(b)(1)(i). In the case of simultaneous transfers, disguised sale treatment is most likely. If the transfers are not simultaneous, then a disguised sale exists if the "but for" test is met and the subsequent transfer (generally the distribution) is independent of the entrepreneurial risks of the partnership. Reg. § 1.707-3(b)(1)(ii). The regulations apply a facts-and-circumstances test to determine whether a disguised sale exists. See Reg. § 1.707-3(b)(2) (listing ten nonexclusive factors). Consistent with the legislative history, the factors listed in the regulations focus essentially on whether the contributing partner has "cashed out" her investment rather than exposed her interest in the transferred property to the economic risks of the partnership's business. If section 707(a)(2)(B) applies, the transaction is recharacterized as a sale for all purposes of the Code. Deferred payments may be subject to the installment sale rules of sections 453, 483, and 1274.

NOTES AND QUESTIONS

1. *Two-year presumptions.* Read Reg. § 1.707-3(c)(1) and (d). What is the purpose of the alternative two-year presumptions in the case of nonsimultaneous transfers? Can both taxpayers and the government rebut these presumptions?

2. *Exceptions.* Special rules exempt certain types of payments, such as guaranteed payments for capital, reasonable preferred returns on capital, distributions from operating cash flow, and certain reimbursed expenses, from disguised sale treatment even if made within two years before or after a contribution. See Reg. § 1.707-4. What is the rationale for these exceptions?

b. Part-Sale, Part-Contribution

If section 707(a)(2)(B) applies, the transaction may be treated as a sale between the contributor and the partnership or between two nonpartners (if no partnership is deemed to exist), or as a part-sale, part-contribution. The following example illustrates the mechanics of the last recharacterization.

Example 9-1: In exchange for equal interests in the newly formed AB partnership, A contributes $75 cash and B contributes land with a fair market value of $100 and a basis of $40 in B's hands. The partnership immediately distributes $25 cash to B. Under section 707(a)(2)(B), B would be treated as selling one-fourth of the land to the partnership and would recognize gain of $15 ($25 amount realized less $10 allocable basis). The rest of the land would be treated as a partnership contribution. See Reg. § 1.707-3(f) (ex. 1). The partnership would take a cost basis in the purchased portion of the land ($25) and a transferred basis in the contributed portion of the land ($30), preserving the remaining built-in gain of $45 (which would all be allocable to B under section 704(c)). Immediately after formation, the partnership would have the following balance sheet:

Assets	*IB*	*BV*	*FMV*	*Capital*	*Tax*	*Book*	*FMV*
Cash	50	50	50	A	75	75	75
Land	55	100	100	B	30	75	75
Total	105	150	150	Total	105	150	150

Problem 9-1: In **example 9-1**, suppose that B instead receives a distribution of $27.50 one year after formation of the partnership and that the discounted present value of the payment (using a discount rate of ten percent) is $25. What are the tax consequences to B and the partnership? See I.R.C. § 1274(a) and (b); Reg. § 1.707-3(f) (ex. 2).

c. Liabilities

Read Reg. § 1.707-5(a). If encumbered property is contributed to a partnership, the simultaneous deemed cash distribution back to the contributor as a result of section 752(b) could automatically cause the transaction to be treated as a disguised sale even though it should not be so characterized. To prevent this result, the regulations generally single out liabilities incurred "in anticipation of the transfer" of property to a partnership ("nonqualified liabilities"). See Reg. § 1.707-5(a)(1). By incurring liabilities shortly before a transfer, a partner may effectively cash out a portion of her investment. To the extent that nonqualified liabilities are shifted to the other partners, the contributing partner is treated as receiving consideration in a part-sale. Any liabilities incurred within two years of a transfer are generally presumed to be incurred in anticipation of the transfer. See Reg. § 1.707-5(a)(7). By contrast, a partnership's assumption of qualified liabilities (i.e., liabilities incurred more than two years before the contribution and certain other liabilities) generally does not give rise to a disguised sale. See Reg. § 1.707-5(a)(1), (5), and (6).

Example 9-2: In exchange for a one-fourth partnership interest, A contributes property with a fair market value of $120 and a basis of $40, subject to an $80 recourse liability. Assume that the partners share the recourse liability according to their percentage interests in the partnership. If A incurred the liability more than two years before the contribution, the qualified liability is disregarded for purposes of the disguised sale rules. Thus, A is not deemed to sell any portion of the transferred property, even though she has net liability relief of $60 (three-fourths of the $80 liability) under section 752. See Reg. § 1.707-5(f) (ex. 5). On the other hand, if the liability were a nonqualified liability, A would be treated as selling one half of the property, thereby recognizing gain of $40 ($60 amount realized less $20 allocable basis). See Reg. § 1.707-5(f) (ex. 2).

The disguised sale rules determine the partners' shares of recourse liabilities under the normal section 752 rules. See Reg. § 1.707-5(a)(2)(i). Nonrecourse liabilities are subject to a special rule: only the partners' overall sharing ratios for excess nonrecourse liabilities are taken into account for purposes of determining the deemed section 752(b) distribution to the contributing partner. See Reg. § 1.707-5(a)(2)(ii). Thus, the section 707 regulations simply ignore section 704(c) gain in allocating nonrecourse liabilities, presumably to avoid excessively generous treatment of the contributing partner. If the liability in **example 9-2** were a nonqualified nonrecourse liability, the disguised sale rules would treat A as having a one-fourth share of the liability (and ignore any priority allocation to reflect section 704(c) gain). Thus, A would be deemed to sell one-half of the property for consideration of $60 ($80 nonqualified nonrecourse liability less A's $20 share of the liability).

NOTES AND QUESTIONS

1. *Corporate tax rule.* In the corporate tax context, section 357(b) addresses a similar problem when property is encumbered shortly before a contribution for the principal purpose of tax avoidance (or not a bona fide business purpose). Section 357(b) is harsher, however, since the entire liability in that case is treated as boot. Is the different treatment under sections 707(a)(2)(B) and 357(b) justified?

2. *More qualified liabilities.* Certain liabilities are considered qualified liabilities even if incurred within two years prior to the contribution. See Reg. § 1.707-5(a)(6)(i)(C) and (D) (liabilities incurred to acquire or improve the contributed property and liabilities incurred in the ordinary course of business if substantially all of the assets of the business are transferred). What is the rationale for these exceptions?

Problem 9-2: In **example 9-2**, above, suppose that A receives $10 cash in addition to the assumption of $80 of qualified liabilities. To what extent is the transfer treated as a disguised sale? See Reg. § 1.707-5(a)(5).

d. Debt-Financed Distributions

Reconsider the facts in *Otey*, where the taxpayer received a distribution from a partnership borrowing equal to the value of the contributed property shortly after the contribution. Congress clearly intended to overrule the holding in *Otey*, but left it to the regulation drafters to determine precisely how to treat this situation. If Otey had borrowed against the property (up to its fair market value) immediately before the contribution, he would have been treated as receiving consideration equal to half the value of the contributed property (the portion of the nonqualified liability shifted to the other 50 percent partner), resulting in a deemed sale of half of the property. The section 707 regulations reach a similar result when a partner contributes unencumbered property and shortly thereafter receives a distribution attributable to a liability incurred by the partnership. In this situation, the distribution is treated as sale proceeds only to the extent that it exceeds the partner's "allocable share" of the partnership liability incurred to finance the distribution. A partner's allocable share of the liability is equal to her share of the liability multiplied by the following fraction:

$$\frac{\text{Amount of distribution attributable to the liability}}{\text{Total amount of liability}}$$

See Reg. § 1.707-5(b), -5(f) (ex. 10). This special rule applies if all or a portion of the debt-financed proceeds are distributed within 90 days after the partnership incurred the liability.

> **Example 9-3:** The facts are the same as in **example 9-2**, except that the property contributed by A is unencumbered. Immediately after the contribution, the partnership incurs a recourse liability of $200 and distributes $80 of the loan proceeds to A. The distribution is treated as sales proceeds only to the extent that it exceeds A's "allocable share of the liability." This share is $20 and is determined by multiplying A's one-fourth share of the $200 liability ($50) by the following fraction: the amount of the distribution attributable to the liability ($80) divided by the total liability ($200), or two-fifths. Thus, only $60 ($80 distribution less $20 allocable share of the liability) is treated as sale proceeds, triggering a deemed sale of one-half of the transferred property. The result is the same as if A had borrowed $80 (the amount distributed) against the property immediately before the contribution and shifted three-fourths of the pre-contribution liability to the other partners.

NOTES AND QUESTIONS

1. *Effect of partnership liabilities*. Recall that the court in *Otey* held that there was no disguised sale because the partners remained jointly and severally liable for the partnership's recourse borrowing, which substantially exceeded the value of the

contributed property. Under the current section 707 regulations, could Otey avoid disguised sale treatment if he agreed to remain personally liable for the entire partnership liability? What difference would it make if the liability were nonrecourse?

2. *Illusory indemnities.* The section 752 regulations contain an anti-abuse rule that disregards a partner's purported payment obligation if the principal purpose of the arrangement is to create the appearance of the partner bearing the economic risk of loss. Reg. § 1.752-2(j)(1). In Canal Corp. v. Comm'r, 135 T.C. 199 (2010), the Tax Court applied the anti-abuse rule to find a disguised sale in a so-called "leveraged partnership" transaction. The taxpayer (Canal) sought to sell the low-basis assets of one of its subsidiaries (WISCO) to another corporation (GP). To defer recognizing gain on the asset sale, Canal's financial and tax advisors suggested an alternative strategy of having WISCO and GP form an LLC (taxable as a partnership), which would borrow from a third party and distribute the proceeds tax free to WISCO. The amount distributed was slightly lower than the previously negotiated sales price for the assets to reflect the tax benefit of deferring gain of $524 million. WISCO agreed to indemnify GP in the event GP made payment on its guarantee of the LLC's recourse debt, thereby hoping to shift the economic risk of loss for the liability to WISCO (and therefore increasing WISCO's share of the liability for purposes of section 752 and the disguised sale rules). After the partnership distribution, WISCO promptly transferred the proceeds to Canal in exchange for an intercompany note, leaving WISCO with no significant assets other than the note (which was later cancelled).

The court found that WISCO's indemnification obligation was economically illusory, noting the absence of any requirement that WISCO maintain any net worth. Indeed, Canal represented to rating agencies that "the only risk associated with the transaction came . . . from the tax risk," not the risk under the indemnity agreement. Id. at 209. Under these circumstances, the court had little difficulty in finding that the anti-abuse rule applied, triggering Canal's deferred gain under the disguised sale rules. For penalty purposes, the taxpayer was not entitled to rely on the opinion of the accounting firm that had helped structure the transaction; the firm wore "too many" hats and its advice was "tainted by an inherent conflict of interest." Id. at 220. Labeling as "exorbitant" the firm's flat fee ($800,000), the court castigated the opinion as "riddled with questionable conclusions and unreasonable assumptions." Id. at 219. Thus, the firm "crossed over the line from trusted advisor for prior accounting purposes" to function essentially as a tax shelter promoter; allowing a penalty shield in this situation would provide "carte blanche to promoters to provide a tax opinion as part and parcel of a promotion." Id. at 220-21. After Canal filed for bankruptcy, the case was settled without an appeal. Do you agree with the court's assessment of the accounting firm's role? Although it is clear that reliance on a promoter's opinion vitiates a good faith defense, it is less clear just who is a promoter for this purpose.

3. *More leveraged partnerships.* The Tribune Co. reportedly used a leveraged partnership transaction to sell the Chicago Cubs. The Tribune Co. (a former C corporation that converted to S status) wanted to defer reporting gain until after the then applicable ten-year recognition period for built-in gains under section 1374.

Because the sole owner of the Tribune Co. was an ESOP, the taxpayer hoped the gain would be exempt from tax at both the corporate and shareholder levels when eventually reported. See I.R.C. § 512(e)(3) (exempting ESOPs owning S stock from tax on "unrelated business taxable income"). The Tribune Co. later filed for bankruptcy; it emerged from bankruptcy in 2012.

In U.S. v. G-1 Holdings Inc., 2010-1 U.S.T.C. ¶ 50,332 (D.N.J. 2009), the court struck down a leveraged partnership transaction structured as a contribution of high-value, low-basis assets followed by a nonrecourse borrowing against the contributor's partnership interest. Although the contributing partner was nominally the borrower, the court found that in substance the partnership was the borrower and distributed the loan proceeds to the contributing partner. In a footnote, the court analogized the transaction to a sale of assets in exchange for an installment note, coupled with a pledge of the installment note for a nonrecourse loan equal to the fair market value of the sold assets. Id. at n.20. The contributor was entitled to priority returns on its capital account to service the interest payments on the nonrecourse loan. Since the partnership agreement guaranteed that the contributor's capital account could not fall below a minimum level, the lender was willing to lend nonrecourse an amount nearly equal to the guaranteed capital account balance.

4. *Too much guidance?* The current section 707 regulations provide much more guidance (too much?) concerning when a contribution and related distribution will be treated as a disguised sale. Now that you have been exposed to some of the mechanics, to what extent do you think that section 707(a)(2)(B) represents an improvement over prior law? Do the provision and accompanying regulations alter or merely codify the prior law? Could it be argued that the regulations actually invite disguised sales along the lines of the leveraged partnership transactions described above? As mentioned in chapters four and five, proposed regulations under section 752 would eliminate some of the flexibility in allocating both recourse and nonrecourse liabilities; proposed regulations were issued simultaneously under section 707 to refine the disguised sale rules. REG-119305-11, 2014-8 I.R.B. 524. These proposed changes are intended partly to address abuses related to leveraged partnership distributions but would also have more far-reaching consequences.

Of course, the culprit underlying the need for rules such as those preventing disguised sales is the general nonrecognition treatment of partnership contributions and distributions. The deemed transfers that result under the disguised sale rules are simply alternative ways of carrying out the identical economic transaction, but with different tax consequences. The extraordinary difficulty in determining whether one set of transfers rather than another has occurred underscores the fundamental tension between the partnership nonrecognition rules and the general tax principle that sales and exchanges are taxable events. The basic question, therefore, is whether the policy rationale for the partnership nonrecognition rules is sufficiently powerful to warrant interjecting such uncertainty and administrative cost.

5. *Disguised sale of tax credits.* In Virginia Historic Tax Credit Fund 2001 LP v. Comm'r, 639 F.3d 129 (4th Cir. 2011), partnerships solicited capital contributions from investors who were allocated state tax credits in exchange for their

contributions. Without deciding whether the investors were partners, the court treated the transactions as, in substance, disguised sales of the tax credits under section 707, generating taxable income to the partnerships. In another recent case involving federal historic rehabilitation tax credits, the court concluded that the investor was not a bona fide partner because it had no meaningful upside potential or downside risk. See Historic Boardwalk Hall, LLC v. Comm'r, 694 F.3d 425 (3d Cir. 2012), cert. denied, 133 S. Ct. 2734 (2013) (noting that the bona fide partner and disguised sale rules both look to whether a purported partner has entrepreneurial risk). Since the court assumed that the transaction had economic substance, it declined to consider whether the transaction would have survived an economic substance inquiry.

B. Other Anti-"Mixing Bowl" Provisions Linking Contributions and Distributions

1. *Overview: Sections 704(c)(1)(B) and 737*

The disguised sale rules demonstrate the need to monitor contributions and related distributions in order to avoid potential misuse of subchapter K's liberal nonrecognition regime. But enactment of section 707(a)(2)(B) alone proved insufficient to thwart other types of "mixing bowl" transactions engaged in by taxpayers. (The term "mixing bowl" connotes a type of transaction in which taxpayers use a partnership as a vehicle to shuffle property back and forth among themselves without recognition of gain.) For example, suppose that section 704(c) property is contributed tax free to a partnership in exchange for a partnership interest. As you know, section 704(c)(1)(A) requires any built-in gain or loss to be specially allocated to the contributor when such gain or loss is recognized by the partnership. But this requirement may be avoided if the link between the contributor and the section 704(c) property is somehow broken prior to the recognition event. The property might be distributed to another partner, or the contributor's interest in the partnership might be completely liquidated, prior to the partnership's recognition of the built-in gain or loss. If the transaction breaking the link is itself a nonrecognition event, the section 704(c)(1)(A) mandate could be circumvented in these situations.

To address this potential problem, Congress enacted sections 704(c)(1)(B) and 737, which generally apply to distributions occurring within seven years of a contribution of section 704(c) property, to the extent that the disguised sale rules do not apply. See Reg. §§ 1.704-4(a)(2), 1.737-1(a)(2). Section 704(c)(1)(B) deals with a distribution of the section 704(c) property to another partner, whereas section 737 generally concerns a distribution of other property that terminates the contributor's tie to the partnership. These two provisions can be viewed as backstopping the section 704(c) built-in gain rules or, alternatively, as expanding the reach of the section 707 disguised sale rules.

2. *Section 704(c)(1)(B)*

Read I.R.C. § 704(c)(1)(B) and Reg. § 1.704-4(a)(1) and (2), (b)(1) and (e)(1)-(3). Section 704(c)(1)(B) provides that if section 704(c) property is distributed to a partner (other than the contributing partner) within seven years of the original contribution, the contributing partner must recognize taxable gain or loss as if the partnership had sold the section 704(c) property at the time of the distribution. (Proposed regulation section 1.704-4(a)(4)(i) reflects the current seven-year statutory period.) Both the contributing partner's outside basis and the partnership's basis in the distributed property are adjusted to reflect any gain or loss recognized. The adjustments to the basis of the distributed property, which occur immediately before the distribution, are taken into account in determining the distributee's basis in the distributed property. See I.R.C. § 732.

Example 9-4: A, B, and C form the equal ABC partnership. A and B contribute $90 cash each and C contributes land with a fair market value of $90 and an adjusted basis of $30 in C's hands. The partnership uses the traditional method of allocating section 704(c) gain or loss. Three years later, the partnership makes a nonliquidating distribution of the land to B when the fair market value of the land is unchanged. Under section 704(c)(1)(B), the partnership is deemed to sell the land for $90, recognizing $60 of built-in gain allocated entirely to C pursuant to section 704(c). C's outside basis (and her tax capital account) is increased from $30 to $90. The distributed property is treated as having a basis of $90 for purposes of determining B's basis under section 732 as well as any basis adjustment under section 734(b). See Reg. § 1.704-4(e)(2) and (3).

Problem 9-3:

(a) Determine the tax consequences to all parties if, in **example 9-4**, the land had declined in value to $30 at the time of the distribution. Construct the partnership's balance sheet immediately after the distribution.
(b) Same as (a), except that the partnership uses the remedial method of allocating section 704(c) gain or loss. See Reg. § 1.704-4(a)(5) (ex. 3).
(c) Suppose in **example 9-4**, the parties simply amend their partnership agreement after three years to provide that substantially all of the benefits and burdens from owning the land are allocated to B and substantially all of the benefits and burdens of the partnership's remaining assets are allocated to A and C. With this arrangement, the partnership continues to own the land and does not distribute it to B until more than seven years after C's contribution. Have the parties

avoided the application of section 704(c)(1)(B)? See Reg. § 1.704-4(f)(1) and (2) (ex. 1).

(d) Suppose in **example 9-4**, the land contributed by C has a fair market value of $90 and an adjusted basis in C's hands of $120. What are the tax consequences if, three years later, the partnership makes a non-liquidating distribution of the land to B when the fair market value of the land is unchanged? See I.R.C. § 704(c)(1)(C), Prop. Reg. § 1.704-3(f)(3)(v)(B) and (D) (ex. 2).

Read I.R.C. § 704(c)(2) and Reg. § 1.704-4(d)(3). Section 704(c)(2) provides an exception to section 704(c)(1)(B) if the contributing partner receives a timely distribution of property of a like kind (within the meaning of section 1031) to the contributed property which is distributed to another partner. (Generally, the distribution to the contributor must take place within 180 days of the earlier distribution.) In this situation, Congress considered it inappropriate to tax the built-in gain or loss immediately to the contributing partner to the extent that she has merely engaged in a section 1031 nonrecognition transaction. The statutory language of section 704(c)(2) is somewhat opaque, however; it treats the contributing partner as if she had contributed the other property distributed to her (rather than the property she actually contributed) to the extent of the value of such other property. The regulations take a different approach for purposes of determining the basis consequences and gain (or loss) recognition. Under this approach, the amount of gain (or loss) that the contributor would otherwise recognize under section 704(c)(1)(B) is reduced by any built-in gain (or loss) preserved in the distributed like-kind property (after taking into account the contributor's basis in the property under section 732).

Example 9-5: The facts are the same as in **example 9-4**, except that the partnership subsequently purchases another parcel of land worth $90. When B receives a distribution of C's land, the partnership also distributes the like-kind purchased land (still worth $90) to C. Under the normal distribution rules of section 732, C properly takes a basis of $30 in the distributed land. Under section 704(c)(1)(B), C would generally recognize section 704(c) gain of $60 on the distribution to B. C's recognized gain is reduced, however, by the amount of the built-gain preserved in the land distributed to C. Since the lurking gain is $60 ($90 fair market value of distributed land less $30 basis in C's hands), C recognizes no gain under section 704(c)(1)(B). See Reg. § 1.704-4(d)(4).

3. *Section 737*

Read I.R.C. § 737 and Reg. § 1.737-1(a), (b) and (c)(1), and -3(a), (b)(1) and (c)(1) and (2). Section 737 may trigger recognition of gain (but not loss) if a partner who contributes section 704(c) property receives a distribution of property (other than cash) within seven years after the original contribution. The recognized gain is limited to the lesser of (i) the "excess distribution," which is the excess of the value of the distributed property (other than cash) over the distributee's outside basis (reduced by any cash distributed) or (ii) the distributee's "net pre-contribution gain." See I.R.C. § 737(a). Net pre-contribution gain is defined as the net gain that the contributing partner would have recognized under section 704(c)(1)(B) if all of the section 704(c) property she contributed within the preceding seven years had been distributed to another partner. See I.R.C. § 737(b). If section 737 applies, both the distributee's outside basis and the partnership's basis in the section 704(c) property are increased to reflect any gain recognized. See I.R.C. § 737(c)(1) and (2); Reg. § 1.737-3(a) and (c).

> **Example 9-6:** The facts are the same as in **example 9-4**, except that the partnership retains the land contributed by C and purchases nonmarketable securities worth $90. Three years after formation, the partnership distributes the securities (now worth $120) to C in liquidation of her partnership interest. At the time of the distribution, the value of the land has increased to $150 and the partnership continues to hold cash of $90. Under section 737, C must recognize gain of $60 on the distribution, i.e., the lesser of the excess distribution of $90 ($120 fair market value of distributed property less C's $30 outside basis) or C's net pre-contribution gain of $60. C's outside basis is increased by the recognized gain of $60 before determining the basis of the distributed securities in C's hands. Thus, C takes a basis in the distributed securities of $90 under section 732(b), i.e., the same as C's basis (after adjustment) in her former partnership interest. The partnership also increases its basis in the land to reflect C's recognized gain.

If the distributee receives a distribution solely of cash, section 737 does not apply. Instead, the distributee's remaining built-in gain will generally be taxed immediately under section 731 (distribution of cash in excess of outside basis). For this reason, section 737 is also inapplicable to a distribution of marketable securities that are treated as cash under section 731(c)(1)(A). See I.R.C. § 737(e). Section 731(c) is described briefly in the next section. Finally, section 737 does not apply to the extent section 751(b) applies or if the transaction is recharacterized as a disguised sale. See Reg. § 1.737-1(a)(2).

NOTES AND QUESTIONS

1. *Overlap.* Sections 704(c)(1)(B) and 737 may *both* apply if section 704(c) property is distributed to another partner and, as part of the same transaction, the contributing partner receives a distribution triggering section 737. In this situation, the contributing partner's net pre-contribution gain and outside basis are both adjusted to reflect any gain recognized under section 704(c)(1)(B) *before* determining

the tax consequences under section 737. This approach serves to minimize any gain recognition under section 737. See Reg. § 1.737-1(c)(2)(iv).

2. *Distributions of cash and other property*. What are the tax consequences if a contributing partner receives a distribution of cash *and* other property in a transaction implicating section 737? See Reg. § 1.737-1(e) (ex. 2). If the cash distribution exceeds the distributee's outside basis, gain may be recognized under both sections 731 and 737.

3. *Why nonliquidating distributions?* Section 737 applies to both nonliquidating and liquidating distributions. But to the extent a distributee retains an interest in the partnership, she has not necessarily avoided section 704(c). Why not limit section 737 to liquidating distributions?

4. *Application to reverse section 704(c) gain or loss*. Sections 704(c)(1)(B) and 737 apply in certain circumstances to a distribution of property if there has been a prior "contribution" of property with a built-in gain or loss to the partnership. Proposed regulations clarify that neither provision applies merely because a partnership holds property subject to a *reverse* section 704(c) allocation, i.e., property with a built-in gain or loss resulting from a partnership revaluation. See Prop. Reg. §§ 1.704-4(c)(7), 1.737-2(e). Thus, suppose A and B contribute $100 cash each for equal shares of new partnership AB and the partnership purchases land for $200. When the land is worth $600 (and the partnership holds no other assets), C contributes $300 cash to the partnership in exchange for a one-third partnership interest. Upon C's admission, the partnership books up the land to $600, thereby specially allocating the $400 of built-in gain to A and B. If, within seven years of C's admission and the revaluation, either the land is distributed to C or other appreciated property is distributed to A or B, neither section 704(c)(1)(B) nor section 737(a) applies.

Although this result may be mandated by the statutory language, is it sensible? Suppose C's admission to the venture had instead been structured as the creation of a new partnership rather than the entry of a new partner to an existing partnership. For example, suppose partnership AB transferred the appreciated land (worth $600) and individual C transferred $300 cash simultaneously to newly formed partnership ABC. In this situation, the land would be section 704(c) property (rather than reverse section 704(c) property), leaving the AB partnership (and indirectly A and B) potentially exposed to sections 704(c)(1)(B) and 737.

C. Distributions of Marketable Securities

You may recall that a cash distribution is taxable to the distributee to the extent the amount distributed exceeds the distributee's outside basis, whereas a distribution of property more often results in the nonrecognition of gain. Solely for purposes of determining the amount of gain recognized on a distribution (and for purposes of section 737), a distribution of "marketable securities" (broadly defined to include actively traded financial instruments and foreign currencies and other similar property) is treated as a distribution of cash equal to the fair market value of the security. Read I.R.C. § 731(c)(1), (2)(A) and (C). This recharacterization of marketable-securities-as-cash is limited, however. The amount of the cash deemed distributed is generally reduced by the distributee's share of net appreciation in such securities. See I.R.C. § 731(c)(3)(B). The basis of the distributed securities is determined under the normal rules of section 732 and increased by any gain recognized by the distributee. See I.R.C. § 731(c)(4)(A); Reg. § 1.731-2(f)(1). Under sections 733 and 734, the distributee's outside basis and any inside basis adjustments are determined as if no gain were recognized. See I.R.C. § 731(c)(5).

Example 9-7: A, whose outside basis is $40, has a one-third interest in each item of partnership ABC. A receives a liquidating distribution of the partnership's only marketable security worth $100 (basis of $10). A is treated as receiving a cash distribution of $70 ($100 fair market value of the security less A's $30 share of unrealized appreciation inherent in the security), resulting in a gain of $30 to A ($70 cash distribution less $40 outside basis) under section 731(a)(1). A takes a basis of $70 in the distributed security ($40 basis under section 732(b) increased by $30 gain recognized), thereby preserving A's one-third share of the pre-distribution unrealized appreciation ($100 fair market value of security less $70 basis in A's hands). If A instead received a nonliquidating distribution, A would still recognize $30 of gain and take a basis of $40 in the distributed security ($10 basis under section 732(a)(1) increased by $30 gain recognized). After the distribution, A's outside basis would be reduced to $30 ($40 less $10 basis allocated to the distributed security under § 732(a)(1)), determined as if no gain were recognized. I.R.C. §§ 733(2), 731(c)(5); Reg. § 1.731-2(j) (ex. 5).

As can be seen from **example 9-7**, section 731(c) bears some resemblance to the dreaded section 751(b): the focus of each provision is on a *disproportionate* distribution of a particular class of partnership property. Like section 751(b), section 731(c) is more complicated when there is a nonliquidating distribution of marketable securities and the partnership continues to hold marketable securities after the distribution. In that situation, there must be a comparison of the distributee's pre- and post-distribution shares of the net appreciation in such securities. (All marketable securities are aggregated for this purpose (Reg. § 1.731-2(b)(1)).) The amount of cash deemed distributed is reduced by the decrease in the distributee's share of the net appreciation in such securities as a result of the distribution. I.R.C. § 731(c)(3)(B).

Example 9-8: Same facts as in **example 9-7**, except that in a pro rata nonliquidating distribution, A receives only one-half of the partnership's marketable securities (worth $50 and with allocable basis of $5). (The other partners receive cash distributions of $50 each.) In this case, A's share of the net appreciation in the partnership's marketable securities is reduced by $15 as a result of the distribution ($30 share prior to distribution less $15 share after the distribution). Therefore, the amount of cash deemed distributed is reduced from $50 (the fair market value of the securities distributed) to $35. Accordingly, A does not recognize any gain (I.R.C. § 731(a)(1)) and her basis in the marketable securities received is $5 (I.R.C. § 732(a)(1)). Following the distribution, her outside basis would be $35. I.R.C. § 733(2).

NOTES AND QUESTIONS

1. *Special allocation.* In **example 9-7**, in order to avoid the impact of section 731(c), could A have claimed, in effect, that all of the appreciation in the marketable security was "hers" by agreeing to a special allocation of such appreciation prior to the distribution? See Reg. § 1.731-2(b)(3)(ii).

2. *Overlap.* If a distribution triggers section 731(c) and one or both of sections 704(c)(1)(B) and 737, the tax consequences are determined by applying section 704(c)(1)(B) first, section 731(c) second, and section 737 last. See Reg. § 1.731-2(g)(1)(i).

3. *Anti-abuse rule.* The regulations contain an anti-abuse rule that allows the IRS to recast a transaction to achieve tax results "consistent with the purpose of section 731(c)" if a principal purpose of the transaction is to achieve a contrary result. Reg. § 1.731-2(h). The anti-abuse rule provides three examples of transactions that might be recast pursuant to this authority. In the following case, the Tax Court refused to apply this regulation to treat certain nontraded private notes as marketable securities for purposes of section 731(c).

Countryside Limited Partnership v. Commissioner

95 T.C.M. 1006 (2008)

HALPERN, J.: [Much simplified, *Countryside* involved a distribution of recently purchased nontraded private notes (worth $12 million) issued by AIG in liquidation of two partners (Mr. Winn and Mr. Curtis) who owned nearly 95 percent of the total interests in a real estate partnership. The redeemed partners had essentially a zero basis in their partnership interests (after netting of liabilities) and the liquidating distribution occurred on the eve of a sale of the partnership's appreciated real property. As structured, the partnership hoped that the redemption would be tax free under section 731(a). The partnership also claimed a $12 million step-up in the basis of the real property (pursuant to sections 754 and 734(b)(1)(B)), eliminating most of the built-in gain. (Under the normal rules of subchapter K, the basis of the notes would have been stepped down from $12 million (their cost basis) to zero to match the redeemed partners' outside basis. Through a complicated tiered-partnership arrangement and inconsistent use of section 754 elections, however, the taxpayers sought to avoid any step-down in the basis of the notes but still obtain the step-up in the basis of the real property, thus duplicating the $12 million basis in both the notes and the property.) In part, the government argued that the AIG notes should be treated as marketable securities for purposes of section 731(c). Had the government prevailed on this issue, the distribution would have triggered $12 million of gain (the fair market value of the notes) under section 731(a)(1) and (c)(1). Other issues relating to the larger Countryside transaction were subsequently resolved by a stipulated decision.]

. . . Section 731(c)(1) provides that, for purposes of section 731(a)(1), the term "money" includes "marketable securities," which are to be taken into account at fair market value as of the distribution date. Section 731(c)(2)(A) defines the term "marketable securities" to mean "financial instruments . . . which are, as of the date of distribution, actively traded (within the meaning of section 1092(d)(1))." Section 731(c)(2)(B)(ii) . . . includes in the meaning of the term "marketable securities" (1) "any financial instrument which, pursuant to its terms or any other arrangement, is readily convertible into, or exchangeable for, money or marketable securities.". . .

Section 1.731-2(h) . . . provides in pertinent part:

> [I]f a principal purpose of a transaction is to achieve a tax result that is inconsistent with the purpose of section 731(c) and this section, the Commissioner can recast the transaction for Federal tax purposes as appropriate to achieve tax results that are consistent with the purpose of section 731(c) and this section.

. . . Participating partner's position that neither Mr. Winn nor Mr. Curtis recognized gain on the liquidating distribution is dependent upon his argument that the AIG notes were not "marketable securities," as defined in section 731(c)(2). In support of that argument, participating partner has submitted two affidavits [indicating that the AIG notes were not listed or traded on an established financial market]. . . . Participating partner also dismisses section 1.731-2(h) . . . as inapplicable on the ground that it is applicable only to circumstances "involving changes in partnership allocations with respect to marketable securities and distributions of nonmarketable securities by a partnership that also owns marketable securities," which, in substance, constitute a manipulation by a partner of "the inherent flexibility of the partnership form to acquire an increased interest in marketable securities from a partnership without effecting a transaction in the form of a distribution [of marketable securities]." Participating partner reasons that "the provision should not have any application to a partnership [Countryside] that owns no marketable securities at all, either directly or indirectly."

. . . Respondent "agrees and would stipulate that the [AIG] Notes . . . were not traded on an established securities market." We interpret that statement as respondent's concession that the AIG notes did not constitute marketable securities on the ground that they were "actively traded (within the meaning of section 1092(d)(1))."

See sec. 731(c)(2)(A). . . . Therefore, the issue regarding the marketability of the AIG notes is whether, pursuant to any term of those notes (or the related documentation) or any "arrangement" . . . those notes were readily convertible into money or marketable securities, thereby causing the notes to be "marketable securities" under section 731(c)(2)(B)(ii). . . . We do not agree that any of the documents [provided by] respondent . . . constitute evidence of an "arrangement" that would render the AIG notes marketable under section 731(c)(2)(B)(ii).

. . . Participating partner argues, on the basis of the illustrative examples contained in section 1.731-2(h), . . . that "the provision should not have any application to a partnership that owns no marketable securities at all, either directly or indirectly." Respondent describes that argument as expressing "the untenable position" that section 1.731-2(h) . . . does not apply "to situations where partnerships create purportedly nonmarketable securities to distribute in lieu of marketable securities, or cash, to avoid section 731(c)."

. . . [W]e agree with participating partner that each of the three examples contained in section 1.731-2(h), . . . the first of which involves a change in partnership allocations or distribution rights with respect to marketable securities, the second, a distribution of substantially all of the partnership assets other than marketable securities, and the third, a distribution of multiple properties to one or more partners at different times, involves circumstances that are not present in this case. We also note that, in the preamble to the final regulations under section 731(c), the Commissioner, in response to a taxpayer request that there be "examples illustrating abusive transactions intended to be covered by . . . section 1.731-2(h)," stated that "the text of the regulations adequately describes several situations that would be considered abusive . . . , and . . . additional examples are unnecessary." T.D. 8707, 1997-1 C.B. 128, 130. Thus, the examples contained in the regulation, which are the only portion of the text of the regulation describing "situations that would be considered abusive," presumably illustrate the universe of circumstances considered abusive for purposes of section 731(c).

Countryside's . . . distribution of the AIG notes to Mr. Winn and Mr. Curtis was not part of an abusive transaction as described in section 1.731-2(h). . . . We conclude that the liquidating distribution . . . constituted a distribution of nonmarketable securities resulting in nonrecognition of gain to the recipients, Mr. Winn and Mr. Curtis, pursuant to sections 731(a)(1). . . .

NOTES AND QUESTIONS

1. *Purpose of section 731(c).* In *Countryside*, the court refused to invoke the section 731(c) anti-abuse rule, even though the taxpayers conceded that the partnership's purchase and distribution of the AIG notes was intended to circumvent the statutory provision. Should the section 731(c) anti-abuse rule be interpreted so narrowly?

2. *Basis duplication and inconsistent section 754 elections.* The actual *Countryside* transaction was more complicated than the brief summary included with the case. The actual transaction involved a three-tier partnership structure: Countryside, which held a 99 percent interest in another partnership (CLPP), which in turn owned a 99 percent interest in a third partnership (MP). Both Countryside and CLPP made section 754 elections but MP did not. In addition, the property distributed to Messrs. Winn and Curtis in liquidation of their interest in Countryside was not the AIG notes themselves (which were actually held by MP) but rather the 99 percent interest in CLPP (which owned 99 percent of MP). Through this arrangement, the parties hoped that (1) the distribution would result in a reduction in the basis of the distributed CLPP partnership interests received by Messrs. Winn and Curtis (section 732(b)); (2) there would be a corresponding increase in the basis of the real estate held by Countryside and sold shortly thereafter (section 754 election and section 734(b)(1)(B) (the last sentence of section 734(b) was claimed to be inapplicable since CLPP had a section 754 election in effect); and (3) MP would have a cost basis of $12 million in the AIG notes equal to their face amount (no section 754 election by MP). If the larger transaction were respected, the end result would not simply be deferral of gain recognition until the AIG notes were redeemed (about two and a half years after the distribution), but rather potentially unlimited deferral. Under the taxpayer's theory, the redemption of the AIG notes would be tax free because the notes purportedly retained a basis of $12 million equal to their face amount. (The only property with a stepped-down basis (equal to the redeemed partners' zero outside bases) was the CLPP partnership interests held by Messrs. Winn and Curtis; this built-in gain of $12 million was irrelevant, as a practical matter, since the CLPP interests could be held indefinitely.)

If CLPP's existence were disregarded as tax motivated, the absence of a section 754 election by MP would mean that Countryside was not entitled to step up the basis of its real property, triggering $12 million of additional gain on sale of the real property. See I.R.C. § 734(b) (last sentence). If both CLPP and MP were disregarded as tax motivated, the redeemed partners would presumably be treated as receiving a distribution of the notes themselves (rather than partnership interests). The reduction in the basis of the notes would then result in $12 million gain recognition upon redemption of the notes. The Tax Court left open both possibilities (requiring a basis step-down in the notes or disallowing a basis step-up in the real property) for later resolution. In a subsequent stipulated decision resolving the remaining issues, the Tax Court ordered a $12 million step-down in the basis of the AIG notes, applying section 743(b) and the partnership anti-abuse rule. Since the step-up in the basis of the partnership's real property was preserved, the net result was an additional $12 million of capital gain to the redeemed partners when the AIG notes were paid three years later. Thus, the taxpayers' planning and litigation costs resulted in a short-term deferral of the gain that would otherwise have been recognized upon sale of the real property. The taxpayers also agreed to pay a penalty on a portion of their underpayment.

3. *Business purpose and economic substance.* In *Countryside*, the court found that the redemption had a "substantial business purpose," namely, allowing the withdrawing partners to terminate their interests in the partnership. The court criticized the government for "erroneously focusing on the tax-motivated means instead of the business oriented ends." *Countryside*, 95 T.C.M. at 1019. The court's conclusion with respect to business purpose was part of a larger finding that both prongs of the economic substance test were satisfied, i.e., the transaction had a valid business purpose and also altered the partners' economic interests. If the redemption itself served a business purpose, does that mean that all of the steps in the transaction were also imbued with a business purpose? What about substance-over-form principles?

D. Recharacterizations Based on Common-Law Principles

The following case illustrates an attempt to transfer substantial built-in losses by exploiting gaps in the section 704(c) rules prior to the 2004 amendments. In reading the decision, consider how the court uses the various judicially developed doctrines — economic substance, sham, and substance-over-form — to deny the claimed tax benefits.

Southgate Master Fund, L.L.C. v. United States

659 F.3d 466 (5th Cir. 2011)

HIGGINBOTHAM, Circuit Judge: [In a pre-2004 transaction structured to transfer built-in losses, Southgate was formed to hold certain nonperforming loans ("NPLs") contributed by a Chinese government-owned institution (Cinda). Southgate's other partners were Beal, a billionaire Dallas banker and investor in distressed debt, and Beal's long-time associate and accountant, Montgomery, who helped to orchestrate the transaction. Rather than acquire the NPLs directly, Beal purchased most of Cinda's partnership interest in Southgate for $19 million, thereby claiming to step into Cinda's shoes for purposes of obtaining more than $1 billion of paper losses when Southgate disposed of the high-basis, low-value NPLs. To build up his outside basis in Southgate, Beal entered into a complex transaction dubbed "the GNMA basis-build." Beal contributed $180 million of GNMAs — fixed-rate, mortgage-backed securities — to a wholly-owned disregarded entity (Martel) through which Beal had acquired his interest in Southgate. Martel then distributed its interest in Southgate to Beal, so that Beal owned his interest in Southgate directly. Beal then contributed Martel (which owned the GNMAs) to Southgate but on terms that ensured that Beal would retain nearly all of the value of the GNMAs. As a result of the GNMA basis-build, Beal claimed to have an outside basis of nearly $200 million to absorb losses claimed in 2002 that were arguably ordinary in character under sections 724(b), 751(d), and 1221(a)(4). Depending on outside basis, the transaction would purportedly allow Beal to carry forward losses from 2002 and additional losses arising in later years. The district court determined that Southgate was a sham partnership and disallowed the losses, but it denied the government's claim for accuracy-related penalties.]

This appeal requires us to determine the tax consequences of Southgate's formation, Southgate's acquisition of its portfolio of Chinese NPLs, and the GNMA basis-build. The starting point for our analysis is the cardinal principle of income taxation: a transaction's tax consequences depend on its substance, not its form. . . . This foundational principle finds its voice in the judicial anti-abuse doctrines, which "prevent taxpayers from subverting the legislative purpose of the tax code by engaging in transactions that are fictitious or lack economic reality simply to reap a tax benefit." The judicial doctrines empower the federal courts to disregard the claimed tax benefits of a transaction — even a transaction that formally complies with the black-letter provisions of the Code and its implementing regulations — if the taxpayer cannot establish that "what was done, apart from the tax motive, was the thing which the statute intended."

Our disposition of this appeal requires us to make use of three of the judicial doctrines. The first is the economic-substance doctrine. . . . The second is the sham-partnership doctrine. A partnership "may be disregarded where it is a sham or unreal . . . [,] a bald and mischievous fiction." A taxpayer must be able to demonstrate that there was some nontax business purpose for his use of the partnership form. Finally, [the] substance-over-form doctrine allows a transaction to be recharacterized so that its taxable form corresponds to its economic substance.

. . . Our de novo application of the judicial doctrines to the facts as found by the district court leads us to three conclusions. First, Southgate's acquisition of its portfolio of Chinese NPLs had economic substance. Second, Southgate itself was a sham partnership. This second conclusion finds substantial support in our determination that the GNMA basis-build lacked economic substance. Third, Southgate's acquisition of the NPLs should be recharacterized under the substance-over-form doctrine as a direct sale from Cinda to Beal and Montgomery.

. . . With little difficulty, we affirm the district court's conclusion that Southgate's acquisition of the portfolio of NPLs had economic substance. . . . This is not an instance of a taxpayer's engaging in an exotic, one-off transaction that bears no resemblance to its ordinary business activities. Beal and Montgomery specialize in buying stressed debt. They had previously identified a growth opportunity in foreign NPL markets. As the district court found, the acquisition of the NPLs fit squarely within Beal and Montgomery's core business. The district court also found that Beal and Montgomery would have done the deal regardless of whether it had any tax benefits. . . . The acquisition of the NPLs did not, by itself, generate any tax benefits. It was the funneling of that acquisition through the partnership structure that generated massive deductions for Beal. The fact that an economically substantial transaction comes wrapped in a dubious form is not a reason to disregard the transaction; it is a reason to disregard the form. Once the acquisition of the NPLs is recharacterized as a direct sale, it becomes apparent that the tax benefits it created were not disproportionate to its expected profitability. As a result, we affirm the district court's conclusion that Southgate's acquisition of a portfolio of Chinese NPLs was an economically substantial transaction motivated by a genuine business purpose.

. . . We are also persuaded that the district court was correct to determine that Southgate was a sham partnership that must be disregarded for federal-income-tax purposes. As the Supreme Court explained in *Comm'r v. Culbertson*, whether a partnership will be respected for tax purposes depends on whether "the parties in good faith and acting with a business purpose" genuinely "intended to join together for the purpose of carrying on the business and sharing in the profits and losses." . . . Because so many abusive tax-avoidance schemes are designed to exploit the Code's partnership provisions, our scrutiny of a taxpayer's choice to use the partnership form is especially stringent. We are not compelled to conclude that a partnership must be respected for tax purposes "merely because the taxpayer can point to the existence of some business purpose or objective reality in addition to [the partnership's] tax-avoidance objective." Rather, a taxpayer's formation of a partnership must, on balance, display good "common sense from an economic standpoint."

The fact that a partnership's underlying business activities had economic substance does not, standing alone, immunize the partnership from judicial scrutiny. The parties' selection of the partnership form must have been driven by a genuine business purpose. This is not to say that tax considerations cannot play any role in the decision to operate as a partnership. It is only to say that tax considerations cannot be the *only* reason for a partnership's formation. If there was not a legitimate, profit-motivated reason to operate as a partnership, then the partnership will be disregarded for tax purposes even if it engaged in transactions that had economic substance.

In this case, an application of *Culbertson's* totality-of-the-facts-and-circumstances test demonstrates that the Southgate partnership was a sham that need not be respected for tax purposes. Montgomery, Beal, and Cinda did not intend to come together to jointly conduct the business of collecting on the NPLs. The structure of the GNMA basis-build underscores their lack of such an intent. The parties also lacked any genuine business purpose for their decision to form Southgate.

. . . In light of the vise grip that Beal maintained on all economic benefits flowing from the GNMAs, the district court was correct to conclude that the GNMA basis-build lacked objective economic reality. . . . Beal reserved for himself all loan proceeds, principal payments, interest income, and built-in gain. He contributed the right to share in any post-contribution gain in the event the GNMAs were sold, but he retained an unconditional right to decide whether to sell the GNMAs in the first place, and he had no intention of selling them. Stripped to its essentials, Beal's putative contribution of the GNMAs was no contribution at all. . . .

For present purposes, the economically insubstantial nature of the GNMA basis-build is important primarily because of what it reveals about the intentions of Beal, Montgomery, and Cinda. . . . Beal's decision to structure the basis-build as he did, Montgomery's willingness to accede to such one-sided terms, and Cinda's total lack of participation in the transaction are inconsistent with their professed intent to share, as partners, in Southgate's profits and losses.

. . . Finally, *Culbertson* instructs us to ask whether the partners were "acting with a business purpose" when they made the decision to form the partnership. . . . Southgate was a redundancy, "a meaningless and unnecessary incident" inserted into the chain of entities, transactions, and agreements through which the NPL acquisition took place. Southgate served no function whose accomplishment was not already assured by other means or could not have been equally well assured by alternative, less tax-beneficial means. . . . [O]ur analysis . . . trains exclusively on the question whether there was a nontax business purpose that necessitated the partnership's existence. Discerning none, we affirm the district court's holding that Southgate was a sham partnership that must be disregarded for federal-income-tax purposes. . . .

Because we have concluded that the acquisition of the NPLs had economic substance but that the formal partnership structure through which that acquisition took place was a sham, we are left to determine what transactional form most neatly maps onto the substance of that acquisition. The outcome of our analysis under the substance-over-form doctrine is dictated by the outcomes of our economic-substance and sham-partnership analyses. Beal paid Cinda $19.4 million in exchange for an interest in a portfolio of NPLs. That interest was not properly classified as a partnership interest. It is most naturally classified as an ownership interest. We hold that Southgate's acquisition of the portfolio of NPLs should be recharacterized as a direct sale of those NPLs by Cinda to Beal. . . .

AFFIRMED.

NOTES AND QUESTIONS

1. *Legislative response.* In 2004, Congress responded to the attempted shifting of built-in loss by adding section 704(c)(1)(C) and requiring mandatory basis adjustments under sections 734(b) and 743(b) in certain circumstances. If applicable, how would these provisions have frustrated the claimed tax benefits in *Southgate*?

2. *Sorting out judicial doctrines.* In *Southgate*, the court uses three judicial doctrines to reach its decision. Although the acquisition of the NPLs had economic substance and profit potential, the court nevertheless found that the partnership was a sham and recharacterized the underlying transaction as a direct sale of the NPLs, rather than a contribution to Southgate and a purchase of an interest in that partnership. Should *Southgate* be viewed as a straightforward application of substance-over-form principles or, more broadly, as imposing a business-purpose requirement for a taxpayer's use of the partnership form?

3. *Other distressed asset/debt (DAD) shelters.* In Superior Trading, LLC v. Comm'r, 728 F.3d 676 (7th Cir. 2013), the court applied the sham partnership doctrine to disallow losses in a DAD shelter, citing *Southgate* and *Culbertson*. Even if the partnership "had been an actual rather than fake partnership," the transaction would have given rise to a disguised sale under section 707(a)(2)(B), "leaving no losses for the shelter investors to claim." Id. at 681. The court also imposed accuracy-related penalties at the partnership level.

4. *Taxation of partnership distributions (in retrospect).* Now that you have learned the special exceptions and rules described in chapter eight and this chapter—including section 751(b), the disguised sale and anti-"mixing bowl" rules, and section 731(c)—how accurate is it to describe partnership distributions as "generally" resulting in the nonrecognition of gains and losses? Would the law be simplified if this general rule were instead turned on its head by treating partnership distributions generally as recognition events, except perhaps in narrowly specified circumstances?

Chapter 10

Compensating Partners for Services or the Use of Property

A. Introduction

This chapter concerns the tax consequences of compensation provided by a partnership to a partner in exchange for services or the use of property. Specific issues that arise include the amount, character, and timing of any income earned by the partner and the consequences of the transaction to the other partners. As we shall see, resolution of these issues may be affected by several factors, including whether compensation is received for past or future services rendered to the partnership, the nature of the compensation, and finally, whether the compensated party is acting in the capacity of a "partner."

Part B deals with the consequences of compensation consisting of an interest in the partnership and part C concerns the taxation of so-called "guaranteed payments." Part D describes certain compensation arrangements that are recharacterized for tax purposes under section 707(a)(2)(A) as payments to one who is not a partner.

B. Receipt of a Partnership Interest

1. *Introduction*

Suppose that after toiling for ten years as a law associate at the Ox & Nox firm, the partners invite you to become a member of the firm and you agree. You are promised a percentage of the firm's profits with the specific share based on your total billable hours for the year, the amount of business you are able to attract to the firm and your promotional activities, your firm management responsibilities and seniority, and other factors. What are the tax consequences of this agreement to you and the firm?

A threshold question is whether you may be viewed as providing "property" instead of "services" to the firm. Review I.R.C. § 721. As discussed in chapter eight, section 721 generally provides nonrecognition treatment to all parties when "property" is contributed to a partnership in exchange for a partnership interest. In addition to items such as cash, installment obligations, accounts receivable and goodwill, the term sometimes encompasses certain service-flavored property. See, e.g., U.S. v. Frazell, 335 F.2d 487 (5th Cir. 1964), cert. denied, 380 U.S. 961 (1965) (geological maps prepared by the taxpayer constituted property).

Assuming that you will be performing services, a further question is the nature of the partnership interest received. The tax treatment to you and the firm depends upon whether the partnership interest includes a right to capital (a capital interest) or is a "mere" right to share in future profits (a profits interest).

The difference between these two types of interest is described in Rev. Proc. 93-27, excerpted at p. 305. The test is whether the service partner would receive anything if the firm hypothetically sold all of its assets for fair market value and liquidated immediately after grant of the interest. If so, then the service partner has received a capital interest (and presumably a right to participate in future profits as well). If not, then the service partner has merely received a profits interest (and no present right to share in partnership capital). Many arrangements with professional firms start out as a mere profits interest, with the service partner gradually building up a capital interest through accumulations of undistributed profits and other capital contributions to the firm.

The following sections describe the tax consequences when a capital or profits interest is received in exchange for services. The tax consequences may also depend on whether the interest received — capital or profits — is vested or is subject to a substantial risk of forfeiture (within the meaning of section 83) at the time of the exchange.

2. *Receipt of a Vested Capital Interest*

Read Reg. § 1.721-1(b)(1). As the regulation indicates, if a taxpayer receives a vested capital interest in exchange for services, section 721 does not apply and the taxpayer must include in income the fair market value of the interest transferred. See I.R.C. §§ 61(a)(1), 83(a). The following case illustrates the application of this rule upon the formation of a firm and explores some collateral consequences.

McDougal v. Commissioner

62 T.C. 720 (1974), acq. 1975-2 C.B. 2

FAY, J.: . . . F. C. and Frankie McDougal . . . were engaged in the business of breeding and racing horses. Gilbert McClanahan was a licensed public horse trainer who rendered his services to various horse owners for a standard fee. He had numbered the McDougals among his clientele since 1965.

. . . [A] horse of exceptional pedigree, Iron Card, [was owned by] [t]he Ratliffs and Burnett [who] entered Iron Card in several races as a 2-year-old; . . . although the horse enjoyed some success in these contests, it soon became evident that he was suffering from a condition diagnosed by a veterinarian as a protein allergy.

When, due to a dispute among themselves, the Ratliffs and Burnett decided to sell Iron Card for whatever price he could attract, McClanahan (who had trained the horse for the Ratliffs and Burnett) advised the McDougals to make the purchase. He made this recommendation because, despite the veterinarian's prognosis to the contrary, McClanahan believed that by the use of home remedy Iron Card could be restored to full racing vigor. Furthermore, McClanahan felt that as Iron Card's allergy was not genetic and as his pedigree was impressive, he would be valuable in the future as a stud even if further attempts to race him proved unsuccessful.

The McDougals purchased Iron Card for $10,000 on January 1, 1968. At the time of the purchase McDougal promised that if McClanahan trained and attended to Iron Card, a half interest in the horse would be his once the McDougals had recovered the costs and expenses of acquisition. This promise was not made in lieu of payment of the standard trainer's fee; for from January 1, 1968, until the date of the transfer, McClanahan was paid $2,910 as compensation for services rendered as Iron Card's trainer.

McClanahan's home remedy proved so effective in relieving Iron Card of his allergy that the horse began to race with success, and his reputation consequently grew to such proportion that he attracted a succession of offers to purchase, one of which reached $60,000. The McDougals decided, however, to keep the horse and by October 4, 1968, had recovered out of their winnings the costs of acquiring him. It was therefore on that date that they transferred a half interest in the horse to McClanahan in accordance with the promise which McDougal had made to the trainer. A document entitled "Bill of Sale," wherein the transfer was described as a gift, was executed on the following day.

Iron Card continued to race well until very late in 1968 when, without warning and for an unascertained cause, he developed a condition called "hot ankle" which effectively terminated his racing career. From 1970 onward he was used exclusively for breeding purposes. That his value as a stud was no less than his value as a racehorse is attested to by the fact that in September of 1970 petitioners were offered $75,000 for him; but after considering the offer, the McDougals and McClanahan decided to refuse it, preferring to exploit Iron Card's earning potential as a stud to their own profit.

On November 1, 1968, petitioners had concluded a partnership agreement by parol to effectuate their design of racing the horse for as long as that proved feasible and of offering him out as a stud thereafter. Profits were to be shared equally by the McDougals and the McClanahans, while losses were to be allocated to the McDougals alone. . . .

ULTIMATE FINDINGS OF FACT

The transfer of October 4, 1968, gave rise to a joint venture to which the McDougals are deemed to have contributed Iron Card and in which they are deemed to have granted McClanahan an interest in the capital and profits thereof, equal to their own, as compensation for his having trained Iron Card. . . .

OPINION

Respondent contends that the McDougals did not recognize a $25,000 gain on the transaction of October 4, 1968, and that they were not entitled to claim a $30,000 business expense deduction by reason thereof. He further contends that were Iron Card to be contributed to a partnership or joint venture under the circumstances obtaining in the instant case, its basis in Iron Card at the time of contribution would have been limited by the McDougals' cost basis in the horse, as adjusted. Respondent justifies these contentions by arguing that the transfer of October 4, 1968, constituted a gift.

In the alternative, respondent has urged us to find that at some point in time no later than the transfer of October 4, 1968, McDougal and McClanahan entered into a partnership or joint venture to which the McDougals contributed Iron Card and McClanahan contributed services. Respondent contends that such a finding would require our holding that the McDougals did not recognize a gain on the transfer of October 4, 1968, by reason of section 721, and that under section 723 the joint venture's basis in Iron Card at the time of the contribution was equal to the McDougals' adjusted basis in the horse as of that time.

We dismiss at the outset respondent's contention that the transfer of October 4, 1968, constituted a gift, and we are undeterred in so doing by the fact that petitioners originally characterized the transfer as a gift. . . . A gift has been defined as a transfer motivated by detached and disinterested generosity, *Commissioner v. Duberstein*, 363 U.S. 278 (1960). The presence of such motivation is belied in this instance by two factors. The relationship of the parties concerned was essentially of a business nature, and the transfer itself was made conditional upon the outcome of an enterprise which McDougal had undertaken at McClanahan's suggestion and in reliance upon McClanahan's ability to render it profitable. These factors instead bespeak the presence of an arm's-length transaction.

With respect to respondent's alternative contention, we note firstly that the law provides no rule easy of application for making a determination as to whether a partnership or joint venture has been formed. . . .

While in the case at bar the risk of loss was to be borne by the McDougals alone, all the other elements of a joint venture were present once the transfer of October 4, 1968, had been effected. Accordingly, we hold that the aforesaid transfer constituted the formation of a joint venture to which the McDougals contributed capital in the form of the horse, Iron Card, and in which they granted McClanahan an interest equal to their own in capital and profits as compensation for his having trained Iron Card. . . . However, this holding does not result in the tax consequences which respondent has contended would follow from it. See sec. 1.721-1(b)(1), Income Tax Regs.

When on the formation of a joint venture a party contributing appreciated assets satisfies an obligation by granting his obligee a capital interest in the venture, he is deemed first to have transferred to the obligee an undivided interest in the assets contributed, equal in value to the amount of the obligation so satisfied. He and the obligee are deemed thereafter and in concert to have contributed those assets to the joint venture.

The contributing obligor will recognize gain on the transaction to the extent that the value of the undivided interest which he is deemed to have transferred exceeds his basis therein. The obligee is considered to have realized an amount equal to the fair market value of the interest which he receives in the venture and will recognize income depending upon the character of the obligation satisfied.[1] The joint venture's basis in the assets will be determined under section 723 in accordance with the foregoing assumptions. Accordingly, we hold that the transaction under consideration constituted an exchange in which the McDougals realized $30,000, *United States v. Davis*, 370 U.S. 65 (1962). . . .

In determining the basis offset to which the McDougals are entitled with respect to the transfer of October 4, 1968, we note the following: that the McDougals had an unadjusted cost basis in Iron Card of $10,000; that they had claimed $1,390 in depreciation on the entire horse for the period January 1 to October 31, 1968; and that after an agreement of partnership was concluded on November 1, 1968, depreciation on Iron Card was deducted by the partnership exclusively. . . .

In determining their adjusted basis in the portion of Iron Card on whose disposition they are required to recognize gain, the McDougals charged all the depreciation which they had taken on the horse against their basis in the half in which they retained an interest. This procedure was improper. As in accordance with Reg. § 1.167(g)-1, we have allowed the McDougals a depreciation deduction with respect to Iron Card for the period January 1 to October 4, 1968, computed on their entire cost basis in the horse of $10,000; so also do we require that the said deduction be charged against that entire cost basis under section 1016(a)(2)(A).

As the McDougals were in the business of racing horses, any gain recognized by them on the exchange of Iron Card in satisfaction of a debt would be characterized under section 1231(a) provided he had been held by them for the period [six months — EDS.] requisite under section 1231(b) as it applies to livestock acquired

1. For example, if the obligation arose out of a loan, the obligee will recognize no income by reason of the transaction; if the obligation represents the selling price of a capital asset, he will recognize a capital gain to the extent that the amount he is deemed to have realized exceeds his adjusted basis in the asset; if the obligation represents compensation for services, the transaction will result in ordinary income to the obligee in an amount equal to the value of the interest which he received in the joint venture.

before 1970. In that as of October 4, 1968, Iron Card had been used by the McDougals exclusively for racing and not for breeding, we do now hold that they had held him for a period sufficiently long to make section 1231(a) applicable to their gain on the transaction. This is the case although the McDougals may have intended eventually to use Iron Card for breeding purposes. . . .

The joint venture's basis in Iron Card as of October 4, 1968, must be determined under section 723 in accordance with the principles of law set forth earlier in this opinion. In the half interest in the horse which it is deemed to have received from the McDougals, the joint venture had a basis equal to one-half of the McDougals' adjusted cost basis in Iron Card as of October 4, 1968, i.e., the excess of $5,000 over one-half of the depreciation which the McDougals were entitled to claim on Iron Card for the period January 1 to October 4, 1968. In the half interest which the venture is considered to have received from McClanahan, it can claim to have had a basis equal to the amount which McClanahan is considered to have realized on the transaction, $30,000. The joint venture's deductions for depreciation on Iron Card for the years 1968 and 1969 are to be determined on the basis computed in the above-described manner.

When an interest in a joint venture is transferred as compensation for services rendered, any deduction which may be authorized under section 162(a)(1) by reason of that transfer is properly claimed by the party to whose benefit the services accrued, be that party the venture itself or one or more venturers, Reg. § 1.721-1(b)(2). Prior to McClanahan's receipt of his interest, a joint venture did not exist under the facts of the case at bar; the McDougals were the sole owners of Iron Card and recipients of his earnings. Therefore, they alone could have benefitted from the services rendered by McClanahan prior to October 4, 1968, for which he was compensated by the transaction of that date. Accordingly, we hold that the McDougals are entitled to a business expense deduction of $30,000, that amount being the value of the interest which McClanahan received. Respondent has contended that a deduction of $30,000 would be unreasonable in amount in view of the nature of the services for which McClanahan was being compensated. But having found that the transaction under consideration was not a gift but rather was occasioned by a compensation arrangement which was entered upon at arm's length, we must reject this contention. . . .

NOTES AND QUESTIONS

1. *What were the stakes involved in this case?* This case is confusing because of the similarity in the names of the principals involved (the *McDougals* were the purchasers and *McClanahan* was the trainer) and the numerous tax consequences flowing from the characterization assigned to their transaction. To understand the tax consequences, assume the following simplified facts: (1) the McDougals purchased Iron Card for $10,000 on January 1, 1968; (2) the horse was depreciable over five years on a straight-line basis (ignore any half-year convention), with the

owner entitled to one-twelfth of the annual depreciation deduction for each month of ownership ($166.67 each month); (3) the McDougals and McClanahan formed a partnership for the purpose of racing Iron Card on November 1, 1968, or five-sixths of the way into 1968, when the horse was worth $60,000; (4) the McDougals, McClanahan, and the partnership were all calendar-year taxpayers; (5) the parties agreed to share all partnership items equally except as otherwise required by the tax law (including use of the traditional method under section 704(c)); and (6) the partnership had $1,000 of ordinary income in 1968 prior to taking into account any depreciation deductions. Based on these simplified facts, determine the tax consequences to the partners and the partnership under the following alternative characterizations of their arrangement. How much income or loss must be reported by the parties under each scenario, and what is the timing and character of those items? What is the partnership's basis in the horse after 1968?

a. *Government's first position.* Just prior to forming the partnership on November 1, 1968, the McDougals made a gift of a half-interest in the horse to McClanahan. In the formation of the partnership, the parties transferred their respective one-half interests in the horse in exchange for equal capital and profits interests in the partnership.
b. *Government's second position.* In forming the partnership on November 1, 1968, the McDougals transferred their entire interest in the horse, and McClanahan agreed to perform services, in exchange for equal capital and profit interest in the partnership. Assume that, as contended by the government, section 721 applied to this transaction and that it was therefore a nonrecognition event to each of the parties.
c. *Court's holding.* Same as (b), except that the tax law consequences of the transaction were as determined by the Tax Court.

2. *Was a partnership formed on January 1, 1968?* What is the significance of the court's finding that a partnership between the McDougals and McClanahan was not formed until October 4, 1968? Should the government have argued that a partnership resulted on January 1, 1968 at the outset of the parties' arrangement? Under this theory, should McClanahan be treated as receiving merely a profit interest?

3. *Transfer of a vested capital interest in a new or existing firm. McDougal* involved a transfer in exchange for services of a vested capital interest in a newly formed partnership. The court held that the transaction should be taxed as if the McDougals had transferred a part-interest in their property directly to McClanahan immediately prior to the formation of the partnership, followed by the joint transfer of their respective interests in that property to the partnership upon formation. If an entity disregarded for tax purposes (such as a single-member LLC not electing corporate status) transfers a vested capital interest in the entity to a service provider, the tax consequences are the same as in *McDougal.* Thus, the transfer of the vested capital interest results in recognition of gain or loss to the service recipient, who is treated as transferring a proportionate interest in the underlying assets of the disregarded entity

to the service provider. The addition of the new member converts the disregarded entity into a partnership for federal tax purposes. See Rev. Rul. 99-5, 1999-1 C.B. 434.

When a vested capital interest in an *existing* partnership is issued to a service provider, the transaction is generally treated as an exchange between the partnership and the service provider. The service provider still recognizes income (under I.R.C. §§ 61 and 83) equal to the fair market value of the capital interest received, and takes an initial basis in the transferred interest equal to its cost, i.e., the amount included in income.

The consequences to the partnership are somewhat more complicated. Assuming that the services are performed for the partnership (rather than another partner), the partnership deducts under section 162 (subject to the capitalization requirement of section 263) the fair market value of the transferred interest. The regulations characterize this compensatory transfer as a "guaranteed payment" under section 707(c) which, as discussed in part C of this chapter, permits the partnership to deduct (or capitalize) the amount. See Reg. § 1.721-1(b)(2). In general, any deduction is allowed only in the year in which the service provider includes the amount in income. See I.R.C. § 83(h). Moreover, the deduction (or capital expenditure) should be specially allocated to the non-service partners. See I.R.C. § 706(d)(1). Under proposed regulations issued in 2005, the timing rules of section 83 override the timing rules under section 707(c) to the extent they are inconsistent.

Under the prevailing view prior to issuance of proposed regulations in 2005, the partnership recognizes gain or loss in the exchange. The partnership is deemed to transfer an undivided interest in each of its assets to the service provider, who then recontributes such assets to the partnership in exchange for her capital interest. The partnership recognizes gain or loss equal to the difference between the fair market value of the assets deemed transferred and the partnership's basis in the assets. Any gain or loss must be specially allocated to the non-service partners. See I.R.C. § 706(d)(1). The deemed re-contribution of the assets to the partnership is treated as a tax-free section 721 transaction. Under section 723, the partnership takes a cost basis in the recontributed assets equal to their basis in the service partner's hands. Thus, the partnership winds up with a fair-market-value basis in the recontributed assets. If the partnership revalues its assets upon the admission of the new partner (and the deemed contribution of assets by her), then any remaining gain or loss inherent in the partnership's assets is specially allocated to the non-service partners pursuant to section 704(c) principles. See Reg. § 1.704-1(b)(2)(iv)(*f*)(*5*)(*i*).

As discussed below, the 2005 proposed regulations generally reach the same result but would not require the non-service partners to recognize gain or loss on the exchange; instead, under section 704(c) principles, any built-in gain (or loss) in the partnership property would be preserved for later recognition by the non-service partners. These proposed regulations are controversial and have not yet been finalized.

4. *Should the partnership recognize gain or loss?* Some commentators have argued that no gain or loss should be recognized by an existing partnership when it transfers

a capital interest in exchange for services. Compare I.R.C. § 1032(a) (transfer of corporate stock does not result in recognition of gain or loss to the issuing corporation). Under this view (sometimes referred to as the "circle of cash"), the partnership should be viewed as transferring cash compensation to the service provider who then recontributes the cash to the partnership in exchange for the capital interest. This characterization does not affect the tax treatment of the service provider, who continues to recognize ordinary income equal to the cash deemed received. Since the issuing partnership is deemed to transfer cash (rather than appreciated or depreciated property) in satisfaction of its obligation, however, the transfer does not result in recognition of gain or loss to the partnership or the non-service partners. Even if the partnership in fact has an insufficient amount of cash, it could avoid recognizing gain by borrowing enough cash to pay the service provider. The partnership could then repay the debt with the cash transferred to the service provider and recontributed to the partnership.

While the 2005 proposed regulations do not explicitly adopt the circle-of-cash concept, they provide that a partnership generally recognizes no gain or loss when a "compensatory partnership interest" is transferred or becomes vested (within the meaning of section 83). See Prop. Reg. §§ 1.721-1(b)(2); 1.83-6(b). For this purpose, a compensatory partnership interest is an interest in the transferring partnership that is transferred in connection with the performance of services for that partnership (either before or after formation of the partnership). See Prop. Reg. § 1.721-1(b)(3). It also includes a compensatory partnership option, i.e., an option to acquire an interest in the partnership in connection with the performance of services. Id.

Without much explanation, the preamble to the 2005 proposed regulations asserts that a nonrecognition rule is "more consistent with the policies underlying section 721 — to defer recognition of gain and loss when persons join together to conduct a business — than would be a rule requiring the partnership to recognize gain on the transfer of these types of interests." Although the practicing bar has generally applauded nonrecognition treatment, some commentators maintain that the result cannot be reconciled with the legislative history and statutory structure of section 721. Leaving aside the policy implications, what are the constraints on the Treasury's ability to reinterpret a 50-year-old statute? What is the policy rationale, if any, for requiring a partnership to recognize gain on issuing a capital interest if this taxable event can be so easily avoided by employing the circle of cash transfers? Why might a partnership prefer to issue a partnership interest to a service partner rather than provide cash compensation? What valuation problems might arise in connection with such a transfer?

Problem 10-1:

(a) A and B contribute $75 each to a general partnership, which purchases land worth $150. When the land has appreciated in value to $450, C receives a vested one-third capital interest in the partnership worth

$150 in exchange for services performed for the partnership. What are the tax consequences of this transaction to A, B, and C? Assume that the partnership revalues its property immediately before transfer of the interest and that the transfer is treated as a recognition event for both the service partner and non-service partners.

(b) Same as (a), except that the partnership borrows $150 cash to compensate C, who contributes the cash to the partnership in exchange for a one-third interest. The recontributed cash is then used to repay the debt.

3. *Receipt of a Vested Profits Interest*

If a service provider receives a "mere" profits interest, the issue is whether she should be taxed immediately upon receipt of the profits interest or instead be taxed only on her share of profits when realized by the partnership. Sections 61 and 83 would seem to support taxing the service provider immediately, analogous to receipt of a vested capital interest. Given the often speculative nature of future profits, however, immediate taxation of a profits interest is likely to raise difficult valuation issues. Moreover, if the service provider is taxed immediately, some mechanism would be necessary to avoid double taxation when she is subsequently allocated a distributive share of partnership income. To avoid valuation difficulties and potential double taxation, it may be preferable to treat receipt of a vested profits interest as an "open" transaction, i.e., to defer taxation of the service provider until her share of partnership profits is actually earned.

Prior to *Diamond*, excerpted below, commentators viewed the negative implication of the parenthetical in Reg. § 1.721-1(b)(1) (distinguishing a transfer of a capital interest) as support for not taxing receipt of a "mere" profits interest. *Diamond* upset this conventional wisdom by holding that receipt of a profits interest might be taxable under certain unusual circumstances.

Diamond v. Commissioner

492 F.2d 286 (7th Cir. 1974)

FAIRCHILD, Circuit Judge: This is an appeal from a decision of the Tax Court upholding the commissioner's assessment of deficiencies against Sol and Muriel Diamond for the years 1961 and 1962. . . . The Tax Court concluded that Diamond realized ordinary income on the receipt of a right to a share of profit or loss to be derived from a real estate venture (the 1962 partnership case). . . .

During 1961, Diamond was a mortgage broker. Philip Kargman had acquired for $25,000 the buyer's rights in a contract for the sale of an office building. Kargman asked Diamond to obtain a mortgage loan for the full $1,100,000 purchase price of the building. Diamond and Kargman agreed that Diamond would receive a 60% share of profit or loss of the venture if he arranged the financing.

Diamond succeeded in obtaining a $1,100,000 mortgage loan. . . . On December 15, 1961 Diamond and Kargman entered into an agreement which provided:

> (1) The two were associated as joint venturers for 24 years (the life of the mortgage) unless earlier terminated by agreement or by sale;
> (2) Kargman was to advance all cash needed for the purchase beyond the loan proceeds;
> (3) Profits and losses would be divided, 40% to Kargman, 60% to Diamond;
> (4) In event of sale, proceeds would be devoted first to repayment to Kargman of money supplied by him, and net profits thereafter would be divided 40% to Kargman, 60% to Diamond. . . .

The purchase proceeded as planned and closing took place on February 18, 1962. Kargman made cash outlays totaling $78,195.33 in connection with the purchase. Thus, under the terms of the agreement, the property would have to appreciate at least $78,195.33 before Diamond would have any equity in it.

Shortly after closing, it was proposed that Diamond would sell his interest and one Liederman would be substituted, except on a 50-50 basis. Liederman persuaded Diamond to sell his interest for $40,000. This sale was effectuated on March 8, 1962 by Diamond assigning his interest to Kargman for $40,000. Kargman in turn then conveyed a similar interest, except for 50-50 sharing, to Liederman for the same amount.

On their 1962 joint return, the Diamonds reported the March 8, 1962 $40,000 sale proceeds as a short term capital gain. This gain was offset by an unrelated short term capital loss. They reported no tax consequences from the February 18 receipt of the interest in the venture. Diamond's position is that his receipt of this type of interest in partnership is not taxable income although received in return for services. He relies on § 721 and Reg. § 1.721-1(b)(1). He further argues that the subsequent sale of this interest produced a capital gain under § 741. The Tax Court held that the receipt of this type of interest in partnership in return for services is not within § 721 and is taxable under § 61 when received. The Tax Court valued the interest at $40,000 as of February 18, as evidenced by the sale for that amount three weeks later, on March 8.

Both the taxpayer and the Tax Court treated the venture as a partnership and purported to apply partnership income tax principles. It has been suggested that the record might have supported findings that there was in truth an employment or other relationship, other than partnership, and produced a similar result, but these findings were not made. . . . It has also been suggested (and argued, alternatively, by the government) that although on the face of the agreement Diamond appeared to receive only a right to share in profit (loss) to be derived, the value of the real estate may well have been substantially greater than the purchase price, so that Diamond may really have had an interest in capital, if the assets were properly valued. This finding was not made. The Tax Court suggested the possibility that Diamond would not in any event be entitled to capital gains treatment of his sale of a right to receive income in the future, but did not decide the question.[2]

Taking matters at face value, taxpayer received, on February 18, an interest in partnership, limited to a right to a share of profit (loss) to be derived. In discussion we shall refer to this interest either as his interest in partnership or a profit-share.

The Tax Court, with clearly adequate support, found that Diamond's interest in partnership had a market value of $40,000 on February 18. Taxpayer's analysis is that under the regulations the receipt of a profit-share [on] February 18, albeit having a market value and being conferred in return for services, was not a taxable event, and that the entire proceeds of the March 8 sale were a capital gain. The Tax Court analysis was that the interest in partnership, albeit limited to a profit-share, was property worth $40,000, and taxpayer's acquisition, thereof on February 18 was compensation for services and ordinary income. Assuming that capital gain treatment at sale would have been appropriate, there was no gain because the sale was for the same amount.

There is no statute or regulation which expressly and particularly prescribes the income tax effect, or absence of one, at the moment a partner receives a profit-share in return for services. The Tax Court's holding rests upon the general principle that a valuable property interest received in return for services is compensation and income. Taxpayer's argument is predicated upon an implication which his counsel, and others, have found in Reg. § 1.721-1(1)(b), but which need not, and the government argues should not, be found there.

[Section 721] is entitled "Nonrecognition of gain or loss on contribution," and provides: "No gain or loss shall be recognized to a partnership or to any of its partners in the case of a contribution of property to the partnership in exchange for an interest in the partnership." Only if, by a strained construction, "property" were said to include services, would § 721 say anything about the effect of furnishing services. It clearly deals with a contribution like Kargman's, of property, and prescribes that when he contributed his property, no gain or loss was recognized. It does not, of course, explicitly say that no income accrues to one who renders services and, in return, becomes a partner with a profit-share.

Reg. § 1.721-1 presumably explains and interprets § 721, perhaps to the extent of qualifying or limiting its meaning. Subsec. (b)(1), particularly relied on here, reads in part as follows:

> Normally, under local law, each partner is entitled to be repaid his contributions of money or other property to the partnership (at the value placed upon such property by the partnership at the time of the contribution) whether made at the formation of the partnership or subsequent thereto. To the extent that any of the partners gives up any

2. Because of the decision we reach, it is also unnecessary for us to consider this possibility and we express no conclusions concerning it.

> part of his right to be repaid his contributions (as distinguished from a share in partnership profits) in favor of another partner as compensation for services (or in satisfaction of an obligation), section 721 does not apply. The value of an interest in such partnership capital so transferred to a partner as compensation for services constitutes income to the partner under section 61. . . .

The quoted portion of the regulation may well be read, like § 721, as being directly addressed only to the consequences of a contribution of money or other property. It asserts that when a partner making such contributions transfers to another some part of the contributing partner's right to be repaid, in order to compensate the other for services or to satisfy an obligation to the other, § 721 does not apply, there is recognition of gain or loss to the contributing partner, and there is income to the partner who receives, as compensation for services, part of the right to be repaid.

The regulation does not specify that if a partner contributing property agrees that, in return for services, another shall be a partner with a profit-share only, the value of the profit-share is not income to the recipient. An implication to that effect, such as is relied on by taxpayer, would have to rest on the proposition that the regulation was meant to be all inclusive as to when gain or loss would be recognized or income would exist as a consequence of the contribution of property to a partnership and disposition of the partnership interests. It would have to appear, in order to sustain such implication, that the existence of income by reason of a creation of a profit-share, immediately having a determinable market value, in favor of a partner would be inconsistent with the result specified in the regulation.

We do not find this implication in our own reading of the regulation. It becomes necessary to consider the substantial consensus of commentators in favor of the principle claimed to be implied and to look to judicial interpretation, legislative history, administrative interpretation, and policy considerations to determine whether the implication is justified.

The Commentators: There is a startling degree of unanimity that the conferral of a profit-share as compensation for services is not income at the time of the conferral, although little by way of explanation of why this should be so, or analysis of statute or regulation to show that it is prescribed. . . .

One of the most unequivocal statements, with an explanation in terms of practicality or policy, was made by Arthur Willis in a text:

> However obliquely the proposition is stated in the regulations, it is clear that a partner who receives only an interest in future profits of the partnership as compensation for services is not required to report the receipt of his partnership interest as taxable income. The rationale is twofold. In the first place, the present value of a right to participate in future profits is usually too conjectural to be subject to valuation. In the second place, the service partner is taxable on his distributive share of partnership income as it is realized by the partnership. If he were taxed on the present value of the right to receive his share of future partnership income, either he would be taxed twice,

or the value of his right to participate in partnership income must be amortized over some period of time.[3]

Judicial Interpretation: Except for one statement by the Tax Court no decision cited by the parties or found by us appears squarely to reach the question, either on principle in the absence of the regulations, or by application of the regulations. In a footnote in *Herman M. Hale*, 24 T.C.M. 1497, 1502 (1965) the Tax Court said: "Under the regulations, the mere receipt of a partnership interest in future profits does not create any tax liability. Sec. 1.721-1(b), Income Tax Regs." There was no explanation of how this conclusion was derived from the regulations.

Legislative History: The legislative history is equivocal.

An advisory group appointed in 1956 to review the regulations evidently felt concern about whether the provision of Reg. § 1.721-1 that the value of an interest in capital transferred to a partner in compensation for services constitutes income had a statutory basis in the light of § 721 providing that there shall be no recognition of gain or loss in the case of a contribution of property. The group proposed enactment of a new section to provide such basis, and legislation introduced into the 86th Congress in 1959 incorporated this recommendation. The bill, H.R. 9662, would have created a new § 770 providing specifically for the taxation of a person receiving an interest in partnership capital in exchange for the performance of services for the partnership. However, neither proposed § 770 nor anything else in H.R. 9662 dealt with the receipt merely of a profit-share. The lack of concern over an income tax impact when only a profit-share was conferred might imply an opinion that such conferring of a profit-share would not be taxable under any circumstances, or might imply an opinion that it would be income or not under § 61 depending upon whether it had a determinable market value or not.

Several statements in the course of the hearings and committee reports paralleled the first parenthetical phrase in Reg. § 1.721-1(b) and were to the effect that the provision did not apply where a person received only a profit-share. There was, however, at least one specific statement by the chairman of the advisory group (Mr. Willis) that if the service partner "were to receive merely an interest in future profits in exchange for his services, he would have no immediate taxable gain because he would be taxed on his share of income as it was earned." H.R. 9662 passed the House of Representatives, and was favorably reported to the Senate by its finance committee, but never came to a vote in the Senate. Even had the bill become law, it would not have dealt expressly with the problem at hand.

Administrative Interpretation: We are unaware of instances in which the Commissioner has asserted delinquencies where a taxpayer who received a profit-share with determinable market value in return for services failed to report the value as income, or has otherwise acted consistently with the Tax Court decision in *Diamond.* Although the consensus referred to earlier appears to exist, the Commissioner

3. Willis on Partnership Taxation 84-85 (1971). . . .

has not by regulation or otherwise acted affirmatively to reject it, and in a sense might be said to have agreed by silence.

Consideration of partnership principles or practices: There must be wide variation in the degree to which a profit-share created in favor of a partner who has or will render service has determinable market value at the moment of creation. Surely in many if not the typical situations it will have only speculative value, if any.

In the present case, taxpayer's services had all been rendered, and the prospect of earnings from the real estate under Kargman's management was evidently very good. The profit-share had determinable market value.

If the present decision be sound, then the question will always arise, whenever a profit-share is created or augmented, whether it has a market value capable of determination. Will the existence of this question be unduly burdensome on those who choose to do business under the partnership form?

Each partner determines his income tax by taking into account his distributive share of the taxable income of the partnership. 26 U.S.C. § 702. Taxpayer's position here is that he was entitled to defer income taxation on the compensation for his services except as partnership earnings were realized. If a partner is taxed on the determinable market value of a profit-share at the time it is created in his favor, and is also taxed on his full share of earnings as realized, there will arguably be double taxation, avoidable by permitting him to amortize the value which was originally treated as income. Does the absence of a recognized procedure for amortization militate against the treatment of the creation of the profit-share as income?

Do the disadvantages of treating the creation of the profit-share as income in those instances where it has a determinable market value at that time outweigh the desirability of imposing a tax at the time the taxpayer has received an interest with determinable market value as compensation for services?

We think, of course, that the resolution of these practical questions makes clearly desirable the promulgation of appropriate regulations, to achieve a degree of certainty. But in the absence of regulation, we think it sound policy to defer to the expertise of the Commissioner and the Judges of the Tax Court, and to sustain their decision that the receipt of a profit-share with determinable market value is income. . . .

NOTES AND QUESTIONS

1. *The stakes.* Whether a service provider is taxed upon receipt of a profits interest affects both the timing and character of the taxpayer's income. In *Diamond*, the timing issue was not very important because the taxpayer sold his interest shortly after receiving it. When no sale is contemplated, however, not taxing the initial receipt of the interest means that the service provider may defer reporting income until profits are realized by the partnership and allocated under the usual scheme of subchapter K.

Diamond illustrates how the character of the service provider's income may be affected by failure to tax receipt of the interest. In the *Hale* case referred to in the opinion, however, the Tax Court concluded that if a sale of a profits interest is simply a disposition of a right to receive future ordinary income, the seller's gain is properly characterized as ordinary income. See Hort v. Comm'r, 313 U.S. 28 (1941). The Seventh Circuit specifically did not reach this issue in *Diamond* (see footnote 2 of the court's opinion).

Entity-level interpretation of section 702(b) may also affect the character of the service partner's income. If a continuing service partner is not taxed on receipt of a profits interest initially, the character of the partner's share of future partnership income is determined at the partnership level. Thus, the service partner's future income may or may not be ordinary income. For example, a partner who performs services in exchange for a share of an investment partnership's future profits will be taxed on passthrough income based on the partnership-level character of that income. Recall that the application of this rule was at issue in both *Wheeler* (p. 7) and *Podell* (p. 45).

The narrow holding of *Diamond* is that a partnership profits interest is taxable upon receipt only if the interest has a readily ascertainable fair market value. This test was satisfied because Diamond's services had all been rendered, the prospect of partnership income "was evidently very good," and Diamond was able to sell the interest promptly after receipt for $40,000. Note the court's statement that "[s]urely in many if not the typical situations [a profits interest] will have only speculative value, if any."

2. *Capital vs. profits interest.* Diamond claimed that he received a mere profits interest and that Reg. § 1.721-1(b)(1) precludes the taxation of such an interest. The government challenged the first claim by asserting that "the value of the real estate may well have been substantially greater than the purchase price." Assuming the real estate was worth more than the partnership's borrowing ($1,100,000) and Kargman's cash outlay ($80,000), Diamond would have been entitled to 60 percent of that excess value if the partnership liquidated before any profits were received. Under this assumption, should Diamond's right to receive a 60 percent profit share (after Kargman's recovery of his $80,000 capital investment) have been properly characterized as a capital or profits share of the partnership?

The court did not resolve this factual claim because it disagreed with Diamond's interpretation of the regulation. Do you think the court's interpretation was correct?

3. *Was Diamond a partner?* The court assumed that Diamond was in fact a partner. Do you agree? How would the outcome have been affected if the court had instead found that Diamond had an employment or similar relationship with the partnership?

Following *Diamond*, the issue of taxing a profits interest enjoyed benign neglect for nearly two decades. An internal IRS memorandum prepared during this period contained a draft (but never issued) Revenue Ruling indicating that the *Diamond* holding should be limited to situations in which the service provider in fact received a *capital* interest in the partnership. See GCM 36346 (July 23, 1975) (analogizing a true profits interest to an "unfunded, unsecured promise to pay deferred compensation," which is not treated as "property" for purposes of section 83 and thus not immediately taxable). Moreover, in light of valuation uncertainties, courts proved reluctant to treat receipt of a profits interest as a taxable event. See, e.g., St. John v. U.S., 84-1 U.S.T.C. ¶ 9158 (C.D. Ill. 1983) (profits interest constituted property for purpose of section 83 but had a value of zero under the hypothetical liquidation approach); Kenroy, Inc. v. Comm'r, 47 T.C.M. 1749 (1984) (same).

This period of relative calm ended with the Tax Court's decision in Campbell v. Comm'r, 59 T.C.M. 236 (1990), rev'd 943 F.2d 815 (8th Cir. 1991). The Tax Court held that the taxpayer, who received "special limited partnership interests" as compensation for his activities in connection with the formation and syndication of several real estate tax shelter partnerships, was taxable immediately on the fair market value of the profits interests. It determined the value of the profits interests by discounting the present value of projected future tax benefits and cash flow from the ventures, even though investors had been warned about the likelihood that some or all of the claimed deductions and allocations might not withstand scrutiny from the IRS upon audit.

The Tax Court's decision sparked a lively discussion among tax experts concerning the practical and policy implications of taxing profits interests. While some maintained that receipt of a profits interest should receive no more favorable treatment than other types of compensatory transfers of property, others argued that taxing profits interests immediately was inconsistent with the underlying framework of subchapter K. Despite the continuing murkiness of the theoretical issues, two intervening events largely laid to rest (at least temporarily) most practical concerns about the taxability of a profits interest. First, the Eighth Circuit reversed the Tax Court's *Campbell* decision, holding that the profits interests were "without fair market value" because of their speculative nature. Second, the IRS issued Rev. Proc. 93-27.

Rev. Proc. 93-27

1993-2 C.B. 343

SEC. 1. PURPOSE

This revenue procedure provides guidance on the treatment of the receipt of a partnership profits interest for services provided to or for the benefit of the partnership.

SEC. 2. DEFINITIONS

The following definitions apply for purposes of this revenue procedure.

.01 A capital interest is an interest that would give the holder a share of the proceeds if the partnership's assets were sold at fair market value and then the proceeds were distributed in a complete liquidation of the partnership. This determination generally is made at the time of receipt of the partnership interest.

.02 A profits interest is a partnership interest other than a capital interest.

SEC. 3. BACKGROUND

Under Reg. § 1.721-1(b)(1), the receipt of a partnership capital interest for services provided to or for the benefit of the partnership is taxable as compensation. On the other hand, the issue of whether the receipt of a partnership profits interest for services is taxable has been the subject of litigation. Most recently, in *Campbell v. Commissioner*, 943 F.2d 815 (8th Cir. 1991), the Eighth Circuit in dictum suggested that the taxpayer's receipt of a partnership profits interest received for services was not taxable, but decided the case on valuation. Other courts have determined that in certain circumstances the receipt of a partnership profits interest for services is a taxable event under section 83 of the Internal Revenue Code. See, e.g., *Campbell v. Commissioner*, T.C.M. 1990-236, rev'd, 943 F.2d 815 (8th Cir. 1991); *St. John v. United States*, No. 82-1134 (C.D. Ill. Nov. 16, 1983). The courts have also found that typically the profits interest received has speculative or no determinable value at the time of receipt. See *Campbell*, 943 F.2d at 823; *St. John*. In *Diamond v. Commissioner*, 56 T.C. 530 (1971), aff'd, 492 F.2d 286 (7th Cir. 1974), however, the court assumed that the interest received by the taxpayer was a partnership profits interest and found the value of the interest was readily determinable. In that case, the interest was sold soon after receipt.

SEC. 4. APPLICATION

.01 Other than as provided below, if a person receives a profits interest for the provision of services to or for the benefit of a partnership in a partner capacity or in anticipation of being a partner, the Internal Revenue Service will not treat the receipt of such an interest as a taxable event for the partner or the partnership.

.02 This revenue procedure does not apply:

(1) If the profits interest relates to a substantially certain and predictable stream of income from partnership assets, such as income from high-quality debt securities or a high-quality net lease;
(2) If within two years of receipt, the partner disposes of the profits interest; or
(3) If the profits interest is a limited partnership interest in a "publicly traded partnership" within the meaning of section 7704(b) of the Internal Revenue Code.

4. *Receipt of an Unvested Capital or Profits Interest*

So far, we have considered the receipt by a service provider of a *vested* interest in the partnership. Particularly when the compensation is for future services, however, there are often strings attached to the interest received. For example, the interest may be forfeitable if the service provider fails to work for at least three years. What are the tax consequences of this arrangement?

Read I.R.C. § 83(a)-(c) and (h). In general, the taxable event to the service provider (and the deduction and other consequences, if any, to the partnership) is deferred until such time as the partnership interest is either "transferable" or "not subject to a substantial risk of forfeiture." See Reg. § 1.83-6(a)(1) and (b). Thus, in the above example, the taxable event may be deferred until the interest vests after three years. Importantly, the determination of the amount of the service provider's income (and other tax consequences) is also deferred until vesting.

> **Example 10-1:** In exchange for services, C is provided in Year 1 with a one-third interest in the capital and profits of a partnership, contingent on C's satisfactory performance over the next two years. C performs satisfactorily and the interest vests in Year 3. Assume that the interest is worth $1,000 in Year 1 and $5,000 in Year 3.

In this example, absent a section 83(b) election, C must report ordinary income of $5,000 in Year 3 on vesting of the partnership interest. The partnership's potential deduction is also deferred until Year 3. To avoid this result, C may make a section 83(b) election. In this case, C will report income of $1,000 in Year 1 equal to the value of the interest at that time (but no additional compensation income when the interest vests). If the section 83(b) election is made, the partnership's deduction will also be determined in Year 1 when C reports income. If C sells her interest in Year 4 for $5,000, the $4,000 of subsequent appreciation in the value of the partnership interest may therefore be taxed to C at preferential capital gains rates. One disadvantage of the section 83(b) election is that, if the interest never vests, C is denied a deduction to offset the $1,000 of income reported in Year 1. See I.R.C. § 83(b) (flush language).

The partnership may also be required to recognize gain or loss if it transfers an unvested capital interest to C in exchange for services. If the section 83(b) election is made, the partnership's recognition of gain or loss will occur in Year 1; if not, the partnership's recognition of gain or loss will be deferred until Year 3 when the interest vests. If the 2005 proposed regulations become final, the partnership would not be required to recognize gain or loss upon transfer (or vesting) of a compensatory partnership interest (whether a capital or profits interest). See Prop. Reg. §§ 1.721-1(b)(2); 1.83-6(b). Any built-in gain (or loss) inherent in the partnership property at the time of transfer (or vesting) would be preserved for later recognition by the non-service partners through the application of section 704(c) principles.

Suppose in **example 10-1**, C receives an unvested "profits only" interest in the partnership to which Rev. Proc. 93-27 applies. Now, the granting of the interest to

C in Year 1 is not a taxable event by virtue of both section 83(a) and the position taken in the Revenue Procedure. But suppose the interest evolves into a capital interest by the time it vests in C. For example, C might be promised in Year 1 a share of the future profits of the partnership as well as any appreciation in the partnership's assets accruing after Year 1. If, when the interest vests in Year 3, C is entitled to a share of the partnership's undistributed profits and unrealized gains accrued since Year 1, then her interest should be considered a capital interest in the firm. Upon a hypothetical liquidation of the firm immediately after the vesting of the interest, she would be entitled to a share of the liquidation proceeds. What are the tax consequences of this arrangement with respect to C?

A straightforward reading of section 83 and the other pertinent authorities might suggest that there is a taxable event in Year 3. In general, absent a section 83(b) election, section 83 defers determination of the relevant tax consequences until vesting, i.e., Year 3 in the example. If C is therefore deemed to receive a taxable capital interest (rather than a profits interest) at that later date, then C should arguably be required to report income based on the then value of the interest (with any consequences to the partnership determined at the later date as well). In Rev. Proc. 2001-43, however, the IRS reached a different conclusion.

Rev. Proc. 2001-43

2001-2 C.B. 191

. . . This revenue procedure clarifies Rev. Proc. 93-27 by providing that the determination under Rev. Proc. 93-27 of whether an interest granted to a service provider is a profits interest is, under the circumstances described below, tested at the time the interest is granted, even if, at that time, the interest is substantially nonvested (within the meaning of Reg. § 1.83-3(b)). Accordingly, where a partnership grants a profits interest to a service provider in a transaction meeting the requirements of this revenue procedure and Rev. Proc. 93-27, the Internal Revenue Service will not treat the grant of the interest or the event that causes the interest to become substantially vested (within the meaning of Reg. § 1.83-3(b)) as a taxable event for the partner or the partnership. Taxpayers to which this revenue procedure applies need not file an election under section 83(b) of the Code.

SECTION 4. APPLICATION

This revenue procedure clarifies that, for purposes of Rev. Proc. 93-27, where a partnership grants an interest in the partnership that is substantially nonvested to a service provider, the service provider will be treated as receiving the interest on the date of its grant, provided that:

.01 The partnership and the service provider treat the service provider as the owner of the partnership interest from the date of its grant and the service provider takes into account the distributive share of partnership income, gain, loss, deduction, and credit associated with that interest in computing the service provider's income tax liability for the entire period during which the service provider has the interest;

.02 Upon the grant of the interest or at the time that the interest becomes substantially vested, neither the partnership nor any of the partners deducts any amount (as wages, compensation, or otherwise) for the fair market value of the interest; and

.03 All other conditions of Rev. Proc. 93-27 are satisfied.

NOTES AND QUESTIONS

1. *No reasoning (again).* Once again, the lack of reasoned analysis in the Revenue Procedure makes it difficult to ascertain the parameters of the IRS's position and the precise meaning of its conditions. The first condition seems contrary to Reg. § 1.83-1(a)(1) which provides that, until the property is substantially vested, the party transferring the property to the service provider (and not the service provider) is regarded as the owner of the property. By treating the service provider as the owner prior to vesting, the Revenue Procedure allows the service provider to benefit from the partnership-level character of any income earned prior to vesting. The service provider's share of such passthrough income, thus, may not be ordinary income.

The Revenue Procedure may also lull some taxpayers into erroneously forgoing a section 83(b) election. Distinguishing between a capital and profits interest is a function of the value of the interest at the time of the exchange, an inherently uncertain determination in many cases. If a service provider relies upon Rev. Proc. 2001-43 but is subsequently determined to have received a capital interest, she will have lost the opportunity to make the section 83(b) election.

2. *Changes on the horizon?* The 2005 proposed regulations and Notice 2005-43, 2005-1 C.B. 122, generally reach the same result as under Rev. Proc. 2001-43 but require a different procedure. Under the proposed regulations, a service provider who receives an unvested profits interest would be required to make *two* elections: the section 83(b) election, which would establish the time of the grant as the taxable event, and the liquidation-value election. Since a "profits only" interest has a zero liquidation value at the time of the grant, these two elections would allow the service provider to avoid having to pay any tax either at the time of the grant or at the later time of vesting. The purpose of the liquidation-value election would be to ensure that all other partners are taxed in a manner consistent with the nontaxation of the service provider. For example, neither the partnership nor any of the other partners would be entitled to any compensation deduction. See Rev. Proc. 2001-43, § 4.02. These results would be subject to the same conditions set forth in Rev. Proc. 2001-43 and the same exceptions identified in Rev. Proc. 93-27. The proposed regulations reiterate the general rule under current law that, in the absence of a section 83(b) election, the service provider is *not* the owner of the partnership interest and is therefore *not* a partner. See Prop. Reg. § 1.761-1(b); Reg. § 1.83-1(a)(1).

Accordingly, until vesting of the interest, the partnership's income and loss must be allocated entirely to the non-service partners, and any distributions to the service provider are treated as additional compensation.

As noted, Rev. Proc. 2001-43 provides a more lenient way to reach the same result. Until the 2005 proposed regulations become final, the recipient of an unvested profits interest will be treated as a partner if *either* a section 83(b) election is made *or* the taxpayer qualifies under the revenue procedure (even if no election is made).

3. *Forfeiture allocations*. If a section 83(b) election is made, the holder of an unvested compensatory partnership interest (whether a capital or profits interest) may be allocated partnership items that are "contingent" on vesting of the interest. Because there is no assurance that the service partner will eventually receive the amounts credited to her capital account, the allocation of such items cannot have economic effect. See Prop. Reg. § 1.704-1(b)(4)(xii). Proposed regulations treat the allocation as having economic effect so long as the partnership agrees to make "forfeiture allocations" in the event the interest is later forfeited. The purpose of a forfeiture allocation is to reverse the prior allocations to the service partner when the interest is forfeited. For example, if the service partner was previously allocated $300 of income which is later forfeited, a forfeiture allocation of $300 of deductions to the service partner in the year of forfeiture would reverse the partner's capital account credit for the prior income. (The special allocation of deductions in the year of forfeiture has a similar effect as retroactively reallocating the $300 of income to the non-service partners, although the identity of the partners may have changed between the year the income was earned and initially allocated and the year the forfeiture occurs.)

As we have seen, Rev. Proc. 2001-43 does not treat either the grant or the vesting of an unvested profits interest as a taxable event to a service provider or the partnership. Moreover, the service provider is treated as the owner of the interest from the date of its grant as long as she takes into account the distributive share of partnership items associated with the interest during the entire period the interest is held. Addressing an issue of first impression, the following case describes the tax consequences when an unvested *capital* interest is granted to a service provider (and no section 83(b) election is made).

Crescent Holdings, LLC v. Commissioner

141 T.C. 477 (2013)

RUWE, Judge. [In exchange for his services as president and CEO of Crescent Resources (an LLC taxable as a partnership), the petitioner (Arthur Fields) received a two percent interest in Crescent Holdings (another LLC taxable as a partnership) that was the sole owner of Crescent Resources. The interest was forfeitable if petitioner terminated his employment within three years and could not be transferred until the interest vested. Because petitioner, who did not make a section 83(b) election with respect to the restricted property, resigned his position within the three-year period, the interest never vested. Nevertheless, for each of the two years following grant of the interest, petitioner was allocated two percent of Crescent Holdings' income (but received no distributions). One of the other partners of Crescent Holdings intervened in the litigation to oppose the petitioner's claim that he was not taxable on any of Crescent Holdings' income.]

The issues for decision are: (1) whether petitioner should be treated as a partner owning a 2% interest in Crescent Holdings for purposes of allocating its profits and losses for the . . . years at issue; and (2) if not, how the profits and losses attributable to the 2% interest should be allocated to the other partners. . . .

[Applying the "liquidation-value" test described in Rev. Proc. 93-27 and Rev. Proc. 2001-43, the court concluded that petitioner was granted an unvested capital interest (rather than a profits interest) in Crescent Holdings and, therefore, the tax consequences of the transaction were not controlled by those two revenue procedures.]

PROVISIONS GOVERNING A NONVESTED PARTNERSHIP CAPITAL INTEREST

Petitioner and respondent argue that Reg. § 1.83-1(a)(1) provides that petitioner was not the owner of the interest for purposes of income recognition. Intervenor argues that Reg. § 1.721-1(b)(1) provides that petitioner was the owner. We must first decide whether section 83 applies to the transfer of a partnership capital interest in exchange for services.

SECTION 83

Section 83(a) generally provides that where property is transferred to a taxpayer in connection with the performance of services, the fair market value of the property, less the amount paid for the property, shall be included in the taxpayer's gross income in the first taxable year in which the taxpayer's rights in the property are "transferable or are not subject to a substantial risk of forfeiture." Section 83(a) is a deferral provision that allows a taxpayer to defer recognition of income to the taxable year in which his interest in the property is transferable or no longer subject to a substantial risk of forfeiture.

Reg. § 1.83-1(a)(1) provides that "[u]ntil such property becomes substantially vested, the transferor shall be regarded as the owner of such property.". . .

Section 83 governs the timing of income recognition when property is transferred in exchange for services. Section 721 provides that the contribution of *property* to a partnership in exchange for an interest in the partnership is a nonrecognition event for the partner and partnership. Section 83 does not conflict with section 721.

We have previously applied section 83 to partnership capital interests. . . . Nothing in the language of section 83 or its legislative history indicates that Congress did not intend for section 83 to apply to partnerships. Accordingly, we hold that section 83 applies to the transfer of a partnership capital interest in exchange for the performance of services.

ALLOCATION OF UNDISTRIBUTED PARTNERSHIP INCOME

Reg. § 1.83-1(a)(1) states that "any income from [the restricted] property received by the employee or independent contractor . . . constitutes additional compensation and shall be included in the gross income of such employee or independent contractor for the taxable year in which such income is received . . . ." As a result, if the transferee receives an actual distribution of income from the property before his right is substantially vested, then this income is treated as additional compensation and the transferee must include it in his gross income in the year received. Reg. § 1.83-1(a)(1) creates a dichotomy for ownership between the property and income actually received from the property: it treats income the transferee actually received from the property as owned by the transferee and treats property that is not substantially vested as owned by the transferor.

In addition to the dichotomy created by [the regulation] . . . , there exists another stream of potential income recognition — income attributable to property (such as a partnership interest) but not actually distributed. Section 83 does not specifically address whether recognition of undistributed income attributable to the property is also deferred. Similarly, Reg. § 1.83-1(a)(1) does not address whether income attributable to the property, but not actually received by the transferee, is included in the gross income of the transferee or the transferor. Particular to this case, Reg. § 1.83-1(a)(1) is silent as to whether the distributive share of partnership income attributable to the nonvested 2% partnership interest is included in the income of the transferor or the transferee (petitioner).

Petitioner and respondent argue that Reg. § 1.83-1(a)(1) provides that petitioner was not the owner of the 2% interest for purposes of income recognition. Therefore, they argue that petitioner should not have been allocated any of the partnership profits or losses attributable to the 2% interest. In its opening brief intervenor notes that if this regulation applies to the 2% interest, then petitioner would not be treated as the owner of the interest for income recognition purposes until the interest is substantially vested. However, intervenor argues that Reg. § 1.83-1(a)(1) is in conflict with Reg. § 1.721-1(b)(1). Intervenor argues that Reg. § 1.721-1(b)(1) applies to the 2% interest; therefore, petitioner should be allocated the partnership profits and losses attributable to the 2% interest. This appears to be an issue of first impression as no case has specifically decided whether the transferor or the transferee of a nonvested partnership capital interest must include in gross income the undistributed partnership profit or loss allocations attributable to the partnership capital interest. . . .

Although neither section 83 nor Reg. § 1.83-1(a)(1) specifically address this issue, for the reasons below we hold that the transferor of a partnership capital interest must recognize in income the undistributed partnership profit or loss allocations attributable to a nonvested capital interest.

The Purpose of Section 83 Is to Defer Recognition of Income When Property Is Subject to a Substantial Risk of Forfeiture

Section 83 is a deferral provision that delays the recognition of income to the taxable year in which the transferee's interest in the property is either transferable or not subject to a substantial risk of forfeiture. The policy underpinning section 83 is that it would be unfair to require a taxpayer to recognize the fair market value of property in income if the taxpayer may never own the property. . . .

Petitioner's right to receive the undistributed income allocations attributable to the 2% interest was subject to the same substantial risk of forfeiture as his right to the 2% interest. If petitioner forfeited his right to the 2% interest, then he would also forfeit his right to receive any benefit from the undistributed income allocations. In other words, petitioner's right to eventually receive any benefit from the undistributed income allocations was entirely dependent on whether his right vested in the 2% interest. When petitioner resigned from his position with Crescent Resources, he forfeited his right to the 2% interest, which resulted in him losing any rights he would have had to the undistributed income attributable to the 2% interest. Therefore, we find that the undistributed income allocations were subject to the same substantial risk of forfeiture as the 2% interest in Crescent Holdings. The 2% interest was not recognized in petitioner's income because it was subject to a substantial risk of forfeiture. Consistency requires that the undistributed partnership income allocations attributable to the 2% interest, which were subject to the same risk of forfeiture, should also not be recognized in petitioner's income.

If petitioner had continued his employment with Crescent Resources [for the minimum three years], then his interest would have vested. If this had occurred, then under section 83(a) petitioner would have recognized the fair market value of his partnership interest in gross income in the year [it vested]. The fair market value of the interest is measured at the time the property becomes substantially vested. . . . The fair market value of petitioner's interest [when it vested] would have been enhanced by income allocable to his interest for which no distributions had yet been paid.

Since petitioner forfeited his right to the 2% interest before it substantially vested, he never owned the interest. Petitioner never received any of the economic benefits from the undistributed partnership income allocations to the 2% interest.

Requiring petitioner to recognize the partnership allocations in his income is inconsistent with the fact that he received no economic benefit from the allocations.[4] When petitioner's interest was forfeited to Crescent Holdings, his right to the 2% interest and to receive any benefit from the partnership income allocations reverted to Crescent Holdings. As a result, . . . the remaining partners [of Crescent Holdings] received [the] economic benefits attributable to the undistributed income allocations.

Reg. § 1.83-1(a)(1) Does Not Conflict with Reg. § 1.721-1(b)(1)

Intervenor argues that Reg. § 1.83-1(a)(1) conflicts with Reg. § 1.721-1(b)(1) and since [the latter] specifically applies to partnerships we should apply that regulation to determine who should be allocated the partnership profits and losses attributable to the 2% interest.

Section 721(a) provides that "[n]o gain or loss shall be recognized to a partnership or to any of its partners in the case of a contribution of *property* to the partnership in exchange for an interest in the partnership." (Emphasis added.) Section 721 applies to contributions of property; it does not apply to contributions of services. Reg. § 1.721-1(b)(1) provides that the nonrecognition treatment for contributions of property to a partnership provided by section 721 does not apply to contributions of services. . . . This regulation provides no statements regarding who is treated as the owner of the partnership capital interest prior to the capital interest becoming substantially vested. As a result, the provision in Reg. § 1.83-1(a)(1) providing that the transferor of the property is treated as the owner of the property until it becomes substantially vested, does not conflict with Reg. § 1.721-1(b)(1) or with section 721.

We hold that under Reg. § 1.83-1(a)(1) undistributed partnership allocations attributable to a nonvested partnership capital interest are to be recognized in the gross income of the transferor.

IDENTITY OF THE TRANSFEROR

Reg. § 1.83-1(a)(1) provides that the transferor of petitioner's interest in Crescent Holdings will be treated as the owner of petitioner's interest. We must first

4. We note that Crescent Holdings filed [a document in bankruptcy court stating that] "Fields chose to terminate his employment, forfeiting any interest in Crescent Holdings, and negating his income tax liability arising out of the forfeited interest." . . . It is inconsistent for intervenor to have argued to the bankruptcy court that petitioner's tax liability for the allocations to his forfeited interest was negated and then argue to this Court that petitioner should be liable to pay tax on the income allocated to his forfeited interest.

determine who the transferor was in order to determine who is allocated the profits and losses associated with petitioner's 2% interest for the years at issue. . . .

Section 2.2 of the [LLC] Agreement clearly provides that Crescent Holdings was the transferor of petitioner's 2% interest in Crescent Holdings. Both respondent and intervenor agree that if Crescent Holdings was the transferor of petitioner's 2% interest, then the partnership profits and losses associated with the 2% interest for the years at issue should be allocated on a pro rata basis to [the other partners of Crescent Holdings]. Furthermore, the 2% interest was forfeited to Crescent Holdings . . . owned by [those partners]. Therefore, [they will] receive . . . the economic benefits attributable to the 2% interest. . . .

NOTES AND QUESTIONS

1. *What did the parties intend?* Although the court found that Fields received an unvested capital interest, the intent of the parties is unclear. The intervenor maintained that Fields received a profits interest governed by Rev. Proc. 93-27 and Rev. Proc. 2001-43. If the conditions of the revenue procedures were satisfied, Fields was the "owner" of the profits interest and a section 83(b) election was unnecessary. Although Fields was upset about the allocation of income to him, he nevertheless reported the amounts on his individual return.

2. *Unvested capital or profits interest?* In determining the nature of Fields' interest, one of the key issues was whether his right to a liquidating distribution was subordinated to return of the other partners' capital (and any priority return on such capital). The intervenor pointed to a provision of the partnership agreement under which Fields arguably would not have received any amount on liquidation immediately after receiving the restricted interest. The court, however, found that liquidating distributions were governed by a different provision, under which Fields was entitled to share distributions in accordance with his percentage interest; accordingly, he received a capital interest rather than a (subordinated) profits interest.

3. *Why might Fields wish to avoid a section 83(b) election?* Based on other evidence in the case, the value of Fields' interest (had it been unrestricted) would have been approximately $17 million (ignoring potential discounts for lack of marketability, etc.) at the time of grant. Thus, Fields would potentially have faced significant federal income and employment taxes if he had made a section 83(b) election at that time. Moreover, he apparently would not have been entitled to any distributions to cover these taxes. If the partnership had been successful, however, Fields might have been taxed on a larger amount when his (capital) interest vested. Instead, by terminating his employment and forfeiting his interest (on the eve of Crescent Holdings' bankruptcy), he avoided the prospect of an income inclusion coupled with a potential (capital) loss on his partnership interest.

4. *Outcome under the 2005 proposed regulations.* The 2005 proposed regulations conform the treatment of capital and profits interests by treating the recipient of an unvested interest as a partner only if a section 83(b) election is made. See Prop. Reg.

§ 1.761-1(b); Reg. § 1.83-1(a). Absent a section 83(b) election, the proposals would not treat Fields as owning either a capital or profits interest; partnership income would be allocated solely to the other partners (and Fields would be taxed only if he received distributions as additional compensation). The 2005 proposals also clarify that section 83 applies to profits (as well as capital interests), an issue that the court did not address.

5. *Potential "whipsaw" of Fields.* As noted in the footnote, the court clearly viewed the intervenor's argument in the tax proceedings that Fields was liable for tax on the distributive share as inconsistent with its argument in the bankruptcy proceedings that Fields had "negated his income tax liability" by terminating his employment and forfeiting his interest. Although Fields received no distributions in the years at issue, he received over $2 million from the LLC in subsequent years to cover his tax payments on the income reported earlier on his individual return.

5. *Tax Treatment of "Carried Interests"*

Controversy surrounding the tax treatment of "carried interests" earned by managers of private equity and hedge funds (usually organized as limited partnerships) illustrates nicely how potentially unsettled and unsatisfactory the current state of the law is. Such managers provide services to manage the fund's investments for the investor-partners of the fund, and the managers typically receive an annual fee equal to two percent of the fund's capital plus a 20 percent interest in the profits of the fund. The 20 percent interest is known as the "carried interest" and can represent huge amounts of money depending upon the success of the fund. Even if the interest they receive is vested upon receipt, managers do not report the "profits only" 20 percent interest as income at that time under the authority of Rev. Proc. 93-27. The character of their subsequent share of the partnership's profits is then determined by the character of the partnership's income by reason of section 702(b); in the case of managers of private equity funds which may seek out appreciation in longer-term investments, most or all of that income is long-term capital gain. The specter of enormous sums of money being earned from the performance of labor yet not taxed as ordinary income has understandably aroused much interest on Capitol Hill and in the media. A profits share is also potentially exempt from the Medicare portion (3.8 percent for certain high-income earners) of employment taxes, which is not subject to an income cap. (The profits share may, however, be subject to the 3.8 percent tax on net investment income (NII) (I.R.C. § 1411).) The controversial treatment of carried interests is, as we have seen, an outgrowth of the IRS's favorable ruling policy since the early 1990s as well as the basic difficulty the tax system often has in differentiating between ordinary income and capital gains.

The tax advantage of the current treatment of carried interests depends in part on the managers and investors of the fund being in different tax situations. If, for example, the profit share of the managers were treated as ordinary income for services rendered, then the other investors should generally be entitled to an ordinary deduction for the compensation paid to the managers. These two consequences would offset each other if the managers and investors had the same tax profile and the deduction were fully allowed. But whereas many managers are high-paid individuals, many investors are tax-exempt entities or foreign persons taxed only to a limited extent by the U.S. Other investors are taxable entities, such as financial institutions, that are subject to preferential tax regimes. And fully taxable U.S. investors are often subject to rules, such as the alternative minimum tax, that restrict or deny their deduction for this type of expense. Finally, there would be no complete offset if the managers were required to pay the Medicare tax on their share of profits.

As previously discussed, a theoretical case could be made for taxing the fair market value (not liquidation value) of a profits interest received by a service partner as ordinary income upon receipt. Immediate taxation would mean that the service partner could be treated as investing that amount in the partnership, with any additional returns (above the amounts already taxed) simply taxed under the general conduit rule of section 702(b). The service partner could be viewed as providing both services and capital to the venture, with taxation of the return from those inputs treated as ordinary income or capital gain based on general principles. This "front-end" approach of taxing a profits interest when granted would require an acceptable valuation method that could be applied in different situations in which carried interests arise. Also, there might be legitimate concern that service partners would significantly understate the value of the carried interest when granted.

It might be more practical instead to defer the taxable event until the stream of future profits is allocated to the service partner. Regardless of the character of the partnership's income, the profits allocated to the service partner could be treated as ordinary income. Since the fair market value of a profits interest upon receipt is equal to the discounted present value of the future income stream, taxing that stream of future profits as ordinary income when earned and allocated should roughly replicate taxing the value of the profits interest as ordinary income upon grant. Such a "back-end" approach would eliminate the potential double taxation of the service partner on the same income that might arise under the front-end approach — once at the time of grant and then again as earned — while also avoiding liquidity problems for the service partner. The back-end approach may also avoid some difficult issues involving the tax treatment of the non-service partners if the discounted present value of a profits interest were taxed at the front end.

To illustrate how the back-end approach might work, consider a private equity fund with $1 billion of investments under management and a service partner with a 20 percent carried interest. If the fund's investments grow in value to $1.5 billion and are then sold (generating $500 million of long-term capital gain), the service partner would be entitled to a $100 million share of profits (20 percent of the $500 million gain). Rather than treat such profits as long-term capital gain under the normal passthrough rule, the service partner would instead report ordinary income of $100 million. At a 39.6 percent tax rate, the service partner would therefore owe taxes of $39.6 million, rather than only $20 million (plus the NII tax of $3.8 million) if the profits were taxed as long-term capital gain. The service partner's $100 million might also be subject to self-employment taxes. Meanwhile, the investor partners would report all $500 million of long-term capital gain but also be entitled to claim an ordinary deduction (or capital expenditure) of $100 million. Thus, leaving aside the character of the income, the service partner would still report $100 million of income (20 percent) and the investor partners would still report $400 million of income (80 percent). But, of course, the character of the income and the availability of any deduction may be important to both the service partner and the investor partners.

In theory, if carried interests were taxed along the lines described above, it might be appropriate to extend this treatment to other types of arrangements in which a service provider receives a "profits only" interest, e.g., when a new partner is admitted to a law firm. But as a practical matter, the tax stakes may be less important when partners and partnerships earn principally or exclusively ordinary income. Thus, it would be possible to exempt service partners who work for non-capital intensive firms from any proposed changes.

NOTES AND QUESTIONS

1. *Guaranteed payments and section 707(a)(2)(A) payments.* As explained in the remaining two parts of this chapter, current law would treat the non-service partners correctly under the back-end approach if the service partner's share were considered either a "guaranteed payment" or a "section 707(a)(2)(A) payment." To encompass the typical carried interest, however, these provisions would need to be broadened considerably.

2. *Alternative approaches.* It may be helpful to consider other ways of characterizing a carried interest transaction for tax purposes. For example, the service partner could be viewed as receiving an option to acquire 20 percent of the partnership at a strike or exercise price equal to 20 percent of the value of the firm at the time of the grant. Thus, in the example in the text, the service partner's exercise of the option when the fund's investments are worth $1.5 billion would entitle her to receive a $300 million interest in exchange for a payment of $200 million (20 percent of the value of the fund when the option was granted). Under this view, the service partner would be taxed in the same manner generally as a recipient of a compensatory partnership option. If the option were treated as restricted property under section 83, the result would be $100 million of ordinary income to the service partner at the time of exercise.

Yet another approach would treat the investor partners as making a nonrecourse loan to the holder of the carried interest who would be obligated to invest the capital in the partnership and potentially earn long-term capital gain from the investment. In the example in the text, the service partner would be treated as borrowing and investing $200 million (20 percent of the $1 billion of initial fund capital) that would eventually grow in value to $300 million. The service partner would then pay off the $200 million loan and retain the $100 million balance which would be treated as long-term capital gain. Under this approach, the key tax question would be the consequences of the implicit borrowing by the service partner and any imputed interest on such borrowing. By analogy to section 7872(a)(1), the forgone interest might be treated as first transferred by the investors to the service partner (presumably as compensation) and then retransferred by the service partner to the investors (as interest). Tax results would then depend upon the consequences of these two deemed transfers as well as the rate of imputed interest. Would an imputed interest rate equal to the Treasury rate, as specified for purposes of section 7872 (see I.R.C. § 7872(e)(2) and (f)(2)), be appropriate in this case?

3. *Possible taxpayer responses.* Once the dynamics of tax planning are taken into account, it quickly becomes quite tricky to amend the partnership tax rules to ensure that the profits attributable to a carried interest are taxed as ordinary income rather than long-term capital gain. If, for example, Congress enacted the back-end approach, there would be an incentive for the partnership to distribute appreciated property (before the fund's realization of any gain) to the service partner in order potentially to avoid ordinary-income treatment. In the example described in the text, assume that when the fund's investments are worth $1.5 billion, the fund distributes $100 million in-kind (with an allocable basis of $67 million) to the service partner in liquidation of the partner's interest. Assume further that the service partner's outside basis is zero immediately before the distribution, the fund has a section 754 election in effect, and the distributed property is not treated as a marketable security under section 731(c). How should the service partner be taxed? What are the tax consequences to the investor partners?

4. *Publicly traded private equity funds.* As mentioned in chapter one, certain private equity funds organized as partnerships have become publicly traded, relying on the "qualifying income" exception to avoid corporate classification. See I.R.C. § 7704(c). If such firms were treated as corporations for tax purposes, perhaps because of a statutory amendment, then the favorable tax treatment of carried interests would no longer be available to the managers of the funds going forward.

5. *Nonqualified deferred compensation under section 457A.* Section 457A may require immediate inclusion in income of amounts deferred under a nonqualified deferred compensation plan to the extent a service provider's right to such compensation is not subject to a substantial risk of forfeiture. Section 457A is aimed primarily at deferral of fees by U.S.-based managers of investment funds when such compensation is paid by a tax-indifferent party (such as a foreign corporation located in a tax haven whose income is not subject to U.S. tax). In this situation, deferral of the service-provider's income is not offset by any tax detriment to the payor.

6. *Partnership Options and Debt-Equity Exchanges*

The use of options (both compensatory and noncompensatory) to acquire partnership interests presents challenging issues under subchapter K, as does an exchange of debt for a partnership interest. A compensatory partnership option is an option to acquire an interest in the issuing partnership that is granted in connection with the performance of services for that partnership. See Prop. Reg. § 1.721-1(b)(3). For example, suppose A and B contribute $75 each to partnership AB, which purchases land for $150. When the land is still worth that amount, the partnership grants to C in exchange for services an option to acquire a one-third interest in the capital and profits of the partnership for $90. The option may be exercised at any time during the next ten years and is not transferable by C except with the consent of the partnership. Assume that C exercises the option after three years when the land is worth $450 (and there are no other partnership assets). What are the tax consequences of these events to the parties?

One possibility is to treat the option granted to C as analogous to an unvested profits interest in the partnership. Like a profits interest, C's rights are limited to a share of future appreciation in the land and other partnership income. On a hypothetical liquidation of the partnership immediately after the grant of the option, C would not receive anything. Thus, if Rev. Proc. 2001-43 applied to this transaction, both the grant and exercise of the option might be nontaxable to C and the partnership. It is not clear, however, what partnership tax items (if any) would be considered "associated with [C's] interest" and thus allocable to C pursuant to the Revenue Procedure.

Alternatively, the option might be treated in the same manner as any other type of "property" transferred to a service provider pursuant to section 83 in a nonpartnership context. For example, nonqualified stock options granted to corporate employees are covered by that provision. In general, if a stock option has a readily ascertainable value at the time of the grant, then there is a taxable event to the employee and the corporation at that time. If value is not readily ascertainable at that time, the taxable event is deferred until the time the option is exercised. See Reg. § 1.83-7(a). Under this view, assuming that the value of C's option is not readily ascertainable when granted, C would have income equal to $90 when the option is exercised, i.e., the excess of the $180 value of the interest received (one-third of the $450 value of the land plus C's $90 payment to the partnership) over the $90 exercise price. Upon exercise of C's option, the partnership may also face tax consequences such as the deduction or capitalization of the compensation paid to C.

The 2005 proposed regulations treat a compensatory option essentially as a transfer of property for purposes of section 83. Thus, the option holder is not treated as a partner until the option is exercised. At the time of exercise, the option holder recognizes compensation income equal to the then liquidation value of the capital interest received (assuming a liquidation-value election is made) less the sum of the amounts paid by the option holder to acquire and exercise the option. The partnership also receives a deduction (allocated entirely to the non-service partners) equal to the amount treated as compensation to the option holder. Except as provided under the 2005 proposed regulations, the partnership may also be required to recognize gain or loss when the option is exercised.

NOTES AND QUESTIONS

1. *Unvested profits interest vs. compensatory option.* The 2005 proposed regulations treat compensatory options more harshly than unvested profits interests, despite their economic similarity. In general, a service provider must recognize income when an option is exercised but not upon the vesting of a profits interest. Why do you think the IRS drew this distinction? How easy is it to structure an unvested profits interest to mimic a compensatory option? Additional uncertainty regarding the tax treatment of compensatory options arises from the impact of C's services on the value of the partnership interest. For example, suppose C's services involve managing the land which appreciates in value in large part due to C's skillful work. How should the parties be taxed in this circumstance?

2. *Noncompensatory options.* Slightly different issues arise if a partnership issues a *non*compensatory option, i.e., an option to acquire a partnership interest other than one issued in connection with the performance of services. From the option holder's perspective, the purchase of a noncompensatory option is merely an investment. Under general tax law principles applicable to investment options, the option holder recognizes no gain when the option is exercised and takes a basis in the investment equal to the amount paid for the option (the "option premium") plus the exercise price. The regulations adopt similar principles in the partnership context. Upon exercise of the option to acquire a partnership interest, the option holder is generally treated as having transferred property, in the form of the option premium and the exercise price, to the partnership in a tax-free transaction under section 721. Reg. § 1.721-2(a)(1). The partnership is also permitted to revalue its property in connection with issuance of a noncompensatory option (other than an option for a *de minimis* partnership interest). Reg. § 1.704-1(b)(2)(iv)(*f*)(*5*)(*iv*).

A challenging issue is whether and how to take such options into account prior to their exercise for purposes of allocating partnership items. Suppose three persons contribute $10,000 apiece and receive equal shares in a new partnership. Suppose a fourth person pays the partnership $1,000 for the right to acquire a one-fourth interest in the partnership for $15,000 anytime during the next year. How should partnership items arising during the next year be allocated? An allocation of tax items only among the three existing partners may overlook economic entitlements belonging to the option holder if the partnership does well during the year and the option holder exercises her right to become a partner. In that case, there will not be the desired one-to-one correspondence between the partnership's tax consequences (split only among the three partners) and economic effects (shared by all four people). On the other hand, an allocation of tax items that includes the option holder may also be incorrect if, for example, the holder eventually allows the option to lapse and never becomes a partner.

Under the regulations, the holder of a noncompensatory option is normally not treated as a partner prior to exercise of the option, unless (1) the rights of the holder are substantially similar to those afforded to a partner, and (2) there is a strong likelihood that the failure to treat the holder as a partner will result in a substantial reduction in the present value of the aggregate tax liability of the option holder and partners. See Reg. § 1.761-3(a)(1). Whether the rights of an option holder are substantially similar to those of a partner would depend principally on whether the option is reasonably certain to be exercised. For example, the holder of an option to acquire an interest in a partnership with a predictable earnings stream and little or no downside risk would potentially be treated as a partner upon the grant of the option if the value of the partnership interest to be acquired by the option holder is expected to exceed the exercise price during the term of the option. Even if it is reasonably certain that the option will be exercised, the regulations do not require the holder to be treated as a partner prior to the exercise of the option unless failure to do so will substantially reduce aggregate tax liabilities.

If an option holder is not treated as a partner, the regulations do not require an allocation of partnership tax items to the holder prior to the exercise of the option. But as noted above, the mere existence of the option still creates uncertainty that tax allocations disregarding the option holder will have economic effect. The regulations create a safe harbor that validates such allocations so long as, in general, corrective adjustments are made to the capital accounts of the partners (and corresponding corrective tax allocations are made) when the option is exercised. The capital account adjustments must give "economic credit" to the former option holder (in her initial capital account balance) to reflect both the economic benefit received by such person in exercising the option and the sum of any amounts paid by the holder to acquire and exercise the option. In certain cases, this mandated economic credit will require a shifting of capital away from the other partners in the form of a reduction in their capital account balances. Corrective tax allocations must then be made consistent with these capital account adjustments. See Reg. § 1.704-1(b)(4)(*x*) and -1(b)(2)(iv)(*s*).

3. *Debt-for-equity exchanges.* Under section 108(e)(8), a debtor partnership must recognize COD income when it transfers a capital or profits interest to a creditor to the extent that the outstanding indebtedness exceeds the fair market value of the transferred interest. Reg. § 1.108-8(a). The COD income passes through to the partners in proportion to their interests immediately prior to the debt discharge. Under specified conditions, the fair market value of the transferred partnership interest is deemed to be the liquidation value of the interest. Reg. § 1.108-8(b). If the interest is a "profits-only" interest, then the deemed fair market value would be zero. Generally, the creditor recognizes no gain or loss on transfer of the debt (treated as property) to the partnership in exchange for a partnership interest. Reg. § 1.721-1(d)(1). The creditor takes an exchanged basis in the partnership interest and a tacked holding period. I.R.C. §§ 722 and 1223. Even though the partnership is required to recognize debt cancellation, the regulations do not permit the creditor to recognize a loss on the exchange, resulting in deferral and potential conversion from the creditor's perspective. Section 721 treatment does not apply if the creditor receives a partnership interest in exchange for unpaid rent, royalties, or interest.

To illustrate, assume that the AB partnership has $1,000 of outstanding debt owed to C (who has a $1,000 basis in the debt); the partnership used the borrowing to purchase a single nondepreciable asset worth $1,000 that has declined in value to $700. A and B each have an outside basis of $500. C agrees to cancel the debt for an interest in the AB partnership worth $700, the amount C would receive if the partnership sold all of its assets for their fair market value and liquidated. The partnership is treated as satisfying the debt for $700, triggering $300 of COD income (allocated $150 to each of A and B). Since section 721 applies to C's receipt of the partnership interest, C's loss of $300 is deferred but is preserved in the basis of C's partnership interest ($1,000). Following the debt-for-equity exchange, A and B each has an outside basis of $150 ($500 less $500 relief of liabilities plus $150 COD). The partners' aggregate outside basis ($1,300) exceeds the partnership's inside basis ($1,000) by $300 (the amount of C's deferred loss).

C. Guaranteed Payments

In general, most other compensation provided to a partner for services rendered (or the use of property) consists of the partner's distributive share of partnership income. For example, a lawyer who is a partner in a law firm typically performs legal services for the firm's clients and receives a distributive share of the firm's profits. We have already considered in chapter two the general tax consequences of distributive shares.

Sometimes, a partner engages in a transaction with her partnership that is outside of the normal scope of her duties as a member of the firm. For example, a partner of a law firm who also happens to be an astute investor might be hired by the firm for a flat fee to provide investment advice to the other partners and employees of the firm. In this case, the compensation is provided to one of the partners of the firm, but the service provider is acting outside her usual capacity as a lawyer providing legal services. Read I.R.C. § 707(a)(1). The tax law generally treats this transaction as if the partnership paid compensation to an outsider (or "nonpartner"). In that sense, the partnership is viewed as an entity separate from its partners. The distinction between partner and nonpartner payments is not particularly clear, although the focus is usually on whether the particular services provided are within the normal scope of the partner's duties. Further, a partner who loans, rather than contributes, property to her partnership is usually treated as acting in a nonpartner capacity. See Reg. § 1.707-1(a).

So-called "guaranteed payments" represent yet another category of compensatory payments. Read I.R.C. § 707(c). This category includes payments to a partner for services (or property) provided within the scope of the partner's usual duties, but not in the form of a straight distributive share. For example, in consideration of spearheading a major new case, a law-firm partner might be guaranteed special compensation of at least $100,000, regardless of what her share of the firm's profits might otherwise be. The following case explains why this category of guaranteed payments came into the law and then explores some of the tax consequences of such payments. What exactly does section 707(c) mean when it provides that a guaranteed payment shall be treated as a nonpartner payment "but only for the purposes of section 61(a) . . . and, subject to section 263, for purposes of section 162(a)"?

Miller v. Commissioner

52 T.C. 752 (1969)

SIMPSON, J.: . . . The petitioner, a partner in a law firm, spent 2 years abroad as managing partner of the firm's Paris office; the issue for decision is how much of his income from the partnership is excludable from gross income pursuant to section 911 of the Internal Revenue Code of 1954.

FINDINGS OF FACT

. . . In June 1960, White & Case opened a new branch office in Paris, France, of which the petitioner became the managing partner. . . . On June 14, 1960, . . . he and the partnership entered into a letter agreement which provided, in part, as follows:

> . . . In consideration of your services in managing our office in Paris, France, and in performing such other services in Europe as may be requested of you by our Firm, we hereby agree to pay you special compensation at the rate of $20,000 per annum, payable monthly, commencing July 1, 1960. This special compensation is guaranteed to you by the Firm without regard to the income of the Firm and without regard to your share of the partnership profits. You are to remain in charge of the Paris office of the Firm indefinitely until the Firm decides that your services abroad are no longer required.

. . . [T]he purpose of guaranteeing the payment of $20,000 per year to the petitioner, regardless of his share of partnership profits, was to qualify such amount under sections 707(c) and 911 so that, for Federal income tax purposes, the petitioner could treat such amount as compensation for services received by one who was not a partner.

The parties to the letter agreement believed that payment thereunder would be made to the petitioner as long as he continued to perform services as managing partner of the partnership's Paris office. Although the partnership had earned profits substantially in excess of $500,000 per year for the previous 20 years, and the parties to the letter agreement had no reason to expect lesser profits during the taxable years the petitioner might be abroad, it was not impossible for the partnership to incur a loss. Substantial reserve funds were maintained by the partnership against that possibility.

. . . The petitioner received from the partnership, pursuant to the letter agreement of June 14, 1960, $10,000 in 1960, $20,000 in 1961, and $10,000 in 1962, . . . commencing July 1960 and ending June 1962. These amounts were paid to the petitioner on account of his services to the partnership outside the United States. During the period he received them, he performed no services for the partnership other than as managing partner of the Paris office. The amounts paid to the petitioner were treated by the partnership as expenses and were deducted in determining the net income distributable to the partners pursuant to the partnership agreement.

. . . Pursuant to the partnership agreement, each partner, including the petitioner, was entitled to a distributive share consisting of a stated percentage of the partnership's net income (after the deduction of expenses and the payments to partners described previously). The petitioner's percentage was not reduced at any time during the years 1960 through 1962, nor was it increased when he became managing partner of the Paris office. The petitioner's distributive share of the partnership's net income amounted to $42,180.80, $48,929, and $52,463.72 for the calendar years 1960, 1961, and 1962, respectively. Such amounts were in addition to the amounts paid to the petitioner pursuant to the letter agreement of June 14, 1960. . . .

In their Federal income tax returns for the years 1960, 1961, and 1962, the petitioners excluded from gross income the income paid to the petitioner by the partnership pursuant to the letter agreement of June 14, 1960, and the portions of his distributive shares of partnership income which were attributable to the period of time during which he was present and performed services for the partnership outside the United States.

In his notice of deficiency, the respondent excluded from gross income pursuant to section 911 only such percentage of the aggregate income of the petitioner from the partnership each year attributable to his services outside the United States that (1) the net income of the partnership from sources without the United States for such year bore to (2) the total net income of the partnership for such year. . . .

OPINION

. . . As applicable to the years in issue, section 911(a) provides that, in the case of a U.S. citizen meeting certain foreign residence or presence requirements,

> The following items shall not be included in gross income and shall be exempt from taxation under this subtitle:
>
> (1) . . . amounts received from sources without the United States . . . if such amounts constitute earned income . . . attributable to such period . . . .

Earned income is defined in section 911(b) as meaning "wages, salaries, or professional fees, and other amounts received as compensation for personal services actually rendered." Section 862(a)(3) provides that "compensation for labor or personal services performed without the United States" shall be treated as income from sources without the United States.

The respondent makes no distinction between the payments which the petitioner received under the letter agreement and those which he received as his distributive share of the partnership profits. He takes the position that all such payments should be treated alike and that they are excludable only to the extent that they represent the petitioner's share of the firm's income from sources outside the United States.

Although the petitioners have alleged in their pleadings that all income from White & Case is excludable under section 911, they have not seriously urged us to hold that the distributive share is totally excludable. In *Foster v. United States*, 329 F.2d 717 (C.A. 2, 1964), the Court of Appeals for the Second Circuit held that a partner who performed services outside the United States was not entitled to treat his entire share of partnership profits as earned income under section 911; he was limited to excluding that portion of his distributive share which the net income of the partnership from sources outside the United States bore to the total income of the partnership. . . . Accordingly, we hold that the petitioner's distributive share of the White & Case profits is excludable only to the extent that it represents his share of the firm's income from sources outside the United States.

The question remaining for decision is whether the payments received by the petitioner under the letter agreement are totally excludable or whether their excludability is limited in the same manner as the petitioner's distributive share. The petitioners contend that such payments are guaranteed payments within the meaning of section 707(c); that accordingly, such payments are treated as compensation for services; and that since the services of the petitioner were performed outside the United States, such payments are entirely excludable under section 911.

. . . Section 707(c) [pre-1976 version] provides:

> (c) Guaranteed Payments.—To the extent determined without regard to the income of the partnership, payments to a partner for services or the use of capital shall be considered as made to one who is not a member of the partnership, but only for the purposes of section 61(a) (relating to gross income) and section 162(a) (relating to trade or business expenses).

. . . One of the troublesome problems under the [law prior to enactment of section 707(c)] was the treatment of compensation paid to a partner. On the basis of the aggregate theory of partnerships, compensation for a partner's services was treated as part of his distributive share of partnership profits or losses. Accordingly, if partnership profits were sufficiently large, the compensation was treated as a distributive share of profits. . . . However, to the extent that partnership profits were insufficient to cover amounts paid as compensation, the compensation was treated as being paid from each partner's capital. To the extent a partner's compensation was treated as a return of his own capital, there was no tax. However, to the extent he was treated as receiving compensation from the capital of his fellow partners, he was considered to receive taxable income. *Augustine M. Lloyd,* 15 B.T.A. 82 (1929). Congress found this treatment to be "unrealistic and unnecessarily complicated." . . .

The enactment of section 707(c) and this legislative history make clear that Congress intended to permit partners to arrange for the payment of compensation to a partner and to give effect to such arrangement in computing the tax liability of the partners. Of course, for the arrangement to be treated as the payment of compensation, it must in form and in substance meet the conditions of section 707(c). Although in this case the payments were guaranteed to secure the tax benefits of section 911, that fact does not necessarily disqualify them as guaranteed payments; the fact that the petitioner sought a tax benefit does not of itself prevent his achieving it. Nor do the payments fail to qualify as guaranteed payments by reason of the fact that White & Case had a long history of profitable operations and was likely to have sufficient profits out of which to make the guaranteed payments. If the payments were disqualified for these reasons, no profitable partnership could rely on the effectiveness of its arrangements for the payment of guaranteed payments under section 707(c). Such a result would be a severe blow to the certainty and predictability which Congress sought to achieve by the enactment of the partnership provisions.

Whether the payments do qualify as guaranteed payments depends upon what relationships were in fact created. As a result of the letter agreement, the partnership was obligated to pay the petitioner $20,000 a year so long as he continued to manage the Paris office. He thereby acquired a right to such payments, which was not subject to the fortunes of the partnership generally, in contrast to the rights of other partners to receive distributions from the partnership. . . . Despite the profitability of the partnership and the likelihood that the petitioner could be paid the $20,000 out of profits of the partnership, we believe that the guarantee had some significance, and accordingly, we find that the payments were guaranteed payments within the meaning of section 707(c).

Next, the respondent takes the position that even if the payments under the letter agreement are guaranteed payments, they are not totally excludable under section 911. He contends that for purposes of section 911, the guaranteed payments must be treated as payments of a distributive share of partnership income; as such, they do not constitute earned income received from foreign sources under section 911 except to the extent that they represent the petitioner's share of the partnership's foreign source income. . . .

The taxability of the guaranteed payments . . . turns on the meaning of the phrase "but only for the purposes of section 61(a) (relating to gross income) and section 162(a) (relating to trade or business expenses)" in section 707(c). On the basis of this language, the respondent argues that section 707(c) makes the guaranteed payments compensation only for purposes of sections 61 and 162 — not for any other purpose. According to his view, section 707(c) was designed merely to reverse the tax treatment of guaranteed payments established in *Augustine M. Lloyd, supra,* and the only effects of the provision are that the partner receiving the guaranteed payments is taxable on them as compensation and that the partnership is allowed a deduction for the payment of compensation. On the other hand, the petitioners point out that section 61 provides "*Except as otherwise provided in this subtitle*, gross income means all income from whatever source derived." (Emphasis added.) Therefore, they argue that the reference to section 61 in section 707(c) includes the exceptions otherwise provided in the Internal Revenue Code. These different readings of the statute can only be resolved by an examination of the objectives of the provisions.

In describing the reasons for the enactment of section 707, the committee reports indicate that the general approach of the section is to apply the entity theory to the dealings between partners and the partnership. . . . Clearly, section 707(c) makes a guaranteed payment taxable to a partner as compensation, and the committee reports indicate that such payments are not to be treated as a part of his distributive share of the partnership profits. Section 707 includes some express exceptions to the application of the entity theory to transactions involving partners and the partnership. In addition, the conference committee report states:

> No inference is intended, however, that a partnership is to be considered as a separate entity for the purpose of applying other provisions of the internal revenue laws if the concept of the partnership as a collection of individuals is more appropriate for such provisions. . . .

For purposes of section 911, we perceive no reason for not applying the entity theory.

. . . The legislative history of [section 911] indicates that its purpose was to increase foreign trade by removing tax disadvantages of U.S. citizens working abroad. . . . If the petitioner had served as an employee of White & Case while working in Paris, his compensation would have been excludable under section 911. The petitioner seems to be as entitled to tax relief under section 911 as an employee. . . . He was subject to the same French taxes and extra expenses as an employee. The guaranteed payments were received from the law firm as a reward for the services which he rendered the firm, and clearly they were not excessive compensation. Although the distributive share which the petitioner received constituted a share of the entire profits of the partnership and may be considered as more than mere compensation for his services performed in Paris, the guaranteed payments constitute only compensation for his services. . . .

In our opinion, treating the guaranteed payments as compensation for purposes of section 911 carries out the purposes of both that section and section 707(c). Since section 707(c) makes such payments taxable as compensation, it seems reasonable to conclude that other provisions relating to the tax treatment of such compensation are also applicable.

This conclusion does not ignore the effect of the "but only" words. These words were added to section 707(c) . . . to provide that guaranteed payments received by a partner are to be included in his income for his taxable year in which the partnership's taxable year ends. In connection with section 707(c), the Senate committee report indicates that the reason for the change was to provide that guaranteed payments are to be included in income at the same time as a partner's distributive share — not at the time when compensation would ordinarily be included in income. This is the only example in the legislative history of the need for the "but only" words.

Another reason for our conclusion is that if we adopted the respondent's position, we would perpetuate many of the complexities and problems that Congress sought to eliminate by the enactment of section 707(c). These difficulties would arise in determining how to treat the guaranteed payments received by a partner who performs his services outside the United States when the partnership has insufficient profits out of which to make the guaranteed payments. As a result of section 707(c), all of such payments would be taxable as compensation except to the extent that they are excludable under section 911. If the guaranteed payments are treated as a distributive share for purposes of section 911, it would then be necessary to apply the holding of *Augustine M. Lloyd, supra,* and to determine what portion of the payments should be considered as compensation paid by the other partners. We would then have to decide whether all of the payments attributable to the other partners should be treated as foreign-source compensation, or whether they should be allocated in some other manner. It is clear that when Congress enacted section 707(c), one of its purposes was to eliminate such problems, and it appears to us that to hold that the guaranteed payments are to be treated as a distributive share for purposes of section 911 frustrates that legislative purpose. . . .

NOTES AND QUESTIONS

1. *Background.* As briefly described by the court, section 707(c) was enacted to solve both a conceptual and computational problem under pre-1954 law. Based on an aggregate approach, courts generally concluded that a partner could not act as an employee of her own partnership and, therefore, characterized most "salary" payments as a distributive share of partnership income. This approach resulted in complex computations, however, when such fixed payments to a partner exceeded the partnership's taxable income. For example, if White & Case had had an incredibly bad year and ended up with net profits of less than $20,000 (before taking into account the guaranteed payment to the taxpayer), how should the taxpayer and other partners have been taxed if the $20,000 payment were treated as a distributive share? As mentioned by the court in discussing the *Lloyd* case, courts answered this question by treating some part of the payment as a return of the service partner's capital or the capital of the other partners, with differing results. To eliminate this confusion, section 707(c) treats payments to a partner determined without regard to partnership income as payments to an outsider, but only for certain limited purposes.

2. *"Without regard to the income of the partnership."* The key language in section 707(c) that defines a guaranteed payment is that such payment must be determined without regard to the income of the partnership. Compensation based on the *gross* income of a partnership does not qualify as a guaranteed payment. See Pratt v.

Comm'r, 64 T.C. 203 (1975), aff'd in part and rev'd in part on other issues, 550 F.2d 1023 (5th Cir. 1977); accord Rev. Rul. 81-301, 1981-2 C.B. 144 (allocation of gross income was section 707(a) rather than section 707(c) payment).

3. *A nonpartner payment . . . for what purposes?* Even where a guaranteed payment is properly identified as such, there may be controversy regarding its tax consequences. The government argued in *Miller* that section 707(c) should be read narrowly as applying "nonpartner" treatment only for purposes of determining the amount, character, and deductibility of the payment. With respect to the "character" of the payment, the government argued that inquiry was limited to the ordinary-income nature of the payment under section 61, not characterization as foreign-source earned income for purposes of section 911. The court disagreed with the government, drawing a distinction between the taxpayer's distributive share and guaranteed payments for purposes of section 911. Do you think the court interpreted section 707(c) correctly?

4. *More uncertainty*. In an omitted portion of the opinion, the court in *Miller* considered whether a partner receiving section 707(c) guaranteed payments may be treated as an employee for other purposes under the Code. There is lingering uncertainty regarding the proper characterization of such payments. Compare Armstrong v. Phinney, 394 F.2d 661 (5th Cir. 1968) (dicta suggesting that recipient of a guaranteed payment may be treated as an employee who is eligible to exclude the value of meals and lodging under section 119), with Reg. § 1.707-1(c) (partner receiving guaranteed payment is not treated as an employee for purposes of the sick-pay exclusion of former section 105(d), income tax withholding on wages, and deferred compensation plans).

5. *Timing of the income and deduction.* As discussed by the court, the one instance mentioned in the legislative history for which "partner" treatment of a guaranteed payment remains pertinent is the timing of income and deduction (if any). For this purpose, a guaranteed payment continues to be treated as a distributive share. This means that the partnership must first determine the year in which it deducts or capitalizes the payment under its method of accounting. The partner must then include the payment in income in the year in which such partnership year ends. See Reg. § 1.707-1(c); I.R.C. § 706(a). Thus, the partner's method of accounting does not control the timing of the income. As illustrated by the *Gaines* case, excerpted below, the timing rule of section 707(c) can produce particularly harsh results when an accrual-method partnership incurs an obligation to a cash-method partner for a capital expenditure.

Gaines v. Commissioner

45 T.C.M. 363 (1982)

PARKER, J.: [In 1973, certain accrual method limited partnerships accrued and deducted "guaranteed payments" promised to their general partner, Gaines

Properties. The partner, a cash method taxpayer, did not actually receive the payments and therefore did not report any income in that year.]

. . . Respondent disallowed to the limited partnerships [as capital expenditures] portions of the claimed deductions for guaranteed payments. . . . Notwithstanding this partial disallowance of deductions at the partnership level, respondent determined that the entire amount of the guaranteed payments to Gaines Properties, including the portion disallowed as deductions at the partnership level, should be included in Gaines Properties' income [in 1973]. . . . Respondent argues that Gaines Properties' share of these guaranteed payments was includible in its income regardless of the fact that the deduction was partially disallowed at the partnership level and regardless of the fact that Gaines Properties . . . never received the payments. We agree with respondent.

Section 707(c), as in effect in 1973, provided:

> To the extent determined without regard to the income of the partnership, payments to a partner for services or the use of capital shall be considered as made to one who is not a member of the partnership, but only for the purposes of section 61(a) (relating to gross income) and section 162(a) (relating to trade or business expenses).

This case does in fact involve "guaranteed payments" to a partner within the meaning of section 707(c) of the Code. The fact that no actual payments were made does not affect the status of these transactions as section 707(c) guaranteed payments. "[D]espite the use of the word 'payments' in both section 707(c) and the Regulations thereunder, it is clear that no actual payment need be made; if the partnership deducts the amount under its method of accounting, the 'recipient' partner must include the amount in income in the appropriate year." . . . The parties stipulated that each of the four limited partnerships deducted "guaranteed payments." The partnership agreements . . . expressly stated that certain payments to partners "shall constitute guaranteed payments within the meaning of section 707(c) of the Code." While the descriptions of such payments in the partnership agreements are not binding upon us . . . , the payments referred to in those two partnership agreements are clearly fixed sums determined without regard to partnership income. See Sec. 707(c); Reg. § 1.707-1(c). Furthermore, it is equally clear that the payments to the partners were for services in their capacities as partners. Respondent . . . determined that these payments were in fact guaranteed payments under section 707(c), and petitioners did not dispute this determination. Accordingly, we hold that the payments here were guaranteed payments within the meaning of section 707(c).

The statutory language of section 707(c) addresses only the character of the guaranteed payments and not the timing. . . . Reg. § 1.707-1(c) addresses the timing question, as follows:

> Payments made by a partnership to a partner for services or for the use of capital are considered as made to a person who is not a partner, to the extent such payments are

> determined without regard to the income of the partnership. However, a partner must include such payments as ordinary income for his taxable year within or with which ends the partnership taxable year in which the partnership deducted such payments as paid or accrued under its method of accounting. See section 706(a) and paragraph (a) of § 1.706-1.

As the regulation makes clear, the statutory authority for the timing of the inclusion of these guaranteed payments is section 706(a), which provides:

> In computing the taxable income of a partner for a taxable year, the inclusions required by section 702 and section 707(c) with respect to a partnership shall be based on the income, gain, loss, deduction, or credit of the partnership for any taxable year of the partnership ending within or with the taxable year of the partner.

The separate reference of section 707(c) guaranteed payments in the timing provisions of section 706(a) was explained by the Senate Report as simply:

> to make clear that payments made to a partner for services or for the use of capital are includible in his income at the same time as his distributive share of partnership income for the partnership year when the payments are made or accrued. . . . (S. Rept. No. 1622, to accompany H.R. 8300 (Pub. L. No. 591), 83d Cong., 2d Sess. 385 (1954)).

In *Cagle v. Commissioner*, 63 T.C. 86 (1974), affd. 539 F.2d 409 (5th Cir. 1976), we held that includibility and deductibility of guaranteed payments are two separate questions, and specifically that guaranteed payments are not automatically deductible simply by reason of their being included in the recipient's income. In *Cagle*, we stated 63 T.C. at 95:

> We think that all Congress meant was that guaranteed payments should be included in the recipient partner's income in the partnership taxable year ending with or within which the partner's taxable year ends and in which the tax accounting treatment of the transaction is determined at the partnership level. S. Rept. No. 1622, supra at pp. 94, 385, 387.

We believe our statement in *Cagle* is an accurate description of the Congressional intent. We have found nothing in the statutory language, regulations, or legislative history to indicate that includability in the recipient partner's income was intended to be dependent upon deductibility at the partnership level.

Petitioners seem to argue that there is a patent unfairness in taxing them on nonexistent income, namely income that they have neither received nor benefitted from (e.g. through a tax deduction at the partnership level). Their argument has a superficial appeal to it, but on closer analysis must fail. Except for certain very limited purposes, guaranteed payments are treated as part of the partner's distributive share of partnership income and loss. Reg. § 1.707-1(c). For timing purposes guaranteed payments are treated the same as distributive income and loss. Sec. 706(a); Reg. §§ 1.706-1(a) and 1.707-1(c). A partner's distributive share of partnership income is includible in his taxable income for any partnership year ending within or with the partner's taxable year. Sec. 706(a). As is the case with a partner's ordinary distributive share of partnership income and loss, any unfairness in taxing a partner on guaranteed payments that he neither receives nor benefits from results from the conduit theory of partnerships, and is a consequence of the taxpayer's choice to do the business in the partnership form. We find no justification in the statute, regulations, or legislative history to permit these petitioners to recognize their income pro rata as deductions are allowed to the partnership. . . .

NOTES AND QUESTIONS

1. *Worst case. Gaines* represents the worst possible outcome from the taxpayer's perspective — the guaranteed payment is includible in the taxpayer's income immediately, even though the partnership is required to capitalize the expenditure. The net result is income to the partner without any actual receipt of cash, while the partnership's deduction is deferred. How should the taxpayer report the guaranteed payment when received? Will the same amount be taxed twice? Is the guaranteed payment reflected in the recipient's capital account?

2. *Is section 707(c) now superfluous?* In *Gaines*, the taxpayer tried to take advantage of the difference between its accounting method and that of the partnership's. Had the compensation been treated as a deductible nonpartner payment, the accrual method partnerships would have accrued and deducted the amount in 1973 (and passed through a portion of the deduction to the taxpayer in that year) even though the cash method taxpayer would not report the income until a later year. For this reason, Congress provided in section 707(c) that nonpartner treatment of guaranteed payments does not extend to the timing of income and deduction. Rather, treatment of the guaranteed payment as a distributive share links the timing of the income and any resulting deduction, with both being controlled by the partnership's method of accounting.

In 1984, Congress eliminated the potential timing advantage in the case of nonpartner payments. Read I.R.C. § 267(a)(2), (e)(1) and (2). Under current law, an accrual method partnership's deduction (if any) for compensation owed to a partner is deferred until such compensation is included in the recipient's income. Since nonpartner payments now also require a matching of the timing of income and deduction, section 707(c) is arguably superfluous. A guaranteed payment could simply be treated as a nonpartner payment for *all* purposes. The only question, then, would be whether the compensation is a partner payment (taxable as a distributive share for all purposes) or a nonpartner payment (taxable under section 707(a) as a payment to an outsider for all purposes).

3. *Treatment of the partnership.* Rev. Rul. 2007-40, 2007-1 C.B. 1426, is consistent with the trend toward treating guaranteed payments more broadly as

nonpartner payments. The ruling concludes that the transfer of appreciated property by a partnership to a partner in satisfaction of the latter's guaranteed payment is a sale or exchange to the partnership under section 1001(a) and is not controlled by the partnership distribution rule of section 731(b).

4. *Organization and syndication expenses.* Read I.R.C. § 709. One common type of partnership expense that may be a guaranteed payment to a partner is an amount paid in connection with the organization and syndication of a partnership. In general, these amounts are not immediately deductible by the partnership. Rather, under section 709(b)(1), a partnership is generally deemed to elect to amortize certain organizational expenses over a 15-year period, the same period provided for the amortization of section 197 intangibles. See Reg. § 1.709-1(b)(2). A limited amount of such expenses incurred by small ventures may be deducted immediately.

5. *Guaranteed minimum.* Read Prop. Reg. § 1.707-1(c) (ex. 2). As that example illustrates, guaranteed payments are sometimes provided in the form of a guaranteed minimum. In this situation, the entire minimum amount is treated as a guaranteed payment under section 707(c), regardless of the amount of income allocated to the partner. Thus, only the income allocation in excess of the guaranteed minimum is subject to entrepreneurial risk and hence treated as a section 704(b) distributive share.

Review Reg. § 1.707-1(c) and do the following problems.

Problem 10-3:

(a) In Year 1, PS, an accrual-basis, calendar-year partnership, agrees to make a $10,000 payment to partner Q in exchange for services performed by Q in that year. The services are within the scope of Q's normal duties as a partner of the partnership. Q also is entitled to a ten percent share of the partnership's profits and losses (determined after taking into account any guaranteed payments). The $10,000 payment is not actually received by Q, who is a cash-basis, calendar-year taxpayer, until Year 2. Determine the amount, character, and timing of Q's income in the following alternative circumstances:

(i) the $10,000 expense is deductible by PS and before taking the expense into account, PS has $500,000 of profits (all ordinary income) in both Years 1 and 2;

(ii) the $10,000 expense is deductible by PS and before taking the expense into account, PS has $6,000 of profits (all ordinary income) in both Years 1 and 2;

(iii) the $10,000 expense is deductible by PS and before taking the expense into account, PS has $500,000 of profits (all long-term capital gain) in both Years 1 and 2.

(b) Assume the same basic facts as in (a), except that the $10,000 expense relates to interest owed to Q as a result of a loan made by Q to the partnership at the beginning of Year 1. The principal of the loan is repaid at the end of Year 1 but the $10,000 interest is not paid until Year 2. Before taking the $10,000 expense into account, PS has $500,000 of profits (all ordinary income) in both Years 1 and 2. What is the amount, character, and timing of Q's income?

(c) Assume the same basic facts as in (a), except that the expense is for $75,000 and represents compensation for Q's services in connection with organizing the PS. The payment again is not actually received by Q until Year 2. Before taking the $75,000 expense into account, PS has $100,000 of profits (all ordinary income) in both Years 1 and 2. What is the amount, character, and timing of Q's income?

Problem 10-4: In exchange for services within the scope of her normal duties as a partner, D agrees to receive 25 percent of the partnership's taxable income or loss but not less than $10,000. Assume that any amount treated as a guaranteed payment is immediately deductible by the partnership.

(a) If the partnership has $60,000 of ordinary income before the guaranteed payment, what is the amount D receives? How is the payment characterized? See Prop. Reg. § 1.707-1(c) (ex. 2).

(b) Same as (a), except that the partnership has taxable income of $4,000 (before the guaranteed payment) consisting entirely of ordinary income.

D. Compensation Recharacterized as Nonpartner Payments

Compensation provided to a partner in the form of a special allocation of partnership income (and a related distribution of cash) is sometimes recharacterized under section 707(a)(2)(A) as a payment to an outsider. The purpose of this provision is primarily to prevent avoidance of the capitalization requirement of section 263.

To understand the problem, consider the situation in which an architect-partner (A) is to receive compensation of $50,000 for architectural services in connection with the construction of property owned by the partnership. If the $50,000 is a guaranteed payment, the partnership would be required to capitalize the entire amount, while A would receive ordinary income for services. Instead, the partnership specially allocates and distributes to A the first $50,000 of the partnership's taxable income of $60,000. If respected, the special allocation reduces the other partners' distributive share of taxable income to $10,000, the same result as if the expense for architectural services were immediately deductible. A continues to receive $50,000 of ordinary income. Since the special allocation and distribution offset each other, there is no net effect on A's outside basis or capital account.

To prevent such circumvention of the capitalization requirement, section 707(a)(2)(A) disregards a purported special allocation and distribution that is, in substance, a disguised fee for nonpartner services. Thus, section 707(a)(2)(A) would recast this transaction as a section 707(a)(1) payment of $50,000 to A, resulting in ordinary income to A. The partnership would be required to capitalize the $50,000 fee for A's services, restoring the partnership's taxable income to $60,000. Thus, the principal effect of the disguised payment rules is to increase the other partners' distributive share of the partnership's taxable income.

The legislative history lists five factors to be considered in determining whether a special allocation and related distribution is a nonpartner payment under section 707(a)(2)(A). The most important factor is whether the service provider is subject to a "significant entrepreneurial risk" concerning the amount and fact of payment. To the extent that a service provider is not insulated from risk, she is more likely to be acting in a partner capacity and the distributive share arrangement should be respected. Other factors indicating a disguised payment for services include: (i) transitory partner status, (ii) proximity in time between the services rendered and the allocation/distribution, (iii) tax motivation for the arrangement, and (iv) the relative size of the purported allocation/distribution in relationship to the service partner's overall interest in the partnership.

The legislative history makes clear that Congress did not intend section 707(a)(2)(A) to affect nonabusive transactions that properly reflect the parties' economic arrangement. Thus, section 707(a)(2)(A) is limited to those special allocations and related distributions that are properly characterized as substantively equivalent to nonpartner payments. To discern the distinction, consider the following example from the legislative history.

Staff of the Joint Committee on Taxation, General Explanation of the Revenue Provisions of the Deficit Reduction Act of 1984

98th Cong., 2d Sess. 229-230 (1984)

A commercial office building constructed by a partnership is projected to generate gross income of at least $100,000 per year indefinitely. Its architect, whose normal fee for such services is $40,000, contributes cash for a 25-percent interest in the partnership and receives both a 25-percent distributive share of net income for the life of the partnership, and an allocation of $20,000 of partnership gross income for the first two years of partnership operations after lease-up. The partnership is expected to have sufficient cash available to distribute $20,000 to the architect in each of the first two years, and the agreement requires such a distribution.

The purported gross income allocation and partnership distribution in this example should be treated as a fee under section 707(a), rather than as a distributive share because as to those payments the architect is insulated from the risk of the joint enterprise. Factors which contribute to this conclusion are (1) the special allocation to the architect is fixed in amount and there is a substantial probability that the partnership will have sufficient gross income and cash to satisfy the allocation/distribution; (2) the distribution relating to the allocation is fairly close in time to the rendering of the services; and (3) it is not unreasonable to conclude from all the facts and circumstances that the architect became a partner primarily for tax reasons.

If, on the other hand, the agreement allocates to the architect 20 percent of gross income for the first two years following construction of the building, a question arises as to how likely it is that the architect will receive substantially more or less than his imputed fee of $40,000. If the building is pre-leased to a high credit tenant under a lease requiring the lessee to pay $100,000 per year of rent, or if there is low vacancy rate in the area for comparable space, it is likely that the architect will receive approximately $20,000 per year for the first two years of operations. Therefore, he assumes limited risk as to the amount or payment of the allocation and, as a consequence, the allocation/distribution should be treated as a disguised fee. If, on the other hand, the project is a "spec building," and the architect assumes significant entrepreneurial risk that the partnership will be unable to lease the building, the special allocation might (even though a gross income allocation), depending on all the facts and circumstances, properly be treated as a distributive share and a genuine partnership distribution.

NOTES AND QUESTIONS

1. *Payments contingent on partnership income.* Normally, payments contingent on partnership *net* income will not be treated as section 707(a)(2)(A) payments, since the service provider bears a significant entrepreneurial risk. Some net income allocations may be so short-lived or provide a sufficiently fixed stream of income, however, as to be considered nonpartner payments. Payments that are not contingent on partnership net income, including *gross* income allocations, are likely to run afoul of section 707(a)(2)(A). Moreover, even contingent arrangements may be recast as nonpartner payments if the service partner performs similar services for others and, under such circumstances, third parties would normally be compensated on a contingent basis.

2. *Disguised payments for property.* Section 707(a)(2)(A) also applies to recharacterize a special allocation and distribution as, in effect, a disguised payment for *property*, and one of the factors included in the legislative history relates exclusively to that application of the rule. Because a partner's capital account must reflect the fair market value of contributed property under the section 704(b) regulations, however, a purported allocation/distribution is unlikely to constitute a disguised payment for property. In effect, the income allocation would cause the partnership to pay twice for the property, assuming that the partner's capital account has already been credited with the full fair market value of the property. Contrast the disguised *sale* rules in

section 707(a)(2)(B), which recharacterize a tax-free contribution and distribution as a sale of property between the partnership and partner. We considered the disguised sale rules in chapter nine.

3. *Guaranteed payments vs. nonpartner payments vs. distributive shares.* Reconsider the facts and holding in *Gaines.* The guaranteed payment in that case was treated as income to the partner in 1973, the year the partnership accrued and capitalized the expense, even though actual payment was not made until a later year. What would the tax result have been if the payment were instead classified as a section 707(a) payment or, alternatively, as a distributive share of partnership income for all purposes?

4. *Proposed regulations under section 707(a)(2)(A).* More than 30 years after the 1984 legislation, the Treasury in 2015 issued proposed regulations under section 707(a)(2)(A). REG-115452-14, 2015-32 I.R.B. 158. The proposed regulations confirm that lack of significant entrepreneurial risk is the most important factor in determining whether an arrangement constitutes a nonpartner payment for services. Under the proposed regulations, waiver of a fee for services in exchange for an additional profits interest may be treated as a nonpartner payment under section 707(a)(2)(A) if there is a high likelihood that the service provider will receive an allocation of net profits equal to the waived fee. See Prop. Reg. § 1.707-2(d) (exs. 5, 6) (management fee waiver not recharacterized under section 707(a)(2)(A) if allocation of net profits is subject to substantial risk). As discussed earlier (p. 308, note 7), receipt of a profits interest in conjunction with waiver of a right to a substantially fixed amount for performance of services would also fall outside of the safe harbor under Rev. Proc. 93-27, potentially triggering immediate taxation under section 83.

Problem 10-5:

(a) A partnership formed to invest in stocks admits a stockbroker as a partner. The broker contributes 25 percent of the partnership's capital and is entitled to a 25 percent share of the partnership's residual profits and losses. The broker, who forgoes her normal commission for performing stock trades, is also entitled to a gross income allocation and priority distribution that is computed in a manner that approximates the amount of the forgone commissions. The partnership expects to have ample gross income. How should the allocation/distribution be taxed?

(b) An open-end investment company formed to invest in municipal bonds admits an investment advisor as a partner, who is entitled to ten percent of the partnership's daily gross income for managing its investments. The investment advisor's services are substantially similar to those she provides to third parties on a contingent fee basis. Will the investment advisor's share of partnership income be treated as tax-exempt income or ordinary income?

Chapter 11

Termination of Partnership Interests and Partnerships

A. Introduction

This chapter concerns the tax consequences of two final transactions: the termination of a partner's interest in a partnership and termination of a partnership itself. For the most part, the tax consequences of these two transactions follow from rules already described in prior chapters.

A partner may terminate her interest in a partnership by either selling the interest to a new or existing partner or receiving a liquidating distribution from the partnership. Conceptually, there may be little economic difference between these two approaches since the receipt of a liquidating distribution is functionally equivalent to a sale of the interest to all of the remaining partners. Consequently, as explained in chapters seven and eight, the partnership tax law generally tries to equate the tax consequences of the two alternative approaches. In spite of these efforts, there remain important differences in the tax treatment of sales of partnership interests and liquidating distributions.

This chapter introduces yet another distinction in how these two transactions are taxed. Section 736 sometimes permits the proceeds from a liquidating distribution, but not from the sale of a partnership interest, to be treated as a distributive share of (or guaranteed payment to) the terminated partner or such partner's successor in interest (including such partner's estate). Part B of this chapter describes the operation of section 736 and also discusses some special considerations if a partnership interest is terminated by reason of the death of a partner.

The termination of a partnership interest may or may not be accompanied by a termination of the partnership. In general, under section 708, partnerships are treated as continuing for tax purposes except in certain specified circumstances. Even the dissolution of a partnership under state law, such as upon the death or withdrawal of the sole general partner of a limited partnership, does not necessarily result in a termination for tax purposes. Part C of this chapter outlines the conditions and principal ramifications of a partnership termination for tax purposes.

B. Termination of Partnership Interests

1. *The Statutory Pattern of Section 736*

Suppose that a partnership makes payments to a partner in liquidation of the partner's interest in the venture. Such payments should ordinarily reflect the partner's share of partnership property at the time of the liquidation, including accounts receivable, unbilled works in progress, and goodwill. How should such payments be taxed?

Read I.R.C. § 736. While section 736 may seem quite baffling upon an initial reading, its fundamental purpose is simply to classify liquidating payments as either (i) payments in exchange for the withdrawing partner's interest in partnership property (section 736(b) payments) or (ii) all other payments (section 736(a) payments). Payments in the first category are subject to the normal distribution rules studied in chapter eight (sections 731-737), while payments in the second category are treated as either a distributive share (section 702) or guaranteed payment (section 707(c)).

Payments received in exchange for two types of property are specifically excluded from section 736(b) and therefore are not subject to the normal distribution rules. Thus, these payments are taxed under section 736(a) as distributive shares or guaranteed payments. Payments excluded from section 736(b) are amounts received by a general partner in a service partnership in exchange for the partnership's (i) traditional unrealized receivables, such as accounts receivables held by a cash-method partnership, and (ii) unstated goodwill. An amount received for "unstated goodwill" refers to an amount received for goodwill that is not specifically stated as such in the partnership agreement. See I.R.C. § 736(b)(2) and (3).

What are the stakes of this classification? As we have previously seen, liquidating payments classified as "distributions" under section 736(b), if taxable, generally result in capital gain or loss to the distributee. See I.R.C. § 731(a) and (b). The term "generally" is important here; remember that section 751(b) (as interpreted by the proposed regulations) results in the distributee (or other partners) recognizing ordinary income to the extent the distribution reduces such partner's share of hot asset gain. Distribution treatment of section 736(b) payments determines the distributee's basis in the distributed assets and also may affect the partnership's basis in its retained assets by reason of section 734(b).

In contrast, a section 736(a) payment treated as a distributive share or guaranteed payment may result in ordinary income to the terminating partner. Since ordinary income allocated to one partner is necessarily allocated away from the other partners, ordinary income treatment to the terminated partner results in the equivalent of an ordinary deduction for the partnership and the other partners. Section 736(a) payments are not subject to section 751(b). I.R.C. § 751(b)(2)(B).

The following example illustrates the basic application of section 736:

Example 11-1: A, a one-third general partner whose outside basis is $55, retires from the ABC service partnership in exchange for a liquidating payment of $90, when the partnership has the following balance sheet:

Assets	*Basis*	*FMV*
Cash	120	120
Accounts Receivable	30	90
Securities	15	30
Goodwill	0	30
Total	165	270

Section 736 divides the liquidating payment to A into two categories. The portion representing A's share of the partnership's cash ($40) and securities ($10) constitutes a section 736(b) payment in exchange for A's interest in partnership property. In addition, the portion equal to A's share of the partnership's basis in the accounts receivable ($10) is also a section 736(b) payment. See Reg. § 1.736-1(b)(2) and (3). The portion attributable to A's share of the unrealized appreciation in the accounts receivable ($20) is classified as a section 736(a) payment. The remainder of the payment attributable to A's share of the partnership's zero-basis goodwill ($10) is also classified as a section 736(a) payment unless the partnership agreement specifically provides for a payment with respect to goodwill (stated goodwill). Assuming that the partnership agreement does not so provide, A is treated as receiving total section 736(a) payments of $30 ($20 payment for accounts receivable in excess of A's share of their basis plus $10 payment for unstated goodwill) and total section 736(b) payments of $60. The liquidating payment of $90 to A may be made in a lump sum or spread over time.

Once the total amount of the section 736(a) payments is determined, it is still necessary to assign them to section 736(a)(1) (distributive share) or section 736(a)(2) (guaranteed payment). If a section 736(a) payment is linked to the partnership's income, it is classified under section 736(a)(1) as a section 702 distributive share of partnership income and decreases the distributive shares reportable by the continuing partners. The payment retains the same character in the hands of the retiring partner as the partnership items comprising the distributive share. If a section 736(a) payment is not dependent on the partnership's income, it is classified under section 736(a)(2) as a section 707(c) guaranteed payment. Section 736(a)(2) payments are taxed as ordinary income to the retiring partner and are deductible to the continuing partners under section 162(a). The capitalization requirement of section 263 is evidently not applicable to section 736(a)(2) payments. Cf. Reg. § 1.707-1(c).

NOTES AND QUESTIONS

1. *The convoluted statute.* It should be abundantly clear that section 736 is drafted in a remarkably byzantine manner. Consider the following quote from

Judge Raum concerning the "distressingly complex and confusing nature of subchapter K":

> If there should be any lingering doubt on this matter one has only to reread section 736 in its entirety . . . and give an honest answer to the question whether it is reasonably comprehensible to the average lawyer or even to the average tax expert who has not given special attention and extended study to the tax problems of partners. Surely, a statute has not achieved "simplicity" when its complex provisions may confidently be dealt with by at most only a comparatively small number of specialists who have been initiated into its mysteries.

Foxman v. Comm'r, 41 T.C. 535, 551 n.9 (1964), aff'd, 352 F.2d 466 (3d Cir. 1965) (p. 352). How might the provision be redrafted to improve its clarity?

2. *Payments for property vs. payments for future income from property.* Reg. § 1.736-1(b)(2) and (3) makes clear that section 736(a) treatment applies to payments for a partner's share of unrealized receivables and unstated goodwill only to the extent that the fair market value of such items exceeds their bases. Why is a retiring partner's share of the partnership's basis in such items treated as a section 736(b) payment? Is this result clear from the statutory language?

3. *Unrealized receivables.* For purposes of section 736, the term "unrealized receivables" does not include "nontraditional" unrealized receivables (e.g., depreciation recapture). See I.R.C. § 751(c) (flush language). Thus, section 736(a) treatment is available only for traditional unrealized receivables consisting of rights to payment for certain goods delivered or services rendered, to the extent such amounts have not been included in income. See I.R.C. § 751(c)(1) and (2).

4. *Some terminology.* In this area, the terms "retiring," "withdrawing," "liquidating," or "terminating" partner are generally used interchangeably to refer to a partner whose interest in a partnership is completely terminated. Section 736 does not apply to distributions to a continuing partner even though the distribution may reduce the partner's interest in the partnership. In addition, section 736 applies only to payments by a partnership to a partner in termination of a partner's interest, not to transactions between partners such as a sale of one partner's interest to another partner. Reg. § 1.736-1(a)(1)(i).

2. *The Significance of Section 736*

Although the regulations refer to liquidating payments that are in the nature of mutual insurance (such as a provision in the partnership agreement to pay a lump sum of money to the family or estate of the "first partner to die") or compensation for the deferral of payments, most liquidating payments generally represent the value of the withdrawing partner's interest in the partnership's assets (including billed receivables, unbilled works in progress, and goodwill) at the time of the liquidation. Thus, the principal effect of the classification scheme set forth in section 736 is to except from the normal distribution rules (and thus to tax as distributive shares or guaranteed payments) amounts paid to a general partner in a service partnership for two specific types of partnership property. As previously noted, those two types of property are the unrealized income element of traditional unrealized receivables and unstated goodwill. Hence, liquidating payments to limited partners as well as payments to all partners of capital-intensive firms should be classified almost exclusively as section 736(b) payments taxable under the distribution rules.

In many situations, the tax significance of treating the amount received for the income element of a service partnership's traditional unrealized receivables as a distributive share or guaranteed payment (rather than as a partnership distribution) may be relatively minor. As a distributive share or guaranteed payment, the amount would generally be ordinary income to the liquidated partner and produce an ordinary deduction for the other partners. In contrast, if the amount were taxed as a partnership distribution, section 751(b) would likely come into play. Under that provision, the amount received would also generally represent ordinary income to the liquidated partner, with the other partners obtaining a basis increase in the receivables. (As previously noted, section 751(b) is specifically barred if the payments are taxed under section 736(a). See I.R.C. § 751(b)(2)(B).) If traditional receivables of a service partnership are collected relatively quickly, section 736(a) classification merely accelerates slightly the tax benefit to the other partners.

Section 736(a) treatment of amounts paid to a general partner in a service partnership in exchange for unstated goodwill presents more complex considerations. As a distributive share or guaranteed payment, the amount again would generally be ordinary income to the liquidated partner and produce an ordinary deduction for the other partners. As a partnership distribution, the amount would potentially produce capital gain to the distributee, thereby triggering an increase in the partnership's basis in goodwill under section 734(b)(1) if the partnership has a section 754 election in effect. This additional basis may in turn produce amortization deductions that reduce the partnership's ordinary income over a 15-year period. I.R.C. § 197(a). The relative advantage of these two alternatives — section 736(a) or section 736(b) treatment — typically depends upon the particular tax situations of the distributee and other partners. In effect, section 736 allows the partners to elect the most favorable tax consequences among themselves by including in the partnership agreement a provision for payment for goodwill (stated goodwill) or by failing to include such a provision (unstated goodwill).

Since 1993, this elective treatment is no longer available for payments for traditional unrealized receivables and goodwill if the retiring partner is a limited partner or the partnership is a capital-intensive partnership. See I.R.C. § 736(b)(3). In this situation, any payment for goodwill (stated or unstated) will be treated as a section 736(b) payment and taxed under the distribution rules. The enactment of section 197 may mitigate any adverse tax consequences, however, provided the partnership has a section 754 election in effect to adjust inside basis.

The following case involves a version of section 736 that preceded enactment of section 197. It illustrates nicely, however, some of the complexity arising from the "effective election" allowed by section 736.

Commissioner v. Jackson Investment Co.

346 F.2d 187 (9th Cir. 1965)

BARNES, J.: . . . The question presented for our consideration involves the construction of Section 736 of the Internal Revenue Code of 1954. That section [was] drafted as part of a series of provisions intended to clarify and simplify the tax laws with respect to partnerships. . . .

The intended purpose of [Section 736] was to permit the participants themselves to determine whether the retiring partner or the remaining partners would bear the tax burdens for payments in liquidation of a retiring partner's interest. Thus, under the general approach of subsection (a), the tax burden is borne by the retiring partner — he recognizes the payments as taxable income, and the remaining partners are allowed a commensurate deduction from partnership income. Under subsection (b), the general rule conceives an approach of nonrecognition of ordinary income to the retiring partner, but places the tax burden on the partnership by denying a deduction from income for the payments. This latter subsection, however, adopts a special rule — (b)(2)(B) — in an express effort to assist the participants to decide inter sese upon the allocation of the tax burden. This special rule lies at the heart of the present controversy. Under this rule, payments for the good will of the partnership are deductible by the partnership (and hence recognizable as ordinary income to the retiring partner) "except to the extent that the partnership agreement provides for a payment with respect to good will." If the partnership agreement provides for a payment with respect to good will, the tax burden is allocated to the partnership — no deduction is allowed and the retiring partner need not recognize the payments as ordinary income. In the present case, petitioner contends that this exception under Section 736(b)(2)(B) applies, and thus the deductions taken by the partnership should be disallowed. We must determine, therefore, whether the parties intended to place the tax burden on the partnership by expressly incorporating into the partnership agreement a provision for payment to the retiring partner with respect to good will.

It is undisputed that the original Partnership Agreement did not contain a provision for partnership good will or a payment therefor upon the withdrawal of a partner. On May 7, 1956, however, the three partners executed an instrument entitled "Amendment of Limited Partnership Agreement of George W. Carter Co." . . . This instrument provided for Ethel Carter's retirement, and bound the partnership to compensate Ethel in the amount of $60,000.00 in consideration for her withdrawal. After the necessary adjustment of the figures, it was determined that $19,650.00 of the amount was in return for Ethel's "15% Interest in the fair market value of all the net assets of the partnership." The other $40,350.00, the amount in controversy here, was referred to as "a guaranteed payment, or a payment for good will." . . . The $40,350.00 was paid by the partnership in three annual parts, and deductions were made for good will expense in the partnership net income for each of the years. It is these deductions that petitioner challenges.

The decision of the Tax Court (six judges dissenting), concluded that the document entitled "Amendment of Limited Partnership Agreement of George W. Carter Co." was not a part of the partnership agreement, and therefore, the exception of Section 736(b)(2)(B) was not applicable. As a result, the court held that the amounts in question were legitimate deductions from the partnership income under the terms of Section 736(a)(2). The court founded its conclusion on the fact that the "Amendment" was solely designed to effect a withdrawal of one of the partners; it was not at all concerned with any continued role for Ethel in the partnership affairs.

We cannot agree with the interpretation of the majority of the Tax Court. We find this view unduly interferes with the clear objective of the statute, i.e., to permit and enable the partners to allocate the tax burdens as they choose, and with a minimum of uncertainty and difficulty. If a partnership agreement such as the one involved here, had no provision regarding the withdrawal of a partner, and the partners negotiated to compensate the retiring partner with payments that could be treated by the recipient at capital gain rates, the statutory scheme should not be read to frustrate the parties' efforts. An amendment to the partnership agreement which incorporates the plan of withdrawal and which designates the amount payable as being in consideration for the partnership good will seems clearly to be an attempt to utilize Section 736(b)(2)(B), affording capital gain rates to the retiring partner but precluding an expense deduction for the partnership. Simply because the subject matter of the amendment deals only with the liquidation of one partner's interest, we should not thwart whatever may be the clear intent of the parties by holding the amendment is not part of the partnership agreement. The Internal Revenue Code of 1954 expressly touches upon modifications of partnership agreements, and it gives no support to the thesis that an amendment dealing with the withdrawal of a partner cannot be considered a part of the partnership agreement. Section 761(c) provides:

> *Partnership Agreement.* — For purposes of this subchapter, a partnership agreement includes any modifications of the partnership agreement made prior to, or at, the time prescribed by law for the filing of the partnership return for the taxable year (not including extensions) which are agreed to by all the partners, or which are adopted in such other manner as may be provided by the partnership agreement.

We hold, therefore, in harmony with the intent of the parties to the partnership, that the "Amendment of Limited Partnership Agreement of George W. Carter Co." was a modification of the partnership agreement within the meaning of Section 761(c). As such, the requirement of a provision in the partnership agreement as specified in Section 736(b)(2)(B) is satisfied.

There remains, however, an additional requirement to call into operation Section 736(b)(2)(B), viz., that the provision for payment in the partnership agreement be *with respect to good will.* As noted above, the payment of the $40,350.00 was inartistically described in the Amendment as a "guaranteed payment, or a payment for good will." The "guaranteed payment" terminology seems to expressly incorporate Section 736(a)(2), which would permit an expense deduction to the partnership, while recognizing the payments as ordinary income to the retiring partner. The "good will" language, on the other hand, would appear directed to Section 736(b)(2)(B), which results in the opposite tax consequences. In resolving this conflict, we feel the most helpful guide is to pay deference to what we may determine was the revealed intent of the parties. An examination of the entire amendment leads us to conclude that, notwithstanding the use of the words "guaranteed payment," the parties intended to invoke Section 736(b)(2)(B), not Section 736(a)(2). The Amendment expressly states the following (which we find impossible to harmonize with the majority opinion of the Tax Court or the arguments advanced by respondents in their brief):

> It is recognized by all the parties hereto that the prior agreements among the partners do not provide for any payment to any partner in respect to good will in the event of the retirement or withdrawal of a partner, but George W. Carter Company will nevertheless make a payment to Ethel M. Carter *in respect to good will* as herein provided in consideration of her entering into this agreement and her consent to retire from the partnership upon the terms herein expressed. . . . (Emphasis added.)

The meaning of this language as well as the words chosen to express it leads to the conclusion that the $40,350.00 was to be a payment "in respect to good will," with the parties intending to be governed by the tax consequences of Section 736(b)(2)(B). The concluding paragraph of Judge Raum's dissenting opinion in the Tax Court, joined in by five other judges, expresses in our judgment sound reasoning, and we incorporate it here as a summary statement of our viewpoint:

> To fail to give effect to the plain language thus used by the parties is, I think, to defeat the very purpose of the pertinent partnership provisions of the statute, namely, to permit the partners themselves to fix their tax liabilities inter sese. Although the May 7, 1956, agreement may be inartistically drawn, and indeed may even contain some internal inconsistencies, the plain and obvious import of its provisions in respect of the present problem was to amend the partnership agreement so as to provide specifically for a goodwill payment. This is the kind of thing that section 736(b)(2)(B) dealt with when it allowed the partners to fix the tax consequences of goodwill payments to a withdrawing partner. And this is what the partners clearly attempted to do here, however crude may have been their effort. I would give further effect to that effort, and would not add further complications to an already overcomplicated statute. . . .

The decision of the Tax Court is reversed, and the matter is remanded to that court for further proceedings consistent with this opinion.

NOTES AND QUESTIONS

1. *Policy of section 736.* The court notes that section 736 is intended to allow the partners "to allocate the tax burdens as they choose . . . with a minimum of uncertainty and difficulty." What is the policy basis for that objective? Would it be preferable if the law simply provided that all liquidating payments are taxed under the distribution rules?

2. *Drafting inconsistencies.* While *Jackson* obviously demonstrates the need for careful drafting, what do you think accounts for the inconsistent language in the parties' agreement?

3. *Should there be an explicit election? Jackson* arguably illustrates the inherent limitations of relying on the parties' choice of language in the partnership agreement to classify goodwill payments. If any elective treatment concerning the tax consequences of liquidating payments is retained, should an election be provided explicitly, analogous to the check-the-box rules?

4. *General partners of service partnerships.* Section 736(b)(3) provides that liquidating payments for traditional unrealized receivables and unstated goodwill are excluded from section 736(b) treatment only in the case of general partners of partnerships where "capital is not a material income-producing factor." According to the legislative history, this determination is to be made by reference to criteria developed under other provisions employing similar terminology. See, e.g., I.R.C. § 761(b) (2d sentence). Most professional partnerships will qualify as long as any substantial capital investments are merely incidental to the performance of services. Since the statutory rule is limited to general partners, it is also important to determine whether a member of an LLC or similar entity will be considered a general partner for this purpose.

5. *Nontraditional unrealized receivables.* In 1993, Congress eliminated section 736(a) treatment for a partner's share of nontraditional unrealized receivables such as depreciation recapture. See I.R.C. § 751(c) (flush language). As in the case of goodwill, section 736(a) treatment under prior law allowed the continuing partners to, in effect, immediately expense payments for depreciation recapture amounts (rather than capitalize such amounts) at the cost of ordinary income (rather than capital gain) to the retiring partner. Under current law, all payments for a partner's share of nontraditional unrealized receivables will be classified as nondeductible section 736(b) payments regardless of the nature of the partnership. Thus, the continuing partners will be entitled to additional depreciation deductions attributable to recapture amounts only if a section 736(b) payment triggers an inside basis adjustment under section 734(b).

3. *Installment Payments*

If liquidating payments are deferred, section 736 may produce quite beneficial results to the retiring partner. While an installment sale governed by section 453 generally requires ratable basis recovery, a retiring partner may recover her entire outside basis before reporting any gain from section 736(b) payments (except to the extent that section 751(b) applies). Moreover, deferred section 736 payments are not subject to the imputed interest rules of sections 483 and 1272, and deferral is permitted even though the partnership owns assets that would not qualify for installment-sale treatment.

The regulations describe the consequences of a deferred-payment liquidation involving both section 736(a) and section 736(b) payments. Unless the parties agree otherwise, fixed payments are generally allocated proportionately between the two categories; contingent payments are allocated first to section 736(b) payments to the extent of the entire value of the retiring partner's share of section 736(b) property. See Reg. § 1.736-1(b)(5).

> **Example 11-2:** The facts are the same as in **example 11-1**, except that A receives the liquidating payment of $90 in three equal annual installments (ignore any adjustment to reflect interest on the deferred installments). Two-thirds of each annual installment ($20) would be treated as a section 736(b) payment and the remaining one-third ($10) would be treated as a section 736(a) payment based on the ratio of fixed payments in each category. In the first year, A would reduce her outside basis from $55 to $35 to reflect the section 736(b) payment of $20 and would report ordinary income of $10 immediately as a result of the section 736(a) payment. During the second year, A would again have $20 of basis recovery (reducing her outside basis to $15) attributable to the section 736(b) payment and $10 of ordinary income attributable to the section 736(a) payment. In the third year, the section 736(b) payment would trigger $5 of capital gain ($20 payment less $15 remaining outside basis), while the section 736(a) payment would again produce ordinary income of $10. Thus, A would report total of ordinary income of $30 and total capital gain of $5 over the installment period.

NOTES AND QUESTIONS

1. *Timing of gain recognition to retiring partner.* If the total amount of section 736(b) payments is fixed, the retiring partner may elect to recover her outside basis ratably (assuming that section 751(b) does not apply). See Reg. § 1.736-1(b)(6). Why might a retiring partner elect to accelerate taxation of section 736(b) payments?

2. *Timing of partnership basis adjustments.* Receipt of a section 736(b) payment may result in the recognition of gain (or loss) to the retiring partner. In turn, the partnership may be permitted (or required) to adjust its basis in partnership assets under section 734(b) to reflect any recognized gain (or loss). To offset the deferral benefit to the retiring partner, however, any basis adjustment is postponed until such gain (or loss) is recognized. See Rev. Rul. 93-13, 1993-1 C.B. 126.

4. *Partnership Liabilities*

A partner's share of section 736(b) property is equal to the gross fair market value of such property (i.e., without any reduction for partnership liabilities). See Reg. § 1.736-1(a)(2). Thus, section 736(b) payments include the amount of any deemed distribution under section 752(b) resulting from a decrease in the partner's share of partnership liabilities. The taxation of the deemed distribution, however, may be deferred until the partner's entire interest is liquidated.

Example 11-3: The ABC capital-intensive partnership agrees to pay A three equal installments of $20 each in liquidation of her one-third general partnership interest (ignore any adjustment to reflect interest on the deferred installments), when A has an outside basis of $60 and the partnership has the following balance sheet:

	Basis	*FMV*		*Book*	*FMV*
Assets			*Recourse Liabilities*	75	75
Cash	105	105	*Capital*		
Accounts Receivable	15	15	A	35	60
Land	60	105	B	35	60
Goodwill	0	30	C	35	60
Total	180	255	Total	180	255

Since ABC is a capital-intensive partnership, all of the liquidating payments to A are classified as section 736(b) payments. A's share of section 736(b) property is $85 (one-third of $255). A's outside basis of $60 includes her $25 share of the partnership's recourse liabilities. If A agrees to remain liable for her share of the partnership's debt until her interest is completely liquidated, the deemed section 752(b) distribution will be deferred until the final year of payments. During the first and second years, A receives total installment payments of $40, reducing her outside basis to $20. In the third year, A receives a final installment payment of $20 and a deemed section 752(b) distribution of $25 attributable to relief of her one-third share of the partnership's liabilities, triggering capital gain of $25 ($45 distribution less $20 remaining outside basis).

5. *Liquidating Distributions vs. Sales*

Rather than avail themselves of the flexibility allowed by section 736 for liquidating distributions, partners can bypass section 736 entirely by structuring a transaction as a sale of the withdrawing partner's partnership interest to the continuing partners (or new partners). The following case illustrates the difficulty of distinguishing between these two alternative ways of accomplishing essentially the same economic result, albeit with potentially quite different tax consequences.

Foxman v. Commissioner

352 F.2d 466 (3d Cir. 1965)

WILLIAM F. SMITH, Circuit Judge: . . . As the result of agreements reached in February of 1955, and January of 1956, Foxman, Grenell and Jacobowitz became equal partners in a commercial enterprise which was then trading under the name of Abbey Record Manufacturing Company, hereinafter identified as the Company. They also became equal shareholders in a corporation known as Sound Plastics, Inc. When differences of opinion arose in the spring of 1956, efforts were made to persuade Jacobowitz to withdraw from the partnership. . . . Thereafter the parties entered into negotiations which, on May 21, 1957, culminated in a contract for the acquisition of Jacobowitz's interest in the partnership of Foxman and Grenell. The terms and conditions, except one not here material, were substantially in accord with an option to purchase offered earlier to Foxman and Grenell. . . .

The contract, prepared by an attorney representing Foxman and Grenell, referred to them as the "Second Party," and to Jacobowitz as the "First Party." We regard as particularly pertinent to the issue before us the following clauses:

> WHEREAS, the parties hereto are equal owners and the sole partners of ABBEY RECORD MFG. Co., a partnership, . . . , and are also the sole stockholders, officers and directors of SOUND PLASTICS, INC., a corporation organized under the laws of the State of New York; and
>
> WHEREAS, the first party is desirous of selling, conveying, transferring and assigning all of his right, title and interest in and to his one-third share and interest in the said ABBEY to the second parties; and
>
> WHEREAS, the second parties are desirous of conveying, transferring and assigning all of their right, title and interest in and to their combined two-thirds shares and interest in SOUND PLASTICS, INC., to the first party;
>
> NOW, THEREFORE, IT IS MUTUALLY AGREED AS FOLLOWS:
> First: The second parties hereby purchase all the right, title, share and interest of the first party in ABBEY and the first party does hereby sell, transfer, convey and assign all of his right, title, interest and share in ABBEY and in the moneys in banks, trade names, accounts due, or to become due, and in all other assets of any kind whatsoever, belonging to said ABBEY, for and in consideration of the following. . . .

The stated consideration was cash in the sum of $242,500; the assignment by Foxman and Grenell of their stock in Sound Plastics; and the transfer of an automobile, title to which was held by the Company. The agreement provided for the payment of $67,500 upon consummation of the contract and payment of the balance as follows: $67,500 on January 2, 1958, and $90,000 in equal monthly installments, payable on the first of each month after January 30, 1958. This balance was evidenced by a series of promissory notes, payment of which was secured by a chattel mortgage on the assets of the Company. This mortgage, like the contract, referred to a sale by Jacobowitz of his partnership interest to Foxman and Grenell. The notes were executed in the name of the Company as the purported maker and were signed by Foxman and Grenell, who also endorsed them under a guarantee of payment.

The down payment of $67,500 was by a cashier's check which was issued in exchange for a check drawn on the account of the Company. The first note, in the amount of $67,500, which became due on January 2, 1958, was timely paid by a check drawn on the Company's account. Pursuant to the terms of an option reserved to Foxman and Grenell, they elected to prepay the balance of $90,000 on January 28, 1958, thereby relieving themselves of an obligation to pay Jacobowitz a further $17,550, designated in the contract as a consultant's fee. They delivered to Jacobowitz a cashier's check which was charged against the account of the Company.

In its partnership return for the fiscal year ending February 28, 1958, the Company treated the sum of $159,656.09, the consideration received by Jacobowitz less the value of his interest in partnership property, as a guaranteed payment made in liquidation of a retiring partner's interest under § 736(a)(2) of the Internal Revenue Code of 1954, Title 26 U.S.C.A. This treatment resulted in a substantial reduction of the distributive shares of Foxman and Grenell and consequently a proportionate decrease in their possible tax liability. In his income tax return Jacobowitz treated the sum of $164,356.09, the consideration less the value of his partnership interest, as a long term capital gain realized upon the sale of his interest. This, of course, resulted in a tax advantage favorable to him. The Commissioner determined deficiencies against each of the taxpayers in amounts not relevant to the issue before us and each filed separate petitions for redetermination.

The critical issue before the Tax Court was raised by the antithetical positions maintained by Foxman and Grenell on one side and Jacobowitz on the other. The former, relying on § 736(a)(2), supra, contended that the transaction, evidenced by the contract, constituted a liquidation of a retiring partner's interest and that the consideration paid was accorded correct treatment in the partnership return. The latter contended that the transaction constituted a sale of his partnership interest and, under § 741 of the Code, 26 U.S.C.A., the profit realized was correctly treated in his return as a capital gain. The Tax Court rejected the position of Foxman and Grenell and held that the deficiency determinations as to them were not erroneous; it sustained the position of Jacobowitz and held that the deficiency determination as to him was erroneous. The petitioners Foxman and Grenell challenge that decision as erroneous and not in accord with the law.

It appears from the evidence, which the Tax Court apparently found credible, that the negotiations which led to the consummation of the contract of May 21, 1957, related to a contemplated sale of Jacobowitz's partnership interest to Foxman and Grenell. The option offered to Foxman and Grenell early in May of 1957, referred to a sale and the execution of "a bill of sale" upon completion of the agreement. The relevant provisions of the contract were couched in terms of "purchase" and "sale." The contract was signed by Foxman and Grenell, individually, and by them on behalf of the Company, although the Company assumed no liability thereunder. The obligation to purchase Jacobowitz's interest was solely that of Foxman and Grenell. The chattel mortgage on the partnership assets was given to secure payment.

Notwithstanding these facts and the lack of any ambiguity in the contract, Foxman and Grenell argue that the factors unequivocally determinative of the substance of the transaction were: the initial payment of $67,500 by a cashier's check issued in exchange for a check drawn on the account of the Company; the second payment in a similar amount by check drawn on the Company's account; the execution of notes in the name of the Company as maker; and, the prepayment of the notes by cashier's check charged against the Company's account.

This argument unduly emphasizes form in preference to substance. While form may be relevant "the incidence of taxation depends upon the substance of a transaction." *Commissioner of Internal Revenue v. Court Holding Co.*, 324 U.S. 331, 334 (1945); *United States v. Cumberland Pub. Serv. Co.*, 338 U.S. 451, 455 (1950). The "transaction must be viewed as a whole, and each step, from the commencement of negotiations" to consummation, is relevant. Ibid. Where, as here, there has been a transfer and an acquisition of property pursuant to a contract, the nature of the transaction does not depend solely on the means employed to effect payment. Ibid.

It is apparent from the opinion of the Tax Court that careful consideration was given to the factors relied upon by Foxman and Grenell. It is therein stated, 41 T.C. at page 553:

> These notes were endorsed by Foxman and Grenell individually, and the liability of [the Company] thereon was merely in the nature of security for their primary obligation under the agreement of May 21, 1957. The fact that they utilized partnership resources to discharge their own individual liability in such manner can hardly convert into a section 736 "liquidation" what would otherwise qualify as a section 741 "sale". . . .
>
> [T]he payments received by Jacobowitz were in discharge of their [Foxman's and Grenell's] obligation under the agreement, and not that of [the Company.] It was they who procured those payments in their own behalf from the assets of the partnership which they controlled. The use of [the Company] to make payment was wholly within their discretion and of no concern to Jacobowitz; his only interest was payment.

We are of the opinion that the quoted statements represent a fair appraisal of the true significance of the notes and the means employed to effect payment.

When the members of the partnership decided that Jacobowitz would withdraw in the interest of harmony they had a choice of means by which his withdrawal could be effected. They could have agreed inter se on either liquidation or sale. On a consideration of the plain language of the contract, the negotiations which preceded its consummation, the intent of the parties as reflected by their conduct, and the circumstances surrounding the transaction, the Tax Court found that the transaction was in substance a sale and not a liquidation of a retiring partner's interest. This finding is amply supported by the evidence in the record. The partners having employed the sale method to achieve their objective, Foxman and Grenell cannot avoid the tax consequences by a hindsight application of principles they now find advantageous to them and disadvantageous to Jacobowitz.

The issue before the Tax Court was essentially one of fact and its decision thereon may not be reversed in the absence of a showing that its findings were not supported by substantial evidence or that its decision was not in accord with the law. . . . There has been no such showing in this case.

The decisions of the Tax Court will be affirmed.

6. *Special Considerations upon the Death of a Partner*

This section considers some special issues that arise when a partner's interest terminates by reason of her death.

a. Taxable Year and Outside Basis

Read I.R.C. §§ 706(c)(2)(A), 2031; Reg. §§ 1.742-1(a), 1.1014-1(a). Upon the death of a partner, the partnership's taxable year automatically closes with respect to the deceased partner. See I.R.C. § 706(c)(2)(A). Thus, the deceased partner's pre-death share of partnership income and deductions will be reported on the decedent's final return (or a joint return filed by the decedent's surviving spouse). The deceased partner's gross estate must generally include the fair market value of the decedent's partnership interest (net of liabilities). See I.R.C. § 2031. Under section 1014, a person acquiring a decedent's partnership interest takes a basis equal to the amount included in the decedent's estate, increased by the successor's share of partnership liabilities. Thus, the decedent's successor will generally receive an outside basis equal to the gross fair market value of the partnership interest (including her share of liabilities) as of the date of death (or alternate valuation date). See Reg. §§ 1.742-1, 1.1014-1(a).

b. IRD Attributable to Partnership Interests

"Income in respect of a decedent" (IRD) generally refers to income to which the decedent was entitled at death but which was never properly includible by the decedent prior to death under her method of accounting. See Reg. § 1.691(a)-1(b). For example, IRD of a cash-method decedent includes accounts receivable, rights to deferred payments for services, and unrealized gain from installment sales.

By virtue of section 1014(c), items of IRD includible in a decedent's estate are not entitled to a basis step-up at death; moreover, such items must be reported for income-tax purposes, under section 691(a), by the decedent's successor upon receipt (subject to any deduction allowable under section 691(c)). The denial of a section 1014 basis step-up for IRD items ensures that such items will not escape income tax entirely. A downward adjustment to a successor partner's outside basis is required to the extent that the value of the decedent's partnership interest at death is attributable to IRD. See Reg. § 1.742-1.

In the partnership context, two categories of IRD are of particular concern. The first category of IRD items is statutory (section 753) while the second category is derived from case law. Section 753 provides that all section 736(a) payments in liquidation of a deceased partner's interest are IRD. Thus, section 736(a) payments by service partnerships to the successor of a deceased general partner for accounts receivable or unstated goodwill will automatically be treated as IRD under section 753, provided that there was a binding obligation to purchase the decedent's interest at the time of death. This treatment may have distinctly unfavorable tax consequences for the decedent's successor, since goodwill payments will be taxed to her as ordinary income as a result of the operation of sections 736(a) and 753. By contrast, if section 736(a) were inapplicable, the decedent's successor would receive a section 1014 basis step-up equal to her share of the partnership's goodwill and would be entitled to recover her additional basis upon liquidation.

The courts have created a second category of IRD payments where a successor receives a decedent's partnership interest rather than a right to liquidating payments. In this situation, courts found it necessary to determine whether section 753, which refers only to section 736(a) payments, should be construed narrowly to preclude IRD treatment of other types of partnership items. As illustrated by the two cases excerpted below, courts have been willing to look through the partnership to treat as IRD those items that would constitute IRD if held directly by the deceased partner rather than by the partnership.

George Edward Quick Trust v. Commissioner

54 T.C. 1336 (1970), aff'd per curiam, 444 F.2d 90 (8th Cir. 1971)

TANNENWALD, J.: . . . When Quick died he was an equal partner in a partnership which had been in the business of providing architectural and engineering services. In 1957, the partnership had ceased all business activity except the collection of outstanding accounts receivable. These receivables, and some cash, were the only assets of the partnership. Since partnership income was reported on the cash basis, the receivables had a zero basis.

Upon Quick's death in 1960, the estate became a partner [in the former two-person partnership] and remained a partner until 1965 when it was succeeded as a partner by petitioner herein. The outstanding accounts receivable were substantial in amount at that time. In its 1960 return, the partnership elected under section 754 to make the adjustment in the basis of the partnership property provided for in section 743(b) and to allocate that adjustment in accordance with section 755. On the facts of this case, the net result of this adjustment was to increase the basis of the accounts receivable to the partnership from zero to an amount slightly less than one-half of their face value. If such treatment was correct, it substantially reduced the amount of the taxable income to the partnership from the collection of the accounts receivable under section 743(b) and the estate and the petitioner herein were entitled to the benefit of that reduction.

The issue before us is whether the foregoing adjustment to basis was correctly made. Its resolution depends upon the determination of the basis to the estate of its interest in the partnership, since section 743(b)(1) allows only an "increase [in] the adjusted basis of the partnership property by the excess of *the basis to the transferee partner of his interest in the partnership* over his proportionate share of the adjusted basis of the partnership property." (Emphasis added.) This in turn depends upon whether, to the extent that "the basis to the transferee partner" reflects an interest in underlying accounts receivable arising out of personal services of the deceased partner, such interest constitutes income in respect of a decedent under section 691(a)(1) and (3). In such event, section 1014(c) comes into play and prohibits equating the basis of Quick's partnership interest with the fair market value of that interest at the time of his death under section 1014(a).

Petitioner argues that the partnership provisions of the Internal Revenue Code of 1954 adopted the entity theory of partnership, that the plain meaning of those provisions, insofar as they relate to the question of basis, requires the conclusion that the inherited partnership interest is separate and distinct from the underlying assets of the partnership, and that, therefore, section 691, and consequently section 1014(c), has no application herein.

Respondent counters with the assertion that the basis of a partnership interest is determined under section 742 by reference to other sections of the Code. He claims that, by virtue of section 1014(c), section 1014(a) does not apply to property which is classified as a right to receive income in respect of a decedent under section 691 and that the interest of the estate and of petitioner in the proceeds of the accounts receivable of the partnership falls within this classification. He emphasizes that, since the accounts receivable represent money earned by the performance of personal services, the collections thereon would have been taxable to the decedent, if the partnership had been on the accrual basis, or to the estate and to petitioner if the decedent had been a cash basis sole proprietor. Similarly, he points out that if the business had been conducted by a corporation, the collections on the accounts receivable would have been fully taxable, regardless of Quick's death. Respondent concludes that no different result should occur simply because a cash basis partnership is interposed.

The share of a general partner's successor in interest upon his death in the collections by a partnership on accounts receivable arising out of the rendition of personal services constituted income in respect of a decedent under the 1939

Code. . . . Petitioner ignores these decisions, apparently on the ground that the enactment of comprehensive provisions dealing with the taxation of partnerships in the 1954 Code and what it asserts is "the plain meaning" of those provisions render such decisions inapplicable in the instant case. We disagree.

The partnership provisions of the 1954 Code are comprehensive in the sense that they are detailed. But this does not mean that they are exclusive, especially where those provisions themselves recognize the interplay with other provisions of the Code. Section 742 specifies: "The basis of an interest in a partnership acquired other than by contribution shall be determined under part II of subchapter O (sec. 1011 and following)." With the exception of section 722, which deals with the basis of a contributing partner's interest and which has no applicability herein, this is the only section directed toward the question of the initial determination of the basis of a partnership interest. From the specification of section 742, one is thus led directly to section 1014 and by subsection (c) thereof directly to section 691. [I]nsofar as this case is concerned, section 691 incorporates the provisions and legal underpinning of its predecessor (sec. 126 of the 1939 Code). . . .

Thus, to the extent that a "plain meaning" can be distilled from the partnership provisions of the 1954 Code, we think that it is contrary to petitioner's position.[1] In point of fact, however, we hesitate to rest our decision in an area such as is involved herein exclusively on such linguistic clarity and purity. . . . However, an examination of the legislative purpose reinforces our reading of the statute. Section 751, dealing with unrealized receivables and inventory items, is included in subpart D of subchapter K, and is labeled "Provisions Common to Other Subparts." Both the House and Senate committee reports specifically state that income rights relating to unrealized receivables or fees are regarded "as severable from the partnership interest and as subject to the same tax consequences which would be accorded an individual entrepreneur." See H. Rept. No. 1337, 83d Cong., 2d Sess., p. 71 (1954); S. Rept. No. 1622, 83d Cong., 2d Sess., p. 99 (1954). And the Senate committee report adds the following significant language.

> *The House bill provides that a decedent partner's share of unrealized receivables are* [sic] *to be treated as income in respect of a decedent.* Such rights to income are to be taxed to the estate or heirs when collected, with an appropriate adjustment for estate taxes. . . . *Your committee's bill agrees substantially with the House in the treatment described above* but also provides that other income apart from unrealized receivables is to be treated as income in respect of a decedent. [See S. Rept. No. 1622, supra at 99; emphasis added.]

In light of the foregoing, the deletion of a provision in section 743 of the House bill which specifically provided that the optional adjustment to basis of partnership

1. We note that petitioner's position has been the subject of extensive legal analysis and that it has some support among the legal pundits. See Willis, Handbook of Partnership Taxation, 389-395 (1957); Ferguson, "Income and Deductions in Respect of Decedents and Related Problems," 25 Tax L. Rev. 5, 100 et seq.

property should not be made with respect to unrealized receivables is of little, if any, significance. H.R. 8300, 83d Cong., 2d Sess., sec. 743(e) (1954) (introduced print). The fact that such deletion was made without comment either in the Senate or Conference Committee reports indicates that the problem was covered by other sections and that such a provision was therefore unnecessary. Similarly, the specific reference in section 753 to income in respect of a decedent cannot be given an exclusive characterization. That section merely states that certain distributions in liquidation under section 736(a) shall be treated as income in respect of a decedent. It does not state that no other amounts can be so treated.

Many of the assertions of the parties have dealt with the superstructure of the partnership provisions — assertions based upon a technical and involuted analysis of those provisions dealing with various adjustments and the treatment to be accorded to distributions after the basis of the partnership has been determined. But, as we have previously indicated . . . , the question herein involves the foundation, not the superstructure, i.e., what is the basis of petitioner's partnership interest?

Petitioner asserts that a partnership interest is an "asset separate and apart from the individual assets of the partnership" and that the character of the accounts receivable disappears into the character of the partnership interest, with the result that such interest cannot, in whole or in part, represent a right to receive income in respect of a decedent. In making such an argument, petitioner has erroneously transmuted the so-called partnership "entity" approach into a rule of law which allegedly precludes fragmentation of a partnership interest. But it is clear that even the "entity" approach should not be inexorably applied under all circumstances. See H. Rept. No. 2543, 83d Cong., 2d Sess., p. 59 (1954). Similarly, the fact that a rule of nonfragmentation of a partnership interest (except to the extent that the statute otherwise expressly provides) may govern sales of such an interest to third parties . . . does not compel its application in all situations where such an interest is transferred. In short, a partnership interest is not, as petitioner suggests, a unitary res, incapable of further analysis.

A partnership interest is a property interest, and an intangible one at that. A property interest can often be appropriately viewed as a bundle of rights. . . . Viewed as a bundle of rights, a major constituent element of that interest was the right to share in the proceeds of the accounts receivable as they were collected. This right was admittedly not the same as the right to collect the accounts receivable; only the partnership had the latter right. But it does not follow from this dichotomy that the right of the estate to share in the collections merged into the partnership interest. Nothing in the statute compels such a merger. Indeed, an analysis of the applicable statutory provisions points to the opposite conclusion.

Accordingly, we hold that section 691(a)(1) and (3) applies and that the right to share in the collections from the accounts receivable must be considered a right to receive income in respect of a decedent. Consequently, section 1014(c) also applies and the basis of the partnership interest must be reduced from the fair market value thereof at Quick's death. The measure of that reduction under section 1014 is the extent to which that value includes the fair market value of a one-half interest in the proceeds of the zero basis partnership accounts receivable. See sec. 1.742-1, Income Tax Regs. It follows that the optional adjustment to basis made by the partnership under section 743(b) must be modified accordingly and that respondent's determination as to the amount of additional income subject to the tax should be sustained.[2] See Rev. Rul. 66-325, 1966-2 C.B. 249.

Petitioner would have us equate the absence of statutory language specifically dealing with the problem herein and purported inferences from tangential provisions with an intention on the part of Congress entirely to relieve from taxation an item that had previously been held subject to tax. We would normally be reluctant to find that Congress indirectly legislated so eccentrically. . . . In any event, as we have previously indicated, we think the enacted provisions prevent us from so doing herein. . . .

NOTE

The scope of the judicially created category of IRD payments is uncertain. For example, a successor partner's interest in installment obligations held by the partnership might fall within this category if such obligations would constitute IRD in the decedent's hands. On the other hand, items such as depreciation recapture should not be treated as IRD for purposes of the judicial exception or section 753; since depreciation recapture is a nontraditional unrealized receivable, it can never fall within the category of section 736(a) payments under current law.

Woodhall v. Commissioner

454 F.2d 226 (9th Cir. 1972)

CHOY, J.: W. Lyle Woodhall died on January 20, 1964, leaving Mrs. Woodhall as his sole heir and executrix. For 1964, Chrissie Woodhall filed a joint income tax return as surviving spouse. She also filed a fiduciary income tax return for the estate of W. Lyle Woodhall for part of 1964. For 1965, she filed an individual tax return and a fiduciary return.

The Commissioner of Internal Revenue determined deficiencies against [Mrs.] W. Woodhall for the years 1964 and 1965. The ground was that she had not declared as income certain amounts that came to her from the sale of her husband's interest in a partnership. Mrs. Woodhall petitioned the Tax Court for a declaration that she did not owe the deficiencies. The Tax Court upheld the . . . Commissioner's determination and Mrs. Woodhall appeals. We affirm.

2. We reached a similar result in *Chrissie H. Woodhall*, T.C. Memo. 1969-279; that case involved a sale of the partnership interest by the decedent's successor in interest.

From January 1958 until his death, Woodhall was equal partner with his brother, Eldon Woodhall, in a lath and plaster contracting business known as Woodhall Brothers.

In December 1961, the brothers executed a written buy-sell agreement, which provided that "upon the death of either partner the partnership shall terminate and the survivor shall purchase the decedent's interest in the partnership." The price was to be determined according to a formula set out in the agreement. The formula defined accounts payable and included certain valuations for fixed assets, inventory, accounts receivable and other assets. It is the accounts receivable item that generates this controversy over Mrs. Woodhall's income for 1964 and 1965.

Because the partnership reported income on a cash basis, Woodhall had not paid taxes on his share of the accounts receivable which were outstanding at the time of his death. Mrs. Woodhall, in filing her tax returns as an individual and as executrix of her husband's estate, did not report as income the amounts allocated to the accounts receivable. Instead Mrs. Woodhall's tax returns stated that no gain had been realized by the sale of her husband's partnership interest because the tax basis of the interest was the fair market value at the time of death and this was the same as the sale price.

The issue presented is whether portions of payments received by Mrs. Woodhall, as executrix of the estate and as surviving spouse, constitute income in respect of a decedent under § 691(a)(1) of the Internal Revenue Code and are therefore subject to income taxes to the extent that such portions are allocable to unrealized receivables.

Generally, the sale of a partnership interest is an occasion for determining the character of gain or loss "to the transferor partner" as provided by § 741. In the case at bar, however, there was technically no "transferor partner" to accomplish the sale. The Woodhall Brothers partnership terminated automatically upon the death of Woodhall by operation of the buy-sell agreement, as well as under common law. Mrs. Woodhall, as executrix of the estate and as holder of a community property interest, was the transferor.

[Regulation § 1.741-1(b)] recognizes that § 741 applies when the sale of the partnership interest results in a termination of the partnership. The question arises whether a termination of the partnership by operation of a written agreement of the parties upon the death of one partner has the same effect.

The legislative history of § 741 explicitly deals with this question. The House report reads as follows:

> Transfer of an interest in a partnership (§§ 741-743, 751)
>
> General rules.—Under present decisions the sale of a partnership interest is generally considered to be a sale of a capital asset, and any gain or loss realized is treated as capital gain or loss. It is not clear whether the sale of an interest whose value is attributable to uncollected rights to income gives rise to capital gain or ordinary income. . . .

> Unrealized receivables or fees. . . . In order to prevent the conversion of potential ordinary income into capital gain by virtue of transfers of partnership interests, certain rules have been adopted . . . which will apply to all dispositions of partnership interests. . . .
>
> A decedent partner's share of unrealized receivables and fees will be treated as income in respect of a decedent. Such rights to income will be taxed to the estate or heirs when collected. . . .
>
> The term "unrealized receivables or fees" is used to apply to any rights to income which have not been included in gross income under the method of accounting employed by the partnership. The provision is applicable mainly to cash basis partnerships which have acquired a contractual or other legal right to income for goods or services. House Report No. 1337, to accompany H.R. 8300 (Pub. L. 591), 83rd Cong., 2d Sess., pp. 70-71 (1954) (emphasis added); U.S. Code Cong. & Admin. News, p. 4096.

The Senate report is similar, with only technical amendments which do not alter the basic statement of purpose in the House report. Senate Report No. 1622, to accompany H.R. 8300 (Pub. L. 591), 83rd Cong., 2d Sess., p. 396 (1954).

Mrs. Woodhall's approach to the issue was much different. On the sale of her husband's partnership interest, she attempted to elect to establish the tax basis as the fair market value on the date of her husband's death. By this means, the sale price would be the same as the fair market value; there would be no gain and so no income to be taxed.

Mrs. Woodhall contends that the payments she received for the accounts receivable do not come within § 691(a), pertaining to income in respect of a decedent. Section 691(f), she points out, makes cross-reference to § 753, for application of § 691 to income in respect of a deceased partner. Section 753, in turn, refers to § 736 which provides that payments by a partnership for a deceased partner's interest in unrealized receivables shall be considered income in respect of a decedent under § 691. Mrs. Woodhall argues that a payment by a surviving partner is distinct from a payment by a partnership. Thus, she would have us interpret § 753, in conjunction with § 736, exclusively. In effect, this means that no payment other than one by a partnership which continues after one partner's death could constitute income in respect of a deceased partner. We reject this reading of the statutes.

The approach suggested by Mrs. Woodhall is not an appropriate characterization of the transfer of funds to her. Reading § 691 in the light of § 741, it is clear that Congress intended that the money Mrs. Woodhall received as an allocation from the unrealized accounts receivable be treated as income in respect of a decedent.

The Court of Appeals for the Eighth Circuit has just recently ruled that accounts receivable of a partnership shared in by a successor in interest of a deceased partner constituted income in respect of a decedent. *Quick's Trust v. Commissioner of Internal Revenue*, 444 F.2d 90 (8th Cir. 1971). The instant case is substantially the same.

We hold that the Commissioner rightly determined deficiencies against Mrs. Woodhall in the tax years 1964 and 1965. . . .

c. Special Basis Adjustments

A deceased partner's successor may be required to adjust her share of the partnership's inside basis to match her outside basis as determined under section 1014. As explained in chapter seven, the amount of the section 743(b) adjustment is equal to the difference between the successor's outside basis and her proportionate share of the partnership's common inside basis. Since IRD items are excluded from the section 1014 basis step-up, presumably no portion of the section 743(b) adjustment may be allocated to such items. See Rev. Rul. 66-325, 1966-2 C.B. 249.

In the absence of an optional (or mandatory) inside basis adjustment, a successor's outside basis will generally be greater than her unadjusted share of the partnership's common basis. Such a disparity may be detrimental to the successor. For example, if the partnership holds substantially appreciated inventory and the successor subsequently sells her partnership interest, she must report ordinary income under section 751(a) and a corresponding capital loss under section 741. The successor will be similarly disadvantaged if she retains her interest and the partnership later sells the inventory, since she will then be taxed on a distributive share of ordinary income that accrued prior to her predecessor's death and should have been eliminated by virtue of section 1014.

To a limited extent, the continuing partners may be able to take advantage of the successor's high outside basis at no cost to the successor. Thus, the partnership may distribute low-basis property to the successor in liquidation of such partner's partnership interest. Under certain circumstances, the basis of the distributed property in the hands of the successor will be stepped up under section 732(b) to match her high outside basis without any corresponding downward adjustment to the partnership's inside basis. In effect, the continuing partners will have achieved the equivalent of a basis step-up for a portion of the partnership's retained property, even though section 1014 is inapplicable to them. Under current law, such planning is possible only if there is no section 754 election in effect and the amount of the otherwise resulting downward basis adjustment does not exceed $250,000. If the downward adjustment exceeds the statutory threshold, inside basis must be reduced. I.R.C. § 734(b) and (d).

Problem 11-1:

(a) A, a one-third general partner in the ABC service partnership, dies when the partnership has the following balance sheet:

	Basis	*FMV*		*Book*	*FMV*
Assets			*Liabilities*	300	300
Cash	600	600	*Capital*		
Accts. Rec.	0	300	A	150	400
Land	150	450	B	150	400
Goodwill	0	150	C	150	400
Total	750	1,500	Total	750	1,500

(b) A's death triggers the partnership's buy-sell agreement, entitling D (A's successor) to a liquidating payment of $400 cash. The partnership agreement contains no provision concerning goodwill.

(i) Determine the tax consequences of the liquidating payment with respect to D and the continuing partners.
(ii) In (i), what difference would it make if the partnership agreement specifically allocated a portion of the liquidating payment to goodwill?

(c) The facts are the same as in (a), except that the partnership does not have a buy-sell agreement and D becomes a successor partner to A.

C. Partnership Terminations

1. *Events Causing a Partnership Termination*

Read I.R.C. § 708(a) and (b)(1). In general, a partnership is treated as continuing for tax purposes unless (1) no part of its business continues to be carried on by any of its partners in a partnership or (2) within a 12-month period, there is a sale or exchange of 50 percent or more of its capital and profits interests. Since the definition of a "partnership" for tax purposes does not depend upon its recognition under state law, the dissolution of a partnership for state law purposes does not necessarily terminate the partnership for tax purposes.

The "business cessation" test under section 708(b)(1)(A) can be satisfied by an actual or deemed termination of the partnership's business. For example, a partnership may completely cease its business activities, wind up its affairs, and distribute all of its remaining assets to its partners in complete liquidation. Alternatively, a transfer of a partnership interest may leave a state-law partnership with only a single owner. A single-owner entity cannot qualify as a partnership for tax purposes, see Reg. § 301.7701-2(c)(1); therefore, even if the business is continued by the remaining owner, there is no longer any business carried on by any "partner" in a "partnership." See Reg. § 1.708-1(b)(1). Similarly, a partnership is deemed to terminate if it elects to be classified as an association under the check-the-box rules. See Reg. § 301.7701-3(g)(1) and (2). Continued conduct of some nominal amount of business activity by a partnership may suffice to prevent a business cessation.

Although the "sale or exchange" test under section 708(b)(1)(B) may also result in a deemed termination, a partnership and its business activities generally continue following the requisite transfer of interests. Section 708(b)(1)(B) was included in the law apparently to prevent trafficking in partnerships with advantageous taxable years, a concern that has now largely been curbed by the rules in section 706. The tax consequences of a partnership termination are described in the next section.

Changes in partnership interests as a result of gifts, bequests, distributions, or contributions do not count for purposes of the 50 percent test in section 708(b)(1)(B). Reg. § 1.708-1(b)(2). Thus, the devise of a 50 percent (or greater) interest of a deceased partner does not cause a partnership termination. Even if the firm had only two members prior to the death of one of them, it is treated as continuing so long as the deceased partner's estate or other successor continues to share in profits and losses. If liquidating payments are made to the holder of the deceased partner's interest, the partnership continues to exist for tax purposes until the interest has been completely liquidated. See Reg. §§ 1.708-1(b)(1)(i), 1.736-1(a)(6). But if the partnership agreement includes a buy-sell provision obligating the remaining partners to purchase the interest of any deceased partner, a sale of a 50 percent (or greater) interest causes a termination. The following ruling further illustrates the scope of the sale or exchange requirement.

Rev. Rul. 84-52

1984-1 C.B. 157

ISSUE

What are the federal income tax consequences of the conversion of a general partnership interest into a limited partnership interest in the same partnership?

FACTS

In 1975, X was formed as a general partnership under the Uniform Partnership Act of state M. X is engaged in the business of farming. The partners of X are A, B, C, and D. The partners have equal interests in the partnership.

The partners propose to amend the partnership agreement to convert the general partnership into a limited partnership under the Uniform Limited Partnership Act of State M, a statute that corresponds in all material respects to the Uniform Limited Partnership Act. Under the certificate of limited partnership, A and B will be limited partners, and both C and D will be general partners and limited partners. Each partner's total percent interest in the partnership's profits, losses, and capital will remain the same when the general partnership is converted into a limited partnership. The business of the general partnership will continue to be carried on after the conversion.

... Under the facts of this revenue ruling, A, B, C, and D, will remain partners in X after X is converted to a limited partnership. Although the partners have exchanged their interests in the general partnership X for interests in the limited partnership X, under section 721 of the Code, gain or loss will not be recognized by any of the partners of X except as provided in section 731 of the Code.

HOLDINGS

(1) Except as provided below, pursuant to section 721 of the Code, no gain or loss will be recognized by A, B, C, or D under section 741 or section 1001 of the Code as a result of the conversion of a general partnership interest in X into a limited partnership in X.

(2) Because the business of X will continue after the conversion and because, under section 1.708-1(b)(1)(ii) of the regulations, a transaction governed by section 721 of the Code is not treated as a sale or exchange for purposes of section 708 of the Code, X will not be terminated under section 708 of the Code. . . .

NOTES

1. *Basis for the ruling.* This cryptic ruling treats the conversion as resulting from a distribution of new interests to the converting partners in exchange for a contribution of the old interests under section 721. Since neither transaction counts for purposes of the "sale or exchange" requirement, there is no deemed termination under section 708(b)(1)(B). Because the business continues in the form of a limited partnership, there is also no business cessation under section 708(b)(1)(A). The IRS has reached the same conclusion in connection with the conversion of a partnership into a limited liability company taxed as a partnership. See Rev. Rul. 95-37, 1995-1 C.B. 130.

2. *Capital and profits interests.* For a section 708(b)(1)(B) termination to occur, there must be a sale or exchange within a 12-month period of *both* 50 percent or more of the partnership's capital interests *and* 50 percent or more of its profits interests. Reg. § 1.708-1(b)(2).

3. *The 50 percent test.* All sales or exchanges are aggregated during a 12-month period to determine whether the 50 percent threshold has been met, but successive sales of the same interest are only counted once. For example, suppose A, B, and C are each one-third partners in partnership ABC. If, during a 12-month period, A sells his entire interest to new partner D and B sells her entire interest to new partner E, the partnership terminates under section 708(b)(1)(B). On the other hand, if during the same period, A sells his entire interest to D and then D sells the same interest to E, the partnership does not terminate because only a single one-third interest in the partnership is sold during the 12-month period. Reg. § 1.708-1(b)(2).

4. *Planning possibilities.* For purposes of section 708(b)(1)(B), changes in partnership interests resulting from sales or exchanges are counted, but not those resulting from contributions and distributions. Thus, it may be fairly simple to avoid a partnership termination by combining sales with distributions that redeem a partner's interest. For example, assume that A owns 80 percent and B owns 20 percent of the interests in the AB partnership. A, who wishes to terminate her interest, sells half

of her interest (40 percent) to C and has the partnership redeem the remaining half of her interest. Following the sale and redemption, C winds up with two-thirds and B with one-third of the partnership. Even though C's interest increased from zero to two-thirds during a 12-month period, the increase in C's interest resulting from the redemption of A's interest is ignored and the partnership does not terminate under section 708(b)(1)(B).

2. *Tax Consequences of a Partnership Termination*

If a sale or exchange of interests causes a partnership to terminate under section 708(b)(1)(B), the terminated partnership is deemed first to contribute all of its assets and liabilities to a new partnership in exchange for all of the interests of the new partnership. The terminated partnership is then treated as distributing the interests of the new partnership to the purchasing partner and the remaining partners of the terminated partnership in complete liquidation of the terminated partnership. Reg. § 1.708-1(b)(4). This characterization generally minimizes any adverse tax consequences resulting from the termination. The principal tax consequences are as follows:

(1) closing of taxable year — the taxable year of the terminated partnership closes with respect to all persons who were partners immediately before the termination event (I.R.C. § 706(c)(1); Reg. § 1.708-1(b)(3));
(2) deemed contribution of assets to new partnership — this transaction should generally be a nonrecognition event (I.R.C. § 721(a)) with the new partnership receiving the same basis, character, and holding period in such assets as the terminated partnership (I.R.C. §§ 723, 724, 1223(2)). Any property contributed to the new partnership is treated as section 704(c) property only to the extent it was section 704(c) property in the hands of the terminated partnership immediately prior to the termination (Reg. §§ 1.704-3(a)(3)(i), 1.708-1(b)(4) (ex. (iii)). The partnership also continues to amortize any start-up or organizational expenses over the terminated partnership's remaining amortization period (Reg. § 1.708-1(b)(6));
(3) deemed distribution of new partnership interests to partners — this transaction should also generally be a nonrecognition event (I.R.C. § 731(a) and (b); Reg. §§ 1.704-4(c)(3), 1.731-2(g)(2), 1.737-2(a)) with the partners receiving the same basis and holding period in the new interests as in their former partnership interests (I.R.C. §§ 732(b), 1223(1)). A subsequent distribution of property by the new partnership is subject to sections 704(c)(1)(B) and 737 to the same extent a distribution by the terminated partnership would have been subject to those provisions. Reg. §§ 1.704-4(c)(3), 1.737-2(a). Thus, a termination under section 708(b)(1)(B) does not restart the seven-year period in those two provisions (Reg. § 1.704-4(a)(4)(ii));

(4) effect on capital accounts — the capital accounts of the remaining partners of the terminated partnership carry over to the new partnership, and the purchasing partner inherits the capital account of the selling partner (Reg. §§ 1.704-1(b)(2)(iv)(*l*), 1.708-1(b)(4) (ex. (ii));

(5) elections — in general, elections of the terminated partnership, including a section 754 election, do not carry over to the new partnership. However, a special basis adjustment belonging to a partner with respect to an asset of the terminated partnership carries over to the same asset held by the new partnership with respect to such partner even if the new partnership does not make a section 754 election (Reg. § 1.743-1(h)(1)). If the terminated partnership has a section 754 election in effect, a partner whose purchase caused the termination is entitled to a section 743(b) adjustment. Reg. § 1.708-1(b)(5). Similarly, if the new partnership has a section 754 election in effect, the deemed distribution of partnership interests may result in a section 743(b) adjustment with respect to all of the partners. See I.R.C. § 761(e); Reg. § 1.761-1(e).

The following ruling explains the tax consequences of a termination resulting from a "business cessation" under section 708(b)(1)(A).

Rev. Rul. 99-6

1999-1 C.B. 432

ISSUE

What are the federal income tax consequences if one person purchases all of the ownership interests in a domestic limited liability company (LLC) that is classified as a partnership under § 301.7701-3, causing the LLC's status as a partnership to terminate under § 708(b)(1)(A) of the Internal Revenue Code?

FACTS

In each of the following situations, an LLC is formed and operates in a state which permits an LLC to have a single owner. Each LLC is classified as a partnership under § 301.7701-3. Neither of the LLCs holds any unrealized receivables or substantially appreciated inventory for purposes of § 751(b). For the sake of simplicity, it is assumed that neither LLC is liable for any indebtedness, nor are the assets of the LLCs subject to any indebtedness.

Situation 1. A and *B* are equal partners in *AB*, an LLC. *A* sells *A*'s entire interest in *AB* to *B* for $10,000. After the sale, the business is continued by the LLC, which is owned solely by *B*.

Situation 2. C and *D* are equal partners in *CD*, an LLC. *C* and *D* sell their entire interests in *CD* to *E*, an unrelated person, in exchange for $10,000 each. After the sale, the business is continued by the LLC, which is owned solely by *E*.

After the sale, in both situations, no entity classification election is made under § 301.7701-3(c) to treat the LLC as an association for federal tax purposes.

LAW

Section 708(b)(1)(A) and § 1.708-1(b)(1) provide that a partnership shall terminate when the operations of the partnership are discontinued and no part of any business, financial operation, or venture of the partnership continues to be carried on by any of its partners in a partnership.

. . . In *Edwin E. McCauslen v. Commissioner*, 45 T.C. 588 (1966), one partner in an equal, two-person partnership died, and his partnership interest was purchased from his estate by the remaining partner. The purchase caused a termination of the partnership under § 708(b)(1)(A). The Tax Court held that the surviving partner did not purchase the deceased partner's interest in the partnership, but that the surviving partner purchased the partnership assets attributable to the interest. As a result, the surviving partner was not permitted to succeed to the partnership's holding period with respect to these assets.

Rev. Rul. 67-65, 1967-1 C.B. 168, also considered the purchase of a deceased partner's interest by the other partner in a two-person partnership. The Service ruled that, for the purpose of determining the purchaser's holding period in the assets attributable to the deceased partner's interest, the purchaser should treat the transaction as a purchase of the assets attributable to the interest. Accordingly, the purchaser was not permitted to succeed to the partnership's holding period with respect to these assets. . . .

ANALYSIS AND HOLDINGS

Situation 1. The *AB* partnership terminates under § 708(b)(1)(A) when *B* purchases *A*'s entire interest in *AB*. Accordingly, *A* must treat the transaction as the sale of a partnership interest. Reg. § 1.741-1(b). *A* must report gain or loss, if any, resulting from the sale of *A*'s partnership interest in accordance with § 741.

Under the analysis of *McCauslen* and Rev. Rul. 67-65, for purposes of determining the tax treatment of *B*, the *AB* partnership is deemed to make a liquidating distribution of all of its assets to *A* and *B*, and following this distribution, *B* is treated as acquiring the assets deemed to have been distributed to *A* in liquidation of *A*'s partnership interest.

B's basis in the assets attributable to *A*'s one-half interest in the partnership is $10,000, the purchase price for *A*'s partnership interest. Section 1012. Section

735(b) does not apply with respect to the assets *B* is deemed to have purchased from *A*. Therefore, *B*'s holding period for these assets begins on the day immediately following the date of the sale. See Rev. Rul. 66-7, 1966-1 C.B. 188, which provides that the holding period of an asset is computed by excluding the date on which the asset is acquired.

Upon the termination of *AB*, *B* is considered to receive a distribution of those assets attributable to *B*'s former interest in *AB*, *B* must recognize gain or loss, if any, on the deemed distribution of the assets to the extent required by § 731(a). *B*'s basis in the assets received in the deemed liquidation of *B*'s partnership interest is determined under § 732(b). Under § 735(b), *B*'s holding period for the assets attributable to *B*'s one-half interest in *AB* includes the partnership's holding period for such assets (except for purposes of § 735(a)(2)).

Situation 2. The *CD* partnership terminates under § 708(b)(1)(A) when E purchases the entire interests of *C* and *D* in *CD*. *C* and *D* must report gain or loss, if any, resulting from the sale of their partnership interests in accordance with § 741.

For purposes of classifying the acquisition by *E*, the *CD* partnership is deemed to make a liquidating distribution of its assets to *C* and *D*. Immediately following this distribution, *E* is deemed to acquire, by purchase, all of the former partnership's assets. . . .

E's basis in the assets is $20,000 under § 1012. *E*'s holding period for the assets begins on the day immediately following the date of sale.

NOTE

Aggregate vs. entity approach. In the case of a deemed termination under section 708(b)(1)(B) by reason of a sale or exchange of partnership interests, the basis, character, and holding period of all of the terminated partnership's assets generally continue in the hands of the new partnership. Thus, in the absence of a section 754 election, a purchasing partner whose purchase may have caused the termination generally succeeds to those attributes. This result is consistent with an entity conception of a partnership. In contrast, as Revenue Ruling 99-6 indicates, a purchasing partner who causes a termination under the business cessation rule of section 708(b)(1)(A) does not inherit the terminated partnership's attributes with respect to the portion of the assets deemed acquired in the purchase. Since there is no longer any "entity" after the purchase, the tax law must apply aggregate principles in determining the tax consequences of the transaction.

3. *Mergers and Divisions of Partnerships*

Read I.R.C. § 708(b)(2). When a partnership merges or consolidates with one or more other partnerships or divides itself into two or more partnerships, the transaction raises issues concerning partnership termination. In the case of a merger or consolidation, any resulting partnership is treated as a continuation of a prior partnership if members of the prior partnership own more than 50 percent of the capital and profits interests of the resulting partnership. Any other partnership involved in the transaction terminates. If all of the partnerships involved in a merger or consolidation terminate, a new partnership results. See I.R.C. § 708(b)(2)(A); Reg. § 1.708-1(c)(1).

> **Example 11-4:** Partnership AB is owned equally by partners A and B, and partnership CD is owned equally by partners C and D. The two partnerships merge forming partnership ABCD. Ownership interests in the new partnership are as follows: A (30%), B (30%), C (20%) and D (20%). In this situation, partnership ABCD is treated as a continuation of partnership AB since the former members of AB (A and B) own more than 50 percent of the resulting partnership. Partnership CD terminates. If, as a result of the transaction, each partner owned an equal interest in partnership ABCD, then both partnerships AB and CD would terminate, and a new partnership ABCD would result.

Taxpayers have a choice of two forms for characterizing the manner in which a merger or consolidation occurs for tax purposes, with the tax consequences flowing from the form chosen. If taxpayers structure a merger or consolidation using an "assets-up" form under state law, the form of the transaction will be respected for tax purposes. Under the "assets-up" form, any terminated partnership distributes all of its assets to its partners in complete liquidation of their interest in such partnership and, immediately thereafter, the partners of the terminated partnership contribute those same assets to the resulting partnership in exchange for interests in that partnership. If the merger or consolidation is structured in any other way under state law, the transaction will be treated for tax purposes as having followed the "assets-over" form. Under this default form, any terminated partnership is treated as contributing all of its assets and liabilities to the resulting partnership in exchange for an interest in such partnership and immediately thereafter, the terminated partnership is treated as distributing to its partners the interests in the resulting partnership in complete liquidation of the terminated partnership. See Reg. § 1.708-1(c)(3). The "assets-over" form should already be familiar, since it is the same form employed when a partnership is deemed to terminate under section 708(b)(1)(B).

The analysis of a partnership merger or consolidation adopts a "forward-looking" approach, which focuses on whether the members of a partnership involved in the transaction own a greater than 50 percent interest in the resulting partnership. By contrast, the analysis of a partnership division adopts a "backward-looking" approach, which focuses on whether the members of any resulting partnership previously owned more than 50 percent of the prior partnership. If this backward-looking test is met, the resulting partnership is treated as a continuation of the prior partnership; otherwise, any resulting partnership is treated as new partnership. Any prior partnership other than a continuing partnership is treated as terminated. See I.R.C. § 708(b)(2)(B); Reg. § 1.708-1(d)(1).

Example 11-5: Partnership ABCD, involved in two lines of business, is owned by four partners with the following interests: A (40%), B (20%), C (20%), and D (20%). The partners decide to divide the partnership into two partnerships, each operating one of the businesses. After the division, the two resulting partnerships are partnership AB (A and B partners) and partnership CD (C and D partners). Because A and B previously owned a greater than 50 percent interest in partnership ABCD, partnership AB is treated as a continuation of partnership ABCD. Partnership CD is treated as a new partnership. If the four partners originally had equal interests in partnership ABCD, then resulting partnerships AB and CD would both be treated as new partnerships, and the prior partnership ABCD would terminate.

As in the case of partnership mergers and consolidations, the parties have a choice of two tax forms for a division with the tax consequences flowing from the form chosen. Thus, in general, if the parties carry out a partnership division under state law using an "assets-up" form, the form of the transaction will be respected for tax purposes. In all other cases, the partnership division will be taxed in accordance with the "assets-over" form. Reg. § 1.708-1(d)(3). These tax constructs offer the parties considerable flexibility in determining the direction in which assets are deemed to move for tax purposes. Such flexibility may be beneficial, for example, in minimizing local transfer taxes or avoiding restrictions on actual asset transfers.

NOTE

Application of section 704(c) in an assets-over merger. Although an assets-over merger of partnerships follows the same form as that deemed to occur when a partnership terminates under section 708(b)(1)(B), the two transactions have different section 704(c) implications. A partnership merger usually results in a change in sharing ratios because ownership of the resulting partnership is now split among the former members of the two merging partnerships. When sharing ratios change, section 704(c) principles generally must be applied to prevent a shifting of any built-in items among the different partners as a result of the merger. In contrast, a section 708(b)(1)(B) termination as a result of a sale or exchange of partnership interests does not alter sharing ratios, and therefore section 704(c) principles are not needed. Instead, the purchasing partner simply inherits the share of any built-in items belonging to the selling partner.

In 2007, the IRS proposed controversial regulations dealing with the consequences under section 704(c) (and sections 704(c)(1)(B) and 737) when partnerships combine in an assets-over merger. With respect to the terminated partnership, a merger generally gives rise to two layers of section 704(c) built-in items. "Original" section 704(c) gain or loss refers to any remaining built-in amount inherent in the terminated partnership's property that is attributable to the initial contribution of such property to the terminated partnership. "New" section 704(c) gain or loss refers to any built-in items of the terminated partnership at the time of the merger, but only to the extent that such items are not already taken into account as original section 704(c) gain or loss. For purposes of sections 704(c)(1)(B) and 737, the distinction may be important. The merger starts a new seven-year period with respect to any new section 704(c) gain or loss (but not original section 704(c) gain or loss) of the terminated partnership. See Prop. Reg. §§ 1.704-4(c)(4)(ii)(A) and (B), and 1.737-2(b)(1)(ii)(A) and (B). These rules place a premium on properly identifying which partnership is treated as continuing or terminating as a result of the merger. See Notice 2009-70, 2009-34 I.R.B. 255 (requesting comments on layering of section 704(c) gain (or loss) in mergers).

Example 11-6: At the beginning of Year 1, A and B contribute $300 cash each for equal shares of new partnership AB. On the same day, C contributes land worth $200 (basis of $100) and D contributes $200 cash for equal shares of new partnership CD. At the beginning of Year 5, partnerships AB and CD merge in a transaction treated as an assets-over merger for tax purposes. At the time of the merger, AB holds cash and assets worth $1,200, and CD still holds the land (now worth $600) and $200 cash. Following the merger, A and B own 60 percent (30 percent each) and C and D own 40 percent (20 percent each) of partnership ABCD. At the beginning of Year 9 when the land is still worth $600, partnership ABCD distributes the land to partner A in complete liquidation of her interest.

Because A and B end up with over 50 percent of the interests of partnership ABCD, partnership AB is treated as continuing and partnership CD is treated as terminating. At the time of the merger, CD (the terminated partnership) had $100 of original section 704(c) gain inherent in the land (the remaining built-in amount attributable to C's contribution) and $400 of new section 704(c) gain (the $500 total built-in amount less the $100 treated as original section 704(c) gain). Since partnership ABCD's distribution of the land, in Year 9, occurs more than seven years after C's contribution of the land to partnership CD but within seven years of the merger, section 704(c)(1)(B) applies with respect to the $400 of new section 704(c) gain (but not the $100 of original section 704(c) gain). Accordingly, C and D, as the "contributing partners," must each recognize $200 of gain on the distribution, triggering a corresponding adjustment to the partnership's basis in the distributed land. See Prop. Reg. § 1.704-4(c)(4)(ii)(F) (ex. 1). Under section 737, the result would be similar if, instead of distributing the land to partner A, partnership ABCD distributed other appreciated property to C and D in Year 9.

If the merging partnerships are owned by the same persons in the same proportions (or any differences in ownership are *de minimis*), the proposed regulations provide that no new section 704(c) gain or loss arises as a result of the merger. See Prop. Reg. §§ 1.704-4(c)(4)(ii)(E) and 1.737-2(b)(1)(ii)(E). As in the case of a section 708(b)(1)(B) termination, the partners of the continuing or new partnership simply inherit any section 704(c) gain or loss attributable to the terminated partnership, without the starting of a new seven-year period for built-in items.

4. *Incorporation of a Partnership*

Now that you have been introduced to partnership mergers and divisions, consider similar issues of form that arise in connection with incorporation of a partnership.

Rev. Rul. 84-111

1984-2 C.B. 88

ISSUE

Does Rev. Rul. 70-239, 1970-1 C.B. 74, still represent the Service's position with respect to the three situations described therein?

FACTS

The three situations described in Rev. Rul. 70-239 involve partnerships X, Y, and Z, respectively. Each partnership used the accrual method of accounting and had assets and liabilities consisting of cash, equipment, and accounts payable. The liabilities of each partnership did not exceed the adjusted basis of its assets. The three situations are as follows:

Situation 1

X transferred all of its assets to newly-formed corporation R in exchange for all the outstanding stock of R and the assumption by R of X's liabilities. X then terminated by distributing all the stock of R to X's partners in proportion to their partnership interests.

Situation 2

Y distributed all of its assets and liabilities to its partners in proportion to their partnership interests in a transaction that constituted a termination of Y under section 708(b)(1)(A) of the Code. The partners then transferred all the assets received from Y to newly-formed corporation S in exchange for all the outstanding stock of S and the assumption by S of Y's liabilities that had been assumed by the partners.

Situation 3

The partners of Z transferred their partnership interests in Z to newly-formed corporation T in exchange for all the outstanding stock of T. This exchange terminated Z and all of its assets and liabilities became assets and liabilities of T.

In each situation, the steps taken by X, Y, and Z, and the partners of X, Y, and Z, were parts of a plan to transfer the partnership operations to a corporation organized for valid business reasons in exchange for its stock and were not devices to avoid or evade recognition of gain. Rev. Rul. 70-239 holds that because the federal income tax consequences of the three situations are the same, each partnership is considered to have transferred its assets and liabilities to a corporation in exchange for its stock under section 351 of the Internal Revenue Code, followed by a distribution of the stock to the partners in liquidation of the partnership.

LAW AND ANALYSIS

Section 351(a) of the Code provides that no gain or loss will be recognized if property is transferred to a corporation by one or more persons solely in exchange for stock or securities in such corporation and immediately after the exchange such person or persons are in control (as defined in section 368(c)) of the corporation.

Section 1.351-1(a)(1) of the Income Tax Regulations provides that, as used in section 351 of the Code, the phrase "one or more persons" includes individuals, trusts, estates, partnerships, associations, companies, or corporations. To be in control of the transferee corporation, such person or persons must own immediately after the transfer stock possessing at least 80 percent of the total combined voting power of all classes of stock entitled to vote and at least 80 percent of the total number of shares of all other classes of stock of such corporation.

Section 358(a) of the Code provides that in the case of an exchange to which section 351 applies, the basis of the property permitted to be received under such section without the recognition of gain or loss will be the same as that of the property exchanged, decreased by the amount of any money received by the taxpayer.

Section 358(d) of the Code provides that where, as part of the consideration to the taxpayer, another party to the exchange assumed a liability of the taxpayer or acquired from the taxpayer property subject to a liability, such assumption or acquisition (in the amount of the liability) will, for purposes of section 358, be treated as money received by the taxpayer on the exchange.

Section 362(a) of the Code provides that a corporation's basis in property acquired in a transaction to which section 351 applies will be the same as it would be in the hands of the transferor.

Under section 708(b)(1)(A) of the Code, a partnership is terminated if no part of any business, financial operation, or venture of the partnership continues to be carried on by any of its partners in a partnership. Under section 708(b)(1)(B), a partnership terminates if within a 12-month period there is a sale or exchange of 50 percent or more of the total interest in partnership capital and profits.

Section 732(b) of the Code provides that the basis of property other than money distributed by a partnership in a liquidation of a partner's interest shall be an amount equal to the adjusted basis of the partner's interest in the partnership reduced by any money distributed. Section 732(c) of the Code provides rules for the allocation of a partner's basis in a partnership interest among the assets received in a liquidating distribution.

Section 735(b) of the Code provides that a partner's holding period for property received in a distribution from a partnership (other than with respect to certain inventory items defined in section 751(d)(2)) includes the partnership's holding period, as determined under section 1223, with respect to such property.

Section 1223(1) of the Code provides that where property received in an exchange acquires the same basis, in whole or in part, as the property surrendered in the exchange, the holding period of the property received includes the holding period of the property surrendered to the extent such surrendered property was a capital asset or property described in section 1231. Under section 1223(2), the holding period of a taxpayer's property, however acquired, includes the period during which the property was held by any other person if that property has the same basis, in whole or in part, in the taxpayer's hands as it would have in the hands of such other person.

Section 741 of the Code provides that in the case of a sale or exchange of an interest in a partnership, gain or loss shall be recognized to the transferor partner. Such gain or loss shall be considered as a gain or loss from the sale or exchange of a capital asset, except as otherwise provided in section 751.

Section 751(a) of the Code provides that the amount of money or the fair value of property received by a transferor partner in exchange for all or part of such partner's interest in the partnership attributable to unrealized receivables of the partnership, or to inventory items of the partnership that have appreciated substantially in value, shall be considered as an amount realized from the sale or exchange of property other than a capital asset.

Section 752(a) of the Code provides that any increase in a partner's share of the liabilities of a partnership, or any increase in a partner's individual liabilities by reason of the assumption by the partner of partnership liabilities, will be considered as a contribution of money by such partner to the partnership.

Section 752(b) of the Code provides that any decrease in a partner's share of the liabilities of a partnership, or any decrease in a partner's individual liabilities by reason of the assumption by the partnership of such individual liabilities, will be considered as a distribution of money to the partner by the partnership. Under section 733(1) of the Code, the basis of a partner's interest in the partnership is reduced by the amount of money received in a distribution that is not in liquidation of the partnership.

Section 752(d) of the Code provides that in the case of a sale or exchange of an interest in a partnership, liabilities shall be treated in the same manner as liabilities in connection with the sale or exchange of property not associated with partnerships.

The premise in Rev. Rul. 70-239 that the federal income tax consequences of the three situations described therein would be the same, without regard to which of the three transactions was entered into, is incorrect. As described below, depending on the format chosen for the transfer to a controlled corporation, the basis and holding periods of the various assets received by the corporation and the basis and holding periods of the stock received by the former partners can vary.

. . . Recognition of the three possible methods to incorporate a partnership will enable taxpayers to avoid the above potential pitfalls and will facilitate flexibility with respect to the basis and holding periods of the assets received in the exchange.

HOLDING

Rev. Rul. 70-239 no longer represents the Service's position. The Service's current position is set forth below, and for each situation, the methods described and the underlying assumptions and purposes must be satisfied for the conclusions of this revenue ruling to be applicable.

Situation 1

Under section 351 of the Code, gain or loss is not recognized by X on the transfer by X of all of its assets to R in exchange for R's stock and the assumption by R of X's liabilities.

Under section 362(a) of the Code, R's basis in the assets received from X equals their basis to X immediately before their transfer to R. Under section 358(a), the basis to X of the stock received from R is the same as the basis to X of the assets transferred to R, reduced by the liabilities assumed by R, which assumption is treated as a payment of money to X under section 358(d). In addition, the assumption by R of X's liabilities decreased each partner's share of the partnership liabilities, thus, decreasing the basis of each partner's partnership interest pursuant to sections 752 and 733.

On distribution of the stock to X's partners, X terminated under section 708(b)(1)(A) of the Code. Pursuant to section 732(b), the basis of the stock distributed to the partners in liquidation of their partnership interests is, with respect to each partner, equal to the adjusted basis of the partner's interest in the partnership.

Under section 1223(1) of the Code, X's holding period for the stock received in the exchange includes its holding period in the capital assets and section 1231 assets transferred (to the extent that the stock was received in exchange for such assets). To the extent the stock was received in exchange for neither capital nor section 1231 assets, X's holding period for such stock begins on the day following the date of the exchange. See Rev. Rul. 70-598, 1970-2 C.B. 168. Under section 1223(2), R's holding period in the assets transferred to it includes X's holding period. When X distributed the R stock to its partners, under sections 735(b) and 1223, the partners' holding periods included X's holding period of the stock. Furthermore, such distribution will not violate the control requirement of section 368(c) of the Code.

Situation 2

On the transfer of all of Y's assets to its partners, Y terminated under section 708(b)(1)(A) of the Code, and, pursuant to section 732(b), the basis of the assets (other than money) distributed to the partners in liquidation of their partnership interests in Y was, with respect to each partner, equal to the adjusted basis of the partner's interest in Y, reduced by the money distributed. Under section 752, the decrease in Y's liabilities resulting from the transfer to Y's partners was offset by the partners' corresponding assumption of such liabilities so that the net effect on the basis of each partner's interest in Y, with respect to the liabilities transferred, was zero.

Under section 351 of the Code, gain or loss is not recognized by Y's former partners on the transfer to S in exchange for its stock and the assumption of Y's liabilities, of the assets of Y received by Y's partners in liquidation of Y.

Under section 358(a) of the Code, the basis to the former partners of Y in the stock received from S is the same as the section 732(b) basis to the former partners of Y in the assets received in liquidation of Y and transferred to S, reduced by the liabilities assumed by S, which assumption is treated as a payment of money to the partners under section 358(d).

Under section 362(a) of the Code, S's basis in the assets received from Y's former partners equals their basis to the former partners as determined under the section 732(c) immediately before the transfer to S.

Under section 735(b) of the Code, the partners' holding periods for the assets distributed to them by Y includes Y's holding period. Under section 1223(1), the partners' holding periods for the stock received in the exchange includes the partners' holding periods in the capital assets and section 1231 assets transferred to S (to the extent that the stock was received in exchange for such assets). However, to the extent that the stock received was in exchange for neither capital nor section 1231 assets, the holding period of the stock began on the day following the date of the exchange. Under section 1223(2), S's holding period of the Y assets received in the exchange includes the partner's holding periods.

Situation 3

Under section 351 of the Code, gain or loss is not recognized by Z's partners on the transfer of the partnership interests to T in exchange for T's stock.

On the transfer of the partnership interests to the corporation, Z terminated under section 708(b)(1)(A) of the Code.

Under section 358(a) of the Code, the basis to the partners of Z of the stock received from T in exchange for their partnership interests equals the basis of their partnership interests transferred to T, reduced by Z's liabilities assumed by T, the release from which is treated as a payment of money to Z's partners under sections 752(d) and 358(d).

T's basis for the assets received in the exchange equals the basis of the partners in their partnership interests allocated in accordance with section 732(c). T's holding period includes Z's holding period in the assets.

Under section 1223(1) of the Code, the holding period of the T stock received by the former partners of Z includes each respective partner's holding period for the partnership interest transferred, except that the holding period of the T stock that was received by the partners of Z in exchange for their interests in section 751 assets of Z that are neither capital assets nor section 1231 assets begins on the day following the date of the exchange.

NOTES AND QUESTIONS

1. *Three forms.* Note that Rev. Rul. 84-111 allows the parties to select the most favorable tax results (i.e., basis, holding period, and recognized gain) by casting the transaction in one of three possible forms. Two of the forms correspond to those permitted in connection with partnership mergers and divisions — *Situation 1* (Assets-Over Form) and *Situation 2* (Assets-Up Form). Why is the third form (*Situation 3* (Interest-Over Form)) respected in connection with incorporations but not mergers and divisions?

2. *Explicit election?* Why not allow the partners merely to elect a particular form of incorporation by drafting the appropriate documents rather than actually conveying assets or partnership interests?

3. *Section 362(e)(2).* This provision limits the transfer of built-in losses to a corporation in a section 351 transfer. If applicable, the provision generally reduces the transferee corporation's basis in the transferred properties to their fair market value.

Chapter 12

Preventing Abuse of the Partnership Tax Rules

A. Introduction

By this point in the course, you may understandably feel overwhelmed by the complexity of subchapter K. The basic theory of passthrough taxation is fairly straightforward but, as you now know, the implementing details can be excruciatingly difficult. Perhaps the most remarkable feature of subchapter K is that so many of the details have been worked out as thoroughly as they have.

Such a complicated set of rules inevitably creates opportunities for misuse, as subchapter K amply demonstrates. This final chapter examines certain broad tools that have been developed to prevent abuse of the partnership tax rules.

Part B describes a general anti-abuse regulation, Reg. § 1.701-2, applicable to all of partnership tax. When promulgating this rule at the end of 1994, Treasury justified it in the following way:

> In the past, the IRS and Treasury have attempted to address partnership transactions on a case-by-case basis. However, . . . experience has demonstrated that the case-by-case approach has been inadequate. A case-by-case approach arguably encourages non-economic, tax-motivated behavior by inappropriately putting a premium on being the first to engage in a transaction that would violate the principles of this regulation. The IRS and Treasury believe that [Reg. § 1.701-2] is a reasonable and effective way to reduce the number and magnitude of these abusive transactions. Moreover, the IRS and Treasury believe that proper application of the principles embodied in the regulation will forestall additional complexity in the Code and the regulations, by reducing the pressure for case-by-case legislative or regulatory revisions to prevent inappropriate use of the provisions of subchapter K. [T.D. 8588, 1995-1 C.B. 109, 112.]

Part B considers the two components of the regulation dealing with transactions that are inconsistent with the intent of subchapter K or abuse the treatment of a partnership as an entity for tax purposes.

Part C then briefly examines the "economic substance" doctrine, a general tool potentially available to the courts to prevent abuse of *all* of tax law (and not just the partnership tax rules). This doctrine has common-law origins, but was codified in 2010 in section 7701(o); a sizable, strict liability penalty applies to any underpayment of tax attributable to a transaction lacking economic substance. Finally, part D discusses certain partnership audit rules originally designed to improve the IRS's ability to identify and curb abusive partnership tax transactions.

The following case, ACM Partnership v. Comm'r, 157 F.3d 231 (3d Cir. 1998), gives context to the material presented in this chapter. The case—involving a notorious transaction that illustrated the need for the partnership anti-abuse regulation and eventual codification of the economic substance doctrine—concerned a tax shelter product called a "contingent installment sale" (CINS) transaction, which had been devised and marketed by a brokerage firm (Merrill Lynch). The product was designed to generate capital losses for corporate taxpayers that could be used to shelter their capital gains. Corporations do not benefit from a capital gains preference (I.R.C. § 1201(a)) and, therefore, their capital gains may be taxed at the top statutory rate of 35 percent.

In *ACM*, the Colgate-Palmolive Co., which had recognized a capital gain of over $100 million from the sale of a subsidiary, agreed to participate in a CINS transaction. As simplified, the transaction involved the following steps:

1. On November 2, 1989, Colgate, a foreign bank, and Merrill Lynch formed the ACM partnership by contributing cash in exchange for partnership interests of 17.1 percent, 82.6 percent, and 0.3 percent, respectively. ACM initially deposited the $205 million cash in an account of the foreign bank paying 8.75 percent interest.
2. The day after ACM was formed, it used the $205 million to purchase ten short-term, private placement Citicorp notes paying a floating rate of interest which was initially 8.78 percent, or three basis points higher than the interest rate of the bank account. A "basis point" equals one one-hundredth of one percent.
3. On November 27, 1989, ACM sold $175 million of the Citicorp notes for $140 million in cash plus notes (the "LIBOR notes") promising additional payments over the following five years plus interest at the London Interbank Offering Rate (LIBOR). LIBOR is the primary reference interest rate used in European financial markets. Because payments on the LIBOR notes extended beyond the year of the sale and varied with fluctuations in the LIBOR, the installment sale rules permitted ACM to report gain from the sale over the entire six-year period based on the amount received each year less a ratable (one-sixth) recovery of its basis in the Citicorp notes. See Temp. Reg. § 15A.453-1(c)(3)(i). Accordingly, in the year of the sale, ACM reported gain of about $111 million, which equaled the $140 million in cash received less $29 million (one-sixth of its roughly $175 million basis in the Citicorp notes sold). This gain was allocated

proportionately to the partners, including about $91.5 million to the foreign bank and $19 million to Colgate. The foreign bank was not subject to U.S. tax on its share of the gain. Following the reporting of this gain, ACM's basis in the LIBOR notes (worth about $35 million) was about $146 million ($175 million basis in Citicorp notes sold less $29 million basis recovered in year of sale).

4. During the next two years, ACM used its cash to purchase long-term, fixed-rate Colgate debt. The claimed purpose was to rebalance Colgate's outstanding debt profile which had become heavily weighted with long-term, fixed-rate obligations, thereby making Colgate vulnerable to an anticipated drop in interest rates. If interest rates fell, Colgate's return from its short-term deposits would decline yet it would still owe the above-market interest payments on its outstanding long-term, fixed-rate debt. According to Colgate, ACM's purchase of some of this debt enabled Colgate to reap part of the benefit of earning the above-market interest payments, thereby offsetting some of Colgate's burden as a debtor on these obligations. Colgate did not simply retire a portion of its fixed-rate debt because it wanted to remain highly leveraged to avoid becoming an attractive target for a hostile takeover. Because ACM was a partnership not controlled by Colgate, ACM's assets, including its purchase of the Colgate debt, did not have to be included in Colgate's financial statements.
5. In late 1991, ACM completely liquidated the partnership interest held by the foreign bank, so that Colgate and Merrill Lynch increased their percentage interests in ACM to approximately 99 percent and one percent, respectively. Thereafter, ACM sold its remaining LIBOR notes, producing a substantial capital loss allocated to Colgate and Merrill Lynch in proportion to their percentage interests. Colgate used its portion of the loss to offset its gain from the sale of its subsidiary as well as its share of ACM's gain in 1989 from sale of the Citicorp notes. The total net loss claimed by Colgate as a result of its involvement in ACM was almost $100 million. The Commissioner disallowed the loss claimed by Colgate and his position was upheld by the Tax Court. The Third Circuit's opinion on appeal follows.

ACM Partnership v. Commissioner

157 F.3d 231 (3d Cir. 1998), aff'g 73 T.C.M. 2189 (1997)

Greenberg, Cir. J.: . . . We must decide whether the Tax Court erred in disallowing ACM's claimed . . . capital gain in 1989 and its . . . capital loss [in 1991] which the court characterized as a "phantom loss from a transaction that lacks economic substance." . . . The inquiry into whether the taxpayer's transactions had sufficient economic substance to be respected for tax purposes turns on both the "objective economic substance of the transactions" and the "subjective business motivation" behind them. . . . For the reasons that follow, we find that both the objective analysis of the actual economic consequences of ACM's transactions and the subjective analysis of their intended purposes support the Tax Court's conclusion that ACM's transactions did not have sufficient economic substance to be respected for tax purposes. . . .

2. Objective Economic Consequences of ACM's Transactions

. . . [The Tax Court's] findings . . . demonstrate a lack of objective economic consequences arising from ACM's offsetting acquisition and virtually immediate disposition of the Citicorp notes. On November 3, 1989, ACM invested $175 million of its cash in private placement Citicorp notes paying just three basis points more than the cash was earning on deposit, then sold the same notes 24 days later for consideration equal to their purchase price, in a transaction whose terms had been finalized by November 10, 1989, one week after ACM acquired the notes. These transactions, which generated the disputed capital losses by triggering the application of the ratable basis recovery rule, offset one another with no net effect on ACM's financial position. . . . Viewed according to their objective economic effects rather than their form, ACM's transactions involved only a fleeting and economically inconsequential investment in and offsetting divestment from the Citicorp notes. . . . [W]e find that ACM's intervening acquisition and disposition of the Citicorp notes was a mere device to create the appearance of a contingent installment sale despite the transaction's actual character as an investment of $35 million in cash into a roughly equivalent amount of LIBOR notes. Thus, the acquisition and disposition of the qualifying private placement Citicorp notes . . . had no effect on ACM's net economic position or nontax business interests and thus, as the Tax Court properly found, did not constitute an economically substantive transaction that may be respected for tax purposes.

ACM contends that the Tax Court was bound to respect the tax consequences of ACM's exchange of Citicorp notes for LIBOR notes because, under *Cottage Sav. Ass'n v. Commissioner*, 499 U.S. 554 (1991), an exchange of property for "materially different" assets is a substantive disposition whose tax effects must be recognized. We find *Cottage Savings* inapposite. The taxpayer in that case, a savings and loan association, owned fixed-rate mortgages whose value had declined as interest rates had risen during the preceding decade. The taxpayer simultaneously sold those mortgages and purchased other mortgages which were approximately equal in fair market value, but far lower in face value, than the mortgages which the taxpayer relinquished. The Court found that the exchange for different mortgages of equivalent value afforded the taxpayer "legally distinct entitlements," and thus was a substantive disposition which entitled the taxpayer to deduct its losses resulting from the decline in value of the mortgages during the time that the taxpayer held them.

The distinctions between the exchange at issue in this case and the exchange before the Court in *Cottage Savings* predominate over any superficial similarities between the two transactions. The taxpayer in *Cottage Savings* had an economically substantive investment in assets which it had acquired a number of years earlier in the course of its ordinary business operations and which had declined in actual economic value by over $2 million from approximately $6.9 million to approximately $4.5 million from the time of acquisition to the time of disposition. The taxpayer's relinquishment of assets so altered in actual economic value over the course of a long-term investment stands in stark contrast to ACM's relinquishment of assets that it had acquired 24 days earlier under circumstances which assured that their principal value would remain constant and that their interest payments would not vary materially from those generated by ACM's cash deposits.

. . . [T]he disposition in *Cottage Savings* precipitated the realization of actual economic losses arising from a long-term, economically significant investment, while the disposition in this case was without economic effect as it merely terminated a fleeting and economically inconsequential investment, effectively returning ACM to the same economic position it had occupied before the notes' acquisition 24 days earlier. . . . Tax losses such as [involved in this case], which are purely an artifact of tax accounting methods and which do not correspond to any actual economic losses, do not constitute the type of "bona fide" losses that are deductible under the Internal Revenue Code and regulations. . . . In order to be deductible, a loss must reflect actual economic consequences sustained in an economically substantive transaction and cannot result solely from the application of a tax accounting rule to bifurcate a loss component of a transaction from its offsetting gain component to generate an artificial loss which, as the Tax Court found, is "not economically inherent in" the transaction. Based on our review of the record regarding the objective economic consequences of ACM's short-swing, offsetting investment in and divestment from the Citicorp notes, we find ample support for the Tax Court's determination that ACM's transactions generated only "phantom losses" which cannot form the basis of a capital loss deduction under the Internal Revenue Code.

3. Subjective Aspects of the Economic Sham Analysis

In making its determination that it did "not find any economic substance" in ACM's transactions, the Tax Court relied extensively on evidence that the transactions were not intended to serve any "useful nontax purpose" and were not reasonably expected to generate a pre-tax profit. . . . [W]e turn to the question of whether the court erred. . . .

4. Intended Purposes and Anticipated Profitability of ACM's Transactions

Before the Tax Court, ACM conceded that there were tax objectives behind its transactions but contended that "tax-independent considerations informed and justified each step of the strategy." ACM asserted that its transactions, in addition to presenting "a realistic prospect that ACM would have made a profit" on a pre-tax basis, also served the tax-independent purposes of providing an interim investment until ACM needed its cash to acquire Colgate debt and a hedge against interest rate risk within the partnership. . . .

a. Interim Investment

ACM contends that it invested in the Citicorp notes . . . because they served as an appropriate interim investment until ACM could invest in the Colgate debt whose acquisition, according to ACM, was a central objective of the partnership. The Tax Court, however, rejected this contention on the grounds that ACM did not acquire the Citicorp notes as an interim investment "to accommodate the timing of the acquisition of Colgate debt; rather, it was the reverse: The acquisition of the Colgate debt was timed so as to accommodate the requirements of the [CINS] strategy" which required ACM to acquire and dispose of private placement notes. This conclusion finds abundant support in the record. . . . [W]e agree with the Tax Court's finding that any delay preceding the opportunity to acquire Colgate debt was of ACM's own deliberate making and was intended so that ACM could engage in the tax-motivated acquisition and disposition of qualifying short-term notes in the contingent installment sale that had been contemplated since before Merrill Lynch and Colgate devised the concept of incorporating debt acquisition objectives into Merrill Lynch's initial tax reduction proposal.

Even if ACM had faced a delay before it could purchase Colgate debt and thus needed to locate a suitable interim investment, the Citicorp notes ill served the professed purpose of holding cash assets in anticipation of an impending purchase. The notes, which in order to qualify for treatment in a contingent installment sale could not be traded on an established market, see I.R.C. § 453(k)(2)(A), were highly illiquid and thus could not be converted back into the cash needed to purchase Colgate debt without significant transaction costs in the form of the bid-ask spread which Merrill Lynch deemed necessary to market the notes to third parties. These transaction costs rendered the illiquid Citicorp notes paying 8.78% significantly less advantageous as an interim investment than the fully liquid cash deposit account paying 8.75%. Accordingly, we find no error in the Tax Court's conclusion that ACM's brief investment in the Citicorp notes was motivated by the pursuit of the tax advantages of a contingent installment sale rather than by a need for an interim investment pending its acquisition of Colgate debt.

b. Hedge Against Interest Rate Risk

The Tax Court also rejected ACM's contention that it invested in LIBOR notes . . . because they were an appropriate hedge against the interest rate exposure brought about by ACM's investment in Colgate debt issues. . . . While the acquisition of Colgate debt furthered this professed goal of decreasing the exposure associated with Colgate's fixed rate long term debt structure outside of the partnership, the acquisition of the LIBOR notes, whose value would decline as interest rates declined, conversely increased ACM's exposure to falling interest rates, offsetting the desired effect of the debt acquisition program which purportedly was a fundamental partnership objective. Accordingly, the LIBOR notes, by hedging against the Colgate debt issues acquired within the partnership, negated the potential benefit of ACM's acquisition of these issues as a hedge against Colgate's interest rate exposure outside the partnership. . . . [W]e find no error in the Tax Court's determination. . . .

c. Anticipated Profitability

. . . [T]he Tax Court also rejected ACM's contention that its transactions were reasonably expected to yield a pre-tax profit because the court found ACM had planned and executed its transactions without regard to their pre-tax economic consequences. The evidence in the record overwhelmingly supports this conclusion. The documents outlining the proposed transactions, while quite detailed in their explication of expected tax consequences, are devoid of such detailed projections as to the expected rate of return on the private placement notes and contingent payment notes that were essential components of each proposal.

Moreover, ACM's partners were aware before they entered the partnership that the planned sequence of investments would entail over $3 million in transaction costs. Yet Colgate, which effectively bore virtually all of these costs pursuant to the terms of the partnership agreement, did not attempt to assess whether the transactions would be profitable after accounting for these significant transaction costs. Furthermore, while ACM planned to dispose of the Citicorp notes after a brief holding period for an amount equal to their purchase price, its proposed transactions contemplated holding for two years the LIBOR notes whose principal value would decline in the event of the falling interest rates which ACM's partners predicted.

Thus, while the Citicorp note investment which was essential to structuring the transaction as a contingent installment sale was economically inconsequential, the LIBOR note investment which was equally essential to achieving the desired tax structure was economically disadvantageous under the market conditions which Colgate predicted and which actually transpired. ACM's lack of regard for the relative costs and benefits of the contemplated transaction and its failure to conduct a contemporaneous profitability analysis support the Tax Court's conclusion that ACM's transactions were not designed or reasonably anticipated to yield a pre-tax profit. . . .

Because ACM's acquisition and disposition of the Citicorp notes in a contingent installment exchange was without objective effect on ACM's net economic position or nontax objectives, and because its investments in the Citicorp notes and LIBOR notes did not rationally serve ACM's professed nontax objectives or afford ACM or its partners a reasonable prospect for pre-tax profit, we will affirm the Tax Court's determination that the contingent installment exchange transactions lacked economic substance and its resulting decision providing that the capital gain and loss at issue will not be recognized and thus disallowing deductions arising from the application of the contingent installment sale provisions and the ratable basis recovery rule. . . .

McKee, Cir. J., dissenting: By finding that ACM's sales of the Citicorp notes for cash and LIBOR Notes "satisfied each requirement of the contingent installment sales provisions and the ratable basis recovery rule," yet, simultaneously subjecting these transactions to an economic substance and sham transaction analysis, the majority has ignored the plain language of IRC § 1001, and controlling Supreme Court precedent. We have injected the "economic substance" analysis into an inquiry where it does not belong. Therefore, I respectfully dissent.

. . . Here, the sales of the Citicorp Notes for cash and LIBOR Notes were clearly "legitimate" sales in the nontax sense. Under IRC § 1001, the tax consequences of a gain or loss in the value of property are deferred until the taxpayer realizes the gain or loss. The concept of "realization" is implicit in IRC § 1001(a), and the realized gain is recognized when the property is sold or exchanged. IRC § 1001(c). In *Cottage Savings*, the Court held that a sale or exchange of property is a realization event "so long as the exchanged properties are 'materially different' — that is, so long as they embody legally distinct entitlements." . . . ACM's sales of the Citicorp Notes for cash and LIBOR Notes resulted in the exchange of materially different property. I believe our inquiry should proceed no further, and reverse the holding of the Tax Court. . . .

I can't help but suspect that the majority's conclusion to the contrary is, in its essence, something akin to a "smell test." If the scheme in question smells bad, the intent to avoid taxes defines the result as we do not want the taxpayer to "put one over." However, the issue clearly is not whether ACM put one over on the Commissioner, or used LIBOR notes to "pull the wool over his eyes." The issue is whether what ACM did qualifies for the tax treatment it seeks under § 1001. The fact that ACM may have "put one over" in crafting these transactions ought not to influence our inquiry. Our inquiry is cerebral, not visceral. To the extent that the Commissioner is offended by these transactions he should address Congress and/or the rulemaking process, and not the courts.[1] . . .

NOTES

1. *The meaning of the "economic substance" doctrine.* In *ACM*, the Third Circuit refused to give tax effect to the transactions undertaken by the partnership because they lacked "economic substance." The underlying transaction antedated both codification of the doctrine in section 7701(o) (discussed in part C) and promulgation of

---

1. . . . [T]he Commissioner apparently realized the possible "loophole" in the regulations and enacted Treas. Reg. § 1.701-2(a) in an apparent effort to curb such tax driven transactions as the ones here.

the partnership anti-abuse regulation. As we shall see, one reason for codification of the doctrine was to clarify its meaning, given slightly differing judicial interpretations. As discussed in the case excerpt, the common-law doctrine generally involved both an "objective" inquiry — does a transaction have a sufficient nontax economic effect? — and a "subjective" inquiry — does a transaction have an adequate business purpose apart from the avoidance of taxes? Courts differed, however, regarding whether both inquiries — or only one — had to be answered in the affirmative in order for a transaction to be respected for tax purposes. In *ACM*, the Third Circuit took essentially a middle ground when it stated that the two inquiries

> do not constitute discrete prongs of a "rigid two-step analysis," but rather represent related factors both of which inform the analysis of whether the transaction had sufficient substance, apart from its tax consequences, to be respected for tax purposes. [157 F.3d at 247.]

The court further tried to distinguish the economic substance inquiry from the question of taxpayer motivation. It noted that if the "transaction [had] objectively affect[ed] the taxpayer's net economic position, legal relations, or nontax business interests, it [would not have been] disregarded merely because it was motivated by tax considerations." Id. at 248 n.31.

2. Cottage Savings. In Cottage Savings Ass'n v. Comm'r, 499 U.S. 554 (1991), a bank exchanged one group of mortgages for another in order to recognize a tax loss in the mortgages surrendered. The exchange was economically so insignificant that the overseeing federal regulatory agency did not require the bank to recognize the loss for financial accounting purposes. Nevertheless, the Supreme Court respected the bank's loss for tax purposes, finding that even a very minor change in a taxpayer's position constitutes a realization event. Does the majority opinion in *ACM* adequately distinguish *Cottage Savings*?

3. *What losses are deductible?* Suppose the foreign bank in *ACM* had been a domestic bank fully subject to U.S. tax. Or suppose the foreign bank had never been a partner at all, and that the only two partners throughout each of the transactions undertaken by the partnership were Colgate and Merrill Lynch. In either of those situations, would ACM's loss upon sale of the LIBOR notes have been respected for tax purposes? Bear in mind the Third Circuit's admonition that

> [i]n order to be deductible, a loss must reflect actual economic consequences sustained in an economically substantive transaction and cannot result solely from the application of a tax accounting rule to bifurcate a loss component of a transaction from its offsetting gain component to generate an artificial loss. . . .

4. *Subsequent cases.* As noted in chapter one, the government has prevailed in several other cases involving the tax consequences of the same CINS transaction. In these cases, all decided by the D.C. Circuit, the court disregarded for tax purposes the purported partnership arrangement itself (rather than merely the transaction

undertaken by the partnership) because of the absence of any business purpose for the arrangement apart from tax avoidance. See ASA Investerings Partnership v. Comm'r, 210 F.3d 505 (D.C. Cir.), cert. denied, 531 U.S. 871 (2000), Saba Partnership v. Comm'r, 273 F.3d 1135 (D.C. Cir. 2001), and Boca Investerings Partnership v. U.S., 314 F.3d 625 (D.C. Cir.), cert. denied, 540 U.S. 826 (2003).

Problem 12-1: Read Reg. § 1.701-2(d) (ex. 7), which is modeled on the CINS transaction. Based on that example, verify that the partners would have the following capital accounts and outside bases following the distribution to X and the allocation of the loss to Y and Z. Steps 7 and 8 are included in the example simply to make sure Y and Z have enough outside basis to claim the loss allocated to them. Under current law, consider the application of section 734(b) and (d). Would a mandatory inside basis adjustment eliminate any tax benefit to Y and Z, without the uncertain application of the economic substance, business purpose, or sham transaction doctrines or the partnership anti-abuse regulation?

	X			*Y*			*Z*		
	Tax	*Book*	*OB*	*Tax*	*Book*	*OB*	*Tax*	*Book*	*OB*
1. initial contributions	9,000	9,000	9,000	990	990	990	10	10	10
2. income from sale of leasehold interest	8,100	8,100	8,100	891	891	891	9	9	9
3. revaluation prior to liquidation of X	-0-	(8,100)	-0-	-0-	(891)	-0-	-0-	(9)	-0-
4. balance prior to liquidation of X	17,100	9,000	17,100	1,881	990	1,881	19	10	19
5. liquidation of X for $9,000	(9,000)	(9,000)	(9,000)						
6. tax loss to X from liquidation			(8,100)						
7. partnership borrows $8,000						7,920			80
8. balance after borrowing				1,881	990	9,801	19	10	99
9. loss from sale of equipment				(8,910)		(8,910)	(90)		(90)
10. balance after sale				(7,029)	990	891	(71)	10	9

B. The Partnership Anti-Abuse Regulation

1. *Transactions Inconsistent with the Intent of Subchapter K*

The first part of the anti-abuse regulation deals with transactions that are inconsistent with the intent of subchapter K. Read Reg. § 1.701-2(b), which contains the general rule. This provision authorizes the Commissioner to recast a partnership transaction for tax purposes if two conditions are satisfied:

(1) a principal purpose of the transaction is "to reduce substantially the present value of the partners' aggregate federal tax liability"; and
(2) the tax savings is accomplished "in a manner that is inconsistent with the intent of subchapter K."

If these two conditions are met, the Commissioner has broad authority to modify the tax consequences of the transaction. A transaction may be recast even though it complies with the literal words of a particular statutory or regulatory provision.

The potential breadth of this general rule is apparent from the fact that much partnership tax planning involves minimizing the partners' tax liabilities. Thus, the critical question in many cases is whether any tax savings achieved is "inconsistent with the intent of subchapter K." Read Reg. § 1.701-2(a) and (c) which together provide some guidance regarding the meaning of this phrase. According to the first provision, the intent of subchapter K is to facilitate joint business activities through a flexible economic arrangement without incurring an entity-level tax. General principles, largely of common-law origin, are "implicit in the intent of subchapter K." The partnership must be bona fide, each partnership transaction must have a substantial business purpose and be respected under substance-over-form principles, and the tax consequences of each transaction must be consistent with its underlying economics and clearly reflect each partner's income. The provision clarifies that the clear reflection of income requirement is not violated simply as a result of tax consequences clearly contemplated by partnership rules adopted for administrative convenience and other reasons, such as the value-equals-basis rule or the elective nature of section 754.

Regulation § 1.701-2(c) explains that application of the anti-abuse rule to a particular transaction depends upon all of the facts and circumstances, including a comparison of the purported business purpose of the transaction and its claimed tax benefits. The provision sets forth seven non-exclusive factors that may indicate that a principal purpose of the transaction is to reduce taxes in the prohibited manner. Most of the factors listed are fairly general and do not clearly differentiate between permissible and impermissible tax reduction arrangements. One specific factor, perhaps included with the *ACM* transaction in mind, indicates that special scrutiny will be paid to partnerships that specially allocate income or gain to partners that may be legally or effectively exempt from U.S. taxation.

Finally, Reg. § 1.701-2(d) includes a series of examples illustrating the general rule. The utility of these examples is, unfortunately, limited due in part to changes in the underlying substantive law since promulgation of the regulation. For example, the anti-abuse rules apply a facts-and-circumstances test to determine when the tax consequences flowing from the absence of a section 754 election violate the "proper-reflection-of-income" test. Compare Reg. § 1.701-2(d) (ex. 8) (absence of section

754 election deemed abusive because the partnership was formed for the purpose of duplicating a built-in loss inherent in contributed property) with id. (ex. 9) (absence of section 754 election was nonabusive because the partnership was formed for a bona fide business purpose and the ultimate tax consequences were clearly contemplated under subchapter K). These examples do not reflect recent amendments to sections 704(c), 734 and 743 targeting duplication of loss. Because of these statutory amendments, there should be less need to invoke the anti-abuse rules to prevent duplication of loss (and less reason for taxpayers to structure such abusive transactions in the first place).

In addition, the anti-abuse examples are highly fact-specific and do not contain much careful analysis. To illustrate, in example 5, two corporations formed a partnership to invest in the stock of a third corporation. The nontax economic objective of one of the investing corporations was to obtain a return on its investment based on the LIBOR, i.e., an interest-rate return. By investing through the partnership, the corporation claimed that its investment return constituted dividend income that was largely tax free due to the dividends-received deduction. Had the corporation invested instead in a debt instrument paying interest equal to the LIBOR, the corporation would not have been entitled to a dividends-received deduction. The example concludes that the claimed treatment will be respected for tax purposes but, unfortunately, offers little analysis to explain this conclusion.

The following case involves a mass-marketed tax shelter that the IRS targeted in Notice 2000-44 (p. 115). Partly as a weapon against the offsetting-option shelter at issue here, the IRS revised regulations under section 752 clarifying the definition of the term "liability." See chapters four and six. As you read the case, consider the outcome under the anti-abuse rule if the government had lost its argument concerning the retroactive force of the revised regulations under section 752.

Cemco Investors, LLC v. United States

515 F.3d 749 (7th Cir.), cert. denied, 555 U.S. 823 (2008)

EASTERBROOK, Chief Judge: [Cemco Investors, LLC (Cemco) was one of three entities involved in the underlying transactions that occurred in December, 2000. The other two entities were a grantor trust, Cemco Investors Trust (Trust), and a general partnership, Cemco Investment Partners (Partnership). Both Cemco and Partnership had only two partners, an individual investor (Steven Kaplan) and a shell company (Forest Chartered Holdings, Ltd.) owned by the tax lawyer (Paul Daugerdas) who designed the tax shelter. Trust's only beneficiaries were Kaplan and the shell company, and its trustee was Daugerdas. Working with Deutsche Bank (Bank), the Trust simultaneously purchased from the Bank a long option (the "long" or "purchased" option) and sold to the Bank a short option (the "short" or "sold" option) involving foreign currency. The options had virtually identical terms so that except for a minute chance that the Trust would be entitled to receive a large payoff ($7.2 million) if the euro was trading within a very narrow price range on a particular future date, the obligations of the Bank to the Trust and the Trust back to the Bank would be offsetting. The options eventually did offset and expired unexercised, and the only money that actually changed hands was $36,000 (paid by the Trust to the Bank), the difference between the premiums for the two options. The Bank refunded $30,000 to the Trust when the options expired.

The tax shelter was designed to produce an inflated basis and a corresponding loss of $3.6 million for the benefit of Kaplan and Daugerdas, based on an aggressive interpretation of case law and the pre-2003 version of the section 752 regulations. The shelter consisted of several prearranged steps: (1) the Trust contributed the paired options to the Partnership along with $50,000 cash (which the Partnership used to buy $50,000 worth of euros), and claimed a basis in its partnership interest of $3.6 million (the premium allegedly paid for the purchased option unreduced by the corresponding obligation under the sold option); (2) after the options expired unexercised, the Partnership liquidated and distributed its assets (the $50,000 worth of euros) to the Trust, which claimed a $3.6 million basis in the distributed assets; (3) the Trust contributed the inflated-basis euros to Cemco, which claimed the same basis in the euros as their basis in the Trust's hands; and (4) Cemco sold the euros for $50,000 and claimed a $3.6 million loss, which passed through to Daugerdas and Kaplan.]

Paul M. Daugerdas, a tax lawyer whose opinion letters while at Jenkins & Gilchrist led to the firm's demise (it had to pay more than $75 million in penalties on account of his work), designed a tax shelter for himself, with one client owning a 37% share. Like many tax shelters it was complex in detail but simple in principle, and to facilitate exposition we cover only its basics, rounding all figures. . . .

One would think . . . that the Trust (and the Partnership as its assignee) suffered a loss of $6,000 — the net premium paid for options that cancelled each other out and hence lacked value on the exercise date — while Cemco had neither profit nor loss. Yet Cemco filed a tax return for 2000 showing a loss of $3.6 million! Its theory was that the Partnership's euros (later contributed to Cemco) had the same $3.6 million basis as the long option, and that a loss could be recognized once the euros had been sold. Cemco passed the loss to Daugerdas and his client, who reported it on their tax returns. What of the $3.6 million [rounded] that Deutsche Bank "paid" the Trust for the short option, which almost exactly offset the long option? Well, Cemco took the view that this stayed with the Trust — and would never be taxed *to* the Trust, which, after all, had a net loss of $6,000 — or if assumed by Cemco may be ignored because the options offset in the end. The purchase and sale of euros was the device used to transfer the basis of one option to Cemco while consigning the other option to oblivion.

A transaction with an out-of-pocket cost of $6,000 and no risk beyond that expense, while generating a tax loss of $3.6 million, is the sort of thing that the Internal Revenue Service frowns on. The deal as a whole seems to lack economic substance; if it has any substance (a few thousand dollars paid to purchase a slight chance of a big payoff) then the $3.6 million "gain" on one premium should be paired with the $3.6 million "loss" on the other; and at all events the deal's nature ($36,000 paid for a slim chance to receive $7.2 million) is not accurately reflected by treating [the euros] as having a basis of $3.6 million. The IRS sent Cemco a Notice of Final Partnership Administrative Adjustment [FPAA] disallowing the loss and assessing a 40% penalty for Cemco's grossly incorrect return. In the ensuing litigation, the district court sided with the IRS. . . .

Cemco says that in treating $50,000 of euros as having a $3.6 million basis, which turned into a loss when the euros were sold for exactly what they had been worth all along, it was just relying on *Helmer v. CIR*, T.C. Memo 1975-160, 34 T.C.M. 727 (1975), and a few similar decisions. That may or may not be the right way to understand *Helmer*; we need not decide, for it is not controlling in this court — or anywhere else. The Commissioner has a statutory power to disregard transactions that lack economic substance. Compare *Gregory v. Helvering*, 293 U.S. 465 (1935), with *Frank Lyon Co. v. United States*, 435 U.S. 561 (1978). And the IRS has considerable latitude in issuing regulations that specify [the] sorts of transactions that may be looked through. (These regulations avoid the need to litigate, one tax shelter at a time, whether any real economic transaction is inside the box.) A few months before Daugerdas set up this tax shelter, the IRS had issued Notice 2000-44, 2000-2 C.B. 255, alerting taxpayers to its view that *Helmer* could not be relied on, that purported losses from transactions that assigned artificially high basis to partnership assets would be disallowed, and that formal regulations to this effect were on their way. One of the transactions covered in Notice 2000-44 is the offsetting-option device.

Getting from a warning to a regulation often takes years, however, and did so here. Treasury Regulation § 1.752-6 was issued in temporary form in 2003. . . . Two more years passed before the temporary regulation was made permanent. . . . This sets the stage for Cemco's principal argument. It concedes that Notice 2000-44 and Treas. Reg. § 1.752-6 scupper the entire class of offsetting-option tax shelters. The regulation does this by subtracting, from the partnership's basis in an asset, the value of any corresponding liability. Thus if Cemco's basis in the euros comes from the premium for one option, then the premium for the offsetting option must be subtracted. That gets the basis back to roughly $50,000 (the value of the euros) +$6,000 (the difference in the premiums). But as Cemco sees things the notice lacks legal effect, while the regulation cannot be applied retroactively. One district court has held that Treas. Reg. § 1.752-6 does not affect transactions that predate it. *Klamath Strategic Investment Fund, LLC v. United States*, 440 F. Supp. 2d 608 (E.D. Tex. 2006). We disagree with that conclusion.

The regulation could not be more explicit: "This section applies to assumptions of liabilities occurring after October 18, 1999, and before June 24, 2003." Treas. Reg. § 1.752-6(d)(1). (Transactions after June 23, 2003, are governed by the more elaborate 26 C.F.R. § 1.752-7.) Why October 18, 1999? Because, although regulations generally do not apply to transactions that occur before the initial publication date of a draft regulation, see 26 U.S.C. § 7805(b)(1)(C), the norm of prospective application "may be superseded by a legislative grant from Congress authorizing the

Secretary to prescribe the effective date with respect to any regulation." 26 U.S.C. § 7805(b)(6). Section 309 of the Community Renewal Tax Relief Act of 2000, Pub. L. 106-554, 114 Stat. 2763A-587, 638 (2000), enacts basis-reduction rules for many transactions and authorizes the IRS to adopt regulations prescribing similar rules for partnerships and S corporations. Section 309(d)(2) of the 2000 Act adds that these regulations may be retroactive to October 18, 1999. That's the power the Commissioner used when promulgating Treas. Reg. § 1.752-6.

The district court in *Klamath* did not doubt that retroactivity *could* rest on the 2000 Act; Treas. Reg. § 1.752-6 applies to partnerships (and LLCs treated as partnerships) a rule "similar" to the approach that Congress adopted for other business entities. *Klamath* held, however, that when promulgating Treas. Reg. § 1.752-6 the IRS had not availed itself of that power. But if the IRS was not using that authority, why in the world does the regulation reach back to October 18, 1999? Retroactivity requires justification; to make a rule retroactive is to invoke one of the available justifications; and the choice of date tells us that the justification is the one supplied by the 2000 Act (in conjunction with § 7805(b)(6)). A regulation's legal effect does not depend on reiterating the obvious. So Treas. Reg. § 1.752-6 applies to this deal and prevents Cemco's investors from claiming a loss. Cemco is scarcely in a position to complain — not only because this tax shelter was constructed after the warning in Notice 2000-44, but also because all the regulation does is instantiate the pre-existing norm that transactions with no economic substance don't reduce people's taxes. See *Coltec Industries, Inc. v. United States*, 454 F.3d 1340 (Fed. Cir. 2006). . . .

AFFIRMED.

NOTES AND QUESTIONS

1. *The "economic substance" doctrine.* In *Cemco*, the court notes that the transaction "as a whole seems to lack economic substance" and that the 2003 temporary regulations merely "instantiate the pre-existing norm" that transactions lacking economic substance will not be respected. Although *Cemco* was decided on other grounds, another court found that a similar offsetting-option shelter lacked economic substance and disallowed the claimed losses on that ground. See Jade Trading, LLC v. U.S., 80 Fed. Cl. 11 (2007), aff'd on this issue, 598 F.3d 1372 (Fed. Cir. 2010). There, the court found that:

> In sum, this transaction's fictional loss, inability to realize a profit, lack of investment character, meaningless inclusion in a partnership, and disproportionate tax advantage compared to the amount invested and potential return, compel a conclusion that the spread transaction objectively lacked economic substance. [Id. at 14.]

Although in *Cemco*, the Trust had a slight chance of a large payoff, what was its economic downside under the option sold to the Bank?

2. *The partnership anti-abuse rule.* Since use of the partnership form was essential to claim an inflated basis in the euros, could the government have denied the purported losses on the ground that the Partnership and Cemco should be disregarded under the anti-abuse rule? When should a court apply the partnership anti-abuse rule rather than the codified economic substance doctrine?

3. *Administrative procedure and penalties.* In *Cemco*, the court rejected the taxpayer's claim that the IRS's proposed tax adjustment should have been issued to the Partnership and not to Cemco. According to the court, it was both proper and sensible to issue the adjustment to Cemco, since "Cemco's return is what matters to what real taxpayers owe." 515 F.3d at 753.

The government also successfully imposed the 40 percent penalty applicable to the portion of a tax underpayment "attributable to one or more gross valuation misstatements." I.R.C. § 6662(h)(1). According to the government, the grossly excessive basis in the euros qualified as such a misstatement. The taxpayer argued unsuccessfully that the penalty was inapplicable because there was no valuation dispute, but rather only a legal issue concerning whether the sold option had to be taken into account as a liability.

In Woods v. U.S., 134 S. Ct. 557 (2013), the Supreme Court addressed a split in the Circuits concerning the meaning of the phrase "attributable to" for purposes of the 40 percent penalty for gross valuation misstatements. It rejected the position of the Fifth and Ninth Circuits that the penalty does not apply if there is an independent cause (such as lack of economic substance) for an underpayment in addition to the gross valuation misstatement. See Bemont Invs., LLC v. U.S., 679 F.3d 339 (5th Cir. 2012); Keller v. Comm'r, 556 F.3d 1056 (9th Cir. 2009). Other Circuits had upheld the 40 percent penalty even if a valuation misstatement was only one of multiple reasons for an underpayment. See Fidelity Int'l Currency Advisor A Fund, LLC v. U.S., 661 F.3d 667 (1st Cir. 2011); Alpha I L.P. v. U.S., 682 F.3d 1009 (Fed Cir. 2012) (same). In *Woods*, the Supreme Court "had no difficulty concluding that any underpayment resulting from [the partners'] tax shelter [was] attributable to the partners' misrepresentation of outside basis (a 'valuation' misstatement)." *Woods*, 134 S. Ct. at 568. According to the Supreme Court:

> The economic-substance determination and the basis misstatement are not "independent" of one another. This is not a case where a valuation misstatement is a mere side effect of a sham transaction. Rather, the overstatement of basis was the linchpin of the [tax shelter] transaction and the mechanism by which [the taxpayers] sought to reduce their taxable income. [Id. at 567.]

Since the partnership was disregarded as a sham, the partners were precluded as a matter of law from establishing any outside basis in their purported partnership interests. To the extent the partners claimed an outside basis greater than zero to generate the disallowed loss, the resulting underpayment was necessarily attributable to a basis overstatement that would automatically be considered gross for purposes of the 40 percent penalty. See I.R.C. § 6662(e)(1) and (h); Reg. § 1.6662-5(g).

In *Woods*, the Supreme Court also resolved an important jurisdictional issue concerning partnership-level penalty determinations under the TEFRA rules (discussed at p. 409).

4. *Statute of limitations.* In U.S. v. Home Concrete & Supply, LLC, 132 S. Ct. 1836 (2012), the Supreme Court handed a victory to tax shelter participants on statute-of-limitations grounds. Relying on Colony, Inc. v. Comm'r, 357 U.S. 28 (1958), taxpayers claimed that an overstated basis resulting from contingent liability shelters did not constitute a substantial omission of gross income that triggered the extended six-year statute of limitations. I.R.C. § 6501(a) and (e)(1)(A). After losing several cases on this question, the government issued regulations affirming its litigating position, and the Supreme Court intervened. In a 5-4 decision, the Supreme Court concluded that *Colony* was controlling and the contrary regulations were invalid. In 2015, Congress reversed the holding of the Court in *Home Concrete.* I.R.C. § 6501(e)(1)(B)(ii) (after 2015 amendment).

In 2004, Congress added a new provision (section 6501(a)(10)) applicable to taxpayers that fail to disclose a "listed transaction." The provision extends the statute of limitations prospectively until one year after the earlier of the date on which the taxpayer or a material advisor discloses the relevant information. Should it make any difference that many taxpayers in these tax shelter transactions used aggressive strategies to disguise the offsetting gains and losses on their returns? Should courts accord less deferential treatment to "fighting" regulations intended to influence the outcome of litigation?

2. *The Abuse of Entity Rule*

Read Reg. § 1.701-2(e). The other aspect of the anti-abuse regulation authorizes the Commissioner to treat a partnership as an aggregate of its partners for purposes of a tax provision outside of subchapter K unless entity treatment of the partnership is clearly contemplated by that provision. Application of this rule does not turn on the presence or absence of a tax avoidance purpose. While this rule was promulgated largely in response to the following controversy involving the interplay of subchapter K with the subpart F provisions of international taxation, similar issues may arise in many different contexts.

Under current law, U.S. corporations are taxed by the U.S. on their worldwide income. In contrast, a foreign corporation with insufficient contacts in the U.S. is not taxed by the U.S. on its business income. The combination of these two rules has long provided U.S. corporations with a tax incentive to conduct their business activities outside the U.S. through a foreign subsidiary organized in a country that imposes little or no income tax. In general, subpart F of the U.S. tax law eliminates the tax advantage if the subsidiary is classified as a "controlled foreign corporation" (CFC) (meaning that it is controlled by certain U.S. shareholders) and the subsidiary's income is considered "subpart F income" (representing certain types of income for which deferral of U.S. taxation is not permitted). In that situation, the

CFC is essentially treated as if it were a conduit for tax purposes, with its controlling U.S. shareholders being taxed currently on the subpart F income of the CFC. With this background, read the following case.

Brown Group, Inc. v. Commissioner

77 F.3d 217 (8th Cir. 1996), rev'g 104 T.C. 105 (1995), nonacq. 1996-2 C.B. 209

GARTH, Senior Circuit Judge: [Brown Group, a U.S. corporation, was the parent of BCL, a Cayman Islands subsidiary and a "controlled foreign corporation." BCL was an 88 percent partner in Brinco, a foreign partnership, which operated in Brazil and purchased Brazilian footwear on behalf of Brown Group for resale in the U.S. Brown Group paid Brinco commissions which Brown Group deducted for U.S. income tax purposes. The commissions were Brinco's only income in 1986, the year in issue. If BCL had earned Brinco's commission income directly, such income would have been "subpart F income" and therefore taxable to Brown Group.]

[Under section 954(d)(1), "subpart F income" includes:]

> Income . . . derived in connection with the purchase of personal property from any person and its sale to [or on behalf of] a *related person*. . . .

. . . Under the version of section 954(d)(3) in effect for the taxable year of 1986, a "related person" is defined as:

> (A) an individual, *partnership*, trust, or estate which *controls* the controlled foreign corporation; or (B) a corporation which *controls*, or is *controlled by*, the controlled foreign corporation; . . .

The present case boils down to a very discrete question of law: whether BCL's distributive share of Brinco's partnership earnings (commissions) constituted "Subpart F income," under section 954(d)(3), given that the commissions did not constitute "Subpart F income" when earned by Brinco. . . .

We hold that the Tax Court erred in ignoring the partnership entity in characterizing BCL's earnings as taxable "Subpart F income." . . .

It is not disputed that under section 954(d)(3), as that statute existed in 1986, Brinco was not a "related person" to [Brown Group] or BCL. Moreover, this conclusion is supported by the plain language of the statute. Brinco is not a corporation. Hence, the only portion of the "related person" definition that could apply to Brinco is that of a "partnership . . . which controls the controlled foreign corporation." 26 U.S.C. § 954(d)(3)(A). However Brinco did not *control* BCL but rather was *controlled by* BCL. Thus, Brinco was not a "related person" to [Brown Group]. . . .

Because Brinco earned its commission income on behalf of an unrelated person, [Brown Group], that income was not [Subpart F income]. Given that partnership income is characterized at the partnership level, the income earned by Brinco retained its character of being not "Subpart F income" when distributed to BCL. Accordingly, [Brown Group], under the pre-1987 version of section 954(d)(3), cannot be assessed income tax on Brinco's partnership earnings which were distributed to BCL.

We find this analysis to be consistent with the well-established principle that income is to be characterized at the partnership level and that such income retains its character when distributed to the individual partners.

. . . The [Supreme] Court in [United States v. Basye, 410 U.S. 441 (1973),] stated that:

> While the partnership itself pays no taxes, 26 U.S.C. § 701, it must report the income it generates and such income must be calculated in largely the same manner as an individual computes his personal income. For this purpose, then, the partnership is regarded as an independently recognizable entity apart from the aggregate of its partners. Once its income is ascertained and reported, its existence may be disregarded since each partner must pay a tax on a portion of the total income as if the partnership were merely an agent or conduit through which the income is passed. [Id. at 448.]

"The legislative history indicates, and the commentators agree, that partnerships are entities for purposes of calculating and filing informational returns but that they are conduits through which the taxpaying obligation passes to the individual partners in accord with their distributive shares." Id. at 448 n.8. . . .

Although our holding may result in a tax windfall to the Brown Group due to the particularized definition of "related person" under the pre-1987 version of section 954(d)(3) of the Internal Revenue Code, such a tax loophole is not ours to close but must rather be closed or cured by Congress. . . . Indeed, Congress has done just that. It closed this loophole the following year, in 1987, when it amended section 954(d)(3) to broaden the definition of "related person" to include not only partnerships that *control* CFC's but also those that *are controlled* by CFC's or their parents.

Furthermore, for transactions occurring on and after December 30, 1994, Congress for the first time has apparently permitted, in special circumstances not relevant here, the recasting of partnership income under Subpart F. Treasury Regulation § 1.701-2 . . . , characterized as the "anti-abuse rule," permitted the IRS to recast partnership transactions that make inappropriate use of Subchapter K rules. In particular § 1.701-2(e) provided that the IRS can treat a partnership as an aggregation of its partners in whole or in part as appropriate to carry out the purpose of any provision of the Code or regulations. However, because section 1.701-2 is effective only for transactions on or after May 12, 1994, and section 1.701-2(e) is effective only for transactions on or after December 29, 1994, those provisions cannot apply to this case. Indeed, as we read the regulations, the IRS does *not* have the power to recast partnership transactions or apply the aggregate approach for transactions occurring prior to these effective dates.

Because the "loophole" in Subpart F taxable income has been closed, the issue that arises in the present case is unlikely to occur again. Under the pre-1987 law applicable to the instant case, however, the Brown Group cannot be held taxable on BCL's distributive share of Brinco's partnership earnings. . . .

NOTES

1. *Case history.* The initial Tax Court decision in this case favored Brown Group and the IRS immediately moved for reconsideration, arguing that the decision had effectively repealed virtually all of subpart F. The court subsequently decided 9-3 in favor of the government, stating:

> Congress chose to minimize (perhaps even eliminate) the entity character of the CFC in order to tax U.S. shareholders as if they had earned directly the subpart F income earned by the CFC. It would be ironic, indeed, if one could defeat the clearly expressed intent of Congress to tax the income from the activities involved here by engaging in those activities [through] a form of doing business that not only is taxed on a conduit basis but whose non-tax-law character often resembles an aggregate of persons doing business together (as mutual agents) rather than an entity. [104 T.C. 105, 114-15 (1995).]

Following the Eighth Circuit's reversal of the second Tax Court decision, the IRS issued Notice 96-39, 1996-2 C.B. 209, which expressed its continuing disagreement with the result in *Brown Group* and announced its intention to issue regulations clarifying the interplay between subpart F and subchapter K. These regulations are briefly described in note 4 below. As previously noted, the *Brown Group* controversy also figured prominently in the promulgation of Reg. § 1.701-2(e).

2. *The IRS's position.* The Eighth Circuit treated *Brown Group* as a relatively simple case. The IRS's counterargument in the case was also quite straightforward. First, given Brown Group's 100 percent ownership of BCL, the IRS considered BCL and Brown Group to be "related persons" within the meaning of section 954(d)(3) (excerpted in the opinion). Thus, had BCL purchased the Brazilian footwear on behalf of Brown Group, any commission income of BCL would have constituted "subpart F income" currently taxable to Brown Group. See section 954(d)(1), pertinent portions of which are also excerpted in the opinion. The question was whether BCL and Brown Group could avoid that consequence simply by having BCL form a partnership to carry out the business activity.

The IRS argued that the subpart F provisions could not be circumvented so easily. The IRS's basic theory is explained in Rev. Rul. 89-72, 1989-1 C.B. 257:

> For purposes of section 954(a) of the Code, the character of an item of income included in a CFC partner's distributive share includes such attributes of the income

> as would make it subpart F income if realized directly by the CFC partner, including whether the person [to] whom the goods are [sold] is a related person with respect to the CFC partner. . . .

In making this argument, the IRS urged a somewhat different interpretation of section 702(b) than adopted and applied in *Podell* (p. 45). As you may recall, *Podell* concerned the character of income earned on the purchase, renovation, and sale of residential property. The Tax Court interpreted section 702(b) as requiring that the character of the income be determined exclusively at the partnership level and passed though as such to the partners. Can you think of a policy rationale that might justify applying this provision differently in the *Brown Group* and *Podell* situations?

3. *Does closing the loophole end the controversy?* As noted in the opinion, Congress has since amended section 954(d)(3) to specify that the U.S. parent (Brown Group) and the foreign partnership (Brinco) are related persons and therefore the partnership's commission income was earned as a result of purchases made on behalf of a related person. If the revised statute had applied to this case, would it have ended the controversy? Apparently not, at least according to the Eighth Circuit. At oral argument, the IRS claimed that even under the pre-amended version of section 954(d)(3), Brinco and Brown Group should have been viewed as related persons. In a portion of the opinion not excerpted above, the Eighth Circuit responded, "even if we were to accept the IRS's broad interpretation of 'related person,' it is irrelevant to the present inquiry because Brinco is not a controlled foreign corporation, and therefore its income, whether earned on behalf of a 'related person' or not, cannot be characterized as Subpart F income." 77 F.3d at 221 n.5.

4. Brown Group *regulations*. Regulations finalized in 2002 clearly reject the Eighth Circuit's position noted immediately above. The regulations state that "[a] controlled foreign corporation's distributive share of any item of income of a partnership is income that falls within a category of subpart F income . . . to the extent the item of income would have been income in such category if received by the controlled foreign corporation directly." Reg. § 1.952-1(g). Thus, the regulations reverse the normal interpretation of section 702(b) as requiring the character of income to be determined at the partnership level. In the preamble to the final regulations, the Treasury justified a partner-level determination as follows:

> To allow a CFC to avoid subpart F treatment for items of income through the simple expedient of receiving them as distributive shares of partnership income, rather than directly, is contrary to the intent of subpart F. . . . The IRS and Treasury believe that the approach set out in these regulations (which treats the partnership as an entity for certain purposes and as an aggregate for certain purposes) best achieves the purposes of subpart F and is consistent with the policies underlying subchapter K. [T.D. 9008, 2002-2 C.B. 335.]

Unfortunately, this "results-oriented" explanation does not clarify when section 702(b) should be interpreted similarly in other situations.

3. *Evaluation of the Partnership Anti-Abuse Regulation*

Read the following brief commentary written shortly after Reg. § 1.701-2 was finalized.[2] Do you agree with its rather pessimistic assessment of the regulation? More generally, how should subchapter K be revised if its policy objective is to facilitate joint business activities through flexible economic arrangements, while simultaneously discouraging transactions like the ones described in *ACM Partnership* and *Cemco*?

> [T]he IRS proposed, and then finalized . . . a general, "anti-abuse" regulation in the partnership area. The regulation expressly grants the Commissioner authority to recast a partnership transaction if a principal purpose of the transaction is to reduce substantially the present value of the partners' aggregate federal income tax liability in a manner that is inconsistent with the intent of subchapter K. The recharacterization may take place "even though the transaction may fall within the literal words of a particular statutory or regulatory provision." In addition, regarding the intersection between the partnership provisions and other aspects of the Internal Revenue Code, the regulation authorizes the Commissioner to treat a partnership as "an aggregate of its partners" if appropriate to carry out the purpose of such other parts of the Code. "Aggregate" treatment apparently means that the partners are deemed to own directly the assets, and participate directly in the activities, of the partnership.
>
> There continues to be some disagreement as to the meaning and scope of the regulation, as well as its wisdom and validity. At this point, we might make three brief observations. First, the final version of the regulation has succumbed somewhat to the same disease it was designed to cure. The final version is both longer and more narrowly tailored than the original [proposed] version, and offers a series of "good" and "bad" examples (mostly "good") that attempt to illustrate the application of both objective and subjective tests to particular fact patterns. Unfortunately, there is no clear theme, aside from political expediency, that explains why certain examples are "good" or "bad." In the foregoing respects, the regulation follows somewhat the general trend of regulatory projects in subchapter K. Yet, in a sense, it is the failure of those other regulations, as well as of course, the basic statute, to deal adequately with problems inherent in subchapter K that necessitated the anti-abuse regulation in the first place. Given the modifications made to the regulation, it is unclear how useful it will be in accomplishing the objectives originally sought by the IRS. At a minimum, there will be ample basis for future controversy and litigation in interpreting the parameters and interstices of the broad regulatory prohibition.
>
> More broadly, the proposed and final regulations seem to represent a recognition by the IRS that the operating rules in subchapter K, the most developed set of pass-through entity operating rules presently existing, are dysfunctional, at least in certain cases. Indeed, some of the commentary published in response to the proposed regulation, complete with examples of transactions meeting the literal terms of the statute and/or regulations yet reaching seemingly nonsensical results, would appear to

---

2. American Law Institute Reporters' Study, Taxation of Pass-Through Entities, Memorandum No. 1 (Oct. 12, 1995), pp. 5-9.

confirm that conclusion. The approach of the final regulation is to modify the result of dysfunctional cases only where that result was the motivating factor for the parties to the transaction.[3] Yet it is unclear why tax results should turn on one's state of mind, even if that state could be accurately ascertained. Put another way, the dysfunctional rule would seem to be the source of the problem, not the taxpayer's state of mind.

Finally and most broadly, whatever one might think of the merits of the regulation given the present state of current law, it is evident that if one were writing on a clean slate, one would not adopt a set of operating rules that first touts their flexibility, then proceeds to restrict that flexibility with a series of highly complex mechanical and sometimes subjective tests, and then overlays on top of those tests a relatively amorphous supertest authorizing the disregard of the consequences of earlier tests despite plain compliance with them. Indeed, the general anti-abuse rule may apparently apply to negate a taxpayer's successful navigation of other anti-abuse rules adopted to monitor particular types of partnership-related transactions.[4] Something very fundamental must be awry in the basic structure of the rules for the law to have evolved into this unhappy state.

C. Codification of Economic Substance Doctrine

After more than a decade of debate, Congress in 2010 codified the economic substance doctrine. It also enacted a strict liability penalty to be added to any tax underpayment attributable to a violation of the doctrine (or any "similar rule of law"). Read I.R.C. §§ 7701(o), 6662(a), (b)(6), and (i), and 6664(a), (c)(1) and (2), and the following legislative description of the new provision.

Staff of the Joint Committee on Taxation, Technical Explanation of the Revenue Provisions of the "Reconciliation Act of 2010," as Amended (2010)

The provision clarifies and enhances the application of the economic substance doctrine. Under the provision, new section 7701(o) provides that in the case of any transaction[5] to which the economic substance doctrine is relevant, such transaction is treated as having economic substance only if (1) the transaction changes in a meaningful way (apart from Federal income tax effects) the taxpayer's economic position, and (2) the taxpayer has a substantial purpose (apart from Federal income tax effects) for entering into such transaction. The provision provides a uniform

3. Compare Reg. § 1.701-2(d), Exs. (8) and (9), and (10) and (11).
4. See Reg. § 1.701-2(d), Ex. (8)(iii) (general anti-abuse rule may recast transaction already subject to (and presumably satisfying the requirements of) anti-abuse disguised sale rule in section 707).
5. The term "transaction" includes a series of transactions.

definition of economic substance, but does not alter the flexibility of the courts in other respects.

The determination of whether the economic substance doctrine is relevant to a transaction is made in the same manner as if the provision had never been enacted. Thus, the provision does not change present law standards in determining when to utilize an economic substance analysis.[6]

The provision is not intended to alter the tax treatment of certain basic business transactions that, under longstanding judicial and administrative practice are respected, merely because the choice between meaningful economic alternatives is largely or entirely based on comparative tax advantages. Among these basic transactions are (1) the choice between capitalizing a business enterprise with debt or equity; (2) a U.S. person's choice between utilizing a foreign corporation or a domestic corporation to make a foreign investment; (3) the choice to enter a transaction or series of transactions that constitute a corporate organization or reorganization under subchapter C; and (4) the choice to utilize a related-party entity in a transaction, provided that the arm's length standard of section 482 and other applicable concepts are satisfied. Leasing transactions, like all other types of transactions, will continue to be analyzed in light of all the facts and circumstances. As under present law, whether a particular transaction meets the requirements for specific treatment under any of these provisions is a question of facts and circumstances. Also, the fact that a transaction meets the requirements for specific treatment under any provision of the Code is not determinative of whether a transaction or series of transactions of which it is a part has economic substance.

The provision does not alter the court's ability to aggregate, disaggregate, or otherwise recharacterize a transaction when applying the doctrine. For example, the provision reiterates the present-law ability of the courts to bifurcate a transaction in which independent activities with nontax objectives are combined with an unrelated item having only tax-avoidance objectives in order to disallow those tax-motivated benefits.

Conjunctive analysis — The provision clarifies that the economic substance doctrine involves a conjunctive analysis — there must be an inquiry regarding the objective effects of the transaction on the taxpayer's economic position as well as an inquiry regarding the taxpayer's subjective motives for engaging in the transaction. Under the provision, a transaction must satisfy both tests, i.e., the transaction must change in a meaningful way (apart from Federal income tax effects) the taxpayer's economic position and the taxpayer must have a substantial non-Federal-income-tax purpose for entering into such transaction, in order for a transaction to be treated as having economic substance. This clarification eliminates the disparity that exists among the Federal circuit courts regarding the application of the doctrine, and modifies its application in those circuits in which either a change in economic

6. If the realization of the tax benefits of a transaction is consistent with the Congressional purpose or plan that the tax benefits were designed by Congress to effectuate, it is not intended that such tax benefits be disallowed. . . .

position or a nontax business purpose (without having both) is sufficient to satisfy the economic substance doctrine.[7]

Non-Federal-income-tax business purpose—Under the provision, a taxpayer's non-Federal-income-tax purpose for entering into a transaction (the second prong in the analysis) must be "substantial." For purposes of this analysis, any State or local income tax effect which is related to a Federal income tax effect is treated in the same manner as a Federal income tax effect. Also, a purpose of achieving a favorable accounting treatment for financial reporting purposes is not taken into account as a non-Federal-income-tax purpose if the origin of the financial accounting benefit is a reduction of Federal income tax.

Profit potential—Under the provision, a taxpayer may rely on factors other than profit potential to demonstrate that a transaction results in a meaningful change in the taxpayer's economic position or that the taxpayer has a substantial non-Federal-income-tax purpose for entering into such transaction. The provision does not require or establish a minimum return that will satisfy the profit potential test. However, if a taxpayer relies on a profit potential, the present value of the reasonably expected pre-tax profit must be substantial in relation to the present value of the expected net tax benefits that would be allowed if the transaction were respected. Fees and other transaction expenses are taken into account as expenses in determining pre-tax profit. In addition, the Secretary is to issue regulations requiring foreign taxes to be treated as expenses in determining pre-tax profit in appropriate cases.

Personal transactions of individuals—In the case of an individual, the provision applies only to transactions entered into in connection with a trade or business or an activity engaged in for the production of income.

Other rules—No inference is intended as to the proper application of the economic substance doctrine under present law. The provision is not intended to alter or supplant any other rule of law, including any common-law doctrine or provision of the Code or regulations or other guidance thereunder; and it is intended the provision be construed as being additive to any such other rule of law.

As with other provisions in the Code, the Secretary has general authority to prescribe rules and regulations necessary for the enforcement of the provision.

Penalty for underpayments and understatements attributable to transactions lacking economic substance—The provision imposes a new strict liability penalty under section 6662 for an underpayment attributable to any disallowance of claimed tax benefits by reason of a transaction lacking economic substance, as defined in new section 7701(o), or failing to meet the requirements of any similar rule of law.[8] The penalty rate is 20 percent (increased to 40 percent if the taxpayer does not adequately

---

7. The provision defines "economic substance doctrine" as the common law doctrine under which tax benefits under subtitle A with respect to a transaction are not allowable if the transaction does not have economic substance or lacks a business purpose. Thus, the definition includes any doctrine that denies tax benefits for lack of economic substance, for lack of business purpose, or for lack of both.

8. It is intended that the penalty would apply to a transaction the tax benefits of which are disallowed as a result of the application of the similar factors and analysis that is required under the provision for an economic substance analysis, even if a different term is used to describe the doctrine.

disclose the relevant facts affecting the tax treatment in the return or a statement attached to the return). An amended return or supplement to a return is not taken into account if filed after the taxpayer has been contacted for audit or such other date as is specified by the Secretary. No exceptions (including the reasonable cause rules) to the penalty are available. Thus, under the provision, outside opinions or in-house analysis would not protect a taxpayer from imposition of a penalty if it is determined that the transaction lacks economic substance or fails to meet the requirements of any similar rule of law. . . .

NOTES

1. *Scope of section 7701(o).* The Code and regulations are already replete with anti-tax-avoidance provisions applicable in specific cases. Section 7701(o) may be viewed as imposing a substance-over-form principle broadly throughout the tax law, even outside those contexts in which the principle has traditionally been invoked. Many tax shelter claims have involved the unanticipated consequences of interactions among different tax provisions; section 7701(o) presumably will now be available to determine whether those consequences will be respected.

A broad provision, of course, runs the risk of affecting too many transactions, including ones whose tax advantages are fully intended by Congress. The statute, for the most part, is silent as to its scope. Other than excluding certain personal transactions of individuals, the statute leaves to the courts to determine whether the doctrine is "relevant" and should be applied. Indeed, the relevance determination is to be made as if the provision had never been enacted. The Joint Committee explanation identifies a few transactions that should generally be immune from challenge under the new provision. Given the "unofficial" nature of this legislative history, some have urged the IRS to compile and publish "angel lists" of permissible transactions in regulations.

Compilation of an angel list would be a monumental task and might even contravene the intended prophylactic effect of the new statute. In Notice 2010-62, 2010-2 C.B. 411, the IRS provided interim guidance on how it intends to apply the new provision:

> [T]he IRS will continue to analyze when the economic substance doctrine will apply in the same fashion as it did prior to the enactment of section 7701(o). If authorities, prior to the enactment of section 7701(o), provided that the economic substance doctrine was not relevant to whether certain tax benefits are allowable, the IRS will continue to take the position that the economic substance doctrine is not relevant to whether those tax benefits are allowable. The IRS anticipates that the case law regarding the circumstances in which the economic substance doctrine is relevant will continue to develop. Consistent with section 7701(o)(5)(C), codification of the economic substance doctrine should not affect the ongoing development of authorities on this issue. The Treasury Department and the IRS do not intend to issue general

administrative guidance regarding the types of transactions to which the economic substance doctrine either applies or does not apply.

2. *Transaction.* Identifying the proper "transaction" to be analyzed is a crucial aspect of section 7701(o). Section 7701(o)(5)(D) provides that the term includes a series of transactions, and the Joint Committee explanation leaves open the possibility of a court aggregating, disaggregating, or otherwise recharacterizing a transaction when applying the economic substance doctrine. In Notice 2014-58, 2014-44 I.R.B. 746, the IRS announced that "'transaction' generally includes all the factual elements relevant to the expected tax treatment of any investment, entity, plan, or arrangement; and any or all of the steps that are carried out as part of a plan." Thus, if a plan generating a tax benefit involves a series of interconnected steps with a common objective, the "transaction" generally includes all of the steps. The IRS cautioned, however, that "when a series of steps includes a tax-motivated step that is not necessary to achieve a non-tax objective, an aggregation approach may not be appropriate. In that case, the 'transaction' may include only the tax-motivated steps." This warning seems designed to maximize the IRS's flexibility in applying the economic substance doctrine, and provides little guidance in understanding the parameters of the new provision. For example, a purely tax-motivated step that does not change in a meaningful way the taxpayer's economic position or lacks a substantial nontax business purpose may apparently run afoul of the economic substance doctrine even though the step is embedded in a larger transaction satisfying both conditions. This interpretation might suggest that a step undertaken merely to satisfy some tax law condition (including, for example, the making of a tax election) could jeopardize respect for a larger transaction incorporating that step.

3. *Penalties.* The penalty structure accompanying section 7701(o) helps to explain taxpayer demands for increased certainty. In general, tax underpayments attributable to a violation of the provision are subject to a 40 percent penalty, which is reduced to 20 percent only if the taxpayer adequately discloses the challenged transaction. I.R.C. § 6662(a), (b)(6), and (i). Moreover, the strict liability penalty is not abated, for example, if there was reasonable cause for the underpayment and the taxpayer acted in good faith. I.R.C. § 6664(c)(1) and (2). As a practical matter, this means that taxpayers cannot be shielded from the penalty even if they obtain advice of counsel prior to carrying out the transaction. Proponents of a tough, strict liability penalty argue that it enhances the deterrent effect of codifying the doctrine, discouraging all but the most audacious taxpayers from entering into questionable transactions. Opponents assert, however, that a penalty has a useful deterrent effect only when the activity triggering the penalty is reasonably clear. Otherwise, the penalty may operate erratically, deterring some legitimate business activity and potentially punishing innocent violators. Congress presumably did not intend to require taxpayers to engage in transactions in the *least* tax-efficient manner possible in order to avoid the penalty. A stringent penalty may also backfire; the IRS and the courts may be reluctant to assert and apply the economic substance doctrine if they know that such a penalty would automatically follow. Finally, courts will need

to determine whether the penalty, applicable to tax underpayments "attributable to" a violation of section 7701(o), should be imposed if that provision is only one of multiple causes for an underpayment.

The penalty applies if the taxpayer's claimed tax benefits are disallowed by reason of section 7701(o) or failure to meet the requirements of any "similar rule of law." I.R.C. § 6662(b)(6). In Notice 2014-58, the IRS clarified that "'similar rule of law' means a rule or doctrine that applies the same factors and analysis that is required under section 7701(o) for an economic substance analysis," even if a different term or terms, such as the "sham transaction doctrine," is used. Importantly, the IRS indicated that it would not apply the strict liability penalty unless it also raises section 7701(o) to support the underlying tax adjustment. Thus, if the Service relies solely on common-law doctrines such as the substance-over-form and step-transaction doctrines, the strict liability penalty will apparently not apply.

The uncertain scope of section 7701(o) creates the possibility of the new provision being used strategically by the IRS as a bargaining chip in settlement negotiations. Courts may be hard pressed to ignore the economic substance doctrine if the IRS raises it. Yet, if the position is raised and considered, the penalty may significantly increase the stakes of the disagreement. The IRS's announcement in Notice 2010-62 of its plan to centralize the decision-making process for asserting the doctrine (and penalty) was intended to moderate such concerns. Notice 2014-58 may also provide some comfort to taxpayers, but it remains to be seen how the law will evolve.

4. *Partnership anti-abuse rule in retrospect.* Although it has apparently not had much impact in litigation, courts often cite the partnership anti-abuse rule as an alternative ground for disallowing a transaction. See Fidelity Int'l Currency Advisor A Fund, LLC v. U.S., 747 F. Supp. 2d 49 (D. Mass. 2010), aff'd, 661 F.3d 667 (1st Cir. 2011) (describing anti-abuse rule as a complement to common-law doctrines). In a stipulated settlement of the larger transaction in *Countryside* (p. 280), the court applied the partnership anti-abuse rule to prevent manipulation of the basis adjustment rules under section 743. The IRS has also expressly referenced the anti-abuse rule in other regulations. See, e.g., Reg. § 1.704-3(a)(1). In partnership audits and administrative announcements challenging abusive transactions, the IRS routinely invokes the anti-abuse rule.

Codification of the economic substance doctrine in section 7701(o) raises the issue whether the anti-abuse rule continues to serve a useful function. Despite considerable overlap — both provisions require a substantial business purpose and compare the nontax aspects of a transaction with the claimed tax benefit — the anti-abuse rule and the economic substance doctrine are clearly not wholly congruent. For example, the "clear-reflection-of-income" principle under the anti-abuse rule has no counterpart under the economic substance doctrine. Moreover, the economic substance doctrine may not be considered "relevant" to a transaction that nevertheless violates the anti-abuse rule.

Some commentators claim that Treasury should revoke the anti-abuse rule as either redundant or preempted by section 7701(o). This position may be premised on an overly broad reading of section 7701(o), which codifies only the strand of the economic substance doctrine related to transactions that lack a business purpose or that produce no meaningful change in the taxpayer's economic position. By contrast, the anti-abuse rule embodies traditional substance-over-form principles and focuses on transactions that seek to manipulate the mechanical provisions of subchapter K to produce unintended consequences. The IRS's guidance in Notice 2014-58 (see note 3) apparently means that it will not assert the strict liability penalty for violation of the partnership anti-abuse rule unless section 7701(o) is also invoked. Although the Notice does not explicitly mention the anti-abuse rule, it states that "Treasury regulations, other than section 7701(o) and the regulations under that section, that disallow tax benefits are not similar rules of law for purposes of [the strict liability penalty]."

Ironically, section 7701(o) may actually suggest an invigorated role for the anti-abuse rule, especially if courts are reluctant to impose strict liability penalties for lack of economic substance. The anti-abuse rule provides courts with an alternative, specific ground for disallowing abusive partnership transactions, without invoking the economic substance doctrine. Moreover, challenges to the IRS's authority to issue the anti-abuse rule are less credible in light of the Supreme Court's *Mayo* decision according deference to Treasury regulations. See Mayo Foundation for Medical Ed. and Res. v. U.S., 562 U.S. 44 (2011). On balance, the anti-abuse rule may continue to play a useful role even if only as a salutary reminder to overly aggressive planners of the importance of business purpose, economic substance, clear reflection of income, and substance over form.

D. Partnership Audit Rules

1. *TEFRA Audit Rules*

In response to mass-marketed tax shelters in the early 1980s, Congress enacted unified partnership audit and litigation procedures in the Tax Equity and Fiscal Responsibility Act of 1982 (TEFRA). Prior to TEFRA, an audit of a single partnership could often lead to multiple proceedings against many partners and potentially inconsistent treatment of partnership items among partners. To promote more efficient use of IRS resources, the TEFRA procedures effectively provide for a single proceeding at the partnership level to determine the appropriate treatment of all partnership items. I.R.C. §§ 6221-6234. A "partnership item" is generally any item required to be taken into account for the partnership's taxable year that, as provided in Treasury regulations, is "more appropriately determined at the partnership level than at the partner level." I.R.C. § 6231(a)(3). Penalties and other additions to tax that "relate to an adjustment to a partnership item" are also determined at the partnership level. I.R.C. § 6221. The TEFRA procedures apply to all partnerships, except for certain "small partnerships" (consisting generally of ten or fewer individual partners) and electing large partnerships with 100 or more partners. I.R.C. §§ 6231(a) and 6240-6255. The Service must provide notice to affected partners concerning the beginning of a partnership audit and any proposed adjustments (a notice of "final partnership administrative adjustment," or FPAA). I.R.C. § 6223. Within 90 days of the mailing of the FPAA, the tax matters partner (TMP) may file a notice for judicial review. I.R.C. § 6226(a).

Once the partnership-level proceeding is completed, a second partner-level proceeding may be necessary to determine adjustments to "affected items," which are items that are not themselves partnership items but are affected by partnership items. I.R.C. § 6231(a)(5). If no partner-level determinations are needed, any change in a partner's tax liability to properly reflect the partnership item may be assessed directly through a "computational adjustment." I.R.C. §§ 6230(a)(1) and 6231(a)(6). Otherwise, the normal deficiency procedures apply. I.R.C. § 6230(a)(2)(A)(i); see I.R.C. §§ 6212 and 6213. Penalties determined in the partnership proceeding may be assessed directly and any partner-level defenses may be raised only in a refund suit. I.R.C. §§ 6221 and 6230(c)(4); Reg. § 301.6221-1(c) and (d). Congress believed that centralizing penalty determinations was efficient and justified because the relevant conduct underlying the penalty often occurred at the partnership level. After much litigation, it is generally settled that a reasonable cause defense can be asserted in a partner-level proceeding only if it involves factors unique to the partner's own situation.

The TEFRA amendments focused on helping the IRS deal with "middle class" tax shelters involving hundreds of investors, but the current tax shelter wave poses quite different challenges. These tax shelter transactions are often sold to only a few wealthy individuals, but often involve multiple entities—including trusts, S corporations, and tiers of entities taxed as partnerships. But for these "impermissible partners," the TEFRA procedures might be inapplicable because of the small partnership exception. Ironically, from the government's perspective, avoiding the TEFRA procedures might actually be preferable: these procedures have proven to be cumbersome and potential sources of procedural error. In a recent case, the Tax Court noted that:

> [The TEFRA audit rules are] fiendishly complicated. Significant procedural problems arise from the complexity introduced by two levels of proceedings . . . at the partnership level and the partner level. There are situations in which the two levels fail to fit perfectly together. . . . These situations have allowed or created the potential for taxpayers to escape liabilities for tax deficiencies that would have been due if the Commissioner had asserted the correct arguments and positions at the correct level.

Tigers Eye Trading LLC v. Comm'r, 138 T.C. 67, 94 n.29 (2012).

Partnership-level penalties imposed in *Cemco*-type transactions have also come under challenge in TEFRA proceedings. In Woods v. U.S., 134 S. Ct. 557, 562 (2013), the Supreme Court held that, under the TEFRA provisions, a court has jurisdiction in a partnership proceeding to determine the "applicability" of any penalty that "relates to" an adjustment to a partnership item. The sham-partnership determination was clearly a "partnership item" and the penalty for misstatement of basis related to the sham finding. As the Supreme Court noted, the penalty determination is "inherently provisional," since the final determination of a partner's liability for a penalty (and the amount of the penalty) must ultimately be made at the partner level. Id. at 564. *Woods* opens the door to assessing penalties in numerous pending offsetting-option cases.

NOTES AND QUESTIONS

1. *Procedural complexity—sham entities.* The offsetting-option cases have forced courts to explore the complexities lurking in the TEFRA procedures as applied to entities that are shams or lack economic substance. Since the owners of the entity are not partners and do not hold partnership interests in the disregarded entity, how should transactions between the purported entity and purported partners be characterized? Does it make sense to apply the TEFRA procedures to sham partnerships?

2. Woods' *aftermath.* In offsetting-option shelters, the taxpayers' disallowed losses depended on the partners' purported outside basis (in the nonexistent) partnership. As *Woods* affirms, outside basis is an affected item (not a partnership item) that may require further partner-level findings. Nevertheless, *Woods* found it "not apparent why additional partner-level determinations would be required before adjusting outside basis in a sham partnership." Id. at 565 n.2. Thus, the Supreme Court left open the possibility that the government could directly assess the underlying tax liability (as well as penalties). If so, a shelter investor would be forced to bring a refund action (after payment of the tax (and penalties)) before asserting any defense unique to the partner's own situation. Does this procedure seem unfair?

2. *Post-TEFRA Audit Rules*

In the Bipartisan Budget Act of 2015, Congress replaced the TEFRA rules and the special rules for electing large partnerships with a new partnership audit regime, which generally is effective for partnership taxable years beginning in 2018. As described in a 2014 GAO report, the cumbersome nature of the TEFRA process—designed to address a class of tax shelters that have largely disappeared—has led to few IRS audits of large partnerships with most audits yielding little change in tax liability. Auditing partnerships with tiers of other partnerships as direct or indirect partners has proven especially challenging because of the difficulty in tracing and determining the ultimate tax effect of required adjustments to the audited partnership's tax items. In enacting the new regime, Congress evidently hoped that both the number and efficiency of audits would increase, potentially generating an estimated $9 billion of revenue during the ten years following enactment. Unfortunately, due to the hasty adoption of the provisions, there remain numerous technical problems that will need to be resolved through statutory amendments or regulations. It seems likely that most partnerships eligible to elect out of the new regime will do so, and that any partnerships subject to the new rules will need to amend their agreements to take into account the new procedures.

Under the new regime, the default rule is entity-level collection and assessment of taxes from all partnerships — not just widely held or publicly traded partnerships — subject to an annual election out for certain partnerships with 100 or fewer partners. I.R.C. § 6221(a) and (b)(1). To be able to elect out of the new rules, a partnership must generally have only partners that are individuals, a C corporation (or certain foreign entities), an S corporation, or an estate of a deceased partner. Thus, a partnership with another partnership or a trust as a partner may not elect out no matter how few additional partners it has. A special look-through rule applies for partnerships with an S corporation partner for purposes of determining the 100-partner threshold. I.R.C. § 6221(b)(2).

If the entity-level regime applies, the partnership must pay any "imputed underpayment" stemming from the audit adjustments; any penalties are also determined at the partnership level. I.R.C. §§ 6225(a), 6233(a). The additional tax is due for the partnership taxable year of the adjustment (the "adjustment year"), even though the adjusted items relate to a prior partnership taxable year (the "reviewed year"). I.R.C. §§ 6225(d), 6232(a). For example, if the IRS determines in 2021 that there was an underpayment for a calendar-year partnership's 2018 taxable year, the partnership would owe additional tax on its return for 2021. The tax due is determined by multiplying the net adjustment by the highest corporate or individual tax rate in effect for the reviewed year (currently 39.6%) regardless of the partners' actual tax rates. I.R.C. § 6225(b)(1). If an adjustment involves merely a reallocation of a partnership item from one partner to another partner (such as a reallocation of $100 income from partner A to partner B), only the adjustment producing a tax increase (B's additional income in this example), and not the net adjustment (which would be zero in this example), is taken into account. I.R.C. § 6225(b)(2). The statute also provides for modification of the imputed underpayment under certain circumstances, such as when partners file amended returns and pay the additional tax directly or the partnership has tax-exempt partners. I.R.C. § 6225(c)(2) and (3). The imputed underpayment may also be reduced to reflect a lower tax rate applicable to corporate partners and capital gains or qualified dividends of partners who are individuals. I.R.C. § 6225(c)(4).

The statutory default rule would seem to upend the notion that partnerships do not pay tax. It may also frequently give rise to economic mismatches, since the tax burden on underpayments is shifted from the historic partners (those partners who were partners during the reviewed year) to the current partners, leading to potential abuses and acrimony among partners. The partnership can avoid paying an entity-level tax by electing, within a 45-day period after a final IRS notice of adjustment, to issue amended schedule K-1s (or the equivalent) to its partners in the reviewed year. I.R.C. § 6226(a). This election (commonly referred to as a "push-up election") effectively shifts the tax obligation of the partnership to its historic partners who must take their share of the adjustment (and any penalties and interest) into account on their individual returns for the current year. I.R.C. § 6226(b) and (c). The tax liability of these partners is equal to the additional amount that would have been due if the original K-1 had included the corrected partnership information (with appropriate adjustments for any collateral effects in the intervening years). I.R.C. § 6226(b). Unless payment of an entity-level tax is less onerous, the push-up election seems likely to be the default rule in practice.

Appendix
Form 1065 and Schedule K-1

Form **1065** Department of the Treasury Internal Revenue Service

U.S. Return of Partnership Income

For calendar year 2015, or tax year beginning ______, 2015, ending ______, 20 ____.

▶ Information about Form 1065 and its separate instructions is at *www.irs.gov/form1065*.

OMB No. 1545-0123

2015

A Principal business activity	Type or Print	Name of partnership	D Employer identification number
B Principal product or service		Number, street, and room or suite no. If a P.O. box, see the instructions.	E Date business started
C Business code number		City or town, state or province, country, and ZIP or foreign postal code	F Total assets (see the instructions) $

G Check applicable boxes: **(1)** ☐ Initial return **(2)** ☐ Final return **(3)** ☐ Name change **(4)** ☐ Address change **(5)** ☐ Amended return **(6)** ☐ Technical termination - also check (1) or (2)

H Check accounting method: **(1)** ☐ Cash **(2)** ☐ Accrual **(3)** ☐ Other (specify) ▶

I Number of Schedules K-1. Attach one for each person who was a partner at any time during the tax year ▶

J Check if Schedules C and M-3 are attached . . . ☐

Caution. *Include **only** trade or business income and expenses on lines 1a through 22 below. See the instructions for more information.*

Income	1a	Gross receipts or sales	1a		
	b	Returns and allowances	1b		
	c	Balance. Subtract line 1b from line 1a		1c	
	2	Cost of goods sold (attach Form 1125-A)		2	
	3	Gross profit. Subtract line 2 from line 1c		3	
	4	Ordinary income (loss) from other partnerships, estates, and trusts (attach statement)		4	
	5	Net farm profit (loss) (attach Schedule F (Form 1040))		5	
	6	Net gain (loss) from Form 4797, Part II, line 17 (attach Form 4797)		6	
	7	Other income (loss) (attach statement)		7	
	8	**Total income (loss).** Combine lines 3 through 7		8	
Deductions (see the instructions for limitations)	9	Salaries and wages (other than to partners) (less employment credits)		9	
	10	Guaranteed payments to partners		10	
	11	Repairs and maintenance		11	
	12	Bad debts		12	
	13	Rent		13	
	14	Taxes and licenses		14	
	15	Interest		15	
	16a	Depreciation (if required, attach Form 4562)	16a		
	b	Less depreciation reported on Form 1125-A and elsewhere on return	16b	16c	
	17	Depletion **(Do not deduct oil and gas depletion.)**		17	
	18	Retirement plans, etc.		18	
	19	Employee benefit programs		19	
	20	Other deductions (attach statement)		20	
	21	**Total deductions.** Add the amounts shown in the far right column for lines 9 through 20		21	
	22	**Ordinary business income (loss).** Subtract line 21 from line 8		22	

Sign Here

Under penalties of perjury, I declare that I have examined this return, including accompanying schedules and statements, and to the best of my knowledge and belief, it is true, correct, and complete. Declaration of preparer (other than general partner or limited liability company member manager) is based on all information of which preparer has any knowledge.

▶ Signature of general partner or limited liability company member manager ▶ Date

May the IRS discuss this return with the preparer shown below (see instructions)? ☐ **Yes** ☐ **No**

Paid Preparer Use Only				
Print/Type preparer's name	Preparer's signature	Date	Check ☐ if self-employed	PTIN
Firm's name ▶			Firm's EIN ▶	
Firm's address ▶			Phone no.	

For Paperwork Reduction Act Notice, see separate instructions. Cat. No. 11390Z Form **1065** (2015)

Form 1065 (2015) Page **2**

Schedule B **Other Information**

		Yes	No
1	What type of entity is filing this return? Check the applicable box: **a** ☐ Domestic general partnership **b** ☐ Domestic limited partnership **c** ☐ Domestic limited liability company **d** ☐ Domestic limited liability partnership **e** ☐ Foreign partnership **f** ☐ Other ▶		
2	At any time during the tax year, was any partner in the partnership a disregarded entity, a partnership (including an entity treated as a partnership), a trust, an S corporation, an estate (other than an estate of a deceased partner), or a nominee or similar person?		
3	At the end of the tax year:		
a	Did any foreign or domestic corporation, partnership (including any entity treated as a partnership), trust, or tax-exempt organization, or any foreign government own, directly or indirectly, an interest of 50% or more in the profit, loss, or capital of the partnership? For rules of constructive ownership, see instructions. If "Yes," attach Schedule B-1, Information on Partners Owning 50% or More of the Partnership		
b	Did any individual or estate own, directly or indirectly, an interest of 50% or more in the profit, loss, or capital of the partnership? For rules of constructive ownership, see instructions. If "Yes," attach Schedule B-1, Information on Partners Owning 50% or More of the Partnership		
4	At the end of the tax year, did the partnership:		
a	Own directly 20% or more, or own, directly or indirectly, 50% or more of the total voting power of all classes of stock entitled to vote of any foreign or domestic corporation? For rules of constructive ownership, see instructions. If "Yes," complete (i) through (iv) below		

(i) Name of Corporation	**(ii)** Employer Identification Number (if any)	**(iii)** Country of Incorporation	**(iv)** Percentage Owned in Voting Stock

b	Own directly an interest of 20% or more, or own, directly or indirectly, an interest of 50% or more in the profit, loss, or capital in any foreign or domestic partnership (including an entity treated as a partnership) or in the beneficial interest of a trust? For rules of constructive ownership, see instructions. If "Yes," complete (i) through (v) below		

(i) Name of Entity	**(ii)** Employer Identification Number (if any)	**(iii)** Type of Entity	**(iv)** Country of Organization	**(v)** Maximum Percentage Owned in Profit, Loss, or Capital

		Yes	No
5	Did the partnership file Form 8893, Election of Partnership Level Tax Treatment, or an election statement under section 6231(a)(1)(B)(ii) for partnership-level tax treatment, that is in effect for this tax year? See Form 8893 for more details		
6	Does the partnership satisfy **all four** of the following conditions?		
a	The partnership's total receipts for the tax year were less than $250,000.		
b	The partnership's total assets at the end of the tax year were less than $1 million.		
c	Schedules K-1 are filed with the return and furnished to the partners on or before the due date (including extensions) for the partnership return.		
d	The partnership is not filing and is not required to file Schedule M-3 If "Yes," the partnership is not required to complete Schedules L, M-1, and M-2; Item F on page 1 of Form 1065; or Item L on Schedule K-1.		
7	Is this partnership a publicly traded partnership as defined in section 469(k)(2)?		
8	During the tax year, did the partnership have any debt that was cancelled, was forgiven, or had the terms modified so as to reduce the principal amount of the debt?		
9	Has this partnership filed, or is it required to file, Form 8918, Material Advisor Disclosure Statement, to provide information on any reportable transaction?		
10	At any time during calendar year 2015, did the partnership have an interest in or a signature or other authority over a financial account in a foreign country (such as a bank account, securities account, or other financial account)? See the instructions for exceptions and filing requirements for FinCEN Form 114, Report of Foreign Bank and Financial Accounts (FBAR). If "Yes," enter the name of the foreign country. ▶		

Form **1065** (2015)

Form 1065 (2015) Page 3

Schedule B **Other Information *(continued)***

		Yes	No
11	At any time during the tax year, did the partnership receive a distribution from, or was it the grantor of, or transferor to, a foreign trust? If "Yes," the partnership may have to file Form 3520, Annual Return To Report Transactions With Foreign Trusts and Receipt of Certain Foreign Gifts. See instructions		
12a	Is the partnership making, or had it previously made (and not revoked), a section 754 election? . . . . See instructions for details regarding a section 754 election.		
b	Did the partnership make for this tax year an optional basis adjustment under section 743(b) or 734(b)? If "Yes," attach a statement showing the computation and allocation of the basis adjustment. See instructions		
c	Is the partnership required to adjust the basis of partnership assets under section 743(b) or 734(b) because of a substantial built-in loss (as defined under section 743(d)) or substantial basis reduction (as defined under section 734(d))? If "Yes," attach a statement showing the computation and allocation of the basis adjustment. See instructions		
13	Check this box if, during the current or prior tax year, the partnership distributed any property received in a like-kind exchange or contributed such property to another entity (other than disregarded entities wholly owned by the partnership throughout the tax year) . . . . ▶ ☐		
14	At any time during the tax year, did the partnership distribute to any partner a tenancy-in-common or other undivided interest in partnership property?		
15	If the partnership is required to file Form 8858, Information Return of U.S. Persons With Respect To Foreign Disregarded Entities, enter the number of Forms 8858 attached. See instructions ▶		
16	Does the partnership have any foreign partners? If "Yes," enter the number of Forms 8805, Foreign Partner's Information Statement of Section 1446 Withholding Tax, filed for this partnership. ▶		
17	Enter the number of Forms 8865, Return of U.S. Persons With Respect to Certain Foreign Partnerships, attached to this return. ▶		
18a	Did you make any payments in 2015 that would require you to file Form(s) 1099? See instructions		
b	If "Yes," did you or will you file required Form(s) 1099?		
19	Enter the number of Form(s) 5471, Information Return of U.S. Persons With Respect To Certain Foreign Corporations, attached to this return. ▶		
20	Enter the number of partners that are foreign governments under section 892. ▶		

Designation of Tax Matters Partner (see instructions)

Enter below the general partner or member-manager designated as the tax matters partner (TMP) for the tax year of this return:

Name of designated TMP ▶		Identifying number of TMP ▶	
If the TMP is an entity, name of TMP representative ▶		Phone number of TMP ▶	
Address of designated TMP ▶			

Form **1065** (2015)

Form 1065 (2015) Page 4

Schedule K		Partners' Distributive Share Items		Total amount
Income (Loss)	1	Ordinary business income (loss) (page 1, line 22)	1	
	2	Net rental real estate income (loss) (attach Form 8825)	2	
	3a	Other gross rental income (loss) 3a		
	b	Expenses from other rental activities (attach statement) 3b		
	c	Other net rental income (loss). Subtract line 3b from line 3a	3c	
	4	Guaranteed payments	4	
	5	Interest income	5	
	6	Dividends: a Ordinary dividends	6a	
		b Qualified dividends 6b		
	7	Royalties	7	
	8	Net short-term capital gain (loss) (attach Schedule D (Form 1065))	8	
	9a	Net long-term capital gain (loss) (attach Schedule D (Form 1065))	9a	
	b	Collectibles (28%) gain (loss) 9b		
	c	Unrecaptured section 1250 gain (attach statement) 9c		
	10	Net section 1231 gain (loss) (attach Form 4797)	10	
	11	Other income (loss) (see instructions) Type ▶	11	
Deductions	12	Section 179 deduction (attach Form 4562)	12	
	13a	Contributions	13a	
	b	Investment interest expense	13b	
	c	Section 59(e)(2) expenditures: (1) Type ▶ (2) Amount ▶	13c(2)	
	d	Other deductions (see instructions) Type ▶	13d	
Self-Employment	14a	Net earnings (loss) from self-employment	14a	
	b	Gross farming or fishing income	14b	
	c	Gross nonfarm income	14c	
Credits	15a	Low-income housing credit (section 42(j)(5))	15a	
	b	Low-income housing credit (other)	15b	
	c	Qualified rehabilitation expenditures (rental real estate) (attach Form 3468, if applicable)	15c	
	d	Other rental real estate credits (see instructions) Type ▶	15d	
	e	Other rental credits (see instructions) Type ▶	15e	
	f	Other credits (see instructions) Type ▶	15f	
Foreign Transactions	16a	Name of country or U.S. possession ▶		
	b	Gross income from all sources	16b	
	c	Gross income sourced at partner level	16c	
		Foreign gross income sourced at partnership level		
	d	Passive category ▶ e General category ▶ f Other ▶	16f	
		Deductions allocated and apportioned at partner level		
	g	Interest expense ▶ h Other ▶	16h	
		Deductions allocated and apportioned at partnership level to foreign source income		
	i	Passive category ▶ j General category ▶ k Other ▶	16k	
	l	Total foreign taxes (check one): ▶ Paid ☐ Accrued ☐	16l	
	m	Reduction in taxes available for credit (attach statement)	16m	
	n	Other foreign tax information (attach statement)		
Alternative Minimum Tax (AMT) Items	17a	Post-1986 depreciation adjustment	17a	
	b	Adjusted gain or loss	17b	
	c	Depletion (other than oil and gas)	17c	
	d	Oil, gas, and geothermal properties—gross income	17d	
	e	Oil, gas, and geothermal properties—deductions	17e	
	f	Other AMT items (attach statement)	17f	
Other Information	18a	Tax-exempt interest income	18a	
	b	Other tax-exempt income	18b	
	c	Nondeductible expenses	18c	
	19a	Distributions of cash and marketable securities	19a	
	b	Distributions of other property	19b	
	20a	Investment income	20a	
	b	Investment expenses	20b	
	c	Other items and amounts (attach statement)		

Form 1065 (2015)

Form 1065 (2015) Page **5**

Analysis of Net Income (Loss)

1	Net income (loss). Combine Schedule K, lines 1 through 11. From the result, subtract the sum of Schedule K, lines 12 through 13d, and 16l	1	

2 Analysis by partner type:	(i) Corporate	(ii) Individual (active)	(iii) Individual (passive)	(iv) Partnership	(v) Exempt Organization	(vi) Nominee/Other
a General partners						
b Limited partners						

Schedule L **Balance Sheets per Books**

	Beginning of tax year		End of tax year	
Assets	(a)	(b)	(c)	(d)
1 Cash				
2a Trade notes and accounts receivable				
b Less allowance for bad debts				
3 Inventories				
4 U.S. government obligations				
5 Tax-exempt securities				
6 Other current assets (attach statement)				
7a Loans to partners (or persons related to partners)				
b Mortgage and real estate loans				
8 Other investments (attach statement)				
9a Buildings and other depreciable assets				
b Less accumulated depreciation				
10a Depletable assets				
b Less accumulated depletion				
11 Land (net of any amortization)				
12a Intangible assets (amortizable only)				
b Less accumulated amortization				
13 Other assets (attach statement)				
14 Total assets				
Liabilities and Capital				
15 Accounts payable				
16 Mortgages, notes, bonds payable in less than 1 year				
17 Other current liabilities (attach statement)				
18 All nonrecourse loans				
19a Loans from partners (or persons related to partners)				
b Mortgages, notes, bonds payable in 1 year or more				
20 Other liabilities (attach statement)				
21 Partners' capital accounts				
22 Total liabilities and capital				

Schedule M-1 **Reconciliation of Income (Loss) per Books With Income (Loss) per Return**

Note. The partnership may be required to file Schedule M-3 (see instructions).

1	Net income (loss) per books		6	Income recorded on books this year not included on Schedule K, lines 1 through 11 (itemize):	
2	Income included on Schedule K, lines 1, 2, 3c, 5, 6a, 7, 8, 9a, 10, and 11, not recorded on books this year (itemize):		a	Tax-exempt interest $	
3	Guaranteed payments (other than health insurance)		7	Deductions included on Schedule K, lines 1 through 13d, and 16l, not charged against book income this year (itemize):	
4	Expenses recorded on books this year not included on Schedule K, lines 1 through 13d, and 16l (itemize):		a	Depreciation $	
a	Depreciation $		8	Add lines 6 and 7	
b	Travel and entertainment $		9	Income (loss) (Analysis of Net Income (Loss), line 1). Subtract line 8 from line 5	
5	Add lines 1 through 4				

Schedule M-2 **Analysis of Partners' Capital Accounts**

1	Balance at beginning of year		6	Distributions: **a** Cash	
2	Capital contributed: **a** Cash			**b** Property	
	b Property		7	Other decreases (itemize):	
3	Net income (loss) per books				
4	Other increases (itemize):		8	Add lines 6 and 7	
5	Add lines 1 through 4		9	Balance at end of year. Subtract line 8 from line 5	

Form **1065** (2015)

651113

☐ Final K-1 ☐ Amended K-1 OMB No. 1545-0123

Schedule K-1 (Form 1065) **2015**

Department of the Treasury
Internal Revenue Service

For calendar year 2015, or tax year beginning ________, 2015 ending ________, 20____

Partner's Share of Income, Deductions, Credits, etc.

▶ See back of form and separate instructions.

Part I Information About the Partnership

A Partnership's employer identification number

B Partnership's name, address, city, state, and ZIP code

C IRS Center where partnership filed return

D ☐ Check if this is a publicly traded partnership (PTP)

Part II Information About the Partner

E Partner's identifying number

F Partner's name, address, city, state, and ZIP code

G ☐ General partner or LLC member-manager ☐ Limited partner or other LLC member

H ☐ Domestic partner ☐ Foreign partner

I1 What type of entity is this partner? ________

I2 If this partner is a retirement plan (IRA/SEP/Keogh/etc.), check here . . . . . ☐

J Partner's share of profit, loss, and capital (see instructions):

	Beginning	Ending
Profit	%	%
Loss	%	%
Capital	%	%

K Partner's share of liabilities at year end:

Nonrecourse . . . . $ ________
Qualified nonrecourse financing . $ ________
Recourse . . . . $ ________

L Partner's capital account analysis:

Beginning capital account . . . $ ________
Capital contributed during the year $ ________
Current year increase (decrease) . $ ________
Withdrawals & distributions . . $ (________)
Ending capital account . . . . $ ________

☐ Tax basis ☐ GAAP ☐ Section 704(b) book
☐ Other (explain)

M Did the partner contribute property with a built-in gain or loss?
☐ Yes ☐ No
If "Yes," attach statement (see instructions)

Part III Partner's Share of Current Year Income, Deductions, Credits, and Other Items

1	Ordinary business income (loss)	15	Credits
2	Net rental real estate income (loss)		
3	Other net rental income (loss)	16	Foreign transactions
4	Guaranteed payments		
5	Interest income		
6a	Ordinary dividends		
6b	Qualified dividends		
7	Royalties		
8	Net short-term capital gain (loss)		
9a	Net long-term capital gain (loss)	17	Alternative minimum tax (AMT) items
9b	Collectibles (28%) gain (loss)		
9c	Unrecaptured section 1250 gain		
10	Net section 1231 gain (loss)	18	Tax-exempt income and nondeductible expenses
11	Other income (loss)		
		19	Distributions
12	Section 179 deduction		
13	Other deductions	20	Other information
14	Self-employment earnings (loss)		

*See attached statement for additional information.

For IRS Use Only

For Paperwork Reduction Act Notice, see Instructions for Form 1065. IRS.gov/form1065 Cat. No. 11394R **Schedule K-1 (Form 1065) 2015**

Schedule K-1 (Form 1065) 2015 Page **2**

This list identifies the codes used on Schedule K-1 for all partners and provides summarized reporting information for partners who file Form 1040. For detailed reporting and filing information, see the separate Partner's Instructions for Schedule K-1 and the instructions for your income tax return.

1. Ordinary business income (loss). Determine whether the income (loss) is passive or nonpassive and enter on your return as follows.

	Report on
Passive loss	See the Partner's Instructions
Passive income	Schedule E, line 28, column (g)
Nonpassive loss	Schedule E, line 28, column (h)
Nonpassive income	Schedule E, line 28, column (j)
2. Net rental real estate income (loss)	See the Partner's Instructions
3. Other net rental income (loss)	
Net income	Schedule E, line 28, column (g)
Net loss	See the Partner's Instructions
4. Guaranteed payments	Schedule E, line 28, column (j)
5. Interest income	Form 1040, line 8a
6a. Ordinary dividends	Form 1040, line 9a
6b. Qualified dividends	Form 1040, line 9b
7. Royalties	Schedule E, line 4
8. Net short-term capital gain (loss)	Schedule D, line 5
9a. Net long-term capital gain (loss)	Schedule D, line 12
9b. Collectibles (28%) gain (loss)	28% Rate Gain Worksheet, line 4 (Schedule D instructions)
9c. Unrecaptured section 1250 gain	See the Partner's Instructions
10. Net section 1231 gain (loss)	See the Partner's Instructions
11. Other income (loss)	
Code	
A Other portfolio income (loss)	See the Partner's Instructions
B Involuntary conversions	See the Partner's Instructions
C Sec. 1256 contracts & straddles	Form 6781, line 1
D Mining exploration costs recapture	See Pub. 535
E Cancellation of debt	Form 1040, line 21 or Form 982
F Other income (loss)	See the Partner's Instructions
12. Section 179 deduction	See the Partner's Instructions
13. Other deductions	
A Cash contributions (50%)	See the Partner's Instructions (A–G)
B Cash contributions (30%)	
C Noncash contributions (50%)	
D Noncash contributions (30%)	
E Capital gain property to a 50% organization (30%)	
F Capital gain property (20%)	
G Contributions (100%)	
H Investment interest expense	Form 4952, line 1
I Deductions—royalty income	Schedule E, line 19
J Section 59(e)(2) expenditures	See the Partner's Instructions
K Deductions—portfolio (2% floor)	Schedule A, line 23
L Deductions—portfolio (other)	Schedule A, line 28
M Amounts paid for medical insurance	Schedule A, line 1 or Form 1040, line 29
N Educational assistance benefits	See the Partner's Instructions
O Dependent care benefits	Form 2441, line 12
P Preproductive period expenses	See the Partner's Instructions
Q Commercial revitalization deduction from rental real estate activities	See Form 8582 instructions
R Pensions and IRAs	See the Partner's Instructions
S Reforestation expense deduction	See the Partner's Instructions
T Domestic production activities information	See Form 8903 instructions
U Qualified production activities income	Form 8903, line 7b
V Employer's Form W-2 wages	Form 8903, line 17
W Other deductions	See the Partner's Instructions
14. Self-employment earnings (loss)	

Note: If you have a section 179 deduction or any partner-level deductions, see the Partner's Instructions before completing Schedule SE.

A Net earnings (loss) from self-employment	Schedule SE, Section A or B
B Gross farming or fishing income	See the Partner's Instructions
C Gross non-farm income	See the Partner's Instructions
15. Credits	
A Low-income housing credit (section 42(j)(5)) from pre-2008 buildings	See the Partner's Instructions (A–G)
B Low-income housing credit (other) from pre-2008 buildings	
C Low-income housing credit (section 42(j)(5)) from post-2007 buildings	
D Low-income housing credit (other) from post-2007 buildings	
E Qualified rehabilitation expenditures (rental real estate)	
F Other rental real estate credits	
G Other rental credits	
H Undistributed capital gains credit	Form 1040, line 73; check box a
I Biofuel producer credit	See the Partner's Instructions (I–P)
J Work opportunity credit	
K Disabled access credit	

Code	*Report on*
L Empowerment zone employment credit	See the Partner's Instructions (I–P)
M Credit for increasing research activities	
N Credit for employer social security and Medicare taxes	
O Backup withholding	
P Other credits	
16. Foreign transactions	
A Name of country or U.S. possession	Form 1116, Part I (A–C)
B Gross income from all sources	
C Gross income sourced at partner level	
Foreign gross income sourced at partnership level	
D Passive category	Form 1116, Part I (D–F)
E General category	
F Other	
Deductions allocated and apportioned at partner level	
G Interest expense	Form 1116, Part I
H Other	Form 1116, Part I
Deductions allocated and apportioned at partnership level to foreign source income	
I Passive category	Form 1116, Part I (I–K)
J General category	
K Other	
Other information	
L Total foreign taxes paid	Form 1116, Part II
M Total foreign taxes accrued	Form 1116, Part II
N Reduction in taxes available for credit	Form 1116, line 12
O Foreign trading gross receipts	Form 8873
P Extraterritorial income exclusion	Form 8873
Q Other foreign transactions	See the Partner's Instructions
17. Alternative minimum tax (AMT) items	
A Post-1986 depreciation adjustment	See the Partner's Instructions and the Instructions for Form 6251 (A–F)
B Adjusted gain or loss	
C Depletion (other than oil & gas)	
D Oil, gas, & geothermal—gross income	
E Oil, gas, & geothermal—deductions	
F Other AMT items	
18. Tax-exempt income and nondeductible expenses	
A Tax-exempt interest income	Form 1040, line 8b
B Other tax-exempt income	See the Partner's Instructions
C Nondeductible expenses	See the Partner's Instructions
19. Distributions	
A Cash and marketable securities	See the Partner's Instructions (A–C)
B Distribution subject to section 737	
C Other property	
20. Other information	
A Investment income	Form 4952, line 4a
B Investment expenses	Form 4952, line 5
C Fuel tax credit information	Form 4136
D Qualified rehabilitation expenditures (other than rental real estate)	See the Partner's Instructions
E Basis of energy property	See the Partner's Instructions
F Recapture of low-income housing credit (section 42(j)(5))	Form 8611, line 8
G Recapture of low-income housing credit (other)	Form 8611, line 8
H Recapture of investment credit	See Form 4255
I Recapture of other credits	See the Partner's Instructions
J Look-back interest—completed long-term contracts	See Form 8697
K Look-back interest—income forecast method	See Form 8866
L Dispositions of property with section 179 deductions	See the Partner's Instructions (L–Z)
M Recapture of section 179 deduction	
N Interest expense for corporate partners	
O Section 453(l)(3) information	
P Section 453A(c) information	
Q Section 1260(b) information	
R Interest allocable to production expenditures	
S CCF nonqualified withdrawals	
T Depletion information—oil and gas	
U Reserved	
V Unrelated business taxable income	
W Precontribution gain (loss)	
X Section 108(i) information	
Y Net investment income	
Z Other information	

Table of Authorities

Principal cases are indicated by italics.

Cases

Notices

Revenue Procedures

Revenue Rulings

Treasury Decisions

Other Administrative Guidance

Other Reference Material

Index